The fragility of goodness

The fragility of goodness
Luck and ethics in Greek tragedy and philosophy

Martha C. Nussbaum

*Professor of Philosophy and Classics,
Brown University*

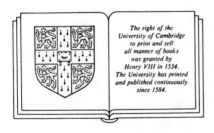

The right of the
University of Cambridge
to print and sell
all manner of books
was granted by
Henry VIII in 1534.
The University has printed
and published continuously
since 1584.

Cambridge University Press

Cambridge

New York   Port Chester   Melbourne   Sydney

Published by the Press Syndicate of the University of Cambridge
The Pitt Building, Trumpington Street, Cambridge CB2 IRP
40 West 20th Street, New York, NY 10011, USA
10 Stamford Road, Oakleigh, Melbourne 3166, Australia

First published 1986
Reprinted 1986, 1987, 1988 (twice), 1989 (twice), 1991

Printed in the United States of America

British Library cataloguing in publication data
Nussbaum, Martha C.
The fragility of goodness: luck and ethics in
Greek tragedy and philosophy. – Cambridge
paperback library)
1. Ethics, Greek
I. Title
170'.938   BJ161

Library of Congress cataloguing in publication data
Nussbaum, Martha Craven, 1947 –
The fragility of goodness.
Bibliography.
Includes indexes.
1. Ethics, Greek. 2. Greek drama (Tragedy)–
History and criticism. 3. Chance in literature.
4. Ethics in literature. I. Title
BJ192.N87 1986   170'.938   85-7912

ISBN 0-521-25768-9 hardback
ISBN 0-521-27702-7 paperback

For Rachel

Some pray for gold, others for boundless land.
I pray to delight my fellow citizens
until my limbs are wrapped in earth – a man
who praised what deserves praise
and sowed blame for wrong-doers.
But human excellence
grows like a vine tree
fed by the green dew
raised up, among wise men and just,
to the liquid sky.
We have all kinds of needs for those we love –
most of all in hardships, but joy, too,
strains to track down eyes that it can trust.

Pindar, Nemean VIII.37–44

He will see it as being itself by itself with itself, eternal and unitary,
and see all the other beautifuls as partaking of it in such a manner
that, when the others come to be and are destroyed, it never comes
to be any more or less, nor suffers any alteration...In this place, my
dear Socrates, if anywhere, life is livable for a human being – the
place where he contemplates the beautiful itself...Do you think life
would be miserable for a person who looked out there and
contemplated it in an appropriate way and was with it? Or don't
you understand that there alone, where he sees the beautiful with
that faculty to which it is visible, it will be possible for him to give
birth not to simulacra of excellence, since it is no simulacrum he is
grasping, but to true excellence, since he is grasping truth? And as
he brings forth true excellence and nourishes it, he will become
god-loved, and, if ever a human being can, immortal?

Plato, Symposium 211B–212A

SOCRATES: Well, then, what is a human being?
ALCIBIADES: I don't know what to say.

Plato, Alcibiades I, 129E

Contents

Preface

This book can be read in two ways. Except in the case of Aristotle, I have made each chapter an essay on a single work, in order to respect the complex philosophical/literary structure of each. This means that I have given readings of single tragedies (in the case of Chapter 2, of significant portions of two related tragedies), rather than a systematic account of fifth-century moral thinking. It also means, in the case of Plato, that I have made overarching systematic claims only with caution (as in Chapter 5), trying for overall connectedness across chapters only insofar as this accords with the requirements of the philosophical/literary interpretation of particular dialogues. I believe that this way of proceeding is more adequate to the complexity of the material than a topic-by-topic systematic approach. Each chapter is, then, relatively self-sufficient; each sheds its own light on the problems that I identify in Chapter 1. Readers can, then, feel free to turn directly to the chapter or chapters that seem most pertinent to their own concerns. But there is also an overall historical argument, concerning the development of Greek thought on our questions; this is closely linked to an overall philosophical argument about the merits of various proposals for self-sufficient life. Because the work-by-work structure I have chosen makes the thematic connections have more the shape of a Heraclitean spider's web (see pp. 68–9) than of a linear measuring stick, I have also provided a number of different types of guides for the reader interested in tracing my discussion of some single theme through the chapters: (1) the outline of the overall argument in Chapter 1; (2) the detailed analytic table of contents; (3) frequent cross-references within the chapters; and (4) a detailed thematic index.

Most of the close scholarly discussions of the interpretations of others, all references to secondary literature, and a number of more peripheral philosophical points have been kept in notes at the back of the book. The asterisked notes on the page are those that provide material of essential importance to the reader.

Acknowledgements

My earliest work planning this book was supported by a leave from Harvard University and by a Humanities Fellowship from Princeton University in 1977–8. A National Endowment for the Humanities Summer Grant supported my first work on the Aristotle section in 1979. A Guggenheim Fellowship in 1981 allowed me to complete a draft of the entire book; and the Bunting Institute of Radcliffe College provided a stimulating environment for the work.

I have read many portions of this book in many places; I have published several sections separately and distributed copies of others. I therefore have an unusually large number of people to thank for helpful suggestions and criticism. Most of my particular debts are acknowledged in the notes to the individual chapters. Here I gratefully acknowledge the invaluable assistance of Julia Annas, Myles Burnyeat, Sissela Bok, Geoffrey Lloyd, Hugh Lloyd-Jones, Nancy Sherman, Gregory Vlastos, and Bernard Williams, all of whom read the entire manuscript at a near-final stage and most generously gave me detailed comments. I owe a more intangible and general debt to several people whose encouragement and conversation have nourished my work over the years – especially to Stanley Cavell, Arnold Davidson, Robert Nozick, Hilary Putnam, David Wiggins, Susan Wolf, and Richard Wollheim. The entire project began many years ago in my thoughts, but it first took on concrete form as a possibility in a seminar on Moral Luck given by Bernard Williams at Harvard in 1972–3. Williams's criticisms and his own philosophical work have been especially valuable to me in my work on this subject over the years, not least where we disagree; and I wish to thank him.

I completed this book during a year spent as a Visiting Professor at Wellesley College. I am most grateful to all those who made this appointment possible, and to the College, for providing a serene and supportive atmosphere for this intense period of work; in addition, a Mellon Grant from the College supported the compilation of the alphabetized Bibliography.

I did not write this book at Brown, so I cannot express the usual sort of thanks to my colleagues here. Nonetheless, as I send it to the printer's in the middle of my second term here, I cannot omit some expression of my respect and affection for my colleagues in both Philosophy and Classics. The warm collegiality I have found here, the shared enthusiasm of the two departments for the subject of ancient philosophy, and the harmonious and mutually respectful atmosphere in which plans for the subject have been discussed and implemented between the departments, have convinced me that this is a splendid place for work in ancient philosophy to flourish. I would especially like to thank my two chairmen, Dan

Brock and Kurt Raaflaub, for the unfailing warmth and kindness of their welcome and the stimulus of their conversation.

Chapters 11, 12, and 13 and Interlude 2 were delivered as the Eunice Belgum Memorial Lectures at St Olaf College, Northfield, Minnesota, in February 1983. Eunice Belgum was an undergraduate at St Olaf and then a fellow graduate student with me at Harvard in the early 1970s. Her philosophical concerns included several of the themes of this book: Greek views of passion and action; the relationship between trust and autonomy; the relationship of philosophical theories to literary examples. She committed suicide in 1977, while teaching at William and Mary College. Speaking in her memory and talking with her parents about connections between the subject matter of the lectures and their effort to understand her death, I began to feel that my relation to my topic was far more complicated than I had ever known. For as the writer and speaker of the lectures I felt myself to be not at all passively vulnerable to fortune, but resourcefully capable of self-sufficient activity. It occurred to me to ask myself whether the act of writing about the beauty of human vulnerability is not, paradoxically, a way of rendering oneself less vulnerable and more in control of the uncontrolled elements in life. To Eunice's parents, Joe and Esther Belgum, I would like to dedicate those chapters. To the reader (to myself) I leave the question, what sort of ethical act is the writing of this book?

Having gone through so many stages over such a long period of time, this book has benefited from the skill and dedication of an unusually large number of typists. I would like to extend my very warm thanks to: Cathy Charest, the late Peg Griffin, Lisa Lang, Susan Linder, Leslie Milne, Jan Scherer, Jane Trahan, Martha Yager. Paula Morgan prepared the alphabetized Bibliography, expertly ordering an intractable plurality of references. Russ Landau deserves great thanks and commendation for preparing the two indexes. To my editors, Jeremy Mynott and Pauline Hire, I am most grateful for their rare intelligence and understanding.

M. C. N.

Providence, Rhode Island
February 1985

Portions of this book have been previously published as follows.

Chapter 2 was published in *Ethics* 95 (1985) 233–67; a shortened version was published in a memorial volume for Victor Goldschmidt, ed. J. Brunschwig and C. Imbert (Paris 1984). Material from Chapter 4 was published in my 'Plato on commensurability and desire', *Proceedings of the Aristotelian Society Supplementary Volume* 58 (1984) 55–80. An earlier version of Chapter 6 was published as 'The speech of Alcibiades: a reading of Plato's *Symposium*', *Philosophy and Literature* 3 (1979) 131–72. An earlier version of Chapter 7 was published as '"This story isn't true": poetry, goodness, and understanding in Plato's *Phaedrus*', in *Plato on Beauty*,

Wisdom, and the Arts, ed. J. Moravcsik and P. Temko (Totowa, N.J. 1982) 79–124. A shorter version of Chapter 8 was published in *Language and Logos: Studies in Ancient Greek Philosophy in Honour of G. E. L. Owen*, ed. M. Schofield and M. Nussbaum (Cambridge 1982) 267–93. An earlier version of Chapter 9 was published as 'The "common explanation" of animal motion', in *Zweifelhaftes im Corpus Aristotelicum*, ed. P. Moraux and J. Wiesner (Berlin 1983) 116–56.

Abbreviations used for journals and reference works

AGP	*Archiv für Geschichte der Philosophie*
AJP	*American Journal of Philology*
CJ	*Classical Journal*
CP	*Classical Philology*
CQ	*Classical Quarterly*
CR	*Classical Review*
GR	*Greece and Rome*
GRBS	*Greek, Roman, and Byzantine Studies*
HSCP	*Harvard Studies in Classical Philology*
JHP	*Journal of the History of Philosophy*
JHS	*Journal of Hellenic Studies*
JP	*Journal of Philosophy*
LSJ	*A Greek-English Lexicon*, compiled by H. C. Liddell and R. Scott, revised by H. S. Jones, with Supplement. Oxford, 1968
Mus Helv	*Museum Helveticum*
NLH	*New Literary History*
NYRB	*New York Review of Books*
OSAP	*Oxford Studies in Ancient Philosophy*
PAPA	*Proceedings of the American Philosophical Association*
PAS	*Proceedings of the Aristotelian Society*
PASS	*Proceedings of the Aristotelian Society, Supplementary Volume*
PBA	*Proceedings of the British Academy*
PCPS	*Proceedings of the Cambridge Philological Society*
Phil Lit	*Philosophy and Literature*
PPA	*Philosophy and Public Affairs*
PR	*Philosophical Review*
REA	*Revue des études anciennes*
RM	*Review of Metaphysics*
TAPA	*Transactions of the American Philological Association*
YCS	*Yale Classical Studies*

1   Luck and ethics

'But human excellence grows like a vine tree, fed by the green dew, raised up, among wise men and just, to the liquid sky.'[1] So Pindar displays a problem that lies at the heart of Greek thought about the good life for a human being. He is a poet who has dedicated his career to writing lyric odes in praise of human excellence. This career presupposes, on the part of both poet and audience, the belief that the excellence of a good person is something of that person's own, for whose possession and exercise that person can appropriately be held accountable.[2] He has just been praying to die as he had lived, as one 'who praised what deserves praise and sowed blame for wrong-doers'. His 'but', which might equally well be translated 'and', both continues and qualifies that prayer. The excellence of the good person, he writes, is like a young plant: something growing in the world, slender, fragile, in constant need of food from without.[3] A vine tree must be of good stock if it is to grow well. And even if it has a good heritage, it needs fostering weather (gentle dew and rain, the absence of sudden frosts and harsh winds), as well as the care of concerned and intelligent keepers, for its continued health and full perfection. So, the poet suggests, do we. We need to be born with adequate capacities, to live in fostering natural and social circumstances, to stay clear of abrupt catastrophe, to develop confirming associations with other human beings. The poem's next lines are, 'We have all kinds of needs for those we love: most of all in hardships, but joy, too, strains to track down eyes that it can trust.' Our openness to fortune and our sense of value, here again, both render us dependent on what is outside of us: our openness to fortune, because we encounter hardships and can come to need something that only another can provide; our sense of value, because even when we do not need the *help* of friends and loved ones, love and friendship still matter to us for their own sake. Even the poet's joy is incomplete without the tenuous luck of seeing it confirmed by eyes on whose understanding, good will, and truthfulness he can rely. His joy is like a hunter, straining on the track of an elusive quarry.[4] Much of the poem has been about envy, the way lies can make the world rotten. The one trusted friend invoked by the poet is dead, beyond the reach even of his poetic words. And all these needs for all these things that we do not humanly control are pertinent, clearly, not only to feelings of contentment or happiness. What the external nourishes, and even helps to constitute, is excellence or human worth itself.

The vine-tree image, standing near the poem's end, between the wish to die a praiser of goodness and the invocation of the dead friend, confronts us with a deep dilemma in the poet's situation, which is also ours. It displays the thorough intermingling of what is ours and what belongs to the world, of ambition and vulnerability, of making and being made, that are present in this and in any human life. In so doing, it asks a question about the beliefs that sustain human ethical practices. How can Pindar be a praise poet, if human goodness is nourished, and even constituted, by external happenings? How can we be givers and receivers of praise, if our worth is just a plant in need of watering? The audience is invited to inspect its own self-conception. To what extent *can* we distinguish between what is up to the world and what is up to us, when assessing a human life? To what extent *must* we insist on finding these distinctions, if we are to go on praising as we praise? And how can we improve this situation, making progress by placing the most important things, things such as personal achievement, politics, and love, under our control?

The problem is made more complex by a further implication of the poetic image. It suggests that part of the peculiar beauty of *human* excellence just *is* its vulnerability. The tenderness of a plant is not the dazzling hardness of a gem. There seem to be two, and perhaps two incompatible, kinds of value here. Nor, perhaps, is the beauty of a true human love the same as that of the love of two immortal gods, only shorter. The liquid sky that covers these people and circumscribes their possibilities also lends to their environment a quick, gleaming splendor that would not, we suspect, be the climate of heaven. (A later poet will speak of the moist, 'dewy' freshness of the young Ganymede drying himself after a bath – as a beauty and a sexuality *gone* from him from the moment that the god, out of love, gave him immortality, dooming his own passion.)[5] Human excellence is seen, in Pindar's poem and pervasively in the Greek poetic tradition, as something whose very nature it is to be in need, a growing thing in the world that could not be made invulnerable and keep its own peculiar fineness. (The hero Odysseus chose the mortal love of an aging woman over Calypso's unchanging splendor.)[6] The contingencies that make praise problematic are also, in some as yet unclear way, constitutive of that which is there for praising.

If this picture of the passive vine tree begins to strike us as incompatible with some aspiration we have for ourselves as human agents (and so it is likely to have struck this poem's audience), there is the consolation that, so far, Pindar has apparently left something out. However much human beings resemble lower forms of life, we are unlike, we want to insist, in one crucial respect. We have reason. We are able to deliberate and choose, to make a plan in which ends are ranked, to decide actively what is to have value and how much. All this must count for something. If it is true that a lot about us is messy, needy, uncontrolled, rooted in the dirt and standing helplessly in the rain, it is also true that there is something about us that is pure and purely active, something that we could think of as 'divine, immortal, intelligible, unitary, indissoluble, ever self-consistent and invariable'.[7] It seems possible that this rational element in us can rule and guide the rest, thereby saving the whole person from living at the mercy of luck.

This splendid and equivocal hope is a central preoccupation of ancient Greek thought about the human good. A raw sense of the passivity of human beings and their humanity in the world of nature, and a response of both horror and anger at that passivity, lived side by side with and nourished the belief that reason's activity could make safe, and thereby save, our human lives – indeed, must save them, if they were to be humanly worth living. This need for a livable life preoccupied most of the early Greek thinkers, including some whom tradition calls philosophers and some who usually receive other titles (for example poet, dramatist, historian). Indeed, it was this need above all that seems to have motivated the founders of a human and ethical philosophy to press their search for a new art that would make progress beyond ordinary beliefs and practices; and the Greek philosophical tradition always remained centrally dedicated to the realization of a good human life, even, frequently, in its pursuit of metaphysical and scientific inquiries.

But on the other side of this pursuit of self-sufficiency, complicating and constraining the effort to banish contingency from human life, was always a vivid sense of the special beauty of the contingent and the mutable, that love for the riskiness and openness of empirical humanity which finds its expression in recurrent stories about gods who fall in love with mortals. The question of life-saving thus becomes a delicate and complicated one for any thinker of depth. It becomes, in effect, the question of the human good: how can it be reliably good and still be beautifully human? It was evident to all the thinkers with whom we shall be concerned that the good life for a human being must to some extent, and in some ways, be self-sufficient, immune to the incursions of luck. How far a life can and how far it should be made self-sufficient, what role reason plays in the search for self-sufficiency, what the appropriate kind of self-sufficiency is for a rational human life – these questions elicited and became a part of the general question: who do we think we are, and where (under what sky) do we want to live?

This book will be an examination of the aspiration to rational self-sufficiency in Greek ethical thought: the aspiration to make the goodness of a good human life safe from luck through the controlling power of reason. I shall use the word 'luck' in a not strictly defined but, I hope, perfectly intelligible way, closely related to the way in which the Greeks themselves spoke of *tuchē*.[8] I do not mean to imply that the events in question are random or uncaused. What happens to a person by luck will be just what does not happen through his or her own agency, what just *happens* to him, as opposed to what he does or makes.* In general, to eliminate

---

* The problem of masculine and feminine pronouns has bothered me all through the writing of this manuscript. To use 'he or she' as the unmarked pronoun in every instance seemed intolerably cumbersome. To opt for 'he' everywhere seemed repugnant to my political sensibilities and also false to the current state of the language, where, increasingly, efforts are being made to give 'she' equal time. It also seems clear to me that in the contexts where 'he' most often would so occur in this book (referring back to 'the philosopher', 'the poet', 'the good agent'), its presence is far from being really unmarked: it does encourage the imagination to picture the character in question as male. Nor is this an irrelevant concern in writing about this material. For the tragedians all have a claim to be taken seriously as thinkers about the privileges and the moral status of women; in

luck from human life will be to put that life, or the most important things in it, under the control of the agent (or of those elements in him with which he identifies himself), removing the element of reliance upon the external and undependable that was captured in the plant image. And my general question will be, how much luck do these Greek thinkers believe we can humanly live with? How much *should* we live with, in order to live the life that is best and most valuable for a human being?

This question was, as I have said, central for the Greeks. I have already suggested that I believe it to be important for us as well. But in some periods of history it would have been thought not to be a genuine question at all. The enormous influence of Kantian ethics* on our intellectual culture has led to a long-standing neglect of these issues in work on Greek ethics. When they are treated, it is often suggested that the way the Greeks pose the problems of agency and contingency is primitive or misguided. For the Kantian believes that there is one domain of value, the domain of moral value, that is altogether immune to the assaults of luck. No matter what happens in the world, the moral value of the good will remains unaffected. Furthermore, the Kantian believes that there is a sharp distinction to be drawn between this and every other type of value, *and* that moral value is of overwhelmingly greater importance than anything else.. If these beliefs are all true, then an inquiry such as ours can only serve to uncover false beliefs about the important and true beliefs about the trivial. It can show that Greek thinkers held the false and primitive view that moral value is vulnerable to luck; and it can show that they had the true but relatively unimportant belief that other sorts of value are vulnerable. It will surely reveal, in the process, the

---

each of the plays that we shall discuss, a woman defends her claim to moral and political equality. Plato has a good claim to be called the first feminist philosopher – though his position is more radical still: for it is the denial that the body, therefore gender, is of any ethical significance at all (cf. Ch. 5). He is also the first thinker I know who pointed out that feminism ought to lead to changes in unmarked linguistic gender. At *Republic* 540c, Socrates expresses concern that Glaucon's failure to use both masculine and feminine participles, when referring to the rulers, may give rise to the false impression that they are talking only about males. Aristotle's conspicuous anti-feminism is an issue that we shall discuss. My first idea, as I considered these questions, was to adopt the completely arbitrary 'solution' of using 'he' as unmarked in even-numbered chapters, 'she' in odd. But this proved distracting and harsh to readers of widely varying political beliefs. Nor, clearly, was it a solution that the natural language could ever adopt. I therefore decided, on reflection, to follow Plato's practice in the above-mentioned passage, by using 'he or she' fairly frequently, in order to remind the reader not to think of men only, but reverting (as Plato does) to the masculine in between, in order to avoid cumbersome sentence rhythms. I have also been sensitive to the context – since there is no use pretending that 'he or she' is appropriate when speaking of an Aristotelian ruler as imagined by Aristotle; whereas there is great use in employing this form for Plato.

* There are of course several other post-classical views that would significantly affect the appreciation of these questions: for example Stoic and Christian views concerning divine providence and Christian views concerning the relationship between human goodness and divine grace. I focus on the influence of Kant because, as I shall go on to show (especially in Chapters 2, 11, 12, 13, and Interlude 2), Kantian views have profoundly affected the criticism and evaluation of these Greek texts; and it is the pervasive influence of these views in our time that constitutes the greatest obstacle to a proper estimation of the texts' importance. Except in Chapter 2, where I do discuss Kant's views about conflict of obligation, I speak of 'Kantians' and Kant's influence, rather than of Kant's usually more complex and subtle positions.

primitive character of an ethical thought that does not even attempt to make a sharp distinction between moral value and other types of value. When the truth of these Kantian beliefs, and the importance of the Kantian distinction between moral and non-moral value,* are taken as the starting-point for inquiry into Greek views of these matters,[9] the Greeks do not, then, fare well. There appears to be something peculiar about the way they agonize about contingency, lamenting an insoluble practical conflict and the regret it brings in its wake, pondering the risks of love and friendship, weighing the value of passion against its destructive excesses. It is as if they were in difficulties because they had not discovered what Kant discovered, did not know what we Kantians all know.

But if we do not approach these texts armed with a point of view from which their questions cannot even be seen, it proves difficult to avoid feeling, ourselves, the force of these questions.[10] I begin this book from a position that I believe to be common: the position of one who finds the problems of Pindar's ode anything but peculiar and who has the greatest difficulty understanding how they might ever cease to be problems. That I am an agent, but also a plant; that much that I did not make goes towards making me whatever I shall be praised or blamed for being; that I must constantly choose among competing and apparently incommensurable goods and that circumstances may force me to a position in which I cannot help being false to something or doing some wrong; that an event that simply happens to me may, without my consent, alter my life; that it is equally problematic to entrust one's good to friends, lovers, or country and to try to have a good life without them – all these I take to be not just the material of tragedy, but everyday facts of lived practical reason.

On the other hand, it seems equally impossible, or equally inhuman, to avoid feeling the force of the Platonic conception of a self-sufficient and purely rational being, cleansed of the 'barnacles' and the 'seaweed' of passion, the 'many stony and wild things that have been encrusted all over it',[11] freed from contingent limitations on its power. Plato shows us how Glaucon, an ordinary gentleman, discovers in himself, through conversation with Socrates, an intense love for the pure and stable activity of mathematical reasoning, a love that requires the denigration of much that he had previously valued. Even so, as we read and are gripped by these works, we are likely to recollect an aspiration to purity and to

---

* I shall, in fact, try to avoid not only the Kantian moral/non-moral distinction, but all versions of that distinction and of the related distinctions between moral and non-moral practical reasoning, moral and non-moral practical conflict. The Greek texts make no such distinction. They begin from the general question, 'How should we live?' and consider the claim of all human values to be constituent parts of the good life; they do not assume that there is any one group that has even a *prima facie* claim to be supreme. I believe that their approach is faithful to the way that our intuitive practical reasoning does in fact proceed, and that it recaptures aspects of our practical lives that tend to be obscured in works beginning from that distinction, however understood. In Chapter 2 I describe various versions of the distinction and show why they would be inappropriate starting-points for our inquiry. Our discussions of justice, civic obligation, and religious requirement are, however, intended to satisfy the convinced partisan of the distinction that our points about fragility apply even to values that would, on most versions of the distinction, standardly be considered as central moral values.

freedom from luck that is also a deep part of humanness and stands in a complex tension with other empirical perceptions. And if to feel this tension is not an idiosyncratic or rare experience, but a fact in the natural history of human beings, then good human practical reasoning about the self-sufficiency of the good life seems to require an inquiry that explores both pictures, feeling the power of each.

We shall be investigating the role played by luck in the area of human excellence* and the activities associated with it, leaving aside the countless ways in which luck affects mere contentment or good feeling.† Central to our inquiry will be three questions. The first concerns the role in the human good life of activities and relationships that are, in their nature, especially vulnerable to reversal. How much should a rational plan of life allow for elements such as friendship, love, political activity, attachments to property or possessions, all of which, being themselves vulnerable, make the person who stakes his or her good to them similarly open to chance? These 'external goods' can enter into the excellent life not only as necessary instrumental means to good living but also, if we value them enough, as ends in themselves; their contingent absence, then, may deprive the agent not only of resources but of intrinsic value itself and living well itself. Is all of this reason not to ascribe such value to them or to include them as components in a rational plan?

Closely connected with the question about the individual constituents of the good life is our second question, which concerns the relationship among these

---

* Excellence (*aretē*) should here be understood broadly, not as presupposing any separation of a special group of moral excellences; we so far include all features of persons in virtue of which they live and act well, i.e. so as to merit praise. We thus include, at the least, both what Aristotle would call 'excellences of character' (a group not equivalent to the 'moral virtues', although this phrase is the most common English translation – cf. Ch. 11) and Aristotle's other major group, the excellences of the intellect.

† Some texts we shall discuss are rendered obscure on this point by the common translation of Greek '*eudaimonia*' by English 'happiness'. Especially given our Kantian and Utilitarian heritage in moral philosophy, in both parts of which 'happiness' is taken to be the name of a feeling of contentment or pleasure, and a view that makes happiness the supreme good is assumed to be, by definition, a view that gives supreme value to psychological states rather than to activities, this translation is badly misleading. To the Greeks, *eudaimonia* means something like 'living a good life for a human being'; or, as a recent writer, John Cooper, has suggested, 'human flourishing'. Aristotle tells us that it is equivalent, in ordinary discourse, to 'living well and doing well'. Most Greeks would understand *eudaimonia* to be something essentially active, of which praiseworthy activities are not just productive means, but actual constituent parts. It is possible for a Greek thinker to argue that *eudaimonia* is equivalent to a state of pleasure; to this extent activity is not a conceptual part of the notion. But even here we should be aware that many Greek thinkers conceive of pleasure as something active rather than stative (cf. Ch. 5); an equation of *eudaimonia* with pleasure might, then, not mean what we would expect it to mean in a Utilitarian writer. The view that *eudaimonia* is equivalent to a *state* of pleasure is an unconventional and *prima facie* counterintuitive position in the Greek tradition (cf. Ch. 4). A very common position would be Aristotle's, that *eudaimonia* consists in activity according to excellence(s). In the terms of this view, then, we shall be investigating the ways in which luck affects *eudaimonia* and the excellences that are its basis. Where it is important for clarity of our argument, the Greek word will be left untranslated.

I shall also be leaving aside one part of the question about excellence, namely the luck of birth or constitution – the role of factors the agent does not control in endowing him with the various initial abilities requisite for living humanly well. I shall only assume, as the texts assume, that the answer to this question is not such as to close off all of our other questions.

components. Do they coexist harmoniously, or are they capable, in circumstances not of the agent's own making, of generating conflicting requirements that can themselves impair the goodness of the agent's life? If an agent ascribes intrinsic value to, and cares about, more than one activity, there is always a risk that some circumstances will arise in which incompatible courses of action are both required; deficiency therefore becomes a natural necessity. The richer my scheme of value,* the more I open myself to such a possibility; and yet a life designed to ward off this possibility may prove to be impoverished. This problem is connected with the first in several ways. For a life centered around activities that are always in the agent's power to pursue regardless of circumstances will give few opportunities for conflict; and strategies of reason adopted to minimize conflict will significantly (as we shall see) diminish the fragility of certain important values, taken singly.

We have spoken so far of what we might call 'external contingency'[13] – of luck coming to the agent from the world outside of him, and from his own value system insofar as it links him to the outside. This will be the primary focus of our concern. But we must also raise a third problem, concerning the relationship between self-sufficiency and the more ungovernable parts of the human being's internal makeup. We will be led by our other two problems to ask, in particular, about the ethical value of the so-called 'irrational parts of the soul': appetites, feelings, emotions. For our bodily and sensuous nature, our passions, our sexuality, all serve as powerful links to the world of risk and mutability. The activities associated with the bodily desires not only exemplify mutability and instability in their own internal structure; they also lead us and bind us to the world of perishable objects and, in this way, to the risk of loss and the danger of conflict. The agent who ascribes value to activities connected with the appetites and emotions will *eo ipso* be depending on the external, upon resources and other persons, for his possibilities of ongoing good activity. Furthermore, these 'irrational' attachments import, more than many others, a risk of practical conflict and so of contingent failure in virtue. And even when passional activities are not deemed in themselves valuable, the passions can still figure as sources of disruption, disturbing the agent's rational planning as if from without and producing distortion of judgment, inconstancy or weakness in action. To nourish them at all is thus to expose oneself to a risk of disorder or 'madness'.[14] We need to ask, then, whether a restructuring of the human being, a transformation or suppression of certain familiar parts of ourselves, could lead to greater rational control and self-sufficiency, and whether this would be the appropriate form of self-sufficiency for a rational human life.

To ask any of these three questions is, of course, also to ask about a conception

---

* Anyone who is dubious about the use of the English word 'value' where Greek ethical texts are concerned will, I hope, be reassured as we go along, as it becomes clear why this is an appropriate notion to use to render certain Greek ethical terms. There is no one word for which 'value' is always and only the appropriate translation; but it is frequently the best word for certain uses of '*agathon*', 'good', and especially '*kalon*', 'fine', 'intrinsically good'.[12] Other relevant locutions are 'that which is worthy (*axion*)', 'that which is choiceworthy (*haireton*)', and various verbal locutions involving words of estimating, esteeming, choosing.

of human reason. If it is reason, and reason's art, philosophy, that are supposed to save or transform our lives, then, as beings with an interest in living well, we must ask what this part of ourselves is, how it works to order a life, how it is related to feeling, emotion, perception. The Greeks characteristically, and appropriately, link these ethical questions very closely to questions about the procedures, capabilities, and limits of reason. For it is their instinct that some projects for self-sufficient living are questionable because they ask us to go beyond the cognitive limits of the human being; and, on the other hand, that many attempts to venture, in metaphysical or scientific reasoning, beyond our human limits are inspired by questionable ethical motives, motives having to do with closedness, safety, and power. Human cognitive limits circumscribe and limit ethical knowledge and discourse; and an important topic *within* ethical discourse must be the determination of an appropriate human attitude towards those limits. For both of these reasons our ethical inquiry will find it necessary to speak about first principles, truth, and the requirements of discourse.

This book will describe, usually in historical order, a sequence of interrelated reflections on these problems in works of the three great tragic poets, Plato, and Aristotle. Rather than attempting a systematic account of what every major Greek thinker had to say on this question, I have chosen to study in detail a group of texts that seem to me salient and representative.[15] To summarize briefly, I shall describe the exploration of our problems in several fifth-century tragedies, which will insist on the irreducible role of luck in shaping human life and its value; then, Plato's heroic attempt, in middle-period dialogues, to save the lives of human beings by making them immune to luck; finally, Aristotle's return to many of the insights and values of tragedy, as he articulates a conception of practical rationality that will make human beings self-sufficient in an appropriately human way. But this simple structure is complicated by the fact that all of these works contain within themselves more than one position on the issues. The tragedies characteristically show a struggle between the ambition to transcend the merely human and a recognition of the losses entailed by this ambition. Nor do Plato's dialogues simply argue for their revisionary ethical conception; instead Plato uses the dialogue form to show us a confrontation of positions, making clear to us what any 'solution' risks losing or giving up. And in the later *Phaedrus* we see in addition, as I shall argue, an explicit criticism of the way in which the opposition of positions itself had been conceived in early dialogues. Aristotle's announced procedure is to work through conflicting positions, assessing and responding to their force; nor is his own 'solution' without its inner tensions and divisions. This all means that, although the account will have an overall direction, the movement between ambition and return, transcendence and acceptance, is also present, at the same time, in almost every individual section.

In Chapters 2 and 3, I consider the depiction of human exposure to fortune in three tragedies, particularly with reference to the problem of contingent conflict of values. (Consideration of this problem leads, however, into a discussion of the fragility of certain individual values, since it emerges that the values that most often generate conflict are also among the most vulnerable, taken singly.) Especially in Chapter 2, I try to show ways in which a Kantian approach to problems of luck has impeded our understanding of the Greek texts; I present the Aeschylean characterization of the problems as a compelling alternative to Kantian and related accounts. In Chapter 3, extending these reflections about individual cases of practical conflict, I look at the aspiration to plan the entire course of a life so as to minimize the risk of such conflicts. I find more than one form of this aspiration in Sophocles' *Antigone*. I examine the play's depiction of values as plural and incommensurable, its criticisms of the human ambition to master luck by simplifying our commitments to value. At the same time I try to show the underlying continuity between Aeschylus and Sophocles in their approach to the issues.

In Chapter 4, turning to Plato, I argue that the account of a science of practical reasoning in the *Protagoras* is a response to the same problems that had preoccupied the tragedians and a development of strategies for the defeat of luck that had been proposed within their dramas. This chapter is particularly important not only because it shows this continuity between Plato's motivations and the literary tradition, but also because it displays clearly the interrelationships among our three problems, showing how a strategy adopted for the elimination of incommensurability and conflict among values also renders individual values more stable. Furthermore, by reshaping the nature of our attachments, it transforms the passions, our internal sources of disorder. Chapters 5 and 6 show how Plato develops these ideas in dialogues of his middle period: *Phaedo*, *Republic*, and *Symposium*. (The first transitional Interlude raises questions about the dialogue form as an alternative to tragic drama, showing how Plato's choice of literary form is closely bound up with his views about ethical content.) Chapter 5 analyzes the defense, in *Phaedo* and *Republic*, of a life of self-sufficient contemplation, in which unstable activities and their objects have no intrinsic value. Chapter 6 studies the *Symposium*'s account of these issues in the area of personal love. Although these chapters are most prominently concerned with the vulnerability of individual values, the problem of value conflict is never far away; its relevance to the *Republic*'s arguments is discussed at the end of Chapter 5.

Chapter 6 shows how deeply Plato's account of love responds to the beauty of human fragility, even while motivating us to abandon it for a more stable beauty. In this way it prepares for Chapter 7's argument that the *Phaedrus* questions and modifies Plato's earlier conception of value. I argue that the *Phaedrus* gives a prominent place in the good life, both as instrumental means and as intrinsically valuable components, to passionate relationships between individuals, relationships that are by their very nature fragile. I assess Plato's self-critical arguments and this new account of human goodness.

The Aristotle section begins with a discussion of Aristotle's philosophical method, since his general views about the relationship between philosophical theory and ordinary human belief play an important role in his treatment of ethical problems. Chapter 9 examines Aristotle's account of 'voluntary' motion and action, asking what relationship to happenings in the world our movements must have in order for ethical attitudes and practices to be appropriately directed at them. Chapter 10 looks at the account of practical rationality that Aristotle relies on when he presents his anti-Platonic picture of human self-sufficiency, asking from what standpoint and by what procedures good Aristotelian ethical judgments are made. This chapter is, then, a counterpart to Chapter 5's account of Plato's epistemology of value; we shall see how Aristotle's different epistemology is associated with his different account of the content of human value. We shall also refer back to the Platonic ideal of ethical science first articulated in Chapter 4, asking what Aristotle means by his repeated claim that human practical reasoning is not and should not be scientific. Chapters 11 and 12 deal with the fragility of individual components of the best human life. They ask in what ways the Aristotelian best life is vulnerable to external happenings and how Aristotle argues that a life so vulnerable is, nonetheless, the best. Chapter 11 examines the vulnerability of good human activity in a general way; Chapter 12 looks at two particular cases of vulnerable good activity, namely political activity and personal love. Both chapters contain related discussion of the Aristotelian view of conflict among values. Transitional Interlude 2 then examines the implications of all of this for Aristotle's view of the role of tragedy and the tragic emotions in human learning. Chapter 13 returns to fifth-century tragedy with a reading of the *Hecuba* of Euripides, which shows the vulnerability of good character itself to corruption through chance reversal. Although its argument relies only upon contemporary fifth-century material, its placement at the end of the book will help to show the continuity between Aristotle's enterprise and the tragic tradition to which he himself ascribes such high importance.

The conception of ethical theory on which I rely, as I base this philosophical inquiry on the exegesis of historical texts, is, roughly, an Aristotelian one, the one that is explored and defended in Chapter 8.[16] It holds that ethical theorizing proceeds by way of a reflective dialogue between the intuitions and beliefs of the interlocutor, or reader, and a series of complex ethical conceptions, presented for exploration. (This series, as Aristotle puts it, should ideally include the views of both 'the many' and 'the wise'.) Such an inquiry cannot get started without readers or interlocutors who are already brought up as people of a certain sort. Its aim is to arrive at an account of the values and judgments of people who already have definite attachments and intuitions;[17] these must, ultimately, be the material of the inquiry. And yet this does not mean that the outcome of inquiry will be a mere repetition of the account of his or her view that the reader would have given at the start. For, as Aristotle stresses (and as Socrates showed before him), most people, when asked to generalize, make claims that are false to the complexity and the content of their actual beliefs. They need to learn what they really think. When, through work on the alternatives and through dialogue with one another, they have arrived at a harmonious adjustment of their beliefs, both singly and in community with one another, this will be the ethical truth, on the Aristotelian understanding of truth: a truth that is anthropocentric, but not relativistic.* (In practice the search is rarely complete or thorough enough; so the resulting view will just be the best current candidate for truth.) To bridge the gap between belief and theory, it is frequently valuable to work from texts, leading the interlocutor through an elucidation and assessment of someone else's complex position – or, better, of several alternative positions – on the problem in question. This gives a degree of detachment from our theoretical prejudices; and if we make our selection of texts carefully enough we can hope to have explored the major alternatives.

Since the Greek material, however diverse, presents only some of the available ethical alternatives, and since important rival conceptions, above all Kant's, will not be closely studied here, this project is only a small part of the larger Aristotelian project. It will become clear that the conclusions of this inquiry are conclusions that I find appealing. I believe, on the basis of my thought about these matters so far, that they have a strong claim to ethical truth, in the Aristotelian sense. But I do not claim that they represent the completion of this larger project.

If my method is Aristotelian, doesn't this bias my whole inquiry in the direction of Aristotelian conclusions? If there is, as seems likely, a non-accidental connection between Aristotle's procedures and their outcome, isn't this just a confession that I am going to be heading towards this outcome? There is a deep problem here. The Aristotelian method claims to be fair to all the competing beliefs and conceptions: so in this sense it claims to be fair to Platonism. But Plato does not ascribe much value to this sort of even-handed fairness. He argues, first, that only a very few people are in a position to engage in serious ethical reflection and choice; the others should simply be told what to do. The standpoint from which correct judgments are made is one far removed from the situation of the ordinary human being. And, second, he holds that some ethical positions, for example some of the views developed in tragedy, are so harmful to the soul that they should not be considered at all by anyone in a well-ordered city. So in another sense any procedure that *is* so respectful and even-handed towards so many things and so many people, any procedure that holds his views up to 'the many', and side by side with the views of the tragic poets, cannot, perhaps, be fair to his views as he understands fairness.

My commitment to proceed in an Aristotelian way is as deep as any commitment I have; I could not possibly write or teach in another way.

---

* Both Aristotle and Socrates believe that the best articulation of each individual's internal system of beliefs will also be an account shared by all individuals who are capable of seriously pursuing the search for truth. This is so because they believe that the outstanding obstacles to communal agreement are deficiencies in judgment and reflection; if we are each led singly through the best procedures of practical choice, we will turn out to agree on the most important matters, in ethics as in science. I believe that this position is substantially correct. Although I shall not argue directly for it here, examples of the method at work and further discussions of the method as Aristotle defends it should show its force. Difficulties arising from disagreement concerning 'the best procedures of practical choice' and the threat of circularity these generate are discussed further in Chapters 5 and 10.

Furthermore, I offer, in Chapter 8, a defense of the method that is at least partially non-circular; I defend the remaining circularity as rich and interesting (Ch. 10); and in Chapter 5 I argue that Plato shares more of Aristotle's methodological concerns than this summary indicates. For now, I can only invite the reader to be sensitive, at each stage, to the ways in which my method influences the outcome. In this way, the Platonist challenge against the method itself can be more sympathetically assessed and its connection with Platonist conclusions better understood.

There is one obvious difference between the way in which some recent philosophers, for example Sidgwick and Rawls, have pursued an Aristotelian ethical inquiry and my procedure here. This is that I have chosen to consult certain texts, namely four tragic dramas, that are traditionally considered to be works of 'literature' rather than works of 'philosophy'. It is customary to take these to be texts of quite different sorts, bearing in quite different ways on human ethical questions.[18] This was clearly not the view of the Greeks.[19] For them there were human lives and problems, and various genres in both prose and poetry in which one could reflect about those problems. Indeed, epic and tragic poets were widely assumed to be the central ethical thinkers and teachers of Greece; nobody thought of their work as less serious, less aimed at truth, than the speculative prose treatises of historians and philosophers. Plato regards the poets not as colleagues in another department, pursuing different aims, but as dangerous rivals. His own creation of a way of writing that we deem 'philosophical' is linked with specific views about the good life and the human soul; we do his arguments against tragedy serious injustice by taking the distinction between philosophy and literature for granted and by assuming without argument that literary works are dispensable in an inquiry that aims at ethical truth. We shall discuss Plato's assault on the tragedians below, in the first Interlude; the issues are further pressed in several chapters, especially Chapters 2, 3, and 7, and Interlude 2. But we should make some preliminary remarks now about the importance of literary works for our study. (These remarks should not be read as taking the distinction itself for granted; they address themselves to our conventional grouping of texts, without endorsing it.) The classicist or the literary reader will probably be convinced in advance that these works have a serious claim to human truth and insight. But the reader who approaches the book from the perspective of a philosophical tradition (especially our Anglo-American tradition) will have unanswered questions. Why should this attempt to work through prominent alternative views on an ethical problem turn to dramatic poems instead of confining itself to the works of admitted philosophers? Why should a book that associates itself with the Aristotelianism of Sidgwick and Rawls use texts of a type that neither Sidgwick nor Rawls included within their examination of the ethical tradition? Aren't these texts really dispensable?

First, even if our aim were only to uncover the thought of Plato and Aristotle about our problems, it would be very important to examine the tradition of poetic ethical reflection in which their work takes root and against which they define themselves. Nothing has emerged more clearly for me during my work on this book than the importance of viewing Plato's thought, in particular, as a response to this complex cultural tradition, motivated by its problems and preoccupations. Furthermore, Plato's writing so continually alludes to his poetic context in its choice of image, story, and turn of phrase that the meaning of many salient details is lost on us if we do not try to approach him in awareness of this context.

But I do not intend to study the tragedies only instrumentally, towards the end of a better understanding of Plato. Nor do I intend to study them only in order to record a background of popular thought against which the philosophers sought the truth.[20] My Aristotelian method would in any case make a study of popular thought more directly relevant to the search for truth than many historians of Greek popular morality think it is. But such a systematic and comprehensive historical study, for a culture whose morality survives, for the most part, only through texts of literary excellence, presents enormous problems of evidence and is well beyond the scope of this book. I intend, then, to study the works of the tragic poets as Plato studied them: as ethical reflection in their own right, embodying in both their content and their style a conception of human excellence. In other words, although I shall certainly speak about the relationship of these works to the thought of the 'many' where this can be somehow ascertained, I shall regard them as creations of the 'wise', as works of distinction to which a culture looked for insight. For this procedure I can offer two different types of *prima facie* arguments. The first concerns the value of these texts for work on the particular ethical issues with which I am concerned here; the second will defend the value of texts similar to these for work on any ethical issue whatever.

Tragic poems, in virtue of their subject matter and their social function, are likely to confront and explore problems about human beings and luck that a philosophical text might be able to omit or avoid. Dealing, as they do, with the stories through which an entire culture has reflected about the situation of human beings and dealing, too, with the experiences of complex characters in these stories, they are unlikely to conceal from view the vulnerability of human lives to fortune, the mutability of our circumstances and our passions, the existence of conflicts among our commitments.[21] All of these facts a philosophical work of the type most familiar in our tradition, one that does not focus intently on the stories of concrete characters, can lose from view in the pursuit of systematic considerations or to the end of greater purity. This has frequently happened, both in the Greek tradition and in our own. In order to illustrate this point I shall, in the following chapter, juxtapose the reflections of two Greek tragedies on practical conflict with the purported solutions to this problem offered in several recent philosophical texts, whose influence has combined with the influence of Plato to distance many thinkers from the tragic views. This juxtaposition will help us both to see the tragedies more clearly and to recover for ourselves a motive for turning to tragedy. If our desire is to explore alternative conceptions and if the tragic, by its nature, presents a distinctive perspective concerning these issues, then this is by itself reason to be suspicious of conventional disciplinary boundaries and to consider tragic poetry as, itself, a part of ethical investigation.

It is not, however, a sufficient reason. For the aim of providing reflection about luck with this complex and concrete content might be satisfied by the use, inside traditional philosophical discourse, of *examples* drawn from tragic poetry or myth.[22] We must do more to show why we want, instead, to read the tragedies whole and to discuss them in all their poetic complexity. Is there, then, in the very fact that they are complex tragic poems some possibility for a distinctive contribution to our inquiry? Much of this must emerge from the chapters. But we can say provisionally that a whole tragic drama, unlike a schematic philosophical example making use of a similar story, is capable of tracing the history of a complex pattern of deliberation, showing its roots in a way of life and looking forward to its consequences in that life. As it does all of this, it lays open to view the complexity, the indeterminacy, the sheer difficulty of actual human deliberation. If a philosopher were to use Antigone's story as a philosophical example, he or she would, in setting it out schematically, signal to the reader's attention everything that the reader ought to notice. He would point out only what is strictly relevant. A tragedy does not display the dilemmas of its characters as pre-articulated; it shows them searching for the morally salient; and it forces us, as interpreters, to be similarly active. Interpreting a tragedy is a messier, less determinate, more mysterious matter than assessing a philosophical example; and even when the work has once been interpreted, it remains unexhausted, subject to reassessment, in a way that the example does not. To invite such material into the center of an ethical inquiry concerning these problems of practical reason is, then, to add to its content a picture of reason's procedures and problems that could not readily be conveyed in some other form.

Here again, it is not clear that this constitutes a sufficient argument for the use of tragic poems in our inquiry. For as we examine the Platonic and Aristotelian conceptions (someone might say) we could surely hold them up for assessment, if not only against schematic examples, then also against the data of each reader's own experience. For that experience surely will have all the indeterminacy and difficulty that is relevant for an inquiry that asks how much difficulty there really is in our ethical relationship to luck. (We might put this question in historical terms by asking why Aristotle, who insists on the central role of experience in practical wisdom, should also insist on the importance of tragic poems as a part of each citizen's moral education; this we shall do in Interlude 2.) Certainly an important part of the search for truth here will be each reader's testing of the text against his own ethical experience and intuitions. But, unlike each person's experience, the tragic poem is available equally to all readers as they consult about the good life. It is, furthermore, a carefully crafted working-through of a human story, designed to bring certain themes and questions to each reader's attention. It can therefore advance the conversation among readers that is necessary to the completion of the Aristotelian project, whose aims are ultimately defined in terms of a 'we', of people who wish to live together and share a conception of value.

A tragic poem will be sufficiently distant from each reader's experience not to bring to the fore bias and divisive self-interest; and yet (if we do the hard historical work required to bring out the extent to which we do and do not share the perplexities of the Greeks*) it can count as a shared extension of all readers' experience. It can, then, promote self-inquiry while also facilitating cooperative discussion. In short, it has all the advantages for which we turned to texts, to the 'wise', in the first place, in addition to the special ones that are contributed by its poetic character.

Tragic poetry, then, can bring to an inquiry about luck and human goodness a distinctive content that might be missed if we confined ourselves to conventionally admitted philosophical texts; it will make this contribution best if studied at length in all of its poetic complexity. This content is not separable from its poetic style. To become a poet was not regarded by the Greeks, nor should it be regarded by us, as an ethically neutral matter. Stylistic choices – the selection of certain metres, certain patterns of image and vocabulary – are taken to be closely bound up with a conception of the good. We, too, should be aware of these connections. As we ask which ethical conception we find most compelling, we should ask what way or ways of writing most appropriately express our aspiration to be humanly rational beings.

And this brings us to our second line of argument. For we can now begin to see reasons why poetic works might be indispensable to an Aristotelian ethical project, even independently of our specific ethical questions. Our Anglo-American philosophical tradition has tended to assume that the ethical text should, in the process of inquiry, converse with the intellect alone; it should not make its appeal to the emotions, feelings, and sensory responses. Plato explicitly argues that ethical learning must proceed by separating the intellect from our other merely human parts; many other writers proceed on this assumption, with or without sharing Plato's intellectualistic ethical conception.[23] The conversation we have with a work of tragic poetry is not like this. Our cognitive activity, as we explore the ethical conception embodied in the text, centrally involves emotional response. We discover what we think about these events partly by noticing how we feel; our investigation of our emotional geography is a major part of our search for self-knowledge. (And even this puts matters too intellectualistically: for we shall be arguing that emotional response can sometimes be not just a *means* to practical

---

* The answer to this question cannot be given all at once, but can only emerge out of the work on particular cases. I shall simply assert here my belief that Nietzsche was correct in thinking that a culture grappling with the widespread loss of Judaeo-Christian religious faith could gain insight into its own persisting intuitions about value by turning to the Greeks. When we do not try to see them through the lens of Christian beliefs we can not only see them more truly; we can also see how true they are to us – that is, to a continuous historical tradition of human ethical experience that has not been either displaced or irreversibly altered by the supremacy of Christian (and Kantian) teaching. The problems of human life with which this book deals have not altered very much over the centuries; and if we do not feel required to depict the Greek responses to them as primitive by contrast to something else, we can see how well the Greeks articulate intuitions and responses that human beings have always had to these problems. We will see the element of continuity best, however, if we are careful to point out the respects in which history has altered the face of the problem.

knowledge, but a constituent part of the best sort of recognition or knowledge of one's practical situation.[24])

It is often simply assumed that this fact about tragic poetry in particular, literary texts in general, makes these texts inappropriate for use inside a serious ethical inquiry. Even Iris Murdoch, one of the few contemporary Anglo-American philosophers who is also a distinguished literary writer, claims that the philosophical style, the style that seeks truth and understanding rather than mere entertainment, will be pure of non-intellectual appeals:

Of course philosophers vary and some are more 'literary' than others, but I am tempted to say that there is an ideal philosophical style which has a special unambiguous plainness and hardness about it, an austere unselfish candid style. A philosopher must try to explain exactly what he means and avoid rhetoric and idle decoration. Of course this need not exclude wit and occasional interludes; but when the philosopher is as it were in the front line in relation to his problem I think he speaks with a certain cold clear recognizable voice.[25]

Murdoch seems to assume that there is a philosophical style that is content-neutral, suitable for the fair investigation of all alternative conceptions. She assumes as well that this style is the style of plain hard reason, pure of appeals to emotion and sense. This idea, dominant in our philosophical tradition, can be traced back at least as far as Locke, who writes that the rhetorical and emotive elements of style are rather like a woman: amusing and even delightful when kept in their place, dangerous and corrupting if permitted to take control. But such assumptions simply put aside a question about the nature of the search for wisdom: what parts of the person does, should, it engage, and how are these interrelated? Plato, the main creator of the style that Murdoch describes, did not put aside this question. He believed that the 'plain', 'hard' style expressed a definite ethical conception, and that fairness to a different conception required a different style. If this is true, an Aristotelian inquiry cannot claim to have been fair to all of the alternatives so long as its own style, and its choice of style in texts, expresses, throughout, a conception of rational inquiry in which emotion and imagination play, at best, a decorative and subsidiary role. If we allow these elements of our personality to play a role in the conversation – and we can most easily do this by examining texts that call upon them – then we will be more likely to have a full and balanced assessment of the ethical alternatives.

We encounter here, as we did when we spoke of method, a deep difficulty. For this inquiry is itself a piece of writing and must choose how to make its appeal to, establish its conversation with, the reader. As we read texts that vary in style we must select, ourselves, a way to write about them; this writing, like the choice of texts, will have an important influence on the nature of that conversation. It is tempting to allow ourselves to be drawn into a familiar skeptical argument. If we are to adjudicate between competing conceptions of learning and writing, as embodied in poetic and philosophical texts, we need a criterion, in our own writing, that will allow us to make an unbiased judgment. But in order to know what sort of inquiry, what sort of writing, will provide the criterion of adjudication, we must already have settled the question in favor of one conception or another. We can inquire either in the hard 'philosophical' style or in a mode of writing that lies closer to poetry and makes its appeal to more than one 'part' of the person; or we can use different styles in different parts of the inquiry. But no way is neutral, and it looks as if any choice will prejudice the inquiry in its own favor.

It is obviously fatal to accept this demand for an Archimedean point and for a pure, uninterpretative, translucent art of writing. No such point and no such art are available to us, either here or with respect to other related questions. And yet, as in the case of method, the critic is making a fair request insofar as he or she demands greater self-consciousness as we proceed. If objectivity is to be attained here, it must be by patient explicitness about the possible sources of bias in the inquiry. Too many inquiries into the philosophical value of the literary get derailed at the start by working exclusively, and without examination, in a conventionally philosophical style which strongly indicates that the inquirer knows ahead of time what rationality is and how to express it in writing. The best way of approaching this issue that now seems to me to be within my power as a writer is to attempt to vary the way of writing so that it will be appropriate to the ethical conception to which it responds in each case; to try to show in my writing the full range of my responses to the texts and to evoke similar responses in the reader. There are limits to this. I hope that the writing as a whole exemplifies certain virtues to which I am committed; and I have not, in thinking how to write, tried to give equal time to the opposites of those virtues, for example to stinginess and cautious retentiveness. As in the case of method, some commitments are too deep to be regarded from a perspective of neutrality. The book's stylistic flexibility is limited, too, by the fact that I am obviously writing reflective criticism about poetry, rather than poetry itself (cf. Interlude 2). My writing, then, will remain always committed to the critical faculties, to clarity and close argument. It will also make explicit many connections that remain implicit in the poems. But I also try to deal with tragic (and Platonic) images and dramatic situations in such a way that the reader will feel, as well as think, their force. If, then, I sometimes write 'poetically' it is because I have decided that no other way of writing could at this point be as fair to the claims of the text and the conception being investigated.

The reader who wishes to trace these questions of style through the book will find them discussed in several chapters. Chapters 2 and 3 comment throughout on the contributions made by tragic form and style to the investigation of our problems. Interlude 1 examines Plato's positive debt to tragic drama and his reasons for breaking with this style. Chapter 6 continues these reflections, showing how the *Symposium* links its participants' views of *erōs* with their stylistic views and choices. Chapter 7 argues that in the *Phaedrus* Plato's change of ethical position is accompanied by changes in the theory and practice of writing. This chapter continues the discussion of Plato's explicit criticism of the poets that was begun in Interlude 1, showing how the *Phaedrus* responds to those criticisms. Finally, Interlude 2, in the Aristotle section, returns to these issues, showing how

Aristotle's criticism of Plato's ethical views is closely linked to a high regard for tragic style and tragic action as sources of ethical learning.

We can now sketch, in a proleptic way, some of the concrete results of this juxtaposition of the philosophical texts with some of their literary predecessors. This can most vividly be done by situating them in relation to the claims of two recent studies. In his recent survey of the history of Greek philosophy,[26] Bernard Williams concludes a section on the ethical thought of Plato and Aristotle with some remarks about luck and rational self-sufficiency:

A deeper sense of exposure to fortune is expressed elsewhere in Greek literature, above all in tragedy. There the repeated references to the insecurity of happiness get their force from the fact that the characters are displayed as having responsibilities, or pride, or obsessions, or needs, on a scale which lays them open to disaster in corresponding measure, and that they encounter those disasters in full consciousness. A sense of such significances, that what is great is fragile and that what is necessary may be destructive, which is present in the literature of the fifth century and earlier, has disappeared from the ethics of the philosophers, and perhaps altogether from their minds . . . Greek philosophy, in its sustained pursuit of rational self-sufficiency, does turn its back on kinds of human experience and human necessity of which Greek literature itself offers the purest, if not the richest, expression.

If there are features of the ethical experience of the Greek world which can not only make sense to us now, but make better sense than many things we find nearer to hand, they are not all to be found in its philosophy. Granted the range, the power, the imagination and inventiveness of the Greek foundation of Western philosophy, it is yet more striking that we can take seriously, as we should, Nietzsche's remark: 'Among the greatest characteristics of the Hellenes is their inability to turn the best into reflection.'[27]

Williams's claims fit well with some of the arguments I have already given for the inclusion of tragedies in this study. But if he were right the study could end with those three chapters: for the philosophers, intent upon the pursuit of self-sufficiency in a way that he elsewhere calls 'bizarre', simply fail to feel the force of tragic problems and the pull of tragic values. These problems and values have altogether 'disappeared' from their work.

The continuity between Greek tragedy and Greek philosophy on these questions is, however, far greater than Williams has allowed. On the one hand, inside tragedy itself we find arresting portrayals of the human ambition to rational self-sufficiency; we come to understand the ways in which problems of exposure motivate this ambition. On the other, Plato's philosophical search for a self-sufficient good life is motivated by a keen sense of these same problems. Far from having forgotten about what tragedy describes, he sees the problems of exposure so clearly that only a radical solution seems adequate to their depth. Nor is he naïve about the costs of this solution. I shall argue that in dialogues such as *Protagoras* and *Symposium* he acknowledges that the attainment of self-sufficiency will require giving up much of human life and its beauty, as we empirically know it. I shall argue, too, that in later works Plato develops a deep criticism of the ambition to self-sufficiency itself; this criticism continues the criticism of human ambition that we find in tragedy (cf. Ch. 7, esp. n. 36). In Part III I shall then show how Aristotle attempts to satisfy some of the claims of ambition without a tragic loss in specifically human value. He articulates a conception of self-sufficiency that is appropriate to a limited human life and, with it, a view of human value that is closely related to elements of the picture that we will have discovered in the tragedies. The conclusion ought to be that the Greeks did, *pace* Nietzsche, turn their best into reflection – in all of its range and complexity.

In another recent study of Greek ideas about practical reason, the perspective appears to be reversed. In *Les Ruses de l'intelligence: la métis des Grecs*,[28] Jean-Pierre Vernant and Marcel Detienne agree with Williams that Greek philosophy fails to give an adequate account of the exposure of human value and human reason to luck; they agree with him that certain very important areas of human life are completely absent from the minds of the philosophers, areas that are better characterized in non-philosophical texts. But there the similarity ends. For while Williams believes the philosophical tradition to be obsessed with the pursuit of practical self-sufficiency, Detienne and Vernant believe this to be the obsessive aim of the extra-philosophical tradition. They argue that there are in Greek thought two distinct and opposed conceptions of human reason. There is the speculative reason of the philosophers, which concerns itself with stable objects and with abstract contemplation. This reason does not need to worry about exposure and control, since its objects are from the beginning invulnerably stable. Indeed, it has no practical concerns at all. (They never suggest that practical worries provided the original motivation for the philosophers' position.) On the other hand, there is the practical reason of generations of extra-philosophical texts, a versatile and resourceful type of intelligence that concerns itself with mutable objects and with a world of concrete particulars. The goal of this type of reason, which they associate with the word '*mētis*' (as well as with related words such as '*dolos*' and '*technē*') is, using clever stratagems, to subdue and master the elusive objects of the external world. Salient images for this aim are images of hunting and trapping, fishing and snaring, yoking, binding. This account of the aims of extra-philosophical reason resembles Williams's account of the philosophers' goal: what is sought is self-sufficiency, the elimination of the power of ungoverned luck. Detienne and Vernant do insist on the elusiveness of mastery; the images suggest that, even achieved, it will often be unstable and of short duration. But they insist that for the tradition it is reason's single most valued goal and an unequivocally fine thing.

My account will differ from theirs in two ways. First, I shall argue that the Platonic conception of the life of reason, including its emphasis upon stable and highly abstract objects, is itself a direct continuation of an aspiration to rational self-sufficiency through the 'trapping' and 'binding' of unreliable features of the world that is repeatedly dramatized in pre-Platonic texts. Plato's own images for his philosophical endeavor reveal that he himself saw this continuity of aim. But at the same time I shall argue that this ongoing picture of reason is not, in the

Greek tradition, the only salient model of reason in its relation to luck. What both *mētis* and Platonic self-sufficiency omit is a picture of excellence that is shown to us in the traditional image of *aretē* as plant: a kind of human worth that is inseparable from vulnerability, an excellence that is in its nature other-related and social, a rationality whose nature it is *not* to attempt to seize, hold, trap, and control, in whose values openness, receptivity, and wonder play an important part. We shall find, I believe, that at every stage in the chronological development, the picture of reason as hunter is opposed, criticized, constrained by variants of this other picture, which urge on us the value of just that exposure that *mētis* seeks to eliminate. (This, I believe, is the point that Williams finds in tragedy: the recognition not just of the *fact* of exposure, but also of its *value*.) In this picture hunting and trapping are not merely *difficult*: they are inappropriate aims for a human life (cf. Ch. 7, n. 36).

Lists are no substitutes for argument; these associations will all be further explored in our arguments; but a list may help us to keep our eye on the continuously developing imagery in these two normative conceptions of human practical rationality:[29]

A	B
agent as hunter, trapper, male	agent as plant, child, female (or with elements of both male and female)
agent as purely active	agent as both active and passive/receptive
aim: uninterrupted activity, control; elimination of the power of the external	aim: activity and receptivity; limited control balanced by limited risk; living well within a world in which the external has power
soul as hard, impenetrable	soul as soft, porous, though with a definite structure
trust reposed only in the immutable and altogether stable	trust reposed in the mutable and unstable
intellect as pure sunlight	intellect as flowing water, given and received
solitary good life	good life along with friends, loved ones, and community

If the reader keeps some of these oppositions in mind* they may help to bring together the material in the different parts – showing, among other things, how thoroughly rooted Plato's imagery is in its cultural tradition. My argument will be, very roughly, that tragedy articulates both norms, *A* and *B*, criticizing *A* with reference to the specifically human value contained only in *B*; that Plato, finding the risks involved in *B* intolerable, develops a remarkable version of *A*, and then

---

* It is important to notice that *B* is not the polar opposite of *A*: it is the balanced combination of the elements stressed and cultivated in *A* with the elements that *A* avoids and shuns.

himself criticizes it as lacking in some important human values; that Aristotle articulates and defends a version of *B*, arguing that it meets our deepest practical intuitions about the proper relationship to luck for a being who is situated between beast and god and who can see certain values that are available to neither.[30]

Part I
Tragedy: fragility and ambition

They do not understand that it is by being at variance with itself that it coheres with itself: a backward-stretching harmony, as of a bow or a lyre...One must realize that conflict is common to all, and justice is strife, and all things come to pass according to strife and necessity.

Heraclitus, DK B51, 80

Here we come up against a remarkable and characteristic phenomenon in philosophical investigation: the difficulty – I might say – is not that of finding the solution but rather that of recognizing as the solution something that looks as if it were only a preliminary to it. 'We have already said everything. – Not anything that follows from this, no, *this* itself is the solution!'

This is connected, I believe, with our wrongly expecting an explanation, whereas the solution of the difficulty is a description, if we give it the right place in our considerations. If we dwell upon it, and do not try to get beyond it.

The difficulty here is: to stop.

Wittgenstein, *Zettel* 314

2   Aeschylus and practical conflict

Greek tragedy shows good people being ruined because of things that just happen to them, things that they do not control. This is certainly sad; but it is an ordinary fact of human life, and no one would deny that it happens. Nor does it threaten any of our deeply held beliefs about goodness, since goodness, plainly, can persist unscathed through a change in external fortunes. Tragedy also, however, shows something more deeply disturbing: it shows good people doing bad things, things otherwise repugnant to their ethical character and commitments, because of circumstances whose origin does not lie with them. Some such cases are mitigated by the presence of direct physical constraint or excusable ignorance. In those cases we may feel satisfied that the agent has not actually *acted* badly – either because he or she has not *acted* at all, or because (as in the case of Oedipus) the thing he intentionally *did* was not the same as the bad thing that he inadvertently brought about.[1] But the tragedies also show us, and dwell upon, another more intractable sort of case – one which has come to be called, as a result, the situation of 'tragic conflict'. In such cases we see a wrong action committed without any direct physical compulsion and in full knowledge of its nature, by a person whose ethical character or commitments would otherwise dispose him to reject the act. The constraint comes from the presence of circumstances that prevent the adequate fulfillment of two valid ethical claims. Tragedy tends, on the whole, to take such situations very seriously. It treats them as real cases of wrong-doing that are of relevance for an assessment of the agent's ethical life. Tragedy also seems to think it valuable to dwell upon these situations, exploring them in many ways, asking repeatedly what personal goodness, in such alarming complications, is.

For this attitude Greek tragedy, and especially Aeschylean tragedy, has been repeatedly assailed as morally primitive. The attack begins with the beginning of moral philosophy. Socrates tells Euthyphro (himself enmeshed, we might think, in just such a dilemma)[2] that stories depicting the collisions of competing claims of right are repugnant to reason, since they assert a contradiction: 'By this argument, my dear Euthyphro, the pious and impious would be one and the same' (*Euthyphro* 8A). Such illogical stories cannot provide suitable models for our exploration of what piety is. Since it is a significant feature of traditional Greek theology that it permits such conflicts to occur and even stresses the pervasiveness of their occurrence – for it will frequently be difficult for a single human being to honor simultaneously the claims of gods as different as, for example, Artemis and Aphrodite, and yet each human being is obliged to honor all of the gods[3] –

Socrates (cf. Ch. 4) is in effect conducting an assault upon the old gods in the name of reason, even as he goes to answer the charges against him.

Socrates' objection has by now become so influential that it has convinced many prominent interpreters of Greek tragedy that they have encountered in the tragic depiction of practical conflict an example of primitive, pre-rational thinking. A recent American writer on Aeschylus notes with disapproval:

One *dikē* [claim of justice or right] can be and often is directly challenged by an opposed *dikē*, and in such cases there is no necessity for only one of them to be a true (or 'just') *dikē*... This rather illogical (to our way of thinking) coexistence of valid and opposed *dikai* within an overall process of *dikē* should not be identified with our moral concept of justice... If we equate *dikē* and moral justice, we will undoubtedly be led to make the former more systematic than it really is.[4]

A distinguished German critic, Albin Lesky, goes still further, finding in the Aeschylean depiction of these conflict situations two sorts of logical inconsistency:

If one makes a clear logical distinction, of course, one will say: 'A man who acts under necessity is not acting voluntarily.' But to insist upon logical consistency would mean that we should have to reject considerable parts of Aeschylus' tragedies... In fact, the stumbling-block in the way of any attempt at logical analysis goes much farther... Is not the campaign against Troy a just punishment inflicted on behalf of the highest god, Zeus, who protects the rights of hospitality? Thus, Agamemnon acts on behalf of the god who wills this punishment. And yet the price for this punishment is a terrible guilt, for which the king has to atone with his death. Here there is no logical consistency.[5]

Both in its depiction of the relationship between constraint and choice and in its portrayal of the way in which the conflicting demands are brought to bear on the agent, leaving open no guilt-free course, Aeschylean tragedy is said to commit logical error. Both Gagarin and Lesky (and they are by no means alone) agree, then, that there is a serious confusion in Aeschylus' thought. Both seem to agree that modern thought has progressed beyond these confusions; that, in consequence, Aeschylus' thought would not be helpful to us in exploring our modern beliefs about goodness of choice or our (allegedly systematic) conception of ethical requirement.

I want to investigate these claims, asking why and how some influential modern ethical views have denied that tragic conflict exists and what theoretical influences have led modern critics to belittle the reflections of tragedy. I shall at the same time be asking about the 'we' of whom Gagarin speaks with confidence: whether, that is, in everyday life we *do* avoid these conflicts, and whether the reflections of tragedy might not correspond better than some modern theoretical accounts to our sense of the depth of this problem. Through a study of this problem we will begin to get a sense of the way in which tragic action and the traditional religious thought that lies behind it display the relationship between human goodness and the world of happenings. Since my aim is to ask about the relationship between what tragedy shows and what we find intuitively acceptable,

I shall begin by giving a brief and schematic account of the factors that we usually consider relevant to the assessment of such cases. Next I shall describe several prominent philosophical solutions to the problem, whose influence has greatly contributed to the critics' sense that the tragic non-solution must be primitive. Finally I shall look in detail at two Aeschylean depictions of conflict, arguing that they articulate our practical intuitions better, in fact, than those theoretical solutions.

I

We are considering situations, then, in which a person must choose to do (have) either one thing or another.[6] Because of the way the world has arranged things, he or she cannot do (have) both. (We suspend, temporarily, the question whether by better planning he might have avoided the dilemma altogether. This question will be the subject of our next chapter.) He wants, however, to do (have) both; or, regardless of what he actually wants, he has some reason to do (have) both. Both alternatives make a serious claim upon his practical attention. He senses that no matter how he chooses he will be left with some regret that he did not do the other thing. Sometimes the decision itself may be difficult: his concerns seem evenly balanced. Sometimes he may be clear about which is the *better* choice, and yet feel pain over the frustration of other significant concerns. For it is extremely important to insist from the start that the problem here is not just one of difficult decision – that such conflicts can be present, as well, when the decision itself is perfectly obvious. Aristotle speaks of a captain who throws his cargo overboard in a storm to save his own and other lives.[7] This man sees all too well *what* he must do, once he grasps the alternatives; he would be crazy if he even hesitated very long. And yet he was also attached to that cargo. He will go on regretting that he threw it into the ocean – that things turned out so that he had to choose what no sane person would ordinarily choose, throw away what a sane person would ordinarily cherish.[8]

We have, then, a wide spectrum of cases in which there is something like a conflict of desires (though we have insisted that cases of interest to us can arise even when the agent himself has no occurrent desire for one of the conflicting alternatives): the agent wants (has reason to pursue) x and he or she wants (has reason to pursue) y; but he cannot, because of contingencies of circumstance, pursue both. We want ultimately to ask whether among these cases there are some in which not just contentment, but ethical goodness itself, is affected: whether there is sometimes not just the loss of something desired, but actual blameworthy wrongdoing – and, therefore, occasion not only for regret but for an emotion more like remorse.

A number of distinctions appear *prima facie* to be (and will be recognized inside the tragedies to be) of some relevance to the pursuit of this question. Sometimes what is, of necessity, forgone is a possession, reward, or some other item external to the agent; sometimes it is an activity in which the agent wishes to (has reason to) engage. Sometimes there will simply be an omission or a failure to pursue one of the desired projects; sometimes the course chosen will itself involve acting against the other project or commitment. Sometimes what is omitted is an 'extra' or luxury, peripheral to the agent's conception of value; sometimes it is more central – either a component part of his or her conception of living well or a necessary means to something that is a component. Sometimes what is omitted is peripheral, and sometimes more central, to *our* conception of good living (the conception that obtains in the play as a whole), which may or may not agree with that of the agent whose actions are being assessed. Sometimes what is forgone adversely affects only the agent himself or herself; sometimes there is loss or damage to other people. Sometimes what is forgone is something with regard to which the agent has no commitment or obligation, implicit or explicit; sometimes there is such a commitment. Sometimes the case may be self-contained, affecting little beyond itself; sometimes the choice to forgo *y* now may bring with it far-reaching consequences for the rest of the agent's life and/or other affected lives. Finally, some such cases may be reparable: the agent may have future chances to undo what has been done or to pursue the omitted course; sometimes it is clear that there will be no such chance.

This list is not meant to be either formal or exhaustive; it simply draws our attention to distinctions that we often make. We feel intuitively, I think, that the second alternative in each of these pairs makes matters more serious and, other things being equal, makes it more likely that the presence of conflict will affect our ethical assessment of the agent. These features can combine in many different ways. It would be difficult, and probably misguided, to legislate, in advance of the concrete case, as to what combination of features would be sufficient to make an agent deserving of blame for what he does under circumstantial constraint. No reasonable person will seriously blame Aristotle's captain, who discards a few replaceable possessions to save his own and other lives, even if he had contracted to protect those possessions.[9] Things would look different if the only way to save his ship had been to throw his wife or child overboard; for this loss, which involves harmful activity against another, is also irreparable and of far-reaching consequences for the rest of his life; furthermore, it affects directly what either is, or ought to be, central to his conception of good living. But it seems that it would be difficult indeed, if not impossible, to draw up a firmly fixed set of rules or conditions that will help us determine with precision, in advance, two sharply bounded classes of cases, viz., those in which blame is, and those in which it is not, appropriately attached.

I have said nothing so far about 'moral' conflict; I have included the cases that usually bear this label within this larger and less systematic classification. This is connected with the general mistrust of the moral/non-moral distinction that I articulated in Chapter 1. And grounds for this mistrust can be seen with particular clarity when we consider how talk of 'moral conflict' is sometimes used to sort out the cases in which we are interested. First, it is rarely perspicuous what, exactly, is intended when a conflict is called a 'moral' one (cf. Ch. 1). So many different accounts of the moral/non-moral distinction have been given that the word, by itself, is not self-explanatory. If what is meant is that the case is concerned with other-related values or that it involves the agent's (or our) most serious concerns and commitments, the point can be more clearly brought out by saying this directly. These distinctions are present in our intuitive sketch, although neither by itself seems to offer a complete account of the factors of ethical relevance. If, however, what is meant is that it deals with commitments that are not in the realm of natural contingency and cannot be affected by the 'accidents of step-motherly nature', this will render the distinction a bad starting-point for us, since our purpose is precisely to inquire whether there are any important commitments and concerns that cannot be so affected. Thus understood, the distinction begs our question.

But even if we resolved this problem about the meaning of the distinction, there would be a further difficulty. The use of the two categories, 'moral' and 'non-moral' suggests to numerous writers on the topic that the cases to be investigated fall into two neatly demarcated and opposed categories. They accordingly structure their discussion around this sharp division. Our intuitive sketch, by contrast, suggests that in everyday life we find, instead, a complex spectrum of cases, interrelated and overlapping in ways not captured by any dichotomous taxonomy. If eight features are all of possible relevance to the description and assessment of conflicts, we could well discover that one case exhibits (the second member of) my first, third, fifth, and sixth contrasts; another, (the second member of) the second, seventh, and eighth; and so on. We do not want to rule out or to obscure this possibility. We want to look and see.

Bernard Williams, in an excellent article closely connected with his interest in Greek tragedy,[10] has made an argument of a different kind for the importance of the moral/non-moral distinction in sorting and describing practical conflicts. 'Moral' conflicts, he argues, differ from other conflicts of desires in that we feel that the moral claim is a claim that cannot be avoided by eliminating the desire. Certain claims upon our practical attention are binding, no matter how we feel or what desires we actually have. It is important, he argues, to emphasize this distinction, since it will affect what we want to say about the cases.

This is an important point. I have taken account of it by describing the group of cases so that it will include both cases in which the agent actually desires the two conflicting courses and cases in which, apart from his actual desires, he has some reason to pursue them. Several of my contrasts, furthermore – those concerned with a conception of good living, with harm to others, and with antecedent commitment – express in each case some part of Williams's concern. It is not clear, then, that we *need* the dichotomous division in order to explore these points. Indeed, it may prove seriously misleading for cases in which Williams himself has an interest. For his characterization of moral claims might also correctly describe (and does describe for Williams himself, in recent writings) the force of other practical concerns that are rarely classified as 'moral'.[11] The claims of an intellectual pursuit or a personal emotional relationship, for example, may also be felt as binding, regardless of occurrent desires; and yet the name 'moral' discourages us from considering these cases as central. It seems, furthermore, that what we find in practice is not a sharp contrast between absolute claims and claims that can be avoided with ease, but a messier continuum of claims judged to have various degrees of force and inevitability. For these reasons, it seems to be more perspicuous and more truly in keeping with the spirit of Williams's own project (made explicit in his most recent work) to work with a network of more concrete and informal distinctions, rather than with this dichotomy.[12] If something important has been omitted, we can hope that a precise description of the cases will bring it to light. In order that these conclusions should have force for those who do divide cases in the usual dichotomous way, however, I shall select in tragedy cases of conflict that these people will concede to be central cases of *moral* conflict: cases involving the doing of irreparable harm to another person in violation of a serious antecedent commitment involving major values. Thus, if we show the force of the tragic view about these cases, we will have shown the fragility not just of some part of excellence that is peripheral (in the conventional view) to true *moral* goodness, but, rather, of a part of (what is usually thought to be) moral goodness itself, as it expresses itself in action and choice.

II

We turn now from this intuitive sketch to some philosophical solutions. From the time of the *Euthyphro* onwards, a dominant tradition in moral philosophy has agreed on one central point: these cases of conflict display an inconsistency which is an offense to practical logic and ought to be eliminated.[13] Socrates already makes the crucial move. The conflicting claims in Euthyphro's dilemma (his obligation to respect his father and his obligation to defend human life)[14] are construed as a case of ethical *disagreement*: a conflict of ethical *beliefs* about what is and is not appropriate. But if two beliefs conflict it is only rational to try to find out which is the correct one. At most one can be true; and the other can and should be discarded as false, therefore no longer relevant. This position leads Socrates, later in the dialogue, to question a central element in traditional Greek theology: the idea that the gods impose upon mortals divergent and even conflicting requirements (7E–8E). This idea, together with the belief that it is his duty to honor *all* the gods, generates (or explains), for a typical Greek agent, a sense of the binding force and inevitability of the conflicting requirements, even in a conflict situation. But in Socrates' view, such a picture entails the unacceptable conclusion that at least some of the gods have false beliefs and press unjustified claims. He therefore encourages Euthyphro to revise tradition by considering as binding only those requirements concerning which there is divine unanimity; he expresses, further, his own doubt as to whether gods really do disagree (8E).

Some philosophers, following Socrates' lead, have made his claim concerning all desire or value conflicts: in every case there is at most a single correct answer, and the competing candidate makes no further claim once the choice is made. If the desire persists, the agent must at least regard it as thoroughly irrational. Some, granting that this is not a plausible view of all such conflicts, insist that there is a special group of cases, usually called 'moral conflicts' or 'conflicts of duties', for which the assimilation to disagreement does hold. Such philosophers, being both numerous and from widely varying traditions, have had a direct influence on the criticism of Greek tragedy. And, insofar as they articulate a view to which, at some moments, an ordinary person in their culture could be deeply drawn, they also reveal the presence of more indirect influences. We can, then, hope to get a better understanding of some obstacles in the way of a contemporary evaluation of Aeschylus on this issue if we examine three representative and famous examples.

In *L'Existentialisme est un humanisme*,[15] Jean-Paul Sartre presents us with a striking example of practical conflict. A young man must choose between his patriotic commitment to the French Resistance and his obligation to care for his aging mother. Sartre tells us that we learn from this case of 'inconsistency' that systematic ethical principles are in general inadequate guides for action. The best course will be to discard principle altogether and freely improvise our choices, with lucidity and without regret.[16]

R. M. Hare, in *The Language of Morals*,[17] agrees that the trouble lies with the inconsistent principles, which, again, are taken to clash in a logically unacceptable way. The agent must, then, modify them in the light of the recalcitrant situation, so as to have a new, consistent set that will cover this case without conflict. For example, the moral precept, 'Don't lie', is reformulated, in the light of wartime experience, as the more adequate principle, 'Don't lie, except to the enemy in time of war.' The conflict situation is written into the rule as an exception, limiting the scope of its application.[18]

For Kant, it would be wrong even to say that our principles are at fault here and in need of revision. For, as he argues, it is part of the very notion of a moral rule or principle that it can never conflict with another moral rule:

Because...duty and obligation are in general concepts that express the objective practical necessity of certain actions and because two mutually opposing rules cannot be necessary at the same time, then, if it is a duty to act according to one of them, it is not only not a duty but contrary to duty to act according to the other. It follows, therefore, that a conflict of duties and obligations is inconceivable (*obligationes non colliduntur*). It may, however, very well happen that two grounds of obligation (*rationes obligandi*), one or the other of which is inadequate to bind as a duty (*rationes obligandi non obligantes*), are conjoined in a subject and in the rule that he prescribes to himself, and then one of the grounds is not a duty. When two such grounds are in conflict, practical philosophy does not say that the stronger obligation holds the upper hand (*fortior obligatio vincit*), but that the stronger ground binding to a duty holds the field (*fortior obligandi ratio vincit*).[19]

The requirement that objective practical rules be in every situation consistent, forming a harmonious system like a system of true beliefs, overrides, for Kant, our intuitive feeling (which he acknowledges) that there is a genuine conflict of duties. It appears that our duties may conflict. But this cannot be so, since the very concepts of duty and practical law rule out inconsistency. We must, therefore, find a more adequate way of describing the apparent conflict. Since at most one of the conflicting claims can be a genuine duty, we should call the other merely a *ground* of duty (*Verpflichtungsgrund*). When the stronger 'ground' has prevailed, we see that this alone has all along been our duty in this matter; we drop the conflicting 'ground' as not binding. It quits the field; it no longer exerts any claim at all. To say anything else would, for Kant, be to weaken the strong conceptual bond between duty and practical necessity, and between both and logical consistency. Perhaps even more important, it would be to concede that what contingently happens to an agent (he just happens to be cast into a situation of this sort) could force him to violate duty. For Kant this would be an intolerable thought.[20]

To all this a natural response is that this is not how it *feels* to be in that situation. It does not feel like solving a puzzle, where all that is needed is to find the right answer. If the idea of solving or ending the problem occurs, it is not as the hope of discovery, but as the idea of some more radical break: denial, deliberate callousness, even madness or death. Such intuitive objections have not been ignored by these philosophers, each of whom in some way acknowledges their presence before removing them. (Sartre and Hare contrast ordinary deliberation with a higher or more experienced type of thinking.[21] Kant tells the ordinary person that his own attachment to consistency ought to lead him to reject one of the conflicting principles.) So a defender of the intuitive position cannot simply assert that this is how he ordinarily sees things. He must do two further things, at least. First, he must explore this 'intuitive position' in considerably more detail than is available within many philosophical discussions of the problem, describing the cases as precisely as possible and showing us what about them gives rise to our intuitive sense of their force.* (This would require describing them in such a way that we could feel, as well as intellectually grasp, that force.) Second, and even more important, he must show that, and how, the intuitive picture of the cases is connected with other valuable elements of human ethical life – that we would risk giving up something of real importance if we adjusted our intuitions in accordance with one of these philosophical solutions. I shall now try to show that the 'rather illogical' works of Aeschylus fulfill both of these demands.

III

At the beginning of Aeschylus's *Agamemnon*,[22] there is a strange and ominous portent. The king of birds appears to the kings of the ships. Two eagles, one black, one white-tailed, in full view of the army, devour a pregnant hare with all her

* It is interesting to note that this criticism is not nearly as broadly applicable now (1984) as it was when this section was first mapped out (1973). The tremendous development of 'applied ethics' and the increasing concern of most major (Anglo-American) ethical writers with concrete and complex examples is a welcome development. I do not believe that these examples eliminate the need to turn to works of literature (cf. the arguments of Ch. 1). As examples become increasingly complex, however, we can expect to find not a sharp contrast between example and literary text, but, instead, a continuum.

unborn young (111–20). It is difficult not to connect this omen with the coming slaughter, by this army, of innocent citizens at Troy. It is also difficult for an audience familiar with this story not to connect it with the imminent slaughter of the helpless girl Iphigenia, which will prove necessary for the departure of the expedition. But the omen receives from the prophet Calchas an oddly trivial interpretation.[23] He 'knows the warlike devourers of the hare for the conducting chiefs' (123–4); and yet he predicts only that the army, in laying siege to Troy, will slaughter many herds of cattle before its walls. He finds the appropriate parallel to the eagles' cold-blooded and unreflective slaying of a hare to be human killing of animals, not human killing of other humans. In a sense he is correct. As an eagle kills a hare, so a human being might slaughter cattle: without compunction and to satisfy immediate needs. When the victims are human, we expect deliberations and feelings of greater complexity to be involved. The parallel does, then, have a point. And yet it is clear that this reading of the omen is not to be seen as sufficient. No significant omen merely predicts a beef dinner. Calchas is evasive. If, however, we connect his human/animal parallel with the omen's more sinister references, it does suggest further pertinent reflections. If we think of the omen as pointing towards the war crimes of the Greeks, we are reminded of the way in which circumstances of war can alter and erode the normal conventions of human behavior towards other humans, rendering them, in their indifference to the slain, either bestial or like killers of beasts.[24] If we think of it as pointing to the murder of Iphigenia (for it is she who is 'stopped from her course' before the birth of children, she who is the particular victim of the 'king of ships'), we are introduced already to the central theme in the Chorus's blame of Agamemnon: he adopted an inappropriate attitude towards his conflict, killing a human child with no more agony, no more revulsion of feeling, than if she had indeed been an animal of a different species:

Holding her in no special honor, as if it were the death of a beast where sheep abound in well-fleeced flocks, he sacrificed his own child. (1415–17)

The speaker is Clytemnestra; but she echoes here, as we shall see, the Chorus's own response to the tragic events.

The sacrifice of Iphigenia is regarded by the Chorus as necessary; but they also blame Agamemnon. Critics have usually explained away either the necessity or the blame, feeling that these must be incompatible. Some have introduced, instead, a hypothesis of 'overdetermined' or 'double' motivation that is explicitly said to exemplify Aeschylus's disregard for rational and logical thought.[25] It is, however, possible to arrive at a coherent understanding of both aspects of the situation, if only we look more precisely at the nature and genesis of this necessity and also at what the Chorus finds blameworthy in the conduct of their chief. First of all, it is clear that the situation forcing the killing is the outcome of the contingent intersection of two divine demands and that no personal guilt of Agamemnon's own has led him into this tragic predicament. The expedition was commanded by Zeus (55–62) to avenge the violation of a crime against hospitality.

The Chorus asserts this with as much confidence as they assert anything about these events. In the first stasimon they say of the Trojans, 'They can speak of a stroke from Zeus: this, at least, one can make out.' Agamemnon is, then, fighting in a just cause, and a cause that he could not desert without the most serious impiety.[26] The killing is forced by Artemis, who has in anger becalmed the expedition. Calchas divines that the only remedy for this situation is the sacrifice of Iphigenia.[27] The anger of the goddess, said in other versions of the story to have been caused by a previous offense of Agamemnon's, is left, here, unexplained. Whether we are to infer that her anger is caused by her general pro-Trojan sympathies or by her horror, as protector of the young, at the impending slaughter of Trojan innocents, the force of Aeschylus's omission of a personal offense is to emphasize the contingent and external origin\ of Agamemnon's dreadful dilemma. It simply comes upon him as he is piously executing Zeus's command.[28] (Later the men of the Chorus, singing of their vague foreboding of Agamemnon's death, invoke the image of a man who was sailing his ship on a straight course and came to grief on hidden rocks (1005–7).) There is a background guilt at work in the situation: the guilt of Atreus, which is visited by Zeus upon his offspring. But this fact does not prevent us from asking precisely *how* the familial guilt attaches itself to Agamemnon. And when we do so we must answer that Zeus has attached this guilt to him by placing him, a previously guiltless man, in a situation in which there is open to him no guilt-free course.[29] Such situations may be repellent to practical logic; they are also familiar from the experience of life.

Agamemnon is told by the prophet that if he does not offer up his daughter as a sacrifice, the entire expedition will remain becalmed. Already men are starving (188–9), and winds blowing from the Strymon 'were wearing and wasting away the flower of the Argives' (189–90). If Agamemnon does not fulfill Artemis's condition, everyone, including Iphigenia, will die. He will also be abandoning the expedition and, therefore, violating the command of Zeus. He will be a *deserter* (*liponaus*,[30] 212). It may, furthermore, depending upon our understanding of Artemis's requirements, be an act of disobedience against her. To perform the sacrifice will be, however, to perform a horrible and guilty act. We can see that one choice, the choice to sacrifice Iphigenia, seems clearly preferable, both because of consequences and because of the impiety involved in the other choice. Indeed, it is hard to imagine that Agamemnon could rationally have chosen any other way. But both courses involve him in guilt.[31]

Agamemnon is allowed to choose: that is to say, he knows what he is doing; he is neither ignorant of the situation nor physically compelled; nothing forces him to choose one course rather than the other. But he is under necessity in that his alternatives include no very desirable options. There appears to be no incompatibility between choice and necessity here – unless one takes the ascription of choice to imply that the agent is free to do anything at all. On the contrary, the situation seems to describe quite precisely a kind of interaction between external constraint and personal choice that is found to one degree or another in any ordinary situation of choice.[32] For a choice is always a choice among possible alternatives; and it is a rare agent for whom everything is possible. The special agony of this situation is that none of the possibilities is even harmless.

Agamemnon's first response is anger and grief: 'The Atreidae beat the ground with their staffs, and could not keep back their tears' (203–4). He then describes his predicament, apparently with full recognition of both competing claims. He acknowledges that there is wrong done whichever way he chooses:

A heavy doom is disobedience, but heavy, too, if I shall rend my own child, the adornment of my house, polluting a father's hands with streams of slaughtered maiden's blood close by the altar. Which of these is without evils? How should I become a deserter, failing in my duty to the alliance? (206–13)

Agamemnon's statement of the alternatives shows us his sense that the *better* choice in the situation is the sacrifice: the future indicative in 'if I shall rend my own child' (*ei teknon daïxō*) is not parallel to the weak deliberative subjunctive of 'How should I become a deserter?' (*pōs liponaus genōmai*). But he indicates, too, that both choices involve evil.[33]

So far, Agamemnon's situation seems to resemble the plight of Abraham on the mountain: a good and (so far) innocent man must either kill an innocent child out of obedience to a divine command, or incur the heavier guilt of disobedience and impiety.[34] We might, then, expect to see next the delicate struggle between love and pious obligation that we sense in Abraham's equivocal words to Isaac, followed by a sacrifice executed with horror and reluctance. But something strange takes place. The Chorus had already prepared us for it in introducing their narrative: 'Blaming no prophet, he blew together with the winds of luck that struck against him' (186–8). The bold wind metaphor coined by the Chorus (the word *sumpneō* is used here, apparently, for the first time in Greek) expresses an unnatural cooperation of internal with external forces. Voicing no blame of the prophet or his terrible message, Agamemnon now begins to cooperate inwardly with necessity, arranging his feelings to accord with his fortune. From the moment he makes his decision, itself the best he could have made, he strangely turns himself into a collaborator, a willing victim.[35]

Once he had stated the alternatives and announced his decision, Agamemnon might have been expected to say something like, 'This horrible course is what divine necessity requires, though I embark on it with pain and revulsion.' What he actually says is very different: 'For it is right and holy (*themis*) that I should desire with exceedingly impassioned passion (*orgai periorgōs epithumein*) the sacrifice staying the winds, the maiden's blood.[36] May all turn out well' (214–17). We notice two points in this strange and appalling utterance. First, his attitude towards the decision itself seems to have changed with the making of it. From the acknowledgement that a heavy doom awaits him either way, and that either alternative involves wrongdoing, he has moved to a peculiar optimism: if he has chosen the *better* course, all may yet turn out *well*. An act that we were prepared to view as the lesser of two hideous wrongs and impieties has now become for him pious and right, as though by some art of decision-making he had resolved the conflict and disposed of the other 'heavy doom'. At the same time, we notice that the correctness of his decision is taken by him to justify not only action, but also passion: if it is right to obey the god, it is right to *want* to obey him, to have an appetite (*epithumein*) for the crime, even to yearn for it with exceedingly impassioned passion. Agamemnon seems to have assumed, first, that if he decided right, the action chosen must be right; and, second, that if an action is right, it is appropriate to want it, even to be enthusiastic about it. From 'Which of these is without evils?' he has moved to 'May all turn out well.' The Chorus's repeated refrain is, 'Sing sorrow, sorrow, but may the good prevail' (139, 159). Agamemnon's conclusion, which from one point of view seems logical and even rational, omits the sorrow and the struggle, leaving only the good. If we accept the assimilation of practical conflict to disagreement and of practical claims to beliefs, we ourselves must travel this path with him: for at most one requirement could be legitimate or valid. If we find it, it is the true obligation, and the other one naturally ceases to exert any claim on our attention. And what could be wrong with loving truth and duty?

'And when he had slipped his neck through the yoke-strap of necessity', the Chorus continues, 'blowing his thought in an impious change of direction, from that moment he changed his mind and turned to thinking the all-daring. For men are made bold by base-counselling wretched madness' (219–24). Agamemnon's inference from the necessity of the act to its rightness, and to the rightness of supportive feelings, is called tantamount to putting necessity's yoke-strap on one's own neck,[37] blowing one's own thoughts before the wind. The Chorus does not so much blame the fact of the action, for which they feel the gods bear a primary responsibility, though indeed it is a serious crime; they call upon Zeus here, as if to understand the meaning of his violent intrusions into human life (160ff.). What they impute to Agamemnon himself is the change of thought and passion accompanying the killing, for which they clearly hold him responsible.[38] 'He dared (*etla*) to become the sacrificer of his daughter' (225) – not just *became*, but endured to become. He put up with it; he did not struggle against it. Their description of his behavior in the execution of the sacrifice bears out this charge. Her prayers, her youth, her cries of 'Father', this father 'counted as nothing' (230), treating his daughter, from then on, as an animal victim to be slaughtered. So the eagle omen, as read by the prophet, has its fulfillment. Faithful to his king, he told it the way the king would see it. After the usual prayer, Agamemnon commands the attendants to lift Iphigenia 'like a goat' (232) in the air above the altar. His only acknowledgement of her human status is his command to stop her mouth, so she will not utter inauspicious curses against the house (235–7). And even this command uses animal language: they are to check her voice 'by the force and the voiceless power of the bridle' (238–9). Apparently he does not see what the Chorus sees:

> Her saffron robes streaming to the ground,
> she shot each of the sacrificers with a pitiful arrow from her eye,
> standing out as in a picture,

wanting to speak to them by name –
for often in her father's halls, at the rich feasts given for men,
she had sung, and, virginal, with pure voice,
at the third libation, had lovingly honored
her loving father's paean of good fortune. (239–45)

The shift from report of Agamemnon's commands to the Chorus's own memory brings with it the only note of compassionate humanity in this terrible scene. Never, in the choral narration or subsequently, do we hear the king utter a word of regret or painful memory. No doubt he would endorse the glib summary of his career given by Apollo in the *Eumenides* trial scene: 'He made good bargains, for the most part' (*Eum.* 631–2).

The distinguished historian of Greek religion Walter Burkert has argued for an account of the origins of Greek tragedy that would, if accepted, add a further historical and religious dimension to our reading of this scene.[39] Although in fact I find Burkert's arguments compelling, I do not anywhere rely on their correctness in developing my interpretation of the scene. But it will prove suggestive to juxtapose them with my interpretation.

The ceremony of animal sacrifice, from which Greek tragedy, in Burkert's view, derives its name, expressed the awe and fear felt by this human community towards its own murderous possibilities. By ritually acting out the killing of an animal, not a human victim, and by surrounding even this killing with a ceremony indicative of the killers' innocence and their respect for life, the sacrificers, actors in this 'Comedy of Innocence' (*Unschuldskomödie*)[40] distance themselves from, and at the same time acknowledge, the possibilities for human slaughter that reside in human nature. By expressing their ambivalence and remorse concerning even an animal killing, by humanizing the animal and showing a regard for its 'will', the sacrificers put away from themselves the worst possibility: that they will kill human beings, and kill without pity, becoming themselves bestial. Their ritual actions assert their humanity and at the same time their fear of ceasing to be human. 'Human sacrifice... is a possibility which, as a horrible threat, stands behind every sacrifice.'[41] It is the work of tragedy, song of the goat-sacrifice, to continue and deepen this function of ritual by bringing the hidden threat to light, by acting out, repeatedly, the possibilities for bestiality concealed and distanced by human society.

We can see (as Burkert's work suggests) that the sacrifice of Iphigenia fits precisely into this pattern. Agamemnon's stay at Aulis began with the pitiless killing of one animal by another, interpreted as a non-ritual (therefore remorseless) slaughter of cattle by humans. He now uses (or abuses) the ritual of animal sacrifice to act out the very possibility that this ritual keeps at bay. (Several words in the passage are technical terms in sacrificial rituals well known to the audience: the saffron robe (238) was worn by young girls at the Brauronia, where a goat is sacrificed to Artemis; *ataurōtos*, 'not-bulled' (245) is a technical ritual term designating virginity; the *proteleia* (227) is a sacrifice to Artemis made by Athenian girls before marriage.) Instead of the ritual killing of a 'willing' goat, we see the murder of an unwilling girl, his own child, whom he treats, whom he sees, as if she were a 'willing' goat. We are invited to witness the monstrous ease with which these boundaries are broken down, these substitutions made.[42] We witness, what is more, the clever way in which norms of rationality and consistency are pressed into service when their service will bring safety. We are invited to see how easily, in human lives, with what dexterous sleight-of-hand, human beings substitute human for animal, and animal for human, and stranger for loved one, under pressures endemic to life in a world where choice is constrained by necessity.

Eteocles, king of Thebes, son of Oedipus, faces an invading army led by his brother Polynices.[43] Having already selected six other Theban champions to oppose six of the seven enemy champions at the gates, he now discovers that the seventh opponent is this same brother. At first he cries out, lamenting the curse upon his family (653–5). He then pulls himself up short, declaring that 'it is not fitting to weep or grieve' (656): for against this brother's unjust violence he will station an appropriate champion, himself:

Who else would it be more just (*endikōteros*) to send? Leader against leader, brother against brother, foe against foe, I shall stand against him. Bring me my greaves as quickly as possible, to shield me from the spears and stones. (673–6)

This reasoning looks peculiar: the category of brother does not seem to work the way the other two do, towards justifying Eteocles' decision. He appears to be missing something if he feels no pull in the opposite direction, no tension between his civic and military obligations and his duties as a brother.[44] The evident needs of the city pull against an equally profound requirement. Tears, and not the refusal of tears, would appear to be the more appropriate response. Suppose that in fact only a ruler is equipped to meet a ruler; suppose that the safety of the city really depends on this choice, and that, in consequence, Eteocles' decision is a noble one. Let us say (what the play does not make entirely clear) that nobody could reproach him with having made the wrong actual choice from among the available alternatives.[45] Still, we want to say that there is something wrong with this blank dismissal of the family tie. The Chorus of Theban women, themselves mothers of families, feels this strangeness, reproaching their king not so much for his decision – or at any rate not only for his decision – but, far more, for the responses and feelings with which he approaches the chosen action. 'O child of Oedipus, dearest of men', they implore him, 'do not become similar in passion (*orgēn*) to a person who is called by the worst names' (677–8). He is showing the feelings of a criminal, although he may have reasoned well. Again they implore him: 'Why are you so eager, child? Do not let some spear-craving delusion (*ata*), filling your spirit (*thumoplēthēs*), bear you away. Cast out the authority of this bad passion (*kakou erōtos*)' (686–8). Eteocles, having already shifted, like Agamemnon, from horror to confidence, now replies with an Agamemnon-like inference: 'Since it is clear that the situation is controlled by a god, it is appropriate to go quickly' (689–90). Constraint licenses eagerness. Again the women respond by blaming his enthusiasm: 'Too ravenous is the desire (*himeros*) that goads you on to accomplish a man-killing that bears bitter fruit, shedding blood not to be shed' (692–4). Eteocles' reply grants that he does indeed feel a passionate desire for fratricide (note the use of *gar*); he neither denies this nor regrets it, he simply tries to explain the desire's origin.[46]

Eteocles, like Agamemnon, faces a situation in which he has, it appears, no innocent alternative. Unlike Agamemnon, he may be to some extent to blame for the genesis of the constraining circumstances, though it is clear that forces and coincidences beyond his control are the main governing items.[47] Unlike Agamemnon again, he may or may not have made the better of the available choices. But what we, with the women of the Chorus, feel most clearly is, as in Agamemnon's case, the perversity of the king's imaginative and emotional responses to this serious practical dilemma. He appears to feel no opposing claim, no pull, no reluctance. He goes ahead with eagerness, even passion. It is around these deficiencies of vision and response that the blame of the Chorus centers: his eagerness, his bad *erōs*, his bestially hungry desire. Whether or not they would have him choose differently, they are clear that he has made things too simple. He has failed to see and respond to his conflict as the conflict it is; this crime compounds the already serious burden of his action.

Eteocles has made it his lifelong practical aim to dissociate himself, in imagination and feeling, from the family that bore him, regarding himself simply as a citizen and the city's helmsman (1ff.).[48] He even attempts to believe and to propagate the fiction that all Thebans grew from shoots planted in the earth, extending to the entire population a legend told of a few of the earliest inhabitants. He speaks of his fellow citizens in language appropriate to the life and growth of plants, comparing their bodies to young shoots and calling Earth their 'mother' and 'nurse' (12, 16ff., 557). Even the women of the Chorus, who so often stress their concern for the safety of their families, are addressed as 'You insufferable shoots' (191). It emerges from the later biographies of the champions that only a few living citizens are even descendants of the original 'sown men'; and at least one of these is a generation removed, born from a biological father (cf. 412–14, 473–4). Ironically, it is in connection with the only one of the race of 'sown men' who may in fact be a direct descendant of Earth, without biological parents, that Eteocles invokes 'the justice of consanguinity' (*dikē homaimōn*, 415). This justice, he claims, will send the champion out into the field in defense of the city, 'to ward off the enemy spear from the mother who bore him' (416). Only of Melanippos, in fact, could it be truly said that the justice of consanguinity unproblematically endorses participation in civil war. And yet Eteocles behaves as if all cases were of this same type, calling all young men sons of mother earth, all young women shoots. If he is able to solve the dilemma of brother-killing without pain, it is because he has resolutely refused to acknowledge the existence of families and their importance in human life. Consistency in conflict is bought at the price of self-deception.

We should not think this pattern of response idiosyncratic and merely pathological. In one sense it is the response of a good ruler and patriot. And in one sense it would be the response of every good male citizen in this audience of Athenians. For Athenian males are reared on a mythology of autochthony that persistently, and paradoxically, suppresses the biological role of the female and therefore the family in the continuity of the city. Public political rhetoric frequently calls citizens the children of the city itself, or of her earth. The first parent of Athens, Erichthonius, is said to have been born directly out of the earth, and then reared by Athena, herself born without a biological mother.[49] This mythology is prominent enough in civic political and religious discourse to reflect and reinforce a suppression of the familial, even though in some sense it was not literally believed, and though in other contexts the family received a fuller measure of respect. We now see the civic utility in this stratagem: it teaches citizens to consider that in the eventuality of internecine strife their only serious loyalty is indeed to the city; to feel a conflict will be to misunderstand their own origins. Aeschylus seems to be reflecting, then, on a style of thought, or of avoidance of thought, that is far from idiosyncratic, but on the contrary very fundamental to his way of life. He is showing how such refusals help citizens avoid the tear of conflicting claims. And he is suggesting that the cost of this simplicity may be too high. For it is attended by a false perception of the city and by gravely deficient responses to non-civic ties to which deep respect is owed. By linking these deficiencies with the accursed fratricidal nightmares of Eteocles son of Oedipus (709–11), he may even be suggesting that to fail to cultivate proper non-civic responses is to give encouragement to the bad passions that lurk in the hearts of most members of families. He also shows us that it is possible for the city to cultivate proper acknowledgement: for the messenger who brings the news of Eteocles' death pointedly addresses the Chorus as 'Daughters reared from mothers' (792). Now that the fictions of the king are extinguished, the depth of family ties can be recognized and the family–city conflict seen for what it is.

The play's ending, if it is authentic,[50] seems to show us how the Chorus will acknowledge what Eteocles did not. While Creon and Antigone clash over the burial of Polynices, the Chorus splits in half. In a finale unparalleled in extant tragedy, they exit split, one half following Creon and the corpse of Eteocles, the other half following Antigone and the corpse of Polynices. 'We will go and bury him,' says the other, '…for this is a common grief for our family line, and a city has different ways, at different times, of praising justice' (1068–71). The splitting of what had been single recognizes the claims of both sides. If we think of the Chorus as composed of many individuals, the recognition looks incomplete, since the conflict is once again understood as a form of disagreement, and each individual acknowledges only one of the claims. But if we think of it, as we probably should, as standing in for each one of us, having a single imagination, a single set of feelings, then what we see is a responsive 'individual' acting out the complex reaction to dilemma which Eteocles failed to give. This reading is supported by the final lines of the second half-chorus, which insist that justice, even civic justice, is not a simple thing.

IV

We have now seen two practical conflicts. Each of them is concerned, on both sides, with values that are important within the conception of human excellence held by the Chorus in each play. By reviewing our eight points we can see that in other ways as well they seem strong candidates for the ascription of serious ethical blame. In each case the conflict has forced an action that goes against values seriously held by the Choruses, and, in one case, by the agent as well; in both cases the action also violates a prior obligation of the agent, explicit or implicit; in both cases there is irreparable damage done to another person, in a way that will clearly bring far-reaching consequences for the rest of the agent's life. But we must now look more closely at two particular observations made by the Choruses, as they examine their kings' deficient responses. First, both Choruses insist on the importance to assessment of our distinction between reparable and irreparable crimes, arguing that some offenses are so severe in their effects that their commission, even under situational constraint, must be followed by a serious punishment. The Chorus of the *Seven* emphasizes the distinction between ordinary killing in war, after which one can undertake a ritual purification, and the much more serious crime of killing an irreplaceable member of one's own family: '*That pollution never grows old*' (680–2). The *Agamemnon* Chorus speaks of the difference between a merely economic loss and the loss of a life. The merchant who is forced to throw his cargo overboard escapes drowning. 'His entire house does not founder', and he will have a chance to recover the lost wealth (1007–17). 'But a man's dark blood once it has fallen to the ground, who, by incantation, can call it up again?' (1018–21). They sense, therefore, that their king must and ought to be punished. Even crimes forced by necessity, if they are of this magnitude, cry out for a penalty. The helpless Orestes, forced by a god's command to kill his guilty mother, and far more appropriately reluctant before this awful act, must also have his punishment: the madness of remorse and pursuit by his mother's Furies. The downfall of Agamemnon and the Furies of Orestes answer to our intuitive demand that even the constrained killer should come to regard himself as a killer and should suffer, in his own person, for his deed. These divine interventions into human life are not arbitrary or capricious: they enact a deep ethical response that would be intelligible in the absence of the divine.[51] Even if Orestes did the best thing possible in the circumstances, what he has done, and done intentionally, with his eyes open, is so bad that he cannot go on living his life as if he had not done it. We might say that Orestes is not mad, but at his most sane, when he recognizes that the Furies are in pursuit. The ending of the *Oresteia* (cf. also Ch. 13) shows us that the healthy city does not permit the guilt of such situations to continue indefinitely. The city, under Athena's guidance, devises procedures (which are probably intended to look more than a little arbitrary) in order to permit the full release of such a suffering offender; it also tells us that the guilt will no longer be allowed to descend without limit through the generations. But Athena emphasizes at the same time that the moral fear associated with the Furies will have an important place in her healthy city: they are reformed, but given a place of honor. For there are, she says, times when fear is a good and appropriate thing.[52] These situations of practical conflict look like such times.

The Choruses make a second point. Even if we say that the agent chose and acted under situational constraint, and so may bear a diminished guilt for his or her bad action, this is not the end of the question of praise and blame. If there is much that he cannot help, there is much, nonetheless, that he apparently can: his emotional responses to the dilemma, his thoughts about the claims involved. They seem to believe that a good person, finding him or herself in such a situation, will, first of all, see it as what it is. If he is of good character, he will have brought to the situation a lively imagination and a complex set of responses that will enable him to see the conflict situation as a situation that forces him to act against his character. He will not inhibit these thoughts in the event. Eteocles comes to the situation with an artificially impoverished set of concerns that prevent him from seeing it correctly. Agamemnon seems to repudiate or suppress initially accurate judgments.[53] Once the decision is reached, the case appears soluble, the competing claim 'counts as nothing'. A proper response, by contrast, would begin with the acknowledgement that this is not simply a hard case of discovering truth; it is a case where the agent will have to do wrong.

Such a response would continue with a vivid imagining of both sides of the dilemma, in a conscientious attempt to see the many relevant features of the case as truly and distinctly as possible. For even if the agent comes to the dilemma with good general principles, the case does not present itself with labels written on it, indicating its salient features. To pick these out, he must interpret it; and since often the relevant features emerge distinctly only through memory and projection of a more complicated kind, he will have to use imagination as well as perception. Agamemnon would have to see (as he begins to do) the heavy consequences of disobedience to a god, and, more important, its gross impiety. He would have to think about piety, about his conception of god, about what it really means to him to obey a god, about what it means that his theology recognizes a plurality of divinities who can make conflicting claims. This is what the Chorus does in the hymn to Zeus that interrupts their narrative (160–84). They ask, through mythological imagination, what this god can be like and what he means to show us by his violence. On the other side, Agamemnon would have to allow himself really to *see* his daughter, to see not just the sacrificial goat that he allows himself to see, but all that the Chorus sees: the trailing yellow robes, the prayers, the cries of 'Father', the look of accusation in the silent eyes. He would have to let himself remember, as they remember, her sweet voice, her dutiful and loving presence at his table. Eteocles would have to imagine, as he does, the doom of a city enslaved to an alien enemy; and he would have to let himself see, as a part of this, the tragedy of war-stricken *families*, so vividly depicted throughout by the Chorus, to his annoyance and displeasure. He would also have to allow himself to think of what it means to have grown up with this brother Polynices; to have shared with him not only birth, wealth, power, but also the heavy awareness of a father-brother's crime, the 'seed sown in his mother's holy furrow' (152–3), and, when that came to light, the weight of a father-brother's curse. Perhaps this truthful imaginative seeing would lead to agonizing indecision, or perhaps the decision itself would soon become clear. The correct perception of a conflict need not entail indecision, since there can be such conflicts even where the claims are not evenly balanced. Indecision by itself does not appear to be a virtue or decisiveness a deficiency.

Finally, the good agent will also feel and exhibit the feelings appropriate to a person of good character caught in such a situation. He will not regard the fact of decision as licensing feelings of self-congratulation, much less feelings of unqualified enthusiasm for the act chosen. He will show in his emotive behavior, and also genuinely feel, that this is an act deeply repellent to him and to his character. Though he must, to some extent, *act* like a person 'who is called by the worst names', he will show himself to be utterly dissimilar to such a person in 'passion', in the emotional dispositions that form a part of his character. And after the action he will remember, regret, and, where possible, make reparations. His emotion, moreover, will not be simply regret, which could be felt and expressed by an uninvolved spectator and does not imply that he himself has acted badly. It will be an emotion more like remorse, closely bound up with acknowledgement of the wrong that he has as an agent, however reluctantly, done. (In a legal case with which I am familiar, the defense lawyer permitted his client to express only *regret* in a letter to an inconvenienced bystander, and not to make any apology or to express any emotion that involved the admission of defective action of any kind. The Chorus's point would be that the agent in these cases must go beyond what a good defense lawyer would allow.)

Once we notice the importance of emotional factors in the Chorus's blame, we are led to take a new look at a passage in the *Agamemnon* that has baffled interpreters. In a bold criticism of their returning king, the elders appear to state explicitly that their condemnation is directed at passions, and passions that they regard as 'willing', i.e., as meeting conditions for the reasonable ascription of praise and blame: 'At the time when you were leading the army forth for Helen's sake – I will not conceal it from you – you were drawn unharmoniously in my thoughts, as one who was not wielding well the helm of sense, nourishing a willing boldness of temper (*tharsos hekousion*) on behalf of men who were then dying' (799–804). I have offered a straightforward translation of the Greek of the manuscripts,[54] frequently emended as unintelligible. The phrase *tharsos hekousion*, 'willing boldness of temper', has struck many commentators as impossible: for surely, they argue, only *actions*, not *passions*, can be *hekousion* or *akousion*,[55] open or not open to praise and blame.[56] It has, accordingly, either been removed by emendation or understood as a condemnatory periphrasis for Helen, that 'willing wanton'.[57] (In this case the verb *komizō* must be read as 'bringing back', a translation that involves several serious difficulties.)[58] The references to blame and to dying men clearly recall, however, the events of Aulis. The way in which Agamemnon was 'not wielding well the helm of sense' in their earlier description of those events was a way that the straightforward translation of *tharsos hekousion* captures very well: he nourished and encouraged a monstrous boldness and daring, in accomplishing the sacrifice on behalf of his dying men. Only a prejudice concerning the voluntary nature of the passions, a prejudice deeply rooted in post-Kantian times, with strong backing from Plato, but unknown to Aeschylus and criticized by Aristotle (cf. Chs. 9, 10), has prevented the serious consideration of a reading that would make this later remark the appropriate summary of the Chorus's earlier Aulis narrative. No doubt this suggestion will remain controversial; my argument about the other scenes does not depend on it. But it may prove to be an attractive feature of that argument that it promises to make good sense of the original text of a passage that has puzzled us.

Two further points in these choral reflections call for comment. First, the blameworthy elements of the kings' responses are described as external displays. This is inevitable in a dramatic interaction: the Chorus speaks of what it sees. But we are also made to feel that there would be a great difference for them between the successful counterfeit of appropriate emotion and a genuinely inner response. Agamemnon is accused of cherishing his boldness, of changing his thoughts; Eteocles is said to be like a bad person in passion, not simply in behavior. They bring their charges against his 'spirit-filling delusion', his 'ravenous desire' – although of necessity they infer these from the external behavior. Nor, we are clear, would their demand for imaginative and emotional responsibility be satisfied by counterfeit, by mere unexceptionable behavior. Their words just before the blameful greeting of Agamemnon show that they are very conscious of the possibility of concealing feelings, or feigning sympathy in a case where 'the bite of grief does not penetrate to the liver'; but they dissociate themselves from the 'many men' who prefer seeming to being, calling this preference a transgression of justice. They regard the presence or absence of certain feelings and thoughts as revealing something significant about the character with whom they are dealing. If the person does not have, but only feigns, the responses, whether through hypocrisy or through a sincere desire to do justice to the situation, these men and women will form different judgments, praise and blame in different ways. They are well aware that in practice it is not possible to be certain about this distinction; they stress it nonetheless.

We have been speaking of the conflict situation as a test of character. In fact these cases do give us new information about what the agent's character has been all along. (And thus, to return to the theological background, the guilt of the family works itself out here through assessible features of the agent's own nature.) But we must now add, with the *Agamemnon* Chorus, that the experience of conflict can also be a time of learning and development. The deep meaning of the proverbial *pathei mathos*, repeated both just before and just after the narrative of the slaughter of Iphigenia (177, 250), is that hard cases like these, if one allows oneself really to see and to experience them, may bring progress along with their sorrow, a progress that comes from an increase in self-knowledge and knowledge of the world. An honest effort to do justice to all aspects of a hard case, seeing and feeling it in all its conflicting many-sidedness, could enrich future deliberative efforts. Through the experience of choice, Eteocles might have discovered concerns to which justice had not previously been done; Agamemnon might have come to a new understanding of piety and of the love he owes his family. It is, of course, possible to work towards such a just appreciation of the complexity of the claims upon us in the course of ordinary life, without tragic conflict or tragic suffering. The tragedians, however, notice that often it takes the shock of such suffering to make us look and see. Neoptolemus, in Sophocles' *Philoctetes*, does not know what it is to respect another person's pain until he, too, is made to cry in pain. When, by pain, he learns how his ambitious plan conflicts with his attachment to truth-telling and justice, he ceases to be called 'child', and takes upon himself the responsibility of deciding.[59] Euripides' Admetus does not know until he loses Alcestis what it was to have a wife, indeed what it is to love another separate human being. 'Now I understand', he exclaims in the midst of remorse and self-accusation. And, when his luck turns out to be reversible, 'Now I shall change my life to a better one than before' (1158).

We can say more. So far we have spoken as if the experience of grief is a means to a knowledge of self that is by and in the intellect alone. We have, that is, spoken as if we took *pathei mathos* to mean 'through the means of suffering (experience) comes (intellectual) understanding'. A full and correct understanding of our human practical situation is available in principle to unaided intellect; these people require passional response only because of their deficiencies and blind spots. This reading, which in effect makes the whole experience of tragedy (both in drama and in life) of merely instrumental worth, seems to me to trivialize the poets' claim against the (anti-poetic) philosophers and to skew the debate in a way that is advantageous to the latter. We would do more justice to the Aeschylean claim if we considered another possibility. Here we would see the passional reaction, the suffering, as itself a piece of practical recognition or perception, as at least a partial constituent of the character's correct understanding of his situation as a human being. Neoptolemus's outcry, the Chorus's sleepless agonies, are not means to a grasp that is in the intellect by itself; they are pieces of recognition or acknowledgement of difficult human realities. There is a kind of knowing that works by suffering because suffering is the appropriate acknowledgement of the way human life, in these cases, is. And in general: to grasp either a love or a tragedy by intellect is not sufficient for having real human knowledge of it. Agamemnon *knows that* Iphigenia is his child all through, if by this we mean that he has the correct beliefs, can answer many questions about her truly, etc. But because in his emotions, his imagination and his behavior he does not acknowledge the tie, we want to join the Chorus in saying that his state is less one of knowledge than one of delusion. He doesn't *really know* that she is his daughter. A piece of true understanding is missing (cf. also Ch. 10, Interlude 2). Some may be lucky enough to have this understanding, these accurate responses and recognitions, without extreme tragic situations. Some, like our two heroes, may go through tragic situations in a condition of delusion and denial. Some people might even be coarsened by the painful experience and made worse (cf. Ch. 13). But there are also those for whom good fortune may be a misfortune and tragedy lucky, in that accurate human recognition may for them require the exposure and surprise of the tragic situation. Recognition here may then foster recognition in other areas of life. This may be what the Chorus means when, at the conclusion of their hymn to Zeus, they speak of 'a grace that comes by violence from the gods, as they sit on the dread bench of the helmsman' (182–3).

It is evident, too, that the exploration of such conflicts through our own *pathē* as spectators, our own responses of fear and of pity, is supposed to provide us with, and to help to constitute, just this sort of learning. The poets offer us not simply an alternative route to a contemplative or Platonic type of knowing; their disagreement with Plato is more profound. They claim to offer us an occasion for an activity of knowing that could not even in principle be had by the intellect alone. If their claim is plausible, then their works (or works like theirs) are not optional, but ineliminable in a full investigation of these matters. (We shall pursue their claim further in Interlude 2.)

We have begun to see, by this time, a certain logic in the illogical world of Aeschylus. We have seen, in particular, that a contingent conflict between two ethical claims need not be taken for a logical contradiction; and that the 'inconsistency' between freedom and necessity can, similarly, be seen as a correct description of the way in which natural circumstances restrict the possibilities for choice. In these respects the descriptions of Aeschylus seem to lie very close to our intuitive experience of dilemma. But there is one feature of these descriptions that may continue to appear foreign and strange. It may still be difficult for us to understand how it could be reasonable to praise and blame agents for things about them that do not appear to be under the control of reason or rational will: things like responsiveness, desire, passion, imagination. We have already seen the depth of this difficulty as it affected the interpretation of the Chorus's greeting. Since this is a central issue in Aristotle's view of character and action, we will examine it more fully at a later time.[60] But the tragic examples give us some help with the difficulty. The person who feels a difficulty here does so, we suspect, because he or she assumes that emotional responses are not subject to any sort of control and cannot form part of a character that an agent deliberately forms. But the examples show Agamemnon 'fostering', 'blowing', 'turning' his strange feelings and responses, Eteocles 'stirring himself up', shaping and forming his feelings in keeping with his narrow picture of what matters. They show us, above all, the men and women of these Choruses making themselves look, notice, respond and remember, cultivating responsiveness by working through the memory of these events, until 'the painful memory of pain drips, instead of sleep, before the heart' (*Ag.* 179–80).[61] The presentness of the Chorus before this action, and their patient work, even years later, on the story of that action reminds us that responsive attention to these complexities is a job that practical rationality can, and should, undertake to perform; and that this job of rationality claims more from the agent than the exercise of reason or intellect, narrowly conceived.[62] We see thought and feeling working together, so that it is difficult to distinguish the one from the other: the painful memory of pain, dripping before the heart. We see, too, a two-way interchange of illumination and cultivation working between emotions and thoughts: we see feelings prepared by memory and deliberation, learning brought about through *pathos*. (At the same time we ourselves, if we are good spectators, will find this complex interaction in our own responses.) When we notice the ethical fruitfulness of these exchanges, when we see the *rationality* of the passions as they lead thought towards human understanding, and help to constitute this understanding, then we may feel that the burden of proof is shifted to the defender of the view that only intellect and will are appropriate objects of ethical assessment. Such a conception may begin to look impoverished. The plays show us the practical wisdom and ethical accountability of a contingent mortal being in a world of natural happening. Such a being is neither a pure intellect nor a pure will; nor would he deliberate better in this world if he were.

V

We must now return to the philosophers who assimilate these conflicts to disagreements, asking what light the tragic cases have shed on their arguments. For Sartre, the moral of these hard cases is that it is useless for an agent to form an ordered system of ethical principles and to try to live by that system. What Agamemnon sees is that the principles of obedience to the god and of family obligation can clash irreconcilably, so that one must be violated. This experience is supposed to show him that it is no good living by principled commitment at all; being bound in general to what in extreme cases cannot guide you is foolish bad faith. If Agamemnon were a Sartrean hero, he would, in the moment of conflict, dissociate himself altogether from both of the competing principles, regarding himself as entirely free, unbound, and unsubstantial, asserting his radical liberty in unregretted choice.

This approach to Agamemnon's dilemma has the virtue of regarding it as a serious crisis in his ethical life; but it defuses the crisis by means that seem arbitrary and strange. The case has shown us that two life-guiding commitments may conflict in a particular contingency; it certainly has not shown us that there is any logical contradiction between them, or, more to the point, that they offer bad guidance in the vast majority of deliberative situations.[63] We have not yet asked how much risk of conflict in a set of commitments is sufficient to make them irrational; but we certainly feel that there is nothing irrational about a set of commitments that can clash in a very rare and strange situation. Furthermore, it is not even clear that, in this strange situation, Agamemnon's commitments do offer him bad guidance. The guidance they offer him is that he should feel bound to each of two contingently incompatible actions; and therefore, if they are contingently incompatible, that he should respond and think like a man who is forced to go against that to which he feels bound. But insofar as such thoughts and feelings both express and further strengthen a virtuous and committed character, this guidance seems to be good. It is the Sartrean picture of an agent without character and principles, improvising his freedom, that is difficult for us to grasp. All of our judgments about the appropriateness of certain kinds of emotional and imaginative activity in our two cases has presupposed a background of ongoing character and value-commitments (the agent's own, or, where that proves deficient, the Chorus's) against which action and response can be assessed. The very possibility of moral assessment seems here to be bound up with the idea of ongoing character. We do not know how we would talk about an agent who kept improvising himself from moment to moment and was never willing to identify himself with any general commitments. The Chorus would surely recoil from an Agamemnon who boldly asserted his freedom from principle and proudly claimed the killing as an act of freedom. This is not far from what Agamemnon does; and they call him mad.

Hare's proposal is more moderate. We need not throw out the conflict-generating principles altogether. We must simply revise them so that they do not, after all, produce a conflict in this particular case. By admitting relevant classes of exceptions into the statement of the rules, we make them more precise and we come to future situations better prepared. In Agamemnon's case, Hare would reformulate the principle, 'Don't kill', or 'Don't kill members of your family', until it read, 'Don't kill members of your own family, except when constrained by a god.' *This* should really have been his principle all along. But we feel that our two cases are not the same as Hare's example of lying in wartime. In that case it may well be true that the exception is implicit in the rule and that nothing of great importance is altered by the modification. In our case we feel that the rule was simply 'Don't kill', and that this rule, as we have understood it, admits of no such exceptions. This does not mean that in no circumstances is it the best available course to kill; it does mean that even such rationally justifiable killings violate a moral claim and demand emotions and thoughts appropriate to a situation of violation. When we modify the rule as Hare suggests, there is the very change we noticed in Agamemnon's own deliberation: a change from horror to complacency, from the feeling that wrong must be done to the feeling that right has been discovered. This shift is not compatible with the insights of tragedy.

Finally we must return to Kant, whose demand for consistency among the principles of practical reason led him to defuse what his own view would naturally lead him to see as a deep conflict of practical obligations. The demand for consistency is certainly not a misconceived demand. But we need to distinguish, as Kant (like Sartre) does not in this passage on conflict of duty, a logical inconsistency from a contingent conflict. How far an agent's commitments must avoid the risk of conflict in order to be counted rational remains, as we said, an open question. But most complex sets of commitments risk conflict to some degree, in some possible situations, without looking internally incoherent or irrational. The risk of such conflicts is a fact of the practical life that seems to demand acknowledgement and scrutiny. Kant, however, is not able to agree. Where nothing in the will collides, the 'accidents of step-motherly nature' should not disturb the deliberations of the rational agent. The internal harmony and self-respect of the morally good person, the autonomous maker of his own law, cannot be affected by mere happenings in the world.[64] But let us now think seriously of Eteocles and Agamemnon as Kantian makers of law for their world. What we seem to see is that the recalcitrance of the contingent world to their legislative demands *has* affected their internal harmony. Specifically, it has made them do shameful things, in violation of their own laws, things that demand punishment according to the very standards of their own legislative codes. We could say to Kant that an agent who takes his principles seriously enough cannot but be stricken by the necessity of violating them. If the law is really a law, then the transgression is really a transgression – at least if the agent acts deliberately and in full awareness of what he is doing – no matter whether the situation was of his own making or not. A duty not to kill is a duty in all circumstances. Why should this circumstance of conflict make it cease to be a duty? But if a law is broken, there has to be a condemnation and a punishment. That is what it means to take the law seriously, to take one's own autonomy seriously. Kant's view does, ironically, just what Kant wishes it to avoid: it gives mere chance the power to remove an agent from the binding authority of the moral law. We can claim to be following a part of the deep motivation behind Kant's own view of duty when we insist that duty does not go away because of the world's contingent interventions. Greek polytheism, surprisingly, articulates a certain element of Kantian morality better than any monotheistic creed could: namely, it insists upon the supreme and binding authority, the divinity so to speak, of *each* ethical obligation, in all circumstances whatever, including those in which the gods themselves collide.

Aeschylus, then, shows us not so much a 'solution' to the 'problem of practical conflict' as the richness and depth of the problem itself. (This achievement is closely connected with his poetic resources, which put the scene vividly before us, show us debate about it, and evoke in us responses important to its assessment.) He has, then, done the first thing that needed to be done in order to challenge theoretical solutions to the problem. But if we recognize what he has put before us, we must recognize, too, that the 'solutions' do not really solve the problem. They simply underdescribe or misdescribe it. They fail to observe things that are here to be seen: the force of the losing claim, the demand of good character for remorse and acknowledgement. We suspect that to advance towards a more decisive 'solution' we would have to omit or revise these features of the description of the problem. Aeschylus has indicated to us that the only thing remotely like a solution here is, in fact, to describe and see the conflict clearly and to acknowledge that there is no way out. The best the agent can do is to have his suffering, the natural expression of his goodness of character, and not to stifle these responses out of misguided optimism. The best we (the Chorus) can do for him is to respect the gravity of his predicament, to respect the responses that express his goodness, and to think about his case as showing a possibility for human life in general.[65]

The second significant achievement of the Aeschylean account lies within the first: in the description of these cases Aeschylus has shown us how thoroughly, in fact, the pain and remorse that are a part of the intuitive picture are bound up with ethical goodness in other areas of life; with a seriousness about value, a constancy in commitment, and a sympathetic responsiveness that we wish to maintain and develop in others and in ourselves. He suggests that without the intuitive picture's acknowledgement of the tragic power of circumstance over human goodness we cannot, in fact, maintain other valued features of our goodness: its internal integrity, its ongoing fidelity to its own laws, its responsiveness of vision. If we were such that we could in a crisis dissociate ourselves from one commitment because it clashed with another, we would be less good. Goodness itself, then, insists that there should be no further or more revisionary solving. (This second achievement, like the first, appears to depend on the resources of drama, with its ability to show us an extended pattern of character and choice.)

In this way, these poems return us to the complex 'appearances' of lived practical choice and preserve them. This, we suspected, would be a likely result of a literary contribution to ethics. But to say this is to underrate the tragic poems' complexity. For they display not only the strength of the intuitive position but, at the same time, the power of the motivation to break away from this position for the sake of avoiding its heavy risk of guilt and remorse. The impulse to create a solution to the problem of conflict is not foreign to tragedy, not merely the creation of some odd professional sect. It is present within tragedy as a human possibility: present in the deliberations of Agamemnon, the strategies of Eteocles. Like any works that truly explore the human 'appearances', these tragedies show us, alongside the 'tragic view', the origin of the denial of that view. These two pictures illuminate one another. We have not fully understood the 'tragic view' if we have not understood why it has been found intolerably painful by certain ambitious rational beings. It would, then, be much too simple to regard these plays as works that call for the rejection of theoretical 'solutions' to this problem. They are this. But they also call for a thorough investigation of the birth and the structure of Greek ethical theory, as one fulfillment of the human need to find a solution. The two sides of this investigation are pressed further in Sophocles' *Antigone*, a play that has tempted several eminent philosophers to see in it the adumbration of their own solutions to problems of conflict and contingency.[66]

3 Sophocles' *Antigone*: conflict, vision, and simplification

Agamemnon and Eteocles found themselves, through no fault of their own, in situations where revulsion, remorse, and painful memory seemed, for the person of good character, not only inevitable, but also appropriate. This fact, however, someone might concede while still insisting that it is the part of practical wisdom to avoid such situations as far as possible in planning a life. Agamemnon's was an extreme and unpredictable catastrophe. If human beings cannot make themselves entirely safe against such rare bad luck, at least they can structure their lives and commitments so that in the ordinary course of events they will be able to stay clear of serious conflict. One obvious way to do this is to simplify the structure of one's value-commitments, refusing to attach oneself to concerns that frequently, or even infrequently, generate conflicting demands. The avoidance of practical conflict at this level has frequently been thought to be a criterion of rationality for persons – just as it has frequently been thought to be a condition of rationality for a political system that it should order things so that the sincere efforts of such persons will regularly meet with success. This view was known in fifth-century Athens.[1] It is a prominent theme of tragedy: for the painful experiences recorded in our last chapter naturally prompt questions about their own elimination. And it has become firmly entrenched in modern thought, pressed even by some who defend a 'tragic view' of individual cases of practical conflict.[2] It has profoundly colored modern criticism of ancient tragedy.[3] For the claim is that the human being's relation to value in the world is not, or should not be, profoundly tragic: that it is, or should be, possible without culpable neglect or serious loss to cut off the risk of the typical tragic occurrence. Tragedy would then represent a primitive or benighted stage of ethical life and thought.

To pursue tragedy's treatment of this idea we need, evidently, to interpret an entire play, looking at the way in which it examines an entire 'course of life'[4] and a history of evaluation. Sophocles' *Antigone* seems to be an appropriate choice for this project. For this play examines two different attempts to close off the prospect of conflict and tension by simplifying the structure of the agent's commitments and loves. It asks what motivates such attempts; what becomes of them in a tragic crisis; and, finally, whether practical wisdom is to be found in this sort of strategy or in an entirely different approach to the world.

The *Antigone*[5] is a play about practical reason and the ways in which practical reason orders or sees the world. It is unusually full of words for deliberation, reasoning, knowledge, and vision.[6] It begins with the question, 'Do you know?' (2), asked about a practical crisis, and with a claim about the correct way of viewing its demands. It ends with the assertion that practical wisdom (*to phronein*) is the most important constituent of human good living (*eudaimonia*, 1348–9). It is also a play about teaching and learning, about changing one's vision of the world, about losing one's grip on what looked like secure truth and learning a more elusive kind of wisdom. From a confident claim about what is, in a complicated case, known, it moves to, 'I have no idea where I should look, which way I should lean' and, finally, to the suggestion that a less confident wisdom has, in fact, been learned (1353).

Each of the protagonists has a vision of the world of choice that forestalls serious practical conflict; each has a simple deliberative standard and a set of concerns neatly ordered in terms of this. Each, therefore, approaches problems of choice with unusual confidence and stability; each seems unusually safe from the damages of luck. And yet each, we are made to see, is somehow defective in vision. Each has omitted recognitions, denied claims, called situations by names that are not their most relevant or truest names. One is far more correct in the actual content of her decision; but both have narrowed their sights.[7] We must ask about this narrowing, and how it is criticized.

It will not be enough merely to ask about the ambitions and the deficiencies of the two protagonists, although this will certainly be a necessary beginning. For according to a famous interpretation of this play, that of Hegel, the play itself points beyond their deficiencies to suggest the basis for a conflict-free synthesis of its opposing values. They resolve tensions in the wrong way; but the play shows us how to resolve them in the right way.[8] We must therefore also assess Hegel's claim in the light of the play as a whole – and, in particular, of its choral lyrics. This will require us to ask about Sophocles' treatment of the issues of activity and passivity, making and being made, ordering and responding; in short, to uncover his complex story of the strange adventures of practical reason face to face with the world.

We can find a hint about these adventures in the Greek word *deinon*. No unique English translation for this word is available. Most generally, it is used of that which inspires awe or wonder. But in different contexts it can be used of the dazzling brilliance of the human intellect, of the monstrousness of an evil, of the terrible power of fate. That which is *deinon* is somehow strange, out of place; its strangeness and its capacity to inspire awe are intimately connected. (It is etymologically related to *deos*, 'fear'; we might compare French *formidable*.) *Deinon* frequently implies a disharmony: something is out of keeping with its surroundings, or with what is expected, or what is desired. One is surprised by it, for better or for worse. Because the word's connotations vary so much, it can be used by a character ostensibly to praise, while we are allowed to see in the remark an ironic disclosure of something horrible. 'There are many *deinon* things; but not one of them is more *deinon* than the human being.' This opening of the Chorus's ode on the human being is a deeply ambiguous praise, as we shall see. Equally ambiguous, however, is their apparently despairing conclusion that 'the power of what just happens is *deinon*' (952). The human being, who appears to be thrilling and wonderful, may turn out at the same time to be monstrous in its ambition to simplify and control the world. Contingency, an object of terror and loathing, may turn out to be at the same time wonderful, constitutive of what makes a human life beautiful or thrilling. The word is thus well suited to be central in a drama that will investigate the relationship between beauty and disharmony, between value and exposure, excellence and surprise. We might see the play as an investigation of the *deinon* in all of its elusive many-sidedness.

I

Since we shall be asking about the *Antigone*'s views of deliberation, we begin with a character who is deliberating, who does not know what to do. He walks onto the stage, dragging his feet, reluctance and confusion evident in his simple face and his gestures:

Sir, I won't pretend that I come here breathless from eager haste, with light, agile footsteps. For many times my thinking made me pause and wheel around in my path to go the other way. My soul kept talking to me, saying, 'Fool, why do you go where you will be punished?' 'Wretch, are you delaying? And if Creon learns this from someone else, how will you escape punishment?' Turning this all over in my mind, I gradually made my way, slowly and reluctantly. And so a short road became long. Finally, though, the idea of coming here to you won the victory...I come with a grip on one hope – that nothing can happen to me that is not my lot. (223–6)

This is a vivid picture of ordinary practical deliberation. Most members of the audience would recognize here a part of their own daily lives. This man has trouble making up his mind between two unpleasant alternatives. His soul provides arguments on both sides of the question, and he feels that there is no avoiding them. The two-sidedness of his thinking is mimed in his physical turning, as he walks backwards and forwards along the way. He has no theory of decision, no clear account of his decision process. All he knows is that finally one course 'won the victory'. In his persisting discomfort, his only consolation is the thought that what will happen will happen.

In many ways this man is not permitted to be a representative human being. He is basely cowardly, crudely egoistic. But his narratives full of homely detail return us to ordinary physical realities – heat, dirt, unpleasant smells – about which the heroic characters have been silent. And in a similar way his confusion, his sense that there are two sides to deliberative questions – along with his belief in the importance of what happens – return us to the keenly felt discomfort of ordinary deliberation. A spectator would realize, hearing him just after having listened to Antigone and Creon, that these ordinary ingredients of daily practical thinking have been absent, just like the summer dust and the stench of corruption, from those eloquent deliberations. Both protagonists have made claims to practical knowledge.[9] In both cases this is a knowledge whose 'truths' allow them, in an ongoing way, to avoid the guard's painful turnings. How, one might wonder, have they managed to move so far away from the ordinary, to a point from which daily human cares seem to belong only to a base, comical figure, to a peasant, rather than a king?

II

Creon's first words announce the safety of the city after its great danger and claim knowledge (166) of the Chorus as a group of men faithful, over the years, to the régime and its concerns 'with loyal and healthy reasoning' (169).[10] Like the Chorus (1347–8), like the prophet Tiresias, Creon believes and claims that the most important thing a man can have is practical wisdom, or excellence in deliberation (1050–1); the most harmful thing is lack of wisdom (1051). This praise of the elders' civic loyalty as mental health is no accident: for Creon, the healthy mind just *is* the mind completely devoted to civic safety and civic well-being.[11] Antigone's attack on civic values is taken as a sign of mental incapacity (732); Ismene's sympathy reveals a similar 'mindlessness' (492, 561–2, cf. 281). Haemon is urged not to 'throw out his reason' (648–9) by adopting her 'sick' beliefs. (At a crucial point in the action, Tiresias will turn Creon's language of mental health against itself. Speaking of deficiency in practical wisdom, he says, 'But you yourself have been full of that sickness' (1052, and cf. 1015).) And if, furthermore, we examine the occasions on which Creon claims to *know* something about the world, it appears that there is, for him, no practical knowledge or wisdom outside of the healthy mind's simple knowledge of the primacy of the civic good.[12]

By his own lights, Creon is indeed a healthy-minded man. He has inherited, and uses, a number of different evaluative terms: 'good' and 'bad', 'honorable' and 'shameful', 'just' and 'unjust', 'friend' and 'foe', 'pious' and 'impious'. These are among the most common labels that would be used by an agent in fifth-century Athenian culture to demarcate the world of practice. And to the ordinary member of this play's audience these labels pick out *distinct* and *separate* features of the ethical world. One and the same action or person will frequently possess more than one of the attributes picked out by these words – since in many cases they go together harmoniously. But they can be present separately from one another; and, even when co-present, they are distinct in their nature and in the responses they require. Many friends will turn out to be just and pious people; but what it is to be a friend is distinct from what it is to be just, or pious. The ordinary expectation would therefore be that in some imaginable circumstances the values named by these labels will make conflicting demands. Friendship or love may require an injustice; the just course of action may lead to impiety; the pursuit of honor may require an injury to friendship. Nor would each single value be assumed to be conflict-free: for the justice of the city can conflict, as this Chorus will acknowledge, with the justice of the world below; and piety towards one god may entail offenses against another. In general, then, to *see* clearly the nature of each of these features would be to understand its distinctness from each other, its possibilities of combination with and opposition to each other, and, too, its oppositions within itself.

For a spectator with roughly this view of things, Creon's situation in this play would vividly raise such a question of conflict between major values.[13] For Polynices is a closely related member of Creon's family. Creon has, then, the deepest possible religious obligation to bury the corpse. And yet, Polynices was an enemy of the city; and not simply an enemy, but a traitor. Corpses of enemies may be returned to their kin for honorable burial; traitors are not given this much consideration. Although the law apparently did not prevent the relatives of traitors from arranging for their burial outside of Attica, burial within Attic territory was strictly forbidden; and the city itself charged itself simply with depositing the corpse unburied outside these limits. To do more would, presumably, subvert civic values by honoring treachery. As the city's representative, then, Creon must take care not to honor Polynices' corpse – although he would not be expected to go to the extreme of forbidding or preventing a burial at a considerable distance from the city. And yet, as a family member, this same person would be under an indefeasible obligation to promote or arrange for the burial.[14]

The audience would, then, expect to find in Creon an extremely painful tension between these two roles and requirements. What, to their surprise, they would see is a complete absence of tension or conflict, secured by a 'healthy' rearrangement of evaluations. For if we examine Creon's use of the central ethical terms, what we discover is that he has shifted them around, wrenched them away from their ordinary use, so that they apply to things and persons simply in virtue of their connection to the well-being of the city, which Creon has established as the single intrinsic good. He uses the full range of the traditional ethical vocabulary – but not in the traditional way. These words no longer name features of the world that are separate from and potentially in conflict with the general good of the city; for Creon acknowledges no such separate goods. Through this aggressively revisionary strategy, he secures singleness and the absence of tension. He proceeds as if he can tell things by the names that suit him, *see* only those features of the world that his 'single *ēthos*' requires.

In this way, the good and bad, *agathon* and *kakon*, become for Creon (untraditionally, given their strong link with personal excellence) just those people and things that are good *for* or bad *for* the welfare of the city. The 'worst' (*kakistos*) man is the one who withholds his abilities from the city out of self-interest (181). 'The bad' (*hoi kakoi*) are contrasted with 'whoever is well-minded to the city', as if these were polar opposites (108–9; cf. 212, 284, 288). His one example of a bad (*kakē*) woman is Antigone, whose badness is civic badness. Even among the dead, there are good and bad (cf. 209–10): and the 'best' are the ones who will welcome joyfully the man 'who did the best in every way with his spear' – Eteocles, king and champion of the city. To give burial to the city's enemy would be, he argues, to give equal shares to the good (*chrēstoi*) and the bad (*kakoi*) (520). The gods, he elsewhere insists, surely would not do honor to the bad (*kakous*, 288) – that is to say, to the city's foes.[15]

Honor and respect, too, belong for Creon only to the city's helpers, as such, while shame is associated exclusively with dereliction from public responsibility.

His opening praise of the Chorus for their ongoing respect (*sebein*) is followed by an explicit declaration of his policy in matters of honor:

This is my reasoning – and never will the bad (*kakoi*) get more honor (*timē*) from me than the just (*endikōn*); but whoever is well-disposed to this city will have honor from me (*timēsetai*) alike in life and death. (207–10)

The care with which Creon states this policy indicates that he knows he is saying something new, something that not everyone would readily accept. Later we learn that most of the citizens believe that honor is due even to those who dishonor the city, if it is in pursuit of some other honorable end (730–3). Creon's respect for the civic good and its instruments is seen by them to conflict with other duties of respect. 'Can I be making a mistake in respecting my office as ruler?' asks Creon of his son (744). The answer is, 'Yes, for you are not giving respect (*ou sebeis*) when you trample down the honors (*timas*) of the gods.' Creon, however, assails this conflict-generating view: 'Can it be my job to respect (*sebein*) the disorderly?' (730). He insists that Antigone's disobedience is neither respectful nor worthy of respect, but 'shameful' (510) and 'an impious favor' (514).

We are not, then, surprised to discover that Creon's idea of justice is similarly circumscribed.[16] No claims are allowed to count as claims of justice unless they are claims on behalf of the city, no agents to be called just except in its service. In his speech on respect, 'just' (*endikos*) was used interchangeably with 'well-disposed to this city'. When he warns of trouble for the régime, the prophet Tiresias is accused of injustice; Haemon's charge of injustice against his father is denied by an appeal to the value of respecting the ruler and his power (744).[17] Creon declares to his son, in fact, that the just man in the city is the one who looks out for the welfare of the whole, understanding both how to rule and how to be ruled (662–9). This speech of self-justification concludes with a revealing claim:

And I would be confident that this [sc. the just] man would rule well and be a good willing subject, and in the storm of spears would stand his ground where he was stationed, a just and good helper (*dikaion kagathon parastatēn*, 671).

Here 'just' and 'good' are attributes not of the man simply, but of the man *qua* helper of the city. They have no independent standing; their function is simply to commend attributively, in some vague way, the man's civic dedication. But this, as we have seen, is the way Creon always means them: 'good' is 'good at civic helping', 'just' simply 'doing justice to one's civic obligation'. It is not surprising that ordinary distinctions among the virtues collapse in his speeches (where *kakos* is opposed to *endikos* rather than to *agathos*, and *endikos* is replaced, in turn, with 'well-minded to this city'). There is only one kind of human excellence worth praising: productivity of civic well-being. The function of all virtue-words is to indicate its presence. (The *Protagoras*'s doctrine of the unity of the virtues is, as we shall see, the result of a similar strategy.)

But the boldest part of Creon's revision of the practical world is not his redefinition of the just and the good, both of which already have some strong association with civic values. It is his violent shifting of the values around which the opposition to his policy will center: love[18] and piety. Creon is a member of a family. He has, therefore, binding obligations towards numerous relations or *philoi*.* One of these family *philoi* is a son whom we would expect him to love. He sees Antigone violating a civic ordinance for the sake of a beloved brother. He himself has familial religious duties towards the exposed corpse. And yet he is determined to conceal from deliberative view the claims of both familial and affective ties, at least insofar as they clash with civic interest. In this play about brothers, about obligation to a brother and the opposition between brother and brother, this brother of Jocasta, this brother-in-law of his own nephew, uses the word 'brother' for the first time in a very curious manner. He uses it, in fact, of the close relationship between one civic decree and another: 'And now I will proclaim something that is brother to what preceded' (192). Creon, like Eteocles – but with much greater persuasiveness and subtlety – is attempting to replace blood ties by the bonds of civic friendship. City–family conflicts cannot arise if the city *is* the family, if our only family *is* the city. (Plato was not the first to see the importance of this idea for political theory.) But in the light of this idea, Polynices stands in no particular relation to the family of Creon, except the relation of enmity. And 'an enemy (*echthros*) is never a loved one (*philos*), not even when he dies' (522). Whether our personal ties are ties of blood or of feeling, or both, they are to be acknowledged for deliberative purposes only when they contribute somehow to his supreme good: 'I will never call an enemy of this land a loved one of mine (*philon*)... And as for anyone who considers any *philos* to be more important than his own fatherland, I say that he is nowhere' (187, 182). *Philoi*, for Creon, are *made* (*poioumetha*, 190) in the city's service. He recognizes no bond that he has not himself chosen.[19]

These refusals have been so successful in shaping Creon's moral imagination that they are even able to inform his view of sexual attraction. When Creon advises his son not to let his passion for Antigone delude him into forming an attachment with a 'bad' woman, he does not say that pleasure must be resisted for the civic good. What he says is that, in a healthy man, even sexual pleasure will be found only in association with the civic good. A man who has not 'thrown out his wits' will find an unpatriotic spouse 'a cold armful in his bed' (650–1). There is no reason to suppose that Creon finds Antigone particularly unerotic. Creon's point is that the man who sees the world correctly will just not *see* that, not be moved by that. If you are healthy, you do not allow yourself to be gripped by anything, even sexual response, that might be a source of conflict with civic duty. This, he declares, is practical knowledge (649). The knowing man is the man who refuses to acknowledge things that other, weaker men see plainly.[20] Earlier he implied that a good citizen sees a wife simply as a fertile producer of citizens: if Haemon cannot marry Antigone, 'there are other furrows for his plow' (569). The audience would recognize in this image the language of the Athenian marriage contract:

* On *philos* and *philia*, cf. Ch. 11, p. 328 and Ch. 12, pp. 354ff.

'I give you my daughter for the plowing of legitimate children.' Creon's position grounds itself in familiar and legitimate claims, ignoring others.

Finally, as we might expect, Creon's imagination takes on the gods themselves and remakes them in the image of his demand for order. They have for him, they *must* have, the healthy minds of conscientious statesmen:

> You say something *unbearable* when you say that the gods take kindly forethought for this corpse. Could it be that they tried to cover him out of exceeding honor as if he had done something good, this man who came to burn their temples and shrines, their very land, and to scatter their laws to the winds? Or do you see the gods honoring bad people? It cannot be. (280–90)

The suggestion that the gods have honored Polynices must, Creon feels, be rejected – and rejected not merely as false, but as *unbearable*. It puts too great a strain on deliberative rationality. The mind's demand for orderly life and harmony dictates what religion can and cannot be, forcing the repudiation of the guard's clear story.[21] Respect for Zeus is soon invoked to back a pledge to catch the guilty party (304ff.). The burial of the corpse is an 'impious favor' (514). We suspect that Creon's ambitious rationality is on the way to making itself god.

Creon has, then, made himself a deliberative world into which tragedy cannot enter. Insoluble conflicts cannot arise, because there is only a single supreme good, and all other values are functions of that good. If I say to Creon, 'Here is a conflict: on the one side, the demands of piety and love; on the other, the requirements of civic justice', he will reply that I have misdescribed the case. The true eye of the healthy soul will not *see* the city's enemy as a loved one, or his exposed corpse as an impiety. The apparent presence of a contingent conflict is an indication that we have not been working hard enough at correct vision.[22] Two of Creon's favorite words to describe the world he sees are *orthos*, 'straight', and *orthoō*, 'to set straight' (163, 167, 190, 403, 494; cf. also 636, 685, 706, 994). He likes things to look straight and not (as he will finally see them) crooked (1345) or turning (1111); fixed and not fluid (169); single and not plural (cf. 705); commensurate and not incommensurable (387).[23] By making all values commensurable in terms of a single coin – he is preoccupied with the imagery of coinage and profit in ethical matters – Creon achieves singleness, straightness, and an apparent stability.[24]

What is there about the world, the unreconstructed world, that makes Creon want to pursue this strange and awe-inspiring project? He does offer an argument for his position, backing it with a claim to practical knowledge:

> I would never...make an enemy of this land my friend, knowing (*gignōskōn*) that it is this land that preserves us – and sailing upon her, as she steers straight, we make our friends. With customs of this sort I shall magnify the city. (188–91)

Creon alludes here to an image already established in political rhetoric, one which rapidly became a commonplace of Athenian patriotism.[25] The city is a ship; without her, citizens could do nothing. She must be in good shape for friendship to prosper.[26] So much is unexceptionable; the lines were quoted with approval by Demosthenes as an example of what Aeschines (who apparently acted the role of Creon) would have said to himself offstage as well, had he been a good citizen.[27]

But even if this claim on behalf of the city should be accepted, we have been given no good reason to suppose that it justified Creon's sweeping ethical innovations. For a ship is a tool. It is necessary in order to obtain some goods; its 'health' is necessary for the life and health of the sailors who are on it. But clearly they are not on the ship *just* in order to keep the ship sailing straight. They have other ends, for whose pursuit the ship provides a setting, a conveyance. We would not expect these ends to be definable only in terms of the ship's health. Theognis, one of the earliest users of the image, speaks of a tension between the individual ends of the sailors and the overall good of the ship (670–85). Alcaeus associates the usefulness of the city-ship with the need to give honor to dead kinsmen (6.13–14) – an end which is, plainly, separable from and in potential tension with the health of the ship.[28] As the image develops, the sailor of a ship becomes, in fact, paradigmatic of something that is separable – whose ends and activities come apart from those of his useful and even necessary conveyance.[29] So Creon's use of this image as an argument for a single-ended conception of value is more than a little strange. He might just as well have told us that the fact that I cannot live without a heart shows that my only friends should be specialists in the health of this single organ, entirely dedicated to its welfare. When he affirms the necessity of the city as a condition for other pursuits, he does not yet give any reason for rejecting the claim of the non-civic (even the anti-civic) to be intrinsic goods. Using the ship image, he could attempt to justify the punishment of Antigone and his own refusal to bury the corpse, as impieties and wrongs necessary for the continued life, health, and virtue of all. He could not, on this basis, justify his claim that there is no piety and no justice outside the demands of the civic. The strange gap in his argument makes us want to look for a deeper motivation for his ethical redefinitions. And, in fact, the ship image itself suggests such a deeper motivation.

The image tells us that a city, like a ship, is a tool built by human beings for the subjugation of chance and nature. The city-ship, in the tradition of the image, is something safely water-tight, a barrier against imminent external dangers. Waves beat against its sides, currents toss its hull; clearly its intelligent makers must leave no gap, in the fabric, for the wildness of uncontrolled nature to penetrate.[30] Reflecting on the image in this way, it would be easy to conclude that the task of the city, as life-saving tool, is the removal of ungoverned chance from human life. Ships and cities will recur together in the ode on the human being, as two inventions of this *deinon* creature, 'all-devising', who subdues the world to its purposes. Creon, and the Chorus in their early optimism, believe that human technological resourcefulness can overcome any contingency, short of death itself. But the suppression of contingency requires more than the technology of physical nature: ships, plows, bridles, traps. It requires, in addition, a technology of human nature, a technology of practical reason. Contingency has long caused pain and terror in human life, never more so than when it causes a well-formed plan to generate conflict. Creon is convinced that the human being cannot bear this. His choice of the ship image here expresses his sense of the urgency of the problem. Fortunately, it is not necessary to bear it. The recalcitrant features of the world can be mastered by practical ethical rationality itself: by a constructive rearrangement of practical attachments and ethical language. Creon cleverly effects this adjustment by using the city itself as a standard of the good.

What would it take to make such a strategy work? First, the final good must itself be single or simple: it must not contain conflicts or oppositions within itself. If oppositions between conflicting claims are present within the welfare of the city, properly conceived, then Creon's strategy will have solved nothing. Second, the end must genuinely offer a common coin to which all of the agent's actual interests and values can be reduced. There must be nothing that he sees or loves that cannot be regarded as a function of it, *cashed out* (to use Creon's financial imagery) in terms of it. The end must be protean enough to turn up in everything of value, in such a way that it can plausibly be regarded as the only source of that value. And yet it must be one thing in all the many cases, generating no internal conflicts. (The Socrates of the *Protagoras* will suggest that the parts of virtue are like the parts of gold: qualitatively homogeneous, a single common coin of value.)

The play is about Creon's failure. It ends with his abandonment of this strategy and his recognition of a more complicated deliberative world. The Chorus will compare him to an arrogant animal punished with blows (1350–2) – this man whose linguistic obsession had been the imagery of taming, breaking, punishing (473ff.; cf. 348–52). His plan breaks down, in fact, in both areas: his supreme end, properly conceived, is not as simple as he thinks it is; and it fails to do justice, finally, to all of his concerns. These problems begin to emerge, for us, even in his initial description of his position.

When Creon enters, he speaks first of the affairs of the city; then he addresses the people of the Chorus. The two parts of his assertion are linked by the correlative particles *men* and *de*; this structure indicates the presence of an opposition, or, at the weakest, underlines a distinction, between the city and these citizens. From the first, then, we are asked to wonder whether the city, correctly conceived, has as simple a good as Creon supposes. Later Haemon explicitly tells us that the city understood as a *people* (*homoptolis leōs*, 733) supports Antigone – even though it still seems plausible for Creon to judge that her actions threaten the public safety. A city is a complex whole, composed of individuals and families, with all the disparate, messy, often conflicting concerns that individuals and families have, including their religious practices, their concern for the burial of kin. A plan that makes the city the supreme good cannot so easily deny the intrinsic value of the religious goods that are valued by the people who compose it. Only an impoverished conception of the city can have the simplicity which Creon requires.

This becomes evident, as well, in the area of love and friendship: once again, his simple conception does not do justice to the complexity of the city's own concerns. In Creon's life, all relationships are civic; people are valued only for their productivity of civic good. Thus the bond between husband and wife is simply a means of producing new citizens; the relation between father and son is a civic friendship. This is plainly not the view of these relationships held by the city itself. The closeness of blood ties is a fundamental fact of civic life, as is the passionate love of one individual for another. To Creon's 'there are other furrows for his plow', Ismene replies, 'Not a love like the one that fitted him to her' (570). Creon repudiates this, as he must, with the harsh, 'I hate bad women for my sons.' The Chorus does not repudiate it: their third ode praises the power of *erōs*.

Furthermore, Creon is incapable of seeing any opponent of the city as anything but an obstacle to be overcome. His conception of the wife as merely furrow, of proper civic maleness as the exercise of power over submissive matter (cf. 484–5)[31] already tended to dehumanize the other party to the relationship. With opposition, this is more obvious still. Creon's plan does not permit him to respect a human opponent because of the value of that person's humanity. He or she contains only a single value, productivity of civic good; lacking that, she is 'nowhere'. In a singular conflation of relationships normally kept distinct, Creon expresses his attitude to Antigone:

Understand that excessively rigid reason is the most likely to fall. The toughest iron, hardened in the fire, is the kind you most often see shattered and broken. I know that spirited horses can be disciplined with a small curb; for it is not possible to think proud thoughts when you are your neighbor's slave. (473–9)

Metal-working, horse-taming, slave-owning: all these come to much the same for Creon. And all are appropriate images for the relationship between the dominant male and the *reason* of a stubborn opponent. Can he really mean these images? He is talking to Antigone; he is relying on her ability to understand the language, even to interpret metaphor. But this implicit difference between Antigone and the horse makes it all the more urgent for Creon actively to repudiate her specialness. The human being is a more difficult obstacle than a horse, whom a small curb can tame. Creon needs to efface that special difficulty by denial, in order to tame the human as the human has tamed other obstacles.[32] In the life to which he aspires, there will be only useful objects, and no people to talk back (cf. 757).[33] That is not a city. Haemon, earlier, drew the right conclusion: 'You would rule well in solitude, over a desert space' (739).

Here again, then, Creon's single-ended conception has prevented him from having an adequate conception of the city – which, in the wholeness of its relationships, does not appear to have a single good. Nor does Creon himself manage to sustain the simple view; it does not do justice even to all of his own surviving concerns. In the end, it is his own recalcitrant humanity that he fails to subdue. His education is, the Chorus tells us, a taming; as in Creon's own example, 'blows' must be used to curb the spirit's pride. Unlike horse-taming, however, it ends not in mute obedience, but in understanding (1353). Creon is forced, in particular, to acknowledge his love for his son and to see its separate value. Haemon's first words to him had been, 'Father, I am yours' (634); and his name means 'blood' (as the punning account of his death brings out, 1175).[34] But the father whose name means 'ruler' begins to feel the force of this appeal only later, when the prophet Tiresias warns him, 'Know well that you will not complete many more racing circuits of the sun, before you yourself will give up one from your own loins in exchange, a corpse for corpses' (1064-5). At this moment Creon, who has been seen as *deinon*, awe-inspiring in his power (243, 408, 690), and who has seen himself as a resourcefully controlling being, now finds himself confronted with something beyond his control that commands his awe:

I myself know (*egnōka*) this too, and am shaken in my reason (*phrenas*).[35] To yield is terrible (*deinon*). But to stand against him, striking my spirit with ruin, is also terrible (*deinon*). (1095-7)

It does matter to him that Haemon is his, a child of his loins. To the Chorus's rejoinder that what is needed here is good deliberation (*euboulia*), he replies not with a reassertion of the male theory of the healthy mind, but with a question: 'What am I to do, then?' (1099). He begins to concede that the laws of family piety that he has overridden may still have their force: 'I'm afraid it is best to hold to the established conventions (*nomous*) to the end of life' (1113-14).

When this change proves powerless to prevent the death of his son, Creon, mourning, more radically retracts his old view of practical reason:

O errors of my ill-reasoning reason (*phrenōn dusphronōn hamartēmata*)
unyielding and bringing death.
O you, who look on the killer and the kin he killed.
O how impoverished (*anolba*) my deliberations were.
O son, you were young, you died young.
You have died, you have gone away,
   through my bad deliberations, not your own. (1261-9)

Creon's love for his dead son, a love that can no longer be either denied or accommodated within the framework of the civic theory of the good, forces him to reject this theory. His remorse is specifically directed at his deliberations, especially at their narrowness or impoverishment. Their coin was not coinage enough; it was an impoverished standard because it left things of genuine worth on the outside. This failing is now acknowledged to be his. The suicide of his wife Eurydice (significantly named 'Wide-Justice') confirms and intensifies the bitter learning. 'This blame can be fixed on no mortal man in a way that will acquit me. I, *I* killed you, unhappy that I am – *I*, I say it truly' (1317-20). The old picture of practical knowledge made no room for this; his emphatic truth-claim shows us that his regret is not simply regret at a failure, but a more fundamental reorientation. 'You seem to have seen justice, though late', the Chorus judges (1270). What he sees, precisely, is how 'everything in my hands is crooked'

(1344–5), the helmsman who once (or so he saw it) kept the city's ship 'steering straight'.[36]

III

We have spoken until now only of Creon. And almost all interpreters of this play have agreed that the play shows Creon to be morally defective, though they might not agree about the particular nature of his defect. The situation of Antigone is more controversial. Hegel assimilated her defect to Creon's; some more recent writers uncritically hold her up as a blameless heroine. Without entering into an exhaustive study of her role in the tragedy, I should like to claim (with the support of an increasing number of recent critics)[37] that there is at least some justification for the Hegelian assimilation – though the criticism needs to be focused more clearly and specifically than it is in Hegel's brief remarks. I want to suggest that Antigone, like Creon, has engaged in a ruthless simplification of the world of value which effectively eliminates conflicting obligations. Like Creon, she can be blamed for refusal of vision. But there are important differences, as well, between her project and Creon's. When these are seen, it will also emerge that this criticism of Antigone is not incompatible with the judgment that she is morally superior to Creon.

O kindred, own-sisterly head of Ismene, do you know that there is not one of the evils left by Oedipus that Zeus does not fulfill for us while we live?...Do you grasp anything? Have you heard anything? Or has it escaped your notice that the evils that belong to enemies are advancing against our friends? (1–3, 9–10)

A person is addressed with a periphrasis that is both intimate and impersonal. In the most emphatic terms available, it characterizes her as a close relative of the speaker. And yet its attitude towards the addressee is strangely remote. Antigone sees Ismene simply as the form of a close family relation.[38] As such, she presses on her, with anxious insistence, the knowledge of the family: that 'loved ones' (*philoi*) are being penalized as if they were enemies (*echthroi*). Loving relatives must 'see' the shame and dishonour of 'the evils that are yours and mine' (5–6).

There has been a war. On one side was an army led by Eteocles, brother of Antigone and Ismene. On the other side was an invading army, made up partly of foreigners, but led by a Theban brother, Polynices. This heterogeneity is denied, in different ways, by both Creon and Antigone. Creon's strategy is to draw, in thought, a line between the invading and defending forces. What falls to one side of this line is a foe, bad, unjust; what falls to the other (if loyal to the city's cause) becomes, indiscriminately, friend or loved one. Antigone, on the other hand, denies the relevance of this distinction entirely. She draws, in imagination, a small circle around the members of her family: what is inside (with further restrictions which we shall mention) is family, therefore loved one and friend; what is outside is non-family, therefore, in any conflict with the family, enemy. If one listened only to Antigone, one would not know that a war had taken place or that anything called 'city' was ever in danger.[39] To her it is a simple injustice that Polynices should not be treated like a friend.

'Friend' (*philos*) and 'enemy', then, are functions solely of family relationship.[40] When Antigone says, 'It is my nature to join in loving (*sumphilein*), not to join in hating', she is expressing not a general attachment to love, but a devotion to the *philia* of the family. It is the nature of these *philia* bonds to make claims on one's commitments and actions regardless of one's occurrent desires. This sort of love is not something one decides about; the relationships involved may have little to do with liking or fondness. We might say (to use terminology borrowed from Kant) that Antigone, in speaking of love, means 'practical', not 'pathological' love (a love that has its source in fondness or inclination). 'He is my own brother', she says to Ismene in explanation of her defiance of the city's decree, 'and yours too, even if you don't want it. I certainly will never be found a traitor to him' (45–6). Relationship is itself a source of obligation, regardless of the feelings involved. When Antigone speaks of Polynices as 'my dearest (*philtatōi*) brother' (80–1), even when she proclaims, 'I shall lie with him as a loved one with a loved one (*philē...philou meta*)' (73), there is no sense of closeness, no personal memory, no particularity animating her speech.[41] Ismene, the one person who ought, historically, to be close to her, is treated from the beginning with remote coldness; she is even called enemy (93) when she takes the wrong stand on matters of pious obligation. It is Ismene whom we see weeping 'sister-loving tears', who acts out of commitment to a felt love. 'What life is worth living for me, bereft of you?' (548) she asks with an intensity of feeling that never animates her sister's piety. To Haemon, the man who passionately loves and desires her, Antigone never addresses a word throughout the entire play.[42] It is Haemon, not Antigone, whom the Chorus views as inspired by *erōs* (781ff.). Antigone is as far from *erōs* as Creon.[43] For Antigone, the dead are 'those whom it is most important to please' (89). 'You have a warm heart for the cold', (88) observes her sister, failing to comprehend this impersonal and single-minded passion.

Duty to the family dead is the supreme law and the supreme passion. And Antigone structures her entire life and her vision of the world in accordance with this simple, self-contained system of duties. Even within this system, should a conflict ever arise, she is ready with a fixed priority ordering that will clearly dictate her choice. The strange speech (891ff.) in which she ranks duties to different family dead, placing duty to brother above duties to husband and children, is in this sense (if genuine) highly revealing: it makes us suspect that she is capable of a strangely ruthless simplification of duties, corresponding not so much to any known religious law as to the exigencies of her own practical imagination.[44]

Other values fall into place, confirming these suspicions. Her single-minded identification with duties to the dead (and only some of these) effects a strange reorganization of piety, as well as of honor and justice. She is truly, in her own words, *hosia panourgēsasa*, one who will do anything for the sake of the pious;[45] and her piety takes in only a part of conventional religion.[46] She speaks of her allegiance to Zeus (950), but she refuses to recognize his role as guardian of the city and backer of Eteocles. The very expression of her devotion is suspect: 'Zeus did not decree this, as far as I am concerned' (*ou gar ti moi Zeus...*, 450). She sets herself up as the arbiter of what Zeus can and cannot have decreed, just as Creon took it upon himself to say whom the gods could and could not have covered: no other character bears out her view of Zeus as single-mindedly backing the rights of the dead. She speaks, too, of the goddess *Dikē*, Justice; but *Dikē* for her is, simply, 'the Justice who lives together with the gods below' (457). The Chorus recognizes another *Dikē*.[47] Later they will say to her, 'Having advanced to the utmost limit of boldness, you struck hard against the altar of *Dikē* on high, o child' (852–5). Justice is up here in the city, as well as below the earth. It is not as simple as she says it is. Antigone, accordingly, is seen by them not as a conventionally pious person, but as one who improvised her piety, making her own decisions about what to honor. She is a 'maker of her own law' (*autonomos*, 821); her defiance is 'self-invented passion' (*autognōtos orga*, 875). Finally they tell her unequivocally that her pious respect is incomplete: '[This] reverent action (*sebein*) is a part of piety (*eusebeia tis*)' (872). Antigone's rigid adherence to a single narrow set of duties has caused her to misinterpret the nature of piety itself, a virtue within which a more comprehensive understanding would see the possibility of conflict.

Creon's strategy of simplification led him to regard others as material for his aggressive exploitation. Antigone's dutiful subservience to the dead leads to an equally strange, though different (and certainly less hideous) result. Her relation to others in the world above is characterized by an odd coldness. 'You are alive', she tells her sister, 'but my life (*psuchē*) is long since dead, to the end of serving the dead.' The safely dutiful human life requires, or is, life's annihilation.[48] Creon's attitude towards others is like necrophilia: he aspires to possess the inert and unresisting. Antigone's subservience to duty is, finally, the ambition to be a *nekros*, a corpse beloved of corpses. (Her apparent similarity to martyrs in our own tradition, who expect a fully active life after death, should not conceal from us the strangeness of this goal.) In the world below, there are no risks of failure or wrongdoing.

Neither Creon nor Antigone, then, is a loving or passionate being in anything like the usual sense. Not one of the gods, not one human being escapes the power of *erōs*, says the Chorus (787–90); but these two oddly inhuman beings do, it appears, escape. Creon sees loved persons as functions of the civic good, replaceable producers of citizens. For Antigone, they are either dead, fellow servants of the dead, or objects of complete indifference. No living being is loved for his or her personal qualities, loved with the sort of love that Haemon feels and Ismene praises. By altering their beliefs about the nature and value of persons, they have, it seems, altered or restructured the human passions themselves. They achieve harmony in this way; but at a cost. The Chorus speaks of *erōs* as a force as important and obligating as the ancient *thesmoi* or laws of right, a force against which it is both foolish and, apparently, blameworthy to rebel (781–801).

Antigone learns too – like Creon, by being forced to recognize a problem that lies at the heart of her single-minded concern. Creon saw that the city itself is pious and loving; that he could not be its champion without valuing what it values, in all its complexity. Antigone comes to see that the service of the dead requires the city, that her own religious aims cannot be fulfilled without civic institutions. By being her own law, she has not only ignored a part of piety, she has also jeopardized the fulfillment of the very pious duties to which she is so attached. Cut off from friends, from the possibility of having children, she cannot keep herself alive in order to do further service to the dead; nor can she guarantee the pious treatment of her own corpse. In her last speeches she laments not so much the fact of imminent death as, repeatedly, her isolation from the continuity of offspring, from friends and mourners. She emphasizes the fact that she will never marry; she will remain childless. Acheron will be her husband, the tomb her bridal chamber.[49] Unless she can successfully appeal to the citizens whose needs as citizens she had refused to consider, she will die without anyone to mourn her death[50] or to replace her as guardian of her family religion. She turns therefore increasingly, in this final scene, to the citizens and the gods of the city (839, 843ff.), until her last words closely echo an earlier speech made by Creon (199ff.) and blend his concerns with hers:

O city of my fathers in this land of Thebes. O gods, progenitors of our race. I am led away, and wait no longer. Look, leaders of Thebes, the last of your royal line. Look what I suffer, at whose hands, for having respect for piety. (937–43)

We have, then, two narrowly limited practical worlds, two strategies of avoidance and simplification. In one, a single human value has become *the* final end; in the other, a single set of duties has eclipsed all others. But we can now acknowledge that we admire Antigone, nonetheless, in a way that we do not admire Creon. It seems important to look for the basis of this difference.

First, in the world of the play, it seems clear that Antigone's actual choice is preferable to Creon's. The dishonour to civic values involved in giving pious burial to an enemy's corpse is far less radical than the violation of religion involved in Creon's act.[51] Antigone shows a deeper understanding of the community and its values than Creon does when she argues that the obligation to bury the dead is an unwritten law, which cannot be set aside by the decree of a particular ruler. The belief that not all values are utility-relative, that there are certain claims whose neglect will prove deeply destructive of communal attunement and individual character, is a part of Antigone's position left untouched by the play's implicit criticism of her single-mindedness.

Furthermore, Antigone's pursuit of virtue is her own. It involves nobody else and commits her to abusing no other person. Rulership must be rulership *of* something; Antigone's pious actions are executed alone, out of a solitary commitment. she may be strangely remote from the world; but she does no violence to it.

Finally, and perhaps most important, Antigone remains ready to risk and to sacrifice her ends in a way that is not possible for Creon, given the singleness of his conception of value. There is a complexity in Antigone's virtue that permits genuine sacrifice *within* the defense of piety. She dies recanting nothing; but still she is torn by a conflict. Her virtue is, then, prepared to admit a contingent conflict, at least in the extreme case where its adequate exercise requires the cancellation of the conditions of its exercise. From within her single-minded devotion to the dead, she recognizes the power of these contingent circumstances and yields to them, comparing herself to Niobe wasted away by nature's snow and rain (823ff.).[52] (Earlier she had been compared, in her grief, to a mother bird crying out over an empty nest; so she is, while heroically acting, linked with the openness and vulnerability of the female.) The Chorus here briefly tries to console her with the suggestion that her bad luck does not really matter, in view of her future fame; she calls their rationalization a mockery of her loss. This vulnerability in virtue, this ability to acknowledge the world of nature by mourning the constraints that it imposes on virtue, surely contributes to making her the more humanly rational and the richer of the two protagonists: both active and receptive, neither exploiter nor simply victim.

IV

Both Creon and Antigone are one-sided, narrow, in their pictures of what matters. The concerns of each show us important values that the other has refused to take into account. On this issue Hegel's famous and frequently abused reading is correct. Hegel erred, perhaps, in not stressing the fact that Antigone's actual choice is, in the play's terms, distinctly superior to Creon's; but his general criticism of her neglect of the civic is not, as we have seen, incompatible with this recognition.[53] Hegel, however, locates the deficiency of the protagonists in this narrowness or one-sidedness alone, not in their conflict-avoiding aims. The elimination of conflict is, for Hegel, both an acceptable and a plausible aim for a human ethical conception. From tragedy we learn not to eliminate it in the wrong way, by an exclusive attachment to one value and the disregard of others. But we also learn, by implication, how to avoid it correctly: by effecting a synthesis that will do justice to both of the contending claims. Hegel concludes, 'It is, in short, the harmony of these spheres [sc. the family and the city], and the concordant action within the bounds of their realized content, which constitute the perfected reality of the moral life... The true course of dramatic development consists in the annulment of *contradictions* viewed as such, in the reconciliation of the forces of human action, which alternately strive to negate each other in their conflict.'[54] This approach has recently been echoed by several modern interpreters, who argue that an Athenian audience would understand this play as a challenge to effect a conflict-free harmony among their diverse commitments, neglecting none of them.[55]

Up to a point, this appears to be a promising idea. Certainly it will be one of the proud claims of Periclean Athens to have developed a civic order that incorporates and respects the claims of the 'unwritten laws' of religious obligation (cf. Thucydides II.37). But it is one thing to say that the state will in general respect these claims, and quite another to say, with Hegel, that the very possibility of conflict or tension between different spheres of value will be altogether eliminated. To cancel this possibility requires, it seems, a far more radical reform than Pericles envisaged. Furthermore, we already have reason to think it a dangerous reform, one that involves us in a risk of neglecting some of the richness of the world of value and the separateness of each separate claim within it. From our study of the two protagonists we might infer that to do justice to the nature or identity of two distinct values requires doing justice to their difference; and doing justice to their difference – both their qualitative distinctness and their numerical separateness – requires seeing that there are, at least potentially, circumstances in which the two will collide.[56] Distinctness requires articulation *from*, bounding-off *against*. This, in turn, entails the possibility of opposition – and, for the agent who is committed to both – of conflict. But so far these are only suspicions. To explore them more deeply we must turn now to the thoughts and responses of the Chorus – and, eventually, to those of two of the play's other characters, Tiresias and Haemon.

The *Antigone*'s choral lyrics have an unusual degree of density and compression.[57] Each has an internal structure and an internal set of resonances; each reflects upon the action that has preceded; each reflects upon the preceding lyrics. Already, then, we find that to interpret fully any single image or phrase requires mapping a complex web of connections, as each successive item both modifies and is modified by the imagery and dialogue that has preceded. But once we mention that the succeeding item modifies the preceding or deepens our reading of it, we must then acknowledge that the web of connections to be drawn is much more complex still: for the resonances of a single item will be prospective as well as retrospective. An image in a lyric must be read not only against the background both of dialogue and of lyric that has preceded, but, ultimately, in the light of events and lyrics yet to come. An intrinsically optimistic statement (or, rather – since we do not want to concede that these references are simply extrinsic – one that, taken in isolation, would appear optimistic) may be undercut or qualified in the light of later occurrences of the same images or words; an apparently bleaker image may be shown to have its more hopeful side. The complete understanding of an ode is fuller and deeper than the apparent intentions of the elders as they speak it – as if the odes were their dreams and, like dreams, contained many subtle and compressed allusions to features of their world, far more, perhaps, than the dreamer deliberately placed there, and more than he could easily or readily decipher.[58] Thus the fullest and most complete reading would require the most attentive following-out of connections, as each image and each lyric acquires additional density from its resonances across to other passages, and as the internal density of each lyric contributes to the finding and mapping of these resonances. This structure could be paralleled from other lyric poems, both in and outside of drama. It also bears a strikingly close relation to the compressed, dense, and riddling style of the major ethical thinker of the half-century preceding this play, that is, to the style of Heraclitus.[59]

These features of style need to be mentioned not only as guidelines towards interpretation, but also as signs of this play's view about the nature of human learning and reflection. We have been proceeding on the assumption that the style in which matters of human choice are discussed is likely not to be neutral: it expresses already a view about what understanding is and how the soul acquires it. We might, then, ask, as we embark on the job of decipherment that these lyrics require, what view of these matters seems to be expressed by their dense and enigmatic style; for it is in important ways unlike the model of learning and psychological growth that Platonic philosophy will express and approve. The lyrics both show us and engender in us a process of reflection and (self-)discovery that works through a persistent attention to and a (re)-interpretation of concrete words, images, incidents. We reflect on an incident not by subsuming it under a general rule, not by assimilating its features to the terms of an elegant scientific procedure, but by burrowing down into the depths of the particular, finding images and connections that will permit us to see it more truly, describe it more richly; by combining this burrowing with a horizontal drawing of connections, so that every horizontal link contributes to the depth of our view of the particular, and every new depth creates new horizontal links. The Platonic soul will be directed, in its singleness and purity, to ethical objects that are single-natured and unmixed, themselves by themselves. The Sophoclean soul is more like Heraclitus's image of *psuchē*: a spider sitting in the middle of its web, able to feel and respond to any tug in any part of the complicated structure.[60] It advances its understanding of life and of itself not by a Platonic movement from the particular to the universal, from the perceived world to a simpler, clearer world, but by hovering in thought and imagination around the enigmatic complexities of the seen particular (as we, if we are good readers of this style, hover around the details of the text), seated in the middle of its web of connections, responsive to the pull of each separate thread. (This fact is signaled to us when the Chorus, seeing Antigone enter, a prisoner, says, *es daimonion teras amphinoō tode*, 'looking at this strange portent, I think on both sides' (376).) The image of learning expressed in this style, like the picture of reading required by it, stresses responsiveness and an attention to complexity; it discourages the search for the simple and, above all, for the reductive. It suggests to us that the world of practical choice, like the text, is articulated but never exhausted by reading; that reading must reflect and not obscure this fact, showing that the particular (or: the text) remains there unexhausted, the final arbiter of the correctness of our vision; that correct choice (or: good interpretation) is, first and foremost, a matter of keenness and flexibility of perception, rather than of conformity to a set of simplifying principles. (All this Aristotle, returning to traditional views of choice, will explicitly argue.)

Finally, the Chorus reminds us that good response to a practical situation (or: a text) before us involves not only intellectual appreciation but also, where appropriate, emotional reaction. For their 'readings' of the situation are not themselves coolly intellectual. Like the *Agamemnon* elders, for whom the painful memory of pain is an avenue of learning, these elders allow themselves not only to 'think on both sides' but also to feel deeply. They allow themselves to form the bonds with their world that are the bases for profound fear and love and grief. Immediately after they have spoken of the power of *erōs* (781–801), 'seated beside the laws of right', they align themselves with Haemon over against the non-erotic protagonists by announcing, 'And now I myself, as well, am borne outside of the laws of right (*thesmoi*), seeing this; and I can no longer contain the streams of tears, when I see this Antigone here going to her bridal chamber of eternal sleep' (802–6). Seeing and passionate weeping are, for them, intimately connected; one naturally evokes the other. A purely intellectual perception of this event that was not accompanied by 'being borne' and by the flowing of tears would not, apparently, be a natural or full or good seeing. To perceive the particulars fully it may be necessary to love them. This suggests to us an implicit norm, as well, for our reading and interpreting. If we attempt to impede the flow of tears, if we try too hard not to be carried away, we may not be able to get all that the text offers.

We have spoken so far as if these lyrics were texts for reading. We should not forget that they are, first and foremost, choral elements in a dramatic performance. They are performed by a group working together in word, music, and dance; and they are watched by a group – by an audience that has come together in community at a religious festival and whose physical placement surrounding the action makes acknowledgment of the presence of fellow citizens a major and inevitable part of the dramatic event. This fact deepens our proleptic picture of the contrast with Plato. For these people experience the complexities of the tragedy while and by being a certain sort of community, not by having each soul go off in isolation from its fellows; by attending to what is common or shared and forming themselves into a common responding group, not by reaching for a lonely height of contemplation from which it is a wrenching descent to return to political life. This entire ethical experience, then, stresses the fundamental value of community and friendship; it does not invite or even permit us to seek for the good apart from these.[61]

It seems important to interpret these odes in a style that respects all these suggestions. These interpretations will speak only of certain parts of the lyrics; and they will stress, within these parts, some connections rather than others, some emotional responses rather than others – those, in particular, that advance our inquiry about synthesis and simplification. But they will aim to do this in a way that is appropriate to the material.

> Sun's ray,
> finest light that ever appeared to seven-gated Thebes,
> you appeared then,
> O eye of the golden day,
> rising up above the channels of Dirce

turning to headlong flight, with sharply piercing bit,
the white-shielded man, full-armed, '
the man from Argos.

Polynices sent him to our land,
spurred by a quarrel with arguments on both sides.
Polynices, shrieking sharp,
eagle-like, flew into our land,
closely covered by feathers of white snow,
helmet decked with horse-hair. (100–16)[62]

Entering at sunrise, the Chorus calls upon the sun's emerging rays. This 'eye of the golden day' appears, or is revealed (*ephanthēs*), as before, over the waters of the river. Its light reminds them of its witnessing presence at the Theban victory, whose bloody aftermath it also sees now, outside the safety of their gates. It would have seen, they reflect, the anomalous character of the enemy force where, mixed with the Argive horsemen, lies the Theban eagle Polynices, 'Great Conflict', his helmet decked with horsehair. This eagle plumed with horsehair, his anomalous doubleness indicating the complexities that could be expected to mark their moral dealings with him, lies there still beneath the sun's eye, untended. Their recognition that Polynices had two aspects and that the quarrels that echo his name had arguments on both sides (*neikeōn amphilogōn*, 111) contrasts implicitly with their (and our) knowledge of a simple edict that has refused this enemy and traitor the treatment due to a kinsman and *philos*. The complex tensions of the previous day's revealed world contrast with this day's single-minded strategies.

The lyric begins, then, with an eye opening itself as it opened itself once before, and looking at a scene that presents confusing features. It is articulated in two ways, the simple and the complex. The eye of nature sees a complex and conflict-engendering vision. Creon sees a simpler world. This striking image of the open eye, used just as we ourselves (in the theater, at sunrise) are opening our eyes to the situation that the spreading light unfolds before us, is the first of many images of eyes and seeing in the play. Tracing them helps us to understand the Chorus's unfolding attitude towards practical perception and projects of harmonization.

Creon's talk of seeing implicitly involves a constructing of reality, a refusal of its discordant elements.[63] What he permits to be revealed or to become evident to him is only what accords with his simple picture of value: the present danger of the city (185, cf. 177), the exposed corpse of the traitor (206), the evident guilt of the disobedient one (307, 655), the foolishness of such behavior (562), the terrible efficacy of punishment (581).[64] He calls on 'Zeus who sees all forever' to defend his simple vision (184). The opposition, who see differently, are, in his imagination altogether without vision, people 'contriving in darkness, in no way correctly' (494). Or, if they still dare, like Antigone, to venture into the light, they will shortly be concealed from view (774). Haemon tells him that he has an *omma deinon*, a strange and terrible eye – since he sees only what he wants to see, hears only what he wants to hear. (Antigone similarly, though with less emphasis, insists on keeping before her vision only the ills of the family (6), the revealed force of the laws of the dead (457).) Creon will, in the end, be punished by being deprived of the *sight* of the son whose claims his vision slighted (763–4). The sun's circle will measure his loss (1065); he will come, in pain, to 'look upon' the deaths of members of his family (1264); and, at last, to 'see justice, though too late' (1270).

This *deinon omma* stands in implicit opposition, then, to the sun's eye, which sees the force of two opposing claims – apparently indefeasible without loss, since Zeus backs Thebes, and yet the eagle is his bird. It is opposed to the vision of the Chorus as well. For they have called upon the sun to assist them in their search, asking to see what it saw. They allow themselves to wait for the illumination of an external and non-humanly controlled eye. Their attitude is one of allowing the salient claims to come into view before them from the world, rather than of deciding which ones they will and will not view. The Creonic eye is active, reforming. And Creon's imagery of himself throughout the play is, similarly, active and not passive: the ship's captain, forging his way; the tamer of animals; the toiling worker of metals, the male. The men of the Chorus, from the beginning, see themselves differently. Their call has more the character of a waiting than that of a making or shaping; it asks for something to be opened to them without insisting, from the first, that it be what suits them. It looms out of the dawn, through the mists of the river, and is seen. This same responsiveness of vision is present again at the later moment when their eyes at the same time see and weep, construe and are borne away. It is not an Hegelian attitude.

The position of the audience at a tragic performance has built into it just such a quality of open waiting. Active searching intelligence becomes joined to openness, to a willingness to be surprised and moved, in company with others.

This norm of vision suggests doubts not only about Creon but also, indeed, about projects of harmonizing and synthesizing in general, insofar as a synthesis involves the active modifying of standing commitments backed by Zeus and seen by the eye of nature. Our suspicions that the Chorus's vision is not Hegelian are reinforced by the ode that follows.

There are many *deinon* things, but not one of them is more *deinon* than the human being. This thing crosses the gray sea in the winter storm-wind, making its path along the troughs of the swelling waves. And the loftiest of goddesses, Earth, deathless and unwearied, it wears away, turning up the soil with the offspring of horses, as the ploughs go back and forth from year to year.

And the race of light-headed birds, and the tribes of savage beasts, and the sea-dwelling brood of the deep, he snares with the meshes of his twisted net and leads captive, cunning man. He masters with his arts the beasts of the open air, walkers on hills. The horse with his shaggy mane he tames, yoking him about the neck, and the tireless mountain bull.

Speech, too, and thought (*phronēma*) swift as the wind, and the temper (*orgas*) that builds cities, he has taught himself; and how to escape the arrows of the frost that makes hard lodging under a clear sky, and the arrows of the rain. He has a resource for everything; without resource he comes to nothing in the future. Only against death can he procure no escape; but he has devised escapes from hopeless diseases.

Clever beyond hope is the inventive craft he possesses. It brings him now to ill, now to good. When he fulfills the laws of the land and the oath-sworn justice of the gods, he is a man of lofty city; citiless the person who lives with what is not noble in his rash daring. May he never share my hearth, may he never think as I do, the one who does these things.[65]
(332–75)

By this time, the men of the Chorus have heard Creon's optimistic defense of the supremacy of the *polis*. They have also heard the guard's story of the strange burial. The word *deinon* has occurred twice in the course of the prior experiences that prepare this lyric. Both times it is used by the guard, who finds the burial *deinon* (243), fearful, incomprehensible, and who also thinks it *deinon*, terrible, that Creon should be so proud of his impious views (323). These uses lead us to expect a not unqualified optimism. Having witnessed these events and these ambitions, the men of the Chorus reflect that the human being is, in fact, a *deinon* thing: a wonderful and strange being not at home in, or in harmony with, the world of nature; a natural being who tears up nature to make itself a home, who then modifies its own nature to make itself cities. Nothing is more *deinon*, not even, the text implies, the gods. (This is, presumably, because their life is perfect harmony and control. They cannot be admired in the same way, since they have no obstacles to overcome; nor can they be feared or criticized in the same way, since they have no need to depart from their natures or to become impious in order to fulfill themselves.)

'This thing', they say, using the neuter pronoun, distancing themselves from the strangeness of this creature, attempting to give a dispassionate story of its nature and its behavior, 'crosses the gray sea...' At first reading, it is a history of triumphant progress. We hear enumerated the awesome array of devices invented by this creature to put itself in control of the contingent.[66] The ship and the plow, which appear before and after the ode as political metaphors, now appear literally, as examples of human inventiveness. And this remarkable resourcefulness is not limited to control over the external. For the human being has created itself as a social being, forming thoughts, emotions, institutions, governing the formerly ungovernable aspects of its own inner life. It seems indeed to have a resource for everything. There remains only the ultimate contingency, death. But, the Chorus notes, many sicknesses formerly thought hopeless have been cured by human devices. Death has been pushed back. Will a creature so resourceful really find no escape?

So the surface text of the lyric. But we have said that these images must be pursued backwards and forwards through the play, until we grasp their full web of connections and suggestions. If we do this we undercut this happy story. For every item mentioned, so read, points to some problem in the way of human progress. More specifically, each reveals something about the variety and plurality of human values, casting doubt on attempts to create harmony through synthesis. The ode thus takes us beyond our specific criticisms of the protagonists to a more general criticism of the ambition for the elimination of conflict.

Human beings make ships. They decide to travel across the sea and contrive to do this in safety. But we think now, too, of Creon's ship of state, also a human artifact. This ship, like a literal ship, can be dashed by storms: the gods have shaken Thebes 'in a great sea-storm' (163). And later the Chorus will reflect that 'for those whose house is shaken by the gods...it is just like sea-swell when the fierce-breathing Thracian winds drive it rushing over the dark of the sea, and it rolls up the black sand from the bottom, and the wind-beaten capes give back hollowness' (584–93). These connections make us think, then, not only of the vulnerability of human enterprises to external happenings, but also (insofar as the ship is the Creonic city) of the way in which human beings are so often forced to choose between the value of progress and the value of piety; between the pursuit of well-being or safety and due attention to religious obligations. We are led to think, then, of the central moral conflict of the play and to see it as one not easily defeasible by the art of even the best legislator. For the best legislator will always, and legitimately, be committed to the safety of his people; and in some circumstances this indefeasible commitment may require him to embark upon an impious course. Sometimes there is a Periclean solution; sometimes there is not.

The next image reinforces and extends this reflection. Earth is a source of food for us; and yet the choice to till her seems to involve the human being in an offense against the 'oldest of the goddesses'. Again, progress conflicts with piety; our very survival seems to depend upon a violation. We are led to think in general of the way in which a choice to make technological progress can so frequently involve us in the violation of some natural value, such as integrity, beauty; even the conditions of our own future health and prosperity. These conflicts would not be easily solved by any harmonizing view of the state; even a ruler more Hegelian than Creon will feel a deep conflict. This becomes clearer still when we consider other technological imagery in the play. Creon's talk of mining betrays a determination to control the object at the expense of its integrity and special beauty: the attitude of the miner is in insoluble tension with the attitude of the collector and lover of precious stones. We now recall, as well, Creon's use of plowing as an image for appropriately non-erotic civic sexuality. Here (more generally, in the accepted formulae of Athenian marriage) we see a dangerous ground of conflict harmonized away only by the determined disregard of the divinity of *erōs*. The attitudes necessary for orderly marriage seem to require the neglect of a power which, according to the Chorus, is coeval with and as binding as the ethical norms it endangers.[67] The good civic husband is not permitted to respond to the passion 'that sleeps on a young girl's soft cheeks', to the madness that 'turns men aside from duty'. Thus one divinity opposes another, Demeter is not the friend of Aphrodite, one legitimate claim dwells in tension with another. The Hegelian city will be forced to choose between marriage and *erōs*; it must of necessity choose the former. It must, then, neglect a god, ceasing to be Hegelian. Or, if (like Athens) it makes a serious attempt to honor all the gods, it must house uneasily those who do not honor one another and delight in facing mortals with conflicts; in which case, again, it ceases to be Hegelian.

The imagery of bird-netting and animal-taming which follows can be followed through the play in similar ways with similar results. Speech is next praised as a great invention. But speech, the reshaping of ethical discourse, has been the central tool of Creon's (and Antigone's) simplifications. At the play's end Haemon, the responsive lover, renounces speech altogether to die 'peering with the wild eyes' of an animal, 'making no reply' (1232). We are forced to ask, what sort of discourse would he not refuse? Would it be an Hegelian synthesizing discourse, denying and rising above contradictions? Or would it be more likely to be a discourse in which internal tensions were present and acknowledged? Perhaps, then, it might be the complex discourse of this tragedy taken as a whole.

Phronēma, next praised, is Creon's unusual word of choice for the mind whose health he takes to require simplifying refusals (176, 207, 473; cf. 459). And the 'temper that builds cities' (*astunomous orgas*) is *orgē* indeed: ungovernable rage, violent anger (280, 957, 766; cf. 875).[68] Thus the ode's odd vocabulary invites us to consider that it is, precisely, anger that builds Creon's city: violent rage at our vulnerability before the world is the deep motivation for these strategies of safety. Progress begins to look very like revenge. Even the refined Hegelian attempt to build a harmonized city might be only revenge's subtlest and most clever stratagem. This shows us why the *hupsipolis* and the *apolis*, the lofty-citied and the citiless, lie, in the thought and the wording of the ode, adjacent to one another: the rage for civic control has as its other face the neglect or the harmonizing-away of the special force of each of the separate concerns that fill out the city and give it its substance.[69]

In this way, the statement of human triumphs through reason turns out to be also a compressed document of reason's limitations, transgressions, and conflicts. It suggests that the richer our scheme of values, the harder it will prove to effect a harmony within it. The more open we are to the presence of value, of divinity, in the world, the more surely conflict closes us in. The price of harmonization seems to be impoverishment, the price of richness disharmony. It looks, indeed, like an 'unwritten law' (613) that 'nothing very great comes into the life of mortals without disaster' (613–14). It is at this point that the men of the Chorus say, appropriately, 'looking on this strange portent, I think on both sides'.

The anti-Hegelian intimations of the Ode of Man are developed and made explicit in the play's most darkly pessimistic ode. As Antigone is led away to her rocky tomb, the Chorus reflects on the ways in which optimistic hopes are qualified and undercut by life.

> Danae suffered too.
> She exchanged the light of heaven

for a brass-bound chamber.
Hidden, she was yoked in the tomb-like trunk.
And yet she too was of honorable descent, O child, child.
She even cherished in her body the seed of Zeus,
seed that fell on her in a golden rain.
But the power of a person's portion is terrible (*deina*).
Neither wealth nor war
nor towers nor the dark, sea-beaten
ships can get away from it.

He was yoked too –
the son of Dryas, quick in anger,
king of Edonia – by mocking rage (*orgais*) from Dionysus
bound in a rocky prison.
So the awesome (*deinon*) bursting strength of his madness
trickled away. That man
learned to know the god
he madly assailed with mocking taunts:
for he had tried to stop
the inspired women and the holy fire.
He had angered the flute-loving Muses.

By the black twin rocks of the twofold sea
are the shores of Bosporus and the Thracian strand,
Salmydessus, where Ares, city-neighbor,
saw the cursed wound
that blinded the two sons of Phineas,
wound struck by his savage wife,
bringing darkness to orbs
that looked for vengeance,
ripped by her bloody hands,
by the sharp point of her shuttle.

Melting away, the wretched boys
wept their wretched fate –
those sons of a mother fatefully married.
And yet that mother traced her descent
to the ancient line of the Erechthids.
In far-off caves she grew up, child of Boreas,
with her father's gusts for playmates,
riding with them beyond the steep hills.
But the long-lived Moirai
bore down on her too, my child.[70] (944–87)

We have moved from the human being victorious, traveling over the waves, to human beings immobilized in chambers of rock; from the light of the sun, rising over Thebes, to an airless box like a tomb; from the exuberant lightness of ships to the crushing pressure of Moira; from humans proudly yoking animals to an innocent girl, a guilty man, two helpless boys, a wind-god's daughter, yoked by luck. The expansive openness of the early lyrics has changed to a dense and choking atmosphere. Like Danae, we seem to have exchanged the light of the heavens for a dark prison. The Chorus's open eye saw the power of conflict and constraint; this vision has now become so unbearable that it is like a blinding.

Three prisoners are described in the two strophic pairs. First the Chorus speaks of the entirely innocent Danae, imprisoned by her own father because an oracle told him that her child would slay him. Her good luck of birth, the beauty that made her beloved of Zeus, her innocence, are powerless against darkness and paralysis. She is yoked; human arts offer her no means of escape. In a world where fathers, seeking safety and control, imprison daughters and attempt to prevent the birth of their grandchildren, salvation would have to come from an extra-human source. The Chorus alludes to the story that Zeus managed to impregnate Danae despite her father's safeguards, visiting her prison in the form of a golden rain-shower. When her father set mother and child adrift in the sea, locked tight in a brass-bound trunk, yoked again, we know that again Zeus rescued her. We know that her son was Perseus, that Perseus turned her father into stone with the Gorgon's head, thus appropriately bringing back to its source his mother's pain, rock for rock, ruthless anger for ruthless anger. The Chorus asks us to consider that salvation requires a golden rain, winged sandals, a mirror that enables a hero to conquer the terrible without really seeing it. Antigone, like anyone who has only human things to rely on, will be less fortunate. And even in the happy ending of the myth, deliverance comes about only through the power of anger and revenge, through the turning to stone of a human parent.

Second, the Chorus thinks of a more commanding figure, the king Lycurgus, 'swift in anger', who refused to acknowledge the divinity of Dionysus. Accordingly he, too, was bound to rock and diminished. His mocking rage was yoked by the mocking taunts of the god. This man, like Creon (present on stage during the ode), and, we might add, like Hegel, was apparently guilty of too much faith in human progress, too much pride in the controlling powers of reason and order. He came to know or acknowledge the god whom he had scorned. The price, or the agent, of this knowledge was immobility.

Finally the Chorus speaks of the bleakest case of all. They do not even relate the main features of the story, but simply allude to them, as if to say more would be superfluous, or too painful. It is the story of a girl raised among the swift free winds, daughter of the wind-god; the only caves explicitly mentioned are those in which, as a girl, she played. We are to contrast with these the prison where, the story goes, her husband shut her up because he wanted to marry a different woman. The only mention made of this story is the brief, 'But the long-lived Moirai bore down on her too, my child', which compares her predicament to Antigone's. They focus their attention instead upon the children, blinded by a jealous stepmother because they looked for vengeance (on their mother's behalf) with their eyes. Only Ares, god of war, sees the point of the shuttle pierce the intelligent organs. Through their eyes these children reached out, accused, demanded response and reparation. They demanded that their claim be *seen*; this demand was intolerable to the guilty.

This woman (like Creon) needed to render her opposition inert and inexpressive, because their humanness made itself too keenly felt as a claim upon her. If she allowed herself to respond to that look, she would have been torn between the claims of self and husband and these other just demands. This she could not bear; the other claim had to be forcibly extinguished, the resistance converted into unthreatening matter. Her rage at the way in which they force this tension upon her leads her to take up the shuttle, emblem of wifehood and household management, and to rip out that claim with blood. The children are now held in darkness, able only to weep without seeing. Their melting or yielding is accompanied by no active ordering or seeking.

This lyric bleakly knits together several of the themes that we have been pursuing. We hear of the power of external happenings and the violence of human rage against that power; of stratagem and denial; of the effort to become safe by immobilizing the threatening object; of receptivity and open vision. The choices of the human being seem few indeed; Hegelian progress is not evident among them. Either transgression, or the posture of the victim; the rage of the simplifier, or an openness that gets destroyed. The vision of the *omma deinon*, or the ripped and bloodied eye of a once-receptive child. The eye of the Chorus opened itself to the presence of conflict; it therefore could be swayed by the power of love and moved to tears. Now it pictures the end of this openness in the image of the weeping bloody children, whose just vision was punished by life. Nor do they hold out more hope for the revenger; for Lycurgus, too, is yoked and punished in the end. All humans alike end yoked like animals, whether because of their rage or because of their innocence. Where Hegel sees the hope of a harmony, they see, then, only the terrible power of unconstrained contingency. If you attempt to yoke it you violate and are yoked; if you acknowledge it you melt away.

The choices are unappealing. And we notice, furthermore, as we think of Hegel, that they confront us with a further, higher-order conflict concerning conflict itself. For we must choose, it seems, between active harmonizing or ordering and open responsiveness, between being the makers of a consistent conflict-free world of value and being receptive to the rich plurality of values that exist in the world of nature and of history. Every human forming of a scheme of value seems to involve a balancing of these two values, which have been explored throughout the play. The lyric gives us no confidence that we can have a harmonious synthesis of *these* claims, one that fully does justice to both. For it shows us that active harmonizing or ordering involves denial of something; and the open responsiveness we see here seems to lead to a passive abandonment of the human aim to make an orderly life.

Hegel's optimism has not been justified by the web of associations through which the lyrics have led us. Indeed, we might well think at this point of another writer on tragedy who, like us, objected to Hegel's sanguine extrapolations. For Schopenhauer, a moment of dreadful insight like the one at which we have now arrived is *the* knowledge that tragedy has to give: and the accompanying sense of paralysis is the proper response to this or any tragedy:

The purpose of this highest poetical achievement is the description of the terrible side of life. The unspeakable pain, the wretchedness and misery of mankind, the triumph of wickedness, the scornful mastery of chance, and the irretrievable fall of the good and the innocent are all here presented to us; and here is to be found a significant hint as to the nature of the world and of existence... The motives that were previously so powerful now lose their force, and instead of them the complete knowledge of the real nature of the world, acting as a quieter of the will, produces resignation, the giving up not merely of life, but of the whole will-to-live itself.[71]

This account now sounds more nearly correct than Hegel's as a picture of our experience.

V

But the Antigone does not in fact end with this paralyzing vision. Here, at the darkest moment of the drama, a blind man enters, led by a sighted child. This man, although blind, is walking, not immobilized; this child, though dependent, is active, not passively weeping. Neither of them is solitary in a hostile world; each is in the company of a friend on whom he can rely. From this partnership, this community of response, comes the possibility of action. The boy supports the old man's body; the old man supplies the deficiencies of the boy's immature intellect. In this way, 'two see from one' (989), as they travel a 'common road' (988).

The old man is a priest of Apollo, god associated with ordering and bounding. He is a man of art (*technē*), whose blindness has brought him insight unavailable to the more fortunate. He comes now to teach (992), to give knowledge by showing the 'signs' of his art (998).

His concern, Tiresias tells us, is, above all, with good deliberation, the 'best of possessions' (1050). He urges Creon to heal himself from a sickness of reason that is 'common to all human beings' (1023–5, 1052). This sickness is, presumably, the rage for control, with its attendant impieties; we have seen how justly it might be said to be common to all. But how does Tiresias propose to 'heal' this sickness without falling into the opposite trap of immobility? What healing, indeed, is conceivable without renouncing choice and action altogether?

Tiresias says that good deliberation is connected with 'yielding' (*eike*, 1029), with renouncing self-willed stubbornness (1028), with being flexible (1027). This advice recalls Haemon's speech to his father earlier in the play.[72] Criticizing Creon's *omma deinon* and his singleness of *ēthos*, of concern or commitment (690, 705), his insistence that only his single way is the *correct* one (706, cf. 685), Haemon urges a different policy. To avoids the sheer *hollowness* of Creon's condition (709) he should learn not to *strain* too much (711). Haemon, like Tiresias, connects this not-straining with the ability to learn (710, 723), and with the idea of yielding (718). He gives two examples from nature. By the banks of swift-flowing streams, the trees that bend or give way save their branches; the ones that remain rigid are uprooted and destroyed (712–14). A helmsman who steers his ship, straining, straight into the wind will capsize; the one who gives with the winds and currents steers safely (715–17). Both Haemon and Tiresias, then, press a connection between learning and yielding, between practical wisdom and supple flexibility. What is this conception of practical wisdom, and how does it propose to deal with the problems of one who stands, as does Creon, 'on the razor's edge of luck' (996)?

First of all, we must notice that Haemon and Tiresias do not propose the simple opposite of Creon's actively controlling rigidity. They do not, that is to say, tell him that he had better become completely passive and inert, allowing everything in nature to affect him and to push him this way and that, taking no steps to control or to shape his life. They do not, then, accept the suggestion we found contained in the Danae ode, that the only two alternatives are Creon's violence against the external and complete helpless passivity before the external. A plant has a definite nature; it is this and not that; it requires, 'cares for', responds to, this and not that. It is vulnerable and needy; but it also has its own appropriate ends and, to put it somewhat metaphorically, its own sense of value. The ship, too, is a definite conveyance that takes people somewhere to pursue certain characteristic aims and ends. It does not and cannot simply go with every current and every wind that bears upon it; it has its own orderly way and its own course. Haemon has not, then, urged on Creon an abnegation of the human activity of choosing the good and striving to realize the good. He even accepts from Creon the appropriateness of the ship image for human deliberative life: accepts, that is, the thought that our pursuit of the good must devise ways to keep us safe from natural disaster. What he says is, that it is important, in pursuit of one's human ends, to remain open to the claims and pulls of the external, to cultivate flexible responsiveness, rather than rigid hardness. He urges on Creon (what Aristotle will urge on his Platonist opponents) a practical wisdom that bends responsively to the shape of the natural world, accommodating itself to, giving due recognition to, its complexities. (Aristotle will use the image of an architect who measures a complex column with a flexible strip of metal, contrasting this suppleness to the crude procedures of one who approaches the same column with a straight edge.)[73] This deliberative art appropriately combines activity with passivity, fidelity to its own nature with responsiveness to the world.[74]

These characters suggest, then, as Tiresias's own life suggests, that the bleak alternatives of the Danae ode were too simple: that responsiveness (to other people, to the world of nature) may bring not immobility, but a finer and more supple sort of motion. And it is not simply that this way of proceeding is safer and more prudent. Haemon and Tiresias do say this. But they also indicate (especially Haemon, with his use of nature imagery) that this way is also richer and more beautiful. To be flexibly responsive to the world, rather than rigid, is a way of living in the world that allows an acceptable amount of safety and stability while still permitting recognition of the richness of value that is in the world. Creon's singleness of *ēthos* is not only foolish; it is, as we saw, ugly and impoverished. It began as a civilizing device, but it ends by being fiercely uncivilized.[75] Haemon's advice is that the true way of being humanly civilized requires the preservation of the mystery and specialness of the external, the preservation, in oneself, of the passions that take one to these mysteries. Such a life has room for love; and it also has room, as Tiresias's life shows, for genuine community and cooperation. Only the person who balances self-protection with yielding in this way can be either a lover or a friend: for the completely passive victim cannot act to help another, and the Creonic agent cannot see otherness. The 'razor's edge of luck' requires in this way the most delicate balance between order and disorder, control and vulnerability.

How does this speak to our problem about conflict, and our perception of a higher-level conflict between the value of consistency (freedom from conflict) and the value of richness? We are asked to see that a conflict-free life would be lacking in value and beauty next to a life in which it is possible for conflict to arise; that part of the value of each claim derives from a special separateness and distinctness that would be eclipsed by harmonization. That, as Heraclitus put it, justice really *is* strife: that is, that the tensions that permit this sort of strife to arise are also, at the same time, partly constitutive of the values themselves. Without the possibility of strife it would all fall apart, be itself no longer. The Danae chorus had not comprehended how thoroughly constraint and choice condition one another and are mixed: how anything worth pursuing is worth what it is partly on account of the way it is bounded off against other things, therefore potentially at odds or in tension with them. One would not learn from Haemon to maximize tension or conflict: for the possibility of action itself requires, as his ship imagery suggests, some devising or structuring, therefore, very likely, some refusals or denials. If, for example, we could ever see clearly and be moved by the value of each unique person in the world, we could never without intolerable pain and guilt be able to act so as to benefit any one of them rather than any other – as love, or justice, might in some cases require. (If I saw and valued other people's children as I do my own, my own could never receive from me the love, time, and care that she *ought* to have, that it is just and right for her to have.) But we must stop somewhere in these necessary and even just blindnesses, balancing open responsiveness against order in some appropriate way.

Does the follower of Tiresias know any standard for this balancing? How much simplification is Creonic insult, how much responsiveness is compatible with sanity and justice? Tiresias's 'art' teaches Creon, in fact, to follow convention. 'It is best to keep to the established conventions (*nomous*)[76] to the end of one's life' Creon concludes (1113–14). He suggests, then, that the traditions of a community, built up and established over time, offer a good guide to what, in the world, ought to be recognized and yielded to, what is important and worthy of attention. The conventions preserve a rich plurality of values, and they teach us reverence for gods who protect, together, this plurality. Conventions preserve the special separateness and the importance of each of the gods and the spheres of human life protected by each. They offer no solution in bewildering tragic situations – except the solution that consists in being faithful to or harmonious with one's sense of worth by acknowledging the tension and disharmony. They show how, as Heraclitus said, 'It is in being at variance with itself that it coheres with itself: a back-stretching harmony, as of a bow or a lyre.'

The Chorus responds to this praise of convention with an impassioned invocation of Dionysus,[77] god whose mysterious power has been scorned and mocked by Lycurgus's reason, god neglected (along with Eros) in the strategies of both Creon and Antigone. They imagine the god illuminated or seen by a murky flame that flashes forth in darkness (1126–7). They recall, as well, the flash of lightning that brought to this city, to Semele, the creative force of divine *erōs*, even as it brought danger and death (1139). Dionysus, offspring of this ambiguous union, so linking risk with value, darkness with light, is to be revealed, to come, as watcher or overlooker (1136, 1148–9). Even as he is seen by dark light, so he will be a light in darkness and a watcher to the city, bringing healing (1140–2) by leading the city in nocturnal dances. The witnessing of the god will have as its object a supple, flowing structure that moves in, and takes its character from darkness and mystery; a speech that is humanly artful, and yet responsive to strangeness (*phthegmatōn*, 1148, cf. 353), an orderly and reverent madness (*mainomenai*, 1151).

What healing is in this dance? It surely does not lead to Creon's rigid health. This healing is no vanquishing – but, simply, a communal acknowledgment, in motion and song, of the power of the strange and sudden; of the world's indissoluble intermingling of ecstasy and danger, of light and shadow.

By invoking Dionysus as 'chorus-master of the fire-breathing stars' (1147), the Chorus reminds us that we are watching and responding to just such a choral dance at a Dionysian festival. They suggest that the spectacle of this tragedy is itself an orderly mystery, ambitiously yielding, healing without cure, whose very harmony (as we respond to it in common) is not simplicity but the tension of distinct and separate beauties.[78]

Conclusion to Part I

Our discussions of tragedy so far have started from our second question, about the plurality of the values and the possibility of conflict among them. This has led, in turn, to some discussion of our first question, about the vulnerability of certain values taken singly, and also of our third, about the disrupting power of the passions. For it turns out that some very vulnerable single values are also dangerous grounds of conflict and occasions for passional upheaval; and stratagems for eliminating conflict have also rendered each of these more stable in its own right. (These connections among the problems will be further elaborated in the chapters that follow: especially Chapter 4, pp. 116–17; Chapter 5, §v; Chapter 6, pp. 181 and 196–7; and Chapter 7, p. 221.) It might, however, seem more symmetrical and systematic if, at this point, we devoted an entire chapter to tragedy's perception of the vulnerability of individual values, such as love, friendship, and political commitment. We shall not do this here, for two reasons. First, Chapter 13 is just such a reading of a (Euripidean) tragedy: it asks about the fragility of a good human life through its commitment to love and to social values. This chapter can be read at this point rather than later by any reader interested in pursuing the issues in chronological sequence. Its argument in no way relies on later material. And it further develops several motifs of Chapter 3: the relationship between safety and love, between the ambition to invulnerability and revenge; the importance of eyes, seeing, and blinding in the exploration of human fragility; the ways in which a good person is and is not like a plant. It is placed at the end because it shows very clearly the extent to which Aristotle 'returns' to the conception of the good human life embodied in tragedies.

Second, a conception of vulnerable attachment that is developed in a number of tragedies also finds expression within the Platonic dialogues themselves – especially, as I shall argue, in the *Symposium*. As Plato criticizes tragic values, he allows them to defend themselves with eloquence. Since Chapter 6 develops this conception of love in detail, and since Chapter 7 develops it further, showing Plato 'recanting' aspects of his former criticism, it would be too repetitious to add a chapter on love in tragedy at this point.

For these reasons we shall now turn directly to the role of problems of *tuchē* in motivating the birth of specifically philosophical reflection about human value and choice. We have heard Tiresias speak of *technē*, 'art' or 'science'; we have also heard examples of arts mentioned in the lyric story of human progress. But Tiresias's *technē* enjoined us simply to remain close to established conventions. It did not use the techniques of the newly developing sciences to make progress on our behalf. Plato will feel that this conservatism is insufficient; and he will see in the concept of *technē*, properly developed, the most promising tool for the saving of human lives. *Technē*, properly construed, saves precisely by going beyond convention.

As we turn to Plato and Plato's Socrates, we might think about the following story. Diogenes Laertius reports that Socrates once attended a play of Euripides in which a character, speaking about practical excellence, spoke the lines: 'It is best to let these things go as they will, without management.' Hearing this, Socrates 'got up and left the theater, saying that it was absurd to...let excellence perish in this way' (D. L. II.33).

Part II
Plato: goodness without fragility?

> I hid myself
> Within a fountain in the public square,
> Where I lay like the reflex of the moon
> Seen in a wave under green leaves, and soon
> Those ugly human shapes and visages
> Of which I spoke as having wrought me pain,
> Passed floating through the air, and fading still
> Into the winds that scattered them; and those
> From whom they passed seemed mild and lovely forms
> After some foul disguise had fallen, and all
> Were somewhat changed, and after brief surprise
> And greetings of delighted wonder, all
> Went to their sleep again.
>
> Shelley, *Prometheus Unbound*, III.4

Introduction

We now begin our examination of Plato's radical, stern, and beautiful proposal for a self-sufficient human life. Plato's ethical thought, I shall argue, is continuous with the reflections about *tuchē* that we have uncovered in tragedy, responding to the same urgencies, giving shape to the same human ambitions. It is bolder and more single-minded in its pursuit of progress, but not without its own sense of the human cost of progress.

As we pursue our questions in Plato's works, two major problems confront us: development and dialogue. Plato is a courageously self-critical philosopher; he not only revises previous positions, he even subjects them to criticism within his dialogues themselves. This means that it can be dangerous to make a synthesis of positions from different works; and yet often, clearly, it can also be fruitful, even necessary. In Chapter 5, I defend my procedure in bringing together several dialogues of the 'middle' period as I work on Plato's views about true value. At the end of Chapter 4, I sketch what I see as the most important shifts in Plato's approach to our problems between the early *Protagoras* and the middle-period works; I stress the fundamental continuity between the two approaches. In Chapter 7 I argue that Plato, in the *Phaedrus*, systematically criticizes the middle-period view as insufficiently responsive to the positive role of vulnerable values in the good life. (This criticism is prepared by the *Symposium*'s sympathetic portrayal of the life that it criticizes – Ch. 6.)

A second problem is, clearly, the dialogue form. Plato uses the dialogue to motivate a view, to make us feel the force of a problem, to explain the practical roots and implications of a solution (cf. Interlude 1). A characteristic strategy towards these ends is to show us alternative responses to the same problem and to let them 'examine' one another as the dialogue progresses. If he has done this job well, we will see clearly, at the end, both the nature of the problem and the nature of the choices before us. We do not always so clearly see what choice 'Plato' wants us to make. This makes it dangerous, in such a case, to speak of 'Plato's views', unless we simply mean his view of what the open alternatives are and what the choice of either involves giving up – no trivial view in itself. But we do often want to go further than this and to speak of Plato as defending one alternative over another. It would be a mistake to abandon this way of speaking. His students, Aristotle included, had no doubt that he was defending views in works such as *Republic* and *Phaedo*. They had no hesitation in ascribing to Plato, on the basis of these dialogues, a certain view of the soul, of the best individual and political life. These works are, not coincidentally, dialogues in which there is no deep ongoing opposition to the positions developed by Socrates. I have therefore felt more free in those cases to treat the dialogue form as compatible with the ascription of a single line of argument to Plato. In the *Phaedrus*, I believe that we can still speak with confidence about a view of Plato emerging out of the self-critical work – though here, as I insist, myth and story join with argument in a new way to articulate that view. The most difficult cases are, I now believe, the *Protagoras* and *Symposium*, for similar reasons. In my readings of these I have stressed the way in which one position shows the limitations of another, especially the way in which the deficiencies of the position closer to ordinary belief shows the *need* for the more radical position taken by Socrates. But in both cases the victory of Socrates remains an ambiguous and contested victory, because he is seen to move so far and give up so much. It is probably no accident that both of these contested victories apparently occur just before a significant shift in Plato's thinking. Having described so clearly the loss entailed by each of the Socratic positions, Plato is motivated to work out a new position that will better confront the complexities of the problem.

There are many ways in which a reader who also takes the dialogue form seriously might object to the solutions at which I have arrived. (I confront some of those concerns more explicitly in Interlude 1.) I ask the reader to see these interpretations as plausible attempts to take the dialogue seriously while attending appropriately to the philosophical arguments. I hope that they will inspire further attempts in this same spirit.

The *Protagoras*: a science of practical reasoning

And look: I gave them numbering, chief of all the stratagems.
>   Prometheus, in Aeschylus[?], *Prometheus Bound*

Every circumstance by which the condition of an individual can be
influenced, being remarked and inventoried, nothing...[is] left to chance,
caprice, or unguided discretion, everything being surveyed and set down in
dimension, number, weight, and measure.
>   Jeremy Bentham, *Pauper Management Improved*

They did not want to look on the naked face of luck (*tuchē*), so they turned
themselves over to science (*technē*). As a result, they are released from their
dependence on luck; but not from their dependence on science.
>   Hippocratic treatise *On Science* (*Peri Technēs*), late fifth century B.C.

The *Antigone* spoke of a life lived 'on the razor's edge of luck'. It warned against
overambitious attempts to eliminate luck from human life, displaying both their
internal failures and their problematic relation to the richness of values recognized
in ordinary belief. Its conclusion appeared conservative: human beings had better
stay with 'established conventions' in spite of the risks these leave in place. Both
Aeschylean and Sophoclean tragedy have, in this way, combined a keen sense of
our exposure to fortune with an awareness that some genuine human value is
inseparable from this condition. This recognition left, it seems, little room for
decisive progress on our problems.

The late fifth century in Athens, the time of Plato's youth, was a time both
of acute anxiety and of exuberant confidence in human power. If human life
seemed more than ever exposed to *tuchē* in all its forms, Athenians were also more
than ever gripped by the idea that progress might bring about the elimination
of ungoverned contingency from social life.[1] This hope found expression in an
antithesis and a story: the contrast between *tuchē*, luck,* and *technē*, human art or
science; and the accompanying frequently told story of human progress against
contingency through the reception or discovery of the *technai*.[2] Plato's *Protagoras*,
set in that time, tells the story, criticizes a conservative Athenian interpretation
of it, and proposes a philosophical addition: Socrates argues that really decisive
progress in human social life will be made only when we have developed a new

---

* On *tuchē*, see also Ch. 1, p. 3. *Tuchē* does not imply randomness or absence of causal connections.
  Its basic meaning is 'what just happens'; it is the element of human existence that humans do not
  control.

technē, one that assimilates practical deliberation to counting, weighing, and measuring.

Throughout the dialogues that we shall study here, Plato's elaboration of radical ethical proposals is motivated by an acute sense of the problems caused by ungoverned luck in human life. The need of human beings for philosophy is, for him, deeply connected with their exposure to luck; the elimination of this exposure is a primary task of the philosophical art as he conceives it. His conception of this art in the *Protagoras* differs in certain ways from the conception worked out in dialogues of his 'middle' period.[3] But his sense of the nature and urgency of the problems behind philosophy remains constant. So does the belief that these problems can only be solved by a new kind of expert: one whose knowledge will take practical deliberation beyond the confusion of ordinary practice, fulfilling an aspiration to scientific precision and control already contained within ordinary belief. That is why the *Protagoras*, which takes as its explicit subject the human hope for science and the relationship between science and ordinary belief, is a good place to begin our investigation of Plato's relationship to the problems of *tuchē*, as ordinary belief depicts them.

The dialogue stages a competition between two figures, each of whom claims to be the herald of a social or political *technē* that will add a new chapter to the story of human progress through the *technai*. We should, therefore, prepare ourselves to appreciate the force of their proposals by telling ourselves this story, as a reader of the dialogue would know it.[4]

Once, a long time ago, human beings wandered over the surface of the earth and had no way to make themselves safe. Everything that happened was a threat. Rain drenched their uncovered skin; snow stung; hail slashed. The sun's dry heat brought searing thirst and fever to their unprotected heads. Helpless, they huddled in sunless caves beneath the ground. No hunting or farming skills gave them a stable source of food; no tame animals plowed or carried. No weather-diviner's art prepared them for the next day. No medical science healed their vulnerable bodies. Nor could they turn for help to their fellow human beings, undertaking cooperative projects, communicating in shared language. Speechlessness and wilderness kept them apart. Isolated, silent, naked, they could neither record the past nor plan for the future; they could not even comfort each other in their present misery. 'Like shapes in dreams, they mixed up everything at random as their lives went on.' But so shapeless, without stability or structure, it could hardly have felt like a life.

These proto-humans (for their existence is so far more bestial than human) would soon have died off, victims of starvation, overexposure, the attacks of stronger beasts. Then the kindness of Prometheus (god named for the foresight and planning that his gifts make possible) granted to these creatures, so exposed to *tuchē*, the gift of the *technai*. House-building, farming, yoking and taming, metal-working, shipbuilding, hunting; prophecy, dream-divination, weather-prediction, counting and calculating; articulate speech and writing; the practice of medicine; the art of building dwelling-places – with all these arts they preserved and improved their lives. Human existence became safer, more predictable; there was a measure of control over contingency.

But still, in these cities of human beings (for now we are entitled to call them that), *tuchē* was not defeated. Many of their most cherished pursuits (especially their social pursuits) were vulnerable to uncontrolled happenings. Nor was there any stable harmony among the diverse commitments and values that characterized an ordinary human life. Furthermore, humans regularly found themselves 'overcome', as if by an alien power, by the force of their own passions, which both distorted their view of the good and blocked its effective pursuit. In all these ways their experience threw them into confusion, so that in their actions and choices, both of great things and of small, they felt themselves to be in continual danger. Such a life did not seem worth living for an artful creature like the human being. They searched for another life-saving art.

It is a story of gradually increasing human control over contingency. Its general outlines are familiar to us from the *Antigone*. Socrates and Protagoras will compete to fill out its final chapter. The dialogue presents us with a view of the problems that such a science must solve and offers us two deeply divergent views of what it can and should be. Socrates' proposal, in which numbering and measuring are central, is motivated, I shall argue, by the inability of the Protagorean 'art' to solve pressing problems with which both thinkers are concerned. The dialogue as a whole is a complex reflection about the relationship of sciences to problems, *technē* to *tuchē*; about the way in which science both saves us and transforms us, helps us attain our ends and reshapes the ends themselves. We can begin, then, by seeing how its characters and dramatic setting bring into focus the problems that the new science is supposed to solve. Then (after making some observations about the background conception of *technē*) we shall approach the rival proposals.

I

Plato chooses to set this dialogue right on the 'razor's edge'. It is a time of pride and prosperity – about two years before the outbreak of the Peloponnesian War, three years before the great plague that devastated Athens, both physically and morally.[5] Diseases of the body, diseases of character, the disease of war – all, we know, will shortly strike, unforeseen, this intelligent city that prides itself so much on artfulness and foresight. Since the reader, by hindsight, is aware that a vulnerable moral consensus is soon to be unhinged by external pressures, by the pull of conflicting obligations, by the strength of the appetitive desires, since he knows that among this dialogue's characters some will soon be dead and others will soon be killing, he will feel impatience with the lack of foresight that says that things in Athens are all right as they are. He will look for signs of disease beneath the optimism; he will look for a pessimistic and radical doctor.

In this dialogue Socrates is young – thirty-six in 433, and relatively little-known. His defeat of Protagoras may be his first public 'success'. Plato's dramatic portrait shows that, in other ways as well, he is not the Socrates of the *Symposium* (dramatic date 416) or even of the *Republic* (422).[6] A friend stops him on the road and asks him where he is coming from. Without even waiting for an answer, the friend knows: 'It's obvious that it's from your hunt [the word is the word for giving chase with a pack of dogs] after the beauty of Alcibiades.' (How, we wonder, is it obvious? Because that's his constant preoccupation? Is he distracted from all other pursuits by this hunt, like the characters disdainfully described by Diotima in the *Symposium*?[7]) This friend – not much like later friends of Socrates, but accepted here as a friend nonetheless – now teases him, saying that the boy is past his prime: he's already growing a beard. 'What of it?' Socrates replies, entering into the spirit of erotic gossip. After all, Homer (whose authority he seems happy to cite) says that this is the most delicious age of all. The friend, who seems to be a regular recipient of Socrates' erotic confidences, now presses him: how, then, is the seduction progressing? (For Socrates here is the needy searching *erastēs*, Alcibiades the beautiful *erōmenos*, though, as we shall see in Ch. 6, these roles were later to be reversed.) Socrates is optimistic: Alcibiades is both kind and helpful. We are struck by the degree of Socrates' erotic responsiveness to the particularity of a single bodily individual; such everyday eroticism will figure in his *Symposium* speech only as an unacceptable way of living that philosophy helps us to avoid. Socrates says there that he was *persuaded* by Diotima to undertake the ascent, which promised freedom from the slavish love of unpredictable individuals; he acknowledges that he was different before this persuasion. Here we catch a glimpse of that difference.

But in Socrates' next remarks, we also see evidence that the ascent is in progress. His desire for the (alleged) wisdom of Protagoras made him, he says, completely forgetful of Alcibiades, even in his physical presence. And he considers the beauty of wisdom to be 'more beautiful' than Alcibiades' personal charm. It is important that he is willing already to treat this personal beauty as comparable, apparently along a single quantitative scale, with the beauty of philosophy or understanding. This is a crucial feature both of the *Protagoras* science of measurement and of the *Symposium* ascent, and a salient element of continuity between them. Socrates' remarks are in part ironic, since the conversation with Protagoras has already taken place and he knows that he has nothing to learn from Protagoras. But we do not need to doubt the sincerity of his assertions about the beauty of wisdom and his commitment to its pursuit. Young Socrates, then, is and is not persuaded by Diotima; he goes in and out of focus. But his vestigial love for the individuality of pieces of the physical world seems to be yielding increasingly to the judgments that will ground the science.

Something similar happens in the (dramatically) nearly contemporary *Charmides*.[8] At one point Socrates, inflamed by passion at the sight of Charmides' naked body inside his loose cloak, loses all control over himself and his practical judgments, becoming like a lion in pursuit of a fawn (155D–E, cf. 154B). But both before and after this moment he is pressing the view that beauties of soul and body are similar and commensurable, and that the soul is of far greater importance. Such a view, as we shall see, is good medicine for such losses of control.

Having praised wisdom, the Socrates of the *Protagoras* now takes a seat formerly occupied by a slave-boy (even as his slavish passion for Alcibiades yields place to his love of philosophy) and narrates the rest of the story (310A). It is the story of a competition for a soul. Hippocrates, a well-born, naïve young man, came to Socrates' house before dawn, full of eagerness to go and enroll himself as a pupil of the visiting sophist Protagoras. He is, strikingly, a namesake of the great doctor, leading practitioner and theorist of the new medical science, whose works extol the progress made by this *technē*. The connection of names is prominently stressed by Socrates, who also draws an elaborate parallel between Hippocrates' science and the alleged science of the sophist (331Bff., 313Cff.). After some brief questioning, it emerges that Hippocrates views his relationship to Protagoras as analogous to that of patient to doctor. He and Socrates now agree that there is a therapy of the soul that is analogous to the doctor's therapy of the body: as one goes to a doctor to get physically healed, so the proper end of philosophy (sophistry) is the healing of the soul. Socrates warns Hippocrates of the need for circumspection before he turns over his soul to an alleged expert for cure. Since the treatment will change the soul for better or worse, it is important to ask questions about the doctor's knowledge and the healing it promises.

What diseases of the soul are recognized by these seekers after therapy? For if we can be clear about the dialogue's depiction of human problems we will be better able to assess the competing solutions. (To some extent we must use hindsight, looking in the opening sequence for examples of difficulties that are explicitly recognized later on.) We see here a high degree of confusion about values, about what ought to be pursued and what not. Socrates and his friend disagree about what beauty is and what beauties are important. Socrates himself is confused about his erotic and philosophical motivations. Hippocrates has rushed off in pursuit of wisdom, of which he knows nothing, just because it sounds attractive. He doesn't understand, either, why he did not come earlier to tell Socrates about this runaway slave (310E): he knows he was distracted by something else, but he doesn't seem at any point to have made a deliberate choice in accordance with any clear criterion. We recognize, then, a need later stressed by Socrates (356C–E): the need for an orderly procedure of choice that will save us from being buffeted by the 'appearances' of the moment. Ordinary deliberation looks confused, unsystematic, and consequently lacking in control over both present and future.

This general problem grows out of and is linked to several that are more specific. We notice here, in fact, versions of all three of our problems of *tuchē*. First, we notice the vulnerability of these people to luck through their attachment to vulnerable objects and activities. The love affair with Alcibiades may go well or badly; this is not in Socrates' control. Insofar as he attaches importance to a pursuit and an object that are not in his grasp or even readily manipulable, he puts his own life at the mercy of luck. He does not know or control his future. (He cannot be, as he later is (361D), the new Prometheus.)

We see, too, that the values pursued by these people are plural. They see no clear way of rendering them commensurable or of avoiding serious conflicts among them. The hunt after Alcibiades pulls against the pursuit of philosophical discourse; a competing claim makes Hippocrates lose sight of the problem of the runaway slave. No common coin of value gives them a purchase on these conflicts, making them less stark.

We see, finally, the power of passion and need to derail practical planning. Socrates' pursuit of Alcibiades has often eclipsed all his other pursuits; the friend is more interested in love affairs than in anything else; the erotic and disorderly personality of Alcibiades dominates the scene. Hippocrates is 'overcome' and distracted from his plans by bodily need too: not, in his case, by *erōs*, but by the need for sleep (310C8–D2). Erotic need and the need for sleep are two features of ordinary human life conspicuously absent from the 'cured' Socrates of the *Symposium*.

Those are the diseases. The correct *technē* of practical choice would seem to be the one that could cure them.

II

Protagoras and Socrates agree that we need a *technē* governing practical choice.[9] They differ, at first, concerning the nature of the science required. The argument ends with the agreement of all present that only a practical *technē* of the type favored by Socrates can 'save the lives' of human beings. Before we can assess their proposals we must understand what they are proposals about. What is the common notion of which the two are producing rival specifications? To ask this requires a historical digression, but one necessary for the adequate pursuit of our main line of argument.

The word 'technē' is translated in several ways: 'craft', 'art', and 'science' are the most frequent. Examples of recognized *technai* include items that we would call by each of these three names. There are housebuilding, shoemaking, and weaving; horsemanship, flute-playing, dancing, acting, and poetry-writing; medicine, mathematics, and meteorology. The Greek word is more inclusive than any one of these English terms. It is also very closely associated with the word '*epistēmē*', usually translated 'knowledge', 'understanding'; or 'science', 'body of knowledge' (depending on whether it is being used of the known or of the cognitive condition of the knower). In fact, to judge from my own work and in the consensus of philologists, there is, at least through Plato's time, no systematic or general distinction between *epistēmē* and *technē*.[10] Even in some of Aristotle's most important writings on this topic, the two terms are used interchangeably.[11] This situation obtains in the *Protagoras*.[12]

The best place to begin searching for the ordinary conception of *technē* is the *technē–tuchē* antithesis, which both displays, and, by its pervasiveness, shapes it.[13] Traces of the antithesis are evident already in Homer; by the time of Thucydides and the Hippocratic writer, it is a commonplace. The contrast is between living at the mercy of *tuchē* and living a life made safer or more controlled by (some) *technē*. *Technē* is closely associated with practical judgment or wisdom (*sophia, gnōmē*) with forethought, planning, and prediction. To be at the mercy of *tuchē* where *technē* is available is to be witless (e.g. Democritus B197); indeed, Democritus goes so far as to say that the whole notion of *tuchē*'s power is just an excuse that people have invented to cover up for their own lack of practical resourcefulness (B119).

Technē, then, is a deliberate application of human intelligence to some part of the world, yielding some control over *tuchē*; it is concerned with the management of need and with prediction and control concerning future contingencies. The person who lives by *technē* does not come to each new experience without foresight or resource. He possesses some sort of systematic grasp, some way of ordering the subject matter, that will take him to the new situation well prepared, removed from blind dependence on what happens.[14]

To go further in setting out criteria for *technē* in the fifth and early fourth centuries, we can turn above all to the earlier treatises of the Hippocratic corpus, especially the treatises *On Medicine in the Old Days* (*Peri Archaiēs Iētrikēs*, abbreviated *Vet. Med.*), and *On Science* (*Peri Technēs*, or *De Arte*) – both probably to be dated late in the fifth century. For here we find what we do not find in contemporary literary and philosophical texts, namely a systematic *argument* that some human enterprise, in this case medicine, really deserves the title of *technē*. Criteria that remain implicit elsewhere are here explicitly stated. A similar list of criteria emerges, much later, from Aristotle's reflection on *technē* (especially the medical *technē*) in *Metaphysics* 1.1. I shall refer to this discussion as well, since, though considerably after the *Protagoras* in date, its aim is to articulate a shared ongoing conception, a task which Aristotle here performs with his usual sensitivity. His results agree remarkably well with the medical texts; they may display Aristotle's own medical background. We find, in these sources, four features of *technē* stressed above all: (1) universality; (2) teachability; (3) precision; (4) concern with explanation.

(1) *Universality*. 'A *technē*', writes Aristotle, 'comes into being when from many notions gained by experience a universal judgment about a group of similar things arises' (981a5–7). He contrasts a hypothesis about what helped this particular case of disease with a general theory about a group of cases judged relevantly similar. Only the latter can be *technē*; and in virtue of this universality it can deliver true predictions concerning future cases. The fifth-century evidence stresses this same feature. The *Epidemics*, among the earliest Hippocratic texts, was exciting precisely because it gathered the experience of many similar cases into a general unitary theory of the disease that could provide physicians with an antecedent grasp of the prognosis for a new case. The authors of *On Science* and *On Medicine in the Old Days* answer charges that patients are healed by luck, not *technē*, by pointing to the reliable and general connection between a certain sort of treatment and a certain result: their procedures, they say, are not a series of *ad hoc* manoeuvres, but 'A principle and a charted course' (*Vet. Med.* 1.2; *De Arte* 4). Xenophon, similarly, praises the ability of a person of *technē* to make a systematic unity of disparate elements.[15]

(2) *Teachability*. The universality of *technē* yields the possibility of teaching (Ar. *Metaph.* 981b7–8). Unordered experience can only be *had*, as chance brings it about; but *technē* can be communicated in advance of the experience, since it has grouped many experiences together and produced an account. The Hippocratic doctors make a similar point. The reason that some doctors are good and others are bad is that some have studied something that the others have not (*Vet. Med.* 1); the doctor must say this in order to support the claim of medicine to be a *technē*.

(3) *Precision*. *Technē* brings precision (*akribeia*) where before there was fuzziness and vagueness. The notion of *akribeia* is extremely important in fifth-century debates over *technē*. Originally connected, apparently, with true, precise construction of some manufactured object,[16] *akribeia* comes to be associated, in medical debates, both with lawlike regularity or invariance and with fidelity to data: medicine is precise, *akribēs*, to the extent that its rules hold true, without exception, of all the cases, no matter how many and how varied they are. The acquisition of *akribeia* is frequently linked with the notion of having a *measure* or a *standard*. The carpenter gets a precise fit by measuring correctly; measuring helps him to make his art more artful.[17] The doctor (on the defensive here, as we might expect) apologizes for the lack of *akribeia* in his art by pointing out that the measure to which he must, *faute de mieux*, refer is something far more elusive than number or weight – namely, the perceptions of each patient's body (*Vet. Med.* 9; cf. also the later *On Sterile Women*, which argues that treatment cannot be a matter of weighing). This means that the best he can hope for is to make only small mistakes.

(4) *Concern with explanation*. Finally, *technē* brings with it a concern for explaining: it asks and answers 'why' questions about its procedures (cf. *Vet. Med.* 20, Ar. *Metaph.* 981a28–30). A doctor who has learned the medical *technē* differs from his more *ad hoc* counterpart not just in his ability to predict what will happen if a certain treatment is applied, but also in his ability to explain precisely why and how the treatment works. The person of mere experience could tell you that on various occasions eating a lot of cheese gave the patient a stomach-ache. One stage further on, we find a doctor who says 'Cheese is a bad food, because it gives a stomach-ache to the person who eats a lot of it' (*Vet. Med.* 20). The author of *Vet. Med.*, and Aristotle, insist that this second person's knowledge would still fall short of *technē*: 'He must say what sort of pain it is and why it arises and what part of the human being is badly affected.' In numerous examples this medical author stresses that the doctor must be able to isolate the element *in* the food or the treatment that causes good or harm, and to explain how (through what sort of causal interaction with the body) the effect takes place. This ability, he points out, is closely linked to the goals of prediction and control: for without this information 'he will not be able to know what will result [sc. from a given treatment] or to use it correctly'.

These four features all bear upon the goal of mastering contingency; all are taken to be necessary features of *technē* on account of the relation in which they stand to this goal. Universality and explanation yield control over the future in virtue of their orderly grasp of the past; teaching enables past work to yield future progress; precision yields consistent accuracy, the minimization of failure. A person who says (as many did in the fifth century) that practical reasoning should become a *technē* is likely, then, to be demanding a systematization and unification of practice that will yield accounts and some sort of orderly grasp; he will want principles that can be taught and explanations of how desired results are produced. He will want to eliminate some of the chanciness from human social life.

One reason why it has been necessary to set this background out is that there has recently been an attempt to give the demand for a practical *technē* a much narrower interpretation. This issue must now be confronted, since it will decisively affect the interpretation of the *Protagoras*. In *Plato's Moral Theory*, Terence Irwin has claimed that '*technē*', like English 'craft', includes as a part of its meaning the notion of an external end or product, identifiable and specifiable independently of the craft and its activities.[18] What the craft does is to provide instrumental means to the realization of this independently specifiable end. Any claim that practical deliberation is, or can be, a *technē* – or any analogy between deliberation or virtue and any of the recognized *technai*, whether gymnastics, flute-playing, medicine, or shoemaking – is, on Irwin's reading, the specific, and dubious, claim that there is a human good that can be identified and desired independently of deliberation and the virtues; and that practical rationality is merely the finding of instrumental means to this external good.[19]

It is easy to see how crucial this issue is for a reader of the *Protagoras*. For both characters propose and wish to teach a practical *technē*; and Socrates' proposal, as we shall see, conforms to Irwin's constraints while Protagoras's does not. Irwin's picture implies, then, that Protagoras is not putting forward anything that has even a *prima facie* claim to be *technē*; he, and anyone who takes him seriously, will just be misunderstanding the meaning of the word. Besides the fact that we do not wish a serious interlocutor to be starting from a silly verbal mistake. It is also curious that none of the other highly intelligent characters, not even Prodicus, enamored of verbal fine points, charges him with this error. Nor, on Irwin's account, is the debate for the soul of Hippocrates a genuine debate: for assuming that what is wanted is a *technē* of practical reason, Socrates wins hands down. It will be as if Hippocrates came to an appliance store and, asking for the best vacuum cleaner, was offered, by two salesmen, a choice between a vacuum cleaner and an electric fan. It would be more philosophically interesting, and more worthy of Plato, if Socrates and Protagoras were putting up two serious rival candidates each of which might with some force be defended as a *technē*.

Now in fact the evidence about the ordinary conception of *technē* gives no support to Irwin's claim. No major scholar writing on the subject has even entertained such a theory; intellectual historians of the stature of Dodds, Edelstein, and Guthrie concur in sketching a different story, the one I have attempted to flesh out above.[20] Nor is there a single prominent ancient author who speaks of '*technē*' only in connection with craft production of a separately specifiable product. Even Xenophon, who so often shows sympathy with an instrumentalist view of deliberation, answers a question about the ends of the *technē* of household management by insisting that the activity of managing the house well is itself the end.[21] Aristotle makes a point of saying that there are *some* arts in which the work or *ergon* is a product external to the artist's activities – for example, housebuilding; and *others* in which the activities are themselves ends, for example mathematics, flute-playing, lyre-playing.[22] The Hellenistic divisions of the *technai* tell the same story.

If we now consider not statements about *technē* but examples of recognized *technai*, with ordinary beliefs about them, we find that several types are well represented. There are, first, the clearly productive *technai* such as shoemaking and housebuilding, where the product can indeed be specified (and desired) apart from any knowledge of the craftsman's activities. Even here, however, we note that what makes shoemaking *artful* and *good*, rather than merely adequate, may not be specifiable externally and in advance: for once the art exists, its own activities – fine stitching, elegant ornamentation – tend to become ends in themselves. The Greeks recognized this from the time of Homer. Achilles did not value his shield simply because it served well the requirements he could have set down antecedently. It is an example of high *technē* just because the craftsman has done so much more than Achilles' untutored imagination could have conceived or requested.

Next, there are arts like the medical art, where there is a vague end, health, that the layman can specify as desirable, and towards which, as a product, the practitioner's activity aims. But here one crucial part of the practitioner's work will be to get a more precise specification of the end itself. If he has no theory of what health is, it will be impossible for him to work out instrumental means to health. When a doctor prides himself on his *technē*, he includes his work on the end as well as his investigation of productive means.[23]

Finally, there are arts that seem to have purely internal ends: flute-playing, dancing, athletic achievement. Here there is no product at all: what is valued is the artful activity in itself. And yet, because of the disciplined, precise, and teachable character of these practices, they are unhesitatingly awarded the title of *technē*.[24] They are forms of order imposed upon the previously unordered and ungrasped continua of sound and motion.[25]

There are, then, several varieties of *technē*, with several structures. This digression, necessary to remove an obstacle to reading the *Protagoras* as a serious debate about the varieties of political *technē*, has also prepared us to understand the force of Protagoras's internal-end proposal. But now, surveying the full range of the fifth-century arts in the light of their underlying corporate aim, the elimination of *tuchē*, we can make some observations that will prepare us, too, to understand why Socrates rejects it. Let us ask which arts are, so to speak, the most artful: which best deliver the goods of control, prediction, precise grasp. Now we discover that there may be desiderata towards this goal that are not present in all of the recognized arts. Here the force of Irwin's idea begins to become clear; it is not adequate as an account of the general conception of *technē*, but it singles out an important feature that helps certain arts to make striking advances in subduing *tuchē*. For if there is something *external*, clear, and antecedently specifiable that counts as the end result of an art, its search for procedures can, it seems, be more definite and precise than in the arts where the end consists in acting in certain ways. A competition in shoemaking (abstracting from its aesthetic side) can be adjudicated with precision, because the externality of the end provides a clear measure of the activities' success. A competition in the art of flute-playing is much more elusive, since part of what is at stake is what we shall count as the end. We can easily feel in such cases more as if there is no decisive victory over *tuchē*, no clear progress. Then again, *singleness* in an end appears more tractable than plurality; for if ends are plural we may need some further criterion or measure to adjudicate among them. Finally, an end which permits of *quantitative measure* seems to yield more precision than an end that cannot be so measured. (We shall return to this important idea later.)

If we put all this together, we can say that it is possible to have a *bona fide technē* that will be qualitative, plural in its ends, and in which the art activities themselves constitute the end; but such a *technē* seems unlikely to yield the precision and control that would be yielded by an art with a single, quantitatively measurable, external goal. Someone who was deeply gripped by problems of *tuchē* would naturally prefer a *technē* of this kind, which would promise more decisive progress beyond unsystematized human judgments. Where and to what extent this sort of *technē* is possible and appropriate remains, however, a matter of dispute.[26] Such, I shall now argue, is the shape of the debate in the *Protagoras*. Protagoras, conservative and humanistic, wants a *technē* that stays close to the ordinary practice of deliberation, systematizing it only a little. Socrates, more deeply gripped by the urgency of human practical problems, finds this insufficient. We must go further, be more thoroughly scientific, if we are to 'save our lives' – even if science makes those saved lives different.

	Shoe-making	Flute-playing	Medicine	Land-measuring	Protagorean deliberation	Socratic deliberation
End single	Yes	No	?	Yes	No	Yes
End, external (specifiable apart from the art-activities)	Yes	No	Partly (see above)	Yes	No	Yes
Measure quantitative	Partly	No	No	Yes	No	Yes

This table is offered without further comment as an introduction to the next two sections of this chapter.

III

Protagoras claims to teach a *technē* of practical reasoning.[27] To display the nature of his art, he tells a story of human progress.[28] Its early sections show the power of *technai* to save the lives of living creatures generally; its last describes the progress made (and still being made) by human beings through an art of deliberation and the social excellences. We might at first think that only the last section gives us insight into the progress offered by the sophist himself. But his characterization of progress earlier in the speech reveals his conception of the relationship between arts and ends, life-saving and life-living. This is an important aspect of his teaching, which prepares us for the conservative nature of his social proposal and gives us some questions to ask, on his behalf, about Socrates' more radical strategy.

The story begins with the creation by the gods of mortal creatures, creatures vulnerable to contingency. Formed from a mixture of earth and fire, they live inside the earth until the appointed time for their emergence into the light. At this point, Titans Prometheus and Epimetheus are charged with the task of distributing 'to each kind' powers or capabilities that will enable its members to survive and reproduce. Distinctions among the kinds appear, then, to pre-exist the distribution of arts and capabilities. The gods talk of kinds, even of allotting suitable powers to each kind; but the species, mere lumps of material stuff, are not yet in possession of any of the distinctive capabilities and ways of acting that currently constitute them as the species we know. To these characterless subjects the gods assign the powers that will enable the kind to survive, 'being careful by these devices that no species should be destroyed' (320E–321A). The strangeness of this story – a strangeness which, as we shall suggest below, seems to be intentional – forces closer inspection.

We are asked to imagine an uncharacterized object: a lump of earth and fire, named, let us say, 'horse'. This object now gets made into the speedy, hooved, oat-eating, high-spirited creature we know. We are, then, invited to believe that horses might have been otherwise, had the gods made different decisions. They might, for example, have been timid, seed-eating, nest-dwelling creatures capable of flying through the air. The same goes for the particular species member: the same Bucephalus we admire might have lived in a nest and eaten worms. We discover, as we are meant to, that this is incoherent. A creature that did not have the ability to run in a certain horsy way and to live a characteristic horsy life would not be a horse. If it had the 'arts'[29] of a bird, it would just be a bird. Nor would Bucephalus be one and the same creature if he were to undergo a change with respect to these central characteristics. There might be a Bucephalus in the trees; but it would only be homonymous, not identical, with the one on which Aristotle's pupil rode. When we pick Bucephalus out and trace him through space and time, we pick him out under a kind-concept, not as a bare lump; our practices implicitly rule out his having or coming to have the characteristic capabilities of birds. Central to our conception of his kind are the 'arts', abilities, and ways of life that ostensibly get distributed *to* species already constituted. Before the distribution there was just a lump; after that there is a horse and horsiness. We begin, then, to see, as we try to follow Protagoras' story straight, and fail, to what extent the 'arts', broadly construed as the creature's characteristic abilities and ways of functioning in the world, make living things the things they are.[30]

The incoherence and its moral might, of course, be inadvertent; but there are signs that Protagoras is well aware of the two different ways his account might be read and is deliberately provoking these reflections. For now we encounter this sentence: 'Epimetheus, not being altogether wise, didn't notice that he had used up all the capabilities on the non-rational creatures; so last of all he was left with the human kind (*to anthrōpōn genos*) quite unprovided for.' Here the oddness is blatant and sounds like a deliberate pointer. What can it mean, we wonder, to speak of using powers up on the *non-rational*, so that there is nothing left for *the human being*, when we know (and will be told again) that the human being (or whatever it currently is) is not yet a rational being? The distinction between the rational and the non-rational is presupposed in the very story of the gift of rationality. Protagoras lets us see that there is no coherent way of talking about the human being, and contrasting him with the rest of nature, without mentioning the distinctive capabilities and ways of acting that make him the creature he is. Rationality is not just an instrument given to a creature already constituted with a nature and natural ends; it is an essential element in this creature's nature, a central part of the answer to a 'What is it?' question about that creature; and it is constitutive of, not merely instrumental to, whatever ends that creature forms.

In each of these first two stages, then, 'arts' were given to creatures ostensibly to *save* those creatures' lives. What happened instead was that the art *created* a form of life, and creatures, that had not previously existed. We now must inquire about the status of the 'art' most central to this dialogue, the social or political art. Are the 'gifts of Zeus' a *technē* that merely serves previously existing human ends, or does Protagoras depict them as functions that go to make us what we are? To answer this we must, like Hippocrates, continue to listen to the story.

We now have beings that look something like human beings, living a life that looks something like a human life; they have houses, clothing, farming, religious ceremonies. They are still having trouble about survival. Apparently they do live in clusters – for they use speech, reproduce, and worship. Later references to the role of the 'expert' in these Promethean *technai* suggest even some elementary form of social organization, a simple, art-based division of labor. What they lack are laws, civic education, the institution of punishment. About their emotional and interpersonal lives we are told nothing, except that they wronged one another. We do not know what sorts of feelings and attachments, if any, bound them to one another. We may suppose, as does Hume in his parallel story, that the sexual tie gave rise to some attachments; perhaps also, again with Hume, that there were some ties of affection, even of acknowledged obligation, between parents and children.

We might now feel that we have a great deal, if not all, of our characteristic human nature and ends. At this point, there are two directions that our imaginary history of the arts might take. We might decide that what we have so far given these people is sufficient to make them human beings, their nature and ends human nature and ends. Then we would say that any further arts these creatures discover to help them in the war against contingency will be correctly understood as arts instrumental to a pre-set external end: the maintenance and protection of characteristically human life. The political art is a tool in the service of an end already constituted. Such is Hume's account of the origin and function of justice. Justice figures as an 'artificial virtue' in the service of ends separate from it; it is natural only insofar as it is a necessary means to natural human ends, and it is human nature to be resourceful in devising the necessary means to these.[31] This account tells us that we can coherently imagine a really *human* life in which human beings lack justice and political institutions. Such a life might be full of danger and difficulty, but it would still be recognizably ours. It would have all our natural ends in it. We would treat such people as members of our community; we would recognize in them the nature that we share. The human being is not by nature a political creature.[32]

Protagoras might, on the other hand, give an account of justice that would treat it as more like rationality than like shoemaking. He would then concede that there was a time when creatures bearing some resemblance to human beings lived without political institutions; he might even concede that these institutions arose at some point in history, in response to particular pressures. But he would insist that these institutions and these associated feelings have so shaped the lives of the creatures who have them that we cannot describe their *nature* without mentioning their membership in these institutions and their attachment to them. Nor can we enumerate the ultimate ends of this creature without mentioning his love of his city, his attachment to justice, his feelings of reverence for and obligation to other human beings. Our nature is a political nature.[33] Protagoras's account of justice is of this second kind. His genetic story, far from showing how easy it is to view the various *technai* as instrumental and so separable from human nature, actually shows how difficult it is to describe a recognizably human creature unless one endows him not only with rationality, but also with political aims and attachments.

A Humean view of the 'origin' of justice would characterize it as a means to human survival and flourishing, where these can be completely characterized without reference to the social. The gifts of Zeus are indeed introduced as means to the survival of mankind. Zeus is said to be moved by fear that 'our kind (*genos*) would be totally wiped out' (322C); this implies that a human kind pre-exists the gift of justice. But it is striking that as soon as Zeus's gifts are distributed, even the apparently pre-set end of human survival is no longer characterized in a way that separates survival from the city. Zeus's gifts are now called 'the principles of organization of cities, and the bonds of friendship' (322C); 'cities could not come into being' if they were distributed differently (322D); the lawbreaker is a 'plague on the city' (322D5); if all do not share in the social excellences, 'there can be no city at all' (323A; cf. 324E1, 327A1, A4). What we thought was an external end begins to look internal, as though the arts of Zeus have transformed and now help to constitute this being's nature.

Again, a Humean teacher, if he were to give an honest account of his *ultimate purposes* in dealing with justice, must exclude from the description of the end all reference to social and political virtue, speaking only of whatever pleasure, success, wealth, and happiness are specifiable and desirable apart from the *polis*. But Protagoras's announced goal is, through his *technē*, to 'make human beings good citizens', teaching them good deliberation both about their household and about the affairs of the city. Although Hippocrates desires to become renowned, Protagoras promises him instead that he will be 'better' (*beltiōn*). He claims 'to excel all others in making people fine and good' – never (as was common at the time) to excel in helping people to realize ends that are separable from those of the community. He characterizes 'the excellence of a man' (*andros aretēn*) as a blend of justice, moderation, and piety – all civic excellences and gifts of Zeus.[34]

The rest of his speech fills out this non-Humean picture of social virtue. Moral education is characterized as answering to a need that is part of our nature. Zeus gave us a natural tendency towards justice; but it must be developed by communal training.[35] 'All of human life stands in need of the proper rhythm (*euruthmias*) and harmonious adjustment' (326B5); the adjustment is not natural, but the need for it is. Thus the correction of children is compared to the straightening of wood that is gnarled and bent (325D); the implication is that moral training promotes healthy and natural growth, attacking problems which, left unattended, would blight the child's full natural development. Like Pindar's plant, the child needs external assistance to reach its natural ends. Moral training is the straightening of the tree, moral excellence its straightness – an excellence thoroughly intrinsic to our account of what it is to be a healthy, normal tree. (On a Humean view, the social excellences would be more like sun and rain: necessary but external, and replaceable by other means, should these be found.) Similarly, the punishment of the older offender is said to make him 'better' (*beltiōn*) and more healthy (contrast *aniaton*, 'incurable', 325A). This greater health consists in a reluctance, resulting from learning, to 'commit injustice again'. Social excellence is, then, to our psychological nature as health is to our bodily nature – an intrinsic (non-instrumental) good, which is deeply involved in all our other pursuits: 'what every person must have and with which he must do anything else he wants to learn or to do' (325A).[36] Protagoras's hypothetical citizens say of the person who does not share in them, not that he is stupid, not that he is a public menace, but that he is not one of them; he 'should not be among human beings at all'.[37]

Protagoras's question was, what *technē* do we have, or can we find, that has the power to make human beings good at deliberation and in control of their lives? In answer, he has told us a story about the fundamental role played by arts and capabilities in constituting the characteristic ways of life of living creatures. His story has shown us, in particular, that a capability for social excellence and for its proper development are a deep part of our human nature and way of life. But where, in all this, is the science? What expertise does Protagoras claim to teach? He recognizes that there is a *prima facie* problem about reconciling his insistence that all adults are teachers with his claim to be an expert.[38] But he insists that there need be no contradiction, using, appropriately, an analogy to the learning of language (328A–B). Even if all adults are competent native speakers and teach the language to their children, there is still room for an expert who can take people 'a little further along the road' – presumably by making the speaker more explicitly and reflectively aware of the structures of his practice and the interconnections of its different elements. Even so, an expert ethical teacher can make the already well-trained young person more aware of the nature and interrelationships of his ethical commitments. It seems fair to view this very speech as a contribution to that sort of education. Protagoras's modest claim is not unlike the claim that Aristotle will make on his own behalf; and Aristotle too will insist that this sort of teaching can lead to the improvement of practice. But we must now ask: *how*? What progress could Protagoras's historical and descriptive teaching help us to make with the problems to which the dialogue has already directed our attention?

We can claim on behalf of this speech that it brings to the surface for reflection some important features of our practices of identifying individuals and kinds; in the process it offers us a deeper understanding of the place of the social and political in our own self-conception. It shows us explicitly the arts and orderly practices with which we already, in our cities, save our lives from the pain of conflict and the disorder of passional weakness. By raising current practice to a new level of self-awareness, by giving a general account of human nature and the place of the social excellences in it, Protagoras may fairly claim to be teaching a *technē*, an orderly understanding of a subject matter that displays connections, offers explanations, and has a certain degree of universality and communicability. And to some extent such a *technē*, or such an explicit and general formulation of the implicit *technē* of ordinary practice, can surely help us in the face of the practical dilemmas from which we turned to art.

A clearer articulation of our human self-conception gives us some standards for choice among competing and confusing value alternatives. Far from being relativistic or subjectivistic, this speech provides, in its general account of human nature and needs, some universally fixed points with reference to which we could assess competing social conceptions.[39] It shows us the relationship between a conception of the human being that many of Protagoras's hearers can be expected to share and certain concrete social practices that may be more subject to debate; *if* the listeners agree about the view of humanness, they may be led by his arguments to opt, for example, for one scheme of punishment rather than another. But if practical disagreements are as bitterly divisive as they in fact were in this period of crisis for Greece, they will be very likely to arise concerning the conception of humanness as well; progress is limited. When we turn to our specific problems of *tuchē*, we see its limits even more clearly.

(1) Protagoras allows us to continue to recognize and value vulnerable activities

and objects: friends, families, the city itself. In fact, he insists strongly on the importance of these attachments. (And we shall see that his failure to render different attachments commensurable contributes in no small way to their ongoing vulnerability.) (2) Conflicts of values are made possible, in the first place, by the recognition of a plurality of distinct values. Protagoras's pupils will see more clearly how different major human ends support and in general complement one another. A Protagorean legislator can, further, minimize direct conflict between major components of the city's value system – for example, by structuring civic and religious institutions in such a way as to prevent confrontation between the unwritten laws of family worship and the decrees of civil government. But because Protagoras denies the unity of the virtues, maintaining against Socrates that they are irreducibly heterogeneous in quality, he keeps alive the possibility of tragedy. (3) Finally, the speech recognizes the power of the passions as an ongoing danger for public morality. Here he speaks of the need for punishment; later he will hold that it is a shameful thing if passions can cause people who know the better to choose the worse action (352C–D).[40] The scheme of public and family education which he defends will go a long way towards training the passions and instilling virtuous dispositions; but it will not completely render them innocuous, nor does Protagoras think that it will.

We could say, then, that Protagoras's *technē* follows Tiresias's advice. It leaves our original problems more or less where it found them, making small advances in clarity and self-understanding, but remaining close to current beliefs and practices. He can claim to teach a *technē* that increases our control over *tuchē*; but the internality and plurality of its ends, and the absence of any quantitative measure, seem to leave his art lacking in precision and therefore in potential for decisive progress.

One reason for the conservatism is satisfaction. Protagoras has lived the prime of his life in the greatest age of Athenian political culture. He still seems to us to be a part of this glorious, relatively happy past; he stresses the fact that he is old enough to be the father of anyone else present. He is not gripped by the sense of urgency about moral problems that will soon characterize the writing of younger thinkers, for example Euripides, Thucydides, Aristophanes. The setting, with its allusions to the plague, its metaphors of disease, works to make this jolly conservatism seem anachronistic, inappropriate to the seriousness of impending contemporary problems. We hear it the way we might now hear a speech in praise of the Great Society made at the beginning of the Vietnam War – with our hindsight, and in the knowledge that failures of practical wisdom being made at that very time would erode the moral consensus the speaker was praising. We suspect that young Hippocrates, even without hindsight, will be less contented with things than his would-be mentor, inclined to look for stronger medicine. And if he is still content, the reader cannot be. It is no surprise that the dialogue compares Socrates' interview with these sophists to a living hero's visit to the shades of dead heroes in the underworld. It is a dead generation, lacking understanding of the moral crisis of its own time. Socrates compares himself to artful wily Odysseus,[41] deviser of life-saving stratagems; compared with him, his rivals are without resource.

Protagoras's story however, suggests to us a more serious reason for his conservatism. He has shown us how thoroughly the identity and ways of life of a species are formed by the arts and abilities it possesses. In a time of deep need, feeling that our very survival is at stake, we may turn ourselves over to a new art. Sometimes this art will simply do what we ask of it, providing efficient instrumental means to the ends that we already have. Sometimes, however, as with the gifts of Zeus, the art will so deeply transform ways of life that we will feel that it has created a new type of creature. If, then, we contemplate curing our current ethical diseases by a new art, we must imagine, as well, and with the utmost care, the life that we will live with this new art and the aims and ends that go with it. For we may not want a radical solution, if its cost will be to be no longer human. This would hardly count as saving *our* lives.

IV

There is a *technē* that has made human beings capable of taking things quite different in kind and comparing them with respect to some property in which they are interested. It is a precise and orderly *technē*; it has given them the power to manipulate objects with far greater exactness than would have been available through the exercise of their unaided faculties. It is made by human beings; it appears to be a natural extension of ordinary activities, in the service of standing interests. It thus seems to involve no promise of making our human nature into something else. But it is capable, apparently, of endless progress and refinement. This art is the art or science of weighing, counting, and measuring.

Already in the *Euthyphro*, Socrates sees its attractions as a model for practical deliberation:

> SOC. What sorts of disagreements, my good man, produce enmity and anger? Look at it this way. If you and I disagreed about which of two groups of items was more in number, would this disagreement make us enemies and cause us to be angry with one another? or wouldn't we count them up and quickly be released from our differences?
> EU. Of course.
> SOC. And if we disagreed about the larger and smaller, wouldn't we turn to measurement and quickly stop our disagreement?
> EU. Right.
> SOC. And by turning to weighing, I suppose, we would reach agreement about the heavier and the lighter?
> EU. How else?
> SOC. But what is it that, if we should disagree about it and prove unable to turn to a criterion, would give rise to enmity and anger with one another? Perhaps you don't have the answer ready, but see if you don't agree that it is

the just and unjust, the fine and shameful, the good and bad. Aren't these the things that, when we differ about them, and prove unable to turn to any sufficiently decisive criterion, lead to our becoming enemies to one another, whenever this happens – both you and I and all other human beings? (7B–D)

Evidently, then, a science of deliberative measurement would be an enormous advantage in human social life. And this is an idea for which the tradition of Greek reflection about *technē* and human understanding has by Plato's time prepared the way. The connection between numbering and knowing, the ability to count or measure and the ability to grasp, comprehend, or control, runs very deep in Greek thought about human cognition.[42] Already in Homer, the poet associates knowing with the ability to enumerate: the Muses give him their knowledge of the warring armies by imparting a catalogue of their numbers and divisions. To answer a 'how many?' question is to demonstrate a praiseworthy grasp of that to which one's attention is directed. We find in Homer contrasts between the *andrōn arithmos*, the denumerable company of heroes whose story can therefore be told, and the *dēmos apeirōn*, the mass of the undemarcated, whose lives will never be grasped and set down in a definite way.[43] The denumerable is the definite, the graspable, therefore also the potentially tellable, controllable; what cannot be numbered remains vague and unbounded, evading human grasp.

These connections are old and pervasive; they had more recently been given enormous impetus by the remarkable development in the *technai* of mathematics and astronomy, which became paradigms for science generally. The fifth-century *Prometheus Bound* calls numbering 'chief of all the stratagems', expressing a popular view that number is somehow a, or even the, chief element in *technē*, or the *technē par excellence*. Pythagorean epistemology of the fifth century (of which Plato is known to have been a serious student) explicitly argued that something was graspable only insofar as it was countable or numerically expressible.[44] An examination of fifth- and early fourth-century uses of words associated with measure and quantitative commensurability shows that they come freighted with heavy cognitive and ethical associations: what is measurable or commensurable is graspable, knowable, in order, good; what is without measure is boundless, elusive, chaotic, threatening, bad.[45] The story that Hippasus of Metapontum was punished by the gods for revealing the secret of mathematical incommensurability gives evidence of the fear with which educated Greeks of this time regarded this apparent absence of definite *arithmos* at the heart of their clearest of sciences.[46] (Our own mathematical terms 'rational' and 'irrational' are translations, and give further evidence of the way these things were seen.)

Given this situation, it is hardly surprising that someone who wanted to claim that he had developed a rational *technē* in some area would feel himself obliged to answer questions about number and measurability. Plato reflects this situation when he has Euthyphro, an interlocutor with no special interest in number, respond to Socrates' characterization of the arts as entirely obvious.[47] The author of *On Medicine in the Old Days* recognized, as we saw, that the absence of a quantitative measure in his art doomed it to deficient precision and therefore to error. He was still able to claim *technē* status for it. But some years later it will be forcefully argued that any *technē* at all, to be *technē*, must deal in numbering and measuring. The common concern of all *technē* and *epistēmē* whatever, insofar as it is *technē*, is 'to find out the one and the two and the three – I mean, to sum up, number and calculation. Or isn't it this way with these things, that every *technē* and *epistēmē* must of necessity participate in these?' The author is, of course, Plato; the text is the seventh book of the *Republic*.[48] It is absurd, Socrates there continues, for Aeschylus to represent Palamedes as claiming to have improved the art of generalship by the introduction of number; for surely if enumeration was not there, there could be no generalship at all. The *Epinomis* (977Dff.) develops a similar position with reference to the *technē–tuchē* antithesis: insofar as there is numbering and measuring in a practice, there is precise control; where numbering fails there is vagueness of grasp, therefore guesswork, therefore an element of *tuchē*.[49]

This Platonic argument is the natural development of a long tradition of reflection about the arts and human progress; it is adumbrated in Homer, developed in the *Prometheus Bound*; it haunts the Hippocratic writer. Plato's Pythagorean connections provide additional explanation for his endorsement of the position; or, better, his sense of the urgency of the problems of *tuchē* explains the attractiveness, for him, of Pythagorean arguments.

The idea that deliberation is, or could become, a kind of measuring is not itself alien to ordinary conceptions. It is as common for a Greek as for us to speak of weighing one course against another, measuring the possibilities. Even the Homeric gods, when they need to make a decision, put competing possibilities into the scales, judging by a single standard. Creon spoke of commensurability (387 – cf. n. 54). Aristophanes ends the poetic contest in the *Frogs* with a travesty of this popular picture of deliberation. When he wants to decide which of two great tragic poets to prefer and restore to life, Dionysus's natural response is to put their verses (or rather the things mentioned in their verses) into the scale, weighing their enormously different themes and styles by a single measure. Aeschylus speaks of chariots, corpses, death; Euripides of light ships, speeches, persuasion. Aeschylus, therefore, weighs in as the victor. This is ridiculous. And yet it is a natural extension of a deeply held idea of rationality; the comic hero, surrogate of the ordinary man, goes for it. If deliberating is to become better, surer, more scientific, it is natural to suppose that change must proceed in this direction. (Aristophanes shows the danger of this picture, as well as its power.)

Such a science would offer several important advantages. First, things different in kind would become commensurable, as ungraspable qualitative differences are reduced to quantitative differences. The science presupposes agreement on the scale and units of measure; this achieved, many other things fall into place. Commensurability brings with it, as well, that singleness and externality in the end that promised to make procedures of choice clear and simple. For if we set ourselves to gauge, in each situation, the quantity of a single value and to maximize that, we eliminate uncertainty about what is to count as good activity. Choosing what to do becomes a straightforward matter of selecting the most efficient instrumental means to maximization, not the far messier matter of asking what actions are good for their own sake. And measurement, being precise, will also deliver a definite verdict about the instrumental alternatives, by a clear public procedure that anyone can use.

We readily grasp the relevance of measuremen to the removal of serious value conflict. For instead of choosing, under circumstantial pressure, to neglect a different value with its own separate claims, one will merely be giving up a smaller amount of the same thing. This seems far less serious. And commensurability may be relevant to the elimination of our other problems as well. For if we really saw all ends as different quantities of one and the same thing, we would be likely to *feel* differently about them. This could modify our attachments to the vulnerable and our motivations for acts of passional disorder. This possibility we shall soon explore.

We can begin our examination of Socrates' project by looking at its conclusion, where he tells us what he claims to have shown:

Haven't we seen that the power of appearance leads us astray and throws us into confusion, so that in our actions and our choices between things both great and small we are constantly accepting and rejecting the same things, whereas the *technē* of measurement would have cancelled the effect of the appearance, and by revealing the truth would have caused the soul to live in peace and quiet abiding in the truth, thus saving our life? Faced with these considerations, would human beings agree that it is the *technē* of measurement that saves our lives, or some other *technē*?
Measurement, he agreed.[50] (356D–E)

Socrates claims to have enabled us to see our deep and pressing need for an ethical science of measurement. If we grasp the cost of lacking one and the great benefits of having it, we will, he thinks, agree that it is a matter of the first urgency to do what is needed to get one going. Protagoras, former defender of a plurality of values, proves the point by his agreement. Argument about whether, in fact, our values are commensurable on a single scale is, then, replaced by argument to the conclusion that they *must* be. Underlying the passage is the implicit agreement that what we cannot live with is being at the mercy of what happens, and that what we badly want is peace and quiet. If only measurement can take us from the one to the other, that is sufficient reason for us to 'turn ourselves over to' such a *technē*, whatever else it involves. Measurement is portrayed as the answer to a practical demand and the fulfillment of a pre-scientifically shared ideal of rationality.

Superficially, this agreement about the science follows an agreement that pleasure is the end. But the adoption of this single end is notoriously hasty and unargued. Only Socrates' final conclusion, I now want to claim, reveals the deep motivation behind this maneuver. The *Protagoras* has long been found anomalous among Plato's early and middle dialogues because of Socrates' apparent endorsement of the thesis that pleasure is the only intrinsic end or good.[51] Nowhere else does Socrates appear to be a single-end hedonist; and the nearly contemporary *Gorgias* is devoted, in part, to the refutation of a hedonist thesis.[52] And yet none of the various attempts to explain the hedonism away has been successful. I want to suggest that both the adoption of the hedonistic premise (essential to Socrates' argument) and the vagueness surrounding this strategy can be best understood in the light of Socrates' goal of finding the right *sort* of practical *technē*, one that will do what the arts of Protagoras could not. We will be saved only by something that will assimilate deliberation to weighing and measuring; this, in turn, requires a unit of measure, some external end about which we can all agree, and which can render all alternatives commensurable. Pleasure enters the argument as an attractive candidate for this role: Socrates adopts it because of the science it promises, rather than for its own intrinsic plausibility.[53]

This begins to emerge clearly if we contrast the role of hedonism in this dialogue with the way it figures in later fourth-century thought. Eudoxus and Epicurus both argue for the intrinsic attractiveness of pleasure as the end or good, pointing to the natural pleasure-seeking behavior of animals and children. The *Protagoras* shows no trace of these concerns; nor, indeed, do any texts of the fifth and early fourth centuries. What we do find prominently expressed, as we have already seen in the *Antigone*, is the concern to find *a* standard or measure that will render values commensurable, therefore subject to precise scientific control. The need for measurement motivates the search for an acceptable measure.[54] What we need to get a science of measurement going is, then, an end that is single (differing only quantitatively): specifiable in advance of the *technē* (external); and present in everything valuable in such a way that it may plausibly be held to be the source of its value. Weight, as Aristophanes saw, has singleness, externality, and omnipresence; but it is short on intuitive appeal in the ethical sphere. Pleasure is a far more attractive place-holder. It is one of the few things we value that turns up in just about everything; it is also something to which we might think we could reduce every other value. For these reasons, it has traditionally remained the most popular candidate for the role of single measuring-stick of value, whenever someone has wanted badly enough to find one.

There are textual reasons to believe that pleasure, in the *Protagoras*, plays such a place-holding role. First, the subject of the entire dialogue, as introduced in the beginning of Protagoras's speech, is the *technē* of good deliberation. Our need for such a *technē*, and the various problems standing in the way of our success, have been brought forward before the introduction of hedonism and are its background. Second, the lengthy intervening discussions of the unity of the virtues reveal Socrates' strong interest in showing that there can be a single qualitatively homogeneous standard of choice. He correctly finds in the plurality and apparent incommensurability of the virtues a troublesome feature of Protagoras's so-called *technē*, one that impedes the solution to certain pressing problems. But only the introduction of the science of measurement, which requires and proceeds by way of the hedonistic assumption, shows us how we are to envisage the unity that will solve these problems. We can see, furthermore, that Socrates' introduction of the notion of scientific practical knowledge, and his denial both of conflict and of *akrasia*, in fact precede the introduction of hedonism: in commenting on Simonides' poem, which may well be a reflection on cases of what we have called tragic conflict (certainly it concerns a case where circumstances force a good person to do something shameful against his will), Socrates asserts that 'doing badly is nothing other than being deprived of knowledge (*epistēmē*)' (345B) and that 'all who do shameful and bad things do so involuntarily (*akontes*)' (345D–E). But his only argument to this conclusion turns out to require hedonism (or some other similar premise) for its success.

Finally, we can derive support from a fact that has troubled all commentators: the absence of any sustained exploration of the nature of pleasure and of its suitability as a standard of choice. Problems that trouble Plato not only in the late *Philebus*, but also in the *Gorgias* – the plurality of pleasures, the resistance of subjective feelings to precise measurement – do not even surface here. When Plato does turn to these difficult issues, he concludes that hedonism, as a theory of the good, is deeply defective. Many commentators have, therefore, tried to explain hedonism here as merely an *ad hominem* assumption for use against Protagoras, or as a belief of 'the many', not seriously endorsed by Socrates. But these suggestions are inadequate to explain its role in the argument. It is only with the aid of the hedonistic assumption that Socrates is able to reach conclusions that he clearly claims as his own.[55] It is difficult to see the thesis as *ad hominem*: Protagoras, a defender of the plurality of ends, proves initially quite resistant to Socrates' suggestion. As for the 'many', they and their view of *akrasia* are not introduced until long after the interlocutors agree about hedonism. Where hedonism *is* introduced, the ordinary view, which calls 'some pleasant things bad and some painful things good' is, in fact, *contrasted* with the view of Socrates: 'What I say is, insofar as things are pleasant, are they not to that extent good, leaving their other consequences out of account?' (351C).[56] The summary of the argument again asserts hedonism as Socrates' own view, connecting it with the life-saving project: 'Since we have seen that the preservation of our life depends on a correct choice of pleasure and pain, be it more or less, larger or smaller...' (357A). None of the interlocutors ever doubts that this position is Socrates' own. As the dialogue draws to a close, he expresses in the strongest terms his identification with the figure of Prometheus, saying he takes thought for the entirety of his life in a Promethean fashion (361D). But only the science, based on pleasure, enabled him to do this correctly.[57]

We are, then, in the peculiar position of being unable to get rid of hedonism as a view of the character Socrates without distortion of the text, but unable, also, to see why such a controversial and apparently un-Platonic thesis should be allowed, undefended and even unexplored, to play such a crucial role in a major argument for important and well-known Platonic conclusions. A reading of the argument that takes Socrates' fundamental concern to be the establishment of a deliberative science of measure offers a solution. Knowing in a general way what sort of end we need to get the science going, Socrates, *pro tempore*, tries out pleasure. At the end of the dialogue he concedes that the content of this value has been left unspecified: 'Now *which technē*, and *what epistēmē*, we shall inquire later. But this suffices to show that it is *epistēmē*' (357B–C). If we find it odd that Socrates can feel so confident about the form of the science before establishing that there is a candidate for the end that is unitary and universal in the way required, we might begin to reflect that perhaps Socrates is less interested in our current intuitions about ends than he is in giving us a gift that will save our lives. Zeus did not require that justice be already a central human concern when he decided to make the attachment to justice a linch-pin of his saving *technē*.

It is worth pausing at this point to remark that the drive towards hedonism and utilitarianism in nineteenth-century moral philosophy had a very similar motivation. In both Bentham and Sidgwick,[58] we find that distaste for the plurality and incommensurability of common-sense values gives a powerful push towards the selection of an end that is, admittedly, not believed to be a supreme good in the intuitive deliverances of common sense. Bentham's arguments that only such a science of measure would eliminate contingency from social life show deep Platonic sympathies and are well worth study for any student of this dialogue and of Greek thought about ethical *technē*. Sidgwick's discussion of the reasons for moving beyond common sense to single-standard utilitarianism is of enormous interest to us as well, since it reveals so clearly that the central motivation towards hedonism is a need for commensurability in order to deal with messy deliberative problems. Happiness or pleasure, Sidgwick concedes, is not recognized by common sense to be the single end of choice.[59] But:

> If, however, this view be rejected, it remains to consider whether we can frame any other coherent account of Ultimate Good. If we are not to systematize human activities by taking Universal Happiness as their common end, on what other principles are we to systematize them? It should be observed that these principles must not only enable us to compare among themselves the values of the different non-hedonistic ends which we have been considering, but must also provide a common standard for comparing these values with that of Happiness...[60]

It is, he continues, our 'practical need of determining whether we should pursue Truth rather than Beauty', this value rather than that, that leads us to hedonism, despite its problematic relation to common sense. If it be objected that it is inappropriate to depart to this extent from our intuitions, it can be replied that this is what happens whenever a science is born:

> But it must be borne in mind that Utilitarianism is not concerned to prove the absolute coincidence in results of the Intuitional and Utilitarian methods. Indeed, if it could succeed in proving as much as this, its success would be almost fatal to its practical claims; as the adoption of the Utilitarian principle would then become a matter of complete indifference. Utilitarians are rather called upon to show a natural transition from the Morality of Common Sense to Utilitarianism, somewhat like the transition in special branches of practice from trained instinct and empirical rules to the technical method that embodies and applies the conclusions of science; so that Utilitarianism may be presented as the

scientifically complete and systematically reflective form of that regulation of conduct, which through the whole course of human history has always tended substantially in the same direction.[61]

I want to claim that the *Protagoras* shows a similar motivation towards hedonism and a similar picture of the relation of science to ordinary beliefs. Ethical science is continuous with ordinary belief in that it fulfills an ideal of rationality embodied in ordinary belief: thus there is a 'natural transition' from ordinary belief to scientific practice. To make this transition, clearly, science's choice of an end must also have *some* continuity with ordinary beliefs about ends: this is why hedonism is plausible and Aristophanes absurd. But if it is to be worth something as science, and not 'a matter of complete indifference', it must go beyond the ordinary. To complain about this would be as retrograde as to complain that a Hippocratic doctor does not administer the same old remedies your parents used to make.

We must now confront the argument in which Socrates purports to show us that the phenomenon commonly called *akrasia* does not, as described, occur: scientific knowledge of the overall good is sufficient for correct choice. Much has been written about this argument, whose structure now seems to be rather well understood.[62] It falls into three stages: first, a description of the problem; second, an argument that this problem does not really arise; third, an alternative diagnosis of practical error. The problem is a familiar one. A can do either x or y.[63] A knows that x is better (overall), but chooses y, because he is overcome by pleasure. (The first statement of the problem adds, as alternatives, pain, love, and fear – but Socrates, quite reasonably in light of the hedonist agreement, speaks only of quantities of pleasure in what follows. This is important.) Knowledge, then, is 'dragged around like a slave'.

Protagoras and Socrates have explicitly agreed, from the outset, on two crucial premises:

H: Pleasure is identical with the good.
H_1: A believes pleasure to be identical with the good.

Now, in the crucial second phase of the argument, Socrates uses these premises, substituting 'good' for 'pleasant' to produce an absurdity in the description of what allegedly happens: A knows x is more good than y; A chooses y, because he is overcome by (desire for) the good in y. 'What ridiculous nonsense', Socrates now remarks, 'for a person to do the bad, knowing it is bad [i.e. inferior], and that he ought not to do it, because he was overcome by good.'

At first we do not see clearly what the absurdity is: for isn't this, in a way, just what happens? This other good over here exerts a special kind of pull that draws us to it so that we just neglect our commitment to the good that is better overall. But we get more information when Socrates himself explains the absurdity, showing us what he means by 'overcome'. Is the good in y, he asks, *a match for* the badness involved in missing out on x? No: for this would contradict the description of the case, according to which there is, and is known to be, *more* good in x than in y. But then if y really offers a smaller *amount* of good, an amount that is not *a match for* the good in x, then what A is doing is choosing a smaller package of pleasures and giving up a larger package. But how absurd that A should, with full knowledge, give up the larger package because he was overwhelmed by the smaller amount in the smaller package. It becomes like saying, 'A, offered the choice between \$50 and \$200, chose the \$50, even though he knew that \$200 was more than \$50, because he was overcome by the quantity of the \$50.' And that does seem absurd.[64] In short, notions of *amount* and of qualitative homogeneity seem to be doing some work here in producing the absurd result. We shall shortly see how central their place is.

How could such an absurd mistake occur? Socrates can explain it only as the result of a mistaken judgment about the size of the packages. Just as adverse physical conditions sometimes give rise to false beliefs about size, nearer items appearing taller or larger, so nearer pleasures, too, can strike us as bigger and more important just on account of their nearness. The nearness of the present pleasure produces a false belief about size that temporarily displaces the agent's background knowledge about the real sizes involved. It is clear that, with pleasure as with size, a science of measurement would suffice to put an end to our errors.

Our attention must now be drawn to Socrates' premises in the second, absurdity-producing part of the argument. For the explicit hedonistic assumptions are clearly not enough to get Socrates to his conclusion. He is making tacit use of at least two further assumptions:

> M: Whenever A chooses between x and y, he weighs and measures by a single quantitative standard of value.
> C: A chooses x rather than y if and only if he believes x to be more valuable than y.[65]

M gives us the use of a quantitative standard in each particular case. H gives us the singleness of the standard across all cases. C gives us the reliable connection between the beliefs that are the outcome of the weighing and the agent's actual choices. Together they yield the conclusion Socrates wants: if A's choice is not the result of a correct weighing, and is not made under external duress (ruled out in the description of the case), then it must result from an incorrect weighing. For this is the only reason why someone who could have more would choose to have a smaller quantity of the same thing.

Each of these premises has a certain plausibility as an account of our deliberative procedures *some* of the time. Yet anyone who accepts the initial description of the case as the account of an actual human occurrence should take issue with them. For together they succeed in telling us that a problem by which we are intuitively gripped and troubled does not exist. *Akrasia* was supposed to be a case where ordinary deliberative rationality breaks down. What Socrates has done is not so much to prove that there can never be such breakdowns as to clarify the relationship between a certain picture of deliberative rationality and the *akrasia* problem. If we believe in a single end or good, varying only in quantity, and always deliberate by weighing or measuring (quantitatively), *and* always choose to act in accordance with our beliefs about the greater overall quantity of good, then *akrasia* will not happen. So, we are tempted to say: as long as rationality works it doesn't break down. We didn't need the genius of Socrates to tell us *that*.

At this point, many interpreters dismiss the entire argument. Seeing that the premises are not empirically acceptable as accounts of what we do in all cases (after all, their failure to hold was just what our ordinary belief in *akrasia* articulated), then, so these interpreters say, it looks as if Socrates had better do some more looking at the way people actually live and think. Socrates' conclusion, however, should make us suspect that something more is going on here. What he told us, and Protagoras agreed, is that only an ethical science of measurement will save our lives. If we accept his diagnosis of our problems and their urgency, and agree that we want to save our lives, it may occur to us that we are given, in Socrates' argument, an advertisement, as it were, for its premises. The argument does not rely on the common-sense intuitive acceptability of the premises. (Socrates stresses his disdain for the confused intuitions of the ordinary human being.) It shows us a connection between these premises and the disappearance of more than one problem. An agent who thinks the way these premises describe has no confusion about choice, no possibility of contingent conflict between incommensurables, *and*, it is claimed, no problem of *akrasia*. The whole thing, premises and all, appears to be the Socratic *technē* of practical reasoning, the life-saving art. The most astonishing claim implied by this argument is that the acceptance of the qualitative singleness and homogeneity of the values actually modifies the passions, removing the motivations we now have for certain sorts of irrational behavior. *Akrasia* becomes absurd – not a dangerous temptation, but something that would never happen. To see how this is supposed to be so, we need to return to Socrates' talk of packages and amounts and to enter more deeply into the life and the views of his hypothetical agent.

An ordinary case of *akrasia* looks like this. Phaedra knows that if she eats a bagel just before she goes running she will get a cramp and cut down the distance she can complete. She will be angry with herself later and she will find her health less good than it would have been had she run further and eaten less. She knows, then, let us say, that it is better all things considered not to eat the bagel now, but instead to go running directly. But she is very hungry, and the bagel looks so very appealing, sitting there hot and buttered on its plate. Its appeal to her is quite distinct and special; it does not look like a little bit of exercise or a small package of health. It looks exactly like a buttered bagel. And so (swayed by the desires it arouses) she eats it.

Contrast the following case. Phaedra's rational principle, for some reason, is to maximize her bagel-eating. Standing in the middle of the room, she sees on a table on one side a plate containing two fresh bagels, toasted and buttered. On the other side of the room, on a similar table, is a plate containing one toasted buttered bagel. The bagels are the same variety, equally fresh, equally hot, buttered in the same way. She can go for either one plate or the other, but (for some reason) not both. She knows that, given her rational principle, she ought to eat the two bagels. But, overcome by desire, she eats the one. Now this does seem highly peculiar, in a way that our first case did not. We must comprehend that there is *no* respect in which the single-bagel plate differs from the two-bagel plate, except in the number of bagels it contains. The bagels are in no way qualitatively different. Nor is the arrangement of bagels on plate or plate on table somehow more aesthetically appealing. The single-bagel plate is not even nearer, it is the same distance away. What could make Phaedra's choice anything but absurd, given that she really has the principle we say she has? I find myself imagining, as I try to understand her action, that there must after all be *some* distinguishing quality to that single bagel. It looked so cute, with its little burned spot on the crust. Or: it was from New York, and the other two were not. Or: she remembers eating bagels with her lover at *this* table, and not at that one. Or: she is a mathematician and she thinks that the single bagel in the middle of its plate exhibits a more pleasing geometrical arrangement. Or: it is so funny to see a bagel sitting on an elegant Lenox plate (the others being on a plain kitchen plate): it reminds her of the contradictions of existence. We could go on this way. But I mean to rule out every one of these sources of qualitative specialness in the description of the case. I insist on absolute qualitative homogeneity: the alternatives seem to her to differ in quantity only. And then, I believe, we do get the result Socrates wants. It is absurd. It would never happen; the motivating desires would never arise; nobody who really saw the choice that way would choose that way.

What Socrates gets us to see, if we dig deep enough, is the connection between our *akrasia* problem and the way we ordinarily see things – the enabling role played by our belief in an incommensurable plurality of values in getting the problem going. *Akrasia* as we know and live it seems to depend upon the belief that goods are incommensurable and special: that this bagel, this person, this activity, though in some sense less good over all than its rival, has nonetheless a special *kind* of goodness that pulls us to it, a goodness that we could not get in just the same way by going in the other direction. It's one thing to be unfaithful through passionate desire for a lover whom one sees as a special and distinct individual. But suppose him to be a clone of your present lover, differing qualitatively in no feature (and let us suppose not even in history – as would be true of lovers in the ideal city), and the whole thing somehow loses its appeal.[66]

We might say, then, returning to the premises, that if we really have H_1 and M, C falls out as a natural consequence. C is not true as an empirical description of the workings of desire. It does, however, appear plausible as a description of the desires of agents who really believe to the bottom of their souls in the qualitative homogeneity of all of their alternatives. (For our case is, after all, only the shallowest beginning; what we ultimately must get ourselves to imagine is that Phaedra sees *every one* of her choices this way, *and* that in every choice it is one and the same measure of value that she recognizes. There is no heterogeneity at all, even across cases.) The recognition of heterogeneity, the dialogue tells us, is a necessary condition for the development of irrational motivations; in its absence, they will simply not develop; or, if once developed, will wither away.

In short, I claim that Socrates offers us, in the guise of empirical description, a radical proposal for the transformation of our lives. Like the other gifts mentioned by Protagoras, this science of measurement will enter into and reshape the nature and attachments of the being who receives it. It is now not surprising that he tells us little about the intuitive acceptability of his proposed end: for it may not be something that can be properly assessed from our ordinary viewpoint. From our ordinary viewpoint, things do look plural and incommensurable. But this viewpoint is sick. We want, and know we need, the viewpoint of science.

Now we understand, too, why love and fear drop out when the premises come in: because if we really accept these premises, love and fear, as we know them, do drop out. Here is another benefit of the science: it restructures our attachments so that they are far less fragile, even taken singly. Beautiful Alcibiades, irreplaceable, is a risky thing to love. But if one measure of H goes away to another lover, it is no difficult task to acquire another similar measure. Thoroughgoing commensurability yields a readily renewable supply of similar objects (cf. Ch. 6). The science that eliminated the possibility of contingent conflict and removed *akrasia* did so by eliminating, or denying, just that special separateness and qualitative uniqueness that is also a major source of each single attachment's exposure to fortune. Measurement is even more versatile than we thought.[67] (Cf. also Ch. 5, §v, Ch. 6, pp. 181, 196–7.)

V

This dialogue is deeper than any work of utilitarian or hedonistic moral theory that proceeds as if it *were* straightforwardly describing ordinary beliefs and practices. Such works prove immediately vulnerable to the common-sense objection. Socrates (like Sidgwick) shows us what motivates a movement beyond the ordinary. The common-sense objection does not meet this argument, at least in the form in which I have stated it. How, then, can it be assessed?

Protagoras's myth suggested that a good way to understand the contribution of a new, allegedly life-saving art is to imagine the lives of the creatures to whom it was given, both before and after their receipt of the gift. This thought-experiment allows us to ask who these creatures were when they needed an art, and whether they were the same creatures after the art saved lives. This might help us to see whose lives, what sort of lives, the cure will save. Since Socrates here picks up the motif of life-saving, he invites us to imagine a Socratic conclusion to the Protagorean story, fleshing out the vague ending we sketched at the opening of this chapter. We shall now begin to answer that invitation: although an adequate response would be fuller and more storylike than this brief sketch.

Still human beings lived in confusion in their cities. In spite of the gifts of Zeus, they lacked precise control over their choices and actions. Whenever they disagreed about numbers, lengths, or weights, they could appeal to the arts of counting, measuring, or weighing to settle their disputes. But when they were confused about justice, nobility, or goodness, they had no art to arbitrate their quarrel. They became angry and violent; they insulted and wronged one another. Even when they could agree, the primitive confusion of their value system often gave rise to serious conflicts: piety could seem to dictate one course of action, courage or love another. Then these unfortunate creatures were deeply torn; lamenting, they would cry out, saying things like, 'Which of these is without evils?' And, stricken by after-pain, things like, 'The laborious memory of pain drips, instead of sleep, before the heart.' They had no art that could cure this pain. Worse still, even when they did have settled beliefs about the right course of action, even when there was a single, unconflicted course of action available, they could still, in their disorderly and artless condition, be swayed by the lure of other nearer goods that were the objects of some passion. In their bewilderment they said that they must have been 'overcome' by pleasure, fear, or love. So, frightened and confused, torn by regret and perplexed by uncertainty, they wandered through their cities without understanding of their past actions, without the ability to guarantee their future. They even invented an art form which they called tragedy, in which they explored their pain. From these works one can quickly conclude that they found life not worth living in this state. 'Not to be born is the best of all' – this was the judgment of their most eminent poet and teacher, Sophocles, after surveying these difficulties.

Now Apollo, god of sunlight and rational order, god of numbering and of firm boundaries between one thing and another, the god revered by Pythagoras, looked down at their plight. He did not wish the entire race to perish. So he decided to give them an art that could save their lives. Through his resourceful messenger Socrates, he revealed to them his marvelous gift: the art or science of deliberative measurement, together with the single metric end or good, which is pleasure. With this art, they would be able, in any choice, to calculate precisely the amount of long-term pleasure to be realized by each alternative and so to weigh it against rival alternatives. The human partisans of this art could, then, set themselves, each one, to maximize the long-term pleasure enjoyed in the entire city.

With the gift of this saving art, a wonderful change came over the lives of these creatures, previously so helpless. Thanks to the art, what had seemed to be many and incommensurable values were now truly seen as one. The significance of this new orderliness for all their ways of life was immense. It was as if the clarity of Apollo's sunlight had dispelled all of their troubles. Even the face of the natural world looked different: more open, flatter, clearly demarcated, source of no threatening incommensurables. And the city took on, too, in this way, a new order and beauty. Before this, they had disagreed and quarreled; now they had only to work through the publicly established procedures of pleasure-computation to arrive at an answer in which all good citizens easily concurred. Every circumstance by which the condition of an individual can be influenced being remarked and inventoried, nothing was left to chance, caprice, or unguided discretion. Everything was surveyed and set down in dimension, number, weight, and measure. Before this, again, old-fashioned thinkers like Protagoras had taught that justice was an end in itself; even if it conflicted with another valued end there was no avoiding or denying its claims. Now these beings correctly saw that virtue is all one: justice, courage, and piety are all simply functions of pleasure, and the virtuous action in each case is the one that maximizes total pleasure. Children were raised with a correct, scientific teaching that developed their inner capability to see things in terms of a single measure; by punishing the recognition of incommensurables, civic teachers straightened the young tree towards adult rationality. These children came to see, as they grew, that the 'individuals' around them, parents and teachers, were, all alike, valuable sources and centers of pleasure, entirely comparable one with another.[68] They seemed not separate self-moving souls, but parts of a single system; not qualitatively special, but indistinguishable. Pleasures obtained from them and pleasures rendered to them are all still quantities of pleasure: this is, precisely, the value of persons, that they give so much pleasure to the city's total. If these citizens ever read those tragedies, artifacts of the earlier race, the ways of life depicted seemed strange to them. Here is a character, Haemon, inflamed with what he calls passionate love, killing himself because this one woman, Antigone, whom he loves, has died. This is incomprehensible. Why does he think that she is not precisely replaceable by any other object in the world? Why doesn't he understand that there are other exactly comparable and qualitatively indistinguishable sources of pleasure to whom he can, in return, give a comparable pleasure, thus augmenting the city's sum? In this play Creon is the only character in whom they can recognize themselves: for Creon says of this irrational young man's 'love': 'There are other furrows for his plow.'

And in the light of this change in beliefs and therefore passions, they obtained a further and greater benefit. The deep old-fashioned problem that used to be called *akrasia* is no longer a problem for these people, because in the absence of incommensurable values, and without recognition of the uniqueness of persons, the passions that most gave rise to *akrasia* – love, hatred, anger, fear – no longer have the same nature, or the same force. When everything is seen in terms of a single value, it is enormously easier to control one's desire for a smaller quantity of the same.

So, through science, these creatures have saved their pleasant existence. And if any citizen shows himself unable to perform acts of measurement, if he or she insists on inventing separate sources of value or unique objects of feeling, if he or she manifests desires other than the rational desire for the single good, he or she must be cast aside and put to death as a plague on the city. Each year in spring they celebrate a festival at the time of the old festival of Dionysus, where tragedies were presented. It is called the festival of Socrates. The works of art they present are the clear, reasonable prose dialogues that have taken the place of tragic theatre; they celebrate Socrates' courageous search for the life-saving art.

This dialogue, we see, shows more than a competition for a young soul. It shows us (ironically, since its protagonist wishes to bring about the death of tragedy) a tragedy of human practical reason. For it shows us an apparently insoluble tension between our intuitive attachment to a plurality of values and our ambition to be in control of our planning through a deliberative *technē*. The nature of its arguments is not straightforward. It does not simply try to convince us that such-and-such is the true or correct view of practical reason. It instead displays to us (to Hippocrates) the relationship between certain urgent needs and a certain sort of art or science, showing us at the same time the changes and (from a certain point of view) the losses that this art would entail. We thought that the science of measurement was a science that simply provided instrumental means to an external, agreed-on end. We have now come to see that a deep modification of ends is itself a part of the art – that Socrates' *technē*, like the arts of Zeus, creates new values and new dependencies. We supposed, naïvely, that we could go on recognizing our rich plurality of values and also have the precision and control offered by a quantitative social science. (Some utilitarian works are still naïve in this way, hardly ever asking what a person would be like who really saw the world that way, and more or less assuming that he or she would be just like us.) Plato tells us with his characteristic sternness that this does not look to be the case. Science does change the world. If part of our humanness is our susceptibility to certain sorts of pain, then the task of curing pain may involve putting an end to humanness.

In one way, the dialogue offers us (Hippocrates) a choice, sternly defining the alternatives, but leaving it to us to choose between them. At the end, we do not know whether Hippocrates will choose to make progress with Socrates or to muddle along with Protagoras – or whether he will reject the choice philosophically, by arguing that the alternatives are badly set up, or whether he will reject the choice unphilosophically, by going back to his accustomed thoughts and ways. The argument does not coerce him. It simply clarifies the nature of the situation. He sees more clearly the way the world links cure with disease, progress with cost.

But the argument also forces him to ask, who is he to choose? All the interlocutors agree, by the end, in rejecting Protagoras's 'The human being is the measure of all things', in favor of the Socratic 'All things are *epistēmē*' (361C). Protagoras, earlier, agreed to let the issue be judged by Socratic rationality (cf. 336A); and Socratic rationality insists that the intuitions of the ordinary person are unreliable. Socrates reminded us that in a competition between alternative ethical positions it is crucial to select an appropriate judge. If the judge is inferior to the contending philosophers, that is clearly no good; if he is an equal, why should the rivals take *his* word? So, clearly, it must be the person who is superior to both of them in knowledge or application. This means, for Hippocrates and for us, that ordinary intuitions and attachments cannot carry the day. We are asked by the dialogue to become suspicious of our own Protagorean evaluation and to look, in ourselves or in another, for a way of seeing, intellectually pure and precise. The dialogue allows us to respond with ordinary human judgment, and then reminds us that some types of judgment are higher than that. The troublesome questions raised by this Platonic move will not vanish from view.

*   *   *

We turn now from 'early' to 'middle' dialogues.[69] Plato's diagnosis of our problems and his concern with developing a science to solve them remain constant. Once again, 'All things are *epistēmē*', and the intuitions of the ordinary human being must give way to the judgment of the expert. Again, too, scientific knowledge will concern itself with rendering diverse particulars qualitatively homogeneous and interchangeable.[70] This homogeneity will undo several problems at once, transforming troublesome conflicts, cutting away our motivations for passional excess, and yielding a readily renewable supply of formerly vulnerable items.

There will, however, be some shifts in emphasis. The *Protagoras* used pleasure as a place-holder for the single end of the science. It offered no account of what it is; but the shape of the science seemed to require that it be a homogeneous state or feeling.[71] In the middle dialogues, Plato makes it clear that the ultimate ends of a good life are not feelings, but activities; activities are ranked for their intrinsic worth, not in terms of the states they produce. Nor does pleasure in his view, have, in any case, the singleness that would enable it to provide a common coin of value in terms of which activities could be compared. When 'pleasures' are ranked, this is now a ranking of activities as to their worth.[72] This is not a repudiation of anything explicitly defended in the *Protagoras*; but it does have serious implications for the structure of the ethical *technē*, which now must find a way of ranking activities that is independent of the feelings they produce. The search for an appropriate standpoint of evaluation, accordingly, becomes central.

This brings us to another difference of focus. In the *Protagoras*, Plato focused on problems about conflict and commensurability. Our first problem, the vulnerability of individual pursuits, was dealt with only indirectly, as commensurability altered the nature of our vulnerable attachments. Now the vulnerability and instability of individual human pursuits will be a central focus of Plato's concern, as his adequate judge ranks activities as to their true value.

One final point. The *Protagoras* suggests that the belief in commensurability modifies all our irrational motivations, to the extent to which *akrasia* will no longer occur. It argues, then, that all our irrational desires are, to this extent at least, responsive to teaching. The *Republic* will modify this picture, suggesting that the animal appetites of the soul are 'unqualified desires' that persist and exert their claim regardless of belief or teaching (cf. Ch. 5, p. 139 and n. 5, p. 155). This is so at least for the natural appetites for food and drink; in the *Republic* it is probably true for sexual desire as well, though the *Symposium* gives this desire a more complex treatment, showing it to be responsive to certain changes in belief. To some extent all this will modify the *Protagoras* account of how *akrasia* can be eliminated; it does not undercut it altogether, since the number of those who eat akratically merely in order to pile in an increased amount of food is far smaller than the number who are akratic in matters of food: the desires for novelty and luxury that produce much actual *akrasia* are presumably still modifiable by teaching. But the persistent animal nature of appetite calls for a training more suited to its nature than rational teaching; it calls, in fact, for political control and suppression. We will touch on these issues in Chapters 5 and 6, and return to them at greater length in Chapter 7.[73]

Interlude 1: Plato's anti-tragic theater

We need to pause now to look at this piece of writing, asking in what voice or voices it speaks to an inquiring soul.[1] For we have now seen reflection on our problems taking place in two very different types of texts, one of which, as we shall see both here and in Chapter 7, attacks the other as harmful to the development of the soul. These Platonic criticisms of tragedy, and Plato's own practice of writing, reveal an acute self-consciousness about the relationship between the choice of a style and the content of a philosophical conception, between a view of what the soul is and a view about how to address that soul in writing. Much of our work on these issues will be done in Chapters 6 and 7, as we investigate two dialogues in which questions of writing and truth-telling are especially prominent. Here we cannot hope to raise all of the most interesting questions about the dialogue form as Plato in his middle period develops it, or even to give an exhaustive account of his criticisms of tragic poetry. But it will be useful to provide a sketch of some ways in which his writing defines itself against a literary tradition of ethical teaching; in particular, of the way in which it both acknowledges a debt to tragic poetry and distances itself from it.[2]

We can begin by observing that this is a new kind of writing.[3] Even Aristotle was at a loss about how to respond to it; in the *Poetics* he classifies the dialogues as prose dramas, alongside the realistic urban mimes of Sophron and Xenarchus.[4] Since we see in the dialogue the deliberate structuring of a new literary genre – by a man who was reputed to have spent his youth as an aspiring tragic poet[5] – we can expect to learn something about Plato's views concerning writing and ethical teaching by studying his choices against the background of existing possibilities; and, equally important, against the background of Socrates' rejection of the written word. But in order to begin to see what his choices disclose, we must make ourselves approach the dialogue with the eyes of a contemporary of Plato's, familiar with extant paradigms of ethical reflection in both poetry and prose, but not familiar with our long tradition of philosophical writing about ethical matters. For, all too often, when we ask, 'Why did Plato write in dialogues?', we ask ourselves why the dialogues are not philosophical treatises, not like Mill, say, or Sidgwick, or even Aristotle – rather than, why they are not poetic dramas, not like Sophocles or Aeschylus. We can recover the philosophical thrust of his decisions as he planned them only by approaching them historically, asking how his project is defined by differentiation from its surroundings. This interlude will have succeeded if it at least puts the reader in a better position to begin pursuing these questions. We will begin by briefly situating the dialogue among models of ethical reflection prominent in its time; we will make some observations about the Socratic rejection of writing and Plato's implicit response; finally, we will look at certain features of ethical inquiry in the *Protagoras*, contrasting this dialogue in several ways with the *Antigone*.

Before Plato's time there was no distinction between 'philosophical' and 'literary' discussion of human practical problems.[6] The whole idea of distinguishing between texts that seriously pursue a search for truth and another group of texts that exist primarily for entertainment would be foreign in this culture. One salient distinction among writers that did exist was the distinction between prose writers and poets; there were other distinctions of genre within each of these large divisions; but none of these distinctions by any means corresponds to a distinction between writers who regarded themselves (and were regarded) as serious ethical thinkers and those who did not and were not. It was natural for the reader in this culture to suppose that texts of many different kinds offered instruction in practical wisdom; it is, I think, correct to say that there is no choice of genre that would have signaled to the reader that the text in question had nothing serious to say about human matters. To get a good idea of the situation, we need only look at how those whom we now dignify with the title 'philosopher' conceived of their opposition. Xenophanes (himself a poet) regards himself as the competitor of Homer and Hesiod: he reproves these poets for ascribing human vices inappropriately to the gods. Heraclitus, calling Hesiod 'the teacher of most men', charges him and Homer with purveying false cosmological and ethical views. Again, he announces that Homer and the lyric poet Archilochus deserve a public beating for their inappropriate teaching about value (DK B42). And in a very revealing conflation of genres that a modern reader would usually keep far apart, he writes, 'Information about many things does not teach understanding; if it did, it would have taught Hesiod and Pythagoras, and also Xenophanes and Hecataeus' (B40). In our terms, he has named a didactic poet, a seer and oral philosopher, a philosopher who wrote in verse, and writer of prose geographical and ethnographical treatises; the interesting fact is that all are criticized together (by this aphoristic writer) as searchers for understanding.

If we now consider Plato's own portrayal of the tradition against which he is working, we find that he acknowledges the influence, as sources of ethical teaching, of at least six different kinds of texts: epic, lyric, tragic, and comic poetry; the prose scientific or historical treatise; and oratory. All of these genres are mentioned, discussed, and/or imitated by Plato in his own writing; all are taken seriously – at least initially and provisionally – as possible sources of practical wisdom. Two facts are especially important here. One is that there was, for all practical purposes, no such thing as a tradition of the philosophical prose treatise available to Plato as a model. The prose tradition to which he alludes is the tradition of scientific and ethnographical inquiry exemplified for us in the treatises of the Hippocratic corpus, in lost treatises in other sciences such as mathematics and astronomy, and in the family-related historical writing of Herodotus and Thucydides. Certainly scientific works could contain discussion of ethical issues:

the Hippocratic *On Airs, Waters, Places*, with its account of the climate-relativity of traits of character, had a major influence in fifth-century debates about nature and culture. It is obvious that Herodotus, and especially Thucydides, are major thinkers about value and excellence. But their works do not derive their structure and plan from ethical questions; these are discussed in the course of performing another sort of task, the task of historical inquiry. It seems very likely that there was not available to Plato anything that looked like Aristotle's *Nicomachean Ethics*, that is to say a prose work that sets out to ask and answer our most important questions about virtue and the good life. Our information is incomplete here, so we must be cautious; for example, our lack of knowledge about the ethical writings of Democritus is a serious handicap.[7] But we can confidently say that his background was, in this respect, enormously different from our own.

It is also important to bear in mind that, in the fifth and early fourth centuries, it was the poets who were regarded as the most important ethical teachers. For one thing, some of the major figures whom we call philosophers and include in our histories of Greek philosophy were themselves poets, and wrote placing themselves in a poetic tradition: Xenophanes, Parmenides, and Empedocles are the most salient examples; the first and last are major figures in the history of Greek ethics. But it is equally important to remember that figures whom we usually classify and study as poets were unhesitatingly judged by their contemporaries to be philosophers, if by this one means seekers for wisdom concerning important human matters. Tragic and comic dramas were standardly assessed for their ethical content as well as for other aspects of their construction. In Aristophanes' *Frogs*, characters in search of advice about the city's ethical and political crisis seek out Aeschylus and Euripides in the underworld, arguing that only the return to life of one of these great tragic poets can save the city. Plato's interlocutors, when in search of illumination about virtue or choice, turn naturally to the words of Homer, Hesiod, Simonides, Pindar, the tragic poets;[8] rarely, if ever, to the words of anyone whom we list as a philosopher. It is obvious from the dialogues alone that the well-educated Athenian of the late fifth century has enormous confidence in the wisdom of these figures; Polemarchus, Callicles, and Critias, Protagoras and Prodicus – gentleman and professional sophist alike revere them. Platonic philosophy has to define itself, above all, in opposition to these texts, which embody a deeply shared tradition of reflection about excellence, praise, and blame. It is no surprise that the interlocutors of the *Republic* agree that epic and dramatic poems have the strongest *prima facie* claim to form the center of the new city's curriculum.[9]

It would be foolish indeed to try to say something about the moral voice or persona of the poet in each poetic genre, the way ethical reflection proceeds in each. Fortunately it is also unnecessary, since there is a large and helpful literature on these questions.[10] As we proceed to develop our comparison with tragic poetry we will be mentioning features of other genres that Plato implicitly or explicitly rejects. But simply to have reminded ourselves of these possibilities has cleared the air for a more perspicuous assessment of Plato's project. Before we look at the dialogues as pieces of dramatic writing, however, we have another piece of the background to set in place.

This historical Socrates did not write. He did not write (if we believe Plato's report) because he believed that the real value of philosophizing lay in the responsive interaction of teacher and pupil, as the teacher guides the pupil by questioning (sometimes gentle and sometimes harsh, depending on the pupil's character and degree of resistance) to become more aware of his own beliefs and their relationship to one another.[11] Books (Socrates says in the *Phaedrus*[12]) cannot perform this activity, for they are not 'alive' (275D). They can, at best, remind you of what it is like. At worst, they lull the soul into forgetfulness both of the content and of the manner of real philosophizing, teaching it to be passively reliant on the written word (275A). Worse still, in some readers books can induce the false conceit of wisdom, since they may mistake information about many things for true understanding (275A–B). Books, furthermore, lack the attentiveness and responsiveness of true philosophical teaching. They 'roll around' all over the place with a kind of inflexible inertness (275E), addressing very different people, always in the same way.

We could express these two points by saying that, in Socrates' view, philosophical books are to philosophizing as tennis manuals are to tennis. (We could make the point with other examples: think of child-rearing handbooks, sex manuals, instruction books in navigation.) They can't do it; and they are no substitute for the live activity, although they might, in some circumstances, be more or less useful records of some points, when used by people who already have an experiential sense of what the activity is. If, however, one were to take them for the real thing, to become reliant upon them, rather than upon one's own perceptions and responses – or, worse still, to pride oneself on one's expertise just because one had studied a number of such books – that would be a bad mistake indeed. Such books, furthermore, lack the particularity of really good tennis. They say the same thing to every reader without any regard for the particular characteristics of each reader's game or for the way that game will vary in response to a particular opponent. In one way, the philosophical book is even worse off than the tennis manual. For tennis manuals are neither coercive nor self-important. They do not tell you that you must play, only how you might if you want to; and they typically offer advice in a modest tone of voice. The books of an Empedocles or a Parmenides, by contrast, tell you that you must believe this and not that, act this way and not that way; that this is the way of truth, that the way of loathsome, herdlike error. They shower abuse on the person who does not conform. Their tone is inflated and authoritarian. Even Homer and the lyric poets, though far less strident, do unequivocally praise these deeds and not those, this sort of person and not that. Real philosophy by contrast, as Socrates saw it, is each person's committed search for wisdom, where what matters is not just the acceptance of certain conclusions, but also the following out of a certain path to them; not just correct content, but content achieved as the result of real understanding and self-understanding. Books are not this search and do not impart this self-understanding.

But Plato did write books. What is more, he placed these criticisms of writing inside a written work of his own. The dialogues remind us again and again that Plato lived surrounded by people who had disdain for philosophical activity, people who either cheapened it by making it into sophistry or eristic[13] or totally ignored it. It is not surprising that in such circumstances, especially after the death of Socrates at the hands of those who feared and hated the challenge of real philosophy, he would come to feel the need for written paradigms of good philosophical teaching. (Similarly, in unfavorable political circumstances, the publication of a sex manual or a child-rearing manual could be an enlightened and freedom-engendering act.) A reminder of real philosophical searching, even if it is only that, can still be valuable. But by placing the Socratic criticisms of writing inside his own writing, Plato invites us to ask ourselves, as we read, to what extent his own literary innovations have managed to circumnavigate the criticisms. Let us now ask, more concretely, how the dialogues are written. Two obvious facts about them are (1) that they are a kind of theater, and (2) that they are entirely different from any Greek theater-writing we know. Plato is said to have given up a promising career as a tragic poet to write them; scholars have observed that the dialogues show many traces of his former *métier*.[14] How does he, then, express a positive debt to this cultural paradigm of ethical teaching;[15] and why does he also depart from it?

The Platonic dialogues,[16] like works of tragic theater, but unlike many extant paradigms of ethical discourse (for example the didactic poems of Hesiod, Empedocles, and Parmenides, many of the praise-ascribing works of the early lyric tradition, the prose treatises of Ionian natural scientists and Hippocratic doctors, epideictic oratory) contain more than a single voice.[17] The *Protagoras*, for example, puts before us the responsiveness of dialectical interaction, as tragedy has also shown us concerned moral communication and debate. We see an active, ongoing discussion, rather than a list of conclusions or a proclamation of received truths. Furthermore, the dialogue sets up, in its open-endedness, a similarly dialectical relation with the reader, who is invited to enter critically and actively into the give-and-take, much as a spectator of tragedy is invited to reflect (often along with the chorus) about the meaning of the events for his own system of values. Although, in both cases, our sympathies may turn out to lie with one position (character) rather than another, although sometimes one position emerges as clearly superior, this outcome is not forced upon the spectator/reader by any claim to authority made by a voice inside the text. If there is on one side a decisive victory, it is accomplished by and in the dramatic activity itself, in its relation to the spectator/reader's own deeply-held beliefs. This marks a great difference from many important works of earlier Greek philosophy, where it is usual for the speaker/author to claim to be an initiate (Parmenides), a recipient of wisdom from the gods (Homer, Hesiod), or even, himself, a god on earth (Empedocles). Like the spectator of a tragedy, the dialogue reader is asked by the interaction to work through everything actively and to see where he really stands, who is really praiseworthy and why. Where there is explicit argument, he is invited by the give-and-take to assess what is going on for himself, as the tragic spectator critically assesses the arguments of Creon and Antigone. The sophists used argument, of course, but often as a weapon or a drug: they said it would make a weaker case stronger, or even subdue and overwhelm the soul.[18] Plato, borrowing the critical openness and many-sidedness of good theater, uses argument to show genuine communication taking place and to establish such communication with the reader. Dialogues, then, unlike all the books criticized by Socrates, might fairly claim that they awaken and enliven the soul, arousing it to rational activity rather than lulling it into drugged passivity. They owe this to their kinship with theater.*

A dramatic work, furthermore, can contribute to our understanding of an ethical issue by *motivating* an argument or an inquiry. By showing us how and why characters who are not professional philosophers enter into argument, by showing us what sorts of problems call forth philosophizing, and what contribution philosophy makes to their work on the problems, it can show us, better than a single-voiced work, why and when we ourselves should care about ethical reflection. The *Protagoras* exemplified this function well, as the dramatic setting showed us why Hippocrates, and why we, should worry about diseases of the soul. (The *Republic*, *Symposium*, and *Phaedrus* are no less attentive to the issue.) Sometimes, we might add, Plato stages this issue about motivation explicitly inside the dialogue itself. We are more than once confronted with a scene in which someone wants to leave or drop out of the argument, or says that he does not trust or care about arguments. The ways of dealing with and motivating such an interlocutor show us directly why we should go on doing the hard work required to do what we are doing, reading this dialogue.

We can add that by connecting the different positions on an issue with concretely characterized persons, the dialogue, like a tragedy, can make many subtle suggestions about the connections between belief and action, between an intellectual position and a way of life. (Both *Symposium* and *Phaedrus* will provide us with excellent examples of this.). This aspect of the dialogue form urges us as readers to assess our own individual relationship to the dialogue's issues and arguments. In these ways, again, the dialogue seems to be both less 'silent' and more responsive to individual differences than the books criticized by Socrates.

---

* It is not accidental, however, that it was in fifth-century Athens that this dialectical debate-filled sort of theater got its hold. These aspects of tragedy are thoroughly continuous with the nature of Athenian political discourse, where public debate is everywhere, and each citizen is encouraged to be either a participant or at least an actively critical judge. (See, for example, the debates in Thucydides, which, if not records of actual debates, certainly record a type of activity that frequently took place.) These practices were subject to abuse and manipulation; but at their best they had the characteristics that Plato seeks. Thus Plato's debt to tragic theater is not a debt to some arbitrary aesthetic invention – it is at the same time a debt to the social institutions of his culture. In the same way, his repudiations of tragedy and of Athenian democracy are closely linked (cf. Chs. 5, 6, and below here p. 134).

They are books that each reader can read personally inside his pursuit of self-understanding, exploring the motivations and beliefs of the characters together with his own. There are conclusions here, and views of Plato; we are asked, however, not simply to memorize them, but to find them inside ourselves.

Finally, through its depiction of the dialectical process the dialogue can show us moral development and change taking place. Like a dramatic poem (like the *Antigone*), it can show us the forces that lead to change or increased self-knowledge, and the fruits of change in practical life. Seeing examples of learning is surely an important part of *our* learning from a written text. It is, however, a part of learning that the inertness and the one-voiced structure of non-dramatic didactic moral texts denies us.

In all these ways Plato has learned from his original *métier*, substituting its complexity and its searching, exploratory character for the didactic flatness of much of the earlier philosophizing in his tradition. And in the light of these observations we can now see why, after all, the character Socrates is the real protagonist of the *Protagoras* and the real model for our activity as readers and interpreters, even of the speech of Protagoras. For what Protagoras did was, like a practical epideictic speaker, to give a long speech; what he could not do, or could not do well, was to enter into a responsive exchange of views about its content. He lacked both dedication and humility; and these features of his character were displayed as defects that left him ill-prepared for the activity of self-scrutiny. In fact, everything we have said about the important content of his position he might have said for himself when asked to defend his position against the Socratic challenge; but he didn't. When he could not gratify his vanity by display, he collapsed. Evidently he was more interested in persuasion and effect than in the patient, slow task of sorting things out. His relationship with his audience, like his relationship with his own beliefs, lacked attentiveness, care, and dialectical mutuality. So, although we ourselves got quite a lot of interesting content out of his speech, we did so only by reading it Socratically, asking it what goes with what, what would have to be the case if what was to be so. Even the final thought-experiment which his speech suggested to us was not used by him and owes a lot to our Socratic examination of his earlier speech. Our understanding of the dialogue as a whole, too, required Socratic rather than Protagorean arts: for if the whole is a teaching about what rules out what, and what the cost is of what progress, seeing that will require the clarity, toughness, and flexibility of the Socratic examination, not the vanity of sophistical display.

We have suggested that works of tragic drama share with the dialogues a concern with debate and responsive interaction. We can now deepen the comparison by observing that they share, too, a central structural feature, the *elenchos* or cross-examination. For in the *Antigone*, as in many Socratic dialogues, we begin with the confident assertion of a general position, made by a character over-optimistic about his grasp of and control over practical problems. This general assertion, like so many candidate definitions in the dialogues, turns out not to cover all of Creon's more concrete beliefs about choice and value. The dramatic action consists in the 'separation' of Creon from his false and puffed-up beliefs through painful learning. At the end he arrives at the truth of what he most deeply believes; or at least he becomes able to acknowledge his own deep perplexity. (The spectator should be engaged in a similar sorting process.) But this working-through of the interlocutor's ill-sorted beliefs, this elenctic 'separative' art, is a virtue of Socratic philosophical inquiry to which Plato attaches highest importance, as we can see from his explicit praise as well as by his representations.[19] Even when the interlocutor does not progress beyond perplexity to truth, the *elenchos* separates him, as the *Sophist* puts it, from the tumorous growth of arrogant false belief, preparing the way for healthy growth.[20] We can now see that Plato has used the structure of his former profession to imitate *elenchos* in writing and to engender it in the reader through writing.

But the dialogues are not tragedies. In Plato's view (explicitly argued in *Republic* II–III and X and in the *Laws*) no tragic poem, as his time knew them, could be a good teacher of ethical wisdom. If the dialogues are a kind of theater, owing a debt to tragic models, they are also a theater constructed to supplant tragedy as the paradigm of ethical teaching. We shall say more later, both here and in Chapter 7, about Plato's explicit criticisms of tragedy. Now, to begin to become aware of the deep differences between these two types of dramatic writing, let us approach the *Protagoras* with the expectations with which the Athenians of Plato's time might have approached a tragedy; and let us see how and where these expectations are disappointed.

First we notice its title: *Protagoras*.[21] Like many tragedies (and unlike works from most other known literary genres[22]) this work is named after one of its central characters. But, unlike the *Agamemnon*, the *Oedipus*, the *Antigone*, this work has the name of someone ordinary and close to us. Few readers in Plato's audience could have known him personally; but he will be known to all as a famous cultural figure of the recent past. Certainly he is far from being a mythic king or hero. There is an immediacy, also a flatness and plainness, to the choice: it warns us from the start that we are dealing with figures very like ourselves. (Other titles name figures who are not even famous: *Euthyphro*, *Crito*, *Lysis*, etc.)

Now suppose we (as early fourth-century Greeks) begin to read. The work opens with a dialogue between two characters; this is in itself not foreign to tragic practice. But we are not allowed for a moment to think that we are reading a tragedy. For the work is in prose, a simple conversational Attic prose that is not only unmetrical, but also deliberately anti-rhetorical. We find features of style (frequent hiatus, the absence of certain fashionable prose rhythms) that mark it off unambiguously from the norms of contemporary oratory. Nor, on the other hand, is it any prose style associated with scientific inquiries: we find no affectation of Ionic dialect forms, standard in that literature. We find, deliberately and carefully set down, the plain, unvarnished speech that we might hear in daily life, speech that we are not accustomed to find in any sort of written text:[23]

> FRIEND Hello, Socrates. What have you been doing? But it's obvious. You've been on your dog-hunt after the charms of Alcibiades. Well, when I

saw him a while ago he was still a good-looking man. But a *man* all the same, Socrates, just between the two of us. He's starting to grow a beard.

SOC. What of that? Aren't you an admirer of Homer? He says that the most delicious age of all is when a young man gets his first beard. In fact, just the age Alcibiades is now.

FRIEND Well, how is it going? Have you just been with him? How does he react to you?

SOC. Favorably, I think, especially today. He was very helpful and said a lot of things in my support. In fact, I've only just left him, as you guessed. But I want to tell you something very odd. Even though he was right there, I didn't pay much attention to him. And a number of times I didn't notice him at all.

This speech is deliberately flat and unadorned. It artfully repudiates artfulness. To set such speech on the page is by itself to declare one's difference from the poets and rhetoricians, who deploy the resources of rhythm and figure so as to influence the non-intellectual elements of the soul. This speech is calculated *not* to drug, move, or sway us. It insists on conversing with us calmly.

As we go on reading, we become gradually aware that the *Protagoras* has no *action* of the sort to which we are accustomed in tragic drama (cf. Interlude 2). A tragic drama, as Aristotle puts it, is 'the representation of an action that is serious, complete, and of a certain magnitude'. Even without accepting his theory of tragedy, we can accept this as an accurate descriptive statement. The *Antigone*, for example, tells us the story of a complex action, from its beginning to its end. The implications of its initial situation and problems are worked out in represented actions, with all the reversals of fortune and acknowledgements of error that the interactions of circumstances and characters effect. In the *Protagoras* we hear mention of serious human interactions. Both in the initial dramatic setting and in the course of the discussion there is mention of human dilemmas that could have made suitable material for a tragic plot. But the 'action' of the dialogue is not a working-out of these events: it is not the story of Alcibiades, or of the acts of Prometheus, or even of Hippocrates' runaway slave. At the end of the introductory sequence there is a shift onto the plane of intellect, as the dramatic conflict of the work becomes a competition in *technē*. Concrete experience and personal response to experience are replaced by general argument, questioning, and the search for the best overall account. We find 'reversal' and 'recognition', here as in tragedy: but, again, on the level of intellectual judgment and belief, not personal conduct and response. Socrates and Protagoras 'change places' (or say they do), as Socrates articulates his conception of moral teaching and Protagoras comes to recognize that ethical learning cannot proceed in the way that he has described. What is *not* here that is present in the *Antigone*? Creon, Antigone, their struggle; anger, *erōs*, grief, pity. In short, (1) characters engaged in an action that is of the deepest importance to their entire lives, and (2) the non-intellectual elements of the human soul. Debate is not an outgrowth of and a response to tragic events: debate and discourse *are* the event. Inquiry *is* the action. Hippocrates is led away from his personal worries to the search for an adequate account of practical judgment. Socrates, Odysseus and Prometheus, becomes the hero of a new kind of story, whose ambition it is to rise above the story to the plane of science. It does this in two ways: by moving from particular characters to general accounts, and by moving from the emotions and feelings to the intellect. For it is only by these intellectual gifts that Socrates, as he sees it, can perform his philanthropic Promethean task.

It goes with this that we, as we read the *Protagoras*, find ourselves responding in a way that is very different from the way we would respond to a tragedy. Both works demand our active engagement and response. But the dialogue engages our wits. It demands that we be intellectually active. Its dry and abstract tone positively discourages the arousal of emotions and feelings. If it persuades us of anything, it does so purely by appeal to our powers of reasoning. Dramatic elements are used to engage us initially: once we are engaged, it is intellect that this work claims. We feel that it would be highly inappropriate to weep, to feel fear or pity. The self-possession of the dialogue makes us positively ashamed of these responses. There are, of course, Platonic dialogues in which something humanly moving is taking place: the *Crito* and *Phaedo* are obvious cases. In these dialogues the initial reaction of certain interlocutors is to feel grief or pity. But the dialogue explicitly teaches that these are immature and unhelpful responses. Xanthippe weeps and is escorted out of the room (60A). Socrates reproves Apollodorus for his womanish tears (117D); we are supposed to apply his reprimand to ourselves. Phaedo repeatedly insists that he felt no pity (58E, 59A); nor should we. Socrates leads the interlocutors on from the personal to the general, from the emotional to the intellectual; so the dialogue leads us on. The action of the *Phaedo* is not the death of Socrates; it is the committed pursuit of the truth about the soul. In it Socrates shows us how to rise above tragedy to inquiry. Sir Richard Livingstone, editing an English version of the *Phaedo*, printed the arguments in smaller type 'so that they can be either read or omitted'.[24] This is an exact reversal of Plato's intentions.

There are, it will be said, myths at the end of the *Gorgias*, *Phaedo*, and *Republic*. (There are also the famous allegories of sun, line, and cave in *Republic* VI–VII.) In Chapter 7 I shall argue that the *use* of myth and image in these early/middle works is very different from its both emotionally stirring and philosophically central use in the *Phaedrus*. These myths, unlike the *Phaedrus* myth, are not essential to the philosophical argument; they come after it and reinforce it. Nor are they told in stirring language. In fact, if we compare these myths not with mythless treatises but with the tragic use of myth and image, we will see that Plato is reconstructing myth in much the same way in which he has reconstructed action. He is using it not to entertain in its own right, but to show forth general philosophical truths for which he has already argued; and he is using it to dampen 'mad' passion rather than to arouse it. It would, I think, be a bizarre and quite inappropriate reaction to be moved to love or pity or grief, or even fear, by one of these myths. We do not feel about Er the way we feel about Antigone; in fact, he is incidental, while the general ethical truths of his story are central. His tale does not make us enamored of particulars or arouse our irrational souls.[25]

By now we have some general sense of what Plato is doing to tragedy. What we do not yet know is why he is doing what he does. Why should a work whose aim is to teach practical wisdom avoid engaging the emotions and feelings? Why should it select for itself this lean, plain speech and this intellectualized sphere of activity? Fortunately, answers to these questions are forthcoming from Plato himself. The first and most obvious point, since it is a point stressed by the poets and rhetoricians themselves, is that language that appeals to sense and emotion *can* distract reason in its pursuit of truth. This point is forcefully made by Socrates at the opening of the *Apology*, when he criticizes the diction of his poetically trained opponents:

I do not know what effect my accusers have had on you, gentlemen, but for my own part I am almost carried away by them – their arguments were so persuasive. On the other hand, scarcely a word of what they said was true...I was especially astonished...when they told you that you must be careful not to let me deceive you – the implication being that I am a skillful speaker. I thought that it was particularly brazen of them to tell you this without a blush, since they must know that they will soon be effectively confuted, when it becomes obvious that I have not the slightest skill as a speaker – unless, of course, by a skillful speaker they mean one who speaks the truth...From me you shall hear the whole truth, not, I can assure you, gentlemen, in flowery language like theirs, decked out with fine words and phrases. No, what you will hear will be a straightforward speech in the first words that occur to me, confident as I am in the justice of my cause.

(17A–C, trans. Tredennick)

Here, as in the *Protagoras*, Plato very deliberately creates a speech that will give the impression of not having been deliberately formed.[26] It is not artless; but its art is one that claims to go straight to the truth-telling part of the soul. It is simple rather than flowery, flat rather than emotive or persuasive.[27] Socrates tells us why: he shuns ornamental speech on account of its power to deceive. He strongly implies that the only reason for indulging in such speech would be that one wishes to deceive. He seeks, instead, a transparency and simplicity of diction, free from all disguises.

In this literary context, in which Gorgias and other rhetoricians were explicit about their intention to drug and to captivate, we can see what would motivate this choice. But to justify it Plato must do more than show that poetic speech can deceive. He need not show that it *must* deceive. But he must at least go on to argue that this sort of speech, associated with the increased activity of the emotions, has no important positive role to play in the teaching of ethical truth. For otherwise his poetic opponent might agree with him about the dangers of distortion, but insist that those dangers must be risked for the sake of the good that can be achieved. Plato has certainly not neglected this point. A great deal of the ethical argument in his middle-period dialogues, as we shall shortly see, is devoted to defense of the view that responses of sense and emotion have a powerfully negative and no redeeming positive role to play in the moral and intellectual life of the human being, and that good human development is best promoted by 'separating' the intellectual part of the soul from these responses. From these arguments it would seem to follow, first, that we do not *need* written works that teach by appeal to emotion and feeling; that the most valuable works will be those that make their appeal to the intellectual part in isolation or promote its separation from the other parts. There are, of course, forms of oral instruction that are invaluable in this separation process – first and foremost the study of mathematics (cf. Ch. 5). But a written text like the dialogue can contribute in its own way towards the soul's liberation by actively engaging the intellect, getting it to look beyond the particulars of its own experience towards general accounts, and to be critical of irrational responses.

We might agree with Plato that these features of a written text are of high value and still insist that tragic poetry is a harmless diversion. But in *Republic* x Plato will add that our emotional response to tragic poetry actually strengthens the non-intellectual elements of the soul, making them a source of greater distraction and disturbance to intellect. It 'waters' our emotions, when what a text should above all do is to dry them up (606D). We shall see in Chapter 7 that when Plato modifies his view on this issue he also alters, in a corresponding way, his view and his practice of writing.

What we find in middle-period dialogues, then, is theater; but theater purged and purified of theater's characteristic appeal to powerful emotion, a pure crystalline theater of the intellect. We have said that the dialogue shares with tragic poetry its elenctic structure. We must now return to this claim and qualify it. The *elenchos* of tragedy works above all through the emotions and the sensuous imagination. Creon learns not by being defeated in an argument, but by feeling the loss of a son and remembering a love that he had not seen or felt truly during the loved one's life. As long as Creon remained on the level of intellect and argument, he remained self-confident, not convinced of anything. It took the sudden rush of grief, the tug of loss to make him see an aspect of the world to which he had not done justice. The tragedy even suggests that Creon's feelings were, all along, more deeply rational than his intellect; submerged feeling preserved a balanced scheme of values, while ambitious intellect erred in the direction of one-sidedness and denial. It was one thing to *ask* Creon to describe his views about the family; it was another to confront him with the death of a son. The Platonic *elenchos* is deeply suspicious of this. It teaches by appeal to intellect alone; learning takes place when the interlocutor is enmeshed in logical contradiction. He may, of course, consult his memories and intuitions during the argument; but he approaches them through and for the sake of an intellectual question. No jarring event, no experience that directly awakens feeling, should play any role in these interlocutors' learning. The characters in the *Phaedo* do not learn about the soul by looking to their love for Socrates; they begin to learn only when they are able to put that love away and turn to thought. It is true that in the middle-period dialogues Plato recognizes that the feelings must be given some initial training before Socratic dialectic can take place at all. This is because, as we shall see in Chapters 5–7, he now judges that there are in the soul some genuinely irrational desires that are not at all responsive to teaching about the good; and he also develops a complex understanding of the 'middle', emotional part of the soul in its relation to training and belief. But this training is purely negative, aimed at getting the appetites under control and preventing the birth of inappropriate emotions, such as passionate love and the fear of death.[28] The ascent of the soul towards true understanding, if it uses any texts at all, will surely avoid any with an irrational or emotive character.

There is one more way in which the two sorts of cross-examination are distinct. Platonic inquiry uses particular cases as data towards a general account. By themselves, without a grasp of the general form, particulars cannot be objects of insight. We are urged, always, to look for what is common to all cases which we call by a common name, neglecting (or, refusing to see?)[29] the differences. When we have grasped the single form, the particular judgments with which we began can be regarded as simply one instance of the general. The tragic *elenchos* does not present itself as part of an ongoing search for *the* correct account of anything. We could not learn from it without generalizing to some extent, applying Creon's learning, *mutatis mutandis*, to our own case. But the force of tragedy is usually, too, to warn us of the dangers inherent in all searches for a single form: it continually displays to us the irreducible richness of human value, the complexity and indeterminacy of the lived practical situation. Our primary responsibility is always to the particular rather than the general; although in learning we will generalize to some extent, the test of the adequacy of these accounts will remain their fit with our experienced perception of the cases before us.[30] In the *Symposium*, Plato will indicate both his love and his repudiation of this position by linking it with the character of Alcibiades (Ch. 6).

In Plato's anti-tragic theater, we see the origin of a distinctive philosophical style, a style that opposes itself to the merely literary and expresses the philosopher's commitment to intellect as a source of truth. By writing philosophy as drama, Plato calls on every reader to engage actively in the search for truth. By writing it as anti-tragic drama, he warns the reader that only certain elements of him are appropriate to this search. This, we can now see, is the real meaning of the *Protagoras*'s tension between dialectic and elitism, between its appearance of offering us a choice and its announcement that only a superior being ought to choose. Each of us has the choice, in fact: but it will be an appropriate choice only if it is made by the highest element in us, viz. intellect. We now begin to understand that Plato's style is not content-neutral, as some philosophical styles are sometimes taken to be; it is closely bound up with a definite conception of human rationality.

These observations have been crudely general; they have accounted for only some features of Plato's practice as a writer. They have not, for example, dealt with any of the complexities of comic and tragic speech in the *Symposium*, a dialogue in which the power of the elements beyond which Socrates urges us to ascend will make itself felt with a more than propaideutic force. And, as I have said, they have not accounted for the role of myth, image, and rhythmic language in the *Phaedrus* – where, as I shall argue, Plato criticizes his own ethical conception and the associated conception of writing (Ch. 7). But I hope to have opened here an inquiry into the relationship between the Platonic dialogue form and the content of Platonic ethics, an ethical conception in which much of our ordinary humanity is a source of confusion rather than of insight, and our lives stand in need of transcendence through the dialectical activity of intellect.[31]

5   The *Republic*: true value and the standpoint of perfection

> I am amused, I said, that you seem to be afraid of the many, in case they
> should think that you are prescribing useless studies. It is no trivial matter at
> all, but a difficult one, to realize that there is in the soul of each of us an
> organ or instrument that is purified and rekindled by mathematical studies,
> when it has been destroyed and blinded by our ordinary pursuits, an organ
> whose preservation is worth more than that of ten thousand eyes, for by it
> alone is the truth seen. Those who share this belief will think your proposal
> surpassingly good; those who have never had any perception of these things
> will probably think that you are talking nonsense – for they don't see any
> other advantage worth speaking of in these pursuits.
>
> *Republic* 527D–E

Plato's assault on the goodness of the ordinary opens on a scene of daily Athenian
life. Socrates (who still believes that philosophy can be practiced as one element
in the life of the democratic citizen) goes down from Athens to the Piraeus. With
him is Glaucon, older brother of Plato. The year is probably 421, during the Peace
of Nicias: a time of rest and relative stability. By the time of composition, about
fifty years later, most of the dialogue's principal characters are dead, and few of
them peacefully. Three (Polemarchus, Niceratus, and Socrates) have been executed
on political charges; the first two were brutally murdered for their fortunes by
an oligarchic faction led by members of the family of Plato. We watch these
peaceful interactions, then, with apprehensiveness and a sense of impending
violence – a violence nourished, evidently, by the desires of the appetitive part
of the soul.[1]

They go, Socrates and Glaucon, to observe the festival of Bendis, a recently
imported Thracian goddess. Socrates is at first curious, later admiring. Using
repeatedly the language of *seeming* and *appearing*, he makes a value judgment: both
the local procession and the one sent by the Thracian visitors were 'fine' or
'splendid' (*kalē*)* – or so it seems to him. Later that same evening, furthermore,
there is to be a torch-race on horseback, followed by an all-night festival. And
that, judges Plato's older brother Adeimantus, should be really 'worthwhile to
see' (*axion theasasthai*, 328A).

---

* On the range of meaning of this important aesthetic–ethical term, usually rendered 'beautiful',
  'noble', 'fine', see Ch. 6, p. 178, where I suggest that it comes very close to introducing a unified
  conception of *value* (both moral and aesthetic). For a discussion of Greek terms that are related
  to our 'value', see Ch. 1, p. 7 and n. 12.

Between the procession and the torch-race, then, these Athenian democrats find a little room for philosophical conversation. It is in this space that the entire *Republic* takes place. All the characters but Socrates seem (at first, at any rate) to consider philosophy a diversion like everything else, no more and no less valuable. In the true democratic spirit, they attach equal value to all of their interests and pleasures – each of them, like the democratic man described in Book VIII, 'handing the rule over himself to each appetite as it comes along until it is replenished, as if it had chosen the lot for that office, and then in turn to another, dishonoring none but fostering them all equally' (516B).[2] This attitude to value is linked, clearly, with a lack in both constancy and self-sufficiency. A guardhouse kept in such a way is at the mercy of any ruler that happens along. A soul kept in such a way can all too quickly change its course in obedience to a new mastering desire. And because its desires lead it, so frequently, to attend to vulnerable things, it can all too rapidly be stripped of what it values. We know that the men who here are friends will soon be killing one another for power and property. Of all the dead, only Socrates dies without losing anything that he loves.

The scene shortly shifts to the home of Cephalus (a man whose name means 'head'). This old man's bodily deficiency has brought him, as he tells us, a larger than usual measure of focus and stability. Too infirm to walk easily in the city, his bodily desires dimmed by advancing years, he lacks many of the younger men's distractions; he finds his love of argument correspondingly increased (328C–D). Most of the old men he knows, Cephalus tells Socrates, mourn the coming of old age. They think it has impoverished their lives. Since they attach worth to the bodily appetites and to the activities that satisfy them, they 'long for the absent pleasures of youth. They recall the pleasures of sex and drinking and feasting, and others that go with these, and they are angry, as if they had been deprived of important things – as if they used to live a good life and now aren't even living' (329A). The vulnerability of their good living is – we see again – directly connected with their thought about value. Change and happening are problems for them because they care about chance-governed and changing things. For Cephalus, on the other hand, the change to old age simply means the end of a problem. He reminds Socrates about the poet Sophocles, who, when asked whether he was still capable of making love to a woman, answered, 'Silence, O human being. I am extremely happy to have escaped that, like a slave who has gotten away from a mad and savage master' (329B–C). Cephalus agrees: 'For a great peace and freedom from these things comes with old age. After the tension of the appetites relaxes and ceases, it is just what Sophocles said, an escape from many mad masters' (329C).

The *Republic*'s opening confronts us, then, with a question about value: what is truly worthwhile, worth doing and worth seeing, in a human life? It indicates to us (something that should be no surprise by now) that the answer to this question will be closely connected with our questions about risk and self-sufficiency. The average democratic citizen is maximally unsafe because he attaches value, in his conception of good living, to activities and subjects that are unsafe – that are, in fact, almost certain to fail sooner or later. Cephalus and Sophocles do better. But Cephalus is still tormented by his concern for money and by his fear of death. And we suspect that he has ascribed more importance to appetite than he himself knows: for we shall later see that it is possible, even in one's prime, to live a life much less tormented by 'mad' appetite than his, because less attentive to its objects.[3] By the argument's end, Socrates will have defended as the best human life a life much more extreme in its detachment than Cephalus's: the life of the philosopher, whose soul the *Phaedo* describes as akin to the forms it contemplates: pure, hard, single, unchanging, unchangeable. A life, then, of goodness without fragility. We would like to understand his arguments for the superior value of this life.

As we ask Plato's question about value, we must also be asking, with him, an epistemological question: how, or from what standpoint, are adequate judgments reached about the value of prospective constituents of a life? For it is plain from the dialogue's opening that ordinary people, when asked what *seems* fine to them, will name many activities that the philosopher's argument will in the end judge worthless; and in general, as Socrates will later observe, most people, if asked what is worthwhile, will praise the content of their own lives (581C–D). But Plato is convinced that most of these answers are misguided: the 'eye' of our human souls is 'deeply buried in some barbaric slime' (533D) and cannot see clearly. From what position, then, does this eye see well? And what is the nature of the obstacles to its true vision? Sophocles made a suggestion. With his lofty 'O human being' – words that Plato, at any rate, surely chooses deliberately – he implied that the problem lies with our distinctively human nature; that correct perception would come from a standpoint that is more than human, one that can look on the human from the outside. (*Republic* IX will speak of a 'real above' in nature.) We need to explore, then, not only the account of value but also the account of true vision that goes with it.

We can now begin this search: but in a complicated way. For there is a difficult interpretative problem in our path. We need to set it out and clarify our relation to it before we can properly appreciate Plato's arguments.

I

The *Republic* argues that the best life for a human being is the life of the philosopher, a life devoted to learning and the contemplation of truth. The *Republic* also argues that the best life is a life 'ruled' by reason, in which reason evaluates, ranks, and orders alternative pursuits. Both of these claims about the *Republic*'s theory of the good are generally accepted; what interpreters are less readily able to settle is how, and whether, these two Platonic claims about the good are related. It appears that the conception of 'rule' by reason articulated in the fourth book of the dialogue is a purely formal conception that makes no attempt to specify the content of the life that gets planned and ordered by reason. All that is required there is that the agent harmonize his or her soul, order his or her life plan, in accordance with some orderly conception of the good. The reasoning part of the soul (*logistikon*) determines what has value and how much 'taking thought for the good of the entire soul'.[4] The difference between the reasoning or intellectual part and the other motivational elements of the person is to be found in this capacity for overall evaluation and selection. Appetites merely reach out for objects, without conceiving of them as overall goods.[5] But there is no reason, according to Book iv's formal conception of rational valuation, why the *content* of a life plan should not include appetitive activities as intrinsically valuable components that get selected and arranged alongside the others. There is also no reason to suppose that reason will organize the agent's life around the activity of reasoning. In fact, it seems quite natural to suppose that the reasoning part, in taking thought for the good of the 'entire soul' of a complex human being, will accord intrinsic value to activities that satisfy natural, persisting appetitive needs.[6] Plato does not yet say anything against this; we suppose that any well-ordered content should satisfy his requirements.

And yet, by the time we reach the end of the *Republic*, Plato has said a great deal about content. He has, in fact, rejected many of the most common human activities, including all appetitive activities, as lacking in true or intrinsic value, and he has chosen the life of the philosopher as the best life. In fact, Socrates claims very precisely that this life is 729 times better than the worst life, the life of the tyrant.[7] This move beyond Book iv's purely formal account is prefigured by Socrates' cryptic claim, in Book vi, that the earlier story was insufficient because it stopped with a merely human agreement and used as its measure of value a human, therefore an imperfect, being.[8] The *Protagoras* has already shown us that such a measure will not do for Socrates. Such 'laziness', he now says, is a quality of mind that our city and our philosophers must reject. Similarly, in the *Phaedo*, Socrates defends as the best life a life which he calls a practice for death: a life of philosophical contemplation in which the philosopher dissociates himself or herself as much as possible from the desires and pursuits of the human body, according them no positive value at all.[9]

Recent interpreters are in agreement that Plato's final judgments of the value of lives, in the middle dialogues, cannot be adequately explained by appeal to *Republic* iv's formal argument alone. Clearly Plato has an independent interest in the *components* of lives; overall order is only necessary, and not sufficient, for the highest sort of value. But there is, in the recent literature on this question, a tendency to think of these claims about content as an embarrassment to Plato, and to reconstruct his argument, insofar as possible, so that it relies on the formal considerations alone. One outstanding such attempt is that of Gary Watson in his article 'Free agency', a very persuasive picture of Book iv's account of rational valuation, in which it is explicitly asserted that intrinsic value will, in this account, be attached to activities that satisfy our standing appetitive needs.[10] Watson, however, is not offering an interpretation of the *Republic* as a whole; he is therefore free to ignore the additional questions raised by the later books. In *Plato's Moral Theory*, however, Terence Irwin does offer a reading of the whole *Republic* that develops a position similar to Watson's as an account of the entire work.[11] In his valuable and stimulating book, Irwin argues that Plato's primary interest is in describing a conception of the good as the harmonious adjustment of a number of separate constituents, each possessing intrinsic value. In Irwin's reading, these intrinsic ends will be the personal ideals of each human agent, discovered by the deliberative procedures of recollection (interpreted here as a kind of introspection[12]) and self-criticism. Any life content will be acceptable to Irwin's Plato, provided that it can satisfy, in an orderly way, the agent's own system of desires. In the case of certain lives that Plato rejects, the rejection can be accounted for on grounds of form.[13] But Irwin concedes that Plato does in fact reject, on grounds of content alone, lives whose orderly form seems satisfactory. Irwin also admits that the introspective procedures by which a life content is arrived at on his account are nowhere mentioned in the *Republic* itself; in their place we find a claim that only a life dedicated to contemplation of the truth – a life not everyone can have, or perhaps even want – is fully worthwhile life. But, in Irwin's opinion, this is just a mistake on Plato's part. 'It is regrettable', he writes, 'that Plato leaves us gaps to fill here, because of his interest in contemplative rather than in practical wisdom.' And he attributes this and other 'gaps' to Plato's distance from our contemporary philosophical interests: 'He does not stress the parts of the problem we might like him to stress; but that is because his view of the problem and of the right kind of answer is not the view of some more recent moralists.'[14]

We have turned to Plato as a thinker whose importance is closely linked to the depth and severity of his challenge against prevailing beliefs, both of his day and of our own; so this 'distance' does not, by itself, alarm us. But it would be regrettable – and on Plato's own terms – if vague prejudice and interest had indeed, at this crucial juncture, displaced philosophical argument.[15] Furthermore, it is very important for our particular concerns to determine whether Plato's arguments do or do not support these judgments of content. For if Irwin is correct, only one of our central concerns, the harmonious interrelationship of values, is actually addressed in Plato's arguments; the fragility or instability of individual commitments is not of concern to him – or is of concern only to his prejudice. But if he has arguments for his choice of the philosopher's life these will be likely to tell us why a good life should exclude or minimize our most fragile and unstable attachments, consecrating itself to the more self-sufficient intellectual pursuits. As we pursue this problem we find, as I shall argue in this chapter, that the material about content is not peripheral, but quite central to the *Republic*'s theory of the good. I shall argue that the 'gap' Irwin detects in the *Republic* argument is actually filled by a complex theory of true value and of objective valuation which, far from being built upon prejudice,[16] is well worth our most serious attention. In fact, if we do not consider it, we run the risk of stripping Plato of some of his deepest and most characteristic arguments, of central importance for our own inquiry. In the end we risk turning the *Republic* into a comfortable expression of the liberal principle (mentioned in Book VIII) that it should be 'open to each person to structure an arrangement for his own life, the one that pleases him' (557B) – rather than, what it is, a profound and unsettling attack on that principle as a basis for genuinely good living.

Although the *Republic*'s move from structure to content appears abrupt and puzzling, it is less so once we see that Plato has provided an argument to support it. Towards the end of Book IX, after describing several alternative lives, Socrates introduces a two-part 'demonstration' (580C–D)[17] to show Glaucon that the life of the philosopher is the best (most *eudaimōn*) human life.[18] The complex argument that follows sets up a division of enjoyments or pleasant activities, activities performed with enthusiasm or alacrity, that is related to Book IV's tripartite division of the soul into appetitive, emotional, and intellectual elements. (Although considerations of pleasure appear initially to be separated off from considerations of goodness, it is clear as the argument progresses that the ranking of 'pleasures' is a ranking not of subjective feelings about activities, as to their strength or intensity, but of the activities themselves, as to their true worth or objective desirability. Thus the 'true' pleasures are those activities that are chosen in harmony with *true* beliefs about value or worth, as opposed to those in which agents take pleasure because they falsely believe them to have worth. The latter can and do still give rise to very intense *feelings* of pleasure, as Plato stresses; but they will not be ranked high as pleasures according to Plato's scheme.)[19] Socrates now argues that the activities associated with the 'reasoning part' of the soul, learning and the contemplation of truth, are the best activities in a human life. He argues first epistemologically: the correct criterion of judgment is 'experience combined with wisdom and reason' (581C–583A). The philosopher alone judges with the right criterion or from the appropriate standpoint; he selects his own activities as best. Second, Socrates argues that the philosopher's activities are superior on intrinsic grounds: being concerned, as they are, 'with the unchanging and immortal and with truth', they have a higher worth than the pursuits associated with the other two parts (583Aff.).

Although these two parts of the argument are formally separate, their connection is close: the epistemology of value-judgment underwrites the choice of this content for true value, and the intrinsic merits of the content dispose us to be content with the standpoint that has approved it. (We shall later ask questions about this relationship.) Epistemological considerations continue to be prominent in the second part of the argument, where the ordinary person's errors in value ranking are explained by the observation that his experience has not taken him to the place from which, alone, appropriate judgments of worth can be made. Unlike the philosopher, who has traveled to the 'real above' in nature, this person has only oscillated between the 'below' and the 'middle' (584Dff.).

In this passage, if anywhere, Plato shows us the considerations that would lead a soul 'ruled by reason' in the formal sense to choose a certain specific life content, that of the life devoted to philosophy, rather than some other orderly plan of life. And here, if anywhere, he shows us the standpoint from which true rankings are made. The passage is compressed and difficult; it is not readily evident how Plato moves from his formal ideal to the specification of content through this ranking of activities, or how the ranking itself is produced.[20] Fortunately, however, the theory of activity-value that is cryptically discussed here receives a fuller development in other related dialogues, especially the *Phaedo, Gorgias,* and *Philebus.* If we bring related passages to bear on this one,[21] we shall better appreciate the strength of Plato's position.

In the *Gorgias,* Socrates faces an opponent who grants the importance of having a rational life plan, but wishes to specify the content of that plan in a way that is repellent to the philosopher: the best life is a life organized by reason for the maximal enjoyment of sensual pleasure. The 'naturally noble and just' man, Callicles argues, will allow his appetites to grow very great, in fact, as great as possible. But, because of his superior 'courage and practical intelligence' he will also 'be sufficient to minister to them at their greatest and to satisfy every appetite with what it craves' (492A). Here, then, is a life formally ruled and ordered by reason. But most of its episodes will be episodes of appetitive activity: eating, drinking, sexual indulgence. Socrates' reply should, then, give us some insight into the nature of his argument for the superior value of the content of the philosopher's life.

It should be noticed, first, that Callicles is not at all disturbed by the large element of *need* in the life he describes, the extent to which reason's choices 'minister to' (*hupēretein*) the exigencies of the body.[22] He seems to believe, in fact, that just because we are beings with such-and-such needs, there is a certain positive value attaching to the pursuits that satisfy those needs. He requires only that need remain within the limits of reason's power to procure satisfaction and that the whole life be not haphazard, but under the executive direction of intelligence. Furthermore, Callicles seems to attach a positive value to the very having of these appetitive needs: for Socrates' claim that those who need nothing are living well (are *eudaimōn*) fills him with distaste. 'In that case', he replies, 'stones and corpses would be living superlatively well' (492E). He evidently, then, ascribes positive intrinsic value not to the state of replenishment itself, which even a corpse might exemplify, but far more to the having and pleasant replenish*ing* of the human appetites – and the bigger, apparently, the better: 'the maximum inflow' (494B).[23] It is Socrates' aim to attack both of these claims: both that appetitive activities have value because of the way in which they answer to our needs *and* that there is positive value, for a human being, in the very having of recurring appetitive needs.

The strategy of Socrates' argument is to find some cases of activity bringing satisfaction of an appetitive need for which Callicles will concede that the activity in question is shameful or ridiculous, the need a need any person should wish not to have. Callicles is then pressed to see a close similarity between these cases and his own favored activities; and he is urged to concede that, in his own case as well, the activities are without positive intrinsic value, the needs whose disappearance it would be rational to want. The two text examples presented by Socrates are the pleasure of scratching an itch and the sexual enjoyment of the passive homosexual. Callicles is, in fact, not won over by the first: he tenaciously tries to claim that scratching is a perfectly good component of the ideal life. But the second example so deeply offends his social and sexual prejudices that he is forced to rethink his entire position. 'Aren't you ashamed, Socrates,' he says, 'to lead the argument to things of that sort?'[24]

Socrates' implicit argument about these two cases seems to be as follows. Itching is a need, and scratching an activity answering to and assuaging that need. Scratching has, therefore, what we might call *need-relative* or *replenishment* value. But we can easily see, if we sever the activity from the replenishment context, that we do not ascribe any independent intrinsic value to the activity of scratching. It is nothing that a rational being would include as a component of a plan for the good life.[25] It is valuable as, and only as, the activity that calms a certain sort of troublesome bodily feeling. If we never had itches, we would have no reason at all to scratch. If a person thought scratching a good sort of thing to do and went around scratching whether or not he had an itch, we would think him comical or disturbed.

Furthermore, it is easy to see that we wish, in general, not to be afflicted with the itching that gives rise to the desire for scratching. Perhaps this is just because itching itself is so excruciating; perhaps a further reason is that the activity that relieves it is so undignified and so embarrassing. In any case, we do not value the having of this need or pain; we do not prefer the life with more and greater itches to the life with fewer and smaller.[26] We would think that a person who prayed for the greatest possible itches, provided that he or she always had the power to scratch, was either a maniac or a clown.

The example of the passive homosexual works in a similar way.[27] To take one's sexual pleasure in this manner is, for some people, to satisfy a need. But the activities involved are not, *just* on account of their need-relative value, intrinsically good or valuable activities. They do not make for *eudaimonia*: a life made up of such episodes as components is not a valuable human life (494E). In fact (assuming for the moment the point of view of a Greek of Callicles' class and background[28]), we agree that it is a ridiculous and loathsome way to behave. Callicles would laugh at people who do that, even if he knew they were satisfying a need. And nobody, he assumes, would choose to do that if he did not have that need already. The need, furthermore, is a need that Callicles hopes and prays never to feel. He wishes that no child or friend of his will ever feel it. In this case, the wish not to have the need cannot be explained by the unusual pain of the need itself; this sexual need is, by itself, no more painful than the sexual needs which Callicles values and fosters. The need is wished away, presumably, because it leads to activities that are antecedently and independently classified as disgraceful. The life composed of them is 'terrible and shameful and wretched' (494E). Callicles wishes not to need to do shameful and wretched things.

The examples, then, force Callicles to concede that no activity has positive intrinsic value *merely* because it replenishes a lack or answers to a need. And some needs are themselves hateful just because the activities they prompt are independently judged to be bad, silly, or unmanly. We cannot, then, settle issues of life-content *simply* by looking at what will satisfy the various needs that we happen antecedently to have, or by asking people in the grip of those needs what they think they want. We must look independently at the activities themselves, and ask whether they are noble.

But Socrates does not introduce these two examples as isolated or exceptional cases. He uses them as particularly clear cases that display features shared by all cases of appetitive, or, more generally, need-satisfying activity; and he intends to attack the claim of all these activities to be component parts of the good life. The examples are introduced via a general consideration of the structure of the appetitive element of the soul (493A3, B1); eating to satisfy hunger and drinking to satisfy thirst are agreed to be paradigmatic examples of the type of activity under discussion (494B–C); and the homosexual case is said to be a 'summary' of this entire group (494E3–4). Finally, at the conclusion of the discussion of the examples, Socrates gets Callicles to concede explicitly that 'every need and appetite' has a similarly pain-relative structure (496D, cf. 497C7). The suggestion clearly is that the appetitive pursuits valued by Callicles are all really like itching and scratching: attractive to someone already afflicted with a certain sort of pain, but of no value in themselves. If we can get ourselves to view these common pursuits from outside, not from the distorting perspective of felt need, but objectively, we will, he suggests, find them as ridiculous, as valueless, or perhaps even as loathsome, as we now find the pursuits of the homosexual or the scratcher. We will therefore wish not to have such needs, so that our lives need not be spent in repeated and somewhat absurd attempts to satisfy them. Socrates' stories of the leaky jars and of the 'torrent-bird' told in this same passage, tried to get us to see the futility and squalor of appetitive pursuits. All of us, insofar as we live an appetitive life, are like vessels full of holes, vainly pouring into ourselves, again and again, a satisfaction that as promptly deserts us. Or, worse, we are like an especially loathsome sort of bird that excretes as rapidly as it eats, and is constantly doing both.[29] Overall rational order is not enough: the constituents of a rational life must also be intrinsically choiceworthy.

Socrates' arguments leave us with a number of troublesome questions. It is not clear that Callicles should be so quickly impressed by Socrates' attempted assimilation of his 'naturally noble' person to types that he himself despises. Even if there are *some* activities that have need-relative value without having any separate intrinsic value, it is not clear why we should take the very presence of need-relative value to be evidence of the absence of intrinsic value. Socrates clearly implies this – but clearly his argument will not take him this far. Considerations that would help to fill out the argument – considerations, for example, of the instability and impermanence of appetitive activity – are barely alluded to and not developed. But we will return to these issues later, and turn now to the evidence for a similar theory of value within the *Republic* itself.

Early in the *Republic*'s second book Glaucon presents a tripartite classification of activities with reference to the kind of value or worth they possess. It does not exploit precisely the same distinction that we found in the *Gorgias* and shall find again in the *Republic* ix argument about enjoyings. But it is a related distinction, and one which Plato tends to run together with the one that we have seen; and, equally important, we shall encounter here a number of examples that play a central role in the value-theories of *Republic* ix and the *Philebus*. There are, Glaucon tells us, three kinds of goods (*agatha*), or things we would choose to have. (Although this might look like the introduction to a list of possessions, the members of his lists are all, in fact, activities that we think good and choose to pursue.[30] Glaucon's 'We would choose to have' suggests that what is in question is not the content of all actual pursuits, but only the content of rational choices; or choices made in certain conditions. It invites us to think about good and bad conditions for choice, pointing forward to the epistemological questions of *Republic* ix.) The first group contains activities that are chosen not for their consequences, but for their own sake alone: 'enjoying oneself, and all the harmless pleasures which have no further consequences besides the joy one finds in them' (357A). Second are activities that we choose both for their own sake and for the sake of independently desirable consequences: reasoning, seeing, the healthy functioning of the body. Third are things valuable only for their independently desirable consequences, and not choiceworthy in themselves: exercising, undergoing treatment when one is sick, making money.

Here again, we see that certain pursuits in which we engage have no intrinsic value. We rationally choose them because we have certain needs, pains, or interests, and the pursuits are efficient instrumental means to the desired consequences. A healthy person who took bad-tasting medicine would be irrational. Even exercising, which answers to a standing need of any creature with a bodily nature similar to ours, is held to be one of the things you go through just to be in a state you otherwise want to be in; it has no merit just as an activity. All of these activities look worthwhile in relation to a contingent context; take away the context and the reasons for selecting them will be gone. Contrasted with these cases are the intrinsically valuable components of a life: the good functioning of mind and body that is at once both valuable and useful, the useless but valuable enjoyments. (The latter, to judge from examples in other passages, would include certain aesthetic and sensory pleasures.)

This distinction is not exactly the same one as the *Gorgias*'s distinction between merely need-relative and non-need-relative value. There might be pursuits undertaken as instrumental means to a desired end that were not prompted by any felt pain or lack. Exercise is not always undertaken because bad condition is felt as painful. And it could be argued that not every pursuit that has its value merely, or solely, in relation to some antecedent pain that it assuages is chosen as an *instrument* to the resulting state of relief or replenishment.[31] But the two contrasts are very closely related. Both contrast merely context-relative value with value that would be value in any circumstances whatever; and, more important, they contrast deficiency-relative activities with activities that would be valuable even had we no deficiencies at all. Their 'right-hand' side, the side of intrinsic, non-relative value, is the same in the two cases, and Plato appears to treat the two contrasts as interchangeable for the purposes in which he is interested. This is not, I think, a particularly grave problem for his argument. What is still unanswered in this classification, however, is the question of the *Gorgias*: are we to suppose that every activity whose value derives primarily from its relation to our needs is just for this reason *entirely* lacking in intrinsic value? *Republic* II does not clearly make this claim; indeed, some valuable activities are also useful, though their value does not *derive from* usefulness. But the stronger claim is explicitly advanced, in connection with a similar instrumental/intrinsic contrast illustrated by similar examples, in an early argument of the *Gorgias*. There Socrates and Polus agree that if someone does something for the sake of something else, he does not truly want that which he does, but only that for the sake of which he does it; and that this is true *whenever* someone wants something of instrumental value (467D–468A).[32] Why should we think this? For a deeper understanding of such claims and their consequences for the status of appetitive activity, we must now return to the argument in *Republic* IX with which we began, supplementing it with material drawn from the *Phaedo*, and from the classification of enjoyings in the *Philebus*.

The Book IX argument defends the content of the philosopher's life over the available alternatives by developing a theory of the value of activities whose elements should by now look familiar to us. There are, says Socrates, some activities that people value only because they provide relief from an antecedent pain or lack. The activities are accorded value either (1) because they seem good and pleasant by contrast with the pain that preceded, or (2) because they are means to a pain-free end state that itself seems good by contrast with the preceding pain; or sometimes for both reasons (583C–584A). But, Socrates continues, we can see that neither the activities nor their resultant end states are intrinsically valuable. They are not 'truly pleasant' at all: the judgment that they are worth something is thoroughly based on illusion. For no rational creature would choose to engage in such activities were he or she not in need or pain. Nor is the state of null pain in which these activities culminate anything more valuable than a neutral or zero state (583C–D). It has in itself no positive value; indeed, contrasted with some activity that is intrinsically good or pleasant, this state would look like a state of deficiency, since it is inactive. It is valued highly only by those human beings who have never experienced real intrinsically good enjoyings, people, as Socrates puts it, who have never traveled to the 'above' in nature, but have only oscillated between the 'below' and the 'middle'. The view such people take of the good is a distorted one because of the limitations of their perspective. 'None of these views is healthy with regard to the truth about pleasure – there is a kind of bewitchment' (584A). Socrates' claim (if we now combine these observations with the epistemological claims of the earlier part of the argument) is that a human being who has had the right sort of experience, viz. the philosopher, and who judges from the appropriate standpoint or using the correct criteria, will be in a position to detect the error of the many and to make correct value-ascriptions.

We still lack a clear account of what the reliable perspective or standpoint is, this standpoint of the 'real above' in nature. But the philosopher's ability to judge correctly seems to have less to do with mere quantity of experience than with the fact that experience has taken him to a certain place: a place where reason, free of pain and limitation, can stand alone, above the restrictions imposed upon thought by merely human life. (Socrates' reference to a 'bewitchment' reminds us of a similar passage in the *Phaedo*, in which the most powerful sources of cognitive 'bewitchment' were said to be the needs and appetites of the body (81B).)

We have, then, a fusion of our two familiar contrasts. Intrinsically valuable activities are now divided off both from merely need-relative and from merely instrumental values, both of which are said to lack intrinsic value. (A new point which Socrates adds here is that even the consequences of the instrumental activities in question have, at best, a merely pain-relative and not an intrinsically positive value.) In the latter mixed group, Socrates now argues, belong all of our ordinary appetitive pursuits: eating, drinking, sexual activity. Also, he insists, though without additional argument, the activities associated with the emotional part of the soul, and the enjoyment of anticipating future bodily pleasures (386C, 584C9–11). In the former, intrinsically valuable group we have the pleasures of smell (584B), which are very intense, but neither follow an antecedent pain nor leave pain behind when they depart.[33] But the central example of pure or genuine enjoying is the intellectual activity of the philosopher. (We should never lose sight of the importance of mathematical reasoning and contemplation for Plato as a central case of these pursuits.) Socrates' praise of this activity gives us insight into the features that are, in his view, constitutive of intrinsic value. Both here and in the *Phaedo*'s related discussion of goods of soul and body,[34] he stresses three features.

(1) *Purity*: (a) *of activity*. The activity is chosen itself by itself; it contains no necessary admixture of pain, either as a source of antecedent motivation or as a concomitant experience, by contrast with which the pleasure of the activity is felt as pleasure. So it has its worth by and in itself, without standing in a necessary relation to, being 'mixed up with', something else (584C, 585A–B, 586B–C; cf. *Gorg.* 496C–497D, *Phd.* 66D–E, 60A, 70D). (b) *Of objects*. The objects of intellect are themselves particularly clear and simple paradigms, unmixed with their contraries, existing themselves by themselves (cf. *Phd.* 67B).

(2) *Stability*: (a) *of activity*. The activity can continue in the same way, without cessation, abatement or variation. It is thus very different in structure from the ebb and flow of replenishment-activities, which exhibit an internal sequence of changes and minister to contingent need (585C; cf. *Phd.* 79C–80B). (b) *Of objects*. The objects of intellect are themselves also maximally stable, in fact (in Plato's view) eternal. They never vary or come to be, but are always there and always in the same condition. The objects of the non-philosopher, on the other hand, are the mutable things of this world, 'never the same, and mortal' (585C; cf. *Phd.* 79C, *et al.*).

(3) *Truth*. The activity of the philosopher leads to a grasp of the real truth about the universe and an ability to give fully adequate accounts, not mere half-truths or conjectures (585C; cf. 533B–C). This last point is important because it tells us that the philosopher's life is superior even when he is not directly contemplating the forms, or doing mathematical and scientific thinking, but is going about his political duties. For even then he will 'know each of the likenesses, what they are and of what, because he has seen the truth concerning fine and just and good things' (520C).

The *Republic*, then, develops a theory of value in which no single element predominates, but in which purity, stability, and truth all play a role in the ranking of objects and also of activities that constitute lives. It supports the selection of these marks of value by claiming that human beings who have had the right sort of experience of the available alternatives and who judge from the standpoint of the 'real above' will choose a life that exemplifies these values, and not their opposites. And it argues, further, that the activities that constitute the bulk of most people's lives – eating, drinking, sex – lack these marks of value, possessing a merely specious value because of the way in which they relieve need or distress, and/or the way in which they lead to states of relief. Certain elements of this value-theory – for example Plato's concern for stability and purity of objects – are closely bound up with the *Republic*'s particular theory of truth and of the objects of knowledge. Others, such as the concern with truth *simpliciter* and with stability and purity of activity, look separable from Plato's particular conception of truth and may not even require a realist conception. None of this seems to depend on mere metaphysical prejudice. Constituents of lives, Socrates argues, must be examined for these marks of value. If they lack them, they cannot be called *true* enjoyings, truly valuable pursuits. The philosopher's life is found to be superior not because of bias, but because it exemplifies values which, Socrates argues, all rational beings with the appropriate experience would pursue.

Before we look at the evidence for a similar account of value in the *Philebus*, we have two closely related questions about Plato's account. We have said that the bearers of value are activities that can figure as constituents of lives; but that they have this value both in virtue of what they internally are *qua* activity, and also in virtue of the nature of their objects. Plato does not clearly tell us how these two sets of criteria are to be related: whether, that is, we could have a 'pure' activity directed at 'mixed' or 'impure' objects, a stable activity directed at unstable objects, and, if we could, what we ought to say about the value of such activities. This problem is, in fact, one which enters into the interpretation of the stability-of-activity criterion itself. And this brings us to our second question, which concerns the correct understanding of that criterion. For stability, it seems, can be understood in two rather different ways.[35] On the first account, an activity is unstable if it necessarily involves an internal sequence of changes. Because of its internal structure, it cannot continue in the same way indefinitely. On the second account, an activity is unstable if it relies for its occurrence on contingent circumstances in the world that might fail to be realized. These two interpretations give different accounts of the instability of appetitive activity. For example, on the first, eating is unstable because its internal structure prevents its indefinite continuation; on the second, it is unstable because it depends upon the presence of food, which might fail to be available. If these two accounts are understood as different accounts of what stability and instability *are*, they will also be extensionally non-equivalent: for on the first account, smelling a rose will be stable in spite of the transience of roses, whereas on the second it will not. On the second, the activity will not count as stable unless its objects are permanent or highly stable.

Plato is clearly interested in both of these causes of instability. (We shall see in Chapter 6 how he explores them for the particular case of sexual desire.) Although his position is difficult to determine with precision, I believe that he would regard these as two complementary and compatible accounts of the *causes* of instability, rather than as two rival and incompatible accounts of what instability *is*. (This interpretation may be supported by *Phd.* 79D5–6, where the activity is unstable 'inasmuch as' or 'because' it deals with unstable objects.) Eating and sexual activity are unstable for two reasons: because of their internal structure and because of the nature of their objects. Smelling a rose is stable internally, but its objects can give rise to instability. In fact, however, it is not so badly off in this respect, given that roses are usually readily replaceable and interchangeable. The stability of an activity is thus causally dependent, to some degree, on either the permanence or the ready replaceability of its objects. An activity which has neither source of instability will be better off than one which has the right internal structure but the wrong objects. But this conclusion does not make Plato's defense of philosophy thoroughly dependent on his particular account of the objects of intellect. We can see how the belief that there is a stable truth there to be known in nature, apart from the changing circumstances of human life, would lend force to a Platonic account of activity-value. We can see, too, how a belief in eternal, non-context-dependent paradigmatic objects would tend to support his belief that contemplative activity is maximally stable, unvarying, and context-independent. In fact, the marks that separate true from apparent value bear a striking and non-coincidental resemblance to the marks that separate forms, as objects of knowledge, from other less adequate objects; the *Phaedo* exploits this connection.[36] But stability, purity, and truth may be achieved without separated forms. Even an Aristotelian biologist will be able to insist that what he studies are the stable kinds that replicate themselves in the same way in nature. And the *Symposium* will show us that any scientist or mathematician whatever, with or without eternal objects, is bound to be better off than the lover of unique human individuals.

The *Philebus* supports and expands this account of value, giving further evidence for our reading of Plato's undertaking. Most of this dialogue is explicitly concerned with the critical assessment of prospective constituents of lives and with the construction of a best life out of the acceptable components. In certain ways the account differs from the ethical theory of the middle dialogues; but many important points remain constant. It is quickly agreed that the standard appetitive pursuits – eating, drinking, getting warm, and 'others countless in number' – are mere 'replenishment' activities, chosen only in order to relieve an antecedent lack (32A–B, 46C–D, cf. 54Eff.). They are revealingly compared, all of them, to itching and scratching (46A, D) and held to be impure because inextricably mixed up with pain. Later they are included in the best life only insofar as they are absolutely necessary conditions of the intrinsically valuable pursuits (62E; this means that the 'violent pleasures' are omitted altogether – cf. 63D–E). A great part of the dialogue is then spent in the examination of some troublesome cases on which the *Republic* had spent little time: the pleasures associated with the emotions and the pleasures of anticipation. Socrates attempts to assimilate even these apparently 'pure' psychological pleasures to the replenishments by arguing that all are, in some way, relative to a contingent deficiency, whose removal would remove all reason for choosing them: they are all really pleasures 'mixed with distress' (50D). If you have not been harmed, you have no reason for the 'pleasures' associated with anger and revenge; if you have no lack, you have no reason for the 'pleasures' of love. If you have no false beliefs about the future, you have no reason for the associated false pleasures of anticipation. (And, falsity aside, we could by this argument rule out all the pleasures of hope: for where there is no deficiency in either power or knowledge, there is no room, conceptually, for hope.[37])

Finally, Socrates presents us with his characterization of the 'true' or 'pure' pleasures, arguing that they differ from all that have been rejected. First he describes certain pure aesthetic enjoyings – the contemplation of beautiful shapes and tones apart from all interest in their representational or mimetic content. This contemplation, not attended by antecedent distress, may justly be said to be valuable or good 'in virtue of itself' (*kath' hauto*) and not merely 'relatively to something' (*pros ti*). Smells are included too, 'insofar as they do not have distress as a necessary part of them' (51E).

Turning now to the pleasure of intellectual activity, Socrates insists that both learning and understanding have intrinsic value. He advances reasons for the judgment that are reminiscent of the *Republic*'s account of the marks of value. (1) They are *pure*: preceded by no felt lack, accompanied by a felt pleasure (51B). In no way are they necessarily mixed up with pain, for even the loss of knowledge brings no distress to the agent (52A–B). They are therefore compared to samples of the purest, most unmixed white color. (2) They have *order* and *harmony* (*emmetria*), whereas the intensely pleasant activities directed at replenishment exhibit disorder and disharmony (*ametria*) (52C). This criterion captures at least part of what the *Republic* meant by stability, viz., the absence of internal ebb and flow; at 59C stability is explicitly listed, along with purity (unmixedness) and truth, as a mark of value, and is said to be causally bound up with the stability of an activity's objects. (3) They stand much better than the bodily pleasures with regard to *truth* (52D). Although intellectual activities can be, and later are, further subdivided and ranked according to degrees of precision (*akribeia*), truth, and stability, all of them clearly possess these marks of value to a high degree, and none of the pleasures connected with the body exhibits them at all.

It is important to notice that the *Philebus*, like the *Republic*, speaks of good and

bad, high and low standpoints of value-judgment. The achievement of the dialogue is to convince the young interlocutor that he must reject a fashionable tendency to point to the natural behavior of untutored animals as a criterion of what is worthwhile in a life. He should put his trust in the 'witnessing' of intellect rather than that of our common animality. Socrates says to an acquiescent Protarchus, at the dialogue's end, that bodily pleasure would not be given first place,

> Not even if all the cows and horses and all the beasts in the world spoke for it by their pursuit of pleasure. Although most people, trusting in them as prophets trust their birds, judge that [these] pleasures are the most powerful factors in making a good life for us, and they think that the sexual behavior of beasts is a more authoritative witness than the passion for arguments which have continually prophesied under the inspiration of the philosophic muse. (67B)[39]

II

By this time, we can see Plato's theory of value in its general outlines; we see how it supports the life of the philosopher as against a life devoted primarily to need-relative pursuits. There are certain marks of value which philosophical activity possesses to a particularly high degree and which appetitive activities do not possess at all. Plato has argued that activities possessing these characteristics are the ones that would be selected by a rational being who judges from the appropriate rational standpoint. (He does not tell us whether the marks are jointly necessary conditions of intrinsic value, or individually sufficient; but I think his rankings of lives lend support to the former interpretation.) All this appears to be enough to undermine the 'democratic' conception of enjoying, according to which all enjoyings have an equal claim to inclusion as intrinsic values in the best life (561B).

But little has been said so far about how the valuable activities are related to those which are said to lack intrinsic value. We know that a philosopher must eat and drink enough to live. But we do not yet know whether he or she w' eat and drink *only* enough to live, or whether a moderate, even a high, deg of sensual indulgence will be required instrumentally to foster his philosop' growth. We certainly have no reason yet to think that his life will be partic ascetic.

Both the *Republic* and, to an even more marked degree, the *Phaedo* do, l espouse asceticism for the philosopher. The *Phaedo*, attacking the pleasures' of the body (60B, 64D), tells us that the good person will r activities with active disdain, 'except insofar as he is absolutely comp them' (64E, cf. 54A, 67A, 83B). He not only does not 'honor' them 'dishonors' them (64D–E). He 'stands aside from the body insofar Four reasons for this denial of the body emerge in what follow of the body take up time. The less time we spend on them, th to be spent in intrinsically valuable pursuits (66C–D). Second'

impair not only the quantity, but also the quality of intellectual endeavor. They render it less continuous, less powerful, less regularly able to attain to truth:

[The soul] reasons best, presumably, whenever none of these things bothers it, neither hearing nor sight nor pain, nor any pleasure either, but whenever it comes to be alone by itself as far as possible, disregarding the body, and whenever, having the least possible communion and contact with it, it strives for that which is the case. (65C, cf. 66A, B, D, and *Rep.* 517E, where bodily pleasures and pains disturb the 'better part' and prevent it from attaining truth in dreams)

A further reason to dishonor and disregard the bodily feelings is found in the consideration that they are not accurate or clear, even as indices of real physical need. If we listen to our body every time it registers a lack, we will be deluded into eating and drinking far more than we strictly need for continued life and intellection (65B, D, E; 66D, 67A).[40] The sexual appetite is felt as a very powerful drive; indeed it is clear that Plato views it as the most powerful among the appetites. (The *Republic* speaks of it as their 'chief officer' and as a 'tyrant' in the soul of the person who attends to it − 572E, 573D, E, 574C, 575A.) And yet it is plain that the *Phaedo*'s true philosopher can completely dissociate himself from it with no danger. Finally − what Socrates calls the 'greatest and most extreme of all evils' (83C) − the appetites, whenever we attend to them at all, provide us with a constant very strong incentive to make false judgments about value and worth. They 'bewitch' the soul (81B) into thinking bodily activities more important than contemplation. In this way appetite forces the soul to view everything, as it were, through the walls of a prison which appetite itself has made (82E); the result is that the captive will 'himself be an enthusiastic collaborator in his imprisonment' (82E−83A).

Plato has now defended a way of life that is not only philosophical, but also ascetic.[41] The theory of value gave us a preference for a life with a high philosophy content. Now reflection about the appetitive pursuits and their relationship to reasoning leads us to the conclusion that the philosopher ought to dissociate herself from the body and its needs as far as is compatible with continuing life, setting herself 'at odds with it at every point' (67E), 'practicing for death' (i.e. the separation of the soul from the body), admitting even as instrumentally valuable only those pursuits that satisfy what *Republic* VIII and the *Philebus* refer to as 'necessary' desires. Here, finally, we have reached the position of the end of *Republic* IX, where Socrates expresses his disdain for appetitive activity, declaring that each of us should view ourselves as identical with the intellectual soul alone. In the *Phaedo* we see, similarly, that Socrates is confident that everything that is *him* will survive, unscathed, the death of the body (115C−E) and its desires.

III

We now need to look more carefully at the way in which Plato arrives at his list of the marks of value. Any theory of value that has as its consequences a plan

of life that is so remote from what a normal human being normally pursues and values had better be closely scrutinized. How is so much ordinary value thrown away? From what perspective or standpoint is it that all our eating and drinking look as valueless as scratching an itch?

One thing is very clear: that this standpoint is nothing like that of the ordinary human being. For from the internal viewpoint of the ordinary human being the central appetitive pursuits are in important ways *not* like itching and scratching. If an activity possessed no intrinsic value for us, it would be rational for us to accept any substitute that would procure the same desirable results. We do use lawn-mowers, washing-machines, typewriters, thereby giving evidence that we believe the activities of mowing, washing, and handwriting to have merely instrumental value. But this is not the case with eating. We would choose, most of us, to continue to eat food rather than to take a hunger-capsule, presumably because we find eating to be, to some degree at any rate, valuable in itself, perhaps for the pleasure of taste, smell, texture, and sociability involved. Most of us, again, do not pursue sexual activity merely as a source of release from a painful tension; it is connected with other complex ends such as friendship, self-expression, and communication; there are reasons why most of us do not take the option of becoming eunuchs. The *Republic* seriously underestimates the complexity of our appetitive nature when it ignores the aesthetic side of appetitive activity and the complex connections between such activity and other valuable ends. What we find ridiculous about scratching as an activity is not simply its need-relativity. The source of our condemnation lies elsewhere. It is an indication of bodily disease or poor hygiene; it is futile, because it never completely relieves the annoying pain, but usually makes it worse; and it provides a constant very strong distraction, devoid of all positive pleasure, from other important life-activities like work and sleep. What is more, the activity lacks any positive aesthetic side; we cannot imagine an art of it, or connoisseurs of it. It is, finally, socially unacceptable and embarrassing. Eating isn't like that; sex isn't like that. We do wish to be free of itches all our life long; but how many, even abstracting from considerations of health, really wish to be free of the need to eat? In fact, we tend to be critical of persons who do view appetitive pursuits merely instrumentally, eating merely in order to still a hunger, and to praise those who are capable of entering into such activities in a way that endows them with intrinsic value: the gourmet, the connoisseur of wines, the person who can treat a sexual partner as an end in him or herself, rather than as a mere means to a state of null tension.

Again, the example that so impresses Callicles, the example of the passive homosexual, looks equally unfair. The reason this person's sexual activity is seen by the interlocutors as unfortunate is, even within their point of view, in large part a social and cultural reason. The internal point of view of a Greek gentleman distinguishes sharply between his own manly sexual pleasures (both heterosexual and homosexual) and those of this passive person. The latter is assumed to be acting under some sort of brute compulsion, in large part because the social and political associations of such activity are so strongly negative. We assume that most people wish to avoid ridicule and criticism; we pity them if they have irresistible sexual needs that put them continually at odds with their fellow human beings. For such reasons an Athenian pities the catamite. But this says nothing about sexual activity in general. From the ordinary internal viewpoint of a Callicles, in fact – as Plato was well aware – the ascetic philosopher will seem just as weird and as laughable as the passive homosexual. (In the comedies of Aristophanes, jokes at the expense of the two types are more or less equally distributed.) Furthermore, we ourselves may, as I do, find Callicles' intuitions about the example objectionable and irrational; if we do, then we will not be disposed to grant Plato his point even about this one case.

So if we see Plato's theory of value as an attempt to articulate something like an ordinary human viewpoint concerning the appetites, we must conclude that he has badly failed. He has blurred distinctions that we consider very important, denied intrinsic value where we agree in finding it.

But it is also evident that this is not, in fact, what Plato is trying to do. He readily grants that most people *do* ascribe intrinsic value to the bodily pleasures and to the states that are their objects. The opening of the *Republic* accurately records this fact. What he says is that this is a delusion, resulting from the deficiency of the perspective from which they make their judgments. It is only from the point of view of the 'real above' in nature, i.e. from the viewpoint of the philosopher, who can stand apart from human needs and limitations, that a really appropriate judgment about the value of activities will be made. It is this point of view that he attempts to elucidate.

We know, however, from the *Phaedo* and from the *Republic*'s earlier books that the philosopher, to be that, must first be an ascetic, dissociating him or herself from the body's needs. It is, then, from the viewpoint of one who no longer sees his characteristic human needs as genuine parts of himself that Plato rejects the associated activities as valueless, selecting others as intrinsically good. A striking example of this detached and extra-human viewpoint is found in Socrates' condemnation of the appetitive class at the end of Book IX, where he characterizes their activities using words used elsewhere in the Greek language only of the behavior of sub-human animals:

…Nor have they ever tasted stable and pure pleasure, but, like cattle, always looking downwards and bending over the earth and over their tables, they pasture, grazing and mounting, and, for the sake of getting more of these things they kick and butt one another with iron horns and weapons and kill one another through their insatiability. (586A–B)

This may seem grossly unfair. Surely, one might wish to argue, the pursuits of a species must be assessed from within the ways of life and the standing needs of that sort of creature. If you are such that the typical member of your species looks to you like a member of a species different from yours, then you are not the sort of ethical judge we want or need. Value simply *is* radically anthropocentric, and it should not count against a pursuit that the reasons for choosing it are not evident to a creature who is, or has become, different in nature from those for whom it is a good. The view begins to look dangerously circular: appetitive activity is rejected from a point of view that has already purified itself of appetite.

But Plato's examples have repeatedly shown us to what extent feeling and need can delude or distract the judgments of reason. The person with perverse sexual desires, for example (since most of us will agree that there are some such cases, if not the one that Plato selects) may think that he is engaging in fine or valuable activity; but from the perspective of the average human being these pursuits appear questionable. Appetite's capacity for distortion and self-justification cannot, Plato thinks, be overestimated. The *Phaedo* spoke of 'bewitchment' and of our willing collaboration in a captivity in which the prison walls are made by appetite; the *Republic* depicted appetite as a foul mud that obscures the soul's vision, so long as it has any contact with it at all (533C–D, cf. Ch. 7). Once we realize how severe an obstacle desire is to true judgment we are, as Plato sees it, led inexorably to the conclusion that really adequate judgments can be made only by getting free and clear of appetitive influence altogether. *Each* pleasure or pain to which we attend is like a rivet that binds the soul to a dangerous source of delusion and impurity (*Phd.* 83D). Plato assumes that no reflective person wishes to be the dupe and slave of his appetites. Even the ordinary character Cephalus, in *Republic* I, spoke with relief of his escape from the compulsions and the value-distortions caused by sexual desire. The dialogue's ominous political references remind us of other possibilities for the appetite-inspired distortion of central ethical values. The ordinary person believes that ethical judgment is obscured by the ordinary. The only solution, then, seems to be to get ourselves to a point at which we have no pressing human needs at all and can therefore survey all the alternative activities coolly, clearly, without pain or distraction, 'using pure reason itself by itself' (*Phd.* 66A) – so that eating and love-making *do* eventually look, to our soul's eye, like nothing more interesting than the grazing and copulating of cattle. This would be no solution, clearly, if appetite and emotion had any essential *positive* contribution to make to understanding or to the good life. Then – as the *Phaedrus* will acknowledge – we might have to engage ourselves with them in spite of their dangers. But Plato believes that he has already argued (in *Republic* IV) for an account of the appetites that rules this out: appetites are 'unqualified desires', brutish and unselective, totally unresponsive to judgments about the good; emotions, though somewhat more educable, tend towards dangerous violence without continual supervision.[42]

We find, then, that the interlocutors' sense, and ours, of the obstacles to true judgment has deep roots in human experience; this experience, which does not itself presuppose Plato's standpoint, supports its choice as the best standpoint. Plato does not expect to convince everyone; but he does expect that his arguments will appeal to reflective self-critical adults who are not themselves philosophers or mathematicians. It is, after all, his brother Glaucon, soldier and gentleman, who in *Republic* VII displays enormous zeal for mathematics as a form of training that will purify the soul of the confusing influence of the ordinary. In the passage that I have placed as the epigraph to this chapter, Socrates tells him not to worry if completely unreflective people think mathematics useless: more thoughtful and perceptive people (not just ascetics or experts, plainly) will recognize the merits of his proposal. If there is any sort of circularity here, then, it is a far richer and more interesting circle than the objector has allowed. Plato is not just preaching to the converted. And this sort of circle, in which ethical content, standpoint of judgment, and a sense of the obstacles to correct judgment are all held together, supporting and illuminating one another, is likely to be found in any complex ethical theory. (In Chapter 10 §v, we shall discuss the Aristotelian analogue.)

We can now return to the cryptic transitional moment in *Republic* vi that prepared the way for a move beyond a content-neutral picture of the good. Socrates said there (and the non-philosopher Glaucon agreed) that no imperfect being, *a fortiori* no merely human being, is ever 'good measure' of anything. Anthropocentric 'laziness' is no good basis for an ethical theory. Socrates had already, in the *Protagoras*, replaced 'The human being is the measure of all things' with the uncompromising 'Knowledge [or: science] is the measure of all things' (cf. Ch. 4, pp. 115, 120). Now we learn his considered view about what this requirement comes to: from now on, only the 'perfect' (complete, needless) will be 'good measure' of value for the ideal city: for only from the undistracted viewpoint of perfection can truth be seen. Having agreed as much, the interlocutors move away from their former content-neutral picture of the good life, which rested on a merely human consensus, and strive towards the pure viewpoint of needlessness. Book ix is the result.

This distinction between value relative to a limited being and real intrinsic value (here taken to coincide with that which a perfect, non-limited rational being would select) is, we might now say, the most general and most basic form of the contrast which we have been exploring. It is sufficient to explain the value-distinctions of our other passages, and it can also be invoked to explain judgments, like the *Philebus* judgments of aesthetic value, which could not be explained by appeal to instrumentality or *pain*-relativity alone. Let us digress for a minute to explore that passage.

The *Philebus*, as we saw, rejects all representational painting and sculpture, e.g. the forms of animals, and defends the beauty of the pure, simple shapes and colors. Plato's point here seems to be that insofar as it is the representational features of a painting or sculpture that engage our attention, we are responding from the point of view of anthropocentric interests and needs. Imagine a perfect, disembodied, needless god looking at a Praxiteles statue of an athlete. Its judgments of aesthetic value might turn out to coincide with ours; but we feel that this would be a mere coincidence, so different would be the contexts of the judgment in the two cases. We delight in the fine sensitive depiction of the strength and responsiveness of the human form, the way the sculptor has both captured our likeness and expressed what we find marvelous, strong, or admirable in ourselves. The perfect god would not see anything so wonderful about its being a particular *type* of body. It would be most likely to assess the sculpture as a pure form or shape, judging it successful insofar as it exhibited a composition that was, in the abstract, pleasing or delightful. It would look for the pure qualities of form, color, and arrangement, refusing to value, as such, any of the features of the object that link it with our practical interest in our species and our environment. Plato urges us to see, by assuming, insofar as we can, the standpoint of this god, that our human interest in the representational features of painting and sculpture leads to impure judgment, blinding us to the true or pure value that they offer. Similarly, in music, he urges us to purge ourselves of our interest in human meaning, speech, emotion, and to admire the 'smooth, clear sounds, the ones that produce a single pure tone' (52D). Contingent, species-relative value is not intrinsic value. As the same point is put by the formalist critic Hanslick, 'The beautiful is not contingent upon nor in need of any subject introduced from without, but...consists wholly of sounds artistically combined.'[43]

Plato's standpoint of perfection is not immediately available to any creature who wishes to assume it. It is a long and difficult matter to learn to detach ourselves from our human needs and interests, or to get to a point at which we can do so at will. Therefore, if Plato is really committed to a model of rational evaluation utilizing such a standpoint, we would expect him to provide us with a model of education to accompany it.

This expectation is confirmed. The *Phaedo* describes an entire life that is a 'practice' for the separation of the soul from the body. And the *Republic* is, for more than half its length, a book about education, i.e., about the strategies for 'turning the soul around' from its natural human way of seeing to the correct way. I shall not even attempt here to offer an account of all the stages in the soul's development as it describes them. But I want to point briefly to a feature of Plato's treatment of poetry in the account of early moral education that has, as far as I know, received very little attention, a feature whose importance we can now appreciate in the light of our interpretation.

It is well known that in his purge of poetry in Books II–III, Plato excludes the representation of several of the human emotions most frequently treated by poetic art: grief, passionate love, fear. It is less noticed that these emotions are ruled out by an argument that assumes the standpoint of perfection and asks, from this standpoint, about their value. For the true hero, Socrates argues, or for the god, it is not appropriate to grieve deeply for the death of a mere mortal: no really lofty being will seriously mind the loss of one small portion of the perceptible world. Therefore, since our literature should provide a moral ideal for weaker men, we must not include these and other ungodlike emotions in it (388B–E). In an earlier passage, a similar appeal to what befits the god is used to rule out literature that depicts its lofty or divine heroes as telling falsehoods. Socrates asks his interlocutors what *reasons* a perfect and needless being could have for telling falsehood; concluding that there are none, he concludes also that the figures who are to be models for us should not be depicted engaging in this activity: 'God is altogether simple and true in deed and word, and neither changes himself nor deceives others' (382E). In this appeal to what befits the god, Socrates both uses a standpoint of perfection to determine an aesthetic/moral value and constructs for the young citizens, in speech, a representation of that standpoint as a moral ideal. We should imitate beings who are completely without merely human needs and interests, in order to cultivate our own potential for objective rationality. Therefore our literature should depict those beings and their deliberations.[44]

IV

I have argued that Plato moves beyond Book iv's formal agreement about the shape of rational life plans to provide an independent theory of value that specifies the best content for a rational life. The theory consists, first, of an account of the marks of intrinsic value and of the difference between intrinsic value and merely species-relative value; second, of an epistemology of value, which describes to us the procedures by which genuinely objective judgments of value may be made. The best life will be a life maximally devoted to contemplative, scientific, and aesthetic pursuits, in which all other activities have a merely instrumental value at best.[45] It is important to stress at this point that the activities chosen by the philosopher are supposed to be valuable intrinsically, not just because the philosopher chooses them. His pursuits are good because his choice responds to real value, not just because he judges from the appropriate standpoint. If his choices were constitutive of value in and of themselves, then he and his choices would begin to look arbitrary.[46] But Plato believes that this ideal of the conditions of evaluation offers the best route by which mortal beings can get access to the real value that would be there, and be value, whether they existed or not.

According to this view, the political life of the philosopher can count as intrinsically valuable on the grounds that it realizes and contemplates stability and harmony in the city; also on the grounds that it is occupied with making precise and true judgments concerning the elusive realities of the empirical world. But it is nonetheless no surprise that the philosophers need to be compelled to take it up, since it possesses the marks of intrinsic value to a lesser degree than does their contemplative life. Plato's account of true value does, then, permit one sort of serious contingent value conflict to arise, as the demands of philosophical contemplation pull against the claims of rulership. To this extent its commitments to singleness and unity appear less whole-hearted than those of the *Protagoras*. But we should not conclude that Plato's intense focus on the stability of individual values has led him to ignore problems arising from their interrelationship. We have already spoken of the way in which Book iv constructed an internally harmonious life ruled by reason. Throughout the *Republic*, and especially in Book v, there is enormous emphasis on the internal unity and conflict-free harmony that will be effected for each individual by the city's education. And we can see why this should be so, if we consider once again the relationship between these two problems. A human being who is weaned from all attachment to internally unstable pursuits such as love, sexual activity, power-seeking, and money-making is automatically at the same time rid of many of the most common grounds of value conflict. In part, the superior harmony of the philosopher's life results directly from this reduction in the number of his or her commitments. The pursuit of mathematics and the pursuit of love will not come into conflict for a mathematician who does not care about love or a lover who does not care about mathematics. But the philosopher or mathematician's particular choice of content contributes powerfully, too, to his harmonious condition. He chose these pursuits precisely because they were always available and did not require any special conditions for their exercise. He can think about theorems in all kinds of circumstances; they are always available for his activity, regardless of his political circumstances, regardless of the activities and attachments of other human beings. So how often will he be forced to make a painful choice? The self-sufficiency of individual pursuits leads, then, to a reduction in conflict.

The few potential conflicts remaining in this life are solved by an ingenious combination of moral education and political engineering. In Book V, Socrates turns his attention to the family and to private property, two of the most common grounds of serious value conflict. And he announces his radical and notorious solution. The city will not exactly eliminate either ownership or the family: but it will spread these around in common among members of the city. There is no city–family conflict if, for every young citizen, the whole city simply *is* the family; if any other kind of family tie is unknown to it. Again, there is no conflict between what is 'my own' and what is the city's, if all property is held in common. Plato, unlike Creon, perceives that such radical stratagems cannot simply be imposed upon people who have been brought up another way; he knows that the existing city is not a unity, but a plurality. All of human experience must therefore be transformed, beginning with the baby's experience of the mother's breast. Farmed out to interchangeable wet nurses, prevented from forming special or intimate bonds with particular parental figures, and later with particular sex partners, these citizens will learn in every part of their experience to treat all citizens as 'alike and beloved friends', interchangeable exemplars of the same values.[47] The *Symposium* appears to carry this one step further, showing us how the good person learns to regard the value of persons as itself fully interchangeable with the value of institutions and sciences. And this further move offers not exactly a solution to the philosopher-ruler's dilemma, but at least a marked mitigation: for if his choice between contemplation and rule is just the choice between loving and contemplating two different sources of the same value, then the choice looks far less acutely painful.

These strategies chosen to minimize conflict enhance, at the same time, the stability of single pursuits. For no other type of family attachment, for example, would be as stable, as easily acted on in all kinds of circumstances, as this widespread devotion to an enormous reservoir of citizens, loved for their civic virtue rather than for their personal selves. In this way, Plato, once again solves our two problems together, with a single solution.

There remains one sphere of ineliminable non-interchangeability. The connection that each being has with the feelings of his or her own body cannot be generalized or spread around as can other things formerly 'one's own'. No matter what the legislator does, the sensations of this piece of flesh have a connection with me that is altogether different from the connection I have with that other piece of flesh over there. Plato recognizes this as a deep problem. In the related passage in the *Laws* he tells us that teachers of the young will do whatever lies in their power to undermine this special love of something irreducibly one's own:

> The notion of the private (*idion*) will have been, by every possible stratagem, completely uprooted from every sphere of life. Everything possible will have been devised to make even what is by nature private, such as eyes and hands, common in some way, in the sense that they will seem to see and hear and act in common. (739C–D)

Nature blocks the legislator's full success. The best he can do is to teach us again and again to disregard these special feelings, to remind ourselves that this feeling thing is not really us, this nature not our real nature. That we are single-natured rational souls, only contingently located in that thing. And now we see a further motive for his so teaching. For the body is not only the biggest obstacle to stable life and to true evaluation; it is also the most dangerous source of conflict, and therefore the biggest obstacle to impartial and harmonious civic justice. (Cf. Ch. 6, pp. 181, 196–7; Ch. 7, p. 221; Ch. 12, p. 353).

V

I have said that it is not a strong objection to this value-theory that it does not faithfully reflect the ordinary human's intuitive view of her practices and pursuits, since, according to Plato, no ordinary person, especially in a liberal democracy, has had the education that would sufficiently cultivate his or her potential for objective rationality. But it is, of course, still incumbent on Plato to show us, ordinary as we are, that this ideal of rational valuing and this standpoint of perfection are worthwhile goals for a human being to pursue. He must give us some reason to want to attain his ideal, or to think that it is one to whose pursuit we are already in some way committed. We might object, in particular, that the external god's-eye perspective is neither attractive, in that it requires the denigration of so much that we value, nor important, in that it is not relevant to the living of our *human* lives. Perhaps it is not even available: the world and its value cannot be found and known in isolation from our human interpretations and ways of seeing, shaped as they are by our interests, concerns, and ways of life. Any objectivity about value that is worth talking about, perhaps any about which it is even possible to talk, must be found *within* the human point of view and not by attempting, vainly, to depart from it.

I shall not develop these objections further at this point. They are complex, and a full understanding of them would require, among other things, a detailed examination of Aristotle's ethical views – to which we shall turn in Chapter 8. I shall simply say here that Plato has not in fact ignored this sort of objection; and the question of motivation is one to which he has devoted a great deal of consideration. His answer has what we might call a negative and a positive strand, the two being intimately connected. On the negative side, Plato believes that he can show us that much that is valued in the internal human viewpoint on the world is, if we reflect seriously, a source of intolerable pain for a rational being. Sufficient motivation for the ascent to the philosopher's perspective is already present to us, in the tumult and disorder of our empirical lives. One central task of the philosopher will be to display the intolerable aspects of our lives to us in an unavoidably clear way, at the same time displaying the philosopher's ascent as a remedy for that torment. I believe (and will argue in Chapter 6) that this is the task undertaken in Plato's *Symposium*; and we can see similar considerations at work in *Republic* I, with its ominous foreshadowing of appetitive violence, and VIII, with its devastating portrayal of the unstable lives of those who would have constituted the bulk of Plato's audience.

The positive strand or aspect of Plato's answer to the motivational question is suggested in *Republic* VI. Speaking of the grasp of the truth about the good, a non-perspectival truth that is what it is independent of all human interests, Socrates says, 'This, indeed, is what every soul pursues, and for the sake of this it does everything that it does, divining obscurely what it is' (505E).[48] Again, in the *Philebus*, Socrates urges us to consider 'whether there is in our souls some natural power of loving the truth and doing everything for the sake of that' (58D5–6, cf. 'the passion for arguments', 67B). Mathematical and philosophical reasoning are forms of value to which we, alone among mortal beings, are deeply drawn, by some kind of fortunate innate endowment (cf. *Epinomis* 978B, *Phaedrus* 250A): our psychology has a natural affinity with the truly good. We find mathematics beautiful and exciting because, by good luck, we fit with real beauty.

We might try to see this positive answer as just another way of putting the negative point: we are motivated to seek true, stable value because we cannot live with the pain and instability of our empirical lives. This was Nietzsche's diagnosis of Platonic value-theory. In a fragment entitled 'Psychology of metaphysics', he writes of the motivations underlying the Platonic defense of true value:

It is suffering that inspires these conclusions: fundamentally they are desires that such a world should exist... To imagine another, more valuable world is an expression of hatred for a world that makes one suffer: the *ressentiment* of metaphysicians is here creative.[49]

But this deep and no doubt correct insight into a part of the appeal of Plato's arguments does not do justice to their complexity. Even for Nietzsche this would not have sufficed as an account of Plato's own self-understanding. Plato has argued that the difference between true value and everything else is precisely that it is not simply need-relative, that it is something that a being who had never experienced suffering or lack would still have reason to choose. We are fortunate enough to share with such beings this pure positive motivation, which is, to some extent, independent of our negative motivation. From within our human lives, even disregarding, for the moment, their pain, we have a deep and positive natural desire to get at something more perfect than the merely human. (It is fortunate indeed that we do have this desire; for if we did not we would not have some different good, we would just be cut off from the only good there is.[50]) All of this, Plato would say, is actually a part of the human point of view, since the human being is by nature a being that seeks to transcend, through reason, its merely human limits. What Nietzsche leaves out is that mathematical, scientific, and philosophical reasoning are enormously beautiful and compelling to human souls: and not only to the soul of a mathematical genius like the young Theaetetus, but to the gentleman Glaucon; to Socrates; to every pupil who entered the Academy, over whose door stood (the story goes) the inscription 'Let no one enter here who does not pursue geometry'; to many of us, Plato believes, *if* we will think hard enough about what we really love. To Epicureans who viewed science and philosophy only as means of assuaging human pain, the Platonist Plutarch replied appropriately that they omit what Plato saw, the *joy* and *pleasure* of pure reasoning:

They push the pleasures of mathematics out the door. And yet...the pleasures of geometry and astronomy and harmonics have an intense and manifold lure, in no way less powerful than a love charm; they draw us to them using theorems as their magic spells...No man yet, on having intercourse with the woman he loves, has been so happy that he went out and sacrificed an ox; nor has anyone ever prayed to die on the spot if he could only have his fill of royal meat or cakes. But Eudoxus prayed to be consumed in flames like Phaethon if he could only stand next to the sun and ascertain the shape, size, and composition of the planets; and when Pythagoras discovered his theorem he sacrificed an ox, as Apollodorus records.

(*That Epicurus Makes a Pleasant Life Impossible*, 1093D–1094B, trans. Einarson)[51]

The blessed life, Plato insists, is also blessedly happy. It is not best *because* it is happy; it would be best quite apart from its happiness. But how wonderful it is that we pursue the best with such joy.

If all this is true of us, Plato could now argue, then it may be not he himself, but these criticisms of his work that misrepresent the internal human viewpoint. What the imaginary objector does, Plato would say, is to simplify and flatten human moral psychology by omitting a longing that is in tension with many of the other things that we are and do. What some of Plato's contemporary interpreters do, as they reconstruct Plato's theory, is to ask, in a similar way, whether something acceptable to contemporary democratic humanism might be salvaged if we reject the unfashionable value-talk of the later books. But in doing this, though they may indeed render Plato's thought more palatable to the people who are, and were, Plato's audience, they conceal Plato's powerful defense of a more unsettling view which, as he is prepared to argue, is both more correct and answers more adequately to our deepest desires, the desires which fortunately link us to the true good. If he is right about the complexity of our nature – and I think he has at least a serious chance of being right – when we simplify and flatten Plato's arguments we are at the same time avoiding part of our own psychological complexity. There are a number of dangers in such a procedure. Some of these are historical: we lose sight of some of Plato's views; we cease to understand the force of Aristotle's criticisms of Plato, since Plato will now look very much like Aristotle;[52] we cease, too, to see why and how the *Phaedo* so deeply moved and influenced Kant. Equally deep are the philosophical dangers: by reducing Plato's position to a more familiar one, we lose the chance to work through and seriously examine a distinctive moral position that powerfully questions our own. But perhaps the deepest danger in a criticism that seeks to soften and humanize Plato is that we may, with its help, be encouraged to cease to see and feel what he saw and powerfully recorded, the humanness of denial and dissatisfaction, the depth of our human longing for something better than what we are. Plato would say that to cease to see and feel these things would be to cease, in some way, to be human. And it is striking that Nietzsche, anti-Platonist though he was, supports Plato's intuitions here. His description of the so-called 'last man' in *Zarathustra* predicts for the future of human morality in European bourgeois democracy the extinction of recognizable humanity, precisely through the extinction of the Platonic longing for self-transcendence. 'The time of the most despicable man is coming,' says Zarathustra, 'he that is no longer able to despise himself.' As one might expect, Zarathustra's audience, much like some of Plato's contemporary critics, ignored the fact that his speech was a praise of the 'great longing' and called out, 'Give us this last man'.[53]

*   *   *

In the *Republic*, Plato answered questions about education and motivation by describing an ideal city in which the best possible education for objective rationality could be realized. It was crucial in this city that the 'turning round' of the soul begin 'straight from childhood' (519A), in order that the soul of the young citizen should be freed from the 'leaden weights' of the bodily pleasures that force its vision downward (519B). Plato also concludes, however, that this is a city that will never come into being; and he urges private individuals to aim at the life of the city without its supportive context (591E–592B). In less ideal circumstances, where we begin with adults who already have powerfully fettered souls, the educational and motivational process must be negative as much as positive: it must strike off the lead weights as well as inspiring the soul to look aloft. To commend his account of true non-pain-relative value to democratic readers (ancient or modern), the philosopher, ironically, will need to appeal to their sense of pain and constraint, permitting them to use the pain of the lead weights as a reason for the choice to throw them off. This does not make philosophy itself pain-relative, little more than a convalescence: for it would still be valuable from anywhere in the universe, and to any rational soul at all, regardless of pain. But *we* must be made conscious of *our* pain before we can be brought to a point at which we are ready to pursue a way of life that involves giving up, or radically revising, much that we now value.

All of our appetites are lead weights. But we can have no doubt about which, for Plato, is the heaviest. Sexual desire, the 'chief officer' of the appetites and 'tyrant' of the soul, is singled out again and again. The job of freeing us from the burden of sexual longing and its associated loves of mutable individual persons will be a complicated and difficult one. The therapeutic philosopher will need here above all to work with negative as well as positive appeals, in order to counter the strength of our interest.[54]

6 The speech of Alcibiades: a reading of the *Symposium*

> He had a golden shield made for himself, which was emblazoned not with
> any ancestral device, but with the figure of Eros armed with a thunderbolt.
>
> (Plutarch, *Alcibiades*, 16)

'I'm going to tell the truth. Do you think you'll allow that?' (214E).

He was, to begin with, beautiful. He was endowed with a physical grace and
splendor that captivated the entire city. They did not decline as he grew, but
flourished at each stage with new authority and power. He was always highly
conscious of his body, vain about its influence. He would speak of his beauty as
his 'amazing good fortune', and his 'windfall from the gods' (217A). But this was
not the limit of his natural gifts. Energy and intellectual power had made him
one of the best commanders and strategists Athens had known, one of the most
skillful orators ever to enchant her people. In both careers his genius was his keen
eye for the situation – the way he could discern the salient features of the particular
case and boldly select appropriate action. About all these gifts he was equally vain
– yet also almost morbidly concerned with criticism and gossip. He loved to be
loved. He hated to be observed, skinned, discovered. His heart, generous and
volatile, was rapidly moved to both love and anger, at once changeable and
tenacious. He was, then, a man of great resources who made deep demands on
the world, both emotional and intellectual; and he did what resource and courage
could to guarantee success.

What else? He hated flute-playing, and the flute-playing satyr Marsyas...He
laughed, he staged jokes – at the expense of enemies, of lovers, at his own. He
once arranged for a suitor of his, a resident alien, to win the bid for the local tax
receipts, to the great discomfiture of local suitors and tax-farmers...When he
wanted to win something, he took no chances. He entered seven chariots at
Olympia and walked off with first, second, and fourth prizes. He once sliced off
the tail of his own dog, saying, 'I am quite content for the whole of Athens to
chatter about this. It will stop them from saying any worse about me.'...He
financed extravagant spectacles. The people never had enough of him; he was their
darling, their young 'lion'. Those who hated democratic disorder hated him as
its inspiration...Once he invited a philosopher to dinner and told him the truth
about a particular soul...He betrayed two cities. He said, 'Love of city is what
I do not feel when I am wronged. It is what I felt when I went about my political

business in safety.'... One night he went for a walk through the streets of Athens and defaced the statues of the gods, smashing genitals and faces... The philosopher he loved looked like a snub-nosed Silenus, as he lay on the bed beside him, aloof and self-contained – like one of those toy Sileni you open up to see the shining statues of the gods inside.[1] All these things.

His story is, in the end, a story of waste and loss, of the failure of practical reason to shape a life. Both the extraordinary man and the stages of his careening course were legendary at Athens; they cried out for interpretation, and for healing. The *Symposium* situates itself in the midst of this life and confronts the questions it raises for our thought above love and reason. Alcibiades is, of course, a major character in the dialogue; many details of his life are recounted explicitly in his speech. But there are also more subtle signals. A man who died shot by an arrow will speak of the words of love as arrows or bolts wounding the soul (219B). A man who influentially denounced the flute as an instrument unworthy of a free man's dignity will describe himself as a slave to the enchanting flute-playing of a certain satyr (215B–D, 213C, 219C). A man who will deface holy statues compares the soul of Socrates to a set of god-statues and speaks of the injustice of rubbing out, or defacing, Socratic virtues (213E, 215B, 216D, 217E, 222A). A man who will profane the mysteries puts on trial the initiate of the mystery-religion of *erōs*. These connections suggest that we need to read the work against the background of the already legendary stories of the life, trying to recover for ourselves the Athenian fascination with Alcibiades. Only in this way will we grasp the significance of many apparently casual remarks and, through these, of the whole.

It is commonly charged against Plato that, in the *Symposium*, he ignores the value of the love of one unique whole person for another such whole person. By treating the person as a seat of valuable properties and describing love as directed at those repeatable properties, rather than at the whole person, he misses something that is fundamental to our experience of love. Professor Gregory Vlastos, one of the most eloquent expositors of this view, writes:

We are to love the persons so far, and only insofar, as they are good and beautiful. Now since all too few human beings are masterworks of excellence, and not even the best of those we have the chance to love are wholly free of streaks of the ugly, the mean, the commonplace, the ridiculous, if our love for them is to be only for their virtue and beauty, the individual, in the uniqueness and integrity of his or her individuality, will never be the object of our love. This seems to me the cardinal flaw in Plato's theory. It does not provide for love of whole persons, but only for love of that abstract version of persons which consists of the complex of their best qualities. This is the reason why personal affection ranks so low in Plato's *scala amoris*... The high climactic moment of fulfillment – the peak achievement for which all lesser loves are to be 'used as steps' – is the one farthest removed from affection for concrete human beings.[2]

This is all a bit mysterious. We would like to ask just what this uniqueness and individuality come to. Are they merely a subjective impression we have because we have not yet grasped all the properties? Or is uniqueness perhaps the occurrence of certain properties, each itself repeatable, in a hitherto unexemplified combination? Or is it something more elusive and shadowy than this? And yet, despite our questions, we feel that Vlastos must somehow be right. He is certainly pointing to something that we say and feel about being in love, however unsure we are of what we mean in saying it.

But there is a problem in using this as a criticism of Plato's perceptions. This is that it requires us to treat as Plato's only the view expressed in the speech of Diotima as repeated by Socrates, and to charge him with being unaware of the rest of what he has written. For following that speech is another speech that claims to tell the truth — a speech that ends with these words:

One could find many other wonderful things about Socrates to praise. But these same virtues one might attribute to someone else as well. The really wonderful thing about him is that he is not similar to any human being, past or present... This man is so strange – he himself and his speeches too – that you could look and look and find nobody even near him. (221C–D)

But that is, more or less, what Vlastos was talking about. If a writer describes a certain theory of love and then follows that description with a counterexample to the theory, a story of passion for a unique individual as eloquent as any in literature – a story that says that the theory omits something, is blind to something – then we might want to hesitate before calling the *author* blind.[3] We might want to read the whole of what he has written, and find his meaning emerging from the arrangement of all its parts. I believe that a deep understanding of the *Symposium* will be one that regards it not as a work that ignores the pre-philosophical understanding of *erōs*, but as one that is all about that understanding, and also about why it must be purged and transcended, why Diotima has to come once again to save Athens from a plague. (Perhaps also why she can't save us – or, at any rate, can't save *us*.)

The *Symposium* is a work about passionate erotic love – a fact that would be hard to infer from some of the criticism written about it. Its only speech that claims to tell 'the truth' is a story of complex passion, both sexual and intellectual, for a particular individual. There is, indeed, at its heart a speech that challenges or denies these 'truths' in the name of true goodness. But we can hardly hope to understand the motivation for that challenge, or to assess its force, without first understanding Plato's depiction of our actual attachments and their problems. We have to be willing to explore with this work our own thoughts and feelings about erotic attachment and to ask whether, having done this, we are, like Socrates, ready to be 'persuaded' by the revisionary speech of Diotima. That is why we must turn our attention, as Plato's audience would have done, to the life and character of Alcibiades.

I

This dialogue consists of a series of elaborately nested reports. Like a Chinese box, it gives us a conversation of Apollodorus[4] with a friend, which reports a previous conversation of his own, in which he recalls a speech of Aristodemus, who reports (among others) a speech of Socrates, who reports a speech of Diotima, who reports the secrets of the mysteries. This distancing, continually present to us in the indirect-discourse constructions of the Greek, makes us always aware of the fragility of our knowledge of love, our need to grope for understanding of this central element of our lives through hearing and telling stories. It also reminds us of the fact that Socrates' pupils, inspired by personal love, tend not to follow his advice. Instead of ascending to an equal regard for all instances of value, they, like Alcibiades, remain lovers of the particulars of personal history. In these two ways, the dialogue as a whole is the speech of Alcibiades rather than of Socrates – reminding us that it is as unreformed people that we must learn and judge of the value of Socratic teaching.

The settings of the various conversations are chosen with precision to point us to the dialogue's central themes. Apollodorus, asked by an anonymous friend to repeat the story of the drinking party, replies that he has just had occasion to practice telling it. An acquaintance of his, Glaucon by name, stopped him two days ago in a state of great excitement. He had been looking for Apollodorus all over town in order to hear from him, from start to finish, the story of the party at Agathon's house where Socrates and Alcibiades were guests. Glaucon was extremely eager to hear what their speeches about love were like, but the friend who had informed him of the party, having heard the story at second hand, could not give him a clear account (172A–B). Apollodorus, surprised, had answered that it must have been an unclear account indeed – for this party, which Glaucon seems to think a recent event, took place years ago. Doesn't Glaucon know that Agathon has been out of town for 'a number of years' and that he, Apollodorus, has been a follower of Socrates for only three? The party took place, in fact, back 'when we were boys' (173A5), the day of Agathon's first victory at the tragic festival – for us, in the year 416 B.C.

Now this is, on the face of it, very strange – so strange that it looks as if Plato must be up to something. A busy, active man, apparently sane, goes running all over town to hear a story about a party where some speeches were made about love. And he does not even know that this party took place over ten years ago. (Agathon left Athens in 408 or 407.) He is clearly not an aficionado of either literature or philosophy, or else he would have been aware of the relevant facts about Agathon and Apollodorus. He is characterized as a busy man of action (173A).[5] Perhaps, then, we ought to look to politics for an explanation of his eagerness.

R. G. Bury and other commentators have explored the problem of dating the exchange more precisely.[6] It cannot, Bury persuasively argues, be after Socrates' death in 399, since Apollodorus speaks of his discipleship in the present tense (172E5). It must be 'a number of years' after Agathon's departure, but before his death (probably also 399), since he is described as still 'living out of town'. To make sense of the 'a number of years', Bury argues, we might as well date it as late as possible within this range, therefore in the year 400.

But this ignores politics, and Alcibiades. Alcibiades was murdered in 404. Recalled to Athens in 407 by the restored democracy, he then lost prestige because of the Athenian losses at Notium – for which, however, his subordinates, not he, deserved the blame. He retired to the Chersonese. In 405, his good advice concerning the battle of Aegospotami was disregarded by the commanders. Angry and embittered, he departed to Asia Minor, planning to give his services to the Persian king, Artaxerxes. In 404, while staying in a small village in Phrygia, he was assassinated by a Persian agent, probably as the result of a conspiracy between the Spartan commander Lysander and Plato's uncle Critias, the oligarch.

The date 400 thus becomes impossible as a date for Glaucon's misguided question. No man of affairs would long have remained unaware of the death of Alcibiades. Nor could a reader around 375[7] have believed this possible. (For we must be interested less in the actual facts than in the historical presuppositions and beliefs of Plato's audience.) It would be like supposing that an audience of our day could believe that a drama which mentioned John Kennedy as living could be set in 1968. Some events are indelibly marked on the consciousness of a people; Alcibiades' death is among these. In the last months of his life he was, wherever he traveled, the object of intense, almost obsessive attention.[8] Athens was on the verge of military capitulation to Sparta; internally she was torn by years of struggle between an oligarchic party, now sympathetic to Sparta, and the traditional democratic sentiments, still strong in the hearts of the impotent majority. A moderate oligarchical government led by Theramenes is on the verge of collapse; the extremists, the so-called 'Thirty Tyrants', led by Critias and other associates of Plato's family, promise to obliterate from the city all traces of democratic institutions. The hopes of the defenders of tradition, and freedom, are in disarray. Aristophanes' *Frogs*, produced in 405, testifies to the fear that not only political freedom, but poetic speech as well, are on the verge of extinction. The Chorus pleads for the chance to speak out on serious, as well as comic, matters, asking the god's protection for its truths (384–93).[9]

In the midst of Athenian anxiety and pessimism, there is one hope: that Alcibiades, consenting to return to the city that has mistreated him, may lead a restored democracy to victory and safety. As Plutarch tells us,

In despair they recalled their past mistakes and follies, and they considered that the greatest of all had been their second outburst against Alcibiades...And yet...a faint glimmer of hope remained, that the cause of Athens could never be utterly lost so long as Alcibiades was alive. In the past he had not been content to lead a peaceful or passive existence in exile and now, too,...they believed that he would not look on supinely at the triumph of the Spartans or the outrages of the Thirty Tyrants.[10]

In the *Frogs*, Alcibiades is a central character long before he is mentioned by name (1422). The pivotal test for the two dead poets in Hades, to determine whose moral advice will save the city in its time of trouble, is a test concerning his return. The city 'longs for him, it hates him, and it wants him back' (1425). What should it do? Euripides, using language linked with sophistic and Socratic philosophizing, gives an oligarch's answer: think of him as a self-centered and useless individual, and hate him. Aeschylus, in obscure and noble poetic language, urges the city to take him back.[11] This tough old democrat who fought at Marathon, not the refined comrade of allegedly anti-democratic intellectuals, proves in this way that he is the poet that the soul of Dionysus, god of tragic and comic poetry, desires (1468). He will be brought back from the dead, and, together, tragedy, comedy, and Alcibiades will save Athens from the death of her freedom; also, as they see it, from Socrates.[12]

Glaucon's eagerness now begins to make sense to us. Suppose it is 404, shortly before the assassination, at the height of this frenzy over Alcibiades. (This still satisfies Bury's demand that we remove the setting by several years from the time of Agathon's departure.) Now suppose that a rumor circulates, to the effect that there has been a party, attended by Socrates and Alcibiades, where speeches were made about love. A political man (ignorant of the cultural facts that date this story) would immediately wonder whether the spurned leader had finally agreed to return to Athens, drawn, perhaps, by his famous love for Socrates. He might well drop his ordinary business at such news, pregnant with possibilities for both political parties, and run all over town to pursue the story. If he were a democrat, he would be in a mood of swelling hope and barely suppressed joy. If he were an oligarch, he would be nervous and fearful, annoyed that all the attempts of his party to observe Alcibiades' every movement had miserably failed. Which is Glaucon? His brief questions give us no sign. Since Apollodorus, a disciple of the historical Socrates, is likely, with him, to be opposed to the extreme unconstitutional measures of the Thirty,[13] Glaucon's silence about his deeper concerns may suggest a link with the oligarchs. This Glaucon is not clearly identified; but the two known Platonic characters of this name are both close relatives of Plato and linked with the oligarchs.[14] It is not impossible that this is Plato's brother, the Glaucon of the *Republic*; at any rate, the name, at least, would suggest to a reader these anti-democratic associations.

We have, it appears, a conversation set very shortly before the murder of Alcibiades, between a neutral or sympathetic person and one who may be linked with his murderers. But this is not the conversation that the opening dialogue actually gives us. The dialogue itself takes place two days after the reported Glaucon conversation; and it takes place between Apollodorus and an anonymous 'friend'. We are not told why there should be this two-day gap, or why the conversation should now be repeated. But it leaves room for thought. These baroque complications of discourse are not in themselves pretty or amusing, even if we could believe that Plato invents such things only for amusement's sake. We want a fuller meaning. The 'friend', apparently, is not laboring under Glaucon's delusion that the rumored conversation was recent; and yet he wants to hear it anyway. One sufficient explanation for his greater clarity, which would account also for his desire to hear the story again, would be the death of Alcibiades in Phrygia. This remains conjectural; but in any case we are surely intended to tie the dialogue closely to the death, to think of Alcibiades as dead, or dying, even while 'he' speaks, and to see the oligarch's fear of a love that would reunite Alcibiades and Athens as one of the fears that led to the killing.[15]

But this leaves us with a further question: when, in terms of these events, was the reported banquet, at which speeches are made about love? Here, even more patently, Plato is precise: January of 416.[16] Agathon, the victor, was under thirty. Alcibiades was thirty-four. Socrates was fifty-three. A little over a year later, the Hermae were sacrilegiously mutilated – an incident that was to prove ruinous for Alcibiades' military and political career. Whether or not he was really guilty (in the end, even the official indictment charged him only with the profanation of the Eleusinian Mysteries, not with the desecration of the statues), it remained true that rumor and popular belief, and the general consensus of fourth-century writers, ascribed the incident to his leadership.[17] Not only would Plato himself, as an associate of the oligarchs, very probably have believed it, but so, also, would most of his fourth-century audience. This incident was taken to be the most egregious case of the recklessness and disorder that repeatedly undercut Alcibiades' genius. The dialogue will show us this recklessness as that of a certain sort of lover. The frequent references to statues are probably not accidental. The atmosphere of mock-threat and mock-violence surrounding Alcibiades' speech goes deeper than a game, since we know it to be the speech of a man who will soon commit real acts of violence. When Alcibiades expresses anger, pain, and frustration (e.g. 219C–E, 217E–218A); when Socrates speaks of his fear of Alcibiades' violent jealousy and even appeals for help, should Alcibiades attempt to 'force' him, inspired by 'madness and passion for love' (213D5–6); when Alcibiades says, 'There is no truce between me and you, but I'll get my revenge on you some other time' (213D7–8), we are surely meant to think of another time, and of an assault allegedly made against the stone genitals and the 'wonderful head' (cf. 213E2) of Hermes, god of luck.[18]

II

We can begin with the only one among the original symposiasts who does not praise the speech of Socrates (212C4–5). At the dialogue's end, Socrates attempts to persuade Agathon and Aristophanes that, contrary to popular superstition, one and the same person can be a poet in both the tragic and the comic genres. It is clear, besides, that the comic speech of Aristophanes and the tragic (or tragic-comic) speech of Alcibiades contain the most serious objections raised in the *Symposium* against Socrates' program for the ascent of love. These facts suggest that we should study the two speeches together, asking whether they reveal a shared account of the nature of *erōs* and its value, illuminating both one another and the Socratic alternative. Aristophanes never succeeds in telling us his objections to the ascent story, because Alcibiades' entrance disrupts the dialectic. But perhaps it is this entrance, and the ensuing scene, that make known to us the comic poet's most serious reservations.

The comic poet speaks later than originally scheduled. The orderly plan of the symposium is disrupted by a ridiculous bodily contingency: an attack of hiccups. It makes Aristophanes (and us) wonder at the way in which the good order of the body (*to kosmion tou sōmatos*, 189A3) gives way, as though a willing and desiring victim (*cf. epithumei*, 189A4), to the most absurd of sub-human noises (189A4–5).[19] Recovered, he offers a story about love that wonders, itself, at the power of the body's contingencies to disrupt and subdue the aspirations of practical reason.

We were once, he tells us, perfect and self-sufficient physical beings. We had the circular form, 'similar in every direction', imagined by early philosophy to be the shape of the god.[20] Now punished for our overweening attempt to make ourselves rulers of everything, we are creatures cut in half, severed from our other part and made, by a turning of our heads, to look always at the cut, jagged front side of ourselves that reminds us of our lack (190D–E). And, looking at the contingent loss that cuts us off from the wishes of our imagination, itself still apparently intact, we become preoccupied with the project of returning to the wholeness of our former natures. But to remedy one piece of luck another must happen: we must each find the unique other half from which we were severed. The one hope of 'healing' for our human nature (191D1) is to unite in love with this other oneself and, indeed, to become fused with that one, insofar as this is possible (192B–E). Eros is the name of this desire and pursuit of the whole (192E–193A).

The story is comic because, while it is about us and our deepest concerns, it at the same time distances itself from the inner delight and pain of those concerns, asking us to watch ourselves as we watch a species remote from us and our needs. We think, as humans, that the human shape is something beautiful; the story gets us to consider that, from the point of view of the whole or the god, the circular shape may be formally the most beautiful and adequate. A jagged form, equipped with these untidy folds of skin around the middle (191A), its head turned towards this imperfection and newly expressing, in its searching gazes (191A, 191D), its sense of incompleteness; its exposed and dangling genital members now no longer efficiently, externally, sowing seed into the earth (191B–C), but instead, placed on the side of the 'cutting', attendant upon desire for both reproduction and healing – this looks like the shape of something that is the object of a joke, or a punishment. From the point of view of desire, again, the penetration of a part of one's own body into some opening in the loved one's body is an event of excitement and beauty. From the outside it just looks peculiar, or even grotesque; it certainly seems to be without positive aesthetic value. It is not even functionally efficient as a means of reproduction. Sowing into the earth was both more controlled and more reliably fruitful.

As we hear Aristophanes' distant myth of this passionate groping and grasping, we are invited to think how odd, after all, it is that bodies should have these holes and projections in them, odd that the insertion of a projection into an opening should be thought, by ambitious and intelligent beings, a matter of the deepest concern. How odd that we should have taken as natural, and even fine, this extraordinary fact that our separate bodies actually fit into the insides of other bodies, that bodies are soft and open, not round and shiny-smooth, like stones. (Stone, said Callicles, was the best embodiment of one high ambition.) Finally, from the inside, the disharmony in the nature of these creatures, whose reason still aspires to completeness and control, but whose bodies are so painfully needy, so distracting – from the inside this would feel like torment. From the outside, we cannot help laughing. They want to be gods – and here they are, running around anxiously trying to thrust a piece of themselves inside a hole; or, perhaps more comical still, waiting in the hope that some hole of theirs will have something thrust into it.[21]

And, yet, we are aware that we are those creatures. If the story were told about some completely alien race, in whom we could not see ourselves and our desires, it would be a natural history. If it were told from the inside, it would, as we have said, be tragedy. The comedy comes in the sudden perception of ourselves from another vantage point, the sudden turning round of our heads and eyes to look at human genitals and faces, our unrounded, desiring, and vulnerable parts. It is like those moments in Aristophanes' actual plays, when we are shown some absurd or even base behavior and then, all at once, are made to see that it is our own.*

We seem to have in this story much of what Vlastos wanted from an account of love. The objects of these creatures' passions are whole people: not 'complexes of desirable qualities', but entire beings, thoroughly embodied, with all their idiosyncrasies, flaws, and even faults. What makes them fall in love is a sudden swelling-up of feelings of kinship and intimacy, the astonishment of finding in a supposed stranger a deep part of your own being. 'They are struck in extraordinary fashion by friendly feeling (*philia*) and intimacy (*oikeiotēs*) and passion (*erōs*), and are hardly willing to be apart from one another even a little time' (192B–C). It is a love that is said to be in and of the soul and body both, and of the soul's longings as expressed in the movements and gestures of the body (cf. 192E7–D1).

Nor are love objects interchangeable for these people, as seats of abstract goodness or beauty might be. The individual is loved not only as a whole, but also as a unique and irreplaceable whole. For each there is, apparently, exactly one 'other half' (192B6, 191A6). Although upon the death of the half each will begin a search for a replacement, there is no evidence that this search will bring success. There is nothing like a general description of a suitable or 'fitting' lover, satisfiable by a number of candidates, that could serve as a sufficient criterion of suitability. It is mysterious what does make another person the lost half of you, more

---

* One example will indicate the technique. In the *Clouds*, after some typical jokes at the expense of passive homosexuals, at which the audience has been laughing with superiority, the character mocked turns his mocker around towards the audience and asks him what sort of people, after all, are sitting out there. The answer is unequivocal: 'By the gods, the vast majority are wide-assholes.' 'Well, what do you say to that?' 'I admit defeat. O buggers, by god, take my cloak off, I'm deserting to your side.' And he exits, cloakless, presumably into the audience. Aristophanes, like Plato (cf. Chs. 5 and 7) uses this example to make complex points about passivity and receptivity, dependence on chance, hedonism, democracy.

mysterious still how you come to know that. But there they find it, both body and soul, not like anyone else in the world. (We can see how close we are to a view of *erōs* frequently expressed in tragedy, if we recall a moment in the *Antigone*. Creon argued for the replaceability of love partners with a crude agricultural metaphor: there are 'other furrows' for Haemon's 'plow'. The more conservative Ismene answers, 'Not another love such as the one that fitted him to her.'[22] With their shared emphasis on special *harmonia* (carpenter's 'fit' or musician's 'harmony'), tragedy and Aristophanes seem to capture the uniqueness, as well as the wholeness, that Vlastos found lacking in Plato's view of *erōs*.)

But the picture also shows us problems. First of all, Aristophanes' myth vividly dramatizes the sheer contingency of love, and our vulnerability to contingency through love. The very need that gives rise to erotic pursuit is an unnatural, contingent lack – at least it is seen as such from the point of view of the ambitions of human reason. Here are these ridiculous creatures cut in half, trying to do with these bodies what came easily for them when they had a different bodily nature. The body is a source of limitation and distress. They do not feel at one with it, and they wish they had one of a different sort; or, perhaps, none at all.

Then *erōs*, so necessary to continued life and to 'healing' from distress, comes to the cut-up creature by sheer chance, if at all. His or her other half is somewhere, but it is hard to see what reason and planning can do to make that half turn up. The creatures 'search' and 'come together', but it is plainly not in their power to ensure the happy reunion. It is difficult to accept that something as essential to our good as love is at the same time so much a matter of chance. The creatures would plainly like to believe, with an optimistic modern philosopher, that 'If a person is disappointed in love, it is possible to adopt a vigorous plan of action which carries a good chance of acquainting him with someone else he likes at least as well.'[23] The comic myth doubts it.

And it is not simply that a particular part of the creatures' good seems to resist control by practical reason. For this component, being absent or unhappily present, causes the creature to lose rational control over all the rest of its planning for a life. Before the invention of sexual intercourse, the two halves embraced unsatisfied, until both died of hunger and other needs (191A–B). The possibility of intercourse, a new 'stratagem' provided by the pitying god (191B), brought the procreation of children and a temporary respite from physical tension: 'Satiety might come to be from intercourse, and they might be assuaged and turn to their work and take thought for the rest of their lives' (191C). But this happy possibility indicates to us that the creature remains always in the grip of these recurring needs, which distract him (or her) from work and the rest of life, except where satiety provides a small interval of calm.

It emerges, moreover, that the satisfaction achieved in this way is, even as temporary, incomplete. The aim of desire is more intractable. What these lovers really want is not simply a momentary physical pleasure with its ensuing brief respite from bodily tension. Their erotic behavior expresses a deeper need, one that comes from the soul – a need 'that the soul cannot describe, but it divines, and obscurely hints at' (192D):

Suppose Hephaestus with his tools were to visit them as they lie together and stand over them and ask: 'What is it, mortals, that you hope to gain from one another?' Suppose, too, that when they could not answer he repeated his question in these terms: 'Is the object of your desire to be always together as much as possible, and never to be separated from one another day or night? If that is what you want, I am ready to melt and weld you together, so that, instead of two, you shall be one... Would such a fate as this content you, and satisfy your longings?' We know what their answer would be: no one would refuse the offer. (192D–E, trans. Hamilton)

It is a wish for the impossible. However ardently and however often these lovers may enter one another's bodies, they are always going to remain two. No amount of interpenetration will cause even the smallest particle of flesh to fuse with the other flesh. Their act leads inexorably back to separation and inactivity, never to any more lasting or more thoroughgoing union.

But this impossible story of welding is a far simpler miracle than the one that would have to take place if they were really to become one. For these creatures have souls; and their desire for unity is a desire of the soul, a desire of desires, projects, aspirations. (For the lovers' problem to arise they do not, and we do not, need to be dualists. Aristophanes' *psuchē* is probably not an incorporeal substance, but the 'inner' elements of a person – desires, beliefs, imaginings – however these are, ultimately, to be analyzed and understood. The operative contrast is the one between the 'internal' and the 'external'. The lovers' problem will arise for any people who doubt that the external movements, gestures, and speeches of their limbs, trunk, face, genitals, always fully and adequately express the person that they feel themselves to be.)[24] Hephaestus' tools could do nothing to satisfy their desire – unless their souls, in intercourse, had first become thoroughly fused with their own bodies. What would this mean? That each would have to regard his or her bodily movements as fully expressive of and in harmony with the needs and imaginings of the soul or the 'insides', so that intercourse was at the same time an interpenetration of imagination with imagination and spirit with spirit. Hephaestus can weld only what is engaged in the bodily act of lovemaking and identifies itself with it. If the mind stands to one side, if it asks, even momentarily, 'Is this me?' or 'Is everything that I am in this?' or, 'Does that person moving around inside my body really know anything about *me*?', then the welding will be at best a partial welding. There will be a little detached being left on the outside, who resists the craftsman and remains unengulfed, solitary, proud of its secrets. For these creatures, this is almost certain to be the case. Don't they resent the awkwardness of their bodies, those flawed, imperfect surfaces? Don't they pride themselves on the wholeness and beauty of their natures? Then how will they be willing to identify their proud souls with a cut and jagged face, a set of queerly shaped organs? One miracle presupposes a greater miracle: to get to be the whole, you first have to be willing to be the half.

Let us now suppose that, by a miracle, these two fusions have occurred. Each of the lovers makes himself one with his body, and Hephaestus then makes two soul-bodies into one. Wrapped in each other's arms, there they lie, for the rest of their lives and on into death, welded into one, immobile. (Let us also suppose that the gap between interpenetration and fusion has really been bridged: they can 'die in common' (192E)[25] not just in the sense of simultaneity of experience, but in the sense of unity of experience.) Here we meet, unexpectedly, a second comedy. For what they thought they most wanted out of their passionate movement turns out to be a wholeness that would put an end to all movement and all passion. A sphere would not have intercourse with anyone. It would not eat, or doubt, or drink. It would not, as Xenophanes shrewdly observed, even move this way or that, because it would have no reason; it would be complete (B25; cf. Ch. 5). *Erōs* is the desire to be a being without any contingent occurrent desires. It is a second-order desire that all desires should be cancelled. This need that makes us pathetically vulnerable to chance is a need whose ideal outcome is the existence of a metal statue, an artifact. It is not accidental that the myth speaks of welding, and uses the tools of the smith instead of the instruments of the doctor. Once we see the self-cancelling character of this *erōs*, we are not at all clear that our first, enthusiastic 'yes' to Hephaestus' proposal expressed our deepest wish. (When Hephaestus chained Ares in bed with Aphrodite, Ares was angry, and the gods all laughed at him; only Hermes was willing to risk immobility for love.[26]) But can our deepest wish be to live always in the grip of recurrent needs, and never to reach a stable satisfaction? As Socrates asks in the *Gorgias*, can we choose the life of leaky jars or torrent-birds? We would like to find a way to retain our identity as desiring and moving beings, and yet to make ourselves self-sufficient. It takes considerable ingenuity.

This is only a comedy, and only a myth, about distant beings. We are not sure that it is really our story – whether seen one by one, in detail, and from the inside, our loves really look like that. But we are left with questions.[27] We have a sense that there may be trouble around in the land of 'uniqueness and integrity', that personal affection may not be in control of its world. We turn now to the speech that attempts to restructure that world, making it safe for practical reason.

III

Socrates does not present the account of the ascent of desire in the first person, as a theory of his own developed through experience and reflection. He introduces it, instead, as an account of whose value he was *persuaded* by a woman, and of whose value he will try, in turn, to persuade others (212B). Indeed, when he first heard it, he was, he tells us, dubious about its truth (208B); she, answering 'like a perfect sophist', convinced him. Diotima's teaching depends in a fundamental way on Socrates' own beliefs and intuitions; like Socrates himself when he examines a pupil, she claims to be showing him what he himself really thinks (201E, 202C). But the fact remains that it took an external intervention to convince him that clinging to certain beliefs required abandoning others. Without this, he might have continued living with incompatibles, not seeing how they clash.

Socrates' teacher is a priestess named Diotima. Since she is a fiction, we are moved to ask about her name, and why Plato should have chosen it. The name means 'Zeus-honor'. Alcibiades had a famous mistress, a courtesan whose name history records as Timandra. This name means 'man-honor'. Here, then, Socrates too, takes a mistress: a priestess instead of a courtesan, a woman who prefers the intercourse of the pure mind to the pleasures of the body, who honors (or is honored by) the divine rather than the merely human.[28] Diotima's fictional fame and authority derive, Plato tells us, from her benefits to Athens at the time of the great plague, when she succeeded in postponing the catastrophe for ten years (201D). This invention is also significant. Here, says Plato, is a person who is capable of bringing great benefits to the city, even of averting a dangerous illness, if only we will be persuaded to depart, with her as our guide, from our human-centered, human-honoring ways. Plato's picture of the external guide indicates that our salvation may have to come to us from without – i.e. at the cost of abandoning some beliefs and relationships that we, as humans, now cherish. (The *Protagoras* gave us a vivid sense of our 'diseases'.) And yet the presentation of Socrates' learning as working through his own antecedent beliefs tells us that a need to be so saved is, even now, in us, ready to be awakened (as it was by the *Protagoras*) if we can only be brought to a clear view of our situation.

The crucial pieces of persuasion work their way unobtrusively into the teachings – both into Diotima's teaching of Socrates and into Socrates' teaching of us. We first discover that we believe (or partly believe) that we love individuals for their repeatable properties by following and being (almost) persuaded by an argument that employs this as a hidden premise. In this argument, whose logical form is unusually perspicuous – it is, for example, one of the easiest in all Plato to formalize, and every step is, usually explicitly, universally quantified – Socrates persuades Agathon that *erōs* is not beautiful (199Eff.). (This argument precedes the explicit introduction of Diotima, but it is clearly the fruit of her teaching, and its premises are further explored in her speech.) At the heart of the argument is a difficulty. We have the following steps:

1. For all y, if y loves, then there is an x such that y loves x. (Agreed, 199E6–7)
2. For all y and all x, if y loves x, y desires x. (Agreed, 200A2–4)
3. For all y and all x, if y desires x, then y lacks x. (Agreed, 200A5–7)[29]
4. For all y and all x, if y has x, then y does not desire x. (200E; from 3 by contraposition)[30]
5. For all y and all x, if y has x, y does not love x. (From 2, 4)
6. For all y and all x, if y loves x, x is beautiful. (Agreed, 201A)
7. For all y and all x, if y loves x, y lacks beauty. (201B)
8. For all y, if y lacks beauty, y is not beautiful. (201B6–7)
9. For all y, if y loves, y is not beautiful. (From 1, 7, 8)

The trouble comes, for us (though not for Agathon), at step 7. Even if we grant Socrates' controversial claims about the logic of wanting and possessing, even if we grant him, too, that all love objects must be *kalon* (a claim less implausible if we think of the broad range of the Greek word),* we do not understand how he has reached the conclusion that *y* lacks beauty. We thought that he was talking about people. We had a situation where some *y* – let us say Alcibiades – is in love with beautiful Agathon. He wants to possess this beautiful person, and yet he is aware that he does not possess him. If he is lucky enough to be enjoying at present the charms of Agathon, still he cannot count on fully and stably possessing them for the rest of his life. So there is a beautiful person whom he both loves and lacks. This does not, however, show that he himself lacks beauty, even given the earlier premises of the argument. He may be quite beautiful, for all we know. What he lacks is beautiful Agathon. Socrates' conclusion would follow only if we reinterpret step 6 – which, in the Greek text, was literally the claim '*erōs* is of the beautiful'. From our first interpretation, that the lover's love is for someone (something) that has the property of being beautiful, it follows only that the lover lacks that particular beautiful person (thing). But suppose we now reinterpret step 6 to read:

6'. For all *y* and all *x*: if *y* loves *x*, *x* is a beauty.

– i.e. an instance of beauty, the beauty *of* some person or thing. From this there follows, at least, the conclusion that there is *an* instance of beauty that the lover does not possess, viz., the instance that he (she) loves. (That this is the correct understanding of the ambiguous sentence is suggested by the ensuing claim that 'there cannot be love for the ugly' (201A5): for, as Vlastos remarks, any whole person has uglinesses and faults. To avoid being directed at ugliness, love must be directed at a property of the person, not the whole. 'Love is not for the half or the whole of anything, unless, my friend, that half or whole happens to be good' (205E1–3).)

But we are not yet all the way to Plato's conclusion. So far there is some beauty loved by the lover: Alcibiades loves the beauty of Agathon. From this it follows only that Alcibiades lacks *that* beauty – not that he lacks *all* beauty. He might have some other type of beauty. Or he might even have some other token of the same type. The second possibility may not be relevant: it may be part of the psychological claims of the preceding steps that I will not desire something if I have, stably, something that is qualitatively the same, though a countably different instance.[31] But the first seems important: if Alcibiades is *kalon* in physical appearance, can he not still love and lack the beautiful soul of Socrates? What

---

* In assessing the relationship of this dialogue to the *Protagoras*, we should bear in mind that '*kalon*', which I shall continue to translate as 'beautiful', is here such a broad moral/aesthetic notion that it might be more accurate to render it as 'valuable' and the corresponding noun as 'value'. 201C2 states that (all) good things (*agatha*) are *kala*; and the biconditional is required for the validity of the argument at 201C4–5. It may, then, actually be a single unifying notion of value in terms of which we are to see the special values such as justice and wisdom. It is clear, at any rate, that the *kalon* is supposed to include everything that is relevant to the experience of passionate love, including the love of institutions and sciences – everything that is lovable in the world. Thus a belief in its qualitative homogeneity takes us far along the way to the complete elimination of ethically relevant qualitative differences.

we now see is that Socrates' argument depends on a strong hidden assumption: that all beauty, *qua* beauty, is uniform, the same in kind. All manifestations of the *kalon* must be sufficiently like one another that if you lack one kind it is natural to conclude that you lack them all. The beauty of Alcibiades must be distinct from the beauty of Socrates not qualitatively, but only in terms of contingent spatio-temporal location (and perhaps in *quantity* as well).

And, in fact, this claim about beauty and goodness is explicitly asserted in Diotima's teaching. In her account of the soul's development towards the fullest understanding of the good, the idea of uniformity plays a crucial role. (The section of her speech is introduced as a revelation for the initiate, which will go beyond what Socrates could understand on his own (209E5–210A2).) The young lover beginning the ascent – always under the direction of a 'correct' guide (210A6–7) – will begin by loving a single body, or, more exactly, the beauty of a single body: 'Then he must see that the beauty in any one body is family-related (*adelphon*) to the beauty in another body; and that if he must pursue the beauty of form, it is great mindlessness not to consider the beauty of all bodies to be one and the same' (210A5).

First, he or she sees only one loved one's beauty. Then he must notice a close family resemblance between that beauty and others. Then – and this is the crucial step away from the Vlastos view – he *decides* that it is prudent to consider these related beauties to be 'one and the same', that is, qualitatively homogeneous. He then sees that he 'must set himself up as the lover of all beautiful bodies, and relax his excessively intense passion for one body, looking down on that and thinking it of small importance' (210B). So the crucial step is, oddly, a step of decision, involving considerations of 'senselessness' and good sense. We begin to wonder what sort of need drives this lover. Where, for example, do all these 'must's come from? Why does he think it foolish not to see things in a way that appears, *prima facie*, to be false to our ordinary intuitions about the object of love? What leads us to believe that truth is to be found in the denial of these perceptions? The references to 'excessively intense passion' and to a 'relaxing' raise the possibility that this strategy is adopted at least in part for reasons of mental health, because a certain sort of tension has become too risky or difficult to bear. A kind of therapy alters the look of the world, making the related the same, the irreplaceable replaceable. If one 'must' (by nature) 'pursue the beauty of form', be sexually drawn to bodily beauty, it is most sensible to do it in a way that does not involve this costly tension. And one can do this, if one is determined enough and has the help of a skillful teacher.

At the next stage, once again, the lover makes a decision to consider something the same and to adjust values accordingly: 'He must consider that the beauty in souls is more honorable than that in the body' (210B6–7). This judgment must clearly have been preceded, as was the last, by the perception of a relatedness and a prudent decision to treat the related as intimately comparable. Once again, indications are that he is coming to see a truth that he had not previously seen; but, as before, the negative motivation that comes from his need is at least as prominent as the positive one that comes from the truth. So, in each stage of the ascent, the aspiring lover, aided by his teacher, sees relationships between one beauty and another, acknowledges that these beauties are comparable and intersubstitutable, differing only in quantity. He emerges with a proportionally diminished, though not fully extinguished, regard for those he formerly prized. His vision is broadened to take in the beauty or value of laws, institutions, sciences. We hear talk about comparisons of *size* between one value and another (210B6, 210C5), of a 'vast amount' of value (210D1). (Later Socrates will ascribe to Alcibiades the desire to 'make an exchange of *kalon* for *kalon*' (218E) – and, since Socrates' *kalon* is 'entirely surpassing', Alcibiades stands accused of *pleonexia*, a greedy desire for *more*.)[32] The teacher leads him, makes him see (210C7), until at last he is able to conceive of the whole of beauty as a vast ocean, whose components are, like droplets, qualitatively indistinguishable:

And looking towards the vast amount of the beautiful, he will no longer, like some servant, loving the beauty of a particular boy or a particular man or of one set of customs, and being the slave of this, remain contemptible and of no account. But turned towards the vast sea of the beautiful and contemplating, he gives birth to many beautiful and grand speeches and reasonings in his abundant love of wisdom. (210C7–D5)

Education turns you around, so that you do not see what you used to see.[33] It also turns you into a free man instead of a servant. Diotima connects the love of particulars with tension, excess, and servitude; the love of a qualitatively uniform 'sea' with health, freedom, and creativity. The claim for the change of perception and belief involved in the ascent is not just that the new beliefs are *true*. In fact, questions of truth seem muted; the gap between 'family-related' and 'one and the same' indicates that the ascent may be playing fast and loose with the truth, at least as human beings experience it. (Whatever my brother (*adelphos*) is, he is certainly not one and the same with me.) Its strategy for progress is no less radical than the *technē* of the *Protagoras*, to which it now draws surprisingly close.

It is a startling and powerful vision. Just try to think it seriously: this body of this wonderful beloved person is *exactly* the same in quality as that person's mind and inner life. Both, in turn, the same in quality as the value of Athenian democracy; of Pythagorean geometry; of Eudoxan astronomy. What would it be like to look at a body and to see in it exactly the same shade and tone of goodness and beauty as in a mathematical proof – *exactly* the same, differing only in amount and in location, so that the choice between making love with that person and contemplating that proof presented itself as a choice between having n measures of water and having $n + 100$? Again, what would it be like to see in the mind and soul of Socrates nothing else but (a smaller amount of) the quality that one also sees in a good system of laws, so that the choice between conversing with Socrates and administering those laws was, in the same way, a matter of qualitative indifference? What would it be like, finally, to see not just each single choice, but all choices (or at least all choices involving love and deep attachment) as similarly unvariegated? These proposals are so bold as to be pretty well incomprehensible from the ordinary point of view. We can perhaps, though with difficulty, get ourselves, in imagination, into the posture of seeing bodies as qualitatively interchangeable with one another – because we have, or can imagine having, relevant experiences of promiscuity or of non-particularized sexual desire. We might even imagine the interchangeability of souls, helped by a religious heritage according to which we are all equally, and centrally, children of God. We might even try putting these two together, to get a thoroughgoing interchangeability of persons; and we can see how that sort of replaceability would indeed subvert motivations for certain troublesome and disorder-producing acts. (Think of Epictetus's profound observation that if Menelaus had been able to think of Helen as just another woman, 'gone would have been the *Iliad*, and the *Odyssey* as well'.) But the wide sea of the *kalon* is beyond us. We sense only that to see in this way, if one could do it, would indeed change the world, removing us both from vulnerable attachments and from severe conflicts among them. We can comprehend the extent to which it would erode the motivation for running after Alcibiades, for devoting oneself to a particular beloved person, even for loving one city above all other things. Nor will such commitments collide painfully, since all *kalon* is one thing (cf. Ch. 5, §v). The lover, seeing a flat uniform landscape of value, with no jagged promontories or deep valleys, will have few motivations for moving here rather than there on that landscape. A contemplative life is a natural choice.

At each stage, then, the teacher persuades the pupil to abandon his or her cherished human belief in irreplaceability in the service of his inner need for health. Socrates is among the convinced; and he is now trying to convince us that our human nature could find no better ally or collaborator (*sunergos*) than this sort of *erōs* (212B). An ally comes from another country to help me win my battles. If the ascent appears remote from human nature, that is because, like the *Protagoras* science but more explicitly, it is a device for progress beyond the merely human.

A central feature of the ascent is that the lover escapes, gradually, from his bondage to luck. The Aristophanic lover loved in a chancy way. He or she might never meet the right other in the first place; if he did, the other might not love him, or might die, or leave him. Or he might cease to love; or leave; or retreat; or be tormented by jealousy. Often his passions will distract him from his other plans, and from the good. Even at the best of times he would be trying to do something both impossible and self-defeating. The philosopher is free of all this. His or her contemplative love for all beauty carries no risk of loss, rejection, even frustration. Speeches and thoughts are always in our power to a degree that emotional and physical intercourse with loved individuals is not. And if one instance of worldly beauty fades away or proves recalcitrant, there remains a boundless sea: he will feel the loss of the droplet hardly at all.

But the final revelation to the initiate lover takes him beyond this minimal dependence on the world. Like the other advances, this one comes as a new vision (210E2–3). He sees it 'all at once' (*exaiphnēs*), the culmination of all his efforts:

First of all, it is always, and neither comes to be nor passes away, neither grows nor decays; then it is not beautiful in this respect but ugly in this, nor beautiful at one time and not at another, nor beautiful by comparison with this, ugly by comparison with that, nor beautiful here, ugly there, as though it were beautiful for some, and ugly for others... He will see it as being itself by itself with itself, eternal and unitary, and see all the other beautifuls as partaking of it in such a manner that, when the others come to be and are destroyed, it never comes to be any more or less, nor passively suffers anything... This indeed is what it is to approach erotic matters correctly, or to be led to them by another... In this place, my dear Socrates, if anywhere, life is livable for a human being – the place where he contemplates the beautiful itself. If ever you see that, it will not seem to you to be valuable by comparison with gold and clothing and beautiful boys and youths, the sight of whom at present so inflames you that you, and many others, provided that you could see your beloved boys and be continually with them, are prepared to give up eating and drinking, and to spend your whole time contemplating them and being with them. What do we think it would be like... if someone should see the beautiful itself – unalloyed, pure, unmixed, not stuffed full of human flesh and colors and lots of other mortal rubbish, but if he could see the divine beautiful itself in its unity? Do you think life would be miserable for a man who looked out there, and contemplated it in an appropriate way and was with it? Or don't you understand that there alone, where he sees the beautiful with that faculty to which it is visible, it will be possible for him to give birth not to simulacra of excellence, since it is no simulacrum he is grasping, but to true excellence, since he is grasping truth? And as he brings forth true excellence and nourishes it, he will become god-loved, and, if ever a human being can, immortal? (210E6–212A7)

So ends Diotima's speech of persuasion. I have quoted it at length not only to indicate the powerfully rhetorical character of her discourse, which moves and persuades us as it does Socrates, but also to show, in it, further evidence of the practical motivation lying behind the ascent. The lover's final contemplative activity meets the *Republic*'s standards of true value in every way. Its objects are 'unalloyed, pure, unmixed' (211E); it is itself in no way necessarily mixed with pain. It is a stable activity, giving continuous expression to our truth-loving and creative nature; and one reason why it can be so stable is that it addresses itself to an unvarying and immortal object. We have, at the end, an object of love that is always available, that will to the highest degree satisfy our longing to 'be with' the beloved all the time. Sexual 'being-with' (the word used at 211D6, '*suneinai*', is also the ordinary word for intercourse) cannot be stably prolonged, both because of its internally 'impure' structure of need and repletion, and also because it relies on the presence of an object that is not the lover's to command. Intellectual intercourse ('*suneinai*' is used of the form at 212A2) is free of these defects. Furthermore, as Diotima says, this activity also gets us to the truth, instead of mere simulacra. But considerations of truth are very closely interwoven, in this speech as previously, with motivational appeals based on need. The ascent is true; but it requires us to sacrifice 'truths' that we deeply know. So she must motivate the change in vision for us from where we are. She does so by reminding us of the deep demand of our nature – a demand altogether familiar to us from our empirical lives – for self-sufficient love. The ascent passage accepts Aristophanes' characterization of the misery and the irrational tumult of personal erotic need, agreeing that *erōs* disrupts our rational planning to the point where we would willingly give up everything else, even health, even life. But that is intolerable. Such a life is not 'livable';[34] we must find another way. Instead of flesh and all that mortal rubbish, an immortal object must, and therefore can, be found. Instead of painful yearning for a single body and spirit, a blissful contemplative completeness. It is, we see, the old familiar *erōs*, that longing for an end to longing, that motivates us here to ascend to a world in which erotic activity, as we know it, will not exist.[35]

As Socrates concludes, we are moved to think back through this story (which, we now recall, is being told to us through Aristodemus, a convert and 'lover' of Socrates, as reported by Apollodorus, another formerly wretched person whom philosophy has made happy), and to look at the life and behavior of Socrates as exemplifying the benefits of ascent. It is, first of all, striking that the lives of Socrates and the Socratic narrator appear remarkably orderly and free from distraction. 'I used to rush around here and there as things fell out by chance', Apollodorus remembers, at a distance (172C). And his master too seems at this point in his life to be always remarkably in control of his activities, free from ordinary passions and distractions. He is reliably virtuous – courageous, just, temperate – all without lapses of weakness or fatigue. And this seems intimately connected with his imperviousness to happenings in the world. He cares little about clothing, either for beauty or for comfort. We will hear later of his remarkable endurance of cold and hardship. He walks barefoot over the ice, faces the coldest frosts without any coat or hat. This could be interpreted as the behavior of an arrogant man bent on self-display; so, we are told, it was interpreted by the soldiers (220B). But the correct interpretation seems to be that Socrates has so dissociated himself from his body that he genuinely does not feel its pain, or regard its sufferings as things genuinely happening to him. He is famous for drinking without ever getting drunk, and without the hangovers complained of by the others (176A–B, 214A, 220A). He does not succumb to the most immediate and intense sexual temptation (219B–D). He can go sleepless without ever suffering from fatigue (220C–D, 223D). We cannot explain all this by supposing his physiology to be unique. We are invited, instead, to look for the explanation in his psychological distance from the world and from his body as an object in the world. He really seems to think of himself as a being whose mind is distinct from his body, whose personality in no way identifies itself with the body and the body's adventures. Inside the funny, fat, snub-nosed shell, the soul, self-absorbed, pursues its self-sufficient contemplation. We see him, at the beginning of the walk to the party, 'turning his attention in some way in upon himself' (174D, cf. 220C–D), so that he becomes, at a point, actually forgetful of the world. He falls behind the group; they find him much later, standing in a neighbor's porch, literally deaf to all entreaties. The sounds that enter in at the well-functioning ears never penetrate to the mind. There is a gulf. 'Leave him alone', warns Aristodemus. 'This is a habit of his. Sometimes he stops and stands wherever he happens to be.'

These details have usually been read as intriguing pieces of biography. Perhaps they are. But they are also more than that. They show us what Diotima could only abstractly tell: what a human life starts to look like as one makes the ascent. Socrates is put before us as an example of a man in the process of making himself self-sufficient – put before us, in our still unregenerate state, as a troublesome question mark and a challenge. Is this the life we want for ourselves? Is that the way we want, or need, to see and hear? We are not allowed to have the cozy thought that the transformed person will be just like us, only happier. Socrates is weird. He is, in fact, 'not similar to any human being'. We feel, as we look at him, both awestruck and queasy, timidly homesick for ourselves. We feel that we must look back at what we currently are, our loves and our ways of seeing, the problems these cause for practical reason. We need to see ourselves more clearly before we can say whether we would like to become this other sort of being, excellent and deaf.

IV

The summit of the ascent, Diotima tells us, is marked by a revelation: 'All at once (*exaiphnēs*) he will see a beauty marvelous in its nature, for the sake of which he had made all his previous efforts.' Now, as we begin our reflective descent into ourselves, at this moment when some of the symposiasts are praising Socrates and Aristophanes is trying to remind us again of his view of our nature (212C), we see another sort of revelation, and another beauty. 'And all at once (*exaiphnēs*) there was a loud knocking at the outer door. It sounded like a drunken party; you could hear the voice of the flute girl... And a minute later they heard the voice of Alcibiades in the courtyard, very drunk and shouting loudly, asking where Agathon was and demanding to be taken to Agathon.' The form of the beautiful appeared to the mind's eye alone, looking 'not like some face or hands or anything else that partakes in body' (211A); it was 'unalloyed, pure, unmixed, not stuffed full of human flesh and colors and lots of other mortal rubbish' (211E). Alcibiades the beautiful, the marvelous nature, presents himself to our sensuous imagination, an appearance bursting with color and all the mixed impurity of mortal flesh. We are made to hear his voice, vividly see his movements, even smell the violets that trail through his hair and shade his eyes (212E1–2), their perfume blending with the heavier odors of wine and sweat. The faculty that apprehends the form is preeminently stable, unwavering, and in our power to exercise regardless of the world's happenings. The faculties that see and hear and respond to Alcibiades will be the feelings and sense-perceptions of the body, both vulnerable and inconstant. From the rarified contemplative world of the self-sufficient philosopher we are suddenly, with an abrupt jolt, returned to the world we inhabit and invited (by the parallel 'all at once') to see this vision, too, as a dawning and a revelation.[36] We are then moved to wonder whether there is a kind of understanding that is itself vulnerable and addressed to vulnerable objects – and, if there is, whether the ascent comprehends it, transcends it, or simply passes it by. (The philosopher asks to be taken to the *agathon*, the repeatable universal Good. Alcibiades asks to be taken to Agathon, a not-very-good particular boy.)

Alcibiades takes up this theme at the very opening of his speech. 'You there', says Socrates, 'What do you mean to do?' (A question that reverberates ominously for us in view of our greater knowledge of what this man will soon be up to.) 'Do you mean to give a mock-praise of me? Or what are you going to do?' The answer is a simple one, though difficult to understand. 'I'm going to tell the truth. Do you think you'll allow that?' (Why should anyone, especially a pupil of Socrates, think that philosophy might be resistant to the truth?) When, shortly after, he tells us more about his sort of truth-telling, we begin to understand why he is on the defensive. 'Gentlemen, I shall undertake to praise Socrates through images. He may think that it is a mock-praise, but the image will be for the sake of the truth, not for ridicule.' Asked to speak about Love, Alcibiades has chosen to speak of a particular love; no definitions or explanations of the nature of anything, but just a story of a particular passion for a particular contingent individual. Asked to make a speech, he gives us the story of his own life: the understanding of *erōs* he has achieved through his own experience. (The concluding words of his speech are the tragic maxim *pathonta gnōnai*, 'understanding through experience' or 'suffering' – cf. Ch. 2.) And, what is more, this story conveys its truths using images or likenesses – a poetic practice much deplored by the Socrates of the *Republic*, since images lack the power to provide us with true general accounts or explanations of essences (cf. Interlude 1; Ch. 7 §III). But his opening remarks indicate that Alcibiades is not simply ignorant of these philosophical objections. He anticipates criticism. He anticipates, in fact, that the philosopher will not *allow* his truths, or not allow their claim to be the truth. And he asserts, in the face of this danger, that, nonetheless, what he will tell will be truth – that the truth can and will be told in just this way.

What could lie behind this claim? Perhaps something like this. There are some truths about love that can be learned only through the experience of a particular passion of one's own. If one is asked to teach those truths, one's only recourse is to recreate that experience for the hearer: to tell a story, to appeal to his or her imagination and feelings by the use of vivid narrative. Images are valuable in this attempt to make the audience share the experience, to feel, from the inside, what it is *like* to be that. The comparison of Socrates to the Silenus-statue, for example, takes this man who is not intimately known to the hearer and, by comparing him to something that is part of everyday experience, makes available to the hearer something of the feeling of what it is like to want and to want to know him. We shall examine this and other such cases later on; we shall also see that Alcibiades, drunk, wound round with ivy, presents himself to our understanding as an image that tells the truth.

We now notice that Alcibiades is aligning himself with a tradition that defends the role of poetic or 'literary' texts in moral learning. Certain truths about human experience can best be learned by living them in their particularity. Nor can this particularity be grasped solely by thought 'itself by itself'. As Aeschylus or Sophocles might well have argued, it frequently needs to be apprehended through the cognitive activity of imagination, emotions, even appetitive feelings:[37] through putting oneself inside a problem and feeling it. But we cannot all live, in our own overt activities, through all that we ought to know in order to live well. Here literature, with its stories and images, enters in as an extension of our experience, encouraging us to develop and understand our cognitive/emotional responses.[38]

If this is, indeed, Alcibiades' view, it is not surprising that he is on the defensive in this company. If the symposiasts have anything in common, it is that they seem to believe that *erōs* can and should be praised in the abstract. Particular stories enter in briefly as examples of general principles, but none is described fully or concretely, in a way that would appeal to the sensuous imagination. Aristophanes' myth might be said to teach through an image of human nature; and his poetic gifts are evident in the vividness with which he describes the movements and feelings of the mythic creatures. But the creatures remain anonymous exemplars; and their loved ones, though individuals, are abstractly characterized. We have a hard time seeing ourselves in them, our particular loves in this odd fitting-together. Socrates, meanwhile, has attacked even this limited appeal to lived experience in the name of philosophical wisdom. Nobody loves a half or a whole, unless that half or whole is beautiful and good. Socrates claims to have *epistēmē* of erotic matters (177D); and Socratic *epistēmē*, unlike Alcibiades' *pathonta gnōnai*, is deductive, scientific, concerned with universals. (When Aristotle wants to defend the role, in practical wisdom, of a non-deductive intuition of particulars through feeling and experience, he does so by *contrasting* this intuitive grasp with *epistēmē* – *EN* 1142a23ff.). The Socratic search for definitions embodying *epistēmē* is, throughout the dialogues, the search for a universal account that covers and explains all the particulars. To answer a Socratic 'What is *X*?' question by enumerating particular examples or telling stories is either to misunderstand or to reject his demand. In the early dialogues, examples provide material towards *epistēmē*, material a definition must take into account; they can never on their own embody *epistēmē*.[39] And here in the *Symposium* Socrates' attitude to the particular case seems to be harsher still. Examples are relevant not as complex wholes, but only insofar as they exemplify a repeatable property. And, as for images, the revelation of the beautiful can count as truth for him only because it is *not* a (sensory) image (212A) and does not present itself *through* images. Images are contrasted with truth both as objects and as sources of understanding.[40] Only with the dulling of the 'sight of the body', the senses and the sensuous imagination, does intellect, the 'sight of the mind', begin to flourish (219A).

Socratic philosophy, then, cannot allow the truths of Alcibiades to count as contributions to philosophical understanding. It must insist that the non-repeatable and sensuous aspects of the particular case are irrelevant, even a hindrance to correct seeing. And it is not only the philosophy of Socrates against which Alcibiades must defend his claim to teach. It is also most of the tradition of ethical discourse that got its start with Socrates. Very few moral philosophers, especially in the Anglo-American tradition, have welcomed stories, particulars, and images into their writing on value. Most have regarded these elements of discourse with suspicion (cf. Ch. 1).[41] As a result, contrasts between the mixed and the pure, between story and argument, the literary and the philosophical are as sharply drawn in much of the modern profession of philosophy as they are in this text by Plato – but culpably, because unreflectively, and without Plato's loving recreation of the speech of the other side, his willingness to call into question the contrasts themselves.

The *Symposium* and Alcibiades have fallen victim to these suspicions. Frequently ignored by the philosophers of our tradition (or studied in judiciously selected excerpts), this entire dialogue has been described in its most recent edition as 'the most literary of all Plato's works and one which all students of classics are likely to want to read whether or not they are studying Plato's philosophy'.[42] Which is to say, we will let Alcibiades have his say in some other department, since he clearly has not grasped the way philosophy does things. (And even a piece of critical writing about the *Symposium*, if it responds to Alcibiades' stylistic claims in its own style, will be likely to encounter this resistance. It will be addressed as a literary diversion, or asked to prove Socratically that it, too, is pure enough to tell the truth.)

But to place in this way the burden of proof on Alcibiades – to force him either to argue with Socrates on Socrates' own terms or to take his love stories elsewhere – is simply a refusal to hear him or to enter his world. It is a refusal to investigate and to be affected, where the strangeness of the material calls, above all, for questioning and humble exploration. It is Socrates' response.

Alcibiades' story is, in fact, just a love story. It is, however, not *a* love story, but the story of Socrates, and of the love of Alcibiades for Socrates. Alcibiades, asked to speak about *erōs*, talks about one person.[43] He cannot describe the passion or its object in general terms, because his experience of love has happened to him this way only once, in connection with an individual who is seen by him to be like nobody else in the world. The entire speech is an attempt to communicate that uniqueness. He might have begun his answer by enumerating the excellent qualities of this unlikely figure. This might all have been true, and yet it would not have been sufficient to capture the particular tone and intensity of the love; it might even mislead, by implying that another person turning up with these same repeatable properties would make Alcibiades feel the same way. But he doesn't know that. So Alcibiades tells some Socrates stories; he gropes for images and associations to communicate the inside feel of the experience. He mentions Socrates' virtues in the process of describing the wholeness of a unique personality. The speech, disorganized and tumultuous, moves from imaging to describing, response to story, and back again many times over. It is precisely its groping, somewhat chaotic character that makes it so movingly convincing as an account – and an expression (cf. 'even now' at 215D, 216A) – of love.

Two things in the speech, above all, strike us as strange. Using them as clues we may perhaps be able to understand more fully its teaching and its relationship to Socratic teaching. The first is its confusion about sexual roles. Alcibiades begins as the beautiful *erōmenos*, but seems to end as the active *erastēs*, while Socrates, apparently the *erastēs*, becomes the *erōmenos* (222B). The second is Alcibiades' odd habit of incarnation – the way he speaks of his soul, his reason, his feelings and desires, as pieces of flesh that can experience the bites, burns, and tears that are the usual lot of flesh.

The *erōmenos*, in Greek homosexual custom (as interpreted, for example, in Sir Kenneth Dover's authoritative study),[44] is a beautiful creature without pressing needs of his own. He is aware of his attractiveness, but self-absorbed in his relationship with those who desire him. He will smile sweetly at the admiring lover; he will show appreciation for the other's friendship, advice, and assistance. He will allow the lover to greet him by touching, affectionately, his genitals and his face, while he looks, himself, demurely at the ground. And, as Dover demonstrates from an exhaustive study of Greek erotic painting, he will even occasionally allow the importunate lover to satisfy his desires through intercrural intercourse. The boy may hug him at this point, or otherwise positively indicate affection. But two things he will not allow, if we judge from the evidence of works of art that have come down to us. He will not allow any opening of his body to be penetrated; only hairy satyrs do that. And he will not allow the arousal of his own desire to penetrate the lover. In all of surviving Greek art, there are no boys with erections. Dover concludes, with some incredulity, 'The penis of the *erastēs* is sometimes erect even before any bodily contact is established, but that of the *erōmenos* remains flaccid even in circumstances to which one would expect the penis of any healthy adolescent to respond willy-nilly.'[45] The inner experience of an *erōmenos* would be characterized, we may imagine, by a feeling of proud self-sufficiency. Though the object of importunate solicitation, he is himself not in need of anything beyond himself. He is unwilling to let himself be explored by the other's needy curiosity, and he has, himself, little curiosity about the other. He is something like a god, or the statue of a god. (The *Philebus* (53D) cites the pair *erōmenos/erastēs* as a paradigmatic example of the contrast between the complete or self-sufficient (*auto kath' hauto*) and the incomplete or needy – illustrating its praise of philosophical contemplation with this sexual analogy.)

For Alcibiades, who had spent much of his young life as this sort of closed and self-absorbed being, the experience of love is felt as a sudden openness, and, at the same time, an overwhelming desire to open. The presence of Socrates makes him feel, first of all, a terrifying and painful awareness of being perceived. He wants, with part of himself, to 'hold out' (216A), to remain an *erōmenos*. His impulse, in service of this end, is to run away, hide, stop up his ears – openings that can be entered, willy-nilly, by penetrating words (216A–B). But he senses at the same time that in this being seen and being spoken to, in this siren music (216A) that rushes into his body in this person's presence, is something he deeply needs not to avoid: 'There's something I feel with nobody else but Socrates – something you would not have thought was in me – and that is a sense of shame. He is the only person who makes me feel shame... There are times when I'd gladly see him dead. But if that happened, you understand, I'd be worse off than ever' (216A–C). The openness of the lover brings with it (as Phaedrus has already insisted – 179A) this naked vulnerability to criticism. In the closed world of the *erōmenos*, defects and treasures, both, hide comfortably from scrutiny. Being known by the lover can, by contrast, bring the pain of shame, as the lover's eye reveals one's own imperfections. On the other hand this pain, as he dimly sees it, may lead to some kind of growth.

So Alcibiades is thrown into confusion about his role. He knows himself to be, as an object, desirable. 'I was amazingly vain about my beauty' (217A). He thought of his alliance with Socrates as a decision to grant a favor, while remaining basically unmoved (217A). And yet now he wants and needs, the illumination of the other's activity.

More confusing still, he feels, at the same time, a deep desire to know Socrates – a desire as conventionally inappropriate as his desire to be known. His speech makes repeated and central use of the image of *opening up* the other: an image which is essentially sexual, and inseparable from his sexual aims and imaginings, but which is also epistemic, intended to convey to us his desire 'to hear everything that he knew' (217A) and to know everything that he was. In the early days of his vanity, this longing appears to be confused with personal ambition (217A); but as his love persists and his vanity abates (compare the present tenses of 215D, 216A, etc., with the past tense of 217A), the desire to know and to tell truth about Socrates does not abate. The speech expresses the understanding he has gained, as well as his continuing curiosity.

Socrates, he tells us, is like one of those toy Sileni made by craftsmen. On the outside they look unremarkable, even funny. But what you are moved to do, what you cannot resist doing once you see the crack running down the middle, is to open them up. (They can be opened up because they have this crack or scar, and are not completely smooth.) Then, on the inside, you see the hidden beauty, the elaborate carving of god-statues. We might imagine the effect to be like that of the amazing mediaeval rosary bead in the Cloisters in New York. On the outside, a decorated sphere, nothing remarkable. Then you pry the two halves apart to reveal 'the treasure inside' (216E) – a marvelously wrought scene of animals, trees, and men, all carved with the most delicate precision. That something you thought to be a sphere should contain its own world: that is the surprise, and the reason for awe.

Among our first and best-loved toys are things that can be opened to show something on the inside. Even before we can speak, we are trying to open things up. We spend hours sitting on the floor in rapt attention, pulling our spherical balls of wood or plastic apart into their two halves, looking for the hidden ball, or bell, or family. By using such toys as images, Alcibiades reminds us that the urge to open things up, to get at and explore the inside concealed by the outside, is one of our earliest and strongest desires, a desire in which sexual and epistemological need are joined and, apparently, inseparable. We long to probe and bring to light what is concealed and secret; and when we see a crack, that is, to us, a signal that this aim can be fulfilled in the object. We long to open the cracked object up, to make the other's beauty less rounded and more exposed, to explore the world that we imagine to be there, coming to know it by means of feelings, emotions, sensations, intellect. Alcibiades sees his sexual aim, the fullest fulfillment of which demands both physical intimacy and philosophical conversation, as a kind of epistemic aim, the aim to achieve a more complete understanding of this particular complex portion of the world.

It is easy enough to see structural parallels between sexual desire and the desire for wisdom. Both are directed towards objects in the world, and aim at somehow grasping or possessing these objects. The fulfilled grasp of the object brings, in both cases, satiety and the temporary cessation of desire: no sphere seduces, 'no god searches for wisdom' (204A). (The *contemplation* of truth is, of course, another matter.) Both can be aroused by beauty and goodness, and both seek to understand the nature of that goodness. Both revere the object as a separate, self-complete entity, and yet long, at the same time, to incorporate it. But Alcibiades appears to want to claim something more controversial and anti-Socratic than this parallelism. With his claims that a story tells the truth and that his goal is to open up and to know, he suggests that the lover's knowledge of the particular other, gained through an intimacy both bodily and intellectual, is itself a unique and uniquely valuable *kind* of practical understanding, and one that we risk losing if we take the first step up the Socratic ladder. (The *Phaedrus* will develop this suggestion, confirming our reading.)

Socratic knowledge of the good, attained through pure intellect operating apart from the senses, yields universal truths – and, in practical choice, universal rules. If we have apprehended the form, we will be in possession of a general account of beauty, an account that not only holds true of all and only instances of beauty, but also explains why they are correctly called instances of beauty, and grouped together.[46] Such understanding, once attained, would take priority over our vague, mixed impressions of particular beautifuls. It would tell us how to see.

The lover's understanding, attained through the supple interaction of sense, emotion, and intellect (any one of which, once well trained, may perform a cognitive function in exploring and informing us concerning the other – cf. Ch. 7) yields particular truths and particular judgments. It insists that those particular intuitive judgments are prior to any universal rules we may be using to guide us.[47] A lover decides how to respond to his or her lover not on the basis of definitions or general prescriptions, but on the basis of an intuitive sense of the person and the situation, which, although guided by general theories, is not subservient to them. This does not mean that their judgments and responses are not rational. Indeed, Alcibiades would claim that a Socratic adherence to rule and refusal to see and feel the particular as such is what is irrational. To have seen that, and how, Socrates is like nobody else, to respond to him as such and to act accordingly, is the rational way to behave towards another individual. Nor does it mean that this love neglects the repeatable general features in which Socrates is interested: for Alcibiades sees Socrates' virtues and is moved by them. But his knowledge sees more, and differently; it is an integrated response to the person as a unique whole.[48]

It is tempting to try to understand the contrast between these two kinds of knowledge in terms of the contrast between propositional knowledge and knowledge by acquaintance. This would, I believe, be an error. First of all, Socratic knowledge itself is not simply propositional knowledge. Because of Socrates' constant emphasis on the claim that the man with *epistēmē* is the man who is able to give explanations or accounts, the rendering 'understanding' is, in general, more appropriate.[49] Second, both kinds of understanding, not just the Socratic kind, are concerned with truths. Alcibiades is claiming not just an ineffable familiarity with Socrates, but the ability to tell the truth about Socrates. He wants to claim that through a lover's intimacy he can produce accounts (stories) that are more deeply and precisely true – that capture more of what is characteristic and practically relevant about Socrates, that explain more about what Socrates does and why – than any account that could be produced by a form-lover who denied himself the cognitive resources of the senses and emotions.

Finally, there is much about the lover's understanding that cannot be captured by either model of knowledge, but can be better conceived as a kind of 'knowing how'. The lover can be said to understand the beloved when, and only when, he knows how to treat him or her: how to speak, look, and move at various times and in various circumstances; how to give pleasure and how to receive it; how to deal with the loved one's complex network of intellectual, emotional, and bodily needs. This understanding requires acquaintance and yields the ability to tell truths; but it does not seem to be reducible to either.

Alcibiades suggests, then, that there is a kind of practical understanding that consists in the keen responsiveness of intellect, imagination, and feeling to the particulars of a situation. Of this wisdom the lover's understanding of the particular beloved is a central and particularly deep case – and not only a case among cases, but one whose resulting self-understanding might be fundamental to the flourishing of practical wisdom in other areas of life as well. The lover's understanding obviously has many components that are independent of the success of his or her specifically sexual projects. Alcibiades can tell the truth about Socrates' unique strangeness even though his aims were frustrated. And not just any successful lover would have had his intellectual and emotional grasp. (Indeed, in this case the frustration of sexual vanity is of considerable positive importance.) Aristotle will insist that such intimate personal knowledge arises in the relation of parent to child (cf. Ch. 12). But the speech suggests, as well, that with the failure of physical intimacy a certain *part* of practical understanding is lost to Alcibiades. There is a part of Socrates that remains dark to him, a dimension of intuitive responsiveness to this particular person, an aptness of speech, movement, and gesture, that he can never develop, a kind of 'dialectic' that is missing.[50] Sexuality is a metaphor for personal intimacy; but it is also more than a metaphor, as the *Phaedrus*, with its connections between 'touching' and knowing, will insist.

It is, then, in his openness to such knowing that Alcibiades is revealed as no proper *erōmenos*. To receive the other, he must not be self-sufficient, closed against the world. He must put aside the vanity of his beauty and become, himself, in his own eyes, an object in the world: in the world of the other's activity, and in the larger world of happenings that affect his dealings with the other. Such an object will know more if it has a crack in it.

This gives us a key to our second puzzle: why Alcibiades should persistently speak of his soul, his inner life, as something of flesh and blood like the visible body. Alcibiades has no particular metaphysical view of the person; he makes it clear that he is uncertain about how to refer to what is 'inside' the flesh-and-blood body. What he knows is that this inner part of him is responding like a thing of flesh. He says he feels like a sufferer from snakebite – only he has been 'bitten by something more painful and the most painful way one can be bitten: I've been bitten and wounded in the heart or soul, or whatever one should call it, by the philosophical speeches of Socrates' (217E–218A). And he tries, without success, to treat Socrates' 'whatever' in the same manner, shooting words like lightning bolts in the hope that they will 'pierce' him (219B). Whatever is flesh or fleshlike is vulnerable. The mark of body is its ability to be pierced and bitten, to be prey to snakes, lightning flashes, lovers. Alcibiades, without a philosophical view of mind, gives an extraordinary defense of 'physicalism' for the souls of lovers:

> All and only body is vulnerable to happenings in the world.
> I am inwardly bitten, pierced.
> Therefore this whatever-you-call-it is bodily (or very like body).

It is an argument that appeals to subjective experience, indeed to subjective suffering, to deny a 'Platonic' view of the soul as a thing that is at one and the same time the seat of personality and immortal/invulnerable. The seat of my personality just got bitten by those speeches, so I know it is not 'pure', 'unaffected', 'unmoved'. It is obvious that such a line of argument shows us nothing about the souls of philosophers, for whom the Platonic account may, for all Alcibiades knows, be correct. (This shows us what the *Phaedo* did not make explicit: that the Platonic picture of the soul is not so much a scientific fact as an ethical ideal, something to be chosen and achieved.)

Both the lover's epistemic aim and his felt vulnerability are captured for us in the central image of Alcibiades' story: the lightning bolt. Images of revelation, appearing, and radiance have been seen before. Alcibiades appears before us 'all at once' (212C), just as, for him, Socrates 'is accustomed to appear all at once' (*exaiphnēs anaphainesthai*, 213C), just when he least thinks he is there, and reminds Alcibiades of the inner radiance of his virtues. But now Alcibiades has spoken of the words and gestures of love as things hurled at the other like bolts of lightning. This image knits together, with extraordinary compression, his views about sexual ambition, knowledge, and risk. A lightning bolt strikes all at once, unpredictably, usually allowing no hope of defense or control. It is at one and the same time a brilliance that brings illumination and a force that has the power to wound and to kill. It is, one might say, corporeal light. In the heaven of the philosopher, the Form of the Good, like an intelligible sun, gives intelligibility to the objects of understanding, while remaining, itself unmoving and unchanging.[51] It affects the pure soul only by inspiring it to perform self-sufficient acts of pure reasoning. In the world of Alcibiades, the illumination of the loved one's body and mind strikes like a moving, darting, bodily light, a light that makes its impact by touching as well as by illuminating. (It is rather like what happens to the sun in certain later paintings of Turner. No more a pure, remote condition of sight, it becomes a force that does things in the world to objects such as boats, waves, a just man's eyes – all of which are seen, insofar as they are thus illuminated, to be the sorts of things to which happenings can happen. And the light strikes the beholder's eyes, as well, with a triumphant searing power that refutes, again and again, his belief in his own completeness.) The lover has such light in him to deploy or give, and it is this that he longs to receive, even though it killed the mother of Dionysus. If Socrates had carried a shield, its device would have been the sun of the *Republic*, visible image of the intelligible form -- the sun to which, as Alcibiades tells us, he prayed after a night of sleepless thought at Potidaea (220C–D). Alcibiades, placing on his shield the thunderbolt, marks in his own way the sort of being he claims to be, the sort of understanding he desires.

Our reading has now put us in a position to move from the interpretation of the image *used* by Alcibiades to the interpretation of the image that Alcibiades *is*, as he presents himself before us. He makes his appearance 'crowned with a thick crown of ivy and violets' (212E1–2), making dress itself an image that tells the truth.[52] The crown of violets is, first of all, a sign of Aphrodite (cf. *H. Hom.* 5.18, Solon 11.4). This hardly surprises us, except for the strange fact (of which we shall speak more later) that this aggressively masculine figure sees himself as a female divinity. It is also, further, a crown worn by the Muses. As he begins his truth-telling through images, Alcibiades, then, presents himself as a poet, and an inspiring god of poets (Plato?).

But the violet crown stands for something else as well: for the city of Athens herself. In a fragment from Pindar (only one of the poems that use this apparently well-known epithet) she is addressed:

> O glistening and violet-crowned and famous in song,
> Bulwark of Hellas, glorious Athens,
> Fortunate city.

The crown of violets is the delicate, growing sign of the flourishing of this strange and fragile democracy, now, in the time of Alcibiades, in its greatest danger. By so crowning himself, Alcibiades seems to indicate that his own attentiveness to the particular, to unique persons rather than repeatable properties, intuitions rather than the rules, is the fruit of this city's education. This education values the original and the daring, relies on the ability of gifted leaders to 'improvise what is required' (Thuc. 1.138, cf. Ch. 10, § 111) and, instead of commanding humble subservience to law, asks free men to 'choose, in their nobility of character' (Thuc. 11.41) a life of virtue and service. Doing away, as it does, with rules, it depends on each man's capacity for practical wisdom and the understanding of the lover. Thucydides' Pericles enjoins the citizens to 'look at the city's power day by day and become her lovers' (*erastas autēs*, 11.43). *Erōs*, not law or fear, guides action. But this reliance on *erōs* puts democracy, like Alcibiades, very much at the mercy of fortune and the irrational passions.[53] The violet crown is worn by a gifted drunk, who will soon commit imaginative crimes.

The ivy is the sign of Dionysus, god of wine, god of irrational inspiration (cf. Ch. 3).[54] (Ivy represents the bodily fertility of the inspired lover, who is, and sees himself, as one of the growing things of the natural world, mutable and green.) Agathon appealed to Dionysus to judge the argument between him and Socrates (175E); Alcibiades' arrival answers his request. Dionysus, male in form yet of softly female bearing, exemplifies the sexual contractions of Alcibiades' aspirations. He embodies, too, another apparent contradiction: he is the patron god of both tragic and comic poetry. This is appropriate, since the speech of Alcibiades is both tragic and comic – tragic in its depiction of frustration and its foreshadowing of ruin, comic in the knowing self-humor of the story-teller, who exposes his vanity and illusions with Aristophanic delight. It is already beginning to be evident to us why Socrates should, at the dialogue's end, argue that comedy and tragedy can be the work of a single man. The Aristophanic view of love is of a piece both with the tragic account of *erōs* and with the vision of Alcibiades in its emphasis on the bodily and contingent nature of human erotic aspiration, the vulnerability of practical wisdom to the world. (Socrates charged Aristophanes with being 'exclusively taken up with Dionysus and Aphrodite' (177E).) Tragedy and comedy cherish the same values, value the same dangers. Both, furthermore, are linked through Dionysus to the fragile fortunes of Athenian democracy; both are in danger at the dramatic date, dead, along with Alcibiades, soon after.[55]

Now however, we see a further dimension to the *rapprochement*. Alcibiades is appealing, gripping, and, ultimately, tragic in part *because* he is also the comic poet of his own disaster. If he had told a melodramatic tale of anguish and loss, stripped of the wit, the self-awareness, and the laughter that characterize his actual speech, his story would be less tragic, because we would have less reason to care about him. A self-critical perception of one's cracks and holes, which issues naturally in comic poetry, is an important part of what we value in Alcibiades and want to salvage in ourselves. So it seems not accidental that Dionysus, god of tragic loss, should stand for both.

There is one more feature of Dionysus to which the ivy crown particularly directs us: he is the god who dies. He undergoes, each year, a ritual death and a rebirth, a cutting back and a resurgence, like the plant, like desire itself. Among the gods he alone is not self-sufficient, he alone can be acted on by the world. He is the god who would be no use for teaching young citizens the 'god's eye' point of view. And yet, miraculously, despite his fragility, he restores himself and burgeons. This suggests that an unstable city, an unstable passion, might grow and flourish in a way truly appropriate to a god – a thought that has no place in the theology of the ideal city.

V

We now see a positive case for Alcibiades. But the speech is also, at the same time, Plato's indictment. He has invented a priestess whose job it is to save people from plagues; he has suggested that personal *erōs*, unregenerate, is this plague. We want now to discover in detail the reasons for this condemnation. What makes *erōs* intolerable? What gives rise to this overwhelming need to get above it and away from it?

There are, it must be said, problems for Alcibiades. First there is the problem of what happens to him and what his curiosity finds. His attempt to know the other encounters an obstacle in the stone of Socratic virtue. It is not without reason that Alcibiades compares Socratic virtues to statues of the gods. For, as we have seen, Socrates, in his ascent towards the form, has become, himself, very like a form – hard, indivisible, unchanging. His virtue, in search of science and of assimilation of the good itself, turns away from the responsive intercourse with particular earthly goods that is Alcibiades' knowledge.

It is not only Socrates' dissociation from his body. It is not only that he sleeps all night with the naked Alcibiades without arousal. There is, along with this remoteness, a deeper impenetrability of spirit. Words launched 'like bolts' have no effect. Socrates might conceivably have abstained from sexual relations while remaining attentive to the lover in his particularity. He might also have had a sexual relationship with Alcibiades while remaining inwardly aloof. But Socrates refuses in every way to be affected. He is stone; and he also turns others to stone. Alcibiades is to his sight just one more of the beautifuls, a piece of the form, a pure thing like a jewel.

So the first problem for Alcibiades is that his own openness is denied. He is a victim of *hubris*, pierced, mocked, dishonored[56] (219C, 222B, D). This might have led Alcibiades to philosophy if he had been able to make Diotima's prudent judgments of similarity. But since he remains determined to care for Socrates' individuality, he remains harmed by Socrates' denial. This is, of course, just a story, and the story of a unique problem. It is the story of an especially vain man, a man whose love of honor and reputation is recognized even by him to be an obstacle to goodness of life. There are, furthermore, not many stones like Socrates, his *erōmenos*. But, there are, on the other hand, many varieties of stone. If there is, by luck, responsiveness on both sides now, still there may be change, estrangement bringing painful loss of knowledge. As even Diotima concedes before proposing the method of ascent that will try to remedy the problem, souls, with their thoughts, feelings, and desires, are no more stable than bodies. 'Our understandings come into being and pass away, and we are never the same even in our understandings, but every single understanding suffers this' (207E–208A). Even if there is rare stability in understanding and response, there will surely still be death to put an end to knowledge.

So happenings plague the lover; and we might begin to wonder how contingent these happenings are. But let us suppose, for a moment, that Alcibiades is involved in a mutually passionate love, in which both parties are lovers, each trying to explore the world that the openness of the other makes available. We want to know whether Diotima has reason to see personal *erōs* as, in its nature, a plague, or whether her criticisms work only against the unhappy cases, and speak only to those who either fear or are enmeshed in such experiences. Let us, then, imagine Alcibiades happy in love. Is he, then, in love, truly happy or good? The dialogue makes us wonder. No present fortune is guarantee of its own stability (cf. 200B–E). Therefore, as the dialogue indicates, fears, jealousies, and the threat of loss will be an intimate part of even the best experiences of loving. The playfully threatening banter between Socrates and Alcibiades, the mock violence that points to the real violence to come, are not necessarily to be read against the background of their estrangement. In the best of times such dangerous emotions could be summoned by the fear of the other's separateness. The attribution of value to an unstable external object brings internal instability of activity. There is a strong possibility that Alcibiades *wants* Socrates to be a statue – a thing that can be held, carried, or, when necessary, smashed. There is a possibility that this sort of intense love cannot tolerate, and wishes to end, autonomous movement. The sentimentalized lover of Greek erotic paintings greets the boy by affectionately touching him on face and genitals, indicating in this tender gesture respect and awe for his whole person.[57] The gesture of Alcibiades – the violent smashing of holy faces and genitals – may be, the dialogue suggests, a truer expression of unregenerate *erōs*.

There is also the equally troublesome possibility that it is precisely the stoniness of the other that attracts. The remote, round thing, gleaming like a form, undivided, lures with the promise of secret richness. It's nothing to open something that has a crack. But the perfect thing – if you could ever open that up, then you would be blessed and of unlimited power. Alcibiades loves the stone beauty that he finds: only that temperance is worthy of his pride, because only that cleverly eludes him. So, in yet another way, *erōs*, reaching for power, reaches towards its own immobility. When the light of Socrates 'appears all at once' for Alcibiades, it is the sort of light that, radiantly poured round the aspiring body, may seal or freeze it in, like a coat of ice. That is its beauty.

Furthermore, this happy lover, in loving a particular, loves a standing ground of conflict. For we have seen how Socrates' conception of all value as a homogeneous 'sea' defuses the most troublesome conflicts of value and also removes motives for akratic action. None of his choices is more troublesome than the choice between *n* measures of value and *n*+5 measures. Alcibiades (like Haemon), loving an irreplaceable and incommensurable object – and loving at the same time other distinct things such as honor and military excellence – may be confronted by the world with less tractable choices (cf. Ch. 3, Ch. 4, Ch. 5 §v, Ch. 7, p. 221).

All this leads us to ask most seriously whether personal *erōs* can have, after all, any place in a life that is to be shaped and ruled by practical reason. We tried to think of a life in which *erōs* would play its part along with other component goods – intellectual, political, social. But the nature of personal erotic passion may be such as to be always unstable, both internally and in relation to the lover's whole plan. It fills one part of a life with unstable and vulnerable activity; this, according to the *Republic*, would be sufficient to disqualify it from goodness. And it also threatens, when given a part, to overwhelm the whole. Aristophanes said that the erotic needs of his mythical creatures made them indifferent to eating, drinking, and 'all other pursuits'. We see Alcibiades' jealous passions making him indifferent to truth and goodness. Practical reason shapes a world of value. But the lover, as a lover, ascribes enormous importance to another world outside of his own and autonomous from it. It is not clear that the integrity of his own world can survive this, that he can continue in such circumstances to feel that he is a maker of a world at all.[58] To feel so great a commitment to and power from what is external to your practical reason can feel like slavery, or madness. Alcibiades compares himself to someone who is gripped by something and out of his senses (215C5, 215D5, 218B2–3). His soul is in a turmoil (215E6). He is angry at himself for his slavish condition (215E6). 'I had no resource', he concludes, 'and I went around in slavery to this man, such slavery as has never been before' (219E; cf. 217A1–2). The past is still actual (215D8, 217E6–7). To be a slave is to be without autonomy, unable to live by the plans of your own reason, perhaps unable even to form a plan. But not to do this is not to be fully human. It is no wonder that, as we look on the man who will live, to the end, a disorderly, buffeted life, inconstant and wasteful of his excellent nature, we are tempted to say, with Socrates: 'I shudder at his madness and passion for love' (213D6).

We now begin to understand Plato's strategy in constructing this dramatic confrontation. Through Aristophanes, he raises certain doubts in our minds concerning the erotic projects to which we are most attached. And yet the speech of Aristophanes still praises *erōs* as most necessary, and necessary for the success of practical reason itself. He then shows us, through Socrates and Diotima, how, despite our needy and mortal natures, we can transcend the merely personal in *erōs* and ascend, through desire itself, to the good. But we are not yet persuaded that we can accept this vision of self-sufficiency and this model of practical understanding, since, with Vlastos, we feel that they omit something. What they omit is now movingly displayed to us in the person and the story of Alcibiades. We realize, through him, the deep importance unique passion has for ordinary human beings; we see its irreplaceable contribution to understanding. But the story brings a further problem: it shows us clearly that we cannot simply add the love of Alcibiades to the ascent of Diotima; indeed, that we cannot have this love and the kind of stable rationality that she revealed to us. Socrates was serious when he spoke of two mutually exclusive varieties of vision.

And now, all at once, *exaiphnēs*, there dawns on us the full light of Plato's design, his comic tragedy of choice and practical wisdom. We see two kinds of value, two kinds of knowledge; and we see that we must choose. One sort of understanding blocks out the other. The pure light of the eternal form eclipses, or is eclipsed by, the flickering lightning of the opened and unstably moving body. You think, says Plato, that you can have this love and goodness too, this knowledge of and by flesh and good-knowledge too. Well, says Plato, you can't. You have to blind yourself to something, give up some beauty. 'The sight of reason begins to see clearly when the sight of the eyes begins to grow dim' – whether from age or because you are learning to be good.

But what, then, becomes of us, the audience, when we are confronted with the illumination of this true tragedy and forced to see everything? We are, Alcibiades tells us, the jury (219C). And we are also the accused. As we watch the trial of Socrates for the contemptuous overweening (*huperēphanias*, 219C5) of reason, which is at the same time the trial of Alcibiades for the contemptuous overweening of the body, we see what neither of them can fully see – the overweening of both. And we see that it is the way we must go if we are to follow either one or the other. But so much light can turn to stone. You have to refuse to see something, apparently, if you are going to act. I can choose to follow Socrates, ascending to the vision of the beautiful. But I cannot take the first step on that ladder as long as I *see* Alcibiades. I can follow Socrates only if, like Socrates, I am *persuaded* of the truth of Diotima's account; and Alcibiades robs me of this conviction. He makes me feel that in embarking on the ascent I am sacrificing a beauty; so I can no longer view the ascent as embracing the whole of beauty. The minute I think 'sacrifice' and 'denial', the ascent is no longer what it seemed, nor am I, in it, self-sufficient. I can, on the other hand, follow Alcibiades, making my soul a body. I can live in *erōs*, devoted to its violence and its sudden light. But once I have listened to Diotima, I see the loss of light that this course, too, entails – the loss of rational planning, the loss, we might say, of the chance to make a world. And then, if I am a rational being, with a rational being's deep need for order and for understanding, I feel that I *must* be false to *erōs*, for the world's sake.[59]

The *Symposium* now seems to us a harsh and alarming book. Its relation to the *Republic* and *Phaedo* is more ambiguous than we originally thought; for it does make a case for that conception of value, but it shows us also, all too clearly, how much that conception requires us to give up. It starkly confronts us with a choice, and at the same time it makes us see so clearly that we cannot choose anything. We see now that philosophy is not fully human; but we are terrified of humanity and what it leads to. It is *our* tragedy: it floods us with light and takes away action. As Socrates and Alcibiades compete for our souls, we become, like their object Agathon, beings without character, without choice. Agathon could stand their blandishments, because he had no soul to begin with. We did have souls, and we feel they are being turned to statues.

So they go their ways – Socrates, sleepless, to the city for an ordinary day of dialectic, Alcibiades to disorder and to violence. The confusion of the body conceals the soul of Alcibiades from our sight. He becomes from now on an anonymous member of the band of drunken revellers; we do not even know when he departs. The ambitions of the soul conceal the body of Socrates from his awareness. Just as drink did not make him drunk, cold did not make him freeze, and the naked body of Alcibiades did not arouse him, so now sleeplessness does not make him stop philosophizing. He goes about his business with all the equanimity of a rational stone. Meanwhile, the comic and tragic poets sleep together, tucked in by the cool hand of philosophy (223D). *Those* two – philosophy and poetry – cannot live together or know each other's truths, that's for sure. Not unless literature gives up its attachment to the particular and the vulnerable and makes itself an instrument of Diotima's persuasion. But that would be to leave its own truths behind.

Between one telling of the story and another, or perhaps during the second telling itself – and, for us (in us?) during the time we take to read and experience this work – Alcibiades has died. With him dies a hope that *erōs* and philosophy could live together in the city and so save it from disaster. This was, perhaps, Apollodorus's hope, his companion's hope. It was also ours. Plutarch tells us that the night before his death Alcibiades dreamed that he was dressed in women's clothes. A courtesan was holding his head and painting his face with makeup. In the soul of this proudly aggressive man, it is a dream that expresses the wish for unmixed passivity: the wish to lose the need for practical reason, to become a being who could live entirely in the flux of *erōs* and so avoid tragedy. But at the same time it is a wish to be no longer an erotic being; for what does not reach out to order the world does not love, and the self-sufficiency of the passive object is as unerotic as the self-sufficiency of the god. It is, we might say, a wish not to live in the world. After the arrow had killed him, the courtesan Timandra, 'Honor-the-Man', wrapped his bitten body and his soul of flesh in her own clothes and buried him sumptuously in the earth.

When Alcibiades finished speaking, they burst out laughing at the frankness of his speech, because it looked as though he was still in love with Socrates (222C). He stood there, perhaps, with ivy in his hair, crowned with violets.[60]

7 'This story isn't true': madness, reason, and recantation in the *Phaedrus*

We say indeed that the good man...will be especially sufficient unto himself
for good living, and above all other men will have least need of anyone
else...So then he will mourn least of all, and bear such things very calmly,
when some such occurrence comes his way...So we will be right if we take
laments away from distinguished men and give them over to women – and
to not very good women at that.

Plato, Republic 388A (c. 380–370 B.C.)

Tears were the portion that the Fates spun out
at birth for Hecuba and the Trojan women.
But you, Dion, had built a monument
of noble actions, when the gods spilled
your fair-flowing hopes upon the ground.
You lie there now, in the spacious earth
of your fatherland, praised by citizens. Dion,
you who drove my heart mad with love.[1]

Plato (353 B.C.)

'My dear friend Phaedrus', calls Socrates. 'Where are you going? And where do you come from?' So begins this self-critical and questioning dialogue. Socrates has just caught sight of this impressive young person, whose name means 'Sparkling', and who is clearly radiant with health, good looks, and ability. (And perhaps, catching sight of him, he is struck as if by a 'stream of beauty entering in through his eyes'. Perhaps he feels both warmed and inundated, filled at once with eagerness and awe.[2]) He wants to engage Phaedrus in conversation. He follows him. Phaedrus (who appears so far to be cheerfully unmoved) answers that he has come from talking with Lysias, the son of Cephalus. (We are reminded of *Republic* I, with its stern warning against the 'mad' influence of the passions. Lysias's speech to Phaedrus will be continuous with his father's sane advice.) He is going from the urban house where he has been conversing with Lysias to take a walk, for the sake of his health, outside the city walls, in what we shall see to be a place of burgeoning sensuous beauty. It is also a dangerous place: a place where a pure young girl was carried off by the impassioned wind god, where the mad god Pan (son of Hermes, god of luck) has his shrine, where the traveler risks possession by the power of *erōs* at the hottest hour of the day. In this same way, some important features of Plato's thought, and writing, seem to have left the *Republic*'s city house and to be moving in the direction of greater wildness, sensuousness, and vulnerability. We must ask Socrates' question of Plato: where does he come from here? And where is he going?

We begin with certain facts about the distance traveled.

In the *Republic* and *Phaedo*, the appetites and emotions, particularly sexual feeling and emotion, were held to be unsuitable guides for human action. Only the intellect can reliably guide a human being towards the good and valuable. Nor does the conception of the best human life there ascribe any intrinsic value to the activities associated with these elements. In particular, lasting erotic relationships between individuals are not constituent parts of this life. In the *Symposium*, which develops this picture further, Plato offers us a stark choice: on the one hand, the life of Alcibiades, the person 'possessed' by the 'madness' of personal love; on the other, a life in which the intellectual soul ascends to true insight and stable contemplation by denying the 'mad' influence of personal passion. Alcibiades' madness is, allegedly, incompatible with rational order and stability; its vision is a barrier to correct vision. The life of the philosopher achieves order, stability, and insight at the price of denying the sight of the body and the value of individual love. In the *Phaedrus*, however, philosophy itself is said to be a form of madness or *mania*, of possessed, not purely intellectual activity, in which intellect is guided to insight by personal love itself and by a complex passion-engendered ferment of the entire personality. Certain sorts of madness are not only not incompatible with insight and stability, they are actually necessary for the highest sort of insight and the best kind of stability. Erotic relationships of long duration between particular individuals (who see each other as such) are argued to be fundamental to psychological development and an important component of the best human life.

In the *Republic*, Socrates makes a sharp distinction between poetry and philosophy. He attacks poetry for 'nourishing' the irrational parts of the soul through both its morally dubious content and its exciting style. Repudiating the poet's claim to illuminate the truth, he contrasts that person's cognitive deficiency with the philosopher's wisdom. In the *Symposium*, we see a style that claims to tell the truth through stories and by the use of images. This style (linked with both tragic and comic poetry) is the style of the erotic madman, and its claim to truth is rejected by the philosopher along with Alcibiades' claim. In the *Phaedrus*, the highest human life is described as one devoted to either philosophical or muse-honoring activities. Poetry inspired by 'madness' is defended as a gift of the gods and a valuable educational resource; non-mad styles are condemned as retentive, lacking in insight. The style of Socratic philosophizing now fuses argument with poetry; Socrates presents his deepest philosophical insights in poetic language, in the form of a 'likeness'.

In the *Phaedrus*, Socrates covers his head in shame and delivers a stern prose discourse (modelled on the speech written for Phaedrus by his suitor, the successful orator Lysias) which attacks erotic passion as a form of degrading madness, and characterizes the passions as mere urges for bodily replenishment, with no role to play in our understanding of the good. Then, uncovering his head, he recants, offering (to a Phaedrus newly shaken by the power of feeling) a defense of the benefits of madness. This recantation begins with a poetic quotation. Socrates recites the Palinode of Stesichorus, who slandered Helen of Troy and, struck blind for his insult, composed these verses to regain his sight:

> This story isn't true.
> You did not embark on the well-benched ships.
> You did not come to the citadel of Troy.

What are the connections among these suggestive facts? I shall argue that the *Phaedrus* displays a new view of the role of feeling, emotion, and particular love in the good life, and that this change of view is explored inside the dialogue itself: Plato embodies important features of his own earlier view in the first two speeches, and then both 'recants' and criticizes those speeches. All this is given special immediacy by being set in the context of Phaedrus's personal erotic choice. And the conclusion about the passions will prove to have implications, as well, for Plato's understanding of the role of poetry and of the connections between poetry and philosophy.

There are, then, striking resemblances between the doctrine of Socrates' first speech (together with the speech of Lysias that inspires it) and certain views seriously defended by Socrates in middle-period dialogues. The recantation is a serious recantation of something that Plato has seriously endorsed; the prevailing opinion that finds the two early speeches degraded and disgusting has failed to appreciate their force. They will prove to merit the attention of an aspiring young person of Phaedrus's talent and beauty. But one reason why they have been lightly regarded is that Socrates himself explicitly expresses his shame and disgust. He utters them under a kind of compulsion and quickly recants, claiming that what they said was neither healthy nor true (242C). What, then, within the context itself, could persuade us to think of them as serious competitors for Socrates' own allegiance?

First, respect for their author. I do not believe that Plato ever criticizes a straw man, or that he would spend so much time on a position that he finds self-evidently worthless (or, for that matter, on an interlocutor who is deeply drawn to a self-evidently worthless view). But there is also more concrete evidence. The speeches are criticized above all for their *naïveté* (*euētheia*, 242D7, E5). This is an odd thing to say about a view one thinks to be cynical, debased, and altogether without interest. Second, and more telling, Socrates claims that it was his *daimonion*, his divine sign, that prompted the recantation. The *daimonion* is a serious individual who intercedes infrequently to 'hold back' Socrates when he is about to undertake something wrong (*Phdr.* 242C, cf. *Apol.* 31D). Even making allowances for Socratic irony, we would not expect it to intervene if Socrates were merely role-playing, in no way genuinely tempted to the wrong view. A further indication of seriousness is provided by the fact that Socrates depicts his first speech as inspired by certain Muses. Not, to be sure, the Pan, Nymphs, and other gods of wild nature who guide his later discourse (cf. 279B–C, 262D, 263D–E), but

Muses of the 'Ligurian' or 'Clear-voiced' variety. We might understand these to be the muses of the clear and healthy rationalism to which Phaedrus is now attracted; they might also be the muses of the middle dialogues. As Hackforth points out, the presence of Muses here 'creates a real difficulty' for those who are inclined to be dismissive of the first speech.

Finally, a strange feature of the first speech itself, not readily explicable on the assumption that it is intended as merely worthless, gives us a hint about its relationship to the speech that follows. This speech denouncing *erōs*, like the later speech of recantation, is said to be the speech of a man in love to his beloved boy. This lover, however, here pretends that he is not in love, and speaks slandering *erōs*, urging his beloved not to yield to a lover's importunities (237B). This strange piece of byplay is explained by Hackforth as a sign that the speaker is motivated by real concern for the boy's welfare. 'In fact, we get a glimpse of the *erastēs* par excellence, Socrates himself.'[3] This promising suggestion can be pressed much further if we take the content of the speech more seriously than Hackforth has, as the expression of a real Platonic view. Here we have a lover who tells us, apparently seriously, that *erōs* is a madness and a disease: anyone for whom he cares should avoid its grip and seek to live in reason with reasonable people. It would not be difficult to view the ascetic arguments of the middle dialogues as the speech of such a lover, a lover convinced that, in order to lead towards the good both himself and his readers, he must not only attack the passions but also pretend that he himself is not a humanly erotic personality. He might even decide to adopt the *persona* of Socrates, who was impervious to drink, to cold, to the naked body of Alcibiades. In fact, speaking through this same Socrates, Plato has told us in *Republic* x that a person in love, if he believes that *erōs* is not good for him, will continually rehearse to himself the arguments against *erōs* as a 'countercharm' against its spell. Even so, Plato continues, a lover of poetry should rehearse to himself the arguments against this form of madness – unless and until a defender of poetry should convince him 'in prose without meter, and show that it is not only delightful, but also beneficial to orderly government and all of human life' (*Rep.* 607D–608B).

The *Phaedrus*, I shall argue, is this *apologia* – both for *erōs* and (with qualifications) for poetic writing – following upon some of the most powerful countercharms a philosopher and lover has ever composed. We have sensed all along that Plato has a deep understanding of erotic motivation and its power. The *Phaedrus* would then be a work in which he works out a more complex view of these motivations and accepts some of them as good; a work in which he admits that he has been blind to something, conceived oppositions too starkly; where he seeks, through recantation and self-critical argument, to get back his sight.

I

This is a dialogue about madness, or *mania*. The first two speeches – the speech composed by Lysias and the first speech of Socrates – denounce it, praising rational self-possession, or *sōphrosunē*. The second speech of Socrates argues that *mania* is not, as has been said, a 'simple evil': indeed, it can be a source of the highest goods. This dialogue, furthermore, is a dialogue whose characters go mad. Socrates, for the only time in his life, leaves, his accustomed urban haunts. Following beautiful Phaedrus, he walks to a green place outside the city walls and lies down on the grass by the bank of a flowing stream. He describes himself as 'possessed' by the influence of Phaedrus and the place.[4] Phaedrus, too, yields to the influence of beauty and is moved by wonder (257C). From having been the critical and rationalistic 'speaker' of Socrates' first speech (244A), he becomes the loving and yielding boy to whom the manic second speech is spoken (243E, cf. below). In order to understand what is going on here, and how it is all related to Plato's earlier views, we must, then, go into the question of madness, asking where and on what grounds it was too simply blamed, and how it finds its way back into the good life.

What is madness or possession? Consistently, in pre-*Phaedrus* dialogues,[5] Plato has used '*mania*' and related words to designate the state of soul in which the non-intellectual elements – appetites and emotions – are in control and lead or guide the intellectual part. Consistently, as here, *mania* is contrasted with *sōphrosunē*, the state of soul in which intellect rules securely over the other elements. It is linked particularly with the dominance of erotic appetite.[6] The mad person, then, is one who is in the sway of inner forces that eclipse or transform, for a time at least, the calculations and valuations of pure intellect. The insights of *mania* will be reached not by the measuring, counting, and reckoning of the *logistikon*,[7] but by non-discursive processes less perfectly transparent to the agent's awareness and possibly more difficult to control. He or she is led to action on the basis of feeling and response, by complex receptivity rather than by pure intellectual activity. Even after the fact he may be unable to produce the sort of explicit account that subsumes the action under systematic general principles and definitions. An example of the erotic mad person would be Alcibiades (cf. 215C–E, 213D6, 218B2–3), whose account of his actions is a story concerned with particulars, packed with expressions of and appeals to feeling and emotion. What the *Phaedrus* will be saying, in effect, is that it was over-simple and unfair to use Alcibiades to stand for all mad people: that a lover can deliberate in a mad way without being bad and disorderly in life and choice.

Clearly the pre-*Phaedrus* dialogues do attack *mania* as a 'simple evil', a state of the person that cannot lead to genuine insight and one that, more often than not, produces bad actions.[8] *Mania* is called a species of viciousness at *Republic* 400B2 (cf. *Meno* 91C3, *Rep.* 382C8). In a number of passages it is linked with excessive appetite-gratification, or wantonness (*hubris*, *Rep.* 400B2, 403; *Crat.* 404A4). It is linked with delusion, folly, and the 'death' of true opinion in *Republic* 539C6, 573A–B (cf. 382E2, *Tim.* 86B4, Ps.-Pl. *Def.* 416A22); with the condition of slavery at *Rep.* 329C, *Symp.* 215C–E. And this is not merely a verbal point. For it is unequivocally the view of the *Republic* that any state in which the non-intellectual elements dominate or guide will be characterized, no matter what we call it, by the defects of *mania*: the loss of true insight and a tendency towards excess. The passage about dreaming in Book IX told us, for example, that when the *logistikon* is lulled to sleep the 'bestial' elements will take over and attempt to satisfy their 'own instincts', 'released and let off from all shame and good sense' (571C). Dreams can bring truth *only* if the dreamer can contrive to make them the work of the *logistikon* alone. Before sleep, he or she must lull the other parts so that they 'may not disturb the better part by pleasure and pain, but may suffer that in isolated purity to examine and reach out towards and apprehend some of the things unknown to it, past, present, or future' (571D–572B; cf. *Phd.* 65A–D). It should be stressed that true insight, here, is attained by making the intellect purely active, impervious to influence from outside; forms of passivity or receptivity, like the feelings of pleasure and pain, are held, here as in the *Phaedo*, to be invariably distorting.

This denial of all cognitive value to the non-intellectual elements is not surprising, given Plato's general view of appetition and emotion in middle-period works, as we have set it out in Chapter 5. The *Republic*, we recall, argued that the appetites are merely brute forces reaching out, insatiably and without any selectivity, each for a characteristic object. Such unteachable forces could not be indices of the good. Emotions, though somewhat more responsive to education, require continual control by intellect, and are always potentially dangerous. Genuine insight can therefore best be achieved by a thoroughgoing disengagement of intellect from the rest of the personality; it should go off, pure and clear, itself by itself.[9]

The first two speeches in the *Phaedrus* operate with the dichotomy of the *Republic* and *Symposium*: the boy must choose, simply, between good sense and madness, between good control by intellect and a disorderly lack of control. The speech of Lysias urges the fictional boy (and the speaker urges the real Phaedrus)[10] to give himself sexually, not to the person who is in love with him, but to the person who is not in love with him.* It supports this advice with an argument that contrasts the irrational state of the person in love with the *sōphrosunē* of the person who is not in love: people in love, being 'sick' rather than self-possessed (*sōphronein*), reason badly and cannot control themselves (231D). Lysias the person-who-is-not-in-love, by contrast, is 'not overthrown by love, but in control of myself' (233C); he acts not under passional compulsion but, he says, voluntarily (*hekōn*, 231A) – as if, among the parts of oneself, only the *logistikon* is the author of genuinely voluntary actions, while the other elements are unselective causal forces. The more detailed analysis of the person that is carried out in Socrates' first speech, a speech that introduces itself as an account of the principles of good deliberation (237B7), makes it clear to us that the view in question is strikingly similar to the view of the middle dialogues. There are, Socrates argues, two ruling

---

* The Greek calls these two people *ho erōn* and *ho mē erōn*, 'the person in a condition of *erōs*' and 'the person who is not in a condition of *erōs*'. Hackforth translates, 'the lover' and 'the non-lover'; this is certainly less cumbersome, but (today at any rate) misleading. It is clear that what the *mē erōn* wants is to be the boy's *lover*, in the sexual sense, without being *in love* with him. I shall therefore use the briefer expressions only when the point is absolutely clear.

principles in a human being: 'innate appetite for pleasures' and 'acquired belief about the good'. The state of the person in which belief about the good is in control is called *sōphrosunē*.* The state in which the appetite that draws us towards pleasure is in control is called, simply, *hubris* or wantonness (237D–238A). *Hubris* is said to be 'many-named: for it is many-limbed and many-parted' (238A). (We are reminded of the 'many-headed beast' of *Republic* IX.) When the appetite for food is in control, that is gluttony; when the appetite for drink is in control, drunkenness. *Erōs* is finally defined as the state in which the unreasoning appetite for the sensuous enjoyment of bodily beauty has gained control over true opinion. As with food and drink, it is simply assumed that this is an altogether bad state. Accordingly, in the rest of the speech, the person in love is treated as a 'sick' person in the grip of a 'mindless (*anoētou*) ruling principle' (241A8), 'mindless out of necessity' (241B7). The ex-lover, by contrast, is said to have acquired 'insight (*nous*) and self-possession (*sōphrosunē*) in place of *erōs* and *mania*' (241A). Clarity and true insight require the death of passion. The sane person feels only shame about his former *erōs*-inspired actions.

We can see that this speech succinctly reproduces four central claims of the *Republic* concerning madness and the non-intellectual elements:

(1) The appetites, including the sexual appetite, are blind animal forces reaching out each for a particular object – e.g. food, drink, sex – without either incorporating or being responsive to judgment about the good.[11]

(2) The non-intellectual elements, when in control, tend naturally to excess. (Any state ruled by such an element deserves the name of *hubris*.)

(3) The non-intellectual elements can never, even in a well-trained person, perform a cognitive function, guiding the person towards insight and understanding of the good. They are 'mindless', invariably sources of danger and distortion.

(4) The *logistikon* is a leading element both necessary and sufficient for the apprehension of truth and for right choice. It works better the freer it is from the influence of the other elements. In other words, intellectual purity and clarity is a fundamental prerequisite of genuine insight; sufficiently cultivated it is sufficient for this insight.

Both Lysias and the speaker of Socrates' first speech give the boy moral advice. Briefly put, it is the advice of Diotima and of the *Republic*: cultivate in yourself the state of self-possession, *sōphrosunē*. Develop the clarity of your intellect by exercising strict control over bestial non-intellectual elements. Form only non-mad friendships, and only with other self-possessed, non-mad people. Lysias's speech adds the explicit advice to give yourself sexually to the self-possessed person; this

---

* The language of Socrates' first speech brings it into close connection with the middle dialogues at many points. The definition of *sophrosune* as the state in which reason rules securely over the other elements is the definition of *Republic* IV (431B, 442C–D). The disorderly state is in both cases called a *stasis* or civil war of the soul, and is opposed to a concord (442D1, 237E). The necessity to know 'the being of each thing' at the outset of an inquiry, asking concerning *erōs* 'what sort of thing it is and what power (*dunamin*) it has', so that we can 'look to it' in asking further questions, is a typical Platonic demand couched in language familiar from the *Republic* and other related dialogues (cf. for example *Rep.* 354B–C, 358B). The imagery of appetite 'ruling' and 'tyrannizing' is common in *Republic* I and IX.

advice is not made explicit in Socrates' speech. We shall have more to say about this point, which might seem to tell against our claim that this represents an earlier Platonic view. But now we need to enter more deeply into the world of these two speeches, and this for two reasons. First, because they have usually been so flatly denounced, even by people who view with sympathy the arguments of the middle dialogues. Hackforth, for example, speaks harshly of the 'cold prudential calculation' of the Lysian speaker, his obliviousness to 'romantic sentiment'.[12] This places on us a responsibility to show that, intuitively and on their own terms (not only in comparison with the *Republic*) these speeches offer advice that is plausible and appealing. Second, because this dialogue is, after all, the story of Phaedrus. We are trying to understand his moral development, what choices he faces in his efforts to be rational. The first two speeches embody a moral view to which this able young person is deeply attracted. In fact, Socrates tells us explicitly that we are to view his first speech as a speech *of* or *by* Phaedrus (244A); by this he means, we suppose, that it expresses Phaedrus's current view, what he would say right now if asked to give himself advice. Before we can understand how and on what grounds Phaedrus leaves this view behind, accepting the Socratic recantation, we must, then, do more to show the power of the first view for a certain sort of aspiring young person. We must, in other words, ask ourselves who Phaedrus is.[13]

We must imagine a small city, in which the most able adult citizens all devote their careers to the city's political and cultural life. These leading citizens all know one another and must continue to see and work with one another throughout their adult lives. We now imagine a gifted and ambitious young man beginning a career in this milieu. (Socrates calls him a son of Pythocles, so his whole name becomes 'Sparkling, Son of Man of Pythian Fame'; this otherwise unknown patronymic, like other names in the context, is likely to be a significant fiction, indicating a connection with civic renown.[14]) He is attractive as well as talented. He is sexually inclined towards men of the next older generation, and they are, almost all of them, inclined towards men of his generation. On the verge of an exciting career, surrounded by attractive possibilities (cf. 237B3, where the boy is said to have 'a very large number' of suitors for his favors), he must now decide what sorts of personal relationships he wants to cultivate. And he must consider the implications of this choice for his future in the city.

Although I shall continue to describe the situation using Plato's chosen milieu and characters, I think it will help us to have a sense of the force of Lysias's advice if we imagine the analogous choices faced by a young woman entering a male-dominated profession in which she knows she will be spending the rest of her life. For in our culture it is clearly (in terms of the numbers) such a woman who is most likely to be in Phaedrus's sexual position, more or less surrounded by potential 'suitors' who are more powerful and more established than she is. Such a woman would want to live a full personal life; but she would be seriously concerned, at the same time, to protect her clarity and autonomy, her chance to live and work on reasonable and non-threatening terms with the people with whom she works. Now imagine that the profession is the whole city: everyone she knows is, of necessity, a colleague. There are no other choices. If we imagine what a concerned feminist would say to such a young woman (or what she would say to herself) we will be on the way to understanding what is serious about Lysias. Hackforth and other critics who speak of romance live in a world in which romance naturally terminates in the devotion of the less established female party to the professional ends of the more established male party. This helps them to miss the depth of Phaedrus's dilemma.

The first two speeches tell this young man that, in his search for political, social, and intellectual standing, he must above all protect himself from emotional turmoil and emotional domination. He must remain independent, clear, self-possessed; free internally from psychological conflict, externally from the influence of a 'mad' lover. If he is going to have any sexual relationships at all (and, as we noticed, the first speech of Socrates omits this positive advice) he should certainly avoid the person who is in love with him. The madness of love is unpredictable and dangerous. The person in love does not judge clearly. He will be bad for Phaedrus's career because he will advise him in a way distorted by self-interest and jealous longing. He will be both indiscreet and possessive, preventing the growth of other advantageous friendships. He may even subtly discourage the younger person from excelling because this will keep him more dependent. Transported by passion, this lover so dreads the young person's separateness that he can neither correctly see nor kindly nourish his character and his deepest aspirations. And when the affair ends there will be shame, regret, and even hostility. It will be hard for the two of them to be friends or to see each other calmly in the course of daily life. In short, a person gripped by love, loving out of mad passion and deep need, will prove incapable of genuine kindness and friendliness. He can bring nothing but risk and damage to the person who is involved with him.[15]

On the other side we have the person who is not in love. (And we must remember that it is he who has just given us this description of the person in love.) Let us call him Lysias, son of Cephalus. (It would not be hard to imagine Cephalus offering his son similar advice.) Lysias, we know, is a successful, established man; a prominent defender of democratic freedoms who will soon become famous for his courageous opposition to the oligarchs; an orator renowned for his clarity and simple lucidity.[16] He is urbane, critical, and charming. He prefers a city house to country walks. He sees life very clearly. He dislikes grandiose speeches. Suspicious of powerful emotion, in himself and in others, he is sane, kind, and decent. He offers Phaedrus a well-controlled sensual friendship. If Phaedrus rationally chooses to become involved with him, neither of them will ever see the world differently because of it. Neither of them will 'become someone else', an outcome that Lysias fears and scorns. The affair will be pleasant, full of mutual good will and benefit. Most important, it will enable both of them to preserve autonomy and honesty. And Lysias deeply prides himself on his honesty. (He claims to see and judge Phaedrus without envy, jealousy, passion, or selfish interest.) We see his conception of objectivity in the spare, chaste prose style, pruned of every emotional indulgence, every appeal to feeling through metaphor and rhythm. The message of this style is that rationality is something crisp and cerebral, something of the *logistikon* alone.* With a man like this, Phaedrus can trust that no deep changes or upsets will occur. He will be able to see him for the rest of his life in the market or at meetings, without shame, jealousy, or anger. He will never feel like running away.

Phaedrus, then, seems to be confronted with two starkly defined alternatives: the beneficent detachment of Lysias, the dangerous passion of the mad lover. What choice will he make? He is himself a lucid man, a man attached to the ideal of health and control. He exercises with unusual zeal and worries about the details of his personal bodily regime (227A). It is not surprising that such a young man should fear the person in love and paint for himself in thought and speech a devastating portrait of that sort of madness. Nor is it surprising that a young vulnerable person concerned with fame and autonomy should find Lysias's proposal attractive. We do not need to ask how most feminists would advise a female Phaedrus; and we know that, given a certain picture of the person in love, a picture that is true a good part of the time, they would be right. As Socrates puts it, lovers love boys – the way wolves love lambs (241A). That's a good reason for the lambs to protect themselves as well as possible.

This may appear to have taken us rather far from the ascetic ideal of the *Phaedo*. For here, although there is a related attack on *erōs*, there is also, at least in Lysias's speech, the advice to have a sexual relationship with the person who is not in

---

* The continuing controversy about whether this speech was actually written by the historical Lysias testifies to the shrewdness of Plato's stylistic portrayal (cf. Hackforth *ad loc.*). It is difficult to get from a translation the proper impression of his style, which was famous for simplicity, clarity, and avoidance of feeling. J. F. Dobson, in the article 'Lysias' in the *Oxford Classical Dictionary*: 'Lysias, by his exceptional mastery of idiom, turned the spoken language of everyday life into a literary medium unsurpassed for its simplicity and precision... He avoids rare and poetical words, striking metaphors, and exaggerated phrases, with the result that at times he may seem to lose in force what he gains in smoothness. His blameless style and unimpassioned tones may seem monotonous to some readers... Even when his own personal feelings are deeply concerned he is always moderate.' With these general facts in mind, listen to a few excerpts from the Platonic Lysias (my revision of Hackforth):

> You know how I am situated, and I have told you that I think it is to our advantage that this should happen. Now I claim that I should not be refused what I ask simply because I am not in love with you... Again, a man who is in love is bound to be seen and heard by many people, following his boy around and acting obsessed with him. So whenever they are seen talking together everyone thinks they have either just been in bed or are just going off to bed. With a couple who are not in love, nobody even thinks of this when they are seen together. They know that a man has to have someone to talk to for friendship and entertainment.... And observe this: a man in love usually wants to enjoy your body before he has gotten to know your character or anything about you. This makes it unclear whether he will still want to be your friend when his desire has gone... And now I think I have said enough. If you want anything more or think I have left anything out, let me know.

These bits convey the flavor of the style; the whole speech is, in general, very well done by Hackforth, though here, as we would expect, his choices sound more dated than they do in the rest of the dialogue. The frequent emphasis on the 'clear' and the 'necessary', the general crispness and contemporaneity of the diction, and the repeated use of expressions like 'again' (*eti dē*) and 'and observe this' (*kai dē kai*) are well-known hallmarks of Lysias's style.

love. It is true that this advice is not given in the *Phaedo*. But the *Republic* requires non-passionate sex for purposes of procreation. And Book VIII allows intercourse 'up to the point of health and well-being' – which, given the extreme restrictions attached to procreative sex, almost certainly permits some comfortable and non-passionate homosexual relations.[17] In any case, the distance between abstinence and Lysian sex is not as great as it might seem. The crucial point is that in neither case does the person go mad. There is no deep arousal and ferment of all parts of the personality together, such as we shall see depicted in the defense of *mania*. There is, instead, a friendly agreement to enjoy, in a closely controlled way, a bodily pleasure. Lysias insists that this pleasure never threatens the person's self-control and coolness of vision. Having sex in this spirit might be, for some people, a very good way precisely of distancing oneself from its power and gaining intellectual control. This is likely to be what *Republic* VIII means by 'up to the point of health and well-being'.[18] We need only to recall the prevailing Greek cultural ideal of the self-sufficient *erōmenos* (Ch. 6) in order to become convinced that Phaedrus's sexual life with the Lysian suitor, chosen out of just such an interest in health and self-sufficiency, would be, as far as passion goes, appropriately closed and non-erotic.[19] The difference between this view and the ascetic view of the *Phaedo* is only a difference about means: about whether it is easier to remain intellectually calm by having sex in this non-erotic way, or by abstaining. The answer to that question may vary with the individual, the culture, the time of life: the condemnation of passion remains constant.

We know that Phaedrus will not long remain a devotee of anti-erotic argument. He will soon, in fact, be deeply moved by a speech that attacks Lysias's condemnation of the lover's madness. And it is pretty clear that in the end he will not accept Lysias's offer. So our picture of Phaedrus is not complete. We must add to it the observation that non-erotic purity, attractive though it in one way is, already fails to satisfy him. Now we remember his attraction to the wilder country outside the city walls. It is true that he admires the clear purity of the stream, so suitable for the play of young girls (229B). But he also loves to go barefoot, to get his feet wet; and he rather seductively mentions to Socrates that if they like they can lie down, instead of sitting, on the grass (229B1–2). All this hints at responses and tendencies that are absent from the speech of his thoroughly urban suitor. He excuses this love of the country by mentioning his doctor's orders (227A); but we see enough to suspect, at least, that he longs for madness even as he wards it off, reciting and admiring the 'countercharms' that depict it as a 'simple evil'. And as he accepts Socrates' carefully chosen words of praise for Lysias's speech – 'lucid', 'economical', 'precise and well-crafted' (234E) – he seems to acknowledge already that this elegant and reasonable man lacks access, both in his work and in his human relationships, to sources of creative energy for which the younger man obscurely yearns. For when Socrates playfully suggests that Phaedrus is inspired and awestruck by Lysias's speech, Phaedrus recognizes immediately that this can only be a joke (234C). Such emotions (fundamental, as he will soon grant, to the soul's growth) are not and could not be awakened by this non-mad person, who begins to look retentive and ungenerous.

At the brightest and hottest hour of the day,[20] Socrates finishes his speech against *erōs*. Although Phaedrus tries to convince him to stay and discuss it further, he starts to leave. But it is at this point, as he is crossing the river, that his *daimonion* stops him, forbidding him to leave until he has atoned for his speech, which was both naïve and blasphemous (242B–C). 'If *erōs* is a god or a divine being, as indeed he is, he cannot be something bad; but these two speeches spoke of him as if he were bad. In this way they missed the mark concerning *erōs*' (242E). This claim, we notice, is in direct contradiction to the view of Diotima, who made a great point of denying the divinity of *erōs*.[21] Something is happening. Socrates has to 'purify' himself (243A) by recanting the view that made so much of purity.[22] It is at this point that he recites the Palinode of Stesichorus, applying its 'This story isn't true' to his own first speech and implying that he, like the poet, needs to recover his sight. The speech that follows, as he shortly tells us, finds him speaking in a new persona. Whereas the first speech was the speech 'of Phaedrus a Murrhinousian man', the second will be the speech 'of Stesichorus, son of Euphemus, from Himera' (244A). The names are significant. Euphemus, 'reverent in speech', is clearly connected with the second speech's respectful treatment of *erōs*, against which the earlier speeches had blasphemed (242E–243B). The earlier speeches are now called a slander (*kakēgoria*, 243A6); this one, by contrast, finds Socrates in a state of 'fear and shame before the divinity of *erōs*'. And the pious speech is at the same time the work of a poet, 'Stesichorus', and of a man from Himera – from a place which (the word for passionate, desire – usually for a present object – being '*himeros*') might well be called Desire Town or Passionville.[23] Socrates tells us, then (by the use of a poetic figure of speech) that the reverent speech will be the speech of a poet and a needy lover; and, furthermore, that he is now that lover. He hints that the object of his love is not far away.

This lover is speaking, like the person-not-in-love, to a boy; in this case it is the boy whom he loves. Socrates, assuming the lover's persona, now needs to find a suitably responsive addressee. 'Where', he asks, 'is the boy to whom I was speaking? I want him to hear this speech too, so that he won't run off, through failure to listen, and give himself to the person who is not in love' (243E). The boy who accepts this speech, he implies, will be changed. He asks whether there is a boy who is willing to receive it. The reply is, I think, among the most haunting and splendid moments in philosophy. Phaedrus, the brilliant, self-protective boy, the admirer of the non-lover, answers, simply, 'He is here, quite close beside you, whenever you want him.'

I say that this moment of yielding is a moment in philosophy. I certainly do not say that it is a moment in the literary trimming surrounding the philosophy. Nor, clearly, does Plato. For it is the genius of Plato's philosophical writing to show us here the intertwining of thought with action, of the experience of love with philosophical speech about love, of the philosophical defense of passion with a personal acknowledgment of openness and receptivity. If these characters can bear to experience passion as they do, it is in part because they dare to think and argue as they do, because philosophical speech shows them ways of looking at the world. If, on the other hand, they speak philosophically as they do, it is, too, because they are here lying beside one another as they are, on this grass beside the river, willing to go mad; and this madness leads them to a new view of the philosophical truth. It would be futile, and also perhaps unimportant, to try to say precisely whether experience or thought came first, so thoroughly do they interpenetrate here, illuminating one another. Their entire lives become ways of searching for wisdom; and part of their argument for the new view of madness comes from within their lives. So even within the dialogue and from the viewpoint of its characters, the separation between this moment and philosophical thinking cannot be made. On the level of authorship, furthermore, Plato, who displays to us this fusion of life and argument shows us thereby something serious that is certainly, for him, a deep part of the truth and therefore itself a part of his philosophy. And suppose, as I shall later suggest, this fusion is also a part of Plato's life; suppose he wrote about passion here out of a particular experience of his own. Would this make the *Phaedrus* less philosophical? Surely not. Perhaps more philosophical, if the more philosophical is that which is a deeper part of a thinker's committed search for truth and value, that for which his or her choices, as well as words, constitute the argument.

As we continue to consider the larger design of the dialogue, we now notice yet another way in which it revises the world of the *Symposium*. Stesichorus had told the story believed by everyone, according to which Helen was seduced by Paris and went off adulterously to Troy, causing trouble for everyone. In the Palinode he apologizes to Helen by creating a myth about her, a story that says that all during the war she was instead living peacefully and piously in Egypt. We can now see that the *Phaedrus* as a whole has the form of this Palinode. It has long been observed that a number of internal indications require us to place the dialogue's dramatic date between 411 and 404.[24] But an inscription discovered in this century now shows us that there is a problem about doing this. Phaidros Murrhinousios, this very Phaedrus, was implicated, along with Alcibiades, in the mutilation of the Herms and the profanation of the mysteries; he was forced to go into exile from the city between the years 415 and 404.[25] It is thus historically impossible that Phaedrus should really have been in Athens during this time.

We might take refuge in the claim that Plato does not care for consistency: the setting is an impossible fairy-tale *mélange*.[26] But, given the notoriety of the events and the precision with which Plato dates the dialogue, there is another possibility that deserves to be advanced, at least as a conjecture. In the light of history, we might see the *Phaedrus* as Plato's own Egypt-legend. That story wasn't true. You did not get led into disorder and impiety through your appetitive passions, your devotion to *mania*. You did not have to go into exile. All the time, in spite of appearances, here you were at Athens, living a good and orderly life, *and* living a good life without closing off the influence of *erōs*. Instead of mutilating the holy statues of Hermes, you were saying a reverent prayer at the shrine of Pan, his son (cf. *Cratylus* 407–408). *Erōs* and its madness are not the simple causes of confusion and impiety that we suggested when we used the story of Alcibiades to stand for *mania* in general. We reopen the case. (Recall the judicial metaphors at the end of the *Symposium*.)

'This story isn't true', of course, in the literal historical sense. Alcibiades and Phaedrus *were* both forced into exile. Probably Stesichorus also continued to believe, as his contemporaries did, in the literal historical truth of the received story of the Trojan war. But Plato's Phaedrus-legend and Stesichorus's Egypt-legend attack the deep moral that has been drawn from the stories of Helen and Alcibiades. They claim that, although perhaps literally false, their stories will express, metaphorically, a deeper truth about *erōs*: that it can be a constituent of an orderly and pious life dedicated to understanding of the good.

II

Socrates now begins his second speech, his head uncovered. Madness, he declares, is not, as we had said, a simple evil. The two speeches[27] had operated with a simple dichotomy between *mania* and *sōphrosunē*, treating the former as entirely a bad thing, the latter as entirely good (244A). But in fact neither of these claims is correct. Some kinds of madness can be responsible for 'the greatest of goods for us' (244A); and in some circumstances self-possession can result in narrowness of vision. An irrationally inspired prophetess can accomplish much good for the country, a self-possessed one 'little or nothing' (244B). The inspired kind of divination is 'more perfect and more honorable' that the divination 'of reasonable men' (*tōn emphronōn*), which works 'through discursive reasoning' (*ek dianoias*).[28] Similarly, the poet who is truly possessed and mad can instruct the tender soul of a young person, making it join the bacchic revels; without this madness 'he is imperfect, and he and his poetry, being that of a self-possessed (*sōphronountos*) person, are eclipsed by the work of people who are mad' (245A). Finally, Socrates applies these observations to the case of *erōs*: the 'transported' (*kekinēmenos*) friend or lover (*philos*)[29] should be preferred to the self-possessed (*sōphrōn*, 245B). What follows will be, it is said, a 'demonstration' of the truth of these claims.

There is little doubt that something new is here. Certain states of madness or possession are said to be both helpful and honorable, even necessary sources of the 'greatest goods'. The thoroughly self-possessed person, who subdues emotion and feeling to *technē*, will neither aid his or her city much through prophecy, nor achieve honor and fame as a poetic teacher, nor be the best sort of lover. The ethical thinker cannot, it seems, afford to make sharp and simplistic divisions between bad madness and good *sōphrosunē* as the first two speeches did, as the *Republic* and the *Symposium* did. He must examine the cases more closely, divide artfully, and not, in his divisions, 'hack off a part in the manner of a bad butcher'

(265E). But we must look to the 'demonstration' that follows to find out exactly what the value of madness is and what elements of the previous view are being recanted. Three points emerge above all.

The non-intellectual elements are necessary sources of motivational energy. The image of the tripartite soul in Socrates' mythic account likens the person to a charioteer with two horses. Since the charioteer is clearly the planning, calculating *logistikon*, we are invited by the image to consider that intellect alone is a relatively impotent moving force. Plato's *logistikon* is not, like Hume's reason, a pure means–end calculator, with no role in choosing ends and goals; on the contrary, one of its major functions appears to be that of ranking and valuing.[30] But we are still asked to see that, as we are, we require the cooperative engagement of our non-intellectual elements in order to get where our intellect wants us to go. The power of the whole is a *sumphutos dunamis*, a 'power naturally grown-together' (246A). If we starve and suppress emotions and appetites, it may be at the cost of so weakening the entire personality that it will be unable to act decisively; perhaps it will cease to act altogether. The idea of 'nourishing' the non-intellectual plays an important part in Plato's myth. Even divine beings have horses; even these horses need their food (247E).[31] And the 'food of opinion' (*trophē doxastē*, 248B), though less fine than the gods' food, is both the best we can get for our horses and a necessary item in our search for understanding and the good life. Here Plato seems to grant that the ascetic plan of the *Republic*, which deprives emotion and sense of the nourishment of close ongoing attachments, of the family, of dramatic poetry, may result in crippling the personality even while it purifies it. The starved philosopher may, in his effort to become an undisturbed intellect, block his own search for the good.[32]

The non-intellectual elements have an important guiding role to play in our aspiration towards understanding. The fact that the continuing good health of intellect requires the nourishment of the non-intellectual parts would not show that these could or should ever steer or guide intellect. But Plato's contrast between madness and *sōphrosunē* is a contrast between passion-ruled and intellect-ruled states. He is clearly claiming that certain sorts of essential and high insights come to us only through the *guidance* of the passions. Socrates' story of the growth of the soul's wings shows us what lies behind this claim. The non-intellectual elements have a keen natural responsiveness to beauty, especially when beauty is presented through the sense of sight. Beauty is, among the valuable things in the world, the 'most evident' and the 'most lovable' (250D–E). We 'apprehend it through the clearest of our senses as it gleams most clearly' (D1–3); this stirs our emotions and appetites, motivating us to undertake its pursuit. Earthly examples of justice and practical wisdom, since they do not 'provide a clear visible image' (D5), and so do not engage the guiding appetites and emotions, are harder to discern; they can be grasped only after an initial education in beauty has quickened intellect (250B, D).[33] Sometimes the sight of beauty arouses only a brutish appetite for intercourse, unconnected with deeper feeling (250E). But in people of good nature and training, the sensual and appetitive response is linked with, and arouses,

complicated emotions of fear, awe, and respect, which themselves develop and educate the personality as a whole, making it both more discriminating and more receptive. The role of emotion and appetite as guides is motivational: they move the whole person towards the good. But it is also cognitive: for they give the whole person *information* as to where goodness and beauty are, searching out and selecting, themselves, the beautiful objects. They have in themselves, well trained, a sense of value. We advance towards understanding by pursuing and attending to our complex appetitive/emotional responses to the beautiful; it would not have been accessible to intellect alone. The state of the lover who has fallen in love with someone good and beautiful is a state of passionate inspiration, in which all elements of the personality are in a state of tremendous excitement. Sense and emotion are guides towards the good and indices of its presence:

But when one who is fresh from the mystery, and saw much of the vision, beholds a godlike face or bodily form that truly expresses beauty, first there comes upon him a shuddering and a measure of that awe which the vision inspired, and then reverence as at the sight of a god: and but for being deemed a very madman he would offer sacrifice to his beloved, as to a holy image of deity. Next, with the passing of the shudder, a strange sweating and fever seizes him: for by reason of the stream of beauty entering in through his eyes there comes a warmth, whereby his soul's plumage is fostered; and with that warmth the roots of the wings are melted, which for long had been so hardened and closed up that nothing could grow...Meanwhile [the soul] throbs with ferment in every part, and even as a teething child feels an aching and pain in its gums when a tooth has just come through, so does the soul of him who is beginning to grow his wings feel a ferment and a painful irritation. Wherefore as she gazes upon the boy's beauty, she admits a flood of particles streaming therefrom – that is why we speak of a 'flood of passion' – whereby she is warmed and fostered; then has she respite from her anguish, and is filled with joy. But when she has been parted from him and become parched, the openings of those outlets at which the wings are sprouting dry up likewise and are closed, so that the wing's germ is barred off; and behind its bars, together with the flood aforesaid, it throbs like a fevered pulse, and pricks at its proper outlet; and thereat the whole soul round about is stung and goaded into anguish; howbeit she remembers the beauty of her beloved, and rejoices again. So between joy and anguish she is distraught at being in such strange case, perplexed and frenzied. With madness upon her she can neither sleep by night nor keep still by day, but runs hither and thither, yearning for him in whom beauty dwells, if haply she may behold him. At last she does behold him, and lets the flood pour in upon her, releasing the imprisoned waters; then has she refreshment and respite from her stings and sufferings, and at that moment tastes a pleasure that is sweet beyond compare.

(251A–E, trans. Hackforth)

This moving and extraordinary description of passionate love is obviously the work of the poet from Himera. It takes the same experience described by the earlier two speeches in detached and clinical terms and enters into it, capturing through imagery and emotive language the feeling of being in a state of *mania*.[34] At the same time it shows us how the very madness criticized by the other two speeches can be an important, even a necessary, part of moral and philosophical development. The stimulus of this particular boy's beauty (seen not as a

replaceable piece of the beautiful, but as uniquely linked to his particular presence) proves necessary for the growth of the soul's wings; in the boy's absence the personality dries up, and all parts of it cease, alike, to develop. The ferment of the soul is cognitive: a reliable indicator of beauty's presence and of progress towards true understanding. (This picture becomes a lasting part of Plato's moral psychology; for in the second book of the *Laws*, we are told that the character of young citizens will be tested by putting the intellect to sleep through drunkenness. By observing the choices they make in this 'mad' condition, we will see how their souls are trained with respect to values. It is clear that this test works only given a belief in the independent discriminating power of sense and emotion; in the psychology of the *Republic* the drunken sleep of intellect simply releases bestial urges and could show nothing of moral value.)

The picture of moral and cognitive development in the middle dialogues is one of a progressive detachment of intellect from the other parts of the personality. The more the person can 'prepare for death', i.e. allow the intellect to go off itself by itself, unmixed, unaffected, the more nearly will true philosophical understanding be achieved. The intellect is, ideally, something pure and purely active; it has about it, at its best, no passivity or receptivity. It is 'very similar' to the form (*Phd.* 80B). Its pure lucidity is comparable to the dry clean beams of the sun.[35] The developing soul of the *Phaedrus* is in a very different state. Complex and impure, throbbing with 'ferment in every part', fevered and in constant motion, it depends for its growth on just these impure aspects of its condition. In order to be moved towards beauty, this soul must, first of all, be open and receptive. The stream of beauty that enters in at the eyes must be admitted by the whole soul (251B, C). And a crucial moment in its development is a moment not only of reception but of passivity: the roots of the soul's wings are melted by the warmth of the entering stream. The lover of Diotima's ascent was, like Creon, a hunter, out to immobilize the beauty of his object (203D; cf. *Protag.* 309A), a master of devices and strategems. Now plant imagery is used to characterize the receptivity and growth of the entire soul.[36] All parts of the soul accept and are affected; and they interact with one another in such a way that it becomes impossible to separate them clearly. The growing wings belong to the soul as a whole (232C; cf. 253C, 254C). The deep sensual response to a particular person's splendor, the emotions of love and awe, the intellectual aspirations that this love awakens – all of these flow together, so that the person feels no gap between thought and passion, but, instead, a melting unity of the entire personality. This is no ordinary sexual response to a beautiful body; indeed, the myth suggests that it may happen only once in a lifetime. Like Aristophanes' mythical creatures, these lovers search (262E) for an appropriate soul, and there is no guarantee that the search will be rewarded. But in the rare case of success, we have a response to another individual so deep and complete, involving so fully every part of the self, that it casts doubt on the story of separate parts. All the lover can say is that he or she feels warm and wet and illuminated all at once, everywhere. Instead of being like a dry beam of light looking upon dry light, he receives a mysterious substance that begins by being

light, but transforms itself into fluid. (Its source is not the clear heaven of the *Republic*, but, perhaps, Pindar's 'liquid sky'.)[37] Receiving the other person's soul, allowing to melt the hard or impassive parts of him, he feels the sudden release of pent-up liquid within him, which makes of him another flowing, liquid light. In the 'flowing' of his desire he resembles a person with 'streaming' eyes (255D).[38] So transformed, he begins to have access to insights that are not available within the dry life of the non-lover (cf. 239C8). He would not have had them if he had remained 'very similar' to the form.

What this account achieves is, on the one hand, to make us see human sexuality as something much more complicated and deep, more aspiring, than the middle dialogues had suggested; and, on the other hand, to see intellect as something more sexual than they had allowed, more bound up with receptivity and motion. (These changes were already adumbrated in the *Symposium*'s ascent, which linked the erotic appetite with beauty (cf. n. 11) and stressed the continuity of erotic motivation as the lover ascends towards contemplation. But Diotima's emphasis on self-sufficiency and on the superior value of intellect (cf. 212A1) left her view, nonetheless, quite close to that of the *Phaedo* and *Republic*. Only Alcibiades was able to speak of philosophy as a form of *mania* (218B2–3) – because he had failed to see what Socrates wanted it to be.) The erotic appetite is now not a blind urge for the 'replenishment' of intercourse; as we have seen, it is responsive to beauty and serves as a guide as to where true beauty will be found. Even the basest people look for beautiful objects. And in people of more complex aspiration, *erōs* sets its sights very high, searching for a sensual experience that will lead to a mysterious transformation of the entire soul, including the intellect. When they do fall in love, furthermore, they are moved by emotions of tenderness and awe; these emotions give them new information, both about themselves and about goodness of action. They realize that certain ways of acting towards the other person are good when and if they meet with the approval of these emotions; they reject certain ways of acting when they sense that these do not accord with felt reverence. For example, Plato's lovers choose not to have intercourse with one another, even though they express their love regularly in physical caresses that stop short of this (cf. 255B) – because they feel that the extreme sensual stimulation involved in intercourse is incompatible with the preservation of reverence and awe for the other as a separate person. Appetite is curbed not by contemplative intellect, but by the demands of the passions that it has awakened. The *Republic* had urged that the only reliable moral witness was intellect. The *Phaedrus* has a more complicated view.

On the other side, intellectual activity emerges here as something different in structure from the pure and stable contemplation of the *Republic*. As the philosopher reaches out here towards recollection and truth, his mental aspiration has an internal structure closely akin to that of the lover's sexual yearnings and fulfillments. The account of the growth of the wings uses unmistakably sexual metaphors to characterize the receptivity and growth of the entire soul. Intellect, no longer separated from the other parts, searches for truth in a way that would not meet the demands of the middle dialogues for purity and stability. 'Purity' is compromised by the contrast between pain and replenishment, parched dryness and refreshment. Stability is compromised both by the internal rhythm of the activity, which seems to involve a sequence of changes and could not be imagined continuing ceaselessly in the same way; and by the contingent and mutable nature of the object, which leaves a dryness when it departs. It is not only the fact that the object of intellect's attention is a person; worse still, from the *Symposium*'s viewpoint, is the fact that this person is loved and valued in a unique, or at least a rare and deeply personal way. Such loves are not easily transferable. Even if at the beginning there might have been more than one soul of the appropriate character-type who could answer the lover's inner needs (cf. 252E), it is evident that the history of the relationship, its deepening over time, is one of the sources of its intellectual value as a source of knowledge, self-knowledge, and progress towards recollection. The focus on character takes away much of love's replace-ability; the focus on history removes the rest. Clearly, too, this love's value is closely linked to the fact that this unique person is valued, throughout, as a separate being with his or her own self-moving soul – not as something to be held, trapped, or bound by any philosophical *technē*.[39]

As for Truth, intellect still attains to that. But not all of its most valuable truths will be general accounts or definitions of the sort required by the middle dialogues. Not least of the lover's learning is learning about the other person. Each, through complex responses and interactions, comes, we are told, to understand and honor the 'divinity' of the other person (252D); his effort is to know the other's character through and through. This leads, further, to increased self-understanding, as they 'follow up the trace within themselves of the nature of their own god'. In his state of possession (252E), the lover learns the other person's 'habits and ways', and, through these, his own (252E–253A). If we ask what sort of understanding this is and what truths the lovers can tell, we get a complicated answer. No doubt they will know some general truths about characters of a certain type. But some of their truths may well be more particular and more like stories. And some of their knowledge of habits and ways may reveal itself not so much in speeches as in the intuitive understanding of how to act towards the other person, how to teach, how to respond, how to limit oneself. But Socrates (like the Alcibiades of the *Symposium*) insists that it is insight nonetheless, insight crucial to moral and intellectual development.* The lover owes gratitude for this insight to the beloved, whom gratitude causes him to love all the more. Once 'looking to the lover' was opposed to looking to philosophy (239A–B). Now the lover's soul is a central source of insight and understanding, both general and concrete.

The passions, and the actions inspired by them, are intrinsically valuable components of

---

* The *Statesman* will develop this proto-Aristotelian point. Arguing for the priority of judgments of a person of practical wisdom over standing law, the Stranger (in language very close to that of the *Nicomachean Ethics*) claims that a political *technē* cannot give precedence to fixed rules, because the variety and the temporally changing character of human beings and their actions require a more particularized and contextual knowledge (294Aff.). It has long been noted that this overturns a major element in the political epistemology of the *Republic*.[40]

the best human life. So far, we might believe that Plato has revised only his view of motivation and education, not his view of the best life. Once intellect has been led by mad passion towards the norms of beauty and justice, we can cease to rely on the ferment of madness and clearly contemplate the truth. To say that the highest goods come to us through madness is certainly not to say that madness, or mad actions, are themselves intrinsically good. But the *Phaedrus* gives the passions, and the state of *mania*, much more than a merely instrumental role.

From the beginning of the recantation, this is suggested. The speeches critical of *erōs*, says Socrates, would not be convincing to a listener who was 'of noble and gentle character, who was or had ever been in love with another person of similar character' (243C). This person would think the speeches the work of 'people brought up among sailors, who have never seen a case of free and generous love' (243E). Even if we think that Plato's aristocratic disdain for the unpropertied classes has led him to speak unfairly of the navy, we can see what he has in mind. To him, the person 'brought up among sailors' is likely to take a merely instrumental view of love. He will think of it as calming needs and as yielding positive pleasure. What he will not learn from his experience in this milieu is that love can be a stable and intrinsically valuable part of a good life, a life worthy of a person of free and generous character.

The lovers of the *Phaedrus*, unlike the exploitative sailors of Plato's imagination, live their lives with one another, bound to one another by their erotic passion and by their respect for the other's character, their shared interest in teaching and learning (cf. esp. 252C–253E, 255A–F). Each lover seeks a partner who is similar in character and aspirations (252Cff.). Having found one another, they treat one another with respect for the other's separate choices (252D–E), fostering one another's continuing development towards the flourishing of their deepest aspirations, 'using no envious spite or ungenerous hostility' towards the other (253B), but genuinely benefiting him for his own sake. They are both mutually active and mutually receptive: from the one the other, like a Bacchant, draws in the transforming liquid; and he pours liquid back, in his turn, into the beloved soul (253A). Plato describes their passionate longing and emotion for one another in a way that stirs us (and Phaedrus) with its beauty and strongly indicates that he finds their madness beautiful and good. It is crucial that the lover be 'not one who makes a pretense of passion, but one who is really experiencing it' (255A). All other friends and associates having nothing to offer, Socrates now tells us, in comparison with this inspired lover, whose beneficence moves the beloved to awe. In this speech *erōs* is not just a *daimōn*, but a god: a thing of intrinsic value and beauty, not just a way-station towards the good. The best human life involves ongoing devotion to another individual. This life involves shared intellectual activity; but it also involves continued madness and shared appetitive and emotional feeling. The best lovers are said to deny themselves sexual intercourse. But this, as we have said, is because they feel that in intercourse they risk forfeiting other valuable non-intellectual elements of their relationship: the feelings of tenderness, respect, and awe. Plato still insists that as time goes on they will continue to 'draw near and touch one another, both in the gymnasia and in other places where they meet' (255B). The passage continues with an account of how, apparently during this habitual physical contact, they receive from one another the 'flood of passion' that nourishes their souls. The reference here to the love of Zeus and Ganymede (cf. below) underlines the sexual nature of these metaphors of spiritual growth. And they are more than metaphors, since sexual arousal seems to be an enabling part of the experience of growth. The lovers are, then, encouraged in any sensuous exploration of the other person that stops short of an act which they see as potentially selfish and/or violent. We may feel that here Plato's lovers have allowed the presence of a risk of harm to make them forfeit a further and deep value. We may feel that the old Platonic suspiciousness of the body here reasserts itself in a way that does not accord with the rest of Plato's argument. But Plato's rejection of intercourse, whether justified or not, is a rejection neither of the sensuous, which they continue to explore, nor of sexuality broadly interpreted, which permeates the whole of their madness. And it is prompted by the demands not of pure intellect but of respect and love.

The lover of the *Symposium* also began by loving a single person – or that person's beauty. But he or she soon moved on to a more general appreciation of beauty, relaxing his or her intense love for the one. The pairs of lovers in the *Phaedrus* never do this.[41] Their search for understanding and goodness is accomplished, throughout life, in the context of a particular relationship with an individual whose distinctive character is nourished within it. Instead of loving one another as exemplars of beauty and goodness, properties which they might conceivably lose without ceasing to be themselves, these lovers love one another's character, memories, and aspirations – which are, as Aristotle too will say, what each person is 'in and of himself'. Nothing the lovers learn about the good and beautiful ever makes them denigrate or avoid this unique bond or cast aspersions on anything about it. They do not move from the body to the soul to institutions to sciences. They pursue science or politics in the context of a deep love for a particular human being of similar commitments. (Here it makes no difference whether we refer to the highest human type as 'the one who philosophizes without guile' or 'the one who pursues the love of a boy along with philosophy' (249A); before it would have made a great difference.) They grasp the good and true not by transcending erotic madness, but inside a passionate life.

It is true that the philosophical lovers share an obscure vision of another life, a life better than any available human life (cf. 250B5). It is true that this dim vision contains images of lightness and purity, and that the gods who are its characters seem to lack the tumult of erotic feeling that characterizes human aspiration. But human recollection and human ascent can recover for these human lovers only what their souls have in some previous cycle seen or known; and a careful examination of Plato's myth reveals that the complete divine wisdom is, for a human being, permanently unavailable. The life of the lover's madness is not defended here, then, as the best life for a god or for any living being whatever. It is defended as the best life for a human being, a being with human cognitive limits and prospects. But, what is most striking, Plato here shows himself (as elsewhere in the later dialogues)[42] ready to judge questions about the best life from the point of view of the interests, needs, and limits of the being in question. The best life for a human being is found not by abstracting from the peculiarities of our complex nature, but by exploring that nature and the way of life that it constitutes.

Unlike the life of the ascending person in the *Symposium*, this best human life is unstable, always prey to conflict.[43] The lovers have continually to struggle against inappropriate inclinations, to expend psychic effort in order to hit on what is appropriate. Unlike the ascending person, again, they risk, in the exclusivity of their attachment to a mutable object, the deep grief of departure, alteration, or inevitably – death. This life, unlike Diotima's, seems to admit full-fledged conflict of values as well, since the lovers' devotion to one another is so particular that it might in some circumstances pull against their political commitments or their pursuit of knowledge (contrast Ch. 5, §v, Ch. 6, pp. 181, 196–7). But Plato seems to believe that a life that lacks their passionate devotion – whether or not it had this at some former time – is lacking in beauty and value next to theirs. Socrates concludes his advice to Phaedrus with these unequivocal words: 'Such and so many, my child, are the divine gifts that the love of a person in love will bring you. But a familiarity with the person who is not in love, mingled with mortal self-possession, dispensing retentively its mortal and niggardly benefits, giving birth in your beloved soul to a stinginess that is praised by the many as a virtue, will render it devoid of insight (*anous*) and cause it to roll around and beneath the earth for nine thousand years' (256E–257A). This condemnation is not restricted to the bad person-not-in-love: for Lysias, we know, is an honorable man. Nor is it restricted to the non-lover who has at no former time been passionately in love. *All* lives bereft of madness and the ongoing influence of the other's madness are alike condemned as drab and ungenerous, lacking in depth of insight. Once, in the *Phaedo*, the passions were nails binding the soul to its bodily prison house. Now it is Lysias who appears to be imprisoned, held near and beneath the earth by his lack of generous passion.

If we now return to the four points in Plato's indictment of the passions, we find that he has recanted or seriously qualified all of them.

(1) The appetites are blind animal forces reaching out for their objects without discrimination or selectivity. This has been denied at least for the erotic appetite. Even in its most degenerate form, *erōs* is responsive to beauty; and in aspiring souls it involves a complex, selective response of the entire soul. Phaedrus and Socrates remain critical of certain bodily pleasures (cf. 258E). They do not deny that *some* human appetites conform to the old picture. What they claim is that this picture was too simple and, in particular, that it was a slander against *erōs*.

(2) The appetites tend naturally to excess when not suppressed. Plato still seems to believe that the unruly horse needs constant reining in; it is called a 'companion of *hubris*' (253E). But he also seems to believe that this horse should be well fed and that, properly controlled, it can play a good and a necessary role in motivating

the person, even in teaching the person about the beautiful. The other horse does not tend towards excess at all; in fact it helps prevent excess.

(3) The passions cannot function cognitively. Here, as we have argued, they can and do. They are not invariably sources of distortion; indeed, their information proves necessary for the best insight. A major development is Plato's detailed account of the motivating and cognitive role of certain emotions and his picture of the interaction of sense, emotion, and judgment in *erōs*, which the *Republic* had treated as simply a bodily appetite.

(4) The intellectual element is both necessary and sufficient for the apprehension of truth and for correct choice. Here it is not. Alone, 'itself by itself', it will be doomed to the niggardly life of mortal self-possession. Even its own aspirations are best advanced by a richer ferment of the entire personality, in which it is difficult to separate the contributions of one part from those of the others.

We can use these discoveries to approach what has long been a contested problem in *Phaedrus* interpretation: what to make of the fact that this dialogue uses a conception of the person different from that of the *Phaedo* and the *Republic*. The *Republic* tells me that what I really am is an immortal, intellectual soul, only contingently associated with a body and with appetite. The conflicts that give rise to talk of 'parts' of the soul arise from the soul's union with body; the conflict-free intellectual element, the only one that is immortal, is sufficient to preserve personal identity outside of the body. The *Phaedo*, using a similar picture, urges me to dissociate myself from my bodily nature and from the accompanying passions, and to use my life as a practice for separation. Socrates is convinced that everything that goes to make him Socrates will depart from the body at death. His conception of his identity as an aspiring philosopher gives no part either to appetite or to emotion.[44]

In the *Phaedrus*, as is well known, all souls are tripartite, even the souls of the immortal gods. The proof of immortality does not depend on a premise of non-composition, as in the *Phaedo*, but only on the self-moving nature of soul. Once again, the shift seems to be permanent: for in *Laws* x self-motion is the one essential characteristic of soul as opposed to body, and such things as appetites, hopes, fears, and pleasures are all classified as motions of soul.[45] I think we cannot gloss over this problem by saying that the tripartite gods are just part of the myth.[46] Human beings are tripartite too, before as well as after incarnation; middle-dialogue souls are not. And the list of soul-motions in later dialogues give clear evidence of a change. Besides, the myth is not 'just a myth'; it is Plato's central teaching.

This change should not surprise us by now. The image of the soul is an image of what I value in myself, what I am willing to acknowledge as a part of my identity. The dualism of the *Phaedo* is not prior to that dialogue's moral theory. It expresses it. Neither Plato nor Aristotle thinks of a theory of personal identity as a matter of value-neutral fact. It articulates our deepest values. A way of expressing my repudiation of the passions is to say that that is not really me, not what I really, in my true nature, am. (I could survive after death and be essentially myself without that.) The *Republic*'s myth of Er, which makes my soul out to be a pure, non-composite intellectual substance, albeit crusted over by barnacles and other remnants of my earthly existence, is an image of a view about value which, as we saw in Chapter 5, is carefully defended in that dialogue. Since the *Phaedrus* argues against these arguments, we should expect to find in it a new image of the person. In this respect the agent of the Phaedrus is tolerant. The radiant vision of the myth of Er, a myth that was meant to save us (*Rep.* 621B–C), is laid aside in favor of Socrates' open question: am I a being more complex and puffed up than Typho, or rather some tamer and simpler creature? (230A)[47] And later on this question itself is implicitly rejected as still too much in the grip of the stark dichotomies of the *Republic* and *Symposium*: you can be complex without being Typho, orderly without being simple, a lover of the individual without being Alcibiades.

The action of this dialogue illustrates its view of learning.[48] It begins, as we have seen, when an older man pauses, struck by a younger one; he notices a kinship between the young man's character and his own (228A). Their shared aspirations, like the proverbial carrot held before a hungry animal's nose (230D), lead him to venture, in Phaedrus's company, outside the city walls. Together they pursue their deep concerns, receiving the influence of this wild and sensuous place. Although in some sense Socrates is the leader and the teacher, the process of education that we see – like the one we hear described – involves, on both sides, madness and receptivity, as Socrates, going outside his usual haunts, is transported through Phaedrus's influence (234D, 238D, 231E), and Phaedrus leaves aside the sheltering structure of his *sōphrosunē* to accept the vulnerable position of a lover.[49] On both sides we find emotions of wonder and awe, a careful concern for the other's separate needs and aspirations. Each discovers more about his own aims as he sees them reflected in another soul. (For wasn't it the thought of Phaedrus accepting the proposals of Lysias that made Socrates long to express a more complicated ideal of rationality? Wasn't it Socrates' inspired poetic recantation that led Phaedrus to express his own receptive neediness?) Neither imposes on the other a vision already fixed. Each, responding with awe to the other's soul, elicits from his own a deeper beauty.

III

This is a dialogue about the making of beautiful speeches. Socrates' criticism of Lysias's speech is addressed to its style as well as its content – and shows us how thoroughly interwoven these are. The education of Phaedrus through the second speech is a development of his stylistic tastes as well as his moral imagination. And, as we might expect, Plato's new thought about madness affects his own stylistic choices. It is now time to recognize the implications of this work on madness for the question of philosophy's style and for the status of Plato's ongoing argument with literary or poetic moral teachers.

In a number of dialogues of his 'early' and 'middle' periods (cf. Interlude 1),[50] Plato sharply contrasts the poet and the philosopher, rejecting the claim of the former to genuine understanding. There is, he tells us, 'an old difference' or 'opposition' between poetry and philosophy (*Rep.* 607B). The poet is characterized consistently, in the *Apology*, *Ion*, *Meno*, and the tenth book of the *Republic*, as a person who works in a state of irrational inspiration or transport, and whose creations are expressive of this state. Poets are 'in a state of frenzied enthusiasm' (*enthusiōntes*, *Apol.*, *Meno*); they 'hold their bacchic revels' (*bakcheuousi*, *Ion*), they are 'not in their senses' (*ouch emphrones*, *Ion*), 'inspired' (*epipnoi*, *Ion*), 'god-inspired' (*entheoi*, *Ion*), 'possessed' (*katechomenoi*, *Meno*, *Ion*). Their irrational state is contrasted with the self-possessed good sense of the philosopher.

It comes, then, as no surprise to find that poetic writers are criticized on much the same grounds as other mad people: being possessed and in a state of psychological ferment, they are unable to have access to true insight. As in other cases, madness is taken to be incompatible with understanding: although they might by accident hit upon the truth, the poets 'know nothing of what they say' (*Apol.*, *Meno*).

Furthermore, works that express a poet's madness encourage madness in their audience. Unlike the philosopher, who addresses himself to the pure *logistikon* alone and promotes its separation, the poet addresses himself to, and thereby nourishes, the passional elements in the soul. He finds that the emotions present him with his best opportunities for interesting poetry; displays of intense feeling, especially anger and love, are especially moving to his audience (*Rep.* 604E–605A). But by showing them and moving the audience he feeds and strengthens their passions, jeopardizing their efforts at rational control (*Rep.* 386A–388E, 605B, 696A, D, 607A).[51]

For these two separate reasons, then, the middle dialogues reject the poets who were traditionally the moral teachers of young souls. We have seen in Chapter 5 some of Plato's arguments for a new type of 'literature' which will develop the potential for objective rationality. And in Interlude 1 we began to see the effect of Platonic intellectualism on Plato's own discourse, as he creates a purified theater which, while preserving tragedy's ability to engage the spectator actively as an interlocutor, addresses its claim to the intellect alone. (The mixed appeal of the *Symposium* (cf. Ch. 6) might be called the exception that proves the rule, since Plato here allows himself to engage the sympathies of the non-intellectual parts, but as part of a process of showing the disastrous failure of these elements to guide or make an orderly rational life.) We can see that the earlier dialogues are indeed inspired by the clear-voiced or 'Ligurian' Muses who also inspire the first two speeches of the *Phaedrus*, with their spare, flat, unemotional and unemotive style.

We might expect, then, that any new thoughts on moral psychology would be taken by a writer as serious and honest as Plato to have implications for his own view of his written teaching. The *Phaedrus* reminds us (cf. Interlude 1) that all writing is merely a 'reminder': the real activity of teaching and learning goes on not on the page but in the souls of people.[52] But our view of how a soul learns, and with which parts, will surely affect our view about how a written text should perform its own limited function.

From the very beginning of the *Phaedrus*, we suspect that some such reassessment is taking place. Phaedrus asks Socrates whether he believes in the truth of the myth of Boreas (229C) – in which a virginal girl, who was playing with her companions in the very place where Socrates and Phaedrus now talk, was carried off by the passionate wind-god, who had fallen in love with her. Socrates, in answer, speaks harshly of some 'clever people' who doubt the truth of myths and, 'using a somewhat crude science', ingeniously devise rationalizing explanations for their origin. (In this case, he conjectures, the rationalizer would claim that what happened was not a seduction by Boreas the anthropomorphic wind-god, but simply a gust from the wind we call Boreas, that blew the girl away.) Although Plato has used myths of his own devising to buttress his philosophical arguments, he has, of course, been at the forefront of the attack upon traditional stories of the dubious exploits of the gods. The *Republic* would instantly have rejected the truth claim of this story of a god's *erōs*; and it would have denounced it further for its appeal to the lower parts of the soul. But here Socrates defends the passionate myth as a source of insight, in keeping with the new view of insight that he is about to develop; and the rationalizing attacker is dismissed as an 'excessively clever and hard-working and not entirely fortunate man' (229D4). It is truly entertaining to observe the strategies devised by commentators to accommodate this passage to the views of the *Republic*. Thomson, for example, simply announces that, after all, the story is perfectly harmless.[53] But of course this story of the clear virgin who yields to the overwhelming passion of a divine lover is far from harmless, by the *Republic*'s standards of harmlessness. And it is just this difficult and dangerous psychological material that the *Phaedrus* now urges us to explore.

Our next literary surprise comes in Socrates' criticism of the prose of Lysias – where the orator is praised for his clarity and conciseness, but scolded, among other things, for his lack of *interest* in his subject (235A). Again, we remember that the poets had been criticized precisely because they wrote in a state of passionate arousal. Now Plato seems to be reopening the question about the proper relation between a view and its author.

Most significant, of course, is the role played by poetry in Socrates' second speech. It is said to be the speech 'of' a poet, Stesichorus the son of Reverent from Passionville; and in so saying Socrates assumes a disguise, and tells a lie – things that could not have happened in the heroic literature of Ideal City. (The entire dialogue, we should recall, has the form of a fiction about the actions and character and 'madness' of Phaedrus.) The mad, inspired poet is ranked above the self-possessed craftsmanly poet, and honored as a person whose works instruct and benefit posterity. Socrates presents his own deepest teaching about the soul in the form of a 'likeness' (246A), teaching the truth, like Alcibiades, through sensuous images; and he regards this ability to produce a likeness as sufficient to give him the right to call himself a philosopher and a teacher. Only a god, he implies, could do better (246A). It then comes as no surprise to find that when Socrates later ranks lives in order of their excellence, the first place is occupied by a strange hybrid: 'a person who will be a lover of wisdom or a lover of beauty or some follower of the Muses and a lover' (248D).[54] In the world of the *Republic*, when lives are ranked, the philosopher is alone at the top. Certainly he does not share his berth with unsavory bacchic types like the poet and the (boy)-lover (cf. 249A). His own sort of *erōs* is sharply distinguished from theirs: it is 'correct' just *because* it has nothing to do with 'mania or sexual desire (403A). Now philosopher, image-maker and Muse-follower, lover – all are seen as possessed types, and madness comes at the top.[55]

It is unlikely that these changes would lead to a rehabilitation of the poets whose work Plato knew. Philosophical activity still seems to be necessary for the highest sort of understanding; it is also necessary, as we have seen, for the highest sort of love. The disjunction 'either a lover of wisdom or a lover of beauty or some follower of the Muses' probably does not imply that any one of these, taken without the others, would be sufficient. The point is, rather, that they are taken, as they could not have been before, to be compatible – perhaps even, in their highest realizations, to imply one another. (It doesn't matter which of these names you call him, because if he's one, he's the other too.) The speech about madness has already dismissed the uninspired poet; and in the list of lives the ordinary craftsmanly *poiētēs*, 'maker' (who is not said to be Muse-inspired), comes in sixth place, quite far down the ladder (248E). Later we are told that Homer will be permitted the title of philosopher only if he can show his understanding by answering questions about his writing (278C). But this, as the *Apology* showed, is something that actual poets are unable to do. (This would probably be so even with the more inclusive conception of understanding that seems to be present in the *Phaedrus*.)

So the change implies no softening towards the non-philosophical poet. The really significant point, however, is that philosophy is now permitted to be an inspired, manic, Muse-loving activity. And in this conception it is more intimately related to poetry than Plato has hitherto led us to think. It can, for example, make use of 'literary' devices such as mythic narrative and metaphor in the center of its teaching; and it can, like poetry, contain material expressive of, and arousing, a passional excitation. The rest of the dialogue confirms this close relationship. At the conclusion of Socrates' second speech (a speech which Phaedrus praises as 'more beautiful' than the preceding), Phaedrus is called a 'lover of the Muses' (*philomouson andra*). The myth of the cicadas which follows tells us that philosophy, along with the dance and erotic love, is one of the arts that made its appearance in the world with the advent of the Muses. The philosophical life is said to be a life dedicated to 'Calliope and Urania' – that is, to the Muse traditionally associated with poetry, as well as to the mother of cosmology (259B–C). (We notice that ordinary poetry is not mentioned as an art genuinely inspired by the Muses; this is consistent with the low placement of the mere *poiētēs* before, and with the distinction between this person and the higher *mousikos*: the poet does not genuinely serve the Muses, unless he is both inspired and able to join his art with philosophy.) The last part of the dialogue breaks with the *Gorgias*'s very general condemnation of rhetoric, describing a 'true' rhetorical art in which a central place is given to the knowledge, through experience, of the souls of individuals (268A–B). And, at the dialogue's end, the philosopher's message to Homer tells him that Socrates and Phaedrus have heard the words they relay from the 'stream and Music haunt (*mouseion*) of the Nymphs'. What the nymphs told them, apparently, is that poetry is philosophy if it is combined in the right way with answers and accounts.

What we see emerging, then, is not so much a rehabilitation of the old poetry, as a new understanding of philosophy that reinterprets the distinction between philosophy and poetry; not so much an acceptance of Homer's innocence of *logoi*, as an announcement that philosophy, like Socrates, may have a more complex soul than has been imagined.

But we do not need to rely only on explicit metaphilosophical remarks to know this. For Plato's praise of the inspired poet profoundly affects the shape of his own discourse. The speech of the poet from Himera is still a prose speech. And it does not employ internal dramatic representation in its depiction of the lovers who are its characters. It even contains a section that is in the form of a formal demonstrative argument (245C). But there is no doubt that, more than any other Platonic speech we have so far encountered, this clearly is the speech of an inspired philosopher-poet. It uses metaphor, personification, colorful, rhythmic, and elaborate language. It makes its appeal to the imagination and the feelings as much as to the intellect. And, by calling *all* of this a 'demonstration' of the value of madness, it forces us to question the legitimacy of separating these parts, and these ways of writing, so starkly. Finally, we must acknowledge that the whole of what we read here is a play, a dramatic representation. It is not a representation of ideally good or perfect people; for both characters are self-critical, and both are in the process of growth and change. But it is this sort of representation that is now taken to be what the developing soul requires.[56]

This dialogue may be our first example of the philosophical poetry that Plato has in mind. Nobody else had ever served the two Muses adequately together, combining the rigor of speculative argument with sensitive responses to the particulars of human experience. It demands from us a boldness, and a freedom from set ideas, in our own response. Plato tells us that we cannot throw away the images and the drama as delightful decorations, or lift out his arguments from the 'literary' context for isolated dissection. Still less can we abandon the arguments or relax the demands of our critical faculties. The whole thing is a Music discourse, which asks of us the full participation of all parts of our souls.

IV

We have spoken repeatedly here of change and recantation. So much change, if it is there, calls for explanation. We feel like asking, what happened to Plato? What brought it about that this most intolerant of human beings would decide, at some time around 365 B.C., that he has been too simple in his condemnation of madness?

This is only one of several roughly contemporaneous shifts in Plato's thinking. We have spoken already of changes in his view of the soul and of practical knowledge. Related changes in his political thought have often been discussed. It is generally admitted, too, that his thought about understanding, the forms, and dialectic underwent a development during this period. The *Phaedrus* is apparently the first dialogue of a group that uses a new picture of dialectic, known as the Method of Division; one of the jobs of the second half of the dialogue is to announce and defend this method. In my earlier essay on the *Phaedrus*, I stressed the connection between the newly anthropocentric conception of dialectic that is present in this and other late dialogues and the anthropocentric conception of the good life defended by Socrates' second speech. I traced this conception back to arguments in the *Parmenides* that completely 'unqualified' understanding was unavailable to a human being; I argued that the same position is present in the *Phaedrus* myth.

I still believe that all of these connections are interesting and important; I shall have more to say about them in discussing Aristotle's anthropocentrism. But I would prefer not to stress them here, for two reasons. First, because the complex interpretative issues would have to take us far beyond the *Phaedrus*; they would require a careful examination of the use of the method in *Sophist, Statesman*, and *Philebus*, and of the interactions between epistemology and morality in all of those dialogues. I would rather attempt this on another occasion. But, second, I do not believe that the completion of this project would offer a fully satisfying answer to the question that we are asking here. Suppose Plato did decide that the conception of understanding articulated in the middle dialogues was not, for human beings, viable. It hardly follows from this that he would become better disposed to the limits of a merely human understanding. The new developments would explain what the limitations of inquiry are and why Plato believes that they are there; it would not show us why he defends *anything* as good and valuable, rather than giving way to cognitive/moral despair. Epistemology by itself cannot explain acceptance. And, if anything, the connections, as we saw in Chapter 6, go the other way: a certain sort of object for understanding was required by a view about what has value, what life is worth living, how immune from contingency that life must be.

We would feel happier, then, if we could find something to say about Plato's reevaluations that came from his own practical intuitions and experience. And in fact such a story is forcefully signaled to us by Plato himself. It has frequently been observed that, in discussing the love of his philosophical couple (the pair described in Socrates' second speech), Plato brings the beloved younger one into association, in two ways, with the name of the human being whom he himself most passionately loved. The couple are said to be followers 'of Zeus'; the name of Zeus, as we see clearly in its oblique cases, has the root *Di-*: the genitive 'of Zeus' is '*Dios*'. The soul of the younger man, furthermore, is described at 252E as '*dion*' – 'brilliant' or 'shining' – a word derived from the same root. Plato strikingly juxtaposes the two words in this passage, signaling to us that he wishes us to think of them as etymologically connected: *hoi men dē oun Dios dion tina einai zētousi tēn psuchēn ton huph' hautōn erōmenon*, 'Those who are followers of Zeus seek that the soul of their beloved should be brilliant (Zeus-like).' Interpreters have not hesitated to see in all this a reference to Dion of Syracuse – and, by extension, to see the love described here as an account of Plato's own passionate devotion to Dion.[57] We can now go even further, however: for we notice that the name '*Phaidros*' has the same meaning as the name '*Dion*'. Both mean 'brilliant' or 'sparkling'. Plato is fond of playing with the significance of proper names; this we know from etymologies that occupy most of the *Cratylus*, from his epigram on the boy Aster ('Star'),[58] and not least from the opening of Socrates' second speech in the *Phaedrus*. Given the prominence accorded to the actual name of Dion within this dialogue, it seems impossible that this fact about '*Phaedrus*' could have escaped Plato's attention; it seems virtually certain that Plato is telling us, in this way, that Phaedrus in some sense represents Dion. This complex literary intention would help us to solve two outstanding problems about the dramatic structure of the dialogue. One great problem has always been that at the date when the dialogue must take place, Phaedrus, though portrayed in general as young, is no mere boy. He would, in fact, be nearly forty; and Socrates is clearly about sixty. (A sign of the confusion is that Lysias, about thirty-five, is called Phaedrus's *paidika* ('beloved boy') at 236B.) This does not exactly fit with the conventional expectation about the ages of *erastēs* and *erōmenos*; it does, however, fit precisely with the actual ages of Plato and Dion at the most plausible time of composition, when Dion will be between thirty-five and forty, Plato between fifty-five and sixty. This, then, looks like Plato's way of playfully telling us that the 'boy' to whom he is speaking in this piece of writing is his beloved pupil, like him both a political and a philosophical character. (Both Gilbert Ryle and many other less controversial critics have already closely linked the *Phaedrus* with the time of Plato's second visit to Syracuse.[59]) This would also help us to understand the 'plot' of the dialogue, which puzzles us at the end, in that Socrates and Phaedrus, who have appeared to exemplify the philosophical *erōs* described in Socrates' speech, historically did not go back and spend their lives together. But if we see them as standing in for Plato and Dion, we are free to leave this fact aside and to respond by thinking of two people who did attempt to spend their lives together and to govern a philosophical city. What Plato will then be saying is that his erotic speech, his recantation of former 'slanders' against *erōs*, are truly said '*dia Phaidron*', through Phaedrus – i.e. through Dion and his influence. This dialogue has the character of a love letter, an expression of passion, wonder, and gratitude. (Ryle argues from separate evidence that he wrote it just after leaving Syracuse, on his journey back to Athens.) This is not, of course, to say something so simple as that love made Plato change his mind; for his experience of love was certainly also shaped by his developing thought. The dialogue has explored such interrelationships with too much complexity to allow an oversimple story; but it does ask us to recognize experience as one factor of importance.

We know that the relationship between Plato and Dion was in a number of ways like the relationship described in Socrates' second speech. It was built on complex passion, mutual respect and benefit, a shared devotion to both political and philosophical goals. But we have a piece of evidence that links it even more strikingly with the *Phaedrus*'s rehabilitation of *mania* and its new acceptance of the goodness of the risky and the mutable. Upon the sudden death of Dion at the hands of his enemies (around ten years after the composition of the *Phaedrus*), Plato wrote the elegiac verses that appear as our epigraph here. These verses, which contrast the unrelieved misery of the women of Troy with Dion's surprising and premature death in the midst of happiness, make mention of *erōs*, of *mania*, and of the *thumos* – the 'second' or emotional part of the soul. (The last line reads, literally, 'O Dion, you who drove my *thumos* mad (*ekmēnas*) with *erōs*.') The intense passion expressed in these verses has often been noticed; what has not been noticed is that this passion, and its poetic expression in the form of conventional lamentation, directly contravene the prohibition of the *Republic* against lamentation for the deaths of beloved individuals. Indeed, they contravene the whole moral scheme of the *Republic* and *Symposium*: for if one saw persons, and their value, in the way recommended by these two dialogues, one would have, in the death of an individual, no basis for grief. One 'drop' of the good and beautiful more or less – it should not affect us, if we have correct beliefs. Furthermore, the good person's stable activity should not be risked by the formation of intense particular attachments that would bring the shock of this deep grief. Therefore the *Republic* banishes both grief and poetic lamentation, leaving them, at most, to the 'not-very-good woman' (cf. Ch. 5 §IV, Interlude 2).

In his epigram, and by writing an epigram of this sort, Plato acknowledges himself to be not a self-sufficient philosopher, but a 'not-very-good woman'. He got these verses, clearly, not from the *Symposium*'s ascent, but by 'going down', like Socrates and Phaedrus (279B), into the Muses' Cave. Love has rendered him incomplete in his aspiration. He acknowledges that he feels grief; that he felt, before that, deep passion in his *thumos*; that this passion threw him into a condition of *mania*. But he appears unashamed of this passion. It is unlikely that the Plato of the *Republic* would have published such a poem, even if he had been moved to write it. The *Phaedrus*, I think, tells us why this *mania* is now something that can be praised and acknowledged, and how the experience of *mania* has left the philosopher with an altered view of the good of self-sufficiency.

What happened to Plato, we are invited by his hints to conjecture, was that he discovered that merely human life was more complicated, but also richer or better, than he had imagined. Obviously he had been aware before this of the power of passion; what he had not seen so clearly was its power for goodness. He tells us that he was struck in all parts of his soul by the splendor of another whole person; being struck, he formed, and in this dialogue depicted, a close and exclusive relationship in which wonder, respect, passion, and careful concern all fostered, in both, the growth of philosophical insight. In this love between an older established person and a younger aspiring person, he found access to elements of his own personality as a thinker and writer that he would before have derided as merely womanly, perhaps because they had too much to do with passivity. The complex imagery of Socrates' second speech – in which a flood of liquid entering into the lover brings intense pleasure and the release of his own 'imprisoned waters' – metaphorically expresses a certain type of male homosexual point of view towards sexual experience. (It is significant that the aspects of this experience which Plato selects for emphasis are those that have a great deal in common with the experience of the female, frequently derided for her passivity and emotionality.) It would not be fanciful to see Plato as expressing, both in the *Republic*'s denunciation and in this praise, his complex attitude towards the passive and receptive aspects of his own sexuality, aspects which, for a proud Greek gentleman of this time, could not have been easy to accept. We remember that a central example in the entire argument for the middle dialogues' view of value was the sexual pleasure of the passive homosexual, and that this was the only pleasure that the hedonist interlocutor Callicles agreed with Socrates in finding truly disgusting. Now it appears as a metaphor for the good life. If we doubt that the *Gorgias*'s example is being reconsidered here, we have only to consider the role played in the *Phaedrus* by Ganymede, boy beloved of Zeus, carried off to be cup-bearer of the gods – whose name gives our English word 'catamite' its origin. Socrates tells us that the word '*himeros*' was made up as the name for passionate desire by Zeus himself when he was the lover of Ganymede, after the flowing stream (*rheuma*) of passion that went (*ienai*) from him bearing particles (*merē*) which were received by his beloved (251C, cf. 255B–C). We are to realize, too, that Ganymede, made cup-bearer, became himself, in turn, a pourer of liquids. The central pair of lovers in Socrates' speech are not only both Zeus-like souls (252E, i.e. having the *Dion psuchēn*); they are also both Ganymedes in their receptivity, mutually pouring and receiving. And Ganymede is explicitly connected with Phaedrus through another complex etymological game: for the word '*ganos*', too, means 'bright gleam', and Phaedrus is said to 'gleam brightly' (*ganusthai*) with delight as he reads (234D2–3), while Socrates from Himera is passive (*epathon*, 234B).[60]

What Plato is saying, in all this complicated play, is that the truly blessed life involves the proper cultivation of both activity and passivity, working in harmony and mutuality. A horror of passivity is what lies beyond his culture's (and his own) condemnation of the life of Ganymede; he tells us that this hatred of openness leads to a life impoverished in value and knowledge. (And by presenting these insights in the form of play, he also defends the richness of lovers' play, reminding us that this receptivity expresses itself in jokes, puns, and laughter as well as in the shared pursuit of wisdom.)

But we would surely underestimate the complexity of this work, and its play, if we did not also acknowledge now that Plato, who figures so far in the drama as Socrates the *erastēs*, is also at the same time Phaedrus, the brilliant pupil of Socrates. Phaedrus, we said, is here chronologically forty; he is depicted as a much younger man. This contradiction invites us to recall that at the dramatic date of the dialogue, when Socrates was indeed sixty, Plato himself was around seventeen, a sparkling boy moved and transported by this philosophical influence. (Perhaps Lysias, in the *Republic* his brothers' friend, really was his aspiring lover.) Phaedrus is both forty and seventeen because he stands for two people, just as Socrates stands for Plato, but also for himself. Everything we know about Socrates outside of this dialogue testifies that he never did, in fact, go mad with *erōs*. The passion and wonder of his pupils were answered with a coolly ironic distancing. He was Socrates to Plato's passionate Alcibiades: he remained aloof, stony, self-contained. And if the *Symposium*'s portrait of Alcibiades is in some sense Plato's own self-portrait – a denunciation of his teacher for the overweening of irony and at the same time of himself for love's tumultuous confusion – we might see the *Phaedrus* as a wish, *per impossibile*, for the deep mutual love of teacher and pupil, a wish that Socrates had been a little more mad, receiving and teaching the insight of *erōs*. The double reference also tells us that Plato now claims to be the Socrates that Socrates should have been but refused to be; that he has found what eluded his teacher, a fusion of clarity and passion.[61]

The life of *mania* is not the life of stable contemplation. Plato shows us that it would be safer to choose the closed, ascetic life of the *Phaedo* – or, not so different, the Lysian life of non-involved and painless sexuality. Stinginess is in general more stable than generosity, the closed safer than the open, the simple more harmonious than the complex. But he acknowledges that there are in this risky life (whose riskiness itself is made to seem rather splendid) sources of nourishment for the soul of a complex human being that are not found in any other type of philosophical life. He rejects the simplicity of his former ideal – and its associated conception of insight – in favor of a view of creativity and objectivity that expresses itself in imagery of flowing light and illuminated water, of plant growth, of movement and instability, reception and release.

Such a view about the ethical value of passion is itself an unstable achievement in most human lives, and Plato indicates as much. For he places the poetic quotation, 'This story isn't true', so that it can equally, at any point, be turned against Socrates' *second* speech, or against the whole of the action of the dialogue. (Since it is *not* true that Phaedrus was leading an orderly good life at Athens. And Socrates never talked philosophy on the grass outside the city walls. And Helen went to Troy, not Egypt. And Boreas, anthropomorphic only in stories, did not make love to a human girl. And Lysias the self-possessed found lasting fame in the city, while Phaedrus son of Pythocles, who joined philosophy with madness, was exiled and eclipsed. And Plato and Dion of Syracuse did not succeed in living their adult lives together, bound by philosophical love.) And if the dialogue's end should remind us of the discussion of Pan's name in the *Cratylus* (407E–408B), we would discover this etymological lesson: Speech, says Socrates, 'signifies everything (*to pan*), and rolls about and wanders continually, and is double-natured, both true and false'. (For it is both true and false, perhaps, that love is compatible with order, that passion can be passion and still be rational.) But here, for the present, in this dramatic action and in this mixed piece of writing, the insights stand, published and not denied. This is, perhaps, all that can be asked of a human commitment to a view, or to a passion.

At the dialogue's end, Socrates prays to Pan the mad erotic god, son of Hermes god of luck, and to the other gods of this wild place, asking for a beautiful inside and an outside that will be loved by that inside (279B–C).[62] The prayer expresses both the dialogue's discoveries and also its risks: on the one hand the positive role of guiding divinities associated with passion, not 'pure' intellect; on the other, the standing possibility of conflict – for a prayer for love between soul and body is not a celebration of their oneness. But in the dialogue's discovery of a mutual love of individuals based upon character and aspiration, Socrates has found a powerful resource towards the continued pursuit of these very questions.[63] He now asks Phaedrus whether 'we' need anything more: 'For in my opinion the prayer was appropriate' (279C). And Phaedrus replies, in his turn, with acknowledged need and good will. 'Pray the same for me too. People who love each other share everything.'

'Let's go', says Socrates.[64]

Part III
Aristotle: the fragility of the good human life

We shall not cease from exploration
And the end of all our exploring
Will be to arrive where we started
And know the place for the first time.

T. S. Eliot, 'Little Gidding'

That with which people most continuously associate – the discourse that orders everything – with this they are at variance; and what they encounter every day seems strange to them.

Although the discourse is shared (*xunou*), most people live as if they had a private understanding.

The person who speaks with understanding (*xun noōi*) must insist upon what is shared (*xunōi*) by all, as a city insists upon its law.

Heraclitus, DK 72, 2, 114

Introduction

Aristotle develops a conception of a human being's proper relationship to *tuchē* that returns to and further articulates many of the insights of tragedy. His philosophical account of the good human life is, as I shall argue, an appropriate continuation and an explicit description of those insights. We shall examine his criticisms of Plato's revisionary picture of the good human life and of the Platonic conception of philosophy as radical life-saver.

The structure of this section will differ from the structure of the Plato section, much as Aristotle's philosophical writing differs from Plato's. That is, it will move from problem to related problem, rather than from complex multi-voiced dramatic work to work. And it will attempt to show the interconnections of various apparently separate inquiries in their bearing on our problems. This seems fitting when we are dealing with a philosopher who constantly employs cross-references, and who is known to have rearranged his lectures in several different orderings, depending upon the purpose and the occasion.

Two chapters may at first glance seem extraneous to the purposes of an ethical inquiry. Chapter 8 contains a general discussion of Aristotle's philosophical method, using material from science and metaphysics as well as ethics. Chapter 9 gives an account of human action and the explanation of action, drawing on ethical texts, but also on general discussions of the explanation of animal movement. Why should an account of Aristotle's conception of the good human life begin with such issues?

Chapter 8 first. A central theme in this book so far has been the ambition of human reason to subdue and master *tuchē* through the arts or sciences. Plato took it to be the task of philosophy to become the life-saving *technē* through which this aspiration could be accomplished – through which, then, the human being could make decisive progress beyond the ordinary human condition. Aristotle begins his criticism of Plato's accomplishment in ethics from a very general criticism of this conception of philosophizing. Not only in ethics but in every area, the philosopher must place himself in a balanced relationship to the beliefs and the discourse of existing human beings. To study this conception of philosophy and the arguments by which Aristotle defends it against Platonism thus seems of the first importance for any attempt to understand the apparent conservatism of his ethical conclusions. In the Platonic dialogues that we have studied, concern with reason and its development has rarely been far removed from a concern to describe and to realize a valuable human life. Aristotle's talk about philosophical reason is not always this directly connected to practical questions (except insofar as the pursuit of science is one very important part of our human way of life). We must therefore, in studying his conception of philosophical reason, deal with material that is not explicitly ethical, except in that sense. This will establish a necessary foundation for the pursuit of our more specifically ethical questions.

Plato's middle-period ethical views, furthermore, ascribe supreme value to the pursuit of mathematical and scientific reasoning; these activities are chosen on the grounds that they are pure of pain, maximally stable, and directed at truth. Part of the reason for their superior stability lies in the nature of their alleged objects, which are eternally what they are regardless of what human beings do and say. In assessing Aristotle's response to these ethical arguments, it will thus be important to ask what his conception of these same pursuits is; for his arguments against Plato's conception of them will affect his understanding of their relationship to other more mundanely human activities.

Finally, the acceptance of an anthropocentric conception of ethical truth increases the vulnerability of ethical trust and confidence in situations of upheaval. Chapter 10 on Aristotelian deliberation and Chapter 13 on tragedy will argue that a belief that the fundamental distinctions in the world of practice are human, backed by nothing more eternal or stable than human things, contributes to an agent's sense of ethical risk. For Aristotle this ethical anthropocentrism is a special development of a general argument denying that our belief commitments do, or can, attach themselves to objects that are altogether independent of and more stable than human thought and language. To study that general view, in this way as well, provides essential background for a study of the ethical.

Chapter 9 will also move outside of ethics narrowly conceived, in order to understand Aristotle's reaction to a major element in Plato's attack upon *tuchē*. Again, these related arguments must be pursued in order to grasp the force of his ethical reply. Any inquiry into a human being's relationship to *tuchē* and the world of natural happening must, implicitly or explicitly, give some account of what it means to be a human animal, a being who attempts to control nature, but who is also influenced and acted on by nature. From the beginning of this book we have been brought back repeatedly to the question, how far is a human being like a plant (or a non-rational animal), how far like a god or a solid immutable form? How far are we passive towards the world, and what is the relationship between passivity or receptivity and activity in a human life? How much vulnerability or passivity is compatible with worth and goodness? Aristotle believes that his philosophical tradition has not dealt with these questions well because it has not brought to their study an adequate account of what it is to be a self-moving animal. The richness of ordinary beliefs about action has been lost from view through the influence of bad philosophical theories of action; so it will take an explicitly corrective philosophical account to return us to that complexity, telling us why our passivity is not such as to remove us from ethical assessment, why our animality is not incompatible with our aspirations to goodness. Accordingly, in the *De Anima* and the *De Motu Animalium* he works out a conception of action and of the self-moving animal's causal relation to the world that should provide a better basis for ethics. Chapter 9 describes this project. In the process it will deal with issues in Aristotle's thought about scientific explanation that may seem rather technical for the non-specialist reader, who might prefer to turn directly to the chapter's concluding section (v), where the ethical implications of the explanatory project are described.

We then turn to the ethical treatises more narrowly construed: examining, in Chapter 10, Aristotle's account of a non-scientific picture of practical reasoning and evaluation; in Chapters 11 and 12, his defense of the view that the best human life is vulnerable to catastrophe, and his arguments in favor of including some particularly vulnerable pursuits in that life; in Interlude 2, the implications of these views for the role of poetry and the 'tragic' emotions in human moral learning. Our three original problems of *tuchē* are addressed within these chapters in interconnected ways. The role of 'irrational' passion and desire in the good life is discussed in Chapters 9, 10, and 12 and in Interlude 2; the vulnerability of individual component goods, in Chapter 11 and especially Chapter 12; the plurality of values and the problem of conflict of values in parts of Chapters 10, 11, and 12 and (with reference to tragedy) in Interlude 2.

8   Saving Aristotle's appearances

At the beginning of Book VII of the *Nicomachean Ethics*, just before his discussion of *akrasia*, Aristotle pauses to make some observations about his philosophical method:

Here, as in all other cases, we must set down the appearances (*phainomena*) and, first working through the puzzles (*diaporēsantas*), in this way go on to show, if possible, the truth of all the beliefs we hold (*ta endoxa*) about these experiences; and, if this is not possible, the truth of the greatest number and the most authoritative. For if the difficulties are resolved and the beliefs (*endoxa*) are left in place, we will have done enough showing. (1145b1ff.)

Aristotle tells us that his method, 'here as in all other cases',[1] is to set down what he calls *phainomena*, and what we shall translate as 'the appearances'. Proper philosophical method is committed to and limited by these. If we work through the difficulties with which the *phainomena* confront us and leave the greatest number and the most basic intact, we will have gone as far as philosophy can, or should, go.

This theoretical remark is closely followed by an application of the method. Aristotle first reports some of our most common beliefs and sayings about *akrasia*, concluding his summary with the words, 'These, then, are the things we say (*ta legomena*)' (1145b20). Next he presents the Socratic view that nobody does wrong willingly: we choose the lesser good only as a result of ignorance. Of this theory he says brusquely, 'This story is obviously at variance with the *phainomena*'. He then sets himself to finding an account of akratic behavior that will remain faithful to the 'appearances' in a way that the rejected Socratic account does not.[2]

Here, then, is an ambitious and exciting philosophical view, one that asks us, as we have seen, to revise much of what we ordinarily say and believe. What kind of reply has Aristotle made to this view when he rejects it because it is at variance with the *phainomena* – by which, from the context, he seems to mean our ordinary beliefs and sayings? What sort of philosophical method is this that so thoroughly commits itself to and circumscribes itself by the ordinary?

I have indicated by the title of this chapter that I believe that Aristotle's *phainomena* need saving. This implies that they are in trouble, or under attack. This I believe to be true, on two quite different levels. First, on the level of the text itself, the *phainomena* are in danger of vanishing altogether. Aristotle's word '*phainomena*' receives so many different translations that a reader of the standard English of the passages that I shall discuss would have no clue that they had anything in common. Ross, in the passage from *EN* VII, uses 'observed facts'.[3]

Elsewhere we find 'data of perception', 'admitted facts', 'facts', 'observations' – almost everything *but* the literal 'appearances', or the frequently interchangeable 'what we believe', or 'what we say'. Even G. E. L. Owen, who did so much to salvage the close connection of the *phainomena* with language and ordinary belief, did so, as we shall see, only by charging Aristotle with serious ambiguity of usage.[4] To understand Aristotle's method we must, then, salvage and be more precise about these *phainomena*, which are, as Aristotle tells us in the *Eudemian Ethics*, both the 'witnesses' and the 'paradigms' that we are to use in philosophical inquiry (1216b26).[5]

Second is the deeper problem to which we have alluded. As a philosophical method, the method that announces appearance-saving as its goal was when it was introduced, and still is, in danger of abrupt philosophical dismissal. It can strike us as hopelessly flat, tedious, underambitious. All philosophy does, apparently, is to leave things where they are; when it has done that it has, Aristotle tells us, done 'enough showing'. Enough, we might ask, for what? For whom? For Protagoras, who failed to feel the urgent force of practical problems? For Sophocles? For Plato?

Aristotle was well aware of such questions. In fact, he seems to have chosen the term 'appearances' deliberately, so as to confront them. By using this term for his philosophical 'paradigms', he announces that he is taking a position about philosophical method and limits that is very unusual in his philosophical tradition. 'Appearances' standardly occurs, in pre-Aristotelian Greek epistemology, as one arm of a polarity, on the other side of which is 'the real' or 'the true'. The appearances – by which Plato and his predecessors usually mean the world as perceived, demarcated, interpreted by human beings and their beliefs – are taken to be insufficient 'witnesses' of truth. Philosophy begins when we acknowledge the possibility that the way we pre-philosophically see the world might be radically in error. There is a true nature out there that 'loves to hide itself' (Heraclitus B123) beneath our human ways of speaking and believing. Revealing, uncovering, getting behind, getting beyond – these are some of early Greek philosophy's guiding images for the philosophical pursuit of truth. The Greek word for truth itself means, etymologically 'what is revealed', 'what is brought out from concealment'.[6] Parmenides, the boldest of the philosophers whom Aristotle will be charging with violation of basic appearances, tells us unequivocally that truth is to be found only in a place 'far from the beaten path of human beings', after you depart from 'all the cities'.[7] He puts the contrast between the true and the appearances this way:

> You will learn the unshakeable heart of well-rounded Truth.
> You will, on the other hand, also learn the opinions of mortals, in which
>   there is no true confidence.

The opinions of finite and limited beings provide no good evidence at all for the truth; far less do they provide truth with its 'witnesses' and 'paradigms'.

Plato inherited this tradition and developed it, as we have seen. It is Plato who most explicitly opposes *phainomena*, and the cognitive states concerned with them, to truth and genuine understanding;[8] it is Plato who argues that the *paradeigmata* that we require for understanding of the most important subjects are not to be found in the world of human belief and perception at all. Plato, then, is Aristotle's central target when he tells us that the *phainomena* are our best and only *paradeigmata*. We recall Socrates' attack, in *Republic* VI, against the philosophical adequacy of a method that remains within the human point of view. 'Nothing imperfect is a measure of anything, though sometimes people think that it is enough and that there is no need to search further.' 'They do this', says Glaucon, 'out of laziness.' 'Laziness, however', Socrates replies, 'is a quality that the guardian of a city and of laws can do without.' Nothing imperfect, that is, no limited being, *a fortiori* no human being or human agreement, is ever good measure of anything. Protagoras's anthropocentric dictum is a recipe for inadequacy. The ability to go outside of shared human conceptions and beliefs is here, as in Parmenides' poem, made a necessary condition of access to the real truth about our lives. The perfect god's-eye standpoint is the only reliable one from which to make adequate and reliably true judgments. (And this is so because the aspects of our humanity that separate us from this god, aspects that pervade most of our everyday beliefs and conceptions, have been rejected as distorting and impeding.) The fact that Plato is at pains to show the appeal of his arguments for an ordinary interlocutor such as Glaucon, giving them a deep rootedness in pre-philosophical belief, does not change this picture. For the assent of Glaucon is in no way criterial of their truth; it is only a lucky fact about Glaucon. If neither he nor any other ordinary person had had an interest in contemplation, it would still have been the most valuable activity in the world.*

Nor was Plato's claim concerned with ethics alone. For an adjacent passage criticizes mathematicians on the grounds that they practice their science starting from hypotheses – from something 'laid down' by human beings. They never attain to a pure and unhypothetical point entirely outside these deep human beliefs,[9] a starting-point that is eternal, stable, and not relative in any way to the conditions and contexts of human life and language. Such starting-points are alleged to be the only adequate basis for any science or understanding.

When Aristotle declares that his aim, in science and metaphysics as well as in ethics, is to save the appearances and their truth, he is not, then, saying something cozy and acceptable. Viewed against the background of Eleatic and Platonic philosophizing, these remarks have, instead, a defiant look. Aristotle is promising to rehabilitate the discredited measure or standard of tragic and Protagorean anthropocentrism.† He promises to do his philosophical work in a place from

---

* We should also remember that the world's most valuable activities are this, for Plato, partly because they transcend ordinary experience in the way they do, achieving a superior stability by attaching themselves to objects more stable than the objects we experience in daily life.

† It is important here to bear in mind that anthropocentrism need not imply relativism. Plato's Protagoras, as we have argued, is no relativist (Ch. 4); and the same may well have been true of the historical figure. I an suggesting, then, that Aristotle promises a return from the search for external justification to an *internality* that is deeply rooted in Greek tradition, if at odds with one specifically *philosophical* tradition.

which Plato and Parmenides had spent their careers contriving an exit. He insists
that he will find his truth *inside* what we say, see, and believe, rather than 'far
from the beaten path of human beings' (in Plato's words) 'out there'. When he
writes that the person who orders these appearances and shows their truth has
done 'enough showing', he is replying to the view expressed in *Republic* VI by
insisting that it is not laziness, but good philosophy, that makes one operate within
these limits. I want to arrive at a deeper and more precise account of Aristotle's
method and of his reply to these opponents of anthropocentricity. Three questions
(or groups of questions) will be important:

(1) What are Aristotle's *phainomena*? How is the term '*phainomena*' best translated?
    How are *phainomena* related to observation? to language?

(2) What, more exactly, is the philosophical method described? How does the
    philosopher gather and set down the appearances, and what does he do with them
    then? For what reasons might he throw out some of them, and what has been
    accomplished when he has done that?

(3) Why should we, or our philosophers, be committed to appearances? Where do
    they get their claim to truth? What can Aristotle say to an opponent who claims
    that some of our deepest and most widely shared beliefs are wrong?

I

'*Phainomena*' is a neuter plural of the present participle of '*phainesthai*', 'appear'.
The (*prima facie* unlikely) translation of '*phainomena*' as 'observed facts' comes
out of a long tradition in the interpretation of Aristotelian science. The tradition
ascribes to Aristotle a Baconian picture of scientific/philosophical method that
it also believes to be the most acceptable characterization of the scientist's
procedure. The scientist or philosopher, in each area, begins by gathering data
through precise empirical observation, scrupulously avoiding any kind of
interpreting or theorizing; he or she then searches for a theory that explains the
data. Aristotle's *phainomena* are his Baconian observation-data; the attempt to
'save' them is the attempt to find a comprehensive theory.

It is readily evident that in many contexts this cannot be the meaning of
'*phainomena*'. In our *Ethics* passage, for example, Ross's translation plainly does
not fit. The passage goes directly on to substitute for the word '*phainomena*' the
word '*endoxa*'; *endoxa* are the common conceptions or beliefs on the subject. What
Aristotle actually goes on to collect and set down are, in fact, our common beliefs
about *akrasia*, usually as revealed in things we say. There is no attempt to describe
the incontinent agent's behavior in language free of interpretation; instead
Aristotle looks at the ways we standardly do interpret such behavior. And the
summary of *phainomena* concludes, as we noticed, with the words, 'These, then,
are the things we say (*ta legomena*)' (1145b8–20). Again, Socrates' theory clashes
not with some hard Baconian facts or some theory-neutral description – how could
it? – but with what we commonly say, our shared interpretations.

In his justly famous article, G. E. L. Owen convincingly established that not
only in the ethical works, but also in *Physics*, *De Caelo*, and other scientific works,

Aristotle's *phainomena* must be understood to be our beliefs and interpretations, often as revealed in linguistic usage. To set down the *phainomena* is not to look for belief-free fact, but to record our usage and the structure of thought and belief which usage displays. For example, the *Physics* accounts of place and time begin not with an attempt to gather 'hard' data, but with observations about what we say on this subject, designed to give us a perspicuous view of our current conceptions. By showing us the prominence of conceptual and linguistic considerations in the scientific works, Owen went a long way towards correcting a previously prevalent view, according to which Aristotle makes a sharp distinction between 'science' and 'metaphysics' or *Weltanschauung* – a view in which the *Physics* had always figured as a problematic, or even a confused work.

But Owen did not, I think, go far enough in his criticism of the Baconian picture. He still held on to the view that in certain scientific contexts the Baconian translations are appropriate, and that Aristotle's defense of a method concerned with *phainomena* is, in these cases, a defense of what Owen explicitly calls a 'Baconian picture'. His criticism of the traditional view limits itself to pointing out that it does not fit *all* the evidence; in particular, that it does not even fit all the evidence of all the scientific works. But Owen is then forced to conclude that Aristotle uses the term '*phainomena*' ambiguously. There are two distinct senses – and, we must add, therefore two distinct methods. In one sense, '*phainomena*' means 'observed data' and is associated with a Baconian picture of natural science. In the other, it means 'what we say' or 'our common beliefs', and is associated with a method that aims at sorting out and arranging our descriptions and interpretations of the world.[10]

Owen's article is a major contribution to the study of Aristotle. But its uncharacteristically conservative stopping-place does Aristotle an injustice. First, Owen forces us to charge Aristotle with equivocation concerning his method and several of its central terms.[11] This would be a serious lapse, without any cautionary note, in just the area where Aristotle's precision and attentiveness are usually most striking. Fortunately, however, we do not need to charge him with this. For the entire problem arises only because of a second more serious difficulty in Owen's account, one whose removal will remove this one with it. Owen finds ambiguity because he believes that in biology Aristotle is committed to 'Baconian' empiricism. There is, in fact, no case for crediting Aristotle with anything like the Baconian picture of science based on theory-neutral observation. He was not concerned, in his talk of experience or how the world 'appears', to separate off one privileged group of observations and to call them the 'uninterpreted' or 'hard' data. Such a bounding-off of a part of the data of experience as 'hard' or 'theory-free' was, in fact, unknown to any early Greek scientist. Instead of the sharp Baconian distinction between perception-data and communal belief, we find in Aristotle, as in his predecessors, a loose and inclusive notion of 'experience', or the way(s) a human observer sees or 'takes' the world, using his cognitive faculties (all of which Aristotle calls '*kritika*', 'concerned with making distinctions').[12]

This, I suggest, is the meaning of Aristotle's talk of *phainomena*. It is a loose notion, one that invites (and receives) further subdivisions; but it is neither ambiguous nor vacuous. If we do not insist on introducing an anachronistic scientific conception, the alleged two senses and two methods can be one. When Aristotle sits on the shore of Lesbos taking notes on shellfish, he will be doing something that is not, if we look at it from his point of view, so far removed from his activity when he records what we say about *akrasia*. He will be describing the world *as it appears to*, as it is experienced by, observers who are members of our kind.[13] Certainly there are important differences between these two activities; but there is also an important link, and it is legitimate for him to stress it. We distinguish sharply between 'science' and 'the humanities'. Aristotle would be reminding us of the humanness of good science. Owen correctly emphasizes that Aristotle is composing these methodological remarks in the shadow of Parmenides, who repudiated together, without distinction, both the evidence of sense-perception and the data of shared language and belief; all this he derides as mere 'convention' or 'habit'. Plato, too, repudiates perception and belief together, as 'mired' in the 'barbaric mud' of the human point of view. Aristotle, answering them, promises to work within and to defend a method that is thoroughly committed to the data of human experience and accepts these as its limits.

II

If Aristotle's method simply spoke in vague terms of preserving perceptions and beliefs, it would be no substantial contribution to philosophy. But we can elicit from his theoretical remarks and from his practice a rich account of philosophical procedure and philosophical limits.

First the philosopher must 'set down' the relevant appearances. These will be different (and differently gathered) in each area. But in all areas we are to include both a study of ordinary beliefs and sayings and a review of previous scientific or philosophical treatments of the problem, the views of 'the many and the wise'.[14] To judge from what Aristotle sees fit to set down, the 'we' that bounds the class of relevant appearances is a group whose members share with each other not only species membership, but also some general features of a way of life. The scientific tradition around Aristotle was fascinated by ethnography and by parallels between animal and human customs. Aristotle's practice implicitly denies the relevance of their more remote material for any inquiry into human conceptions or values. We find no mention, in the relevant parts of the *Ethics*, *Politics*, or *Physics*, of the ways in which animals train their young or conceive of time and place. Nor do we find a record of the views and conceptions of the weird primitive communities so lavishly described by Herodotus and his followers. The *phainomena* are drawn from Aristotle's own linguistic community and from several other civilized communities known to him to have recognizably similar general conditions of life, though with different particular institutions. (In other scientific cases, data will be drawn from aspects of the natural world observed or experienced by people from such communities.)[15] Aristotle has often been accused of cultural chauvinism for this selectivity. But there are deeper and more interesting reasons. In *Politics* I he tells us why he omits from his political study both bestial beings and heroic or divine beings. The human being he says (in a passage that we shall also study in Chapter 11) is the only living creature who has experience of the good and bad, the just and unjust, and the other ethical concepts with which this study deals; in consequence only the human being has the capacity to express these conceptions in speech.[16] This unique experience seems to be connected with the fact that humans alone among creatures are both reasonable – capable of association in the institutions that take their form from these articulated conceptions – and lacking in individual self-sufficiency. They are neither beasts nor gods (1253a27–9). It is, then, likely that Aristotle is following a philosophical tradition begun in the writings of Heraclitus, according to which the ability to use the name of justice is based on experiences of need and scarcity that a godlike being would not share.[17] It seems to follow, if we generalize this principle, that data for an inquiry into our conception of F can come only from peoples whose ways of life are similar to ours with respect to those conditions that gave rise to our use of the term 'F'. Other groups and species not so related to us could not have 'F' (or a term closely enough related to our 'F') in their language, and we do not, therefore, need to ask them what they think about it. (We shall see later that these observations derive support from Aristotle's general remarks about discourse.)

The philosopher has now gathered together all the relevant *phainomena*. His next job, Aristotle argues, is to set out the puzzles or dilemmas with which they confront us. The *phainomena* present us with a confused array, often with direct contradiction. They reflect our disagreements and ambivalences. The first step must, therefore, be to bring conflicting opinions to the surface and set them out clearly, marshaling the considerations for and against each side, showing clearly how the adoption of a certain position on one issue would affect our positions on others. Without this serious attempt to describe the puzzles, the philosopher is likely to accept too quickly a solution that disguises or merely avoids the problem. 'It is not possible to resolve anything if you do not see how you are bound; but the puzzles of the intellect show you this about the issue. For insofar as the intellect is puzzled, thus far its experience is similar to that of someone in bonds: it cannot go forward in either direction' (*Metaph.* 995a29–33). Having said this, Aristotle goes on to devote the entire third book of the *Metaphysics* to setting out his most serious puzzles about identity and understanding in preparation for the more positive work of the later books. The scientific works proceed in a similar fashion.

If philosophy simply preserved the *status quo*, it would stop here. Some people think this, but some think this. There are these good reasons for p, these other good reasons for not-p. The Greek skeptic did stop at this point. The conflict of opinion, and the apparently equal weight of opposing beliefs displayed in the puzzles, left him poised in the middle, released from all intellectual commitment.[18]

And he found this experience of dissociation from belief so delightfully pleasant that he sought it out as the human good, designing his arguments, from now on, so as to *produce* this 'equal weight'. Aristotle does not stop here. His imagery of bondage and freedom indicates that *he* found the experience of dilemma anything but delightful. (Here we begin to notice some of the deep human differences that can separate one metaphilosophical position from another.) 'All human beings by nature reach out for understanding', he writes at the opening of the *Metaphysics*. This profound natural desire to bring the matter of life into a perspicuous order will not be satisfied, he believes, as long as there is contradiction. Our deepest intellectual commitment (as we shall see) is to the Principle of Non-Contradiction, the most basic of all our shared beliefs. The method of appearance-saving therefore demands that we press for consistency.

But in resolving our difficulties we are not, Aristotle insists, free to follow a logical argument anywhere it leads. We must, at the end of our work on the puzzles, bring our account back to the *phainomena* and show that our account does, in fact, preserve them as true – or, at any rate, the greatest number and the most basic. Aristotle repeatedly criticizes philosophers and scientists who attend to internal clarity and consistency, ignoring this return. In the *De Caelo* (293a27) he criticizes men who 'look for conviction not out of the *phainomena*, but out of argument'; the context reveals that they have been pressing a theoretical claim which, like Socrates' view of *akrasia*, is seriously at odds with prevalent beliefs.[19] In Book III, he criticizes the Platonist theory that physical bodies are generated from triangular surfaces: 'What happens to these people is that in a discussion about the *phainomena* they say what is not in conformity with the *phainomena*. The reason for this is that they have the wrong notion of first principles and want to bring everything into line with some hard-and-fast theories' (*Cael.* 306a5ff.). Similarly, in *On Generation and Corruption* (325a13ff.), he criticizes the Eleatics for failing to follow the *phainomena* – judgments based on our experience – all the way through their inquiry. They were 'led to overstep' experience, he says, by their view that 'one ought to follow the argument'. What these thinkers did, evidently, was to begin in the right way, with the *phainomena* – in this case, with human perceptual experience of the world. But then they got fascinated by the internal progress of their argument and trusted the argument, even though it ended in a place incredibly remote from, and at odds with, human beliefs. Instead, Aristotle thinks, they should have regarded the strangeness of the conclusion as a sign that something was wrong with the argument. Of the Eleatic conclusion – the denial that distinctions and plurality are genuine features of our world – Aristotle goes on to say, 'Although these opinions appear to follow if one looks at the arguments, still to believe them seems next door to lunacy when one considers practice. For in fact no lunatic seems to stand so far outside as to suppose that fire and ice are one' (*GC* 325a18–22). Theory must remain committed to the ways human beings live, act, see – to the *pragmata*, broadly construed. To follow the Eleatic is to attempt to believe things that not even the abnormal members of our community seem to believe, if we judge from what they do. Even madmen do not generally store butter in the fireplace, or huddle for warmth in front of a block of ice.

But what principles and procedures can we, then, use in deciding what appearances to keep and what to throw out, as we press for consistency? Here Aristotle's procedures vary, as we might expect, with the subject matter and the problem, and it is difficult to say anything illuminating at this level of generality. But we can make a few remarks. First, nothing universally believed is entirely discarded. 'For that which seems so to everyone, this we say is' (*EN* 1172a36). Earlier in the *Ethics*, Aristotle quotes with approval the poetic lines: 'No report is altogether wiped out, which many peoples...' (*EN* 1155b27–8).[20] (Here the context (concerning pleasure) shows that this does not prevent us from qualifying the belief in the light of other beliefs.) Second, nothing that we have to be using in order to argue or inquire can get thrown out. We shall look at that point in the following section.

Beyond this, we must, Aristotle believes, ask ourselves whether, in the inquiry at hand, we share some conception of the good judge, of the person or persons whom we will trust to arbitrate our disputes. Very rarely is truth a matter of majority vote (*Metaph.* 1009b2). Often our idea of the competent judge is more broadly shared among us, and less subject to disagreement, than is our view of the subject matter concerning which this judge is to render a verdict. In ethics, for example, we agree more readily about the characteristics of intellect, temper, imagination, and experience that a competent judge must have than we do about the particular practical judgments that we expect him or her to make. The same is true in other areas as well. In *Metaphysics* IV, Aristotle answers thinkers who create puzzles about perception by pointing out that our practices reveal a set of standards for arbitrating disagreements:

It is worthy of amazement if they create a puzzle about whether magnitudes are of such a size, and colors of such a quality, as they appear (*phainetai*) to those at a distance or to those who are near, and whether they are such as they appear to the healthy or to the sick; and whether those things are quite heavy which appear so to the weak or to the strong; and whether those things are true which appear so to the sleeping or to the waking. It is obvious that they do not really think that these are matters for doubt. At any rate nobody, if, while he is in Libya, he has imagined one night that he is in Athens, [wakes up and] heads for the Odeion.[21] Again, as for the future, as even Plato says, the opinions of the doctor and the ignorant man are not equally authoritative as to whether someone is or is not going to be healthy. (1010b3–14)

Aristotle asks us to look at our practices, seeing, in the different areas, what sorts of judges we do, in fact, trust. The judgment about whom to trust and when seems to come, like the appearances, from us. We turn to doctors because we do, in fact, rely on doctors. This reliance, Aristotle insists, does not need to be justified by producing a further judge to certify the judge (1011a3ff.); it is sufficiently 'justified' by the facts of what we do. The expert, and our reasons for choosing him, are not behind our practices; they are inside them. And yet such experts do, in fact, help us to unravel puzzles.[22]

The importance of the expert emerges clearly if we consider Aristotle's account of our basic linguistic practices of introducing into discourse and defining. In *Posterior Analytics* II.8, Aristotle develops an account of the transition from our initial use of a natural kind term to its scientific definition.[23] The kind term enters our use on the basis of some communal experience or experiences (the pronoun 'we' is used throughout). For example, 'We are aware of thunder as a noise in the clouds, of eclipse as a privation of light, or of the human being as a certain species of animal' (93a22–24). At this point we are able to 'indicate' (*sēmainein*) human beings or eclipses, to introduce them into discourse or refer to them; but we do not yet have the scientific definition that states the nature of things of this kind. We may have sorted our experience and assigned our kind terms very roughly – 'sometimes incidentally, sometimes by grasping something of the item in question' (93a21–2). We move from this rough grouping and this thin account to the full definition only when we have some account or theory that states the nature of the phenomenon: in the case of thunder, he tells us, when we have a theory that tells us that it is the quenching of fire in the clouds, and how this produces the sound we hear. The expert, not the layman, uncovers this theory. In the case of most species of animals, we do not yet, Aristotle believes, have a theory that satisfies our demands. But our broadly shared belief that natural beings are 'things that have within themselves a principle of change' (*Ph.* II.1) implies a commitment to abide by the results of scientific investigation into these inner structures.[24] When the scientist comes up with a theory that offers a satisfactory account of the growth and movement of some type of natural being, we are committed to regarding this theory as defining and bounding (at least *pro tempore*) the nature of this being – even if some individuals whom we have previously tended to include in the extension of the term will have to be excluded. Our agreement in a commitment to scientific exploration proves more basic than our *prima facie* disagreement with the biologist over the extension of the term.

We can use Aristotle's account of defining to make progress on two of our previous problems. First, we can now see more clearly why Aristotle gathers his *phainomena* only from communities relevantly like ours. The suggestion of the *Politics* passage is confirmed by his general account of discourse. We take our evidence about *F*s only from communities where the relevant conditions of experience are similar to those that obtain in our own community, because the very meaning of '*F*' is given by an account couched in terms of laws and conditions of our actual community. Our ability to introduce *F*s into discourse arises from actual experience, and the nature of *F*s is given by a scientific account arrived at by research in and into the world of our experience. In some cases, for example in the case of species terms, the relevant community may be the whole earth; in the case of ethical and political language it may well be much narrower.

We can now also begin to give Aristotle an answer to the charge that his method shuns the hard work involved in making real philosophical or scientific progress. Aristotle can insist that there is no tension – or at least no *simple* tension – between the appearances-method and the scientist's aims. This is so because our practices and our language embody a reliance on such experts, frequently making their judgments constitutive of truth. This method is attempting at once to be seriously respectful of human language and ordinary ways of believing and to do justice to the fact that these very practices reveal an ongoing demand for scientific understanding. The method should not be taken to prevent us from doing what we in fact do. It is, however, also crucial to see that the expert plays here no deeper role than the role that he or she in fact plays. He is normative for our use only to the extent that we in fact agree in accepting his authority. Aristotle shows no tendency to convert these descriptive remarks about discourse into a prescriptive theory of discourse; we, in reading him, should not build in more structure than is present in the text, whose main aim is to argue against those who create specious puzzles by denying an actual feature of our practice.

I have so far said little about how this account of Aristotle's philosophical/scientific method, constructed largely from the *Metaphysics* and the specific scientific treatises, is to be put together with the account of scientific understanding developed in the *Posterior Analytics*. Two pressing questions might be raised at this point. The first concerns the *Analytics'* ideal of a finished science as a hierarchical deductive system: how does this norm cohere with Aristotle's aims and procedures in the appearance-saving passages on which I have drawn? This is clearly a huge question, which can barely be broached here. But we can provisionally say that the appearance-saving method could be fully compatible with the *Analytics'* demand that, in the natural sciences (as opposed to ethics), the expert should in the end be able to validate his claim to understanding by giving systematic demonstrations of the type described. The two aims would be compatible if the deductive ideal were seen as something that arises, itself, from the appearances, a commitment which we believe ourselves to undertake when we do science. And this, in fact, is how Aristotle presents his account of *epistēmē* there: as an articulation of what 'we' believe scientific understanding should be and do. He begins from an account of the conditions under which 'we' 'think we understand' something (*APo* 71b9), and goes on to show what this shared conception requires of the scientist. Similarly, the *Physics* discussion of explanation begins from the ways in which 'we' ask and answer 'Why?' questions, and criticizes earlier scientists for insufficient attention to the variety of our usage. At every step Aristotle is concerned to show how his norm arises out of the appearances and embodies their requirements.[25] In ethics, on the other hand, he takes pains to argue that our beliefs about practice do *not* yield the demand for a deductive system.[26] He is evidently not interested in assimilating the appearances to a theoretical ideal where the appearances themselves do not reveal a commitment to such an ideal.

But a more troublesome question arises when we consider that the first principles of science in the *Analytics* have been thought by centuries of commentators, via the medieval tradition, to be *a priori* truths grasped by special acts of intellectual intuition, apart from all experience. Surely, we might object, the finished structure of an Aristotelian science rests on these, and not, ultimately, on the appearances. Or, if the scientific works do rest on appearances, they depart, in so placing themselves, from the ideal set forth in the *Analytics*.

The objector and I can agree on a number of points about the principles mentioned in the *Analytics*: that they are to be true, indemonstrable, necessary, primary, both prior to and more knowable than the conclusion; that they transmit their truth to the conclusion; even (as it will turn out) that they are *a priori* according to *some* understanding of the *a priori*. But this leaves, it is plain, much scope for disagreement: for a deep and basic human appearance can be all of those things, as I shall show; and to say this about a principle commits us neither to special acts of rational intuition, nor to the notion that the principles are true outside of all conceptual schemes, all language. The objector, it emerges, derives these extra elements of this famous interpretation from an exiguous amount of evidence, especially from some alleged evidence in *Posterior Analytics* II.19. Fortunately (since I have no space here to argue the case in detail) recent work on *nous* (intellect) and *epistēmē* (understanding) in the *Analytics* has convincingly shown that the objector's picture is a misreading of the text. Work by A. Kosman, J. Lesher, and, most recently, an excellent article by Myles Burnyeat, have established that the model of understanding that emerges from this and connected texts does not introduce either intuition or extra-experiential truth.[27] To have *nous*, or insight, concerning first principles is to come to see the fundamental role that principles we have been using all along play in the structure of a science. What is needed is not to grasp the first principles – we grasp them and use them already, inside our experience, as the text of II.19 asserts. As Burnyeat puts it, 'What [the student's belief] is not yet is understanding and that kind of [grasp] that goes with understanding. To acquire this at the level of first principles what we need is greater familiarity, perhaps some more dialectical practice; in short, intellectual habituation.'[28] We move from the confused mass of the appearances to a perspicuous ordering, from the grasp that goes with use to the ability to give accounts. There is no reason to posit two philosophical methods here, one dealing with appearances, one resting on the *a priori*; dialectic and first philosophy have, as Aristotle insists in *Metaphysics* IV.2 (cf. below) exactly the same subject matter. The appearances, then, can go all the way down.

III

But if the *Analytics* does not help the objector, neither does it really answer our remaining questions about the status of Aristotelian first principles. What *is*, then, meant by the claim that they must be both 'true' and 'undemonstrated', and where do we get our conviction of their truth, if undemonstrated is what they are? If they are found in and through experience, it then becomes all the more pressing to inquire how they get their claim to truth and to priority. The *Analytics* tells us some of the characteristics of first principles; it also tells us how, through experience, we can acquire insight into their fundamental status. It does not yet answer our question concerning that status, since it does not encounter any sort of skeptical challenge.[29] Now we must turn, therefore, to *Metaphysics* IV, where we shall see how Aristotle defends their claim against the skeptic's attack.

In *Metaphysics* IV.4, Aristotle considers how we should deal with an opponent who challenges the Principle of Non-Contradiction (contradictory predicates cannot belong to the same subject at the same time). He calls this principle 'The most secure starting-point (*archē*) of all'. How then, are we to deal with the opponent who challenges us to justify our inquiry by demonstrating its truth? Aristotle's answer is revealing. 'They demand a demonstration', he says, 'out of *apaideusia*. For it is *apaideusia* not to recognize of what things you should look for a demonstration, and of what you should not.' Now *apaideusia* is not stupidity, absurdity, logical error, even wrong-headedness. It is lack of *paideia*, the education by practice and precept that initiates a young Greek into the ways of his community; the word is usually translated 'acculturation' or 'moral education'. *Apaideusia* is, for example, the condition of the Cyclopes (Euripides, *Cycl.* 493), humanoid creatures who live in isolation from human community. 'They have no assemblies that make decisions, nor do they have binding conventions, but they inhabit the summits of lofty mountains...and they have no concern for one another' (Hom. *Od.* IX.112–15).[30] It looks significant that the opponent is charged with this defect, rather than with ignorance or dumbness. It is not so much that he is stupid; he just does not know how to do things (or he refuses to do things) the way we do them. He lacks what Burnyeat has called 'intellectual habituation' – the sensitive awareness, produced by education and experience, of the fundamental role this principle plays in all our practices, all our discourse. (Cf. *GC* 316a5: 'The reason for their deficient ability to survey what we all agree on is their inexperience (*apeiria*).') And, for some reason, he has decided to dissociate himself even from the incomplete *paideia* that characterizes the person in the street; for he is assailing a principle that that person *uses* as fundamental, whether he is aware of this or not.

Aristotle now goes on to propose a way of dealing with this objector. First, he says, you must find out whether this person will say anything to you or not. If he will not say anything, then you can stop worrying about him. 'It is comical to look for something to say to someone who won't say anything. A person like that, insofar as he is like that, is pretty well like a vegetable' (1006a13–15). But if he *does* say something, something definite, then you can go on to show him that in so doing he is in fact believing and making use of the very principle he attacks. For in order to be saying something definite he has to be ruling out something else as incompatible: at the very least, the contradictory of what he has asserted.[31]

So if the person does not speak, he ceases to be one of us, and we are not required to take account of him. If he does speak, we can urge him to take a close look at his linguistic practices and what they rest on. In doing this we are giving him the *paideia* he lacks, a kind of initiation into the way we do things. Sometimes the opponent will not listen. 'Some need persuasion, others need violence',

Aristotle remarks somewhat grimly in the next chapter (1009a17–18). Philosophy, at the level of basic principles, seems to be a matter of bringing the isolated person into line, of dispelling illusions that cause the breakdown of communication. Sometimes this can be done gently, sometimes only with violence; and sometimes not at all.

Several things strike us in this reply to the skeptical challenger. First, it is not the sort of reply he demands. In the century after Aristotle, Stoic philosophers answered skeptical attacks against basic beliefs by arguing that these beliefs rest on a perceptual foundation that is absolutely indubitable. The 'cataleptic impression' was a perception that certified its own accuracy; this foundation was, they felt, secure against the skeptic.[32] But Aristotle does not point to this sort of foundation for our knowledge of the world. He says that the principle is true and primary; that we are entitled to assert it; that, in fact, we cannot be wrong about it; that it is what any thinking person must believe. He does not say that this basic principle is true apart from the 'appearances' and from human conceptual schemes, true of the way the world is *behind* or *beyond* the categories of our thought and discourse. In fact, in the next chapter he even refuses to take up the popular contemporary question, which animate species is the standard of truth? All he says is that *we* cannot assail the principle; but neither, he insists, can we demonstrate it in the demanded way. It is, for us, the starting-point of all discourse, and to get outside it would be to cease to think and to speak. So in a very important way Aristotle does *not* answer the opponent's challenge. He does not offer him the exterior, Platonic certainty he wants. And if the opponent does choose to isolate himself from discourse, even the limited 'elenctic demonstration' will not succeed. In a penetrating account of this passage, the third-century A.D. Greek commentator Alexander of Aphrodisias writes that to attempt to converse with such a silent opponent is 'to try to communicate something through discourse to someone who has no discourse, and through discourse to try to establish fellowship with someone who is bereft of fellowship' (272.36–273.1). We cannot satisfy the skeptic's demand for external purity; we can ask him to accept our fellowship. But perhaps, if he is a skeptic bent on securing his equanimity against the risks attendant on community and human involvement, he will refuse that. We cannot, in any harder sense, show him that he is *wrong*. (This is why Aristotle's crucial next step, in *Metaph.* IV.5, is to search for a diagnosis of the opponent's motivations, asking what beliefs and aims might lead an intelligent person to take up this position, and how we might cure the motivating error in each case.)

A similar position is implied in the passage we examined earlier, where Aristotle rejected the Eleatic One on the grounds that not even a lunatic believes in it, if we judge from his actions. Here, too, Aristotle stops short of calling Parmenides' conclusion wrong of the world as it is apart from all conceptualization. All he says is that no human being who undertakes to act in the human world – no human being who does not 'stand so far outside' as not to be acting *among* us at all – can be seriously holding the view. Action, even bizarre and abnormal action, commits itself to the existence of movement and plurality. Aristotle makes this same point later in *Metaphysics* iv.4, extending his discourse argument for the Principle of Non-Contradiction to cover cases in which the opponent, though possibly silent with respect to the argument's verbal demands, reveals his commitment to the principle through his practices:

It is most obvious that nobody really is in this condition [sc. of believing the denial of the Principle of Non-Contradiction], neither those who make the argument, nor anybody else. For why does he go to Megara and not stay put, when he thinks he should go? Why doesn't he go straight out early in the morning and throw himself into a well or off a precipice, if there chance to be one, but instead obviously avoids this, as though he does not actually hold that it is not good and good to fall in? It's clear, then, that he believes one thing better and the other thing not better. (1008b14–19)

The opponent can defeat us, then, only by ceasing to act humanly in our world, as well as by ceasing to speak. As soon as he acts in some definite fashion, he is being responsive to definite features of the world as it strikes a human being, namely himself. He is accepting certain appearances, both perceptions and common human beliefs – e.g. beliefs about the badness of early death, about the danger of being killed if one walks off a precipice, about the fact that he is a mortal, bodily creature with bones that can be broken and blood that can be spilled – as having a bearing on his life and actions. He is not accepting their contradictories as having equal force. He is allowing the humanity that he shares with us to govern his choice.[33] But this Aristotelian reply, once again, comes from within human practices. It makes clear the cost of refusing the principle: immobility as well as silence, the utter loss of community. It does not seek to ground the principle in anything firmer than this. But this is firm enough; this is true, necessary, as firm as anything could be.

Aristotle does not, however, assert that there is *nothing more* to non-contradiction than *paideia* or our practices. He would say, I think, that we are not in a position to judge this; that this claim, like the skeptic's denial of the principle, asks us to stand outside language and life, and is therefore doomed to fail. No argument rules out that some god might be able to say more, or something different. All we can say, however, is that everything we do, say, and think rests on this principle.

Is the principle then for Aristotle an *a priori* principle?[34] This question is frequently raised, but often without sufficient care to define the type of *a priori* principle involved. It is certainly *a priori* if an *a priori* principle is one that is basic or unrevisable, relative to a certain body of knowledge (what has sometimes been called the 'contextual *a priori*'). It is even *a priori* in a somewhat stronger sense: it is so basic that it cannot significantly be defended, explained, or questioned at all from within the appearances, that is to say the lives and practices of human beings, as long as human beings are anything like us. But it is not an *a priori* principle if that is a principle that can be known to hold independently of all experience and all ways of life, all conceptual schemes. This is the question that we are in no position either to ask or to answer. This is what the skeptic wanted to be shown, and this we do not offer him.

We cannot illustrate this point more clearly than by contrasting the Aristotelian and the Platonic notions of the 'unhypothetical' foundations of a science. For Plato, as we said, each science must start from a principle or principles that are 'unhypothetical' in the sense that they are known to hold 'themselves by themselves', entirely independently of all conceptualization and thought. Aristotle also calls his 'most secure principle' an 'unhypothetical' principle; but his account makes clear the difference of his position: 'For that which it is necessary for anyone who understands anything at all to have, this is not a hypothesis' (1005b15–16). A hypothesis is, in his view, quite literally something 'set down beneath' something else. Anything that we must use in order to think at all obviously cannot be posited or 'set down' at will; therefore, we are justified in calling such a principle 'unhypothetical'. But this Kantian kind of non-hypothetical status is all that Aristotle ever endeavors to claim for it. To try to say 'more' would be, in his view, to say less, or perhaps nothing at all. Scientific truths are certainly true *of* or *about* the world of nature; they are not (any more than they were for Kant) all *about* human beings or their mental states. But the status of the basic truths on which science is based is a status of necessity *for* discourse and thought. It is this necessity, and only this, that they can transmit to their dependents.

One further example will show us a connection between Aristotle's replies to skeptical opponents and his views about language. In *Physics* II, Aristotle considers Parmenides' claim that change and motion are merely conventional. As in the *Metaphysics*, he rejects the Eleatic demand that he demonstrate this basic appearance:

To try to show that nature exists is comical; for it is obvious that there are many such [i.e. changing] things. And to show the obvious through the obscure is what someone does who is unable to distinguish what is self-evident from what is not. It's possible to be in that state: a man blind from birth might try to give a proof from premises concerning colors. But it is necessary that the talk of such people will be mere words, and that they will have no *nous* about anything. (193a1ff.)

Once again, we notice that there is a sense in which the challenger goes unanswered. Aristotle says not that the opponent is *wrong* about the way things really are apart from the categories of thought, not that he says what can be decisively falsified by appeal to some foundational evidence, but that what he says is comical. He is trying to say what *he*, at any rate, is in no position to say. Just as a person blind from birth is in no position to use in an argument premises about colors, since he can have had no experience of color, so the Eleatic is in no position to use premises having to do with the unitary, unchanging Being of the universe. Change and plurality are in everything we experience; even Parmenides grants this. They are for him among the very deepest of the facts that form the bounds of our ordinary experience of the world. Even his philosopher-hero is aware of himself throughout the poem as a changing natural being. How then, Aristotle asks, can he make his argument?

These remarks can be better understood if we recall Aristotle's views about linguistic indicating. The Eleatic is 'comical' because he does not succeed in singling out or indicating the unchanging, undivided One. This unity is, by the Eleatic's own story, 'far from the beaten path of human beings'. Neither he nor anyone else in his community can have had experience of it.[35] Therefore, Aristotle would say, he cannot introduce it into discourse; discourse, even when vague and imprecise, is bounded by the experience of the group. Therefore, although the Eleatic believes that he is saying something bold and strange, he is really saying nothing at all. This is why we can say that his talk is 'mere words' without understanding.

And as for the Platonist, who charges with 'laziness' any philosopher who refuses to take the 'longer route' that moves away from appearances to grasp the form of the Good, Aristotle says, elsewhere, that this opponent, too, fails to 'indicate' or refer to his cherished entities. In a remarkable passage in the *Posterior Analytics*, he remarks how queer it is that the Platonist introduces monadic, self-subsistent forms of properties which, like colors, always occur in our experience as the properties of some substance or other. Then, with a burst of exuberant malice that shows us aspects of Aristotle's temperament usually masked by a measured sobriety, he exclaims, 'So goodbye to the Platonic Forms. They are *teretismata*, and have nothing to do with our speech' (*APo* 83a32–4). *Teretismata* are meaningless sounds you make when you are singing to yourself; we might render them as 'dum-de-dum-dums'. Jonathan Barnes's new translation calls them 'noninoes'. But, besides the fact that this suggestion of highbrow musical taste makes the criticism too polite, we also miss the emphasis on solitude and isolation conveyed by the Greek. We are supposed to think not of a madrigal society, but of a completely self-absorbed individual saying to himself what neither anyone else, nor, ultimately, he can understand. When the Platonist speaks of The Good or The White, he is not referring to anything, much less communicating anything to us. He is just crooning away in a corner. For forms are self-subsistent, monadic, where our experience makes properties dependent on substance; forms are non-relational, even where the property (e.g. equality, doubleness) always turns up, in our experience, in a relational context. (In *Metaphysics* I, Aristotle says that Plato's arguments tried to create a non-relative class of relative terms, 'of which *we say* there is no all-by-themselves class' (990b16–17).)

But to say 'goodbye' to the forms is not to assert that they do not exist entirely outside of the world of our experience and thought. That we could not say either. Even the contrast between the world as it is for us and the world as it is behind or apart from our thought may not be a contrast that the defender of a human internal truth should allow himself or herself to make using human language. Here we might say that Aristotle usually maintains his internality more consistently than Kant, refusing, most of the time, even to try to articulate what it is that we cannot say. Aristotelian reason is not so much in bonds, cut off *from* something that we can, nonetheless, describe or point to, as it is committed *to* something, to language and thought, and the limits of these.[36] Appearances and truth are not opposed, as Plato believed they were. We can have truth only *inside* the circle of the appearances, because only there can we communicate, even refer, at all.

This, then – if we may characterize it for ourselves using language not known to Aristotle himself – is a kind of realism, neither idealism of any sort nor skepticism. It has no tendency to confine us to internal representations, nor to ask us to suspend or qualify our deeply grounded judgments. It is fully hospitable to truth, to necessity (properly understood), and to a full-blooded notion of objectivity. It is not relativism, since it insists that truth is one for all thinking, language-using beings. It is a realism, however, that articulates very carefully the limits within which any realism must live. Talk of the eternal or the immortal has its place in such a realism – but, as Aristotle makes clear, only because such talk is an important part of our world. 'It is well to join in by persuading oneself that the ancient beliefs deeply belonging to our native tradition are true, according to which there is something deathless and divine' (*Cael.* 285a1–4; and cf. the preservation of the theistic 'appearances' of 'all human beings' at *Cael.* 270b5ff.). The belief in the divinity and eternity of the heavenly bodies has weight in philosophy because of its depth for us, because it has survived so many changes of social and political belief of a more superficial nature (*Metaph.* 1074a39ff.). But, by the same token, an 'internal' truth is all we are entitled to claim for such beliefs.[37] Even the existence of an unmoved mover is established as one of the conclusions of a physical science, none of whose principles has a deeper status than the Principle of Non-Contradiction, and many of which are obviously less firmly grounded.

To opt out of a basic 'appearance' will not always entail silence or inaction. Appearances come at different levels of depth: by which we mean that the cost of doing without one will vary with the case, and must be individually scrutinized. We notice, for example, that none of the beliefs most central to ethics and politics proves as deeply grounded as the basic logical laws. To deny the prevalent belief in gods will lead to a certain loss of community: there will be a very real sense in which theist and atheist do not inhabit the same world or look at the same stars. But the gulf will not be totally unbridgeable. Similarly, to opt out of very basic communal ethical judgments will lead to a way of life that more normal humans may judge bestial or inhuman. A life of extreme intemperance does bring a communication problem with it, for 'the person who lives according to his impulses will not listen to an argument that dissuades him' (*EN* 1179b26–7); and, at the other end of the spectrum, the extreme ascetic also ceases to be one of us, 'for insensibility of this sort is not human...and if there should be someone to whom nothing is pleasant, he would be far from being a human being' (*EN* 1119a6–10). But the cost of asceticism is not the same as the cost of denying the Principle of Non-Contradiction; presumably this is a life that could be lived among us, though the liver would in significant ways fail to be one of us.

Furthermore, whereas the opponent of the Principle of Non-Contradiction could not find a place from which to argue with us, the opponent of a prevalent but less basic appearance can always try to show us (relying on the Principle) that some other, more basic appearances conflict with this one and ought to lead us to abandon it. For example, a feminist opponent of Aristotle's conservative view about the social role of women could try to show Aristotle that a progresssive position actually preserves certain deep human beliefs about the equal humanity of other human beings better than his own political theory does. If Aristotle agreed about the conflict, and agreed that these other beliefs were deeper (i.e. that the cost of giving them up would be greater, or one we are less inclined to pay), then we would expect him to change his view. The method does not make new discoveries, radical departures, or sharp changes of position impossible, either in science or in ethics.[38] What it does do is to explain to us how any radical or new view must commend itself to our attention: by showing its relationship to our lived experience of the world and giving evidence of its ability to organize and articulate features of that experience. Sometimes it may remain unclear over a long period of time whether a bold hypothesis – including many of Plato's and some of Aristotle's own – has or has not successfully made this return, whether it is the human truth, or just empty words. (This is true in part because it frequently remains unclear which appearances should count for us as deep and regulative and which we may be willing to give up.) It can also remain unclear what *form* the return itself should take – i.e. whether, in a particular subject, we demand the systematic hierarchical grasp that goes with *epistēmē*, or whether we prefer, instead, a more elusive type of perception. In Chapter 10 we shall see Aristotle claim that practical wisdom is not *epistēmē*; and we shall see how he argues, within the appearances, for this conclusion. In general, the role of the marks of Platonic *technē*, such as generality, precision, and commensurability, in the final result must be appropriate to the subject matter; and it is from the appearances themselves that the appropriate criteria must be elicited. The meta-view, like the content of the view, comes from our demands and our practices, and must commend itself as the sort of organization we can live with.

IV

The Platonist has charged the Aristotelian with philosophical laziness. We might now answer this charge in Aristotle's behalf by saying to him that his kind of hard work, struggling for an unconditional vantage point outside the appearances, is both futile and destructive: futile, because such a vantage point is unavailable, as such, to human inquiry; destructive, because the glory of the promised goal makes the humanly possible work look boring and cheap. We could be pursuing the study of ourselves and of our world in ethics, politics, biology, physical science. We could be investigating our human conceptions of place and time, our practices of explaining change, of counting, of individuating. The Platonist encourages us to neglect this work by giving us the idea that philosophy is a worthwhile enterprise only if it takes us away from the 'cave' and up into the sunlight.

The Platonist might now reply that the Aristotelian conception makes of philosophy a flat and unexciting activity, one that makes no distinctive addition to ordinary human life. It seems to destroy philosophy by depriving it of its claim to make decisive progress on our behalf. It is no longer clear why we are doing it, if we have no prospect of going 'outside the beaten path of human beings'. But Aristotle would surely not accept the charge that his conception makes philosophy something unimportant. First, he would insist on the good done by the negative and deflationary aspect of the return to appearances, an aspect that occupies a great part of his own writing. The moment we begin to theorize we are, as Aristotle again and again illustrates, in acute danger of oversimplifying. His historical and critical chapters show the variety of the dangers: materialist reductionism in the philosophy of mind, mechanism in scientific explanation, dominant-end hedonism in ethics, Socratism in talk about language and definition. By returning us, in each case, to the 'appearances', he reminds us that our language and our ways of life are richer and more complex than much of philosophy acknowledges. Insofar as such oversimple theories were, and are, powerfully influential in human life, the return that blocks them can have a corresponding power.

But this answer does not go deep enough to capture the full power of Aristotle's position. So far, it appears that appearance-saving has a point only because a certain tribe of strange professionals, call them philosophers, has somewhat arbitrarily decided to push for severity and simplicity, going beyond and doing violence to ordinary human ways. For the ordinary person in the agora, there is no need for Aristotelian philosophy, because this person has never been gripped by the other kind of philosophy. If philosophy is a neatly demarcated professional activity, appearance-saving would appear to have force only within that profession, and the rest of us can go about our business, knowing what we know.

This is clearly not Aristotle's view. The *Metaphysics* begins, as we saw, with the claim that 'all human beings by nature reach out for understanding'. The discussion that follows these famous words traces the development of philosophy back to a natural inclination, on the part of all human beings, to sort out and interpret the world for themselves, making distinctions, clarifying, finding explanations for that which seems strange or wonderful. Other creatures live by the impressions and impulses of the moment; human beings seek to comprehend and grasp the world under some general principles that will reveal an order in its multiplicity. Our natural desires will not be satisfied so long as something apparently arbitrary eludes us. Philosophy grew up, in fact, as one expression of this hatred of being at a loss in the world:

It is because of wonder that human beings undertake philosophy, both now and at its origins... The person who is at a loss and in a state of wonder thinks he fails to grasp something; this is why the lover of stories is in a sense a philosopher, for stories are composed out of wonders. (*Metaph.* 982b12–19)

Our encounter with the world is, he continues, rather like what happens when we watch a puppet show performed by mechanical marionettes, with no visible human control: we wonder, and we look for an explanation for the apparently wondrous motion. There is a natural continuum between wonder and story-telling, between story-telling and theorizing: continually we seek to expand the comprehensiveness of our grasp.

But if it is a universal human desire to grasp the world and make it comprehensible to reason, then it seems clear that oversimplification and reduction will be deep and ever-present dangers. In seeking to be at home, we may easily become strangers to our home as we experience it. In our anxiety to control and grasp the uncontrolled by *technē*, we may all too easily become distant from the lives that we originally wished to control. The theories that Aristotle attacks as over-simple are not all, or even for the most part, the work of narrow professional sects; many of them come from popular tradition and exercise a great hold over the popular imagination – even the imaginations of those who at the same time, in their daily life and speech, reveal a commitment to a more complicated world. Philosophy answers to a human demand, and the demand is such that we are easily led by our pursuit of it to become estranged from the beliefs that ground our daily lives. Aristotle (like the Heraclitus of our epigraph)[39] believes that most of us have, to one degree or another, through the grip of hedonism, materialism, mechanism, or some other simple picture, become strangers to some aspect of the life we live, the language we use. We need philosophy to show us the way back to the ordinary and to make it an object of interest and pleasure, rather than contempt and evasion.

Sometimes the return encountered resistance; sometimes Aristotle's audience seems to have rebelled against his taste for the ordinary and the worldly, demanding instead the lofty and rarefied concerns to which the philosophical tradition had accustomed them. In the *Parts of Animals* (1.5), he addresses some students who had evidently protested against the study of animals and their form and matter, asking for something more sublime. He tells them that this reluctance is actually a kind of self-contempt: for they are, after all, creatures of flesh and blood themselves (*PA* 654a27–31). That they need to be reminded of this fact is a sign of the depth of Platonism; or, rather, a sign that Platonism appeals to an already deep tendency in us towards shame at the messy, unclear stuff of which our humanity is made. We could generalize Aristotle's point by saying that the opponent of the return to appearances is likely to be a person not at peace with his humanity; and that this is an inner problem for that person, not a defect of the method. Some sorts of philosophizing have their origin in what Aristotle here calls 'childish disgust' (645a16); to undo the edifices built by disgust requires, in turn, another kind of philosophy – much as friends who have become strangers or enemies need a mediator to effect a reconciliation.

Aristotle has a further answer to the students, one that shows us how this therapeutic aim might be connected with positive benefits. He says that we experience joy and exhilaration whenever we discover order or structure in our world, no matter how apparently trivial the sphere of our investigation (*PA* 645a7–11). (This is, we remember, a philosopher who devoted years of his life to the precise description of previously overlooked marine species, making a contribution to biology that went unmatched for centuries. This is also a moral philosopher who speaks with respect of the ability to tell a good joke at the right time, and calls jokes 'the movements of the character' (*EN* 1128a11). Many small animal structures elicited his delight.) Philosophy, inspired by wonder, takes us to the world and its ever more precise description. In so doing it reveals and makes explicit the order that is *in* the appearances: in our view of our natural surroundings, in our beliefs about the universe, in our political and moral lives. In this way it does not simply leave everything where it was: it pursues in a serious and thoroughgoing way the natural human demand for order and understanding. In *Metaphysics* IV.2, after insisting that the dialectician and the philosopher 'range over the same subject matter', Aristotle draws a distinction. 'Dialectic makes conjectures about things concerning which the philosopher seeks understanding' (*Metaph.* 1004b22–6). The philosopher differs from the dialectician, and from the ordinary man as well, not so much in subject matter or even in desire. He differs primarily in the thoroughness and the dedication with which he presses, in each area, the human demand to see order and make distinctions. Empedocles claimed to be a god. Parmenides and Plato's Socrates compare themselves to initiates into a mystery religion. Aristotle's philosopher, by contrast, is what we might call the professional human being. He is the sort of person who, in ethics, gives us a clearer view of the target at which we were aiming all along (*EN* 1094a23–4); who, in logic, describes explicitly the principles that we use in assessing one another's inferences. He is less distracted, more serious, less reluctant than the rest of us. For that reason he can help us to satisfy, appropriately, our natural desires.

There may appear to be an ongoing tension between the therapeutic and the positive aims of the method of *phainomena*. It has sometimes been thought, in our own philosophical tradition, that the therapeutic task can be satisfactorily accomplished only by knocking away all order and structure; therefore one might suggest that Aristotle, whose work obviously presents us with a great deal of structure, cannot be seriously devoted to the human return of which he speaks. Think, for example, of the more purely negative imagery used by Wittgenstein in this well-known passage:

> Where does our investigation get its importance from, since it seems only to destroy everything interesting, that is, all that is great and important? (As it were all the buildings, leaving behind only bits of stone and rubble.) What we are destroying is nothing but houses of cards and we are clearing up the ground of language on which they stand. (*Philosophical Investigations*, I 118)

This paragraph begins with the question we have all along been asking Aristotle. And both Aristotle and Wittgenstein could presumably agree on a part of the answer. Much of the importance of their ways of philosophizing comes from the destruction of philosophical illusion, the careful exploration of language that shows the structures of Platonism to be houses of cards. But the passage is one that could never have been written by Aristotle. For Wittgenstein's image of the result (whether or not this is a reliable indication of his overall view) is a purely negative image. We are left with nothing 'interesting', only with bits of stone and rubble and with the ground to be swept clean of these. Aristotle would speak differently. When we knock down the houses of cards we are still left with a lot of order and structure – the order that is *in* our language and in the world around us as we see and experience it. The order that is in the digestive system of a crayfish; the structure of a well-told joke; the beauty of a close friend's actions and character. What is left would include houses; it would also include laboratories – structures used by human beings in their efforts to know the place where they live. We do not know this place just by living in it and using it; this is clear from our many acts of simplification, our fondness for falsifying theory. The place needs to be perspicuously mapped by serious researchers, so that we will not lose our way in it or from it. And this job is interesting, because human life is interesting, because jokes, and laws, and stars, and rocks, and inferences, and insects, and tragic and epic poems are all interesting and important.

Aristotle's positive task is thoroughly connected with the negative one. Seeing clearly the order that is there helps us to overcome 'childish disgust', so that we will be content to live where we live, 'not making a sour face' (*PA* 645a24). On the other side, we will attend to this order more effectively if the illusory promise of a glorious Platonic order is explicitly demolished. The most serious obstacle to good philosophy is not ignorance, but bad philosophy, which captivates by its pleasing clarity:

There are some people who put forth arguments that are both alien to the matter at hand and empty, and get away with it, because it seems to be the mark of a philosopher to say nothing at random but to use reasoned argument. (Some argue this way out of ignorance and some out of ambitious crookedness.) Even men of experience and practical capability are taken in by these people, who have no capacity for organized or practical thought; this happens to them through *apaideusia*. (*EE* 1217a1–7)

Aristotelian negative work, by removing imposture, makes it possible for the practical person to begin to get, and to appreciate, the positive *paideia* which he or she desires.

Aristotle concludes his appeal to the biology students by telling a story.[40] Some visitors, he tells them, once wanted to be introduced to Heraclitus. When they arrived at his home, they saw the great man sitting in the kitchen, warming himself by the stove. They hesitated. (Presumably they had expected to find him out contemplating the heavens, or lost in reflection – anything but this very ordinary activity.) He said to them, 'Come in. Don't be afraid. There are gods here too' (*PA* 645a19–23).

Aristotelian philosophy, then, like (and as a part of) our human nature, exists in a continual oscillation between too much order and disorder, ambition and abandonment, excess and deficiency, the super-human and the merely animal. The good philosopher would be the one who manages humanly, guarding against these dangers, to improvise the mean. (And 'that's a job, in every area'.[41]) In his lost work *On the Good*, Aristotle is said to have written, 'You must remember that you are a human being: not only in living well, but also in doing philosophy.'[42] Concerning which the ancient author who reports the sentence observes, 'Aristotle must have been a very balanced character.'[43]

9   Rational animals and the explanation of action

> What we are supplying are really remarks on the natural history of man: not
> curiosities however, but rather observations on facts which no-one has
> doubted, and which have only gone unremarked because they are always
> before our eyes.
>
> Wittgenstein, *Remarks on the Foundations of Mathematics* I 141

Our central question has been, how far and in what ways does (and should) the
world impinge upon us as we attempt to live in a valuable way? How far are we
creatures who, like plants, depend passively upon what is outside of us in the world
of nature? How far are we purely active intellectual beings like the souls of Plato's
middle dialogues? And what is, for a human being, the best (most praiseworthy)
way to be? One of the things such questioning demands is, clearly, an account
of human action. We need to consider how our various movements in the world
are caused, if we are going to be able to say what sorts of causal relationships
between world and agent diminish, or remove, the praiseworthiness of a life.
Plato's thought about ethical self-sufficiency has relied implicitly on a picture of
action. In the middle dialogues we are presented with a double story. On the one
hand, there is the self-moving, purely active, self-sufficient intellect, generator of
valuable acts; on the other, there are the bodily appetites, which are themselves
passive and entirely unselective, simply pushed into existence by the world and
pushing, in turn, the passive agent. The *Phaedrus*, as it suggested a new picture
of value, suggested, along with it, a new picture of action. The causality of intellect
was said to involve responsiveness and receptivity as well as pure activity; the
causality of desire was both more active (selective) and less brutishly constraining.

Aristotle, as I shall argue, develops and extends the suggestions of the *Phaedrus*
concerning both value and action.[1] He will argue for a picture of the causes of
action that permits us to see our neediness *vis-à-vis* the world as not inimical to,
but at the very heart of, our ethical value. But Aristotle pursues this ethical project
in his own characteristic way, by looking beyond the ethical question narrowly
construed to develop an account of movement and action in the animal kingdom
as a whole. It is one of his complaints against his fellow philosophers that they
isolate the human being too much in their studies, failing to link the study of the
human with a comprehensive inquiry into the functioning of living beings in
general. This leads, as we shall see, to various failures to preserve deeply shared
appearances concerning our links with other forms of life. It is not surprising,

264

then, that in pursuing his views on the topic of action we need to consult not only the relevant portions of the ethical treatises but also the two texts where he discusses the explanation of animal movement and action in a general way: the third book of *De Anima*, and a work entirely devoted to this question, the *De Motu Animalium*.

Clearly there is a close connection between an account of action and the ethical assessment of persons and lives. We expect that, in deciding what to say about action, Aristotle will be influenced by the ethical implications of his account, its tendency to support or to undermine our evaluative practices. We would be surprised indeed if his account yielded the result that no human animal movement is caused in such a way as to meet our criteria for the ascription of praise and blame. The desire for a livable outcome will constrain – appropriately – his selections.[2] But on the other hand an account of action is, he believes, committed as well to other appearances; it should bring our beliefs in other areas to bear on the finding of this human ethical starting-point. Specifically, we must search for a fit between our understanding of human action and our beliefs about the movements of living things in the universe as a whole. We should not cut off the human, with the result that we say about this case what is not in keeping with the whole range of our beliefs on the subject.

When we turn to the *De Anima* and the *De Motu*, we discover, then, something that is very strange if we are used to Plato's ways of approaching the subject. Instead of Plato's moving accounts of human ethical dilemmas, we find a narrative whose leading characters are fish, birds, and insects as well as humans. Instead of what looks self-evidently important for us, we find what seems – and, we know, seemed to Aristotle's students – trivial and even disgusting. The inquiry into human action is carried out as a part of a larger inquiry into the movements of animals. Human action is very little singled out; instead we find a discussion of sweeping generality that ranges over the entire animal kingdom. It is this generality that we must seek to understand if we are to understand the distinctive contribution this account makes to ethics.

The *De Motu* begins by telling us that we need to consider in general the common explanation (*aitia*) for moving with any movement whatever (698a4–7).[3] The project is restricted explicitly to the movements of animals, implicitly to their movement from place to place. But the remaining subject matter is still oddly general and oddly heterogeneous. Under the rubric of the 'common' we are treated to a mixture of concerns which, from the point of view of a Platonic ethical orientation, and even from the point of view of ordinary belief, might at first seem anomalous. To put the issue succinctly, the 'common' *aitia* seems both too common and not common enough. Not common enough, because, instead of a single account of animal motion, what we seem to find is the juxtaposition of two quite different accounts: an account using the psychological language of perception, thought, and desire, and an account using the physiological language of tendons, sinews, and bones. These two accounts do not have anything obviously in common, and it is not even apparent how they are related. All too 'common', because the project of giving a general account for all sorts of animal motions leads Aristotle to run together explananda which we might think a scientist should keep distinct: the purposive action of human beings, and animal motions such as the swimming of fish, the flying of birds. Any account that tries to take in all of this without spending a lot of time drawing relevant distinctions might turn out to be so 'common' as to be entirely lacking in content. Aristotle himself makes this warning: 'It is humorous to search for the common account (*ton koinon logon*),...which will be the proper account of nothing in the world, if one does not also search according to the peculiar and indivisible species, but abandons the search for such an account.'[4] Does Aristotle escape his own strictures in this case (and in the similar case of *De Anima* III.9–11) and say something with serious content? Or can the *De Motu* be that very rare item, a humorous work of Aristotle?[5]

We must press, then, the following questions:[6]

(1) What is the force of Aristotle's claim that we ought to give a *koinē aitia* for animal motion? And, more concretely, what is the force of the claim made in *MA* 6 that the common account will be one involving reference to the animal's desires and cognitive faculties? What other candidates for the explanation of animal motion does Aristotle intend to rule out here, and on what grounds?

(2) What, more precisely, is this *koinē aitia*? What type of explanation is it, and why is it supposed to be a good one?

(3) What is the connection between this desire/cognition explanation and the physiological account of motion in *De Motu* Chapters 7–9? Do we have alternative answers to the same question here, or answers to different questions?

(4) What sort of basis does this account provide for our practices of ethical assessment?

To pursue these questions we must first do some more historical work; for the force of Aristotle's position can best be grasped as a response to two over-simple philosophical accounts of action, one that attempts to preserve, against them, the complexity of ordinary beliefs on the subject. We shall, consequently, proceed towards Aristotle's account in Aristotelian fashion, considering the views of the 'many' and of the 'wise'.

I

Consider the following accounts of animal movement:

A   He charged like a hill-bred lion, ravenous
for meat, whose proud heart urges him to dare
an attack on the flocks in a close-kept sheepfold.
And even should he find herdsmen there
watching over the sheep with spears and dogs,
he will not think of turning back, empty,
without attacking.

B CHORUS Where has the poor man gone?

    NEOPTOLEMUS It's obvious to me. Because of his need for food he is dragging himself along his painful path, somewhere near here. For the story is that he leads that sort of life, hunting with his winged arrows, poor wretch. Nor does anyone come near him to treat his sickness.

C Holding that vengeance upon their enemies was more to be desired than any personal blessings, and reckoning this to be the most glorious of hazards, they joyfully determined to accept the risk... Thus choosing to die resisting, rather than to live submitting, they fled only from dishonor, but they met danger face to face, and in one brief moment, at the summit of their glory, they were released, not from fear, but from luck (*tuchē*).[7]

In each of these passages (selected more or less randomly, in that hundreds of others could have been used to make the same points) we are given not only a description of some animal movement, but also an aetiology of that movement. The speaker answers not only to the question, 'What did he (it, they) do?' but also to the question, 'Why did he (it, they) do it?' In A, the lion (to whom the human hero Sarpedon is being compared) attacks a sheepfold. He evidently does so *because* he has a very pressing need of food and he sees there what will satisfy that hunger. (Something similar is supposed to be true of Sarpedon: his heart urges him to attack because he needs or wants something (to get across the wall) and sees that attacking is a way to get that.) In B, what Philoctetes has done is to go away from his cave. Neoptolemus does not hesitate to make up an aetiology in terms of the man's desires and beliefs about the possibilities: he must need food, he has nobody to help him, so he (sees that he) has to go out and shoot it himself, painful though it is. C, though grander and apparently more complicated, has a similar structure. What the soldiers did was to stand their ground and fight bravely until death. Why did they do this? Pericles ascribes to them certain desires – for their own personal glory, for civic vengeance, for avoidance of dishonor – and certain beliefs (this is the most glorious of hazards, to flee would bring dishonor) which suffice, in his view, to explain their movements.

The examples form a spectrum, from animal action through animal-like human action to rational virtuous human action. But in all we see the bare bones of a common structure of explanation. In however many ways the cases are distinct, they are alike in four salient points.

(1) The motion of the animal(s) in each case is explained by ascribing to the animal(s) a certain complex of desires and beliefs or perceptions: he (it, they) wanted this, and believed (saw) that this was a way to the object desired. Humans and other animals move about from place to place because there are things that they want or need and things that they see or think that bear on how they are to get them. (This broad agreement in finding a common structure is, in fact, what the Homeric animal simile relies on: for this passage is about Sarpedon as much as about the lion, and Sarpedon is being said to be 'like' the lion concerning the *reasons* for his action.)

(2) The factors cited in the explanation are intentional: (a) the desires and beliefs (perceptions) are directed towards a goal, and (b) the explanation characterizes the goal as it is seen from the animal's point of view.

(3) The desires and beliefs (perceptions) appear to have both a logical and a causal connection with the goal: logical, because we cannot give an account of what the desire (belief) is without mentioning the goal on which it is focused; causal, because they are seen as the things that make the action happen. (The lion's heart *urges*, Philoctetes goes this way 'in virtue of' or 'because of' his need for food.)

(4) If the physiological equipment of the animal is mentioned in the context, it is not introduced in answer to the question, 'Why (on account of what) did it move?', but, at most, in answer to the question, 'How did it move?' or perhaps, 'How (given that it had the desires and beliefs we have mentioned) was it *able* to move?' We see this particularly clearly in the *Philoctetes* example, where later passages dwell on the physiological difficulty involved in his movement and focus on the question: how, given the disability, does he manage to get to what he wants? But try to imagine an animal simile that says, 'He charged like a hill-bred lion, who leaps because he has strong muscles and well-developed sinews...'; or an answer to the Chorus's question that goes, 'It's clear to me that he has gone out because his spine is well-equipped to bend in such-and-such ways, and is connected in turn to the other joints...'; or a funeral oration that says, 'And so, because their gymnastic training had equipped them with firm muscles and because those muscles were firmly anchored to their bones, they did not weaken in the onslaught.' In all these cases (which are certainly not to be found in ordinary pre-philosophical discourse) we would know, once we recovered from the initial hilarity, that something was amiss. Something is parading as an *explanation* which, though not without its own interest, is not the sort of thing we are inclined to count as an explanation of movement. We would feel that we did not yet have an answer to our 'Why?' questions; and I think we would also feel that we did not yet know the real *causes* of this movement, what the factors were that really made this happen. On the other hand, the accounts produced by our speakers do strike us as satisfactory. Speaking in each case to a group of more or less ordinary people, these speakers seem to know the sort of thing they have to say in order to satisfy the hearer's demand for an explanation of what has occurred. Their accounts satisfy not so much because of their truth (for B and C, at least, are clearly conjectural) as because they have the right structure: this is the sort of account which, if true, *would* suffice as an explanation of the movement.[8]

All this, so far, is loose and general, as we might expect. But we also might expect that a Greek philosopher, setting to work on the explanation of animal movement, would set himself in some fruitful relation to these paradigms of explanation, drawing on them and attempting to elucidate their common structure. What happened in fifth- and early fourth-century philosophy was something altogether different. Aristotle is keenly aware of a complex philosophical heritage on the topic of animal motion and its explanation. This heritage confronted him with two prominent models of explanation, both of which – as he says and as we shall see – break sharply with the tradition of discourse about movement exemplified in our three passages; and both of which do so by misrepresenting in some way the relationship between active selectivity and passivity in animal movement. One model, provided by the influential tradition of materialistic natural science, replaced ordinary psychological explanation by physiological explanation, in a way that depicted the animal as a kind of puppet, simply pushed around by the causal forces of nature and contributing nothing to its movement from its own active selectivity. The other (Platonic) model, critical of this scientistic reductionism, restored some of the ordinary psychological categories and the idea that creatures act for reasons – but only in connection with the rational actions of human beings, and at the price of hyper-intellectualizing the explanation of these. If we study, somewhat schematically, this twofold background, we will be in a position to understand why it was philosophically revolutionary and important for Aristotle to lay such stress on what, from the point of view of Sophocles and Thucydides, might look like obvious truisms.[9]

II

The natural science tradition before Aristotle devoted considerable attention to animal movement and its explanation. Aristotle reports that self-motion from place to place was standardly held to be an essential characteristic of the animal; its aetiology must therefore occupy a central place in any account of soul.[10] But in keeping with the rest of their explanatory program these scientists offered as the *aitia* of animal movement an account that made reference only to the interactions of basic constituents of the animal's physiology, both with one another and with the environment. For example, Diogenes of Apollonia said that the soul of all animals was air, that air is what thought really is, and that air is what 'steers and rules' all things, including animals.[11] According to Aristotle, he justified his claim that soul was air by pointing to air's lightness as a property that makes it particularly suitable for producing movement.[12] Democritus explained movement by hypothesizing that the soul (assumed to be that which produces movement) is composed of spherical atoms, whose shape equips them to penetrate everywhere and thereby to impart movement to other things.[13] In these and other similar cases, a demand for the explanation of animal movement is answered not with reference to desires, perceptions, and beliefs, but by mentioning the properties of some physiological entity (or entities) in virtue of which the entity is capable of imparting (causing) movement. The animal is pushed about by this entity, as the entity itself responds to pushes from the environment.

These people are all offering a causal explanation of movement for which they claim a certain importance. What is not so clear is whether they are prepared to do away altogether with the more common explanatory framework or to reduce psychological explanations to physiological ones. The passages I have cited never explicitly insist that the question, 'Why did this animal move from A to B?' *must* be answered (by the scientist) *only* in materialistic terms; it is never said that the physiological account provides the *real* or *genuine* answer to the request for explanation. But we can, I think, infer that this is the attitude of at least Diogenes and the Atomists. Diogenes, in fragment B4, argues directly from the premise that air is necessary for life and thought in animals to the conclusion that air *is* life and thought.[14] This pattern of argument plainly does conflate the question, 'What is it?' with the question, 'What conditions are necessary in order for it to be?', and, similarly, the request for the explanation of certain events with a request for an account of the material necessary conditions for those events. If air-movement is shown to be necessary for thinking, thinking just is air-movement. This is a way of arguing that is typical of reductionist scientism in all ages, not least in contemporary neurobiology, which frequently infers from the necessity of certain brain-functions for certain cognitive activities that the cognitive activities just are these brain functions. There is an enduring temptation to think that our ordinary categories are, as Democritus puts it, 'by convention' only, and that we have gotten at the real or really scientific explanation of some phenomenon only when we have reached the basic building blocks of matter.[15] It seems virtually certain that fifth-century science succumbed to this temptation, treating the animal as an assemblage of material bits that gets pushed (as a whole) by the reaction of some of its bits to other pushes – rather than as a creature that intentionally *does* things, actively and selectively influencing its own motion.

But whatever the real position of these thinkers was, it is plain that Aristotle took them to be offering a replacement for the categories of ordinary discourse, and not simply a supplement. He frequently speaks of their neglect of other sorts of explanation, their belief that material explanation was all the explanation there was.[16] And in the passage in which he describes Democritus's view of animal movement, he says something revealing: 'In general it seems that it is not in this way that the soul moves the body, but through some sort of choice and thinking' (*DA* 406b24–5).[17] This, of course, would be an objection to Democritus only if he is a reductionist of some sort about the explanation of purposive action. What is most relevant for our account of Aristotle's philosophical motivations, however, is that Aristotle plainly believes that this is an appropriate objection.

At first sight this might look like a peculiar remark to make against the physiologist. For it is not as though this person has simply neglected choice and thought. Indeed one of the concerns of this tradition obviously is to give an account of thinking in physiological terms. What, then, can Aristotle mean by his 'not in this way, but through choice and thought'? He certainly does not explain himself in this passage. But his remark does lead us to notice certain peculiar results of the physiologist's project. First, intentionality has been altogether eliminated from scientific explanation. Ordinary explanations of movement referred to the animal's ways of focusing on some external object and described that object as the animal sees, thinks, desires it. The physiologist's account uses the viewpoint of the neutral observer to characterize the animal's physiological states; it picks these out, furthermore, in a way that does not involve any essential reference to an external goal, except perhaps as the stimulus that was the cause of the physiological state. The way in which perception and desire are object-directed, are ways of sorting out and focusing on pieces of the world, drops out. This leads to several further results. One is that we lose crucial distinctions among different internal animal activities. The different types of cognition – perceiving, imagining, thinking – are all being cashed out in exactly similar physiological terms, as the motions of certain sorts of atoms; the same is true of different types of desiring, which we ordinarily distinguish by speaking of their objects and the ways in which they relate to their objects. Furthermore, perceiving and desiring are themselves very closely assimilated. Finally, all of these (formerly) intentional features of the animal are given the same treatment as non-intentional items like blood-circulation and digestion. It is difficult to see how such an account could make room for the richness that is in our ordinary talk, and easy to see that the atomist does not much care about preserving that richness.

Beyond this – and this takes us to the heart, I think, of Aristotle's cryptic criticism – the non-intentional account of movement, by effacing these internal distinctions, also effaces certain distinctions among types of movement that are very important to our practices. Because the external object enters in only as a cause of certain changes, and not also as the object of intentional states and activities, we are left with no way of distinguishing the mechanical physiological response of the organism to a bodily stimulus (reflex motions, for example, or the ongoing processes of digestion) from activity which we generally characterize in intentional terms and assess accordingly. (It is revealing that Diogenes uses going to sleep as an example exactly on a par with movement from place to place.)[18] We lose, in other words, the distinction between movement that has a 'why' in terms of the creature's beliefs and desires and movement for which there is no 'why', but only causal explanatory factors that do not function as reasons. But this *is*, in effect, to do away with the whole idea of chosen action as we ordinarily understand it – and, indeed, with the whole idea, too, of non-chosen intentional action. However much Democritus may use the words 'choice' and 'thinking', he has done away with distinctions crucial to our conception of these. His program would certainly lead to the breakdown of our ordinary distinction between causal explanation *simpliciter* and the giving of reasons, and to the breakdown of such legal and moral institutions and practices as rest upon this distinction. Moral education, for example, would come to look like simply a kind of doctoring or conditioning. The animal is *just* a plant, passive before the causal forces of the world. Aristotle seems right to point to the radical consequences of the scientist's apparently innocuous move.[19]

The physiological model was influential, even among those who, in their discourse, continued to acknowledge a more complicated pattern of distinctions. Plato tells us that 'the many, groping in the dark', fastened on these scientific theories as the real explanations of movement.[20] Since some of the most striking results of the physiological program were in the area of rational human action, it is not surprising that the first objections to it should have focused on this subject rather than on the broader question of intentionality in general. The brief remark of Aristotle which we have just discussed continues a tradition of criticism started by a famous passage in Plato's *Phaedo*. Socrates here takes the natural scientist to task for offering an account of the disposition and interactions of his sinews and bones as the answer to his request for an *aitia* or explanation of why he is sitting in prison. He objects, clearly, not to the mention of these facts, which he allows to be true and even important, but to the scientist's claim that these facts *explain* his action, or answer a 'why' (*dia ti*) question about it. 'To call these items an *aitia* is too out of place.' The real explanation, he insists, is one that makes reference to deliberation and rational choice – in short, he says, to intellect (*nous*, 99A). This is the real explanatory factor (*aition*), and the bones and sinews enter in, properly, only as necessary conditions for the operation of this factor: 'that without which the *aition* would not be an *aition*' (99A4–5, 99B2–4).[21] For it would be true to say that without these bodily parts thus disposed Socrates would not be able to do what seems best.[22]

Plato's criticism is not trivial. We have already seen how hard it is to remember that isolating the bodily condition of an activity does not necessarily amount to isolating that activity itself. But we must now attend carefully to the way in which his interesting criticism is made. Plato here offers us, apparently, a choice between two patterns of explanation: explanation by physiology and explanation by reason and intellect. Having rejected the former, we seem to have decided on the latter. And it is only actions that fit the latter, by which he means rational actions understood as the products of intellectual activity, that are said to be inadequately explained by the former. Nothing is said one way or the other about other sorts of intentional action; nothing is said about the failure of the physiological model to do justice to the intentionality of perception and desire.* Plato does not here explicitly say that a causal physiological account *would* be sufficient in the case of the non-rational intentional movement of animals. (Although I shall not grapple here with the complexities of the *Timaeus* account of explanation, I believe that it shows that he does in fact believe this.) But, by drawing the salient distinction where he does, and by failing to mention that there may be other distinctions and other faculties of the animal at least as relevant to our decision for or against the physiological model as intellect is, Plato encourages an intellectualistic reading of his objection.[23]

Such an intellectualist view would have a number of important consequences. First, it would confront us with a very sharp distinction between human beings and other animals. The motions of the latter would be assimilated to the movements of non-sentient, non-desiring entities and treated as reactions to a push from the environment. Second, it would force a sharp division between those human actions that are motivated by intellect or rational choice, and all other human actions. Again, the latter would be regarded as explicable by necessity alone. Third, we would lose our customary distinction between the movements of animals that are caused and explained by their desires and beliefs, and other movements such as the movements of the digestive system and reflex responses.

---

* The *Republic* complicates this picture, of course, by introducing the middle part of the soul, whose relation to reason is more complex (cf. Ch. 5). Aristotle's criticisms do not, perhaps, take sufficient account of this development; but Plato's account of the middle part is cryptic, and it is not consistently invoked.

We would lose that distinction because we would have lost the distinction between an external intentional object and an external item that functions as a cause without being an object. This reordering of our ordinary distinctions would, like the physiologist's, have serious consequences. It would lead to changes in our treatment of animals, and of our own animality.[24] It would have consequences, as well, for moral training, where the stark division between intellectual judgment and brute reaction would lead in the direction of a division between teaching for the intellect and manipulation or conditioning for everything else.

And in fact we are by now aware that the Plato of the *Phaedo* and the *Republic* is willing, even eager, to pay this price. We have seen in ethical contexts how he does in fact treat desires as brutish unselective reactions that push the creature around; the way in which, while denying to intellect any share in passivity, he starkly opposes its pure activity to the passivity of desire. We have seen that he does in fact draw from this picture its radical consequences for education. All of this confirms Aristotle's judgment that an account of action will have important implications for ethics, especially where questions of our vulnerability and passivity are concerned. And it prepares us to receive Aristotle's claim that all animal action is caused by desire as a claim that might have some serious content.

III

When Aristotle arrives on the philosophical scene, he is, then, confronted, on the one hand, by a model of explanation whose *aitia* is so 'common' that it assimilates all intentional actions both to one another and to other cases of response to an external physical stimulus; on the other, with a model that is not 'common' enough to do justice to our beliefs about what we share with 'the other animals', and about what links together different elements in our own behavior. With an eye to the appearances embodied in our literary examples, we could sum up the situation by saying that we so far lack a general notion of desiring or reaching out for an object – this being the feature with respect to which the movement of all three of our animals differs from a purely mechanical response to a push from the environment. The 'appearances' implicitly contain such a general conception, as a study of animal similes alone would show. But sometimes the absence of a single unifying term in the theoretical language can conduce to a disregard of such an implicit general notion; sometimes, in order to recover and protect what was all along implicit in the appearances, a philosopher will need to step in and create a term of art. Such a term can enable us to recognize the salient features of our antecedent conception and to defend it against superficially attractive philosophical rivals.[25]

To meet this need, Aristotle selects (or, very probably, invents) a word well suited to indicate the common feature shared by all cases of goal-directed animal movement: the word '*orexis*'. Much work has been done on the meaning and origin of other Aristotelian additions to the philosophical language. But the extent to which this word is an item of his own creation goes widely unacknowledged. The word '*orexis*' occurs, in pre-Aristotelian Greek, in only one alleged place:

in the dubious ethical fragments of Democritus.[26] (I believe that this constitutes further evidence in favor of a post-Aristotelian redaction.) The word is altogether absent from the Platonic corpus (except the spurious and late *Definitiones*) and in general from every prose and poetic author. Similarly absent are '*orekton*' and '*orektikon*' (the object of *orexis* and the orectic element). The verb '*oregesthai*' does, of course, occur. But even in Plato (where it is very rare, occurring five times in the *Laws* and only seven times elsewhere[27]) it seems to retain its original sense of 'reach out for', 'grasp at'. At the same time, there is no other word that performs the function for which Aristotle will use '*oregesthai*', the function of introducing a general notion of wanting or desiring. '*Epithumia*' and '*epithumein*' (both of which occur regularly in fifth- and fourth-century authors) are closely linked with the bodily appetites; '*boulesthai*' and '*boulēsis*' (again, both regular items from the late fifth century, though the latter is not terribly common) seem to be more closely linked with judging good and reasoning.[28] It seems worthwhile, then, to examine more closely Aristotle's generic word of choice: its selection looks the more marked for being, apparently, innovative. It may shed some light on his 'common' explanatory project.

The active verb '*oregō*'[29] consistently, from Homer onwards, seems to mean 'stretch out', 'reach out'; it is transitive, and the context is usually one of extending one's hand to somebody or handing an object to somebody. The medio-passive forms have the closely related sense of 'reach out for', 'stretch (oneself) towards', 'grasp at', also 'aim at' or 'hit at'. At a certain point in the Attic use of the word (I have really found this to be clearly true only in certain authors, particularly Euripides and Thucydides), it is transferred to the inner psychological realm and is used in such a way that we could translate it as 'yearn for', 'long for'.[30] But there is no reason why we could not also continue to translate it in the original way and think of it as a metaphorical transferral from the external to the internal realm. For example, in Thucydides, '*oregomenoi tou prōtos hekastos gignesthai*' and '*tou pleonos ōregonto*' can be rendered as 'each one reaching out (or: straining) to become first', and 'they were grasping after more'. The same close association with ideas of (inner or psychological) reaching, striking, or grasping can be observed in Plato. In general we may say two things about this word: (1) It strongly implies directedness towards an object. (The verb occurs only with some sort of object.[31]) It connotes, then, in the inner realm, not a vague state of yearning or being-affected, but a focusing on something, a pointing towards something. (2) It is active more than passive: it is a going for, a reaching after (whether bodily or psychic), as opposed to a being-overwhelmed, or an empty being-in-need. Or rather, it indicates how wanting, which might be taken to be simply a form of passivity, is at the same time active: instead of pure passive being-affected, we have a complex responsiveness that receives from the world and in turn focuses itself outwards towards the world. To find an English translation that brings out these nuances is difficult. The modern German use of 'die Strebung' and 'das Streben' seems pretty good. English 'inclination' has the right directedness, but (compare Kant's use of 'Neigung') too much connotes passivity and being-affected. 'Need' and 'want' are too suggestive of an empty gap or a lack; they lack both the object-directedness and the activity involved in the Greek word. 'Desire' is more appropriate; at least it is clearly object-linked. But it is such an overused and therefore weak and unmarked word that it is very hard to see it as having any definite content or connotation. This is clearly not the case with Aristotle's new choice. In any case, once we recover a sense of the philosophical newness and strangeness of this word, we can begin to see, too, what content there might be to Aristotle's claims that *boulēsis*, *thumos*, and *epithumia* are all forms of *orexis* and that some *orexis* is involved in every animal movement. He is saying, apparently, that they are all forms of object-directed, active inner reaching-out; and that this sort of reaching-out is common to the movements of both human and other animals.

These claims are first made in *De Anima* III.9, where Aristotle turns to the subject of explaining animal movement. He remarks that, as soon as we approach this topic, there is a pressing difficulty about what 'parts of the soul' we ought to recognize. Others, he says, have employed as the basis for their movement-explanations either a bipartite division into the rational and the irrational, or a tripartite division into the calculative, the spirited, and the appetitive. (Having focused on the physiologists in Book I, he now appears to be preoccupied with varieties of Platonism.) Aristotle makes several objections to these as basic explanatory divisions of the soul for this purpose; but the one that will most immediately concern us is that these divisions fail to bring out the unity of the *orektikon*, an element of the animal that is not simply identical to any one of their other 'parts'. 'And indeed it is out of place to carve this up – for wish (*boulēsis*) comes to be in the rational part, and appetite (*epithumia*) and emotion (*thumos*) in the irrational. And if the soul is tripartite, there will be *orexis* in every part.' In the next chapter he repeats his criticism of the Platonist part-divisions, insisting that they fail to indicate what is single and common among *epithumia*, *thumos*, and *boulēsis*: for *orexis*, he insists, is a single thing. Furthermore, by indicating that the rational part is a sufficient origin of movement, they fail to recognize that in every movement, including movement according to intellect, some sort of *orexis* is involved. 'Intellect does not impart movement without *orexis*, for *boulēsis* is a type of *orexis*, and when the creature moves according to reasoning, it also moves according to *boulēsis*.'[32]

What is the content of this assertion that *orexis* is involved in every action? Is it more than a verbal game, seeing that the Platonist conception of reason does not make it an inert contemplative faculty like Hume's reason? The contribution of Aristotle's innovation seems to be precisely that it does enable us to see and focus on what is common to all cases of animal movement, whereas the Platonist structure does not. Aristotle, by choosing this particular word, is saying that the single or common element which Plato fails to recognize is this element of reaching out for something in the world, grasping after some object in order to take it to oneself. Both human and other animals, in their rational and non-rational actions, have in common that they stretch forward, so to speak, towards pieces of the world which they then attain or appropriate. Take a rock on the one hand, the unmoved mover on the other. Neither one moves or acts. What explains this difference between them and all animals? There is nothing for which either of them reaches out – they are complete as they are. Animals, on the other hand, are not self-sufficient, but the sorts of beings that go for items which they see and imagine – and not for any of these, but just for the ones towards which, having a need, they inwardly strain. Moving is seen to be intrinsically connected with a lack of self-sufficiency or completeness, and with the inner movement towards the world with which needy creatures are fortunately endowed. These are points about animals (both human and other) which the Platonist would do well to ponder.[33]

The invention of *orexis* accomplishes several purposes directly. First, it makes us focus on the intentionality of animal movement: both (a) its object-directedness and (b) its responsiveness not to the world *simpliciter* but to the animal's own view of it.[34] Second, it demystifies rational action by asking us to see it as similar to other animal motions. Like them it is a selective reaching-out, and like them it goes after objects that are seen to have a certain relation to the animal's needs. Animals look less brutish, humans more animal.

This gives us some general sense of what Aristotle is up to. But now we must examine in detail the schema of explanation that he himself wishes to defend.

IV

Like the *De Anima* chapters,[35] the *De Motu* begins (i.e. begins this part of its argument, in Chapter 6)[36] by asking for the *archē*, the origin or starting-point, of animal movement. It then quickly asserts that animals all move things and are moved *for the sake of* something. The context makes it plain that what is in question is the explanation of purposive motion towards an intentional object, and not the more general teleological explanation of organic processes such as growth and nutrition. At this point, the more schematic *De Motu* begins to provide a superior clarity. Aristotle lists five items which he calls 'movers of the animal': reasoning and *phantasia* and choice and wish (*boulēsis*) and appetite (*epithumia*).[37] These, he continues, can all be subsumed under two heads: cognition (*noēsis*)[38] and desire (*orexis*). He justifies this (making his lists more complete at the same time) by arguing that *phantasia* and *aisthēsis* 'hold the same place' as intellect, fill the same slot in an explanatory schema, in that all of them are concerned with drawing distinctions (are *kritika*[39]), while *boulēsis*, *thumos*, and *epithumia* are all forms of *orexis*. We now have what the *De Anima* did not clearly supply: (generically) two 'movers' of the animal, both of which will play a vital role in our explanations.

The full story told by *De Motu* Chapters 6 and 7 seems to be as follows. Many objects in the world are presented to the animal by its cognitive faculties. Among these, some will be objects of some sort of *orexis* and some will not. Among the objects of *orexis*, in turn, some will turn out to be available or 'possible': the animal will either see them or reason out some way to get them. The full answer to Chapter 7's question, 'How does it happen that cognition is sometimes accompanied by action and sometimes not?' involves reference not only to the creature's *orexeis* but also to some cognitive activity that will supply the 'premise' 'of the possible'. The cognitive faculties perform, then, a double role. They present the goal to the animal's awareness initially, and they also perform work that gets the animal from *orexis* for the goal to action directed at a specific available object in the world. In many cases, these two operations will not be distinct: the animal's *orexis* may be aroused to activity just by seeing the very item for which it then goes. But in a large number of cases (including many non-human cases, like the 'drink' example), they will be.[40] The final result is that *orexis*, as a 'mover', is absolutely central; but it does nothing alone, without the aid of perception or thought. Animals act in accordance with desire, but within limits imposed by the world of nature, as they see it. The 'good' and the 'possible' must come together in order for movement to result.

What sort of explanation of animal movement is provided by this schema? Aristotle calls the cognitive and orectic factors 'movers'; he uses the active verb 'imparts motion' both for the activity of the object of desire and for the way in which the soul gets the animal going (*kinei*, 700b33, 700b10). He says that animals move 'by' or 'in virtue of' desire and choice (dative, 701a4–6). He also speaks of certain things following thought 'out of necessity' (701a34–5). In the absence of an impediment, the thought (plus *orexis*) and the movement are 'nearly simultaneous' (702a16). He sums up the situation by saying that the cognition 'prepares' the *orexis*, and *orexis* the *pathē* (702a17–19); and it all happens 'simultaneously' and 'rapidly' because of the way in which action and passion are naturally relative to one another.[41] All these remarks certainly lead us to suppose that here, as in *De Anima* III.10 (where *orexis* is 'that which imparts movement (*to kinoun*)', the psychological elements are regarded as efficient causes, as providing an explanation of the type 'from which comes the origin of motion'. It is rather difficult to flesh this out more fully. The background notion seems to be the general one of something that acts in such a way as to make something happen. This is certainly the suggestion contained in active verbs such as '*kinei*' and '*paraskeuazei*', as well as in the dative and in the preposition '*dia*'.[42] It looks, then, as if the orectic element and the cognitive element are, in each case, individually necessary and (in the absence of an impediment)[43] jointly sufficient active causes of the movement.

But I have already said that the connections among *orexis*, cognition, and motion are logical or conceptual. These conceptual links appear to be of two kinds. First, on the level of the particular desire or perception, each is identified, and individuated from other similar items, by reference to the goal or object in view. We cannot give an account of the *orexis* that leads to an action without mentioning the object for which it is an *orexis*. Second, on the general level, Aristotle ascribes the possession of *orexis* and *phantasia* (i.e. the interpretative, selective element in perception, in virtue of which things in the world 'appear' (*phainetai*) to the creature *as* a certain sort of thing)* to a creature just because it is a creature that moves, as a part of unpacking the notion of what it means to be a moving creature. The general notion of *orexis*, if we have been correct so far, is the notion of something going on internally, an inclining towards or reaching for, such that in certain circumstances (in combination with the right sort of perception or thought) action will naturally and swiftly result. Both here and in the comparable passage in *Metaphysics* IX, Aristotle insists that movement *will* result, unless there is some impediment, if the animal really wants something in a decisive way (*kuriōs oregetai*).[44] This seems to be at least in part a remark about what it *means* to have an *orexis* for something, about the conditions under which we are logically entitled to say of an animal that it has an *orexis* for something. If movement does not follow, and we cannot produce any impediment to explain the failure, we will be more likely to withdraw our *orexis*-ascription than to regard it as a counter-example to an empirical thesis about the causes of action.

In my earlier book on the *De Motu* I said more about these conceptual connections. I now believe, however, that I was in error to find Aristotle's assertion of both a logical and a causal connection a serious problem for his account.[45] I suggested that desire and cognition, because of their close conceptual link with action, could not be genuine independent items in a causal explanation of that action. Whether Aristotle realized this or not (so I said), we would have to look for some other description, most likely a physiological one, under which desires and beliefs could be genuine causes. In fact, I speculated that Aristotle might actually be looking for such an independent physiological specification in the second half of Chapter 7.

It is in fact, however, not possible to avoid the fact that the *De Motu* does assert that *orexeis* and cognitive activities, characterized as such and not in some other way, are causes of the movement. This is abundantly clear from the passages mentioned above. Below I shall present a different account of the second part of Chapter 7, and argue that the physiological story not only does not, but, given Aristotle's overall view of explanation, could not, provide a causal explanation of an action. What I want to say here is that it is also quite clear that this is no philosophical problem for Aristotle, who sees the philosophical issues more clearly than his reductionist opponents both ancient and contemporary.[46] Suppose Aristotle does hold (what seems true) that our general conceptions of wanting, perceiving, and moving towards an object are logically interrelated: i.e. that any good story about our conception of one will make reference somehow to the others. Suppose he also holds, as he does and as seems true, that the account of each particular *orexis* and each particular *phantasia* or *aisthēsis* or *noēsis* will involve some essential reference to an object in the world towards which that activity is directed, characterizing it under some intentional description. Nonetheless, none

---

* The standard translation of '*phantasia*' is 'imagination'. In my *Aristotle's De Motu*, Essay 5, I argue (on the basis of a study of all its uses, especially in connection with action) that this is inadequate, and that the best account requires linking it closely with the verb '*phainesthai*', 'appear', in the way I have indicated here.

of this ought to prevent the *orexis* from having the particular sort of logical independence of the goal required in order for it to play its role as moving cause. For the *occurrence* of the desire is obviously (as Aristotle says, and as seems true) entirely independent of the *attainment* or *realization* of the goal in action. Aristotle stresses this independence in several ways. (1) He says that desire must be combined in the right way with perception in order for movement to follow. (2) He insists that the cognitive faculties must come up with a possible and available route to the goal, or else motion will not follow. (3) He makes it clear that the desire must be not just one among others, but *the* one that the agent is acting on at the moment, the 'authoritative' one – however we understand this. (4) He points out that even when all this is true there may be some impediment, in which case motion will not follow.

Indeed, so far from being incompatible, the logical and the conceptual links are, in their explanatory role, closely related. It is just because a desire has the close conceptual relation it does to movement and action that it has the *causal* relation it does to action. It is because what this *orexis* is, is an *orexis* for object *O*, and because what the creature sees before it is this same *O*, that the movement towards *O* can be caused in the way it is by the *orexis* and the seeing. Suppose a dog goes after some meat. It is relevant to the *causal* explanation of its motion that its *orexis* be for meat (or this meat), and that what it sees before it, it also sees *as meat*. If it saw just a round object, or if its *orexis* were simply for exercise, the explanatory causal connections would be undermined. It is just because the goal 'vengeance on the enemies of Athens' figured as a part of the content of the *orexis* and the beliefs of the Athenian soldiers that these items could combine as they did to cause their action towards this goal. They might, for various reasons, not have acted, while having this same desire and belief: in this sense the desire and belief are independent of the goal-directed motion. But their close conceptual relatedness seems very relevant to their causal explanatory role. This, I think, is what Aristotle means when he insists that objects of desire cause motion precisely *by* being seen as the sort of thing that is desired, and when he insists that the 'premises' that are 'productive' of action must mention the goal both as desired and as available.[47]

All of this has an obvious bearing on what we shall want to say about the role of the physiological description. Aristotle, according to my early view, believes that there is, for each token occurrence of each of the psychological causal factors, some physiological realization that might conceivably be captured in a scientist's description. I still believe that there is some truth to this. For perception explicitly, for desire and *phantasia* implicitly, Aristotle seems to believe that such activity is always *realized in* or *constituted by* some matter or other. He even sometimes says that perceptual activities 'are' certain qualitative changes in the body – though it is likely, given his adherence to a principle resembling Leibniz's Law, that this 'is' indicates not identity, but the weaker relation of constitution or realization.[48] In any case, there is no solid evidence that the correlations involved would be of sufficient regularity and precision for any interesting general theory useful to

the scientist to emerge.[49] I recognized this, but then went on to say that we would have a genuine causal explanation only when the physiological factors had, in the particular case at least, been isolated.

This now seems to me unsatisfactory in several ways. First, as we have just seen, the 'only when' is not warranted: we have a perfectly good causal account already, on the psychological level. Second, if the 'two descriptions' are not 'related in any constant or predictable fashion', as I said, then the consequence seems to be that we will never have a genuine causal *explanation*: for explanations, for Aristotle, must be general in order to impart understanding.[50] Third, it is not clear to me on what basis we could ever confidently assert of some physiological condition that it was the bodily realization of this *orexis* or this *phantasia*. At most we could say that it was *necessary* for the occurrence of the *orexis*; and even to say this we would have to be in a position to generalize beyond the particular case. To say this, however, is to fall far short of what we need to say if the physical state is to be explanatory in any way; for example, it could look as if the activities of the heart, being necessary for all *orexis*, thereby constitute every *orexis*. But finally, and most important, the physiological feature, *just because* it lacks both the general and the particular conceptual link with the resulting action, links which the *orexis* does possess, seems to lack the sort of *relevance* and *connectedness* that we require of a cause when we say, 'This was the thing that made that happen.' In other words, to use Aristotle's terminology, it could not be a *proper cause* of the action. Take Aristotle's *Physics* II.3 example of Polyclitus the sculptor. We want to say that not just any attribute of Polyclitus was what caused, brought about, prepared, that statue. It was the skill of sculpting (together, as *Metaphysics* IX makes clear, with the relevant desires). For it is *that* about Polyclitus that has the appropriate conceptual connection with sculpting, although no doubt at every point he had many other properties, and at every point his body was in some physiological condition. There is an intimate connectedness (*oikeiotēs*) to the one factor that is lacked by all the others, which seem, therefore, to be only incidentally connected with the action (*Ph.* 195b3–4; cf. *Cat.* 2b6ff.). This factor, then, seems to answer our 'why' question properly, and the others don't.

It is a tricky matter to know how to unpack this further. Aristotle, in the *Physics* passage, says little more that would help us: only that 'the man builds *because (hoti)* he is a builder', and that the builder builds 'according to *(kata)*' the art of building. Connectedness and efficient causality are closely linked; but we hardly know whether we ought to say that factor A is properly the cause because of its connectedness with the goal, or that its relevance comes from the fact that it, and nothing else, operates as the cause; or perhaps both of these. Furthermore, it remains unclear exactly how this notion of efficient cause itself ought to be fleshed out. We might try a counterfactual analysis: desire D and belief B are the causes of action A and physiological conditions P are not, because we could always have P occurring without A; but D and B could not occur without A, unless there were some impediment. Some of Aristotle's talk of impediments in the *De Motu*

suggests this; and there is strong confirming evidence from *Metaphysics* IX for connecting cause with necessity in this way. But to go any further here would require opening up all the knotted and difficult issues surrounding Aristotle's treatment of cause and necessity, issues that cannot possibly be adequately stated and resolved in this context.[51] We must therefore simply let it remain indefinite exactly what more we are to make of this notion of causing. The central point is that, however it is to be construed, the physiological features are not causes of the animal's movement any more than Polyclitus's having kidneys is the cause of his sculpting the statue.

The proper place for a physiological description seems, in fact, to be what the *Phaedo* said it was. It provides an account of certain necessary conditions for the operation of the causal factors. The story of sinews and bones should be included not as an answer to the *dia ti* question ('*Why* did the dog go after the meat?'), but as the answer to a somewhat different question: '*How* was it able to go after the meat?' In other words, in virtue of what equipment or organization did the desires and the cognitive activities have the power to set in motion this complex bodily creature?[52] This division of questions need not presuppose or imply any form of dualism: it need not imply that *orexeis* are odd sorts of non-physical substances, or that the activities of the animal are not in every concrete case realized in some suitable matter or other. It simply recognizes that desires and cognitions, not physiological states, are the proper causes of the action, the salient items in its causal explanation, therefore the things that really can be said to impart motion or make things happen.

And this is, in fact, exactly the way the *De Motu* and (with its forward reference to the *De Motu*) the *De Anima* divide up the question.[53] The *De Anima* says precisely this: that the answer to the question, 'What imparts movement?' is 'Desire' – desire is the causal factor, the answer to our request for causal explanation. 'But as for the equipment in virtue of which desire imparts motion, that is something bodily' – and there follows a reference to the account of bones and joints in the *De Motu*. We could hardly ask for a clearer articulation of the *Phaedo* picture (without the *Phaedo*'s overemphasis on intellect); but this statement of the issue in *De Anima* would help us little without the *De Motu* to make good on this promise. The *De Motu*, too, makes it very clear to us that two different questions are in view. Chapter 10 clearly distinguishes 'the account that gives the *aitia* of movement' from the specification of the bodily equipment that is necessary in order for *orexis* to function.[54] And the transition to the discussion of physiology in Chapter 7, though less clearly worded, contains indications that it is an answer to the 'how' question about motion (701b7). The question how it is possible for movement to follow so rapidly follows upon the conclusion of the account of the 'origin' of motion, which answered our 'why' question (cf. *dia* at 701a33ff.); it shows how the animal is well equipped for movement in the arrangement of its physiological features. There are certainly unclarities; and sometimes Aristotle's language is compressed and ambiguous in a way that does not satisfy us.[55] But the general picture that emerges seems to be a reasonable one. We can conclude that the *De Motu* provides a basically adequate and rather rich account of the causal and conceptual issues involved in the explanation of animal movement.

V

The *De Motu* has offered us an account of what it, like the ethical works, calls *hekousios* or 'voluntary' movement. This account focuses, more clearly and plainly than the anthropocentric ethical works, on what is evidently there too a matter of central concern: to isolate and characterize a group of movements which, unlike various other movements of the animal – unlike, for example, the automatic movements of the digestive system and the reflex motions of certainly bodily parts[56] – may be said to be the ones for which the animal itself is the explanation, the ones that are done 'through the creature itself', not through some external force that uses the creature as its instrument. This vague notion of the *hekousion*, a notion which is said in the ethical works to be of considerable importance for our practical attitudes and practices – we praise and blame when and only when the creature itself is the origin (*archē*) of the motion or action – has now been further unpacked. The *hekousioi* motions of animals are just those movements which are caused by their own *orexeis* and cognitive activities, their own reachings-out towards objects and their own views of those objects. This account of the *hekousion* seems to be what underlies and explains Aristotle's repeated and entirely consistent ascription of it to other animals and to human children, as well as to human adults: though these less developed creatures lack deliberation, choice, and general principles (cf. further below), they do have in common with human adults that their own view of the world and their own *orexeis*, rather than physical necessity, are the causes of their actions.

Although this positive account of the *hekousion* does not appear at first glance to be the same as the accounts of the ethical works, which characterize the *hekousion* negatively by enumerating the circumstances that make an action *akousios*, 'involuntary' or not appropriate for ethical assessment, we can see upon further inspection that the two accounts are extensionally equivalent and do in effect put forward, though with difference of emphasis, the same criteria.[57] The *De Motu* account is the appropriate unpacking of the ethical works' notion of the agent's being the 'origin' (*archē*) and 'explanation' (*aition* – cf. n. 21) of the action. According to the *De Motu*, an action *A* is *hekousios* if and only if it is caused by the animal's own *orexis* for *A* and cognitive states concerning *A*. This would clearly suffice to exclude one group of *akousioi* actions given prominence in the ethical works, actions performed under external physical constraint. Would it also suffice to rule out the other main group of *akousioi* actions, namely actions done out of ignorance? At first we think not. Oedipus kills an old man at the crossroads. Clearly, as described, this killing is *hekousios* by *De Motu* criteria, caused by his own angry desire to remove this troublesome obstacle and his belief that hitting the man with a stick was a good way to bring this result about.[58] There is the right sort of conceptual connectedness among the contents of desire, belief, and resulting action. But Oedipus's action was a parricide; and, as such, it looks like a paradigmatic case of an action done out of excusable ignorance, and therefore *akousios*. So we have an apparent extensional gap between the *De Motu* and the *EN* criteria.

When we examine the matter further, however, we see that, described as parricide, this action is *akousios* by *De Motu* criteria as well. There is no *orexis* for parricide and no belief concerning parricide that can explain it. Parricide is not the intentional object of any of Oedipus's orectic or cognitive activities, so far as we know. The *EN* puts this point a little circuitously, by saying that the man acted 'out of' ignorance, as if ignorance were the cause of the action. The issue to which this criterion points is more clearly seen in the light of the *De Motu*'s way of putting things: the desires and beliefs of the agent are not directed at that action in such a way as to explain it.[59] We have, then, not a single action, *hekousion* according to the *De Motu* and *akousion* according to the *EN*. We have, instead, two actions, a homicide and a parricide, the former being *hekousion* by both accounts, the latter *akousion* by both accounts. The alleged gap has been removed.

We have spoken of ethical and legal assessment. This brings us to the question with which we began: what does this account of action, constructed with an eye to all our 'appearances' concerning the movements of animals, imply for the ethical problems in which we are interested? Does the combination of vulnerability and activity involved in Aristotelian *orexis* provide a good or a bad basis for our practices of 'praising those who deserve praise and sowing blame for wrong-doers'? We can focus the question by considering a recent objection to the *De Motu*/*De Anima* account, which has a clear connection with what Plato would have said had he had the opportunity to make a criticism of that account. The objection is that by giving this 'common' account of the *hekousion* and thereby admitting to this class many actions of animals and children, Aristotle has failed to provide an adequate basis for an account of ethical responsibility. Terence Irwin is the objector;[60] he has developed this argument eloquently and at length. The conclusions of his very interesting study are as follows: (1) Aristotle has a 'simple theory' of responsibility (which Irwin finds in the *EN* and which is similar to what we have found in the *De Motu*), according to which an action is responsible if and only if it is caused by the creature's own beliefs and desires, functioning as reasons. This view allows the actions of children and animals to count as responsible. (2) But Aristotle also has a 'complex theory' of responsibility (found in other parts of the ethical works) that sets tougher conditions: an action is responsible if and only if it is the voluntary action of a creature capable of effective deliberation, or *prohairesis*.[61] (Much of Irwin's article is devoted to a fruitful exploration of that notion, and I shall not attempt to summarize those results here.) The 'complex theory', however, implies that the actions of children and animals are not responsible. Irwin believes that the complex theory is superior to the simple theory, in that it provides a more adequate basis for our ethical attitudes and practices.

Irwin and I can agree, I believe, more or less, about what Aristotle actually says. We can agree, that is, that there is in Aristotle's text a distinction between *hekousioi* movements and other movements that is not the same, either extensionally or in account, as the distinction, also present in his text, between actions done by agents capable of *prohairesis* and actions done by agents not capable of *prohairesis*. We can agree that both of these distinctions are connected by Aristotle in one way or another with the appropriateness of praise and blame. We can also agree that the two distinctions have different results for the classification of many actions. In particular, we agree that the texts clearly deny deliberation and choice to animals and children, but consistently ascribe *hekousios* action to them.[62]

But here, I believe, our stories will diverge. Irwin believes that the two distinctions are alternative attempts to capture a single notion, the notion of moral responsibility; that there is only one ethically interesting distinction here and that Aristotle ought to have employed only a single contrast, choosing between these two ways of giving an account of it. Irwin clearly believes that Aristotle ought to have opted for the 'complex theory', with the result that animal and child actions will be classified simply as non-responsible acts. He tells us that the 'simple theory' is 'dangerous'[63] in its extension of the voluntary (construed as the responsible) to children and animals; such an extension *seems* reasonable only because the definition of the *hekousion* in the *EN* fails, through oversight, to rule it out. The purpose of a distinction like this, Irwin argues, is to justify our ethical practices and attitudes; but no justification can be found for treating animals and children like responsible agents.

Now Irwin is clearly aware that for Aristotle praise and blame come in several varieties. He produces and stresses the evidence that Aristotle believes it to be inappropriate to speak of flourishing living (*eudaimonia*) or of excellence of character, when praising a creature who lacks the capacity for deliberation and choice, therefore when dealing with an animal or a child. As both Irwin and I can agree, Aristotle nowhere hesitates to say that the most serious sorts of ethical assessments we make, those having to do with judgments of character and of overall goodness of life, are appropriately made only of adults who have formed a character and chosen a way of life, who are capable of *prohairesis*, i.e. deliberation concerning their ultimate ends or values. And yet Aristotle plainly does also say that praise and blame of some sort, and some weaker ethical attitudes, are appropriate so long as the action satisfies certain weaker conditions. This is the heart of the issue: for in Irwin's view nothing short of full adult *prohairesis* ever *could* justify any of these attitudes and practices. If we do apply praise to a child or an animal, he thinks, this can be nothing more than the deploying of a kind of causal force directed at manipulating behavior; and this has very little to do with real praise.[64]

Irwin's is an admirable and serious ethical view. And although it is clearly

Kantian in origin, it corresponds to much in Plato's account of action, as we have sketched it. For Plato, too, clearly thinks that there are two choices only: brutish necessity on the one hand, on the other the purely unaffected self-moving causality of reason. Serious ethical assessments require the capability for intellectual causality; the quickest way to speak of a human being as beyond the pale of ethical assessment is to say that that person does things the way an animal does. And for such people external manipulation is the only sort of training there is. To be passive to natural causality is to be an unselective object, without any active share in choosing the good.

What I now want to argue is that Aristotle's 'common' account offers a serious ethical alternative to this serious view, an alternative that we cannot see or properly appreciate if we demand of Aristotle that he opt for the serious view. To answer Irwin on Aristotle will help us to appreciate Aristotle's own answer to Plato. Aristotle can agree with Irwin (as I believe he does) that certain very high standards must be met in order to justify the most serious of our ethical judgments of persons. And yet, compatibly with this, he can continue to insist (as he plainly does) on the ethical relevance of the different distinction which we have been exploring. The two distinctions seem to be put forward not (what Irwin assumes) as rival accounts of a single notion, but as accounts of two related notions that have complementary roles to play in his ethical theory. Some reasons for keeping both distinctions begin to emerge if we consider how an account of moral development and training might go.

On Irwin's view there is at some point in the development of a child a sudden and mysterious shift. From being the object of a process of behavioral conditioning to which he or she actively contributes little or nothing, the child becomes an adult capable of *prohairesis*, that is, capable of deliberation about values, capable of altering and criticizing his or her own desires. We are not given any account of what, in the child, makes this development possible, or indeed of how an educator might help to bring it about. For Aristotle, centrally concerned as he is with education, and believing, as he does, that the main job of politics is to educate children in such a way that they will become capable of leading good lives according to their own choice, this result would be very unfortunate. But because he retains his 'simple theory' as well as his 'complex theory', he can present a plausible and interesting answer to these questions. The 'common account' (a phrase that I prefer to Irwin's 'simple theory' for several obvious reasons) tells us that we begin the educational process not with a creature who is simply there to be causally affected and manipulated, but with a creature that responds selectively to its world via cognition and *orexis*, and whose movements are explained by its own view of things, its own reachings-out for things as it views them. The 'common account' of the *hekousion* is not meant to be a rival to the account of deliberate choice: it is the account of the animal basis for certain ethical attitudes and practices that are central in the development of an animal creature towards deliberate choice. Because we are dealing with a selective creature who interprets, reaches out, and acts accordingly – because from the very beginning there is a distinction between animal movements that are merely externally caused and movements that are caused by the creature's own point of view – we can embark on a program of habituation and training that is not simply a mindless type of behavioral manipulation. Praise and blame are from the beginning not just pushes, but appropriate modes of communication to an intelligent creature who acts in accordance with its own view of the good. They are attempts to persuade that creature to modify, actively, its view of the good, to reach out for more appropriate objects. If we do not take Irwin's very pessimistic view of animals and children, we do not need to despise the 'simple' *hekousion*: it is the necessary basis for more complicated developments ahead. And if we think of what actually happens when one educates a child, Aristotle's insistence on the centrality of intentionality and selective attention seems far more empirically right than Irwin's behaviorist picture. It offers us an attractive account of the natural animal basis for the development of moral character.[65]

In the ethical works Aristotle goes one step further. We can say not only that a study of our beliefs about *orexis* reveals its intentionality and selectivity; we can also say that the practices of education and exhortation in which we engage would be unintelligible if *orexis* were, as Plato (and Irwin), say, purely mindless:

> The digestive does not partake in reason in any way, but the appetitive and in general the desiderative (*orektikon*) partake of it in a certain way, inasmuch as they are attentive and obedient to it...That the irrational is persuaded in a way by reason is indicated by the practice of giving advice and by all reproof and exhortation. And if we are to say that this element, too, has reason, we must say that there are two sorts of having reason: one being to have it strictly and internally to itself, the other being to have something that is like that which listens to a parent. (*EN* 1102b29–1103a3; cf. *EE* 1219b27ff.)

The existence and the efficacy of certain ethical practices shows that the appetites cannot be as simple and brutish as Plato has alleged, mere pushes responding to other pushes, like the movements of the digestive system. We give advice, injunction, and training to people with respect to appetitive pursuits as well as those that involve the pure intellect. We train children to develop appropriate desires for appropriate sorts of gratification, not by brute suppression of their push towards these activities, but by appealing to them through discourse and motivational interaction to modify their selections. Then there must be a kind of reasonableness to the appetitive forces themselves – something like a listening attentively and responsively to parental injunction. The intentional selectivity of appetite shows us how it can be engaged for positive support in the search for the good. We might say that it is the Plato/Irwin view that fails to justify and give point to the ethical practices in which we actually engage; whereas Aristotle's appears to fit them well.

What we could now do at greater length would be to show how a non-behaviorist account of habituation, which stresses object-relations and selective attention, could chart the child's gradual development from the simple *hekousion* to complex *prohairesis*. The *Politics* provides much of the material for such an account. We shall turn shortly to the job of characterizing the nature and structure of Aristotelian deliberation; so we shall not set out the developmental picture in detail.[66] The general point is, however, clear: that Aristotle's complex ethical views need not be seen as at odds with his account of 'voluntary' animal movement in the *De Motu*, because it is a part of his ethical view that our shared animal nature is the ground of our ethical development. It is our nature to be animal, the sort of animal that is rational. If we do not give a debased account of the animal or a puffed-up account of the rational, we will be in a position to see how well suited the one is to contribute to the flourishing of the other.

This, like much Aristotelian argument inside the appearances, may seem insufficient. For Plato, surely, this description of practices that *in fact* rest upon a distinction between intentional and mechanical causality would not go far towards answering the important question, namely, whether those practices are really *justified* by that distinction. (And this is, of course, the question that would be pressed against Aristotle by Irwin's Kantian view as well.) Just because we *believe* that the distinction justifies the practices, this does not show that they really *are* justified by so little. And Plato is prepared to argue that they are not. As the good judge, the person not deluded by human desire, can see, a purely active causal element, altogether 'unmixed', 'unaffected', is necessary to make our lives worth living, more than brutish.

Aristotle will have several replies to this challenge. First, he has already called into question the distinction between what we all believe and what is really so. We have no access to any truth beyond the deepest and most pervasive appearances. So if his account has succeeded in correctly articulating those appearances, it will have the strongest claim to be the truth. In the strongest sense of justification available within the Aristotelian method, these practices have now been justified by Aristotle's account of motion: that is, they have been shown to be internally in order, to fit with the other things we believe, do, and say.

It is not even clear, furthermore, from what vantage point the Platonist can articulate his challenge. Suspending, as he asks us to do, distinctions and beliefs that are so fundamental to the daily conduct of our lives, he must manage, nonetheless, to motivate the challenge and to make it intelligible within human experience. In posing questions, he must not tacitly trade on the very practices and beliefs he questions; he must, then, put himself outside all relevant commitments and judgments concerning animality, causality, motion. But, on the other hand, he must speak from a position that does not 'stand so far outside' that we will not recognize him as one of us or care about what he says.

Even supposing that he does find an appropriate place from which to address us, and supposing that it is a place in which we recognize him as among us, there is still, furthermore, a deep difficulty about the unmixed and unaffected causal element to which he alludes. If such an element is not familiar to us from our experience, if all our *experience* of causality and motion is of an impure sort, mixing passivity with activity, then Plato's talk of *nous* may fall victim to the same criticism that Aristotle has levelled against his talk of forms (see Ch. 8 above): that it is insufficiently rooted in experience even to be coherent talk.

But since our experience of our own agency is a highly various and variable matter, and since it is not unlikely that some persons in Aristotle's audience would endorse the Platonic description of a split between *nous* and brute necessity as a correct description of experience, Aristotle cannot simply rely on this sort of argument. And implicit in his account of *orexis* is a further line of defense. If we think of his account in connection with the *Phaedrus*, we can suggest that the hard, impassive *nous* of the *Phaedo* is neither necessary nor sufficient for true insight and correct choice. Not necessary, because insight can be reached, as the *Phaedrus* shows and as Aristotle will also show (cf. Ch. 10) through a responsive interaction with the external; not sufficient, because this element lacks the sort of openness and receptivity that seems to be requisite for the best and highest sort of insight. Without being-affected, as Aristotle explicitly reminds us, there will be cleverness and even contemplative wisdom, but not, for example, gentleness, or courage, or love – praiseworthy elements of the person without which a human life would not be a good one (*EE* 1220a11–13). Far from being a way of securing our values and our praiseworthiness, Plato's strategy actually deprives us of many praiseworthy ways of moving, acting, and being, narrowing the ways in which we can be good. (We shall investigate this response in more detail in Chapter 10.)

In short, Aristotle will be ready to claim that a correct and duly subtle articulation of the appearances concerning action will remove the motivation for Plato's strategy, showing that what we want to secure can be not only secured, but better and more fully secured, in his account of action and its causes.

In concluding, we may now return to the appearances with which we began, and ask how the Aristotelian account has preserved them. Let us, then, allow Pericles to conclude his funeral oration in the following way:

You must yourselves realize the power of Athens, and feed your eyes on her from day to day, until love of her fills your hearts. And then, when all her greatness breaks in upon you, you must reflect that it was by courage and knowledge of practical necessities and a sense of shame in action that men were enabled to win all this.... And judging that the good human life is the free life, and the free life the courageous life, do not decline the dangers of war. For this is the way animals move forward to motion and to action: the immediate cause of motion is desire, and this comes into being either through perception or through imagining and thinking. And with creatures that reach out for action, it is sometimes through appetite or emotion and sometimes through rational wish that they create or act.[67]

What would we think of the author of such a conclusion? And what would we take to be his or her motives in so concluding? We would think of him or her, I imagine, as, first of all, a person determined to deflate the pretensions of the intellect: or rather of any view of human action and human rationality that would cut the human being off from its membership in a larger world of nature. This is something implicit in the first sentences of Pericles' conclusion, with their emphasis on the role of perception and love in motivating action; but the last (grafted) sentence, which makes their role explicit, helps to prevent certain sorts of misreading. We would think of this person as someone anxious to stress, on the other hand, the richness and complexity of animal action in the world of nature, refusing to yield to any scientific pressures to see it as a mindless and mechanical matter. Human action and the human being are placed squarely within nature; the human being is taken to be a creature of love and desire, even in his or her rational action. But desire is not something altogether brutish: it involves selective focusing upon objects in the world and an equally selective set of responses to that focusing. Finally, the speaker would be a person who was eager (as both Thucydides and Aristotle usually are) to stress the lack of self-sufficiency that characterizes all animal lives, including our own. Neither inert objects nor perfected gods, neither simply pushed around from without or spontaneously self-moving, we all reach out, being incomplete, for things in the world. That is the way our movements are caused.[68]

10   Non-scientific deliberation

> I was just conscious, vaguely, of being on the track of a law, a law that
> would fit, that would strike me as governing the delicate phenomena –
> delicate though so marked – that my imagination found itself playing with. A
> part of the amusement they yielded came, I daresay, from my exaggerating
> them – grouping them into a larger mystery (and thereby a larger 'law') than
> the facts, as observed, yet warranted; but that is the common fault of minds
> for which the vision of life is an obsession.

> I should certainly never again, on the spot, quite hang together, even though
> it wasn't really that I hadn't three times her method. What I too fatally lacked
> was her tone.

> Henry James, The Sacred Fount, Chapters 1, 14

Aristotle says two anti-Platonic things about practical deliberation. First, that it
is not and cannot be scientific:* 'That practical wisdom is not scientific understanding (*epistēmē*) is obvious' (*EN* 1142a23–4).[1] Second, that the appropriate
criterion of correct choice is a thoroughly human being, the person of practical
wisdom. This person does not attempt to take up a stand outside of the conditions
of human life, but bases his or her judgment on long and broad experience of
these conditions. These two features of Aristotle's view are connected, clearly:
for the reason why good deliberation is not scientific is that this is not the way
this model good judge goes about deliberating; and the reason why this judge
is normative for correct choice is that his procedures and methods, rather than
those of a more 'scientific' judge, appear the most adequate to the subject matter.
Both features are connected, as well, with Aristotle's defense of an anti-Platonic
conception of the good human life. The decision that practical wisdom is not a
technē or *epistēmē*[2] and that the best judge is one who does not use a *technē* both
supports and is supported by the view that the best life is more vulnerable to

---

* When I speak of 'science' in this chapter, I do not ignore the fact that some *technai* were accorded
  that status even without measurement – compare my account of Protagoras in Ch. 4. Aristotle
  himself recognizes the existence of 'stochastic' arts – e.g. medicine, navigation – that are similar
  to (his account of) ethics in their concern for the particular. But when he denies that ethics can
  be an *epistēmē* he is not, I believe, thinking of these examples, but, instead, of Plato's ethical *epistēmē*
  and also of his own (similar) technical notion of *epistēmē* as a deductive system concerned throughout
  with universals. His own account of ethics, being a systematic ordering of appearances, has just
  about as much claim to *technē* status as does Protagoras's proposal; what he means is, that it is not
  technē or *epistēmē* in the sense demanded by either the *Republic* or the *Posterior Analytics*.

ungoverned *tuchē*, more open and less ambitious for control, than Plato said it was.* (These apparent circularities in Aristotle's account will concern us towards the end of this chapter.) Before we move on to the concrete investigation of Aristotle's views about *tuchē* and the good life, we need, then, to look closely at his non-scientific conception of the procedures by which good judgments of value are reached. If we are going to understand on what grounds he refuses to 'save' our lives from certain incursions of *tuchē*, we must understand his refusal of the Platonic aspiration to make ethics into a *technē*.

This chapter will, then, be the Aristotelian counterpart of Chapters 4 and 5, showing how an epistemology of value and an account of the vulnerability of the valuable things go hand in hand. It will ask who the person of practical wisdom is and how he deliberates, how the Platonic aspiration to universality, precision, and stable control is met and criticized in Aristotle's more 'yielding' and flexible conception of responsive perception. We shall begin with an examination of Aristotle's claims that practical deliberation must be anthropocentric, concerning itself with the human good rather than with the good *simpliciter*. Next we shall look at Aristotle's attack on the notion that the major human values are commensurable by a single standard. We shall then give an account of the interplay of universal rule and particular perception in Aristotelian deliberation. Finally we shall examine the role of passional response in good deliberation, showing that the person of practical wisdom both values and allows himself to be guided by these (allegedly) unreliable features of his human makeup. This will give us the materials to put together, finally, a picture of the sort of deliberation that Aristotle finds most appropriate and relevant to our human lives.

I

The Platonic aspiration to an external 'god's-eye' standpoint has already been criticized in our account of the method of appearances (Ch. 8). Aristotle has defended the view that the internal truth, truth *in* the appearances, is all we have to deal with; anything that purports to be more is actually less, or nothing. The standpoint of perfection, which purports to survey all lives neutrally and coolly from a viewpoint outside of any particular life, stands accused already of failure of reference: for in removing itself from all worldly experience it appears to remove itself at the same time from the bases for discourse about the world. Our question about the good life must, like any question whatever, be asked and answered within the appearances.

But ethics is anthropocentric in a stronger sense as well. When we ask about motion or time or place, we begin and end within experience of these items: we say only what has, through experience, entered into the discourse of our group.

* By 'Plato' here I mean the dialogues of the 'middle period' and not the *Phaedrus* (or *Laws* or *Statesman*). Aristotle's writing about *tuchē* is a response to these works and these views; he shows little concern with Plato's later dialogues, possibly as we have suggested, because many of his criticisms antedate them and they are composed in response to these criticisms. On Aristotle's relationship to the arguments of the *Phaedrus*, see this chapter, §IV and Chapter 12, pp. 368–71.

But we may still legitimately aspire to arrive at a unified account of motion or of time or place for the entire universe within which we live and have our experience. The *Physics* does not give one account of human time, another account of time for shellfish, another of time for the heavenly spheres.[3] Animals move in different ways; but there is also a general overarching account of motion in the universe, which has serious content. With the good, things are otherwise. It would in principle be available to Aristotle to attempt a unified account of The Good Life for all beings in the universe, ranking and ordering them in a non-species-relative way. He is familiar enough with projects of this type – above all, with Platonic attempts to discover and articulate an altogether non-context-relative notion of goodness, making it the subject matter of a single science or *epistēmē*. But he devotes considerable space to the criticism of this project – a criticism that is all the more marked for its being, as he acknowledges, personally difficult:

This inquiry is an uphill task, since men who are dear to us have introduced the Forms. But it would seem to be better, in fact to be necessary, to uproot even what is one's own for the sake of preserving the truth – both as a general principle and because we are philosophers. For when both the people and the truth are dear to us, it is fitting to put the truth first. (*EN* 1096a12–17)

Aristotle argues, first, that our notion of goodness falls short of the unity required for the establishment of a single science, since 'good' has application to items belonging in different logical categories.[4] In each case its presence commends the item in question; but we have no reason to think that it singles out a single common nature across all the disparate items. This argument is interesting and deep. We shall not, however, pursue it further here, since the items in which we are most interested – human and other animate *lives* – presumably are logically homogeneous; they might, then, give rise to a Platonic science even if this argument should be accepted. What is of most interest to us, then, is that Aristotle emphatically asserts that the goodness of *lives* is, and must be, a species-relative matter. 'The good is not single for all animals, but is different in the case of each', he writes in *Nicomachean Ethics* VI, contrasting practical value, in this respect, with the theoretical study of nature (1141a31–2). Accordingly, all three ethical works announce that their subject matter is the *human* good, or the good life for a human being. 'We must speak about the good, and about what is good not *simpliciter*, but for us. Not, therefore, about the divine good, for another discourse and another inquiry deals with this' (*MM* 1182b3–5). The *Nicomachean* discussion of the good life begins with an account of the specific and characteristic functioning of the human being, and, in effect, restricts its search for *good* functioning for us to a search for the excellent performance of these characteristic functions.[5] But why should this be so?

First of all, Aristotle emphasizes repeatedly that the goal of his ethical discourse is not theoretical but practical. It follows from this that there is no point to talking about the good life in an ethical inquiry insofar as this life is not practically attainable by beings with our capabilities.[6] The life of a divine being might be ever so admirable; but the study of this life, insofar as it lies beyond our capabilities, is not pertinent to the practical aims of ethics.[7]

Then too, the life we choose must be one that is possible for us in a different and stronger sense. It must be a life that we, as we deliberate, can choose for ourselves as a life that is really a life for *us*, a life in which there will be enough of what makes us the beings we are for *us* to be said to survive in such a life. Therefore, at the very minimum, it must be a life that a *human* being can live, not one which failed to include something without which we think no characteristically human life would be there. We begin an ethical treatise by looking at the characteristic functioning of humans – both its shared and its distinctive elements – because we want a life which includes whatever it is that makes us us.[8] For example, we might attempt to endorse a mindless hedonism, 'choosing the life of dumb grazing animals' (*EN* 1095b19–20); such a life would be possible for us in the first sense. But if we are brought to realize the central importance of practical reason in our conception of characteristic human functioning, we will realize, Aristotle thinks, that no life without this element would be, for us, an acceptable choice. (We shall see in Chapter 12 the role played by this sort of consideration in arguments about politics and friendship.) The beginning of the 'human function argument' makes a useful analogy to the crafts, whose point is as follows. The understanding of *good* shoemaking or lyre-playing must begin from an understanding of what those functions *are*. It could not, logically, turn out that the function of the good shoemaker was to play the lyre: good functioning for any craft practitioner must remain within the boundaries of what that activity, in its nature, *is*. In the same way, it could not, logically, turn out that the best life for a human being was the good living of a life characteristic of ants; that life would contain certain features that human life does not contain, and it would lack certain features that we regard as essential to properly human life. This sort of consideration leads us to the conclusion that a search for the good life for any being O must begin with an account of the essential ingredients of an O-ish life and O-ish activity – those features without which we will not be willing to count a life as O-ish at all. And if the essential features of lives are not the same across the species, as it looks evident to Aristotle that they are not, then the search for the good life must be a species-relative, rather than a general search. I cannot choose for *myself* the good life of an ant, a lion, a god.

Closely connected with the argument is a further consideration. The things that are good and valuable may not be so relatively to all imaginable ways and conditions of life. The good of some genuine values may be context-relative and not any the less good for that. Plato, as we saw in Chapter 5, is committed to the idea that what is *truly* and intrinsically valuable is so always and from a perspective totally severed from particular context; if a value is only species- or context-relative, this disqualifies it from being true intrinsic value. But Aristotle, as we shall see in detail in Chapter 11, questions this notion. Already in his attack upon the singleness of the Platonic Good, he remarks that 'it is not any the more good for being eternal, any more than the longer-enduring item is whiter than the transient one' (1096b3–4). In the same way, it may turn out that what is good only relatively to the contingent conditions of a certain way of life may be no less genuinely good on account of that 'limitation'; it may even turn out (cf. Ch. 11, §vi) that there is no ethical value that is not in this sense context-relative.[9] Aristotle urges that this question cannot be settled in advance, but must be discovered through a deeper understanding of the shared and non-shared features of human life.

II

An anthropocentric ethics could still be scientific. The demands of Platonic *technē* for generality and commensurability could, at least arguably, be met in an account of value that looked for the best and most valuable life for the sort of being we are. The *Protagoras* saw Socrates arguing that a *technē* in which all values were commensurable on a single quantitative scale was still a way of saving the lives of *human beings*. Diotima claimed that the ascent towards a general understanding of beauty, which denies qualitative distinctions in favor of quantitative measuring, the uniqueness of the individual in favor of a grasp of the general, would be the only way of making life 'livable *for a human being*'. We saw that in both cases *questions* of identity were indeed raised by the proposed progress; but it was not self-evident that the answer to these questions ruled out the Platonic life as a life for us. Aristotle rejects both of these salient features of Plato's scientific scheme for ethics. He argues that the values that are constitutive of a good human life are plural and incommensurable; and that a perception of particular cases takes precedence, in ethical judgment, over general rules and accounts. We must now look at the nature of these arguments. For we can see that to answer the Platonic proposal for progress Aristotle must do more (even in terms of his own method) than to say that this is how we currently do things. He must also show the importance and the depth of the aspects of our current practice that we would relinquish by accepting the Platonic proposal.

Commensurability had in Aristotle's time become, for many, a hallmark of the truly scientific.[10] Aristotle pointedly fails to endorse an art of measuring for ethics.[11] First, it is a central concern of the ethical works to assail the most plausible and appealing candidate for the single standard, namely pleasure. There are many difficulties surrounding the interpretation of Aristotle's two accounts of pleasure.[12] What we can confidently say is that they agree in denying that pleasure is a single thing yielded in a qualitatively homogeneous way by many different types of activity. For *EN* vii, my pleasures just *are* the activities that I do in a certain way: the unimpeded activations of my natural state.[13] Pleasures are, then, just as distinct one from another and just as incommensurable as are the different kinds of excellent activity. For *EN* x, pleasure supervenes upon the activity to which it attaches, like the bloom on a young person's cheek, completing or perfecting it.[14] It is not something that can be prised apart from the activity to which it is attached and sought out on its own, any more than blooming cheeks can be genuinely cultivated as such apart from the health and bodily fitness with which they belong.

Pleasures, furthermore, 'differ in kind' as the associated activities differ (1173b28ff.). Some are choiceworthy and some are not, some are better and some worse. Some, furthermore, are pleasant only to corrupt people, while some are pleasant to good people (1173b20ff.). Like (middle-period) Plato, then, Aristotle finds in the qualitative variety and the observer-relativity of pleasure good reasons not to base an ethical science upon it as a single end.

But pleasure does not fall short of the requirements of science by its lack of singleness alone: it also lacks inclusiveness. For, Aristotle insists, 'There are many things that we would eagerly pursue even if they brought no pleasure, such as seeing, remembering, knowing, having the excellences. And even if pleasures follow upon these of necessity, it makes no difference; for we *would* choose them even if no pleasure came from them' (*EN* 1174a4–8). Pleasure, even if firmly linked to excellent activity as a necessary consequence, is not the end for which we act. We choose the action for its own sake alone; and deliberative imagination can inform us that we would do so even if that link with pleasure were broken. This is not simply a counterfactual thought-experiment: for elsewhere Aristotle will insist that a good person will sometimes choose to sacrifice life itself, and therefore all possibility of present and future pleasure, for the sake of acting well or helping a friend (1117b10ff., cf. Ch. 11, p. 336).[15] And in general, the good person chooses to act well even if the world prevents the completion of this activity and its attendant pleasure (Ch. 11, p. 336). The Protagorean science, then, misrepresents the nature of our commitment to the excellences. And Aristotle makes a strong case for the preservation of our current commitments. They protect the continued possibility of personal sacrifice, of disinterested benefit to others, of the committed and non-instrumental pursuit of each value. Insofar as we think these commitments a valuable part of our lives with one another, we will be reluctant to eliminate our disagreements and vexing conflicts by opting for this kind of life-saving art.

Argument against hedonism is strong argument against the science of measurement itself, since no other candidate for the measure was being seriously put forward.[16] But it is also plain that Aristotle's opposition to this sort of *technē* is quite general. One of his arguments in the attack on the Platonic Good insists that 'the definitions of honor and practical wisdom and pleasure are separate and different *qua* goods' (1096b23–4). This fact is supposed to yield the conclusion that there can be no single common notion of good across these things. And in the *Politics* he explicitly repudiates any view that would make all goods commensurable. In this important passage he has been describing a theory about the basis of political claims according to which any and all differences between persons are relevant to political distribution. If A is the same as B in all other respects but excels B in height, A is *eo ipso* entitled to a greater share of political goods than B; if A excels B in height and B excels A at playing the flute, we will have to decide which excels by more. And so on. Aristotle's first objection to this scheme is specific: it recognizes as relevant to political claims many features that are quite irrelevant to good political activity. But his second objection is quite general. The scheme is defective because it involves treating all goods as commensurable with one another: height and musicianship are measured against wealth and freedom. 'But since this is impossible, it is obvious that in politics it is reasonable for men not to base their claim upon any and every inequality' (1283a9–11).

At this point, the proponent of a political *technē* might object that Aristotle is simply describing the *status quo*. But it is no compelling objection to a proposed *technē* that it does not always observe current practice. If it is now impossible to measure freedom against height, musicianship against wealth, the science itself may show us the way to do so tomorrow.[17] What reasons do Aristotle's judgments give us for believing that no *technē* could take us beyond where we currently are in an acceptable way?

Here we must return to Aristotle's remark about difference of definition, interpreting it by considering his actual accounts of the different intrinsic ends of human life. The ethical works display a conception of the best human life as a life inclusive of a number of different constituents, each being defined apart from each of the others and valued for its own sake.[18] Part of the very account of excellence of character, in fact, is the stipulation that the fine actions be chosen in each case for their own sake, not simply for the sake of some further reward or consequence (1105a32). Each excellence is defined separately, as something that has its value in itself. Moreover, Aristotle explicitly asserts that there are many things in life that we choose for their own sake: 'We would choose each of them even if nothing resulted' (1097b3–4, cf. 1096b16–19). But to value each of these separate items, each of which has its separate account, for what it itself is, seems to entail recognition of its distinctness and separateness from each of the others. The student of the *EN* will have, and/or acquire, a good understanding of what courage, justice, friendship, generosity, and many other values are; he will understand how, in our beliefs and practices, they differ from and are non-interchangeable with one another. He will then be in a position to see that to effect the commensurability of the values is to do away with them all as they currently are, creating some new value that is not identical to any of them. The question will then be whether his single-valued world can possibly have the richness and inclusiveness of the current world. A world in which wealth, courage, size, birth, justice are all put into the same scale and weighed together, made in their nature functions of a single thing, will turn out to be a world without any of these items, as now understood. And this, in turn, looks likely to be an impoverished world: for we value these items enough in their separateness not to want to trade them all in.

There is still one outstanding problem for this interpretation. This is that Aristotle explicitly says that deliberation and choice are concerned not with ends, but with the *means* to the end.[19] But if this is so, it will be argued, then the things with which choice concerns itself, including the major values that go to make up a good human life, must, after all, be seen as (comparable) means to something beyond themselves (say, happiness or satisfaction); the end will be some single separate item of which they are productive, in greater and lesser degrees.[20] This seems to bring back the idea of commensurability: for among the productive means to end *E*, the rational agent would select the ones that generate *more* of *E*; and to ask about this requires measuring.

Fortunately, we are not stuck with an insuperable problem here. For Aristotle's text (as a number of critics have by now pointed out) does not say that we deliberate only about *means* to ends.[21] Aristotle actually writes, 'We deliberate not about ends, but about what is *towards* the end' – or, 'what *pertains to* the end'. This looser phrase does not suggest that only instrumental means are in question. Indeed, it is broad enough to accommodate deliberation about what is to *count as* the end, what are the constituent parts of the end – a type of deliberation that Aristotle plainly recognizes elsewhere.[22] Aristotle's point is only that for any given piece of deliberation, there must be something that it is *about*, which is itself not up for question in that particular piece of deliberation. But within that piece of deliberation, I can ask both for means to that end and for a further *specification* of the end.[23] Plainly this demand for a further *specification* of the end or ends need involve no notion of commensurability. Starting, for example, from the valued end of love and friendship, I can go on to ask for a further specification of what, more precisely, love and friendship *are* – requesting, as well, an enumeration of the different types of love – without implying in any way that I regard these different relationships as commensurable on a single quantitative scale, either with one another or with other major values. And if I should ask of justice and of love whether both are constituent parts of *eudaimonia*, the best life for a human being, I surely do not imply by my question that we are to hold them up to a single standard, regarding them as productive of some further value. As Aristotle reminds us, something can be an end in itself and at the same time be a valued constituent in a larger or more inclusive end. The question whether something is or is not to count as a part of *eudaimonia* is just the question, whether something is a valuable component in the best human life. Since it is agreed that the best life must be inclusive of everything that is truly valuable for its own sake (everything without which the life would be incomplete and lacking in value),[24] then this is equivalent to the question whether that item has intrinsic value, is choiceworthy for its own sake. But Aristotle has argued that to choose it for *its own* sake (for the sake of what it itself is) not only does not require, but is actually incompatible with, viewing it as qualitatively commensurable with other valuable items. To view it in that way would not be to have the proper regard for the distinctness of *its* nature.[25] His view of ends seems, then, to be the explicit theoretical articulation of the position about plurality and richness that we found in the *Antigone* – and, more generally, in Greek polytheism. Once again, he 'saves' the appearances of his culture.

III

Aristotle's attack on the scientific aim of commensurability has relied upon the notion of giving an account or definition of each of the values in question. We expect that, like all Aristotelian definitions, such accounts will be universal in form and will not mention particular cases except insofar as they exemplify a universal concept or rule. This makes us wonder whether Aristotle is denying one part of the scientific project only in order to emphasize and affirm another equally important part, the demand for universality. We need to recall what motivates this demand and how its fulfillment would affect our relationship to *tuchē*.

The scientist sees that in the daily business of deliberation we are confused and vexed by the complex particularity of the cases that present themselves to us, ever freshly, for decision. Each new situation can strike us as in certain respects unlike any other; each valuable item can seem qualitatively individual, unlike any other. This way of seeing things has at least two unfortunate consequences. First, we lack comprehensive *understanding* of the practical sphere: we cannot organize it for ourselves, explain in a perspicuous fashion its salient features, bring ourselves to a new situation prepared to find features that we have grasped already.[26] We are, cognitively, at the mercy of each new event, and each presents itself to us as a mystery. This severely limits our attempts to plan a good life and to execute these plans. Insofar as the world of practice *does* make sense to us, is understood by us, it is because we find it exemplifying certain repeatable and therefore general features: we say, 'Here's a case where *courage* is called for', 'Here's an *injustice*', carving up the indeterminate 'matter' of the new by picking out items that we have seen and grasped before. We guide ourselves cognitively by working towards an understanding of these items; meanwhile, we guide ourselves morally by giving ourselves, or being given, precepts or rules in terms of these repeatable items and shaping our desires in accordance with these. The (Platonic) scientist would like to propose that we press this demand for universality as far as we can, trying to get ourselves a system of practical rules that will prepare us before the fact for the demands of the new situation, and also trying to get ourselves to see the new situation in terms of this system, as merely a case falling under its authority. Then we will never be taken by surprise.

The second unfortunate consequence of ethical particularity is vulnerability to loss. We have seen repeatedly how the idea that one valuable item is qualitatively like and replaceable by many others helps us to avoid vulnerability. The shift from seeing a beloved person (an institution, a pursuit) as uniquely valuable to seeing it as just a participant in some general value brings with it, as Diotima says, a relaxing and easing of the tensions of planning a life. If the world does something to one of the items you love, there is a ready supply of other similarly valuable items. Plato's scientific project urges that for this reason as well we ought to press and extend the demand for generality in value.

Aristotle gives general definitions of the excellences. He also defines excellence in general with reference to the notion of a *logos*, a rule or account: 'Excellence is a state of character (*hexis*) concerned with choice, lying in a mean, the mean relative to us, this being determined by a *logos*, the one by which the person of practical wisdom would determine it' (*EN* 1106b36–7a2). So the person whose choices are paradigms for ours is depicted as using a rule or account; and elsewhere, too, Aristotle speaks of the role in practical wisdom of the *orthos logos*, the 'right rule' or 'correct account'.[27] On the other hand, he insists that practical wisdom is not *epistēmē*, not a deductive scientific understanding concerned with universals.[28] He defends this judgment by pointing out that it is concerned with ultimate particulars (*ta kath' hekasta*), which are not in the province of *epistēmē*, but are grasped with insight through experience (1142a11ff.).[29] Thus, although there is some *prima facie* reason for thinking him sympathetic to this part of the scientific project, it is also clear that there are limits to his sympathy. We need to ask, then, what Aristotelian general rules and accounts are and are not, and how the person of practical wisdom uses them.

We can begin by noticing two distinct functions that rules might have in ethical deliberation and justification.* One possibility[30] is that the rules and universal principles are guidelines or rules of thumb: summaries of particular decisions, useful for purposes of economy and aids in identifying the salient features of the particular case. In deciding to work with such principles we would be acknowledging that choices of this sort have, in concrete cases in the past, been judged appropriate by people whom we revere as people of practical wisdom – and appropriate, presumably not simply because they adhere to the rule, but because of their intrinsic character or because of other benefits to which they contribute. Principles are perspicuous descriptive summaries of good judgments, valid only to the extent to which they correctly describe such judgments. They are normative only insofar as they transmit in economical form the normative force of the good concrete decisions of the wise person and because we wish for various reasons to be guided by that person's choices. We note that their very simplicity or economy will be, on this conception, a double-edged attribute: for while it may help the principle to perform certain pedagogical and steering functions, it will also be likely to make it less correct as a summary of numerous and complex choices.

Another possibility is that the universal rules are themselves the ultimate authorities against which the correctness of particular decisions is to be assessed. As the aspiring Platonic philosopher scrutinizes the particular to see the universal features it exemplifies, and considers it ethically relevant only insofar as it falls under the general form, so the aspiring person of practical wisdom will seek to

---

* I add 'justification' because the person of practical wisdom might believe that a rule or system of rules was authoritative in justifying concrete choices without believing that one must explicitly use the rule in each case of deliberation. On both conceptions of rules, some choices will be made as a matter of routine or habit, without conscious deliberation. The important question then is, to what standard would the wise person point in justifying this choice as the correct one? Aristotle plainly believes that the good person decides some things at once, without explicitly going through each piece of deliberation; nonetheless, the correct account of his or her action may make reference to principles that have not been explicitly 'said' (cf. esp. *De Motu*, Ch. 7).

bring the new case under a rule, regarding its concrete features as ethically salient only insofar as they are instances of the universal. The idiosyncratic cannot be relevant.[31] The universal principle, furthermore, is normative because of itself (or because of its relation to higher principles), not because of its relation to particular judgments.

The second picture of rules promises a science or *technē* of practical reasoning, while the first really does not, or not to the same degree.[32] The first allows the contingent features of the case at hand to be, ultimately, authoritative over principle; it thus keeps us in a significant sense at the mercy of *tuchē*. A new, unexpected, or even idiosyncratic feature can cause us to revise the rule: for the rule, to be correct, must correctly describe the cases. There is, thus, room for surprise, room for both the cognitive insecurity and the human vulnerability that the Platonic scientific conception is seeking to avoid. A particular beloved person's particular salient properties can have ethical value when they are not anticipated by the principle – even when they *could not* because of their very nature be captured in any general formulation. Thus we must always be on the lookout for what is there before us in the world: we cannot rest secure in the thought that what we are to see and respond to is something that we have already seen before. And we must also be prepared for loss – for the valuable does not necessarily stay with us just on account of being exemplified in a universal principle that continues to be elsewhere instantiated.

Thus Aristotle's talk of rules and his commitment to the giving of general definitions of the excellences are not necessarily incompatible with his claim that ethical reasoning is not and cannot be an *epistēmē* or *technē*. For his conception of the point, nature, and authority of rules may be the first, non-technical conception. We can now point to some of the textual evidence that this is, in fact, his view.

First, Aristotle says two things about the ultimate criterion of correctness in ethical choice that tell strongly in favor of the non-scientific picture. He says that the standard of excellence is determined with reference to the decisions of the person of practical wisdom: what is appropriate in each case is what such a judge would select. And he says that the 'judgment' or 'discrimination' in ethical matters rests with, or is 'in', something which he calls perception (*aisthēsis*), a faculty of discrimination that is concerned with the apprehending of concrete particulars, rather than universals.[33] The context of this claim makes it clear that he wishes to express grave reservations about universal principles as arbiters of ethical correctness:

The person who diverges only slightly from the correct is not blameworthy, whether he errs in the direction of the more or the less; but the person who diverges *more* is blamed: for this is evident. But to say to what point and how much someone is blameworthy is not easy to determine by a principle (*tōi logōi aphorisai*):[34] nor in fact is this the case with any other perceptible item. For things of this sort are among the concrete particulars, and the discrimination[35] lies in perception. (1109b18–23)

Principles, then, fail to capture the fine detail of the concrete particular, which is the subject matter of ethical choice. This must be seized in a confrontation with the situation itself, by a faculty that is suited to confront it as a complex whole. General rules are being criticized here both for lack of concreteness and for lack of flexibility. 'Perception' can respond to nuance and fine shading, adapting its judgment to the matter at hand in a way that principles set up in advance have a hard time doing.

These two criticisms are pressed repeatedly by Aristotle in order to show that universal statements are posterior in ethical value to concrete descriptions, universal rules to particular judgments. 'Among statements (*logoi*) about conduct', he writes in a nearby passage, 'those that are universal (*katholou*) are more general (*koinoteroi*), but the particular are more true – for action is concerned with particulars (*ta kath' hekasta*), and statements must harmonize with these' (1107a29–32). Rules are authoritative only insofar as they are correct; but they are correct only insofar as they do not err with regard to the particulars. And it is not possible for a simple universal formulation intended to cover many different particulars to achieve a high degree of correctness.[36] Therefore, in his discussion of justice Aristotle insists that the wise judgment of the agent must both correct and supplement the universal formulations of law:

All law is universal; but about some things it is not possible for a universal statement to be correct. Then in those matters in which it is necessary to speak universally, but not possible to do so correctly, the law takes the usual case, though without ignoring the possibility of missing the mark...When, then, the law speaks universally, and something comes up that is not covered by the universal, then it is correct, insofar as the legislator has been deficient or gone wrong in speaking simply, to correct his omission, saying what he would have said himself had he been present and would have legislated if he had known. (*EN* 1137b13ff.)

The law is regarded here as a summary of wise decisions. It is therefore appropriate to supplement it with new wise decisions made on the spot; and it is also appropriate to correct it where it does not correctly summarize what a good judge would do. Good judgment, once again, supplies both a superior concreteness and a superior responsiveness or flexibility.

This requirement of flexibility, so important to our understanding of Aristotle's non-scientific conception of choice, is then described in a vivid metaphor.[37] Aristotle tells us that a person who attempts to make every decision by appeal to some antecedent general principle held firm and inflexible for the occasion is like an architect who tries to use a straight ruler on the intricate curves of a fluted column. Instead, the good architect will, like the builders of Lesbos, measure with a flexible strip of metal that 'bends round to fit the shape of the stone and is not fixed' (1137b30–2). Good deliberation, like this ruler, accommodates itself to what it finds, responsively and with respect for complexity. It does not assume that the form of the rule *governs* the appearances; it allows the appearances to govern themselves and to be normative for correctness of rule.

It might be objected that Aristotle here makes reference only to the defectiveness of actual systems of rules, and says nothing against the idea that an ethical *technē* could come into being if the rules were precise or complicated enough, capturing in a fine-tuned way the complexities of many different types of experienced situations. But this does not, in fact, capture the full force of his criticism of the universal. He points elsewhere to three features of 'the matter of the practical' that show why practical choices cannot, even in principle, be adequately and completely captured in a system of universal rules. These three features are: mutability, indeterminacy, particularity. These three features are not very clearly distinguished by Aristotle, so we must introduce the passages in which they are mentioned and then go on to distinguish them ourselves.

In this same section of *EN* v, Aristotle tells us that practical matters are in their very nature indeterminate or indefinite (*aorista*) – not just so far insufficiently defined (1137b29). The general account of ethical matters is imprecise, he tells us, not because it is not as good as a general account of such matters can be, but because of the way these matters are: 'The error is not in the law or in the legislator, but in the nature of the thing, since the matter of practical affairs is of this kind from the start' (1137b17–19). In Book II, discussing the role of universal definitions and accounts in ethics and preparing to offer his own definition of the excellences, he writes:

Let this be agreed on from the start, that every statement (*logos*) concerning matters of practice ought to be said in outline and not with precision, as we said in the beginning that statements should be demanded in a way appropriate to the matter at hand. And matters of practice and questions of what is advantageous never stand fixed, any more than do matters of health. If the universal definition is like this, the definition concerning particulars is even more lacking in precision. For such cases do not fall under any science (*technē*) nor under any precept, but the agents themselves must in each case look to what suits the occasion, as is also the case in medicine and navigation. (1103b34–1104a10)

Aristotle argues here that the universal account *ought* to be regarded as only an outline, not the precise and final word. (Although some translations write, more weakly, 'have to' or 'must', there is no doubt that the force of *opheilei* is one of obligation.) It is not just that ethics has not yet attained the precision of the natural sciences; it should not even *try* for such precision. As applied to particular cases, which are the stuff of action, general scientific accounts and definitions are woefully lacking, of necessity, in the kind of suitedness to the occasion that good practice would require.

Three different reasons for this deficiency are suggested in this brief passage. First, there is the *mutability* or lack of fixity of the practical. A system of rules set up in advance can encompass only what has been seen before – as the medical treatise can give only the recognized pattern of a disease. But the world of change confronts agents with ever new configurations, surprising them by going beyond what they have seen. Even natural justice for human beings is 'all mutable', i.e. historically rooted, not backed by anything more enduring than the ongoing world of human social practice (*EN* 1134b18–33). And, as he correctly says, if this is true of a general conception of justice it will be all the more true of concrete context-bound requirements of justice, whose shape will be likely to change with economic and social changes. A doctor whose only resource, confronted with a new assortment of symptoms, was to turn to the text of Hippocrates would surely provide woefully inadequate treatment; a pilot who steered his ship by rule in a storm of unanticipated direction or intensity would be, quite simply, incompetent at his task. Even so, the person of practical wisdom must be prepared to meet the new with responsiveness and imagination, cultivating the sort of flexibility and perceptiveness that will permit him (as Thucydides appropriately articulates a shared Athenian ideal) to 'improvise what is required' (cf. Ch. 6, §IV).[38] In several important contexts, Aristotle speaks of practical wisdom as involved in an enterprise of *stochazesthai* at the correct.[39] This word, which originally means 'to take aim at a target', comes to be used of a kind of improvisatory conjectural use of reason. For Aristotle, 'the person who is good at deliberation without qualification is the one who takes aim (*stochastikos*) according to reason at the best for a human being in the sphere of this to be done' (1141b13–14); he associates this norm with the reminder that practical wisdom is concerned with particulars, and not universals (1141b14–16).*

Aristotle also speaks of the *indefiniteness* or *indeterminacy* of the practical. (He mentions this explicitly only in the passage from *EN* v; but in both passages he argues that a practical *technē* is impossible on account of the nature of 'the matter of the practical'; and in *EN* v he tells us that indeterminacy (*to aoriston*) is one of the characteristics of this 'matter' in virtue of which this is true.) It is rather difficult to know what this claim means – but it appears to have something to do with the variety of the practical contexts and the situation-relativity of appropriate choice. One example given elsewhere is revealing. There is no definition (*horismos*) of good joke-telling, Aristotle writes, but it is *aoristos*, indeterminate or indefinable, since it is so much a matter of pleasing the particular hearer, and 'different things are repugnant and pleasant to different people' (1128a25ff.). To extrapolate from this case, excellent choice cannot be captured in universal rules, because it is a matter of fitting one's choice to the complex requirements of a concrete situation, taking all of its contextual features into account. A rule, like a manual of humor, would do both too little and too much: too little, because most of what really counts is in the response to the concrete, and this would be omitted; too much, because the rule would imply that it was itself normative for response (as a joke manual would ask you to tailor your wit to the formulae it contains) – and thus would impinge too much on the flexibility of good practice. The architect's flexible strip of metal is called an *aoristos* ruler, presumably because, unlike such precepts, it varies its own shape according to the shape of what is before it. So, whereas in speaking of the *mutability* of the practical Aristotle had stressed change over time and the importance of surprise,

---

* Here we notice that Aristotle denies that ethics is *epistēmē* in the Platonic or the *Posterior Analytics* sense by pointing to its similarities with stochastic arts that would also be called *technē* in a broader sense, being to some degree general and teachable. Hellenistic divisions of the *technai* will consider the *stochastikai technai* as a separate class, contrasting them with other *technai*.

in speaking of the *aoriston* he stresses complexity and contextual variety. Both features seem to call for responsiveness and yielding flexibility, a rightness of tone and a sureness of touch that could not be adequately captured in any general description.

Finally, Aristotle suggests that the concrete ethical case may simply contain some ultimately particular and non-repeatable elements. He says that such cases do not fall under any *technē* or precept, implying that in their very nature they are not, or not simply, repeatable. This is in part a function of the complexity and variety already mentioned: the occurrence of properties that are, taken singly, repeatable in an endless variety of combinations makes the complex whole situation a non-repeatable particular. But Aristotle also thinks, in speaking of correct choice, of the ethical relevance of particular non-repeatable components of the situation. The moderate diet for Milo the wrestler is not the same as the moderate diet for Aristotle, because Milo's concrete (and presumably unique) size, weight, needs, and occupation are all relevant to determining the appropriate for him. The good friend will, in similar fashion, attend to the particular needs and concerns of his friend, benefiting him or her for the sake of what he or she is in and of him or herself, not for the sake of some general good. Much of this 'in and of himself' will, as we shall see (Ch. 12), consist of repeatable character traits; but in love and friendship features of shared history and family relatedness that are not even in principle repeatable are permitted to bear serious ethical weight. 'Practical wisdom is not concerned with universals only; it must also recognize particulars, for it is practical, and practice concerns particulars' (1141b4–16).

In all of these ways, rules, seen as normative according to the second conception, fail in their very nature to measure up to the challenge of practical choice. Seen according to the first conception, however, they have a distinct though limited usefulness.[40] They are guidelines in moral development: for people not yet possessed of practical wisdom and insight need to follow rules that summarize the wise judgments of others. And even for virtuous adults, they have a function. They guide us tentatively in our approach to the particular, helping us to pick out its salient features (cf. below). When there is not *time* to formulate a fully concrete decision, scrutinizing all the features of the case at hand, it is better to follow a good summary rule than to make a hasty and inadequate concrete choice. Furthermore, rules give constancy and stability in situations in which bias and passion might distort judgment. (This is Aristotle's primary argument for preferring the rule of law to rule by decree.) Rules are necessities because we are not always good judges; if we really were operating ethically as well as we should, we would not have the same need of them.

Finally, as Aristotle stresses in *Politics* II, an anthropocentric ethics will in one sense need to rely on its standing rules more and not less firmly than a Platonic conception. For if there is no divine law or eternal form-grounded *epistēmē* backing ethical judgment – if, as he alleges, human justice is a historically grounded thing that exists only in the human world and if, in consequence, 'the law has no power towards obedience but that of habit' (1268b28ff.), frequent changes in law may conduce to a climate of moral rootlessness. This is not a relativistic claim – for Aristotle can believe compatibly with this, as he plainly does, that there is a single best human way of life. He simply warns us that at no point, in working towards better laws, will we replace the merely human with something harder and more authoritative than the human, something with an extra-human 'power towards obedience'. And if this is so, knowing that humans heed merely human authority best in conditions of stability or slow change, we should not quickly alter our rules, even to improve them.

Practical wisdom, then, uses rules only as summaries and guides; it must itself be flexible, ready for surprise, prepared to see, resourceful at improvisation. This being so, Aristotle stresses that the crucial prerequisite for practical wisdom is a long experience of life that yields an ability to understand and grasp the salient features, the practical meaning, of the concrete particulars. This sort of insight is altogether different from a deductive scientific knowledge, and is, he reminds us again, more akin to sense-perception:[41]

It is obvious that practical wisdom is not deductive scientific understanding (*epistēmē*). For it is of the ultimate and particular, as has been said – for the matter of action is like this. It is the analogue of theoretical insight (*nous*): for *nous* is of the ultimately simple principles, for which there is no external justification;[42] and practical wisdom is of the ultimate and particular, of which there is no scientific understanding, but a kind of perception – not, I mean, ordinary sense-perception of the proper objects of each sense, but the sort of perception by which we grasp that a certain figure is composed in a certain way out of triangles. (1142a23)

  Practical insight is like perceiving in the sense that it is non-inferential, non-deductive; it is, centrally, the ability to recognize, acknowledge, respond to, pick out certain salient features of a complex situation. And just as the theoretical *nous* comes only out of a long experience with first principles and a sense, gained gradually in and through experience, of the fundamental role played by these principles in discourse and explanation, so too practical perception, which Aristotle also calls *nous*, is gained only through a long process of living and choosing that develops the agent's resourcefulness and responsiveness:

...Young people can become mathematicians and geometers and wise in things of that sort; but they do not appear to become people of practical wisdom. The reason is that practical wisdom is of the particular, which becomes graspable through experience, but a young person is not experienced. For a quantity of time is required for experience. (1142a12–16)

And again:

We credit the same people with possessing judgment and having reached the age of intuitive insight and being people of understanding and practical wisdom. For all of these abilities are concerned with the ultimate and the particular,...and all practical matters are concerned with the particular and the ultimate. For the person of practical wisdom must recognize these, and understanding and judgment are also concerned with practical matters, i.e. with ultimates. And intuitive insight (*nous*) is concerned with ultimates in both directions...[There follows a development of the parallel between grasp of first principles and grasp of ultimate particulars.]...This is why we should attend to the undemonstrated sayings of experienced and older people or people of practical wisdom not less than to demonstrations. For since experience has given them an eye they see correctly. (1143a25–b14)[43]

What does experience contribute, if what practical wisdom must see is the idiosyncratic and the new? Here we must insist that Aristotelian practical wisdom is not a type of rootless situational perception that rejects all guidance from ongoing commitments and values.[44] The person of practical wisdom is a person of good character, that is to say, a person who has internalized through early training certain ethical values and a certain conception of the good human life as the more or less harmonious pursuit of these. He or she will be concerned about friendship, justice, courage, moderation, generosity; his desires will be formed in accordance with these concerns; and he will derive from this internalized conception of value many ongoing guidelines for action, pointers as to what to look for in a particular situation. If there were no such guidelines and no such sense of being bound to a character, if the 'eye of the soul' saw each situation as simply new and non-repeatable, the perceptions of practical wisdom would begin to look arbitrary and empty. Aristotle insists that a person's character and value commitments are what that person *is* in and of himself;[45] personal continuity requires a high degree, at least, of continuity in the general nature of these commitments. This continuous basis, internalized and embodied in the agent's system of desires, goes a long way towards explaining what that person can and will see in the new situation: an occasion for courage, for generous giving, for justice. We have insisted that the general background does not *bind* real practical wisdom. The conception is not immune to revision even at the highest level; and this revision may come from the perceptions embodied in new experience. We have also insisted that the general conception is not inclusive of everything that is of relevance – for some relevant features are non-repeatable. Still, it is now time to say that the particular case would be surd and unintelligible without the guiding and sorting power of the universal. (We do not even love particular individuals in the Aristotelian way without loving, centrally, repeatable commitments and values which their lives exemplify.) Nor does particular judgment have the kind of rootedness and focus required for goodness of character without a core of commitment to a general conception – albeit one that is continually evolving, ready for surprise, and not rigid. There is in effect a two-way illumination between particular and universal. Although in the way we have described the particular takes priority, they are partners in commitment and share between them the honors given to the flexibility and responsiveness of the good judge.

IV

The project of constructing a *technē* of practical choice has included as one of its central aspirations the elimination – or at least the reduction – of the troublesome force of the passions. To make our lives safe from *tuchē* was to make them safe, as well, from these internal sources of uncontrolled danger. Commensurability and universality both contributed to the pursuit of this aspiration: for to make objects of desire commensurable is to remove, already, one source of our passional intensity about them; and to see them as instances of a universal rather than irreplaceably particular is so to transform emotions such as love, hate, and grief that their power for damage will be minimized. Aristotle's assault on these two norms thus indirectly reopens the space in which the emotions operate and have their force. But Aristotle's interest in the passions goes deeper than this mild permissiveness. Far from seeing them as obstacles to good reasoning, he makes proper passivity and passional responsiveness an important and necessary part of good deliberation. Since his arguments parallel, in their general outlines, the arguments presented in the second Socratic speech of the *Phaedrus*, it will be helpful to discuss them in an order that corresponds to our discussion of that speech in Chapter 7.

First, as we have seen and shall see further in Chapter 12, the appetites and passions have an essential motivational role to play in human excellence – both in getting a child to excellence in the first place and in motivating continued action according to excellence in the adult. Aristotle agrees with the *Phaedrus* that a model of rationality which suppressed or neglected these elements would starve the soul of nourishment essential for living well.[46] Furthermore, as we saw in Chapter 9, Aristotle devotes considerable attention to developing an account of the appetites and emotions according to which they are selective, responsive to training, and therefore able to play a constructive role in moral motivation, impelling the person towards more appropriate objects in keeping with his or her evolving conception of the appropriate.[47] It is not just that we cannot do without them: it is that they are well equipped (when properly developed) to do well by us. The responsiveness of Aristotelian emotions to developing belief is clear and evident; In Interlude 2 we shall see how emotions are actually individuated with reference to their constitutive beliefs. But even appetites are not, as the *Republic* suggested, as mindless as the automatic workings of the digestive system, mere automatic pushes towards the world that can be directed only by brute suppression. They are responsive intentional elements, capable of a flexible ethical development.

But, like the *Phaedrus*, Aristotle accords to the 'irrational' more than a merely motivational role. Although he does not speak of 'madness', he does recognize and cultivate states in which emotions or appetite, well trained, lead or guide reason in the situation of choice. The intuitive perception that we have seen him praise as the essence of practical wisdom is not an ability of the detached intellect alone. Choice (*prohairesis*) is described as an ability that is on the borderline between the intellectual and passional, partaking of both natures: it can be described as either desiderative deliberation or deliberative desire.[48] So too, practical wisdom functions in close connection with the correctly disposed passions; it is necessarily interdependent with excellence of character, which is, in turn, a disposition concerning appropriate passion as well as appropriate action.[49] The experienced person confronting a new situation does not attempt to face it with the intellect 'itself by itself'. He or she faces it, instead, with desires informed by deliberation and deliberations informed by desire, and responds to it appropriately in both passion and act. Frequently the perception of the salient features will be achieved in a way that relies centrally upon the discriminating power of passion. In the *De Anima* Aristotle tells us that frequently our very view or even imagination of a situation contains, as it were 'marked' or 'determined' in it, elements that correspond to our desires. The pleasurable and painful, the to-be-pursued and the to-be-avoided, are marked out for us in the very way things present themselves to desire;[50] and we might say that it is really desire itself that does the marking, showing us the sort of situation we are dealing with. We do not notice intellectually that there is something here that corresponds to desire; we recognize this with desire itself. We would not have been able to perceive those ethically relevant features without passional reaction.

Aristotle's accounts of the so-called 'practical syllogism',[51] similarly, ascribe to the desires a sorting or discriminatory power: out of the many things presented to the agent by thought and perception, desire will single out some and not others to be foundations of action. Sometimes this selecting role is played by rational desire or 'wish'; but the appetitive forms of desire, too, 'speak', informing the whole creature of its needs and responding directly to the presence of what will satisfy those needs. The emotional desires play an equally important informing or cognitive role, as we shall see in Interlude 2. Aristotle does not dwell, as does the *Phaedrus*, on the special cognitive function of the sense of beauty. His concern is more inclusive. None of the appetites, not even the appetite for food, which Plato seems to hold throughout his life in unmitigated contempt, lacks, properly trained, its cognitive function. A well-formed character is a unity of thought and desire, in which choice has so blended these two elements, desire being attentive to thought and thought responsive to desire, that either one can guide and their guidance will be one and the same.

But Aristotle, like the *Phaedrus* again, does not restrict the role of the non-intellectual elements in deliberation to the instrumental one of showing us how to act well. He completes his non-scientific picture of deliberation by according them intrinsic value in good choice. We can see this in several ways. Proper virtuous choice requires, if it is to be virtue, the combination of correct selection with correct passional response. Without the right 'passion', the very same choice and action will cease to be virtuous. The passion is one constituent of the virtuousness and goodness of the choice, the thing that makes it more than merely self-controlled. If I do generous acts, but only with constant effort, strain, and reluctance, I am not really acting generously; I am not worthy of the same commendation as the person who enjoys his generosity and does the action with his whole heart. If I benefit others but do not love them, I am lacking in practical excellence next to the person who both does and feels good things. It is because the passions are intelligent and educable that they can be assessed in this way: to have serious internal struggle between reason and passion is to be in a condition of ethical immaturity, to be in need of further training.[52]

Furthermore, appetitive activity itself now has full intrinsic value in the best human life. The deliberations of the person of practical wisdom make 'moderation' (*sōphrosunē*) one of the central excellences; its activities are choiceworthy for their own sake. Moderation is appropriate choice with respect to bodily pleasure and pain. And Aristotle makes it very clear that it is not compatible with practical wisdom to seek to minimize the appetites or unduly to dissociate oneself from their claim. 'For this sort of being-without-feeling is not human...If there is someone for whom nothing is pleasant and one thing does not differ from another, he would be far from being a human being' (1119a6–10). Aristotle here goes even beyond the *Phaedrus* in insisting – not just for an isolated case, but quite generally – that the appetitive elements in our nature, which both take us to a world of uɰstable objects and are in themselves difficult to control,[53] must be accorded intrinsic value in the plan of the best human life. Appropriate eating, drinking, and sexual activity has intrinsic value, not in spite of, but because of the way in which it satisfies contingent needs; and to be needy is not a bad, but an appropriate thing for a human being to be. A being without hunger, thirst, and sexual need would not be received into our society, would not be counted as one of us at all.

Finally, we must insist, as we have suggested already, that the 'perception' that is the most valuable manifestation of our practical rationality, and an end in itself, is not merely motivated and informed by the desires. Perception *is* a complex response of the entire personality, an appropriate acknowledgment of the features of the situation on which action is to be based, a *recognition* of the particular. As such, it has in itself non-intellectual components. To have correct perception of the death of a loved one (cf. §vi) is not simply to take note of this fact with intellect or judgment. If someone noted the fact but was devoid of passional response, we would be inclined to say that he did not really *see, take in, recognize*, what had happened; that he did not acknowledge the situation for what it was. (Cf. §vi below, and Interlude 2.)

V

Aristotle has, then, attacked the *technē* conception of practical reason (or its Platonic development) on several fronts. He has insisted upon anthropocentricity, denied the commensurability of the values, shown both the limits (and also the positive contribution) of the general, placed the allegedly ungovernable 'irrational parts' at the heart of rational deliberation. He has developed further a conception of practical reasoning that we saw adumbrated in the *Antigone*, in which receptivity and the ability to yield flexibly to the 'matter' of the contingent particular were combined with a reverence for a plurality of values, for stable character, and for the shared conventions of which character, through moral education, is the internalization. He can claim to have a *technē* of practical reason just in the sense and to the degree that Protagoras can also make this claim: for Aristotelian practical wisdom is, up to a point, both general and (both through early moral education and through reflective material like the *Nicomachean Ethics*) teachable. And this art will in a sense expand our control over uncontrolled *tuchē*: for Aristotle reminds us that we, like archers, will be more likely to hit our target if we try through reflection to get a clearer view of it. But Aristotle warns against pressing such an aim too far: for he shows that each of the strategies used to make practical wisdom *more* scientific and *more* in control than this leads to a distinct impoverishment of the world of practice. Commensurability loses us the distinct nature of each of the values we cherish. Giving priority to the general loses us the ethical value of surprise, contextuality, and particularity. Abstraction of the practical intellect from the passions loses us not only their motivating and informing power but also their intrinsic human worth. Indeed, a creature who deliberated with all the superiority of an acute scientific intelligence but did not allow himself or herself to respond to his surroundings through the passions would both miss a lot that is relevant for practice and be inhumanly cut off from much of the value of our lives. Like James's narrator in our epigraph, he might be ever so strong on method, but he would fall short of the fine responsiveness of 'tone' that is the mark of true practical wisdom.

Detienne and Vernant,[54] whose account of practical intelligence we have followed as we have moved from the tragic poets to the philosophers (cf. Ch. 1, Ch. 7 n. 36), give an account of Aristotelian practical wisdom that will, by contrast, clarify ours. They agree with us that Aristotle's view of practical intelligence constitutes a kind of return from a Platonic conception of truth to pre-philosophical ideas; they agree that one of the primary areas in which a return is made is in the criticism of Platonic generality in favor of an emphasis on the grasping of contingent particulars. They agree in stressing the importance of flexibility and attentiveness to change, in both pre-Platonic and Aristotelian practical intelligence. They correctly emphasize the importance of improvisation in the Aristotelian, as in the earlier, conception. But just as their account of Plato's break with tradition seems to ignore a deep continuity between that tradition's interest in *binding* or *trapping* and the Platonic aspiration to rational self-sufficiency, so too their account of Aristotle seems to ignore the extent to which Aristotle's break with Plato is a rejection of that aspiration. The pre-Aristotelian tradition, we have argued, is not single-mindedly devoted to the ideal of controlling and immobilizing: it is deeply critical of that aim. The *Antigone*, for example, has articulated the idea that the right sort of relationship to have with the contingent particulars of the world is one in which ambition is combined with wonder and openness. Aristotle, we have argued, returns to *this* tradition, in all of its complexity, defending an attitude to contingent particulars that renounces the Platonic aspiration to control and unblemished activity.

As with Plato's conception of 'god's-eye' deliberation, so too with this more immersed and vulnerable human conception we have, it seems, a problem of circularity.[55] The standpoint of the person of practical wisdom is criterial of correct choice. In Aristotle's conception, unlike Plato's, this standpoint is not just heuristic towards a value that would be valuable without this person and his choices; it is definitive of value, and this value would not be value but for its relation to this human person. This makes the circularity even more urgent. For if this person is our standard and his or her judgments and procedures are going to be normative for ours, how do we characterize this person and his procedures in a way that does not already make reference to the good content of his choices? Surely part of what makes this person acceptable to us as a standard is that he chooses the values that we are disposed to think appropriate. He is chosen not from any Archimedean point, but from within the appearances; but the appearances contain, as well, a conception of correct action that is surely at work in some way in this selection. So what point is there to saying that this person is the standard of appropriateness? Just as, in the Platonic case, it was only someone antecedently convinced of the negative role of appetite in judgment, and therefore antecedently sympathetic to a normative view critical of appetite, who would accept the god as a standard of judgment, so here it will only be someone who is committed to the moral relevance of contingent particulars, the value of the passions, and the incommensurability of the values that will tend to approve of this particular sort of judge as a guide. Should we find this problem a fatal one for Aristotle's non-scientific standard?

One route out of this circle is not available to us. In an early article on this very problem, John Rawls proposed a way of characterizing the abilities and procedures of a competent ethical judge that would be non-circular, making reference not to any of the judge's ethical commitments, but rather to value-neutral abilities, such as imagination, empathy, factual knowledge.[56] Aristotle's view of *phronēsis* cannot avail itself of this strategy, for two reasons. First, in the context of his debate with Platonism it becomes very clear that many of the intellectual abilities he cherishes are *not* value-neutral. To emphasize imagination, empathy, perceptiveness, and responsiveness is already to skew the outcome in an anti-Platonic direction. The sight of the body, as Diotima says, just cannot see the same things as are seen by the sight of the pure disembodied intellect; nor can its pure and purely valuable objects be seen by the eyes of Alcibiades. Second, Aristotle would not believe an enumeration of intellectual abilities to be a sufficient characterization of the procedures and nature of the person of practical wisdom. To pick him or her out in an adequate way (even to characterize the full range of his cognitive equipment), we must make reference to character, to well-trained desires, and to the responsive quality of his desire. This, clearly, enmeshes us much more deeply in the circle from which we were trying to escape.

We can, however, point out that Aristotle's argument, like Plato's, starts from an intuitive sense of what the obstacles to correct choice are, an account that has, it would seem, a strong claim to be deeply rooted in the appearances. It aims, by giving an account of these obstacles that is grounded in broadly shared experience, to make the circle at any rate more complex. If we respond as Aristotle hopes we will to the picture of the bad architect or the bad doctor, and agree, as we respond, that there is an analogous picture of a bad ethical judge, then we have reasons that are to some extent independent of the positive characterization of the person of practical wisdom for approving his choice as our judge. We have reasons, that is, for suspecting that the strategies of middle-period Platonism are themselves impediments to correct vision of human matters. Furthermore, to the extent to which Aristotle's choice of a judge issues from the general methods and procedures described in our Chapter 8, Aristotle has, again, enlarged the circle: for his defense of this method, while it would still be said by a confirmed Platonist to have an element of circularity,[57] brings other areas of the appearances, for example a conception of knowledge and reference, to bear on the concrete questions that will confront the philosopher in each area. This method chooses this judge; but the method is chosen partly as a result of independent arguments about language.

Circularity by itself need not dismay us. An element of circularity is probably bound to be present in any complex moral theory (cf. Ch. 5 §IV). But in the end our feeling about the circle, as to whether it is small and pernicious or large and interesting, will depend upon our sense of whether Aristotle has indeed done well what his method dictates: to work through the complexities of our beliefs concerning choice, correctly describing the conflicts and contradictions they present, and to produce the ordering that will save what we most deeply consider worth saving. If the *Symposium* claims that the engagement of pure intellect with non-contingent objects is a paradigm of practical choice and that the ascending philosopher is capable of seeing and responding to everything of beauty and value in the world, Aristotle must answer by showing that this judge is blind to something of genuine value, and blind because of the way in which he or she judges. It is this challenge to which he has directed his efforts; and if he has succeeded the circularity can be viewed with equanimity and interest.

VI

It will be charged that Aristotle's non-scientific view does too little. By refusing so firmly the progress offered by commensurability, universality, and intellectualism it has left itself with no elaborated *theory* of deliberation, no systematic account of good deliberative procedure. Aristotle would be happy to accept this charge: 'Every account concerning practical matters *ought to* be said in outline and not with precision.' His writings give us a sketch, which must be filled in by character and experience. But it still seems important to show the nature of Aristotelian perception in more detail than we have done so far, showing what content there *is* to the claim that choice resides in a perception that responds flexibly to the situation at hand. If a general theoretical account is just what Aristotle is trying to undermine, then it would be in the spirit of his argument to turn for further illumination to complex examples, either from life or from literary texts. Like Alcibiades, he seems to support the claim of concrete narrative to show the truth. We could exemplify Aristotelian perception using texts of many different sorts. I think, above all, of the novels of Henry James.[58] But in order to avoid anachronism, we shall conclude instead with an example from Euripidean tragedy, followed by a commentary.

HECUBA   Achaeans! All your strength is in your spears, not in
the mind. What were you afraid of, that it made you kill
this child so savagely? That Troy, which fell, might be
raised from the ground once more? Your strength meant nothing, then.
When Hector's spear was fortunate, and numberless
strong hands were there to help him, we were still destroyed.
Now when the city is fallen and the Phrygians slain,
this baby terrified you? I despise the fear
which is pure terror in a mind unreasoning.

O darling child, how wretched was this death. You might
have fallen fighting for your city, grown to man's
age, and married, and with the king's power like a god's,
and died happy, if there is any happiness here.
But no. You grew to where you could see and learn, my child,
yet your mind was not old enough to win advantage
of fortune. How wickedly, poor boy, your fathers' walls,
Apollo's handiwork, have crushed your pitiful head
tended and trimmed to ringlets by your mother's hand,
and the face she kissed once, where the brightness now is blood
shining through the torn bones – too horrible to say more.

O little hands, sweet likenesses of Hector's once,
now you lie broken at the wrists before my feet;
and mouth beloved whose words were once so confident,
you are dead; and all was false, when you would lean across
my bed, and say: 'Mother, when you die I will cut
my long hair in your memory, and at your grave
bring companies of boys my age, to sing farewell.'
It did not happen; now I a homeless, childless, old
woman must bury your poor corpse, which is so young.
Alas for all the tendernesses, my nursing care,
and all your slumbers gone. What shall the poet say,
what words will he inscribe upon your monument?
*Here lies a little child the Argives killed, because
they were afraid of him.* That? The epitaph of Greek shame.
You will not win your father's heritage, except
for this, which is your coffin now: the brazen shield.

O shield, who guarded the strong shape of Hector's arm:
the bravest man of all, who wore you once, is dead.
How sweet the impression of his body on your sling,

and at the true circle of your rim the stain of sweat
where in the grind of his many combats Hector leaned
his chin against you, and the drops fell from his brow!

Take up your work now; bring from what is left some robes
to wrap the tragic dead. The gods will not allow us
to do it right. But let him have what we can give.

That mortal is a fool who, prospering, thinks his life
has any strong foundation; since our fortune's course
of action is the reeling way a madman takes,
and no one person is ever happy all the time.

(Euripides, *Trojan Women* 1158–1207)[59]

It seems peculiar to select this speech as an example of deliberation and choice, since Hecuba appears to have no room for choice. What can she do? She is a slave, she has lost this last hope for the restoration of her city and family. We select such a relatively inactive case in order to indicate that proper response, in speech, passion, and circumscribed action, can be just as much a virtuous act as a big heroic deed. Narrowing the scope for movement does not always remove the opportunity for excellent perception.[60] What confronts Hecuba is the death of her grandchild. What she chooses is to mourn for him; to denounce the Greeks; to mourn for Hector; to order the child's fitting burial, despite the evident neglect of these human matters by the gods. These, though confined, are still choices expressing character and exemplifying practical perception. (*EN* I stresses that they are important indices of good character in adversity: cf. Ch. 11.)

The person of practical wisdom inhabits the human world and does not attempt to rise above it. The contrast between the human and the divine pervades Hecuba's speech. She herself speaks from the center of human life, making no attempt at all to distance herself from her merely human values and attachments. In fact, it is one of her major purposes to point out that the point of view of the needless god does not bring with it sufficient concern for very important human things. The perspective of the god – as elsewhere in the play – looks, from the point of view of these tragic events, too detached and cold, lacking in the background of concerns *and* needs that would make possible an appropriate responsiveness.

As a person of practical wisdom, Hecuba brings to the concrete situation of choice a disparate plurality of attachments and commitments, many of which have been nourished by early moral training, long before reflective adulthood. She also brings her *prima facie* reflections about what, for her, will count as a good life for a human being. She brings her love of her son, of her grandson; her love of Troy; her attachment to religious duties and duties to the family; a conception of proper courage, both in battle and in politics; a conception of proper reasonableness. She brings her view that a good life for a human being involves growing up in a family and a city and serving both the city's good and that of one's loved ones in it; that it involves going on to the end of life performing these excellent activities and receiving, at the end of life, a pious burial; that it is a better thing, nonetheless, to die prematurely for these values than to make cowardly compromises. Training in these values has evidently made her well acquainted with her 'target', so that in this new situation she knows what to look for; the intentionality of her desires has a focus. As a result she is adept at sorting out the new situation before her, singling out without hesitation the features of ethical relevance.

Each of the features in the situation is seen by Hecuba as a distinct item with its own separate nature, generating its own separate claims. She does not offer definitions of the values she prizes; but this does not mean that she does not implicitly conceive of each of them as having a distinctive nature. She has a pretty good idea of what piety is, what courage and cowardice are; and it is clear from what she says about them that she takes them to be distinct and incommensurable items. There is not the slightest sign of a measuring scale, or any other reductive device.

Hecuba's deliberation begins from an antecedent conception; but it does not show the inflexible *application* of a pre-set general scheme to this new case. We do not have the impression that Hecuba is bringing forth an arsenal of general rules and conceptions and using them simply to govern the indeterminacies of the new, impressing their order upon it. First of all, we are impressed by the extent to which Hecuba is passive or receptive before the situation. She is simply overwhelmed by response to what she sees, to the mangled body and the sweaty shield. Her discriminatory activity is not, so to speak, prior to her response; it is in and constituted by her response. She does not intellectually perceive that this is the death of a grandson to whom she is committed, and *then* respond with grief. It is the response of overwhelming grief and horror at the sight of those broken bones, those hands, the ringlets shining round the bloodied face, that *is* her perception of the death of a loved one. And we could say that it is in this yielding responsiveness that we find some of the highest value in her deliberation. If we attempt to imagine a Platonic reasoner approaching this same situation with the activity of intellect alone, if we try to imagine what sorts of perceptions and recognitions such a passionless judge would be capable of, what sort of speech he would use, then we begin to have a sense of the cognitive value of her loves and desires, as features that show her the way to and help to constitute a proper practical perception of what she has lost and what the Greeks have done.

We find, as well, that these responses strike us as humanly valuable and constitutive of her goodness even *apart from* their motivational and informational value. Even if she had been able to *see* the same things in the situation without the guidance of feeling, we would feel that a cold criticism of the Argive command, without her extreme anger and deep grief, showed a deficient and even inhuman response. We would find her exceedingly strange if she recognized the death of her grandchild with a cold intellectual eye; we would have a hard time treating her as one of us. We would not praise her for excellent practical perception.

But it is not only in her passivity that Hecuba goes beyond rules. Her deliberative *activity* makes of the situation confronting her far more than an occasion for their application. The features belonging to her antecedent general conception are discovered by and in a response to the particular and are important primarily as they illuminate, for her, its salient features. It is not that a general rule about grandchildren constrains her mourning and has authority over it. Instead, her long commitment to this particular relationship (informed no doubt at some formative stage by rules, but flowing, afterwards, into particular love for this boy) prepares her to respond to this tragedy as she does, with mourning. It is not that she consults some authoritative code in order to denounce the Achaeans for cowardice. Instead, the code of behavior prepares her to perceive before her a concrete situation in which cowardly action is manifested. The background conception contributes preparation and valuable illumination; but the seeing is in the particular, and is not legislated in advance. It has the power to enrich or change the general conception. We have here what we would expect to see in most good examples of Aristotelian deliberation: a flexible movement back and forth between particular and general. She denounces the Achaeans, and then moves to a general reflection about cowardice that is, no doubt, part of her antecedent training, but has now been informed by this new experience. From this she turns to a mourning for the child which itself moves from reflection on the general shape of a good human life to the most vividly concrete mourning over the parts of the body, in which each part conjures up particular memories. The ethical appropriateness of her response is, we feel, inseparable from its concreteness. She might have omitted the general reflections without giving the impression of deficiency. But had she mourned in a purely abstract way, without this vividness of detail, we would have assessed her differently: we would probably have judged her deficient in love. Had she denounced the Achaeans by enumerating general precepts, we would have criticized her for an odd inhuman remoteness.

This talk of the general and the particular informing one another does not, however, do full justice to the importance of what actually happens during this scene. The experience of the particular does not only inform Hecuba further about what her conception of the good life has been all along, showing her more about its constituent values; it can also lead to a shifting or revising of the general conception. The first happens, clearly: for she comes to see more vividly than ever before the importance of her grandchild; the connection between this bond and the future of her city; the incompatibility between true courage and the brutal slaying of a loved one; and so on. She learns more about her concerns taken singly; she also learns more about how they stand to one another. But this is not all: she is led, in at least one case, to revise her conception. For the concrete situation reveals to her an indifference or callousness on the part of the gods that had not figured in her antecedent conception of piety. She has throughout the play been questioning and searching concerning the divine. Now she openly charges the gods with wicked action, with willful obstruction to the moral aspirations of humans. A feature of her *prima facie* conception of the good has now been rejected because the nature of its perceived opposition to other elements makes it not simply in conflict with them but unworthy, itself, of serious respect. The situation is a source of illumination; the illumination becomes the source of a new general account of the human good. In this sense and to this extent, the particular is prior. She improvises what is required.

This deliberation is itself fragile, easily influenced and swayed by external happenings. In its openness to passion and surprise, it risks being overwhelmed by the extreme situation – for appropriate passion, in such a case, can easily become a mind-numbing surge of blind affect, eclipsing deliberation and even coherent discourse. To listen to the passions at all opens up these risks of distortion and derailment. (The approach of the Platonic person, refusing wonder and surprise, cuts off these deep risks also.) Aristotelian deliberation, furthermore, is well suited to the high evaluation of fragile constituents of human life. For in allowing herself to use perception, rather than conformity to rule, as her standard, Hecuba opens herself to the value and special wonder of a particular city, a particular child; therefore to the deep grief she here expresses. There would be little of grief left without the vivid particular vision of the small hands, the loving, childlike face, the stain of Hector's sweat upon the shield. In allowing herself to see and care about these things, using the passions as guides, she binds herself to the possibility of loss.

It is not at all surprising, then, that the heroine who deliberates according to this model should conclude that fortune is madly unstable and that human happiness is a rare and elusive item. We are likely to feel, however, that it would not have been a solution to her problem to have looked upon her deliberative world with the calculative gaze of the *Protagoras*'s measuring scientist, or with the transcendent, supra-human eye of the *Republic*'s god. For these are not the eyes that such a human situation requires.[61]

11   The vulnerability of the good human life: activity and disaster

'Nevertheless, it is evident that *eudaimonia** stands in need of good things from outside, as we have said: for it is impossible or difficult to do fine things without resources' (*EN* 1099a31–3). We have now filled in the background for a study of this claim. We have seen how every Aristotelian philosophical inquiry is conducted within the world of human experience and belief, limited by the limits of that world. We have seen Aristotle defend a conception of action appropriate to a needy animal being vulnerable to influences from its world; he has argued that to view human action as combining activity with passivity in this way is fully compatible with our most serious sorts of ethical assessment. We have, finally, seen him articulate and defend a conception of 'non-scientific' practical deliberation in which proper 'passivity' and responsiveness plays a very important role, and in which the touchstone of correctness is a good person's refined perception of the contingencies of a particular situation. With all of this in place, we must now ask what Aristotle ultimately concludes about our central questions. How far *is* human good living, *eudaimonia*, vulnerable? What external events can disrupt or distract it, and how (and how far) should it attempt to make itself safe? Aristotle clearly regards this as a pressing and a delicate question. For the appearances ascribe to luck considerable ethical importance. 'Most people suppose that the *eudaimōn* life is the fortunate life, or not without good fortune; and no doubt correctly. For without the external goods, which are in the control of luck, it is not possible to be *eudaimōn*' (*MM* 1206b30–5).[1] On the other hand, deeply shared conceptions of practical rationality make luck the natural enemy of human efforts at planning and control: 'Where there is most insight (*nous*) and reason (*logos*), there is the least luck; and where there is the most luck there is the least insight' (*EE* 1207a4–6).[2] How is this tension to be handled in our understanding of what a good human life, lived according to practical reason, might be?

Our strategy will be to examine, first, Aristotle's general view concerning the dependence of the good life upon circumstances and resources, the degree and nature of its vulnerability in conditions of deprivation or calamity. We shall examine, at the same time, his argument for the view that the good life for a human being requires not only a good state of character, but actual activity as well. In a subsequent section of this chapter we shall consider whether the good condition of character is itself, in his view, vulnerable to erosion by uncontrolled events. We shall, finally, examine his argument that the very being and value of certain human virtues is inseparable from, and partly constituted by, conditions of risk,

* On *eudaimonia*, which will remain untranslated, see Ch. 1, p. 6.

deficiency, or impediment. Then, in our next chapter, we shall look at two specific areas in which good living becomes particularly dependent upon externals not under the agent's control – in which externals are not merely instrumentally related to good activity but enter themselves into the specification of what good activity is. All of this will put us in a position to appreciate the importance that Aristotle attaches to tragic poetry as a source of moral learning and to draw some conclusions about the relationship between Aristotelian philosophizing and tragedy.

I

We are asking, then, about the power of luck or fortune* to influence the goodness and praiseworthiness of a human life.[3] Aristotle approaches this question, as he approaches many others, by describing two extreme positions. Some people, he tells us, believe that living well is just the same thing as having a fortunate life (*EN* 1099b7–8). Good living is a gift of the gods that has no reliable connection with effort, learning, or goodness of stable character (*EN* 1099b9ff.). In other words, observing the great power of luck in human affairs, they are led to say that it is *the* single decisive causal factor in achieving a certain sort of life. Nothing else counts for much. *Eudaimonia*, as its name suggests, is just having a good *daimōn* or (external) guardian spirit. In this way, they 'turn what is greatest and best over to luck' (1099b24).

On the other side are those who maintain that luck has no power at all to influence the goodness of a human life. The causal factors relevant to living well, to *eudaimonia*, are all, they claim, within the agent's firm grasp; external uncontrolled happenings can neither significantly enhance nor significantly diminish good living. It is worth noting that these people, as Aristotle describes them, are philosophers determined to establish a thesis, even at the cost of denying some prevalent and obvious appearances. Aristotle makes us aware of two routes by which such opponents have arrived at their denials of luck. One route (associated with Platonism)[4] involves narrowing the specification of the good life, acknowledging as intrinsically valuable only activities that are maximally stable and invulnerable to chance (cf. 1098b24–5). Aristotle deals with this strategy indirectly, by defending, one by one, the claims of more vulnerable values; we shall examine some of these arguments in Chapter 12. The strategy of his other group of opponents[5] is to deny that actual *activity* according to excellence is any part of good living: if one is in a virtuous condition or state, then that is sufficient for *eudaimonia*. This means, for example, that a virtuous person who is enslaved, imprisoned, or even tortured is living just as good and praiseworthy a human life as the person whose activity is unimpeded.

* Here, as before, there is no suggestion that we are dealing with random or uncaused events. For Aristotle, to say that an event happens by *tuchē* is not only not incompatible with, but even requires, concomitant causal explanation (see *Ph.* 11.4–6). As elsewhere, we are asking here about events that influence the agent's life in a way that is not amenable to his or her control.

Aristotle wants to set out these extreme views so that we can ask ourselves what would motivate someone to adopt one of them. This should help us to arrive at a position that does justice to the motivating concerns in each case, while avoiding their excesses and denials. This procedure might be read as a kind of simple-minded conservatism, a mechanical steering of a safe middle course between two dangerous extremes. Carefully examined, it is neither simply a middle course nor mechanically pursued. The strategy is to take each extreme view seriously as a genuine part of the appearances – that is to say, as motivated by something that is really there to be preserved and taken account of. As he remarks of these and other one-sided views, 'Some of these things have been said by many people over a long period of time, others by a few distinguished people; it is reasonable to suppose that none of them has missed the target totally, but each has gotten something or even a lot of things right' (*EN* 1098a28–30). He studies the major accounts of a problem handed down by tradition because he supposes that no view could have gained currency that did not respond to real ethical concerns in a way worthy of serious notice. Now he must show how each extreme position, while seriously grounded, is also defective because of the way in which it forces the rejection of other deep beliefs.

II

The first extreme view on luck[6] receives less extensive consideration than the second; but the manner in which Aristotle dismisses it is of considerable interest. There is, he says, a puzzle about whether the good life is available by some sort of effort, or whether it just comes by luck. He mentions a pervasive belief that goes with the former view: 'The good will be common to many: for it is capable of belonging to all those who are not maimed with respect to excellence through some sort of learning and care' (1099b18–19). He now says something very revealing about this belief: if it is *better* that this view of *eudaimonia*, rather than the luck view, should be true, 'then it is reasonable that things should be so'. For 'to turn what is greatest and best over to luck would strike too false a note' (1099b20–5). In other words, the rejection of the luck-supremacy view is the outcome not of a neutral empirical survey, but of a deliberation in which what we desire to find, what we feel we can live with, enters heavily into practical wisdom's weighing of the alternatives. Given the choice between the two views, we ask ourselves, among other things, which view would make our lives worthwhile. The luck view is rejected not because it has been found to be at odds with scientific fact about the way things are in the universe, discovered by some value-neutral procedure, but because it strikes a false note, i.e., is too much at odds with our other beliefs, and specifically with our evaluative beliefs about what sort of life would be worth the living.[7] For we believe that human life is worth the living only if a good life can be secured by effort, and if the relevant sort of effort lies within the capabilities of most people. (It will emerge that we do not insist that this effort be always sufficient for good living; but in general it must have the most important role.)[8]

This point is further developed in a passage of the *Eudemian Ethics* that deals with suicide. After talking about those who kill themselves because of some chance catastrophe, Aristotle asks what *are*, after all, the things that make life worth the living. In general, he concludes, if you collect together all the things that a person does and suffers because of luck, rather than voluntarily, no combination of these, even prolonged to an infinite term, would suffice to make a person choose living rather than not living (1215b27–31). Life is made worth living for a human being only by voluntary action; and not simply the low-level voluntary action of a child (1215b22–4), but action shaped overall by adult excellence and its efforts. Then if the luck theorist were right in denying to those efforts any important role in living well, we would all be living lives that all of us, including the luck theorist himself, would probably judge to be not worth the living. Such a view indeed 'strikes too false a note' – not just because it clashes with a widely-held belief, but because it clashes with a belief so deep and basic that we hold it to be a condition of our continued willingness to remain in existence.

This is a revealing example of Aristotle's method at work, both because it shows us how an ethical thesis is criticized out of deeper appearances and because it shows us how what we want and think good enters into an ethical inquiry at a basic level. It shows us how Aristotle regards the central questions of this book: not as matters of neutral, discoverable fact, but as matters whose answer is of the deepest concern to us and towards settling which we are accordingly permitted to bring these concerns and desires to bear. Of course Aristotle is not saying that in constructing a view about *eudaimonia* we are free to say anything at all that pleases us; indeed, he is much more cautious than Plato about diverging from the lived 'matter' of our daily lives for the sake of painting a more elegant or beautiful picture. What he is saying is that our most basic beliefs and experiences concerning what is worthwhile constrain what we can discover about the world and about ourselves. Our experience of choice and our beliefs about its value make it unlikely, if not impossible, that we could ever discover that we do not choose or that choice counts for little in this world – just as in Chapter 9 we saw that our deep beliefs about voluntary action made it highly unlikely that we would ever discover that there was no such thing. Certain things are so deep that either to question or to defend them requires us to suspend too much, leaves us no place to stand. If there are any ethical beliefs that approach in this way the status of the Principle of Non-Contradiction, it would be these beliefs concerning *eudaimonia*, voluntary action, and choice. For these are beliefs that we use whenever we act; whenever we engage in ethical inquiry (for if it's all up to luck such inquiry has no point); whenever we argue about a practical decision; whenever we deliberate and choose (for we engage in these practices on the assumption that they make a difference to our *eudaimonia*). To deny them – especially inside an ethical inquiry – approaches the sort of self-refuting position of which Aristotle convicted the opponent of the Prinicple of Non-Contradiction.[9] Such a position does indeed strike too false a note.

III

We said, however, that Aristotle is determined to understand the force and the serious contribution of the luck theorist's proposal. That is, he wants to investigate and in some way to preserve as true the idea that luck is a serious influence in the good life, that the good life is vulnerable and can be disrupted by catastrophe. 'For many reversals and many types of luck come about in the course of a life', he remarks shortly after his criticisms of the luck theorist (1100a5–6). This, presumably, is the deeply shared belief which that opponent had exaggerated and overpressed. We must now examine his articulation and defense of that belief, as he criticizes, in turn, its opponents.

The opponents of luck assert that the good human life is completely invulnerable to *tuchē*. That which we ourselves control is in every case sufficient to secure it. Aristotle clearly sympathizes with their general motivation and wishes to preserve many of the same beliefs. He and the opponents are on common ground when they insist that the good life should be available by effort to the person who has not been ethically 'maimed' (1099b18–19, cf. 1096b34), and when they demand a life that is 'one's own and hard to take away' (1095b25–6), 'stable and in no way easily subject to change' (1100b2–3). But complete invulnerability is purchased, Aristotle will argue, at too high a price: by imagining (as does the Platonist) a life bereft of certain important values; or by doing violence (as does the good-condition theorist) to our beliefs about activity and its worth.[10] The Platonist opponent will concern us in Chapter 12. We turn now to the good-condition opponent and to Aristotle's elaboration, against this opponent, of a view about the value and the vulnerability of excellent activity.

The good-condition theorist argues that *eudaimonia* is invulnerable because it consists simply in having a good ethical state or condition[11] and because this condition is itself stable even under the direst circumstances. To oppose such an opponent Aristotle can, then, adopt more than one strategy. He can argue that states of character *are* vulnerable to external influences. Or he can argue that good states are not by themselves sufficient for good living. If he takes the second course he must, in addition, argue that the further element that must be added to good states is itself not invulnerable. Aristotle's argument, as we shall see, is a complex combination of these two lines of attack. We shall start by following him as he pursues the second line, establishing, first, that *eudaimonia* requires actual activity for its completion, and, second, that good human activity can be disrupted or decisively impeded by various forms of luck. There is, then, a gap between being good and living well. The investigation of this gap will eventually lead Aristotle to the first line as well – since it will turn out that some forms of interfering luck eventually affect the virtuous condition itself.

We agree, Aristotle says, that our end is *eudaimonia*; but we agree on just about nothing concerning it, except the name (1095a17ff.). One further agreement, however, emerges near the beginning of the *Nicomachean Ethics*: it concerns the connection of *eudaimonia* with activity. 'Both the many and the refined... believe that living well and acting well are the same as *eudaimonia*' (1095a19–20). Later he repeats, '*Eudaimonia* has been said to be good living and good acting.' In the *Eudemian Ethics* he brings forward a 'belief held by all of us', the belief that 'acting well and living well are the same thing as *eudaimonein*: both are forms of use and activity' (1219a40–b2). So we can see from the start that the opponent who makes the good life consist in a non-active state or condition, removing it altogether from its realization in activity, is going against beliefs of ours that are as broadly shared as any ever brought forward by Aristotle in the ethical works. This seems to put his thesis in trouble from the start.

But Aristotle must also show the depth and importance of these beliefs; for to show that they are *widely* held is not all that the method of appearances requires. Therefore, instead of contenting himself with this general point, he examines the consequences of the good-condition thesis for concrete types of cases, showing that the thesis has intuitively unacceptable results. We can take, first, the most extreme and therefore clearest case and move towards cases which offer greater potential for controversy.

The starkest and clearest test case for the good-condition view would be one in which there was a good virtuous condition but *no* activity of any kind issuing from this condition. We get such a case if we imagine a person with a well-formed character who, upon becoming an adult (for to imagine this person virtuous we must, in Aristotle's view, imagine him or her as active during the process of formation), goes to sleep and sleeps all through his adult life, doing nothing at all. We could make the case contemporary and plausible by considering a case of irreversible coma – though to match Aristotle's it would have to be one in which the internal structure of goodness was in no way permanently removed or impaired: excellence of character must remain constant. Now our question is, can such a person be said to be living a good life? Can he appropriately be praised and congratulated? According to the good-condition theorist, he can: for the excellent state is the sole appropriate object of these ethical attitudes. Aristotle objects (in both the *EN* and the *EE*) that this just is not in harmony with our practices and our beliefs. We simply do not think that a state or condition that never *does* anything is sufficient for living well. It seems incomplete, frustrated, cut off from its fulfillment. Indeed, we tend to think that having such a condition makes little real difference, if one is never active from it: to sleep through life is like being a vegetable and not a human at all (*EE* 1216a3–5, cf. *EN* 1176a34–5). Just as we do not think a fetus, who lives a purely vegetative existence, without awareness, lives a full human life (*EE* 1216a6–8), so we are not going to be willing to praise and congratulate the life of this hopelessly inactive adult. The *EN* concludes, 'Nobody would say that a person living in such a way was living well, unless he were defending a theoretical position at all costs' (1096a1–2). The case shows us, the parallel passage in *EN* x concludes, that *eudaimonia* cannot be simply a *hexis*, a condition or state (1176a33–5).

Later on in *EN* 1 Aristotle returns to the same point, insisting that, although 'it is possible for a state to be present and accomplish nothing good, as is true for the sleeper and in some cases of waking people as well', nonetheless, such a person will not receive the ethical attitudes of praise and congratulation that we associate with the judgment that someone is living a good human life (1098b33–99a2). He uses an athletic analogy: in a race we applaud, as runners, only those who actually compete, not the ones who might be thought to be in general the strongest and most fit. Just as we will not say of a well-conditioned non-runner that he or she runs well, so we will not praise the virtuous sleeper for living virtuously (1099a3–7). It is important to see that Aristotle does not claim here that the good life is a kind of competition, or that only success is praised. His point is that the endowment and condition are not sufficient for praise: the person has to *do* something, show how he or she can be active. Just as our assessments of people as runners depend upon there being some actual running (though of course they depend, too, on our belief that this good running was caused by their good condition, not by some external force), so too our ethical assessments are based on actual effort and activity, as well as upon the presence of a stable character that is the cause of the activity. Character alone is not sufficient. Furthermore, the opponent's very account of the case may be incoherent: for we do not know what it means to say of someone in irreversible coma that a virtuous condition is retained. At the very least, there is an insuperable epistemological difficulty; but it may be more than that – it may be a logical difficulty as well, given the strong conceptual connection of *hexis* with a pattern of activity. Aristotle points to this problem when he says that 'the good and the bad are not at all distinct in sleep...for sleep is the idleness of that element of the soul in virtue of which it is said to be fine or base' (1102b5–8). It is not clear, then, that it is even appropriate to say of this totally non-active person that he or she has a virtuous character.[12]

We can summarize the general point against the good-condition theorist this way. The good condition of a virtuous character, like good athletic conditioning, is a kind of preparation for the activity; it finds its natural fulfillment and flourishing in activity. To deprive the person of that natural expression of the condition *is* to make a difference in the quality of the person's life. It is to make the condition fruitless or pointless, cut off. Just as a runner who gets into good condition and is then prevented from running would be pitied more than praised, so we pity the virtuous person in situations of impediment. Activity, *energeia*, is the coming-forth of that good condition from its state of concealment or mere potentiality; it is its flourishing or blooming. Without that the good condition is seriously incomplete. Like an actor who is always waiting in the wings and never gets a chance to appear on the stage, it is not doing its job, and, in consequence, is only in a shadowy way itself.[13]

The opponent might grant that *total* cessation of awareness and activity was a diminution or cessation of good living, and yet still try to salvage some of his position by making a distinction between external, worldly activity and a full internal health, or health of condition, that includes thought and awareness. He might say, then, that so long as cognitive functioning and ethical awareness go on in the good person, it does not matter at all that his or her body is altogether prevented from carrying out such projects as the moral imagination forms.[14] So long as he is able to form virtuous intentions and to think good thoughts, so long he is living well – even if he is in prison, enslaved, or tortured. Aristotle needs to argue in reply that the functioning available to a person in such circumstances is not sufficient for acting well and living well. This he does in a passage in *EN* VII:

No activity (*energeia*) is complete if it is impeded; but *eudaimonia* is something complete. So the *eudaimōn* person needs the goods of the body and external goods and goods of luck, in addition, so that his activities should not be impeded. Those who claim that the person who is being tortured on the wheel, or the person who has encountered great reversals of fortune, is *eudaimōn*, so long as he is good, are not saying anything – whether that is their intention or not. (1153b16–21).[15]

Once again, the opponent has specified what *eudaimonia* is in a way that makes it by definition immune to external changes of circumstance: external reversals impede action, not the virtuous state, and the virtuous state (including, presumably, some sort of waking inner life) is sufficient for living well. Once again, Aristotle insists that doing does matter. Being excellent in character is not yet acting according to excellence. But action according to excellence requires certain external conditions: of the body, of social context, of resources. The person on the wheel cannot act justly, generously, moderately; he cannot help his friends or participate in politics. How, then, can he be said to live well? The opponent's case here is more intuitively gripping than the sleeper example was, because we have allowed the person to wake up, restoring at least that awareness of internal goodness that might seem to be a necessary part of goodness itself. But Aristotle argues that, even if we have a richer picture of goodness of character, goodness totally impeded and cut off is not enough to justify our most serious praise and congratulation.

Aristotle suggests a further point as well. Insofar as the opponent's case is initially plausible, it is so because we imagine the tortured person as leading some sort of complex inner life. We might imagine him, for example, as imagining, forming intentions, having appropriate feelings and responses, even reflecting philosophically or proving truths of mathematics. If we pack all of this into 'being good' as opposed to 'acting', then being good looks closer to what might satisfy us than it did in the sleeper's case, where 'being good' was something completely inert and inactive. But now we notice that 'being good' looks like a kind of being active – and, like any being active, it looks itself vulnerable to impediment. Aristotle's talk of impeded activity makes us ask whether the inner activity of the tortured person cannot itself be impeded by pain and deprivation. Thoughts, emotions and reactions, speculative and scientific thinking, are not impervious to circumstance; they can, like projects in the external world, fail to reach completion or perfection. Torture can harm them.[16] In short: the distinction 'inner/outer' is not the same as the distinction 'state/activity'. If the opponent makes the latter the salient distinction, ascribing all value to the state, this will perhaps give him something really immune to luck; but it will make the human being into little more than a vegetable. If he makes the salient distinction the former one, ascribing all value to inner activities, then he will have something richer and more interesting – but something that is, after all, just because it is active, open to chance and upset.

Aristotle does not, in these discussions, set out precise criteria for something's being activity rather than condition or *hexis*. His primary point is to show us that whatever is fulfillment or activity is also, therefore, vulnerable: only the lying-in-wait that is *hexis* can escape disturbance. This is not at all incompatible with the view that some among the activities or *energeiai*, broadly construed, are much more vulnerable and impediment-prone than others. In particular, we might think in this connection of the *Metaphysics* Book IX distinction of the broad class of *energeiai* into two subclasses – the class of *kinēseis*, 'motions', and the (narrow) class of *energeiai*. *Energeiai* (narrowly construed) are activities that are complete at any moment: they 'have their form in themselves'. Whenever it is true to say, 'I am E-ing', it is also true to say (using the Greek perfect), 'I have E'd', or 'I am in the state of having E'd.' For example, whenever it is true to say, 'I am seeing', it is also true to say, 'I have seen.' *Kinēseis*, by contrast, are movements that proceed towards an external completion through time: they can be interrupted in their course, they do not have their completion or form in themselves. Thus, when it is true to say, 'I am building a house', it is *not* at the same time true to say, 'I have built a house.' The process and its completion not only do not imply one another, they are mutually exclusive: only when the building has come to a halt is the house completely built.[17]

This distinction has obvious relevance for the question of impediment. For *kinēseis* permit of interruption and blockage along their path in a way that *energeiai*, narrowly construed, do not. But I have ascribed to Aristotle the view that anything flourishing or active enough to count as *energeia* of either type is vulnerable to impediment. Is this compatible with Aristotle's account of the formal completeness of (narrow) *energeiai*? I believe that it is. For while one *sort* of impediment does not threaten *energeiai* – namely, the sort that would cut it off before it reaches its *telos* or formal completion – they seem, nonetheless, vulnerable to impediment with regard to the quality of the activity. The fact that seeing is 'complete' in a moment is compatible with the evident truth that some people see better than others; and some cases of bad seeing can certainly result from external impediment. The same would clearly be true of the intellectual contemplation of the person on the wheel. (In *EN* VII, Aristotle defines pleasure as the *unimpeded* activity, *energeia*, of the natural *hexis*, implying that sicknesses and other reversals can cramp and impede many types of natural activity.)[18] We might think of activities as like rivers: one way they can be impeded is to be dammed up and prevented from reaching a destination. Another way would be to be filled up with sludge so that their channel would become cramped and muddy, their continuous flow slower, the purity of their waters defiled. It is, I believe, Aristotle's view that anything that is *energeia* broadly construed, and not mere hidden inactive *hexis*, is susceptible to impediment in the second way at least. And, furthermore, there is the obvious and important fact that in the absence of certain external necessary conditions, no *energeia* can get started at all: there is no seeing if there is no light (if a person has been blinded), no river if the sources have dried up.[19] All of this seems sufficient to give Aristotle reason to say that, no matter what *energeiai* are the bearers of value in a human life, luck has the power to obstruct them.

IV

Now, however, Aristotle must describe in more detail the ways in which good activity is vulnerable to circumstances; and he must, in particular, ask to what degree calamities that are temporary or partial should be thought to diminish *eudaimonia*. For while the consideration of extreme cases may suffice to refute the views of the most extreme type of good-condition opponent, they do not go far towards grappling with problems that most of us are likely to face in the course of our lives. The more common practical problems are also, frequently, more subtle and more controversial.

Before we approach Aristotle's treatment of 'tragic' reversal and the case of Priam, we need to point out that there are four rather different ways in which uncontrolled circumstances may, in these cases, interfere with excellent activity. They may (1) deprive it of some instrumental means or resource. This resource, in turn, may be either (a) absolutely necessary for excellent activity, so that its absence altogether blocks the activity; or (b) its absence may simply constrain or impede the performance of the activity. (2) Circumstances may block activity by depriving it, not merely of an external instrument, but of the very object or recipient of the activity. (The death of a friend blocks friendship in this more intimate way.) Here again, the activity may be either (a) completely blocked, if the loss is permanent and complete; or (b) impeded, if the loss is temporary and/or partial. We shall concentrate on (1a) and (1b) here, reserving the loss of an object for the next chapter. But Aristotle does not explicitly draw these distinctions, and his examples are drawn from all groups.

'It is impossible or not easy to do fine things without resources', Aristotle said in the passage with which we began this chapter, as he opened his discussion of the power of luck. He goes on to enumerate various types of necessary 'resources':

For many things are done through *philoi** and wealth and political capability, as through tools. And deprivation of some things defiles blessedness (*to makarion*): for example good birth, good children, good looks. For nobody will entirely live well (be *eudaimonikos*) if he is entirely disgusting to look at, or basely born, or both solitary and childless; still less, perhaps, if he has terribly bad children or *philoi*, or has good ones who die. (1099a33–b6)

Some of these are deprivations of instrumental means towards activity; some (the cases of friends and children) involve the loss both of instrumental means towards further activities (for friends are also 'tools') and of an object for one kind of excellent activity itself. In some cases, we can imagine that the absence of the instrumental means or object will altogether block excellent activity. Lifelong enslavement, severe chronic illness, extreme poverty, the death of all one's loved ones – any of these could make one or more of the excellences impossible to exercise. (Even extreme physical ugliness, as Aristotle elsewhere explicitly says,[20] can altogether block the formation of deep friendships.) In other cases, we imagine that good activity, while not altogether blocked, will be significantly impeded or cut back. The person disadvantaged in social position may lack opportunities for good political activity that are available to the well-placed; the death of a child can cramp the quality or spirit of many types of activity; sickness can do the same. These are not rare disasters, nor does Aristotle here seem to view them that way. They are regular parts of the course of many human lives. Aristotle's list makes us begin to notice the extent to which an average life is hedged round by dangers of impediment. Unconstrained activity begins to look like the rare or lucky item.

Having made these general observations about the power of circumstance to disrupt good activity, Aristotle is ready to test our intuitions against a particular case:

For many reversals and all sorts of luck come about in the course of a life; and it is possible for the person who was most especially going well to encounter great calamities in old age, as in the stories told about Priam in the Trojan war. But when a person has such misfortunes and ends in a wretched condition, nobody says that he is living well (*oudeis eudaimonizei*). (1100a5–10)

The story of Priam is a good test case for Aristotle's ethical theory here. For it begins with a person who had, presumably, developed and maintained a stably virtuous character through life, had acted well and according to excellence – but who was then deprived by war of family, children, friends, power, resources, freedom. In his final pitiable state Priam's capacity to act well is very much diminished; for he cannot, given the constraints upon him, exercise many of the human excellences for which he was previously known. We deeply pity Priam,

---

* In this chapter and the next, *philos* and *philia* (usually rendered 'friend' and 'friendship') will usually remain untranslated; the issues are discussed in Ch. 12. Briefly: *philia* is extensionally wider than friendship – it takes in family relations, the relation between husband and wife, and erotic relationships, as well as what we would call 'friendship'. It is also, frequently, affectively stronger: it is a requirement of *philia* that the partners should be linked by affectionate feeling; and, as we see, *philia* includes the very strongest and most intimate of our affective ties. We can say that two people are 'just friends'; no such thing could be said with *philia*.

feeling that he has lost something of great importance in losing his sphere of activity, something that is deeper than mere contented feeling. On the other hand, even an ethical theorist who rejects the extremes of the good-condition view may wish to maintain here that calamity does not impair the quality of Priam's life, since he has displayed good character in action consistently through the course of a long life. Aristotle's challenge is to sketch a response that will do justice to these competing intuitions.

His strategy here, as elsewhere, is two-pronged. Against the opponent of luck he will insist on luck's real importance, exploring our belief that it is possible to be dislodged from living well. At the same time, he shows us that, given a conception of good living that values stable excellences of character and activity according to these, such drastic upsets will be rare. Making excellences and their activities – rather than, say, honor or success – the primary bearers of value (or, better, acknowledging that we really believe that they *are* the primary bearers of value, for Aristotle argues that those who say something else will change if they think harder about the full range of their beliefs) helps us to avoid seeing ourselves as, and being, mere victims of luck.

Aristotle's remarks about Priam and related cases go against a well-established tradition in moral philosophy, both ancient and modern, according to which moral goodness, that which is an appropriate object of ethical praise and blame, cannot be harmed or affected by external circumstances. For Plato, the good person could not be harmed by the world: his life is no less good and praiseworthy because of adverse circumstances.[21] For the good-condition theorist, the same is evidently true, though for slightly different reasons. For Kant, whose influence upon modern Aristotle commentators and their audiences cannot, here again, be overestimated, *happiness* can be augmented or diminished by fortune; but that which is truly deserving of ethical praise and blame, true moral worth, cannot be.[22] This Kantian view has so influenced the tradition of subsequent ethical theory that it has come to seem to many a hallmark of truly moral thinking. It is not surprising, then, that interpreters under the influence of one or more of these traditions and anxious to make Aristotle look morally respectable have read the Priam passage oddly, so that it no longer says what would be most shocking, namely that ethical praiseworthiness of life, not just happy feeling, can be augmented or diminished by chance reversals. The interpretative view that acquits Aristotle of this immoral doctrine is as follows. Aristotle is, in these passages, drawing a distinction between two of his central ethical notions: between *eudaimonia* and *makariotēs*, living well and being blessed or happy. The former consists in activity according to excellence; the latter in this, plus the blessings of fortune. According to this story, which has been put forward by Kant-influenced commentators such as Sir David Ross and H. H. Joachim,[23] the gifts and reversals of fortune can never diminish *eudaimonia*, i.e., that for which Priam can be praised and blamed; but because they can diminish his enjoyment of his good activity, they do diminish contentment and good feeling. This reading bases itself upon a sentence in the Priam passage that says, 'If things are so, the *eudaimōn* person will never become wretched; nor, however, will he be *makarios*, if he encounters the luck of Priam' (1101a6–7). We shall later investigate this sentence in its context and ask whether it is really making the distinction desired by the interpreter.

It is a famous distinction; and its closeness to the Kantian distinction between moral worth and happiness makes us suspicious of it right away as a reading of Aristotle, especially given the anti-Kantian force of Aristotle's remarks about the person on the wheel. Nor does it give us confidence to find that Aristotle's first remark about Priam's case is, 'As for someone who has luck like that and dies in a wretched condition, nobody says that he is living well (nobody *eudaimonizei* him)' (1100a9–10). Priam is from the beginning denied not just contentment, but *eudaimonia* itself. But perhaps this is an unreflective belief of the many that Aristotle is going to criticize. So we need to look further to see whether the text as a whole supports the interpreters' distinction.

In fact it does not. Aristotle makes no significant distinction, in these passages, between *eudaimonia* and *makariotēs*; and he clearly claims that both can be damaged or disrupted by certain kinds of luck, though not by all the kinds that some of his contemporaries supposed.

The textual evidence can be succinctly set out: first, passages claiming that *eudaimonia* is vulnerable to catastrophe; second, passages indicating that Aristotle here treats '*eudaimon*' and '*makarion*' as interchangeable; those then allow us to draw upon his remarks about the *makarion* for our picture of *eudaimonia*.

(1) As we have already seen, the passage about the person on the wheel from *EN* VII = *EE* VI clearly asserts that external circumstances are required for *eudaimonia*; the same was obviously true of the passage from *Magna Moralia* II.8 that we quoted at the beginning of this chapter. *Eudemian Ethics* VIII.2 argues at length that 'practical wisdom is not the only thing that makes acting well according to excellence (*eupragian kat' aretēn*, the definiens of *eudaimonia*), but we say that the fortunate, too, do well (*eu prattein*), implying that good fortune is a cause of good activity just as knowledge is' (1246b37–42a2). The friendship books will argue that *philoi*, as 'external goods', are necessary for full *eudaimonia* (cf. Ch. 12, and esp. 1169b2ff.). But we do not need to look so far afield. For the very disputed passages in *EN* I tell the same story. Nobody calls Priam *eudaimōn* (1100a7–8). Because it is difficult or impossible to *do fine things* (*ta kala prattein*) without resources, it is obvious that *eudaimonia* stands in need of the external goods (1099a29–31). And at the conclusion of the Priam passage, Aristotle summarizes, 'What, then, prevents us from saying that a person is *eudaimōn* if and only if that person is active according to complete excellence and is sufficiently equipped with the external goods not for some chance period of time, but for a complete life?' (1101a14–15). Here the presence of 'sufficient' external goods is introduced, in a passage as formally definitional as any in the *EN*, as a separate necessary condition for *eudaimonia* itself.

(2) If we now attend to passages in which '*makarion*' and '*eudaimon*' occur together, we find that these passages confirm and do not disrupt this general picture. For the words are, in fact, treated as interchangeable. This is generally true

in the ethical works. To take just a single salient example outside of our present context: in *EN* IX.9, Aristotle reports a debate about the value of *philia*:

There is a debate as to whether the *eudaimōn* needs *philoi* or not. For they say that *makarioi* and self-sufficient people have no need of *philoi*, since they have all good things already... But it seems peculiar to give all good things to the *eudaimōn* and to leave out *philoi*, which seem to be the greatest of the external goods... And surely it is peculiar to make the *makarios* a solitary: for nobody would choose to have all the good things in the world all by himself. For the human being is a political creature and naturally disposed to living-with. And this is true of the *eudaimōn* as well... Therefore the *eudaimōn* needs *philoi*. (1169b3–10, 16–19, 22; for a detailed discussion of the argument of the passage, see Ch. 12)

Nobody could reasonably doubt that the two words are used here with no salient distinction, more or less as stylistic variants. Both in the paraphrase of the opponent's position and in Aristotle's own remarks, this is so. Nor could anyone doubt that the external good of *philia* is held here to be necessary for *eudaimonia*, not just for *makariotēs*.

The same is in fact true of our present context, as we can see if we reexamine its opening passage, part of which we have quoted previously:

Nonetheless, *eudaimonia* evidently needs the external goods as well, as we said. For many things are done through *philoi* and wealth and political capability, as through tools. And deprivation of some things defiles the condition of being *makarion*; for example good birth, good children, good looks. For nobody will entirely be *eudaimonikos* if he is entirely disgusting to look at, or basely born, or both solitary and childless; still less, perhaps, if he has terribly bad children or *philoi*, or has good ones who die. As we said, then, it seems to require this sort of fortunate climate in addition. This is why some have identified *eudaimonia* with good fortune, and others with excellence. (1099a33–b8)

This passage shows very clearly that Aristotle draws no distinction of an important kind between *makariotēs* and *eudaimonia*, and that he is fully prepared to assert that *eudaimonia* itself is disrupted by absence of certain external goods. The entire passage concerns the need of *eudaimonia* for external goods. (The subject of the first quoted sentence is not explicit in the Greek, but must be supplied from the previous sentence, whose last word is '*eudaimonia*'; there is no other candidate subject.) The general point is now further explained (NB 'for') by a passage that speaks of the defilement of the *makarion*; this, in turn, is further explained (another 'for') by a passage that once again speaks in terms of *eudaimonia*. The 'it' in the final conclusion plainly refers to *eudaimonia*: it is this which requires a fortunate climate, as the final sentence of our citation makes clear. The absence of certain necessary conditions for good living impairs good living itself, presumably by impeding the doing of fine actions in which good living consists. So far, '*makarion*' and '*eudaimon*' do not come apart.

Now we must loo' closely at the context of the passage that forms the basis for the opposing inte pretation, the passage in which Aristotle delivers his verdict about the case of Priam. He asks how secure our judgments of *eudaimonia* are during the course of a person's life, given the vulnerability of human good living to reversals in fortune. He then once again reasserts his position that human good living does 'need in addition' (*prosdeitai*, 1100b8) the external goods of luck. But, he goes on, this does not make *eudaimonia* entirely at the mercy of luck, or the *eudaimōn* 'a chameleon and resting on a rotten basis' (1100b6–7). For these goods are not the most important factors in living well: 'the well or badly does not reside in these' (8).[24] They are not the actual constituents of good living: 'activities according to excellence, or their opposites, are what are in charge of[25] *eudaimonia* or its opposite' (1100b8–10). Such activity, though to some degree vulnerable, is just about the most stable and enduring thing in human life, one of the hardest things to lose hold of or forget or have taken away (1100b12ff.). The person who is living and acting well (Aristotle first calls this person the *makarios*, then switches in the next sentence to the *eudaimōn* – 16, 18) will go on doing so throughout his or her entire life. 'For he will always or more than anything else do and consider the things according to excellence; and he will bear luck most nobly and in every way harmoniously, if he is really good and "four-square without blame"' (1100b19–22).

So much is fairly clear. Now the complexities begin, as Aristotle begins to ask in what ways this stable good life, based upon steady character and consisting in activity according to the excellences of character and intellect, *is* vulnerable. Small pieces of either good or bad fortune, he now tells us, will not produce a 'decisive change of life' (*rhopē tēs zōēs*, 22–5). But big and numerous contingencies can, if they happen well, make life more *makarion* because the opportunities they afford will be used nobly and well; on the other hand, correspondingly great misfortunes will 'crush and pollute the (condition of being) *makarion* – for they bring pain and get in the way of many activities' (1100b23–30). So far, then, only the word '*makarion*' has been used, in the immediate context, of that which can be augmented by great good fortune and diminished by great misfortune. But, in addition to our other evidence, the reasons given here, which all have to do with the way fortune augments or impedes excellent *activity*, show us that the *makarion* cannot be some merely supervenient pleasure or feeling of contentment. Aristotle is maintaining, as elsewhere, that some of the component activities in which good living consists can be increased or blocked by external happenings. We are probably supposed to think of both instrumental and more direct effects of fortune. An inheritance gives, instrumentally, scope for fine and generous action; sudden illness impedes good acting in every area by taking away one's energy. Political reversals and deaths of loved ones more directly remove other sorts of good activity, by removing their objects; conversely, the birth of a child or the acquisition of adult political rights makes a direct contribution to excellent action by providing it with an object.

All of this seems to be about *eudaimonia* itself and its constituents, not some supervenient good. Aristotle shortly makes this explicit:

The *eudaimōn* person is not variable and easily changed. For he will not be easily dislodged from his *eudaimonia*, nor by just any misfortune that happens his way, but only by big and numerous misfortunes; and out of these he will not become *eudaimōn* again in a short time, but, if ever, in a long and complete time, if, in that time, he gets hold of big and fine things. (1101a8–14)

(There follows the definitional passage that we have already discussed on p. 330.) Aristotle here very clearly asserts that misfortunes of a severe kind, prolonged over a period of time, impair good living itself. He uses '*eudaimon*' where above he had used '*makarion*', making no distinction. (Several lines later, at 1101a19–20, he paraphrases his concluding definition, now substituting '*makarion*' for '*eudaimon*'.) Such disruptions are rare, he says, since human excellence, once developed, is something stable; but if they are big or deep or frequent enough, catastrophes will 'pollute' good activity, and therefore the good life, so severely that only time and much good luck, if anything, will bring *eudaimonia* back.

Aristotle inserts an important qualification in the intervening section. Since this passage includes the sentence from which we began our criticism of the Kantian interpretation, we should now study its context in full:

If activities are the main thing in life, as we said, nobody who is *makarios* will ever become basely wretched (*athlios*). For he will never engage in hateful and base actions. We think that the really good and reasonable person will bear his luck with dignity and always do the finest thing possible given the circumstances, just as the good general will make the most warlike use of the army he has and the good shoemaker will make the best shoe he can out of the hides he is given – and so on for all craftsmen. If this is right, then the *eudaimōn* person would never become basely wretched; nonetheless, he will still not be *makarios*, if he encounters the luck of Priam. Nor indeed is he variable and easily changed, for he will not be easily dislodged from his *eudaimonia*...etc. (1100b33–1101a10)

Now that we can examine the entire passage some of whose bits we have seen separately, we can understand Aristotle's final judgment concerning Priam. He does concede that such extreme bad luck *could* dislodge a good person from full *eudaimonia*. But he reminds us that a person of good character and practical wisdom will often be able to resist this damage, finding a way to act nobly even in circumstances of adversity. Like a general who does the best he can with the troops he has, or the shoemaker who makes the best shoes he can with the available materials, even so the wise and virtuous person will use life's 'materials' as well as possible, finding for excellence some expression in action. Indeed, part of the 'art' of Aristotelian practical wisdom, as we saw in Chapter 10, seems to consist in being keenly responsive to the limits of one's 'material' and figuring out what is best given the possibilities, rather than rigidly aiming at some inflexible set of norms. Aristotelian practical excellence is prepared for the contingencies of the world and is not easily diminished by them. But none of this will suffice to prevent the loss of *eudaimonia* in a very extreme case such as Priam's.

Finally, Aristotle feels it important to stress that a person of good and stable character will not act diametrically against character just because of continued misfortune; the stability of character will stand between him and really *bad* action. But only bad action makes a person truly *athlios*, if actions are the main thing in life. If *eudaimonia* were constituted by wealth or power, a person could go from the top to the very bottom, from the most praiseworthy condition to the condition most worthy of scorn, as a result of luck. Activity according to excellence may be squeeze or blocked; but the person to whom that happens does not, just on account of this, go to the very bottom of the scale of ethical assessment. Even if we do not wish to grant that the good person on the wheel is living a flourishing and fully praiseworthy life, we can also acknowledge that his life is not evil, despicable, or blameworthy.

In short, an Aristotelian conception of *eudaimonia*, which bases excellent activity on stable goodness of character, makes the good life tolerably stable in the face of the world. But this stability is not limitless. There is a real gap between being good and living well; uncontrolled happening can step into this gap, impeding the good state of character from finding its proper fulfillment in action. We have already mentioned four types of impediment-situations: either complete blockage or constraining of activity through deprivation of an instrumental resource; blockage or constraint through the absence of an object for the activity. Because of our interest in linking these ethical issues with Aristotle's regard for tragedy, we should now, however, add two more situations to this list – situations implicitly recognized by this general account and explicitly recognized by Aristotle in *EN* III and elsewhere. Recalling our discussions in Chapters 2 and 9, we can call these the situation of Oedipus and the situation of Agamemnon.

Oedipus had a good character; but he did a terrible thing that impeded (presumably) his *eudaimonia*. The 'gap' created by luck in his case was not in any simple way one between good character and activity: for he did act and was not in any literal sense impeded. There was, however, a gap, created by circumstances of excusable ignorance, between the act he intended or voluntarily did – the killing of an old man at the crossroads – and the bad act that he involuntarily did, the parricide that dislodged him, if it did, from *eudaimonia*. I now want to suggest that we can see this gap as a variety of the gap between being good and living well. For the intended act was the natural expression of what Oedipus *was* in character. The luck of circumstances caused that intentional description not to be the morally salient description of what took place; indeed, on some interpretations of Aristotle's views about the individuation of actions, that act was not really performed, and only the other one was.[26] So in this sense circumstances impeded and thwarted Oedipus's blameless and appropriate activation of his character, stepping in, so to speak, between the intention and the act and causing the intended act to have at best a merely shadowy existence.

Agamemnon's case is more complex: for here, as we have seen, each of the conflicting alternatives is in one way the natural expression of his goodness of character; yet each has a distressing other face. Pious service to Zeus is inseparable from the murder of his child; protection of that child would have been inseparable from impiety and from cruelty to his suffering soldiers. Unlike Oedipus, Agamemnon chooses and intends the action under both its good and its bad descriptions: no ignorance excuses him.[27] But we might say, in his case as well, that the world, by causing this tragic conflict to arise, has created for him a gap between his good character and its natural unconstrained expression in action. For it is an impediment to his pious activity that piety should be in this case inseparable from murder; the quality of his act, the natural expression of his character, is tarnished by the horror of the crime that is inextricable from it. Aristotle's criticisms of the good-condition theorist and his remarks about impeded activity can, then, accommodate these two further types of case, so central to the appreciation of tragedy.

It appears, furthermore, that Aristotle's text really does give recognition to the existence of Agamemnon-like conflicts. His remark that luck cannot cause a good person to do really bad actions might cast doubt on this. And in the *Magna Moralia* he insists that the excellences, unlike the vices, are in general mutually reinforcing, giving rise to no conflicts.[28] (For example: political justice fits well with moderation and with courage, theoretical pursuits with moderation. The vicious person will not find this harmony: for immoderate appetites pull against crafty injustice, cowardice against excessive power-seeking, and so on.) But in the books on *philia* he allows that obligations to one *philos* may conflict with legitimate obligations to another, in such a way that it is impossible to fulfill both.[29] And in *EN* III.1, Aristotle acknowledges that in certain cases of circumstantial constraint the good person may act in a deficient or even a 'shameful' way, doing things that he or she would never have done but for the conflict situation. He will act as well as he can; and yet he will be doing something bad, something that he would not have chosen. The so-called 'mixed actions' are such cases. Aristotle's examples are, first, a person who throws something overboard in a storm; we discussed this case in Chapter 2. Second, and more central for us, is a case in which a tyrant tells the agent to do something shameful, threatening to kill him and his entire family if he does not. Here we have a case where misfortune will in fact force the sensible agent to do what is shameful and base. But Aristotle argues that the base action is not altogether the agent's own. It is his own in the sense that it is chosen at the time when it is done and the origin of the movement is in him: his beliefs and desires explain it. But our assessment takes into account the element of constraint: the fact that the action, taken by itself, was not one that he voluntarily would have done (1110a18ff.). It is not the action of a shameful or base character. Sometimes, he adds, we admire and praise those who face such conflicts well, making a hard choice for the sake of a valuable end (1110a20–2); Aristotle is no sympathizer with those who, in politics or in private affairs, would so shrink from blame and from unacceptable action that they would be unable to take a necessary decision for the best. But in other cases we simply suspend praise and blame, and pity the agent for having to endure a conflict 'that overstrains human nature and that nobody would be able to withstand' (1110a24–6). Such, we suspect, would be his response to a case like Agamemnon's – had Agamemnon, in it, behaved more like a good character, with more sense of the tension and constraint that was forcing him to go against what he would sanely choose.[30]

Aristotle adds to these remarks about conflict a further observation. This is, that certain valued excellences, particularly courage, political commitment, and love of friends, will take the good agent, far more often than the defective agent, into situations in which the requirements of character conflict with the preservation of life itself – therefore with the continued possibility of all excellent activity. This is a special type of value conflict. The good Aristotelian agent will see it as a choice in which something of real value is forgone – though not, admittedly, one in which evil action is forced. In his discussion of sacrifices for the sake of friendship or love, Aristotle stresses the fact that the person of excellence will think little of comfort or safety or money compared to the chance to do something noble; but he goes on to say that love of friends or country will sometimes call for a sacrifice more intimately connected to good living: a sacrifice of the opportunity to act well, or even of life itself (1169a18–b2).

The good-condition theorist, and other defenders of the view that the good life cannot be diminished by such chance collisions, might try to say that there is no real loss here – for the person's goodness is intact, and the nobility of his choice guarantees that he will suffer no diminution in *eudaimonia*. Aristotle, as we might expect, does not agree. The loss of activity and of life, he argues elsewhere, is even a greater loss to the excellent person than to the base. The more excellent he is, the richer his life is in value – and, therefore, the more painful the choice to risk losing it:

By so much as the courageous person has all of excellence and the more *eudaimōn* he is, so much more will he be pained at the prospect of death. For such a person, above others, has a value worthy of living, and he will be aware that he is being deprived of the greatest goods. That is a painful thing. But he will nonetheless be courageous, and perhaps even more so because he chooses what is fine in war over these other things. In fact we don't have pleasant activity in the case of all the excellences – except insofar as they reach their end. (1117b10–16)

Excellence, in this case and others like it, diminishes self-sufficiency and increases vulnerability: it gives you something of high value and it enjoins that in certain situations of luck you be ready to give it up. But that excellence should bring risk and pain is no surprise, says Aristotle – unless you are in the grip of the false notion that excellence is necessarily linked with having a good time. There is pleasure when the noble activity reaches its end; but if the world should prevent this fulfillment, the good person still chooses to act nobly (cf. also Ch. 10, p. 295).

V

So far, Aristotle's reply to the good-condition theorist has spoken only of impeded activity. It has not spoken of chance-caused damage to the good condition or state of character itself. But Aristotle plainly does believe that our worldly circumstances affect, for better or for worse, adult good character itself, not just its expression. It is obvious that the world, in his view, affects decisively the character-formation of children;[31] the case for adult vulnerability is not as obvious, but it can still be convincingly made out. We can sketch the case by pointing to four pieces of evidence: (1) the Priam passage itself; (2) evidence concerning *philia* and the political context; (3) the *Rhetoric*'s discussion of the relationship between character and time and/or experience of life; (4) the account of the so-called 'goods of fortune' in both *Rhetoric* and *EN*.

The good person, Aristotle said, could not easily be dislodged from *eudaimonia*, but only by 'big and numerous misfortunes'. Once so dislodged, however, 'he will not become *eudaimōn* again in a short time, but, if ever, in a long and complete time, if, in that time, he gets hold of big and fine things'. We must now look more closely into the nature of the damage that dislodges the good person. For misfortunes can 'pollute' good activity in two ways: by disrupting the expression of good dispositions in action, or by affecting the internal springs of action themselves. The former possibility is prominent in the context; but the latter seems important, as well, for the explication of this particular passage. A purely external impediment to good action could be set right *immediately* by the restoration of good fortune. A person who has been enslaved in wartime can be set free in a moment. A sick person can as quickly be cured. A childless person can suddenly conceive or beget a child. What does take time and repeated good fortune to heal is the corruption of desire, expectation, and thought that can be inflicted by crushing and prolonged misfortune. Aristotle's repeated use of words suggesting spoilage or pollution,[32] and his assertion that the damages of luck are reversed, if at all, only over a long period of time, suggest that he is thinking also of this deeper, more internal sort of damage. It takes a long time to restore to the slave a free person's sense of dignity and self-esteem, for the chronic invalid to learn again the desires and projects characteristic of the healthy person, for the bereaved person to form new and fruitful attachments.

This possibility is made more concrete in the books concerning *philia*. For there Aristotle both shows love to be a vulnerable good and ascribes to it an important role in the development and maintenance of adult good character. The same can be said of his discussions of the function of a supporting political context. Since we shall discuss these arguments in detail in our next chapter, we can now turn to the little-known and highly interesting material from the *Rhetoric*.[33]

In *Rhetoric* II.12–14, Aristotle makes a series of observations about the relationship between character and time of life; these show us clearly to what extent the experience of reversal and misfortune can wound character itself. Young people, he tells us, have certain virtues of character of which the elderly are frequently no longer capable. They are of a noble simplicity: they are *euētheis*, open or guileless, rather than *kakoētheis*, guileful or malignant, 'because they have not yet seen much wickedness' (1389a17–18).[34] They are capable of trust because they have not yet been often deceived (1389a18–19). They are courageous because they are capable of high hope, and this makes for confidence (1389a26–7). They are capable of the central Aristotelian virtue of *megalopsuchia*, greatness of soul, 'because they have not yet been humbled by life, but they lack experience of necessities' (1389a31–2). (The *EN*, too, stresses the importance of good luck for this 'crown of the virtues' – 1124a20ff.) They lack excessive concern for money because they have little experience of need (1389a14–15). They form friendships easily because they take pleasure in the company of others and do not calculate everything with an eye to advantage (a35–b2). They are easily moved to pity, since they have a good opinion of others and so easily believe that they are suffering unjustly (b8–9, cf. Interlude 2). They are fond of laughter, so they have the social excellence of *eutrapelia*, charm or ready wit (b10–11). They have certain tendencies to excess as well, Aristotle tells us, which are the outgrowth of their inexperience and their keenness of passion. But what most interests us, in this remarkable set of observations, is that they are capable of certain good and high things just on account of their lack of certain bad experiences.

We see more clearly what this claim means when we turn to the account of the character of the elderly, whose deficiencies result from just that experience of life that the trusting and hopeful young have not yet had. This little known but very important passage deserves to be quoted at length:

Because they have lived many years and have been deceived many times and made many mistakes, and because their experience is that most things go badly, they do not insist upon anything with confidence, but always less forcefully than is appropriate. They *think*, but never *know*; they have views on both sides of a question and are always adding in 'perhaps' and 'probably'; they say everything this way, and nothing unequivocally. And they are malignant (*kakoētheis*): for it is malignant to interpret everything in the worst light. Furthermore, they are excessively suspicious because of their lack of trust (*apistia*), and lacking in trust because of their experience. And they neither love nor hate intensely for these reasons, but, as in the saying of Bias, they love as if they were going to hate tomorrow, and hate as if they were going to love tomorrow. And they are small of soul (*mikropsuchoi*) because they have been humbled by life: for they desire nothing great or excellent, but only what is commensurate with life. And they are ungenerous. For property is one of the necessary things; and in, and through, their experience they know how hard it is to get it and how easy to lose it. And they are cowardly and fear everything beforehand – for they have, in this respect, the opposite character from the young. For they are chilly, and the young are warm; so old age prepares the way for cowardice, since fear, too, is a kind of chilling... And they are self-loving more than is appropriate; for this, too, is a kind of smallness of soul. And they live for advantage and not for the noble, more than is appropriate, because they are self-loving. For the advantageous is good for oneself; the noble is good *simpliciter*... And the elderly, too, feel pity, but not for the same reason as the young: for the young feel it through love of humanity, the old through weakness – for they think every suffering is waiting for them, and this inspires pity. For this reason they are given to grieving, and are neither charming nor fond of laughter. (1389b13–1390a24)

These remarkable observations show us clearly to what extent Aristotle is willing to acknowledge that circumstances of life can impede character itself, making even acquired virtues difficult to retain. Especially at risk are those virtues that require openness or guilelessness rather than self-defensiveness, trust in other people and in the world rather than self-protecting suspiciousness. And it seems to be

Aristotle's view that quite a few of the virtues require this element. Love and friendship require trust in the loved person; generosity is incompatible with continual suspicion that the world is about to take one's necessary goods away; greatness of soul requires high hope and expectation; even courage requires confidence that some good can come of fine action. (In Chapter 13 we shall see the importance of this idea for Aristotle's connection with Euripidean tragedy.) The virtues require a stance of openness towards the world and its possibilities: as the *Antigone* also suggested, a yielding and receptive character of soul that is not compatible with an undue emphasis on self-protection. This openness is both itself vulnerable and a source of vulnerability for the person's *eudaimonia*: for the trusting person is more easily betrayed than the self-enclosed person, and it is the experience of betrayal that slowly erodes the foundation of the virtues. Virtue contains in this way (in a world where most people's experience is that 'things go badly') the seeds of its own disaster.

This is a treatise for orators who will address a mixed group of ordinary people; it therefore aims to say what is so for the average mediocre type, and it does not stress the abilities of the person of superior character.* We can assume, with *EN* I, that such a person would not be corroded by a few bad experiences and that in a wide range of circumstances he or she would be able to act well with the 'materials' at hand, preserving character intact. And yet this passage tells us clearly that character itself can be affected; the mechanisms of its decline are, clearly, present in the good as well as the mediocre life. (Most of the circumstances mentioned are common; some even appear natural and inevitable.) Indeed, we might say that the good are in certain ways more at risk than the bad: for it is the good *euēthēs* person who trusts in uncertain things and therefore risks the pain of disillusionment. We shall see in Euripides' portrait of Hecuba both how difficult it is to sway the character of a really good person *and* how horrible is the spectacle of such a decline, once trust is no longer available.

There follow in the *Rhetoric* three brief chapters concerning the 'goods of luck' and their contribution to character.[35] These chapters flesh out this general story of the vulnerability of virtue, adding the disturbing thought that success can be as corrupting as misfortune. Aristotle considers, in turn, three sorts of advantages that might accrue to an agent by luck: good birth, wealth, and power. He asks of each, what effect does it have upon character? Briefly summarized, his conclusion is that good birth conduces to ambitiousness and disdainfulness; wealth to insolence, arrogance, and a mercenary attitude towards value; power to a somewhat better group of traits – to seriousness and a sober sense of responsibility – but also to some of the same vices as wealth. All the types of good fortune are said to conduce to one virtue: to love of the divine, to whom the

---

* It might be objected, too, that these sections of the *Rhetoric* deal with *endoxa*, prevalent ordinary beliefs not yet sifted and scrutinized. But Aristotle is telling the orator what young and old people are like in part so that he will know how best to persuade them. The success of his teaching here depends on its being right about the way their characters in fact are, not just about how they are *seen*.

fortunate ascribe the origin of their good fortune (1391b4). The opposite situations of bad fortune conduce to opposite states of character in ways that can easily be imagined (1391b5–7).

Aristotle's position here is not that these pieces of luck are sufficient conditions for the states of character named, or that all recipients of such luck will develop these traits. (Indeed, in the *EN* he stresses that the good person will deal with good fortune much more appropriately than the bad or mediocre: 1124a30ff.) He speaks of the luck as a contributory cause, as something that 'pulls towards' these character traits 'along with' other causes (*sunteinousin*, 1391a31). The claim that good fortune 'has' the types of character described (*echei ta ēthē*, 1391a30–1) is probably not to be read more strongly. The luck is one causal factor that has some real effect. The wealthy 'are affected in some way (*paschontes ti*) by the possession of wealth' (1390b33–4); and it is even 'plausible that they should be affected in this way' (1391a7). These causal forces are, then, of the sort that might be resisted by a person of outstandingly firm character in relatively balanced circumstances; but they are real forces, and an ethical account must recognize their power.

We can now summarize Aristotle's argument against the opponent of luck. First of all, he has argued that the good condition of a virtuous person is not, by itself, sufficient for full goodness of living. Our deepest beliefs about value, when scrutinized, show us that we require more. We require that the good condition find its completion or full expression in activity; and this activity takes the agent to the world, in such a way that he or she becomes vulnerable to reversals. Any conception of good living that we will consider rich enough to be worth going for will contain this element of risk. The vulnerability of the good person is not unlimited. For frequently, even in diminished circumstances, the flexible responsiveness of his practical wisdom will show him a way to act well. But the vulnerability is real: and if deprivation and diminution are severe or prolonged enough, this person can be 'dislodged' from *eudaimonia* itself. Aristotle's final point against the good-condition opponent is that even then virtuous condition is not, itself, something hard and invulnerable. Its yielding and open posture towards the world gives it the fragility, as well as the beauty, of a plant.

VI

So far we have spoken of the necessary vulnerability of human *eudaimonia*, given the worldly contingencies of specifically human life. We can see how closely risk and richness of value are connected: for the very same evaluative choices that enhance the quality and completeness of a human life – the choice to value activities rather than just intellectual keenness – open the agent to certain risks of disaster. Our investigation of social values in the next chapter will show this sort of connection even more clearly. But so far it is not evident that one could not imagine these same virtues and this same *eudaimonia* turning up in a risk-free life. The conditions of risk appear to be accidentally, rather than essentially, connected to the structure of virtue itself, however permanent and unavoidable these contingent conditions are. We know from Chapter 10 that the search for the good life must be a search for a human good life – that the notion of a Good abstracted from the nature and the conditions of a certain sort of being is an empty one. But we do not yet know in what way the specifically needy and risky elements of our 'human condition' are going to shape or constitute the virtues that make up our *eudaimonia*.

It is, however, Aristotle's view that certain central human values are available and valuable only within a context of risk and material limitation. A divine or unlimited life could not have those same values, those good things, in it. In the first book of the *Politics* (1253a8ff.), he tells us that certain central ethical notions – including the advantageous and disadvantageous, the just and unjust, the good and bad – are notions that belong to the human being alone among the animals, and that the *polis* is the association of living beings who have these conceptions. He then goes on to point out that the beast and the god are both, in their different ways, non-political creatures, lacking a share in the association that takes its shape from the ethical conceptions – the one because of its savagery and lack of rational capability, the other because of its solitary self-sufficiency (1253a27ff.). It is, then, strongly suggested that a solitary self-sufficient being will not partake, as we humans do, in the understanding and communication of certain basic ethical values. And we can see why this should be so: for the notion of advantage seems to have a close conceptual connectedness with need; and the notion of justice, as Aristotle understands it, is a notion of the equitable distribution of finite and limited resources. Both the meaningfulness of these values and their value or goodness seem to depend upon, be relative to, our human context of limitation.[36] This point is reaffirmed in *EN* VII, where the excellences, whose activities have been held to be ends in themselves for a human being, are denied both to beasts and to gods (1145a25ff.).

Aristotle returns to this point in Book x of the *EN*, making his claim about divine or unlimited beings more explicit.[37] If we really imagine the life of a needless and divine being, he says there, we find that most of the central human ethical values will not be valuable or even comprehensible in such a life.

Will we ascribe to them just actions? Or isn't it evidently ridiculous to imagine them making contracts and returning deposits and so on? Or courageous actions, enduring fearful things and taking risks because it is noble? Or generous actions? To whom will they give? It will be inappropriate for them to have money or anything of that kind. Or moderate actions – what would those be? Isn't that commendation vulgar, since they have no base appetites? (1178b10–16)

It is plain that these central human values – which are, in the bulk of Aristotle's ethical writings, treated as ends in themselves, important constituents of human *eudaimonia*[38] – cannot be found in a life without shortage, risk, need, and limitation. Their nature *and* their goodness are constituted by the fragile nature of human life. (We shall shortly see that the same is true of the value of friendship and of political activity.) What we find valuable depends essentially on what we need and how we are limited. The goodness and beauty of human value cannot be comprehended or seen apart from that context. And the point is not merely epistemological: the persons and actions we now call just and generous simply would not *be* valuable in an animal or a divine context.

Plato had recognized that this was true of very many human values: they were not *kath' hauto*, in and of themselves, but *pros ti*, relative to something, specifically, to the conditions of merely human life. He had argued that the true or superior values would be the few that were *not* context-dependent or need-relative. He equated the truly valuable with that which a perfect non-limited needless being would still have reason to pursue. But Aristotle points out that the perspective of an unlimited being is not necessarily an unlimited perspective: for from this viewpoint many values cannot be seen. Plato suggested that there is available in the universe a pure transparent standpoint, from which the whole truth of value in the universe is evident. Aristotle (in *most* of his writing on virtue – see Appendix) replies that this does not look to be the case. Lack of limit is itself a limit. There may be no single nature to which all of genuine value discloses itself. As Heraclitus wrote, 'Immortals are mortal, mortals immortal, living with respect to one another's death, dead with respect to one another's life.'[39] Immortality closes the god off from the intensity of mortal courage, the beauty of just or generous action. The gods of tradition, we recall, find their own lack of limit constricting: they long after the riskier loves and aspirations of mortals. Even though they are unable to assume the mortal perspective or to understand such lives from the inside, they are drawn to the virtue of the limited being, the quick tense splendor of human excellence aimed against opposition at a difficult goal. Aristotle returns to some of the very deepest 'appearances' of his culture when he insists that the good makes its appearance only within the confines of what some creature is, and that need can be constitutive of beauty.[40]

12   The vulnerability of the good human life: relational goods

Each of the human excellences requires some external resources and necessary conditions. Each also requires, more intimately, external objects that will receive the excellent activity.[1] Generosity involves giving to others, who must be there to receive; moderation involves the appropriate relation, in action, to objects (food, drink, sexual partners) who can fail to be present, either altogether or in the appropriate way. Even intellectual contemplation requires the presence of suitable objects for thought. But this condition, as Plato saw, would rarely, if ever, fail to be met on account of contingencies of circumstance. For something can be an object of thought whether it is physically present or not;[2] as long as there is a universe there will be many things to contemplate everywhere; and, finally, as Aristotle adds, thought can be its own object.[3]

We can see, then, that although all human activities and therefore all candidates for inclusion in a plan for the good human life are in some way relational, some are very much more self-sufficient than others. Aristotle, like Plato, judges that contemplative activity is, among the activities available to us, the most stable and individually self-sufficient (*EN* 1177a25–1177b1, 1178a23–5).[4] Even though he rejects the extremes of the good-condition view, he might, then, like Plato, try to shore up the self-sufficiency of the good life by making those most secure activities its primary, or even its only, components.[5]

There are, however, other important human values that lie at the opposite end of the self-sufficiency spectrum: above all, the good activities connected with citizenship and political attachment, and those involved in personal love and friendship. For these require, and are in their nature relations with, a particular human context that is highly vulnerable and can easily fail to be present. Love requires another loving person. And 'the just person needs those towards whom he will act justly and those with whom' (1177a30–1). (The 'those' must bear the appropriate political relation to the agent: they must be fellow citizens, not fellow slaves.) Furthermore, love and friendship, and the part of political excellence that is a type of friendship or love[6] (if not, indeed, the entirety of political excellence), are in their nature *relations*, rather than virtuous states (*hexeis*)-plus-activities. The central excellences of character reside, so to speak, *in* the person; they are states *of* the person. Activity in the world is their perfection or completion; but if activity is cut off there is still something stably there, an underlying core of good character whose natural expression is in the excellent activity. This core is not invulnerable; but it is relatively stable, even in the absence of activity. Love and friendship, by contrast, are in their very nature contingent relationships between separate elements in the world. Each rests upon and is in complex ways connected with other traits of the person, such as generosity, justice, and kindliness; but there is no trait of being loving or being friendly that stands to love exactly as being courageous stands to courageous action, viz. as its mainspring and, impediments absent, its sufficient condition. To say this would, in Aristotle's view, misrepresent the importance of mutuality and mutual awareness in human love. Love is not simply a loving state of character plus a suitable context for its activation. The object's specific nature and activity enters more deeply into making it itself. Mutual activity, feeling, and awareness are such a deep part of what love and friendship *are* that Aristotle is unwilling to say that there is anything worthy of the name of love or friendship left, when the shared activities and the forms of communication that express it are taken away. The other person enters in not just as an object who receives the good activity, but as an intrinsic part of love itself. But if this is so (and we shall pursue the claim further below), then these components of the good life are going to be minimally self-sufficient. And they will be vulnerable in an especially deep and dangerous way. For luck from the world will be required not just for their adequate expression but for their very existence. And a reversal of fortune will not simply impede their expression; it will strike directly at their root. This special character explains why, in both the ethical works and the *Rhetoric*, Aristotle, in enumerating reversals or pitiable and fearful events, lays particular stress on disasters connected with *philia*.

These 'relational goods' have another distinctive feature: they seem to be dispensable. Many of the other human excellences are identified by focusing on a sphere of activity in which human beings necessarily and more or less inevitably make choices: excellent activity is then defined as appropriate activity within this necessary sphere. Moderation, for example, is appropriate activity with respect to bodily pleasure and pain, especially where food, drink, and sex are concerned. Courage is appropriate activity with respect to situations of risk. To ask, 'Should moderation be included in the good human life?' is not, cannot be, to ask whether the sphere of choice in which moderation figures should be included. Such a question could mean only, 'Should appropriate, rather than inappropriate behavior in this sphere be cultivated?' (We could, of course, go on from this question to ask whether moderation is to be valued as an end *in itself*, or just as a means to other ends.) With friendship, love, and politics, our options and questions are more numerous. For human beings[7] apparently can, and do, live without these relations. Aristotle recognizes as a prominent part of the philosophical tradition the view that the pursuit of self-sufficiency requires us to cultivate a solitary life, one that neither relies upon nor ascribes value to these fragile things.

Aristotle rejects that view, arguing that both social/political relations and *philia* are essential and valuable parts of the good human life. Indeed, he announces quite clearly, towards the beginning of the *Nicomachean Ethics*, that the sort of self-sufficiency that characterizes the best human life is a communal and not a solitary self-sufficiency. 'The complete (*teleion*) good seems to be self-sufficient (*autarkes*). But by self-sufficient we mean not a life for the individual alone, living a solitary life, but for parents as well and children and wife and in general *philoi* and fellow citizens, since the human being is by nature political'* (1097b7–11). This cryptic remark, which seems to stipulate without argument that a solitary life is insufficient for *eudaimonia*, corresponds, in fact, to a complex series of arguments defending that position. We can appropriately conclude our study of Aristotle's views about 'external goods' by examining these arguments. Their strategy, as we might expect, is complex. Against the defender of solitary self-sufficiency Aristotle argues that these vulnerable relationships and their associated activities have both instrumental value as necessary means to, and intrinsic value as component parts of, the best human life. But, he argues, this does not put the best life intolerably at the mercy of fortune. For it is possible to realize each of these values, properly understood, within a life that is not intolerably unstable, one that possesses an appropriately human kind of self-sufficiency.

I

Among the cherished human goods, membership and good activity in a political community are outstandingly vulnerable to chance reversal. This hardly needs to be mentioned. The tragedies on which Aristotle and his audience were raised, and on which he wishes to raise young citizens, focus on themes of defeat in war, enslavement, the loss of political exercise and political freedom. Aristotle's times were times of alarming political instability. His own life exemplified these uncertainties. Forced to leave Athens twice under political pressure, barred because of his resident alien status from owning property or taking an active role in civic, political, and religious affairs, linked by a problematic and uneven relationship to the Macedonian court whose threat to democratic freedoms he probably deplored, he knew all too well that to attach value to the city and one's role in it was to care about something highly unstable.[8] In these unreliable times other philosophers were beginning to urge withdrawal from active engagement in politics. The life of Pyrrho (*c.* 365–275) – or the stories of that life – exemplified for later skeptics a state of freedom from disturbance attained by refusal of commitment to the sources of disturbance.[9] Pyrrho allegedly illustrated the proper state of the human being in the midst of upheavals by pointing to a pig on the deck of a storm-tossed ship: caring nothing for the well-being of the ship and its passengers, it continues to eat contentedly at its trough.[10] Epicurus (341–270) would soon begin to teach a life of contemplative aloofness, in which the philosopher maintains a distance both psychic and physical from civic turmoil. His statues, erected in public places, would give the prospective pupil the message

* I shall translate *politikon* as 'political'; but it is important to notice that it is both more concrete and more inclusive than the English word. More concrete, in that it refers above all to our aptness or suitability for life in a city or *polis* – not in other forms or levels of political organization. More inclusive, because it takes in the entire life of the *polis*, including informal social relations, and is not limited to the sphere of laws and institutions. In this respect, 'social' would be more appropriate; but it would, even more than 'political' lack the concreteness of the Greek word.

that godlike dignity and calm could be his – or hers[11] – with a retreat to the extrapolitical society of the garden.[12] Aristotle, knowing the fragility of the political, and aware of philosophical defenses of the solitary good life,[13] refuses to take this course.

First of all, as he repeatedly stresses, membership and good activity in a political community has a necessary instrumental role in the development of good character generally. Habituation, accomplished both within the family and in the context of a program of public education, is the most decisive factor in becoming good: 'It makes no small difference whether one is brought up in these or those habits from childhood, but a very great difference; or, rather, all the difference' (*EN* 1103b23–4). Teaching and instruction, he argues in *Nicomachean Ethics* x.9, are of no avail unless the soul of the listener has been prepared beforehand by good training in the direction of loving the right things – just as earth must be prepared beforehand if it is to receive seed (1179b23–6).[14] But this preparation can only take place through some orderly system of education; and in this same chapter Aristotle argues that the training that a child receives within the immediate family is not enough. 'To get correct guidance towards excellence from childhood is difficult for someone who is not brought up under such laws' (1179b31–2), for only laws can supply the element of compulsion that is necessary in order to check a young human being's natural hedonism and lack of discipline (1179b34ff.). 'The paternal command possesses neither the forceful nor the necessary; nor indeed does any command from a single person, unless that person is a king or something of the sort. But law has a necessitating power, being a rule (*logos*) from some sort of practical wisdom and insight' (1180a19–22).

Aristotle gives three further arguments for the importance of completing private education with a civic scheme. First, only the civic plan promises the consistency and uniformity that is highly important for the regulation of daily life. Whereas each set of parents might instill a different conception of the good, a common scheme will ensure that people who need to deal with one another throughout life will share values and ends. 'Since the end of the city is one, it is obvious that education as well must be one and the same for all, and that the direction of this should be in common and not private, the way that each person now privately takes charge of his own children, and with a private education, teaching what seems best to him' (*Politics* 1337a21–5). Second, a public scheme has a better chance of getting things *right* about human value, since it will be worked out by a legislator who is a reflective person of practical wisdom and has, let us hope, seriously considered all the alternatives (*EN* 1180a18–22, 29).[15] This may be too much to expect of the average parent (who possesses however, other complementary abilities, in particular the detailed knowledge of the character of the particular child, that make his personal engagement an equally necessary part of the educational process: 1180b7ff., cf. below). Finally, assuming that social excellence is a valuable part of human life, this fact will best be taught by the fostering of a common and not a private scheme: 'It is not good that each one of the citizens should consider himself to be his own: all should believe themselves to belong to the city – for each one is a part of the city' (*Pol.* 1337a27–9). Of these arguments, the third and probably the first depend on the antecedent acceptance of Aristotle's other arguments for the human value of the political: for if it were not otherwise valuable we could choose a life in which we did not have to deal with one another socially and hence would not require a uniform conception of the good; and, again, if it is not valuable it will be bad rather than good for a scheme of education to teach children that it is. But Aristotle shows that our acceptance of this value generates further reasons to value it: only it can best promote its own continuity.

To value a public scheme of education is to value something both vulnerable and difficult to realize. Aristotle's arguments against prevailing custom in *Politics* VIII make it clear that anything approaching adequate general practice is rare. And even if it is possible to become good in less ideal surroundings, cultural instability of a sort familiar in his time will frequently bring practice below the threshold of acceptability. Furthermore, even in a good and stable culture, because of economic necessity there will always be those who, living the life of manual laborers, will be debarred by the exigencies of their daily work from having the education that is requisite for full human excellence. 'If one is living the life of a craftsman or hired servant, it is not possible to practice the things belonging to excellence' (*Pol.* 1278a20–1; cf. 1329a39–41). Even the life of a farmer is not compatible with full excellence, 'for leisure is required both for the coming-to-be of excellence and for political activities' (1329a1–2). But craftsmen, hired servants, and farmers will always be needed for the sake of survival and prosperity. The conclusion that we must draw from these facts is that even in a good city the best human life cannot be open to all, since it requires conditions that cannot at any one time be distributed to all.[16] Aristotle, looking upon these difficult facts, does not conclude that these social conditions cannot, after all, be genuine necessary conditions for excellence. He concludes instead that, even though excellence *should* be available, as he has said, to all who are not naturally unable to attain it, that is not, for all people, the way the world is. Some injustice is required by the exigencies of social life itself under contingent existing economic conditions. To put things this way is, in his view, better than to define the good in terms of the possible: first, because it provides an incentive to the legislator to work against these limitations as much as possible; second, because to aim only at what is, for everyone, 'commensurate with life' is to aim at a lower and impoverished mark.

Suppose now that we have a person who has been well brought up under good laws. His character is well developed, he has generally good attachments. How important is participation in the political community for the continuation of excellence? Here, once again, Aristotle gives the *polis* and our activities in and for it an important role. First of all, moral growth does not come to an abrupt stop when a young person reaches a certain chronological age, or even a certain high developmental stage. In his discussions both of politics and of *philia*, Aristotle depicts growth as an ongoing process that requires continued support from without. This is most urgently true for adults who remain morally immature;

but it appears to be to some extent true even for the very best. 'It is probably not sufficient for people to have correct nurture and attention when they are young, but even when they are grown up they need to practice these things and to go on forming habits. And for this we would need laws – and in general for the entire course of life' (*EN* 1180a1–4). Good character, once well started, is something relatively stable; but we have seen that reversals can corrupt it. The books on *philia* will bear this out in their talk of the character changes, both good and bad, brought about by the influence of associates.

These are ways in which civic activity and the presence of good political surroundings prove instrumentally necessary for the development and maintenance of good character. We may now add that even if we grant the agent a stable good adult character, favorable political conditions are required instrumentally for him or her to *act* well according to excellence. A slave, however good in character, is deprived of choice, therefore of something essential for living well. A slave is a human being who does not live according to his own choice (*Pol.* 1317b3, 13; 1280a32–4). 'Although he is a human being, he is someone else's, not his own' (1254a14–15). For these reasons, Aristotle denies that slaves can share in *eudaimonia*, which requires that excellent activities be chosen by the agent's own practical reason, and chosen for their own sake (1280a33).[17] Nor can they share in the highest sort of *philia*, which is based on mutual respect for choice and character.[18] For these reasons, Aristotle argues that no person who has the natural capacity for practical reason should be held in slavery (1252a32, 1255a25). Although he recognizes that there are some more or less human creatures who might be called 'natural slaves', and might appropriately be held in slavery because they 'do not have the deliberative faculty at all' (1260a12, 1254b20), nonetheless he, in effect, condemns as unjust most of the actual practice of slavery in his culture, since that in fact consisted in holding in bondage perfectly reasonable and reasoning people who simply happened to be captured in war.*

Even less extreme social impediments can diminish *eudaimonia*. Aristotle's remarks about manual labor and leisure probably imply that a well-trained adult who is suddenly thrust into this monotonous and degrading life will not only suffer an impairment of good activity (as is obvious), but will also risk, as time goes on, suffering a decisive impairment of character itself. For a while such a person might 'make the best of' these conditions, in the way that *Nicomachean Ethics* I suggests (cf. Ch. 11). In such a case, the impairment of activity need not dislodge the person from *eudaimonia*, bringing about a 'decisive change of life'. But if the restrictions are severe and prolonged enough, *eudaimonia* will be impeded: either through impairment of activity alone, or through the defilement of excellence itself.

All these are ways in which full participation in a well-functioning *polis* is a

---

* It is not too likely that Aristotle *believes* most actual slaves to be capable of practical reason, hence unjustly enslaved. He sets very stringent criteria for slave-holding, criteria which *in fact* imply that most actual Greek practice is unjust. But his application of his own criteria may be marred by prejudice and xenophobia.

necessary condition for the development and exercise of the individual's other excellences. But we must now add that Aristotle believes the political participation of the citizen to be itself an intrinsic good or end, without which a human life, though flourishing with respect to other excellences, will be incomplete. To some extent we see this in the emphasis he places upon justice and equity in his account of the excellences of character. These excellences are clearly of central importance; and, as with all excellences, their activities must be chosen 'for their own sake', not merely instrumentally. Most of Aristotle's examples of these activities are political in nature. But private life provides at least some scope for the exercise of these virtues; and we might easily imagine that a non-citizen, for example a resident alien like Aristotle himself, could live a perfectly full and good human life, so long as his private choices were not unduly constrained. Aristotle's own private autonomy and excellence of life seems to have been little impaired by his failure to participate as a citizen in Athenian public life.

Aristotle does not agree with this suggestion. He apparently does not regard the actual holding of political office as necessary for full adult good living: for he says in the *Magna Moralia* that the good person will frequently yield his opportunity for office-holding to another who might make better use of it (1212a34ff.). But he plainly imagines this man as having a *claim* to office: he actively *yields* this claim to the other. (His name is in the lottery, though he may give away the prize when his name is drawn.) Aristotle does, plainly believe that to be deprived of the *chance* for office is a diminution of good living. He speaks of the resident alien (using an Homeric quotation) as an 'alien without honor (*timē*)', a wanderer in his own country, on the grounds that he 'does not have a share in political office (*timē*)' (*Pol.* 1278a34–8).[19] We must recall at this point that the Greek *polis* was both more pervasive and more immediate than a modern democratic regime. Its values organized and permeated the entire lives of its citizens, including their moral education; and it could truthfully be said that the average individual citizen did have a real share in shaping and controlling these. To be deprived of this chance is, then, not to be deprived of something peripheral to good living, but to be alienated from the ground and basis for good living itself. And this is, Aristotle reasonably concludes, to lack an intrinsic value. He therefore sets himself to plan a city in which citizenship will be available to all those who are not deprived of natural abilities essential for living well, and in which all citizens will have, as single individuals, an active role in the shaping of the institutions that govern them.[20]

Aristotle's defense of the intrinsic value of the political emerges in another context as well. This is in his articulation of the claim that to be political is a part of human nature. It is worth examining these famous passages, asking exactly what they are establishing and by what sort of argument. For it has sometimes been thought that here Aristotle turns aside from the scrutiny of shared human beliefs about ethical value and grounds a normative account of ethical value on a bedrock of value-neutral scientific fact concerning our nature as humans.[21] If this were so it would require some revision in our account of Aristotle's ethical procedures;

so it is worth getting clear about just how an appeal to our nature really works in the context of an ethical argument.

The force and point of the arguments in the *Politics* and the *EN* that appeal to the political nature of the human being is to defend the intrinsic value of the political against an opponent who has conceded it only instrumental value. The opponent says that a solitary or apolitical life is entirely sufficient for human *eudaimonia* if one has no *need* for the good things that the political supplies. Aristotle replies that the political is itself one of the good things, something without which a human life would be incomplete. The claim that the political is a part of our *nature* appears to be equivalent to the claim that a life without it is lacking in an important good, is seriously frustrated or incomplete. It is a conspicuous feature of the style of these passages that they appeal as explicitly and emphatically as any in the corpus to shared belief: 'it appears', 'it seems', 'they say' are used repeatedly, casting doubt at once on the suggestion that we are appealing to a neutral or detached expert. Second, the features of ordinary belief to which appeal is made are in large measure ethical and evaluative in their content. They are beliefs about what is worthwhile, what is praiseworthy, what impoverished.

Two passages in the *EN* defend the naturalness of interpersonal association against the claim that the self-sufficient solitary is fully *eudaimōn*. Of these, the first speaks only of the naturalness of *philia* (1155a16–23). The second speaks of the naturalness of the *politikon*, but in the context of defending the importance of personal *philia*. We shall therefore examine it in more detail later on. But we can now examine the sentence in which the political claim is made:

And surely it is peculiar to make the *makarios* a solitary: for nobody would choose to have all the good things in the world all by himself. For the human being is a political creature and naturally disposed to living-with (1169b16–19).

Aristotle appeals here, clearly, not to some separate realm of natural fact, but to our deepest judgments of value: the solitary life is insufficient for *eudaimonia* because we would not find such a life choiceworthy or sufficient for us. The solitary view of *eudaimonia* is at odds with the choices we make and the beliefs that we share. If *eudaimonia* is to include every value without which a life would be judged incomplete, it must include the political as an end in its own right. The sentence about our political *nature* indicates to us, furthermore, that political choices and concerns lie so deep that they are a part of what we *are*. The solitary life would not only be less than perfect; it would also be lacking in something so fundamental that we could hardly call it a human life at all. The appeal to nature thus underlines the depth and importance of the element in question. Without it we are not even ourselves. To choose a life without it is to depart so much from ourselves that we could hardly say that *we* still go on in such a life. To find out about our nature seems to be one and the same with finding out what we believe to be the most important and indispensable elements of our lives.[22]

The appeal to the political nature of the human being in *Politics* I seems to tell the same story. Again, the claim that the *polis* exists by nature works to defend the intrinsic value of this constituent of human life. Aristotle states the general principle that if X is part of the nature of creature C, then no account of the ends of C's life would be complete without mention of X, and no account of the sort of self-sufficiency appropriate for Cs could omit X (1252b31–1253a1). An argument that the political is a part of our nature would, then, rule out (as in the *EN*) the view that the solitary life can be sufficient for *eudaimonia*, provided that this life has no further instrumental needs. Aristotle next advances some reasons for thinking that to be *politikon* is a part of our nature:

...It is evident that...the human being is by nature a political animal, and that the person who is citiless through nature (*apolis dia phusin*) and not through luck is either an inferior creature or greater than a human being: just like the person denounced by Homer as 'clanless, without customs, without a hearth' – for this person is in his very nature (*hama phusei*) of such a sort and a lover of war, being 'unyoked' like a piece in the dice-game. (1253a1–7)

Shortly before this, Aristotle had made reference to Homer's Cyclopes, whose specific difference from us is constituted by their lack of social and political concern alone (1252b20–4; cf. *EN* 1180a28–9). He thus reminded his audience of the depth of a tradition of thought about the human being according to which an anthropomorphic being who lacked social concerns would not be classified as human.[23] Now he goes a step further, considering a Homeric line that in fact refers to a being whom any modern scientist would classify as, technically, a member of the species *homo sapiens* – not, then, a mythical creature like the Cyclops – and reminds his audience of the way in which their greatest sage Nestor (and their most authoritative poet Homer) denounces this being and relegates him to a distant place of inferiority. If it is really his *nature* to be a solitary and to love war for its own sake, not just as a means, then, Aristotle says, he is either below or above our kind, but he is not of it. If we encountered such a being, asocial not through accident or frustration but in his natural inclinations, we would not count him as one of us, accord to him the treatment we accord our fellow humans. And if all this is so, then it seems likely that to act politically is an end in itself for human beings and a constituent of human *eudaimonia*. Deprived of this, we are leading a life that does not suit us; we are frustrated and cut off from a part of what we are. All of this is drawn, clearly, from deep and prevalent ordinary beliefs, the beliefs that are reflected and further explored in our most cherished myths and stories.[24]

In *EN* v (1129b26ff.), Aristotle goes one step further. Investigating the nature of justice, *dikaiosunē*, he tells us that in one sense it is the 'most authoritative' of the excellences and is the same as 'complete excellence' itself, in that all excellence has an other-related or social aspect. *Qua* other-related, all excellence deserves the name of justice. Aristotle seems to be claiming that with only solitary concerns, without the excellence that consists in having an appropriate regard for the good of others, a human being will lack not just one important human end, he will lack all of the excellences – for each is, as he says, a thing 'in relation to others' (*pros heteron*) as well as 'in relation to oneself' (*pros hauton*). Aristotle here uses Platonic terminology in a deliberately anti-Platonic way: where Plato had insisted that no true value is a relational (*pros heteron*) item, Aristotle now insists that all true excellence of character has a relational nature: without making political and other-related concerns ends in themselves, one will lack not only justice but also true courage, true moderation, true generosity, greatness of soul, conviviality, and so forth. For a creature whose conception of the ultimate good made mention only of his own good would not be able to possess any of these items in the true sense (as the *Rhetoric* discussion of trust and excellence has indicated already). The idea seems to be something like this. True courage (as opposed to mere brashness) requires an appropriate, which is to say more than merely instrumental, concern for the well-being of one's country and fellow citizens; true moderation (as opposed to crafty pleasure-seeking) requires the proper (and this is non-instrumental) respect for standing norms of convivial and sexual interaction; true generosity a non-crafty concern for the good of the recipient; and so forth. In each case, one cannot choose these excellent activities as ends in themselves (as the definition of excellence requires), without also choosing the good of others as an end. Deprived of this end, then, we lack not a part of our good, we lack the whole.

Aristotle has, then, argued that an investigation of the 'appearances' reveals that social and other-related activity possesses both instrumental and intrinsic value for human beings. He does not regard the evident riskiness and instability of these values in the world as a reason to rule them out of the best life by fiat, or to conclude, against the evidence of intuitive beliefs and poetic stories, that the person who loses them has lost nothing of serious value. Instead he views these facts about politics and society as giving a reason for competent and serious people to turn their attentions to legislation and political planning. Instead of reducing our demands on the world so that they will more consistently be met, we ought, he believes, to increase our activity in and towards the world so that it will more regularly meet our high demands. Instead of decreeing in advance that the only important things are the ones that are already under human control, we try to increase our human control over the important things. This would be the proper way for a human being to pursue self-sufficiency.[25]

We should notice, however, that Aristotle's interest in stability in political life is tempered by his concern for other social values, such as the autonomy of individual choice and civic vitality. Among the available conceptions of the *polis* he does not opt for one that would seek to maximize stability and unity by turning over all choice-making to a single person or a small group. Against Platonic efforts to eliminate conflict and instability through minimizing the legislative engagement of separate wills, Aristotle defends a conception of the city as a 'plurality', an association of 'free and equal' citizens who rule and are ruled by turns.[26] He defends this conception on grounds of justice, pointing to the fundamental role played by separateness and personal choice in any good human life; and he also claims that such an association will possess a superior vitality and richness, since human beings are more profoundly motivated to attend to and care about things by the thought that the object of care is in some important way *theirs* (*Pol.* 1262b22ff., 1261b16ff.). Finally, he does not urge cities to cultivate stability at the expense of a commitment to excellence, avoiding noble endeavors or large projects because of the risks these entail. His evident admiration for the policies of Periclean Athens reveals a preference for ambitious endeavor over conservative safety. As in the private sphere, where he defends the nobility of self-sacrifice for an excellent end, so, too, in the public he is willing to put achievement over safety.

In one further way, Aristotle's city refuses to eliminate risk. We have spoken so far here of his defense of the fragility of individual components of the good life. We should now add that in his good city the possibility of contingent conflict of values is preserved as a condition of the richness and vigor of civic life itself. Plato attempted to eliminate the risk of conflict between family and city by making the only family the city. Aristotle defends the importance of the intimate bonds of family love, as we shall shortly see, arguing that interpersonal bonds in a city that lacked this possibility for conflict would be simply 'watery' (1262b15ff.). Plato attempted to eliminate, as grounds of conflict, both private property and the exclusiveness of sexual relations (cf. Ch. 5 §v, pp. 158–60). Aristotle, here again, argues that to do this is to deprive civic life of sources of motivation and concern that could be found in no other way. Plato he aptly says, tried to make the city a unity in the way that a single organic body is a unity: with a single good, a single conception of 'one's own', a single pleasure and pain (1261a16ff.). Aristotle argues at length that this sort of conflict-free unity is not the sort of unity appropriate to the *polis*, since it destroys personal separateness, an essential ingredient of human social goodness. A city is by nature a plurality of separate parts (1261a18–22). To make it one in the Platonic way is to eliminate the bases of political justice and of *philia*, two of its central goods. For there is no justice between the elements of a single organic whole. The idea of justice as distribution presupposes the separateness of the parties and of their interests (cf. *MM* 1194b5–23, *EN* 1134b1ff.). Therefore, even if it were possible to eliminate the bases of conflict, making all citizens say 'mine' and 'not-mine' as a single body, we should not do this: it would mean the destruction of the values proper to the city (1261b25–6, 31–2, 1332a36–7).

We find, then, in Aristotle's thought about the civilized city, an idea we first encountered in the *Antigone*: the idea that the value of certain constituents of the good human life is inseparable from a risk of opposition, therefore of conflict. To have them adequately is to have them plural and separate (cf. Ch. 10 §ii); to have them in this way is to risk strife. But to unify and harmonize, removing the bases of conflict, is to remove value as well. The singleness of Creon's simplification or even Hegel's synthesis – even if successful – impoverishes the world.

II

Philoi, says Aristotle, are 'the greatest of the external goods' (*EN* 1169b10). To the topic of *philia* he devotes one-fifth of each of his two major ethical works – more space than is devoted to any other single topic.[27] We need to begin our study of this external good with two verbal points. We have indicated (cf. Ch. 11, p. 328) that we are not going to follow the usual practice of translating *philia* as 'friendship', *philos* as 'friend'. We now need to give more fully the reasons for this. The first reason is extensional: *philia* includes many relationships that would not be classified as friendships. The love of mother and child is a paradigmatic case of *philia*; all close family relations, including the relation of husband and wife, are so characterized. Furthermore, our 'friendship' can suggest a relationship that is weak in affect relative to some other relationship, as in the expression 'just friends'. Aristotle deals with relationships of varying degrees of intimacy and depth; a few of them may be weak in affect. But *philia* includes the very strongest affective relationships that human beings form; it includes, furthermore, relationships that have a passionate sexual component. For both of these reasons, English 'love' seems more appropriately wide-ranging. So where we translate, we shall speak of love. But we must notice from the start that Aristotle's choice of a central word reveals something about what he values in human relationships. For the emphasis of *philia* is less on intensely passionate longing than on disinterested benefit, sharing, and mutuality; less on madness than on a rare kind of balance and harmony.

A second translation problem is more intractable. In English, partners to a love relationship are linguistically divided into the active and the passive: we have 'lover' or 'person who loves', and we have 'loved one'.[28] Greek *philos* makes no active/passive distinction. And mutuality will in fact be an important part of Aristotle's conception of *philia* and the *philos*. (In this respect, English 'friend' is better off.) I shall, therefore, frequently use transliteration, in order to preserve the unity of active and passive elements.

Love is, in its very nature, a relationship with something separate and external.[29] This externality, which Aristotle sees as essential to the benefits and value of love, is also, plainly, a source of great vulnerability. And yet it is to this external-dependent and risky part of human life that Aristotle devotes more sustained attention than to any other of the human excellences. He devotes to love, furthermore, not only space, but tremendous emphasis. He insists that *philia* is 'most necessary for life' (*EN* 1155a4). And not only necessary but also intrinsically good and fine – for 'we praise those who love their *philoi*, and having many *philoi* seems to be one of the intrinsically fine things. Indeed, we think the very same people are good people and good *philoi*' (1155a28–32). We need to characterize the relationship that is the subject of these large claims, and then to examine each of the claims in more detail.

Not every case in which a person likes or even intensely loves something or someone is, Aristotle insists, a genuine case of *philia*. For example, the lover of wine may really love the wine; but he or she is not a *philos* of the wine, for two reasons: 'There is no return of love, and there is no wishing the good for the other's own sake. For it is surely ridiculous to wish the good for the wine – or if one does, what one wants is for it to be preserved so that one can have it. But they say that the *philos* must wish the good for the other's own sake' (1155b27–31). We find in this passage two requirements for *philia*. The first is mutuality: *philia* is a relation, not a one-way street; its benefits are inseparable from sharing and the return of benefit and affection. The second is independence: the object of *philia* must be seen as a being with a separate good, not as simply a possession or extension of the *philos*; and the real *philos* will wish the other well for the sake of that separate good. The connoisseur loves the wine as his own possession, as a part of his good. *Philoi*, by contrast, should be separate and independent; they ought to be, and to see one another as, separate centers of choice and action. Elsewhere Aristotle tells us that for these reasons there is no genuine *philia* between master and slave: the slave is like 'something of' the master, an extension of the master's own good. He or she is not regarded as a separate seat of choice, whose *eudaimonia* it is the business of the relation to promote.

Philia requires, then, mutuality in affection; it requires separateness and a mutual respect for separateness; it requires mutual well-wishing for the other's own sake and, as the *Rhetoric* definition tells us, mutual benefiting in action, insofar as this is possible (*Rhet.* 1380b35–1381a1).[30] Aristotle completes his general sketch of *philia* by adding that there must be mutual awareness of these good feelings and good wishes: *philia* must be distinguished from the sort of mutual admiration that could obtain between people who had no knowledge at all of one another.[31] These people know each other, feel emotion for one another, wish and act well towards one another, and know that these relationships of thought, emotion, and action obtain between them (1155b28–1156a5).

A number of different types of love meet, after a fashion, these conditions.[32] For the persons involved may wish one another well on the basis of various different specifications or conceptions of one another. They may each, for example, think of the other simply, or primarily, as someone who is pleasant or fun to be with; in this case they will take no further or deeper interests in one another's character and aspirations. Or they may think of one another as useful to their other projects (as might be the case between business partners), and still have, again, no deeper mutual knowledge or attachment. Such relationships will not be merely exploitative: for we recall that without mutuality of genuine well-wishing for the other person's own sake the relationship will not deserve the title of *philia* at all.*

---

* Here it is important to distinguish three things: the *basis* or *ground* of the relationship (the thing 'through (*dia*) which' they love); its *object*; and its *goal* or *end*. Pleasure, advantage, and good character are three different bases or original grounds of *philia*; they are not the goal or final (intentional) end of the relationship. In other words, the two people are friends 'through' or 'on the basis of' these, but the goal they try to achieve in action will still be some sort of mutual benefit. Pleasure and advantage-friendships, while not perfect, are importantly distinct from exploitative relationships, in which the parties aim each at their own pleasure, and not at all at the other's good. The *object* of the relation in all cases is the other person; but the person will be conceived of and known in a way bounded by the basis: as someone who is pleasant to be with, as a person well-placed for useful dealings, as a person of good character. Thus the two inferior types aim at benefit for the other only under a thin and superficial description of the other.

There can be genuinely disinterested mutual benefit in cases where the basis of attachment is shallow and partial. Business partners may give one another gifts and entertain one another; young lovers, knowing only one another's pleasantness, may still genuinely contribute, unselfishly, to one another's good. But then, Aristotle says, the relationship will be connected only incidentally to the central aims and aspirations of each member. It will lack depth, since it is not directed at what that other person really is 'in himself', at the goals, values, and characteristics with which he primarily identifies himself. It will also be unstable, since its basis is one that the person could easily cease to have while remaining in deeper ways unchanged (cf. *EN* 1157a8ff.). Business partners frequently care for one another not only as means to profit; but take away the profit context, and the friendship, unless it has deepened into another sort, will falter. Lovers who know only the surface features of one another's pleasantness will, similarly, be easily derailed by a change in looks or by circumstances that put a strain on enjoyment.

The central and best case of love between persons is that of love based upon character and conception of the good. Here each partner loves the other for what that other most deeply is in him or herself (*kath' hauto*), for those dispositions and those patterns of thought and feeling that are so intrinsic to his being himself that a change in them would raise questions of identity and persistence.[33] And of course such a relationship will be richer in goodness if the characteristics that are its basis are themselves good. Such a relationship, Aristotle makes clear, will involve strong feeling. In many cases it will also involve mutual pleasure and advantage. But since its basis is deeper than these transient and incidental features, we can expect it to be stable, enduring, and to have an intimate connection with each person's plans for living well.

Aristotle has by now quite calmly described and praised a relationship whose very existence was called into question by Plato's *Symposium*. For there (most explicitly in Socrates' speeches, but to some extent in the others as well) the desire to possess and control was held to be an intrinsic part of all love, both personal and philosophical. Jealousy and the fear of loss were, in consequence, endemic to even the best loves; they could be controlled only by turning love towards objects stabler and less willful than persons. Aristotle reminds us that there is a kind of human love that really does care for and foster the separate good of another, that desires the independent continued motion, rather than the immobility, of its object. (This kind of love, linking activity with passivity, aspiration with receptivity to the actions of the other, looks close to the love described in the *Phaedrus* – though it lacks, as we shall later observe, that dialogue's emphasis on mad passion.) It is the love of someone who is content to live in a world in which other beings move themselves – who desires to continue to be a part of such a complex world, not controlling the whole, but acting towards and being acted on by its separately moving pieces. In the existence of such moving external pieces, it discovers much of the value and richness of life. It does not aspire to be the only motion there is.

Nor does the Aristotelian lover aspire to the condition of stone, of freedom from affect. He or she is not erotic in the sense given that word by the *Symposium*; for he does not desire not to desire, and not to be in the world of happening. His desire is to remain moving and desiring in the world, and to continue to receive the desiring activity of the other. It is a relationship that expresses, in the structure of its desires, a love for the world of change and motion, for *orexis* itself, and therefore for the needy and non-self-sufficient elements of our condition.[34] As Aristotle movingly reminds us, a *philos* does not wish either himself or his *philos* transformed into a needless god (1159a5ff., 1166a19ff.). First, if only one were transformed, this would put too much distance between them. Second, and more important, the transformation would make the *philos* into a different sort of creature. 'If it was well said that the *philos* wishes the *philos* good things for his own sake, he would have to remain the sort of being he is; so it is as a human being that he will wish him the greatest of goods' (1159a8–12). To be non-godlike, needy, orectic, is seen as a necessary part of what it is to be oneself and a *philos*. *Philia*, loving the whole of another person for that person's own sake, loves humanity and mutability as well as excellence. Platonic *erōs* seeks wholeness; *philia* embraces the half.

The best *philos* does seek repeatable traits of character in the object. But this search is different in several ways from the search enjoined by Diotima. First, he or she seeks out many traits that could have no part in a divine or perfect life: above all, perhaps, virtues which, like justice and generosity, are specifically and only human, and are bound up with our condition of neediness. He knows that to wish away human need would also be to wish away those virtues. Second, he sees and attends to those repeatable traits differently: not as pieces of something homogeneous that turns up in many places in the universe, but as forming the essential core of what that concrete person is. He attends to virtues and aspirations because those are the deepest things that go to make another individual the individual he is. He searches not for isolable bits of a form, but for the combination of traits and aspirations that make the wholeness of a person's character. And he does this because his desire is not to stop with the superficial, but to know that person through and through. Finally, as we shall shortly see, he cares as well about features of the person that do not appear to be repeatable: the pleasure of sharing that person's company; and, above all, the specialness of their shared history of mutual pleasure and mutual activity. Aristotle, then, reminds us that deep love, to be deep, must embrace character and value; that the real individuality of another person is not just something ineffable and indescribable; among its most important constituents are excellences that can be shared by others. Aristotle stresses these shared elements, then, not in order to bypass the individuality in love, but in order to give a richer account of what that individuality comes to.

To these requirements for the best type of love, Aristotle adds one more. To love one another in the best way, the way most relevant to a good human life overall, these *philoi* must 'live together', sharing activities both intellectual and social, sharing the enjoyment, and the mutual recognition of enjoyment, that comes of spending time with someone whom they find both wonderful and delightful. This, he says, is 'the most chosen thing' among *philoi*:

> For love is a sharing... And whatever each of them takes to be living or that for the sake of which they choose living, in this they wish to live with their *philos*. This is why some drink together, some play dice together, some exercise and go hunting together, or do philosophy together – each spending time in that which each particularly loves in life. For they want to live with their *philoi*, and they do these things and share in them with those with whom they want to live. (*EN* 1171b32–1172a8)

What does Aristotle mean by 'living together'? Little has been written about this requirement, so crucial to our understanding of this love's vulnerability. It is sometimes assumed that Aristotle is speaking of 'friendship' as we know it in our fast-moving society – in which little more is frequently required than regular visiting, socializing, discussing. Part of the reason for this reading is that Aristotle's highest *philoi* are, each of them, imagined (by Aristotle himself) as two males, each of whom has a wife and children (who, on account of alleged inequalities, cannot be *philoi* with him in the highest sense); and each clearly *lives with*, in the literal sense, these lower-order *philoi*. But we should notice that Aristotle speaks emphatically of the best *philoi* 'spending their days together' (*sunēmereuein*, 1158a9, 1171a5), of 'going through time together' (*sundiagein*, 1157b22); he speaks of the importance of thorough experience of the other's character and habits (*sunētheia*), developed by regular and familiar association (*homilia*). He also insists that it is the sort of day-to-day association that will be hard to maintain if you do not find the person pleasant and attractive (1157b22–3). In one important passage he contrasts *philoi* with more casual associates: 'Those who receive each other but do not live together are more like well-wishers than like *philoi*. For there is nothing so characteristic of love as living together' (1157b17–19).

This contrast is intelligible only on the understanding that Aristotle means by 'living together' something more than regular social visiting: if not residence in the same household, then at least a regular, even daily association in work and conversation. This would prominently include association in the usually intense political activity of the *polis*. If he had not had his views about female inferiority, he would very likely have preferred this sharing to extend into the sphere of the household as well: thus an even more perfect *philia* would be a good marriage, in which the full range of the aspirations and concerns that make up a human life might be accommodated. The relationships that Aristotle describes may or may not include sexual involvement. Aristotle says little on this point; and, unlike Plato, he does not appear to believe that intense sexual desire or excitement plays any essential role in the values and benefits of love. But he insists that this love does and must include taking pleasure in the physical presence of the other in whatever way one enjoys or values so doing.[35] The ideal is a thoroughgoing and unconstrained sharing in *all* activities that people judge to be pertinent to their human good living. This should, then, include all activities according to the recognized excellences of character; and this would include appropriate eating, drinking, and choosing of sexual pleasures; appropriate distribution of money; appropriate party-giving (*megaloprepeia*); appropriate joke-telling (*eutrapelia*) – as well as appropriate reflecting, legislating, meeting danger. It is one of the distinctions of Aristotle's thought to see in the everyday and the apparently trivial a scene for the expression of human excellence; then humans who love another for their excellence will want to share even in the humble and mundane. It seems, then, that the best way to live with a *philos* is one that allows sharing in all of these activities.

All this makes it abundantly clear that the best sort of love between persons is highly vulnerable to happenings in the world. Indeed, we wonder how often the world has ever allowed such thoroughgoing intimacy to flourish. It is worth pausing to enumerate the sources of that vulnerability. First, there is the luck of finding, in the first place, a loved one to value. Since the most fulfilling loves occur between two people of similar character and aspirations who also find each other physically, socially, and morally attractive and who are able to live in the same place for an extended period of time, this is no small matter. Aristotle calmly points out that people who are physically ugly will have a hard time at this.[36] Nor does he think that good characters are easily found. 'It is probable', he writes, 'that such relationships [sc. between two people of good character] will be rare: for people of that sort are few' (1156b24–5).

Next, the two must find themselves able to trust one another. That is, they must be able to receive one another's expressions of love without suspicion, jealousy, or fearful self-protectiveness. The suspicion of hypocrisy and falsity undermines love (*Rhet.* 1381b28–9); and 'nobody loves the person whom he fears' (1381b33) – presumably because *philia* requires a kind of openness and receptivity that is incompatible with fear. Aristotle repeatedly stresses this requirement of trust as essential to true *philia*. He stresses that it takes time and experience of the other person (*EN* 1156b29, *EE* 1237b12); and it also requires the presence of really good characters on both sides – for bad character does not generally inspire confidence (*MM* 1208b29). We can add, in the spirit of the *Rhetoric* discussion of the young and old, that it appears to require, in addition, generally fortunate circumstances of life, which are not universally available. For a repeatedly betrayed or disappointed person will be fearful and suspicious of everything. Circumstances for which the person is not to blame can, then, inhibit or distort the openness of response that is basic to this valuable relationship.[37] We shall see again in the next chapter how important this fact is, as a source of *philia*'s vulnerability.

Then the basis of the love, and trust in this basis, must remain constant, or the love will be undermined. This is a reasonable hope in love based on knowledge of character – as it would not be in a more superficial sort of love. But even adult character is not altogether fixed and immutable, as Aristotle acknowledges when he speaks of changes for the better and for the worse, of divisions, quarrels, and reproaches – all this within the account of character-love. He speaks of deceptions, of the painful discovery that the two have seriously misinterpreted one another's motives and intentions (1162b5ff., 1165a36ff.). He speaks of the danger that similarity of aspiration may lead to competitiveness and rivalry, undermining the basis of love (*Rhet.* 1381b15). Even if all goes well internally, he continues, two of the people you love may quarrel *with one another*, forcing you to make painful choices (1171a4–6). Finally, there are limits set by contingency to the number of people you can adequately love and to the amount of time and care you can lavish on each. Given our human finitude, our shortness of time, loves compete with one another. 'It is obvious that it is not possible to live with a number of people and parcel oneself out', Aristotle concludes with characteristic simplicity (1171a2–3).[38]

Even a stable ongoing attachment is almost certain to be affected by fortune in one way or another. There are, he tells us, necessary absences, which, at first, 'dissolve not the love *simpliciter*, but its activity' (1157b10–11). This impediment to a valued activity may already diminish *eudaimonia*. Furthermore, 'if the absence is of long duration, it appears to bring about forgetfulness of the love itself'. Aristotelian love is not like romantic infatuation; for it is based on enduring elements of the person. But it has a strong affective element, which is central to its continuity; and it is focused upon the aim to live and act together throughout a shared history. For these two reasons, unlike a Kantian 'practical love' that is based upon the sense of duty, it can be disrupted by departures.

Even if two people who love one another manage to live together all their lives, the damages of old age, which can neither be avoided nor even be precisely foreseen, happening to the two of them either at the same time or at different times, bring about a loss in sensitivity and in enjoyment that can lead to the dissolution or at least the diminution of love. We have seen to what extent the accumulation of worldly experiences can, in elderly people, impair the trust that is *philia*'s necessary basis, and impair, too, the virtues that are at the heart of its conception of its object. Now we can add that, even where this does not happen, age damages the relation. Aristotle has insisted on distinguishing *philia* from the less intimate relationship of mutual well-wishing and mutual helping: the former, requiring living-together, also requires a mutuality in pleasure. He now advances this difference as a reason for believing that elderly people, though they may still wish each other well, will not be likely to form or to maintain the closer relationship of love. 'For their capability for enjoyment is short, and nobody can spend his days with someone who is annoying or not pleasant to be with' (1157b14–16). Later he repeats the point. 'Among elderly people and people of an austere disposition, love does not very often happen, insofar as they are bad-tempered and take rather little pleasure in society...For people do not come to love those whose company they do not enjoy...Such people can be well-disposed to one another, for they wish one another good things and help one another in time of need. But they are not likely to love one another, since they do not spend their days together or take pleasure in one another' (1158a1ff.).[39] Aristotle's insistence on the importance of the non-rational and 'pathological' element in intimate love (both in keeping it going and constituting, itself, a part of its value) leads him to the conclusion that this relationship, which is of the highest ethical importance and value, can be blighted by bodily changes that we cannot control. We can all look forward to the loss of a high value, if we live long enough.

And even if love should survive life's changes, there is always death, which generally comes to some before others, diminishing the goodness of the survivor's life. 'Nobody will entirely live well (be *eudaimonikos*)', Aristotle had said in *EN* I, 'if he is...both solitary and childless; still less, perhaps, if he has terribly bad children or *philoi*, or has good ones who die' (1099b2–4, cf. *Rhet.* 1386a9–11). Such a loss, he now implies, can be so deep that it will make life itself seem not worth living, even if one has all the other goods (1155a5–6). A Kantian or a (middle-period) Platonist would agree with this as an unfortunate psychological fact about many people. Aristotle puts it forward as a rational and appropriate reaction, one that correctly responds to the value of personal affection in a good human life. We consider it a virtue in people, he observes, if they love their *philoi* equally both present and absent, both living and dead (*Rhet.* 1381b24–6). Grief, then, becomes a natural part of the best human life.[40]

By ascribing value to *philia* in a conception of the good life, we make ourselves more vulnerable to loss. And we can add one further point: we also, through our attachments, make ourselves susceptible to losses that are not, properly speaking, our own. A person with no strong attachments has only his or her own health, virtue, and success to worry about. A person who loves another will be grieved or made anxious by a double number of events and becomes doubly susceptible to luck, 'being pleased together by good things and grieved together by painful things, for no other reason than on account of the *philos* himself' (*Rhet.* 1381a4–6). 'To say that the fortunes of one's descendants and *philoi* do not have any impact seems excessively unloving (*aphilon*) and contrary to what we think' (*EN* 1101a22).

The middle-period Platonist (and the modern Kantian) might reply to this that the relationship described and praised by Aristotle cannot, then, be a central part of a morally good life, and cannot, therefore, be a source of high value and praiseworthiness in life. Any relationship in which emotional and physical response figures so prominently, any relationship that attends so thoroughly to the unique characteristics and histories of single persons, above all any relationship in which and because of which we are so thoroughly at the mercy of 'step-motherly nature' cannot be the sort of love on which we wish to build the good human life. The Kantian distinction between pathological and practical love[41] is intended to develop a conception of personal relations in which the moral good will reign supreme: to show us a love between persons that is still recognizably *love*, and yet is free of the elements that make Aristotelian love so fragile. Aristotle is, plainly, aware of attempts by Plato and others to replace deeply personal love by a more will-governed or reason-governed relationship, or by the solitary pursuit of goodness. If we cannot expect to find in his text answers to all of Kant's questions, at least we can expect of him some response to those questions that were already raised by his own contemporaries: What *is* the value of a close and intimate relationship between particular human beings? Why should we cultivate such relationships and give them a place in our conception of *eudaimonia*? What human value is it that only this fragile sort of love can provide?

Here again, we may divide Aristotle's arguments into two categories: those that defend the instrumental benefit of *philia* and those that defend its intrinsic value. We take the instrumental arguments first. First of all, close personal love plays a central instrumental role in the development of good character and appropriate aspiration. We have spoken already of the importance of a nurturing political context; but we can now add that Aristotle believes this context to be motivationally ineffective without the closer bonds of love that link members of a family with one another. The two strongest sources of human motivation, he tells us in Book II of the *Politics*, in criticism of Plato, are the idea that something is your own and the idea that it is the only one you have (1262b22ff., cf. *EN* 1180a3ff.). The intensity of concern that binds parents and children in the enterprise of moral education cannot simply be replaced by a communal system, though it must work, as we said, within one: for it is the thought that it is *your own* child, not someone else's, together with the thought that you are unique and irreplaceable for that child and that child for you, that most keenly spurs the parent to work and care for the education of the child, the child to work and care for the parent.[42] Love, furthermore, eases the difficult task of the educator: for gratitude and affection enhance the forcefulness of the parental command. 'Just as in cities customs and ways have force, so too in households do parental arguments and habits, and even more so because of relatedness and beneficence. For there is present beforehand a context of grateful love and a natural openness to persuasion' (*EN* 1180b3–7). Take intimacy and felt love away and you have, Aristotle concludes, only a 'watery' sort of concern all round, without the power to mold or transform a soul. The intimacy of *philia* will be so dispersed in a political scheme that does away with the nuclear family that its flavor will hardly be noticeable, and the resulting mixture will not have the character belonging with that flavor (*Pol.* 1262b15ff.).

EN x.9 adds to these considerations a further argument. Parental training has a superior ability to respond to the individuality of the child, achieving in this way a superior 'accuracy' (1180b7ff.): 'Each in this way will be more likely to receive what is beneficial.' This accuracy looks inseparable not only from closeness, but also from affective involvement: for it is surely through felt love that the parent is able to hit on what is appropriate for the particular child, not through a detached scientific scrutiny.

This special importance of the unique and irreplaceably close figures, as well, in adult love. Aristotle insists that people who love one another's character have a strong influence over one another's moral development, in several ways:

> The love of base people is harmful: for, being unstable, they share in base activities, and they become bad through assimilation to one another. But the love of good people is good and increases with their association. And they seem to become better by their activity and their correction of one another. For they model their tastes and values on one another's – from which we get the proverbial expression 'excellence from excellence'. (*EN* 1172a8–14)

This compressed passage suggests at least three mechanisms of mutual influence; and it is important to notice that all of them depend on the affective character of the relationship. The first and most direct mechanism is that of advice and correction. Aristotle's point here is that the advice of those we closely love has a special power for good or bad; this power is clearly bound up with the pleasure of the association, its shared feelings of concern and affection.

The second mechanism is the levelling or assimilating influence of shared activity: if the person you love loves and values a certain pursuit, you will be inclined to try to spend time sharing in that. This is a good thing if the pursuit is a good one, a bad thing if it is bad. Again, this mechanism operates as described only in an affectionate personal love, not in a Kantian duty-based relationship: for the mechanism requires the unique closeness of 'living-together' and the motivating feelings associated with that. Aristotle's point is that out of the many valuable and not-so-valuable pursuits in the world, we will often fall into certain ones and devote to them our time and concern just because a person whom we love likes to do it and cares about it. Since we love that person and want to share his or her time and activity, we have a strong motivation to cultivate our tastes and abilities in that direction. So if we make good selections of people to love, our own lives will be enriched; if we love impoverished people, they will be impoverished.

The third and final mechanism is one of emulation and imitation. The strong emotions of respect and esteem that are part of Aristotelian *philia* generate a desire to be more *like* the other person. This principle works powerfully in society, where shared public models of excellence play an important motivating role. But Aristotle clearly believes that the intimacy of personal *philia*, with its strong feelings and its history of shared living, has a motivational power through emulation that could not be replaced by a more general social modelling. His point is similar to one made by Phaedrus in the *Symposium*'s first speech, when he argued that an army composed of pairs of lovers would excel all others in excellence because of the strength of emulation and aspiration that can be generated by the presence of a uniquely loved person.

Other contexts contribute several more arguments for *philia*'s instrumental value. Associations of personal *philia*, Aristotle observes, give you a powerful resource towards anything you may wish to do. A loved friend, unlike a stranger, is someone to whom you can turn for help in adversity, care in old age, assistance in any project (1155a9ff.). Then too, sharing makes any valued activity more enjoyable and therefore more continuous. Human beings are not easily able to sustain interest and engagement in solitude: 'with others and towards others it is easier' (1170a5–7). Aristotle seems to be thinking here of the added pleasure and sustaining enjoyment that come from working along 'with others', side by side; he is thinking also of the way in which a kind of conversation, a sharing of the parts of the work, make it a work 'towards others', one in which the mutuality and pleasure of the personal relationship enter deeply into the work itself. The first would be the sort of encouragement you get just from, say, writing philosophy in the same department with a fellow philosopher who is also a personal friend; the second would be the deeper encouragement of philosophical discourse and collaboration with such a friend.[43]

Aristotle mentions one further benefit of friendly love, one that clearly could not be derived without the closeness of 'living together'. This is the increase in self-knowledge and self-perception that comes of seeing and intuitively responding to a person about whom you care. The *Magna Moralia*, which offers the clearest version of this part of Aristotle's argument,[44] says this:

> Now if someone, looking to his *philos*, should see what he is and of what sort of character, the *philos* – if we imagine a *philia* of the most intense sort – would seem to him to be like a second himself, as in the saying, 'This is my second Heracles.' Since, then, it is both a most difficult thing, as some of the sages have also said, to know oneself, and also a most pleasant thing (for to know oneself is pleasant) – moreover, we cannot ourselves study ourselves from ourselves, as is clear from the reproaches we bring against others without being aware that we do the same things ourselves – and this happens because of bias or passion, which in many of us obscure the accuracy of judgments; as, then, when we ourselves wish to see our own face we see it by looking into a mirror, similarly too, when we ourselves wish to know ourselves, we would know ourselves by looking to the *philos*. For the *philos*, as we say, is another oneself. If, then, it is pleasant to know oneself, and if it is not possible to know this without having someone else as a *philos*, the self-sufficient person would need *philia* in order to know himself. (1213a10–26)

Aristotle's argument begins from a fact of human psychology: it is difficult for each of us to see our own life clearly and without bias, assessing its patterns of action and commitment. Often we lack awareness of our own faults, because we are blinded by partiality and by involvement in our own feelings and concerns. It is therefore valuable to study the pattern of good character embodied in another good life: 'It is easier for us to look at someone else than at ourselves' (*EN* 1169b33–4). This reflective look at models of goodness enhances our understanding of our own character and aspirations, improving self-criticism and sharpening judgment. For this to be so, the model in question must be a person similar to ourselves in character and aspiration, someone whom we can identify to ourselves as 'another oneself' for the purposes of this scrutiny.[45]

But what is the significance of Aristotle's claim that this model self must be a *philos*? That is, a person to whom the knowledge-seeker is connected by shared life, and by affective, as well as cognitive, ties? To answer this question we must remind ourselves again of what Aristotelian ethical knowledge is and what sort of experience it requires. This knowledge, we have said, consists, above all, in the intuitive perception of complex particulars. Universals are never more than guides to and summaries of these concrete perceptions; and 'the decision rests with perception'. Perception, furthermore, is both cognitive and affective at the same time: it consists in the ability to single out the ethically salient features of the particular matter at hand; and frequently this recognition is accomplished by and in appropriate emotional response as much as through intellectual judgment. Aristotle repeatedly emphasizes that correct perception cannot be learned by precept, but only through and in one's own experience. If we now think what it would be to understand another person in this Aristotelian way, we begin to see that this understanding could not possibly be acquired through a general description, through reading an encomium or a character-portrait, or, indeed, by any distant and non-engaged relationship. It requires the experience of shared activity and the cultivation, over time and through the trust that comes only with time, of an intimate responsiveness to that person in feeling, thought, and action. This responsiveness is not and could not be purely intellectual. If we imagine a solely intellectual knowledge of another, we see that it would not be able to contain everything that is available to the intimacy of *philia*. *Philia*'s knowledge is guided by the pleasure discovered in that person's company, by the feelings of care and tenderness built up through the association and its shared history. Frequently feeling guides attention and discloses to vision what would otherwise have remained concealed. Only with this ability to perceive and to respond to the nuances of the other person's character and ways will the *seeing* of character that is at the heart of this knowledge come about. This is the knowledge of persons exemplified in the speech of Alcibiades and praised in the *Phaedrus*. It now seems quite reasonable of Aristotle to insist that it can exist, at its finest, only in the intimacy of long-lasting mutual love; its benefits could not be delivered by a more remote or 'watery' association.

Aristotle says much more about the instrumental than about the intrinsic value of love. For the instrumental arguments might convince even someone who was otherwise inclined to banish *philia* from the good life – whereas it is difficult to commend an intrinsic value to someone who does not already respond to its claim. He says, simply, that we *do* in fact love the ones we love for their own sake, not just for the sake of some further benefit to ourselves. (It would be not *philia*, but something else, if it *were* altogether instrumental.) He says that we consider *philia* to be not simply 'most necessary to life' (1155a4), but also something beautiful and valuable on its own: 'It is not only necessary, but fine as well, for we praise those who love their *philoi*, and having many *philoi* seems to be one of the fine things; and, furthermore, we think the very same people are good people and good *philoi*' (1155a29–31). In fact, 'Without *philoi* nobody would choose to live, even if he had all the other goods' (1155a5). The *Eudemian Ethics*, similarly, observes that 'We think the *philos* one of the greatest goods, and lack of *philia* and solitude a very terrible (*deinotaton*) thing, because our entire course of life and our voluntary association is with *philoi*' (1234b32ff.).

Later in the *Nicomachean* discussion, Aristotle turns explicitly to an opponent who claims that the value of *philia* is merely instrumental: the person who is living well in other respects has no need of *philoi*. Once again, Aristotle's answer insists that the benefits of *philia* are intrinsic as well.

There is a debate as to whether the *eudaimōn* person needs *philoi* or not. For they say that *makarioi* and self-sufficient people have no need of *philoi*, since they have all good things already. If then they are self-sufficient, they need nothing further; but the *philos*, being another oneself, provides what he cannot provide by himself. Whence the saying, 'When the *daimōn* gives well, what need is there of *philoi*?' But it seems peculiar to give all good things to the *eudaimōn* and to leave out *philoi*, which seem to be the greatest of the external goods...And surely it is peculiar to make the *makarios* person a solitary; for nobody would choose to have all the good things in the world all by himself. For the human being is a political creature and naturally disposed to living-with. And this is true of the *eudaimōn* as well...Therefore the *eudaimōn* needs *philoi*. (1169b3ff.)[46]

Aristotle says that the opponent has a point *only* if we think of *philoi* as mere means to other solitary goods, and the solitary life which has these goods as a complete life. But in fact we do not think this way. We think that a life without them, even with all other goods, is so seriously incomplete that it is not worth living. So, according to the original agreement, established in Book I, that the self-sufficiency of *eudaimonia* must be such that all by itself the life described will be 'choiceworthy and lacking in nothing' (1097b14–15), *philoi* and *philia* will be *parts* of human *eudaimonia* and constitutive of, rather than just instrumental to, its self-sufficiency.

Here, finally, we have the argument promised in *EN* I, when Aristotle cryptically insisted that the self-sufficiency we were after was communal and not solitary, apparently reserving the exploration of that claim for another time. What sort of argument is it? Indeed, what sort of argument has been presented in any of these passages for *philia*'s intrinsic value? It is conspicuous that in this case, as in the political case (and in fact the two arguments are very closely linked, as the last citation shows), Aristotle refers throughout the argument to prevalent ordinary beliefs. 'We think', 'we praise', 'nobody would choose' – these phrases remind us that we are dealing with the recording of deeply and broadly shared *phainomena*, not with any 'harder' or more external sort of argument.[47] And the *phainomena* reported are not any sort of value-neutral fact about human life; they are not a knock-down argument against the opponent. For perhaps he can reply showing that the solitary conception of self-sufficiency rests upon and answers to even deeper and more pervasive beliefs. Perhaps he can show, as Plato tries to, that from the point of view of these other beliefs, the reported beliefs about *philia* are primitive or mistaken. (In fact, Aristotle goes on in this passage to ask about the origins of the opponent's position, and about the deep beliefs that motivated it in the first place (1169b22ff.).) But the argument reminds the opponent of the depth and power of beliefs that his conception of *eudaimonia* bypasses: it thus places on him the burden of showing why and for the sake of what these beliefs are to be given up.

It does something more concrete than this. For in appealing to a conception of our *nature*, it locates the depth of these beliefs more precisely. It shows them to be beliefs that are so firmly a part of our conception of ourselves that they will affect our assessment of questions of identity and persistence. The opponent has asked us to choose a solitary life; we point out that this goes against our nature, implying in this way that no being identical to us would survive in such a life. To wish the good for oneself or for another, Aristotle has insisted, requires wishing a life in which that sort of person will still exist: not a life which, however admirable or godlike, could not be lived by someone identical with me (*EN* 1159a, 1166a, cf. above, p. 350). In asking whether this solitary life can be the object of our highest wish, the first thing to ask is, whether it can be the object of my wish at all. If it is my nature to be a social being, the happy solitary will not be identical with me; so to wish for a life lacking in the value of *philia* is to wish not for the Protagorean 'saving' of one's own life, but for a (Socratic) transformation to a different life.

This point about nature or identity is not a separate point from the point about intrinsic worth or value. (This our readings of the *Protagoras* and the *Phaedrus* have already prepared us to see.) It is introduced and defended by remarks about what we think and deeply believe about matters of value. It is just another way of putting the point that a life without *philia* is radically lacking in essential human values. Not all reasons for non-survival will be reasons of value, of course; but here we are stipulating that a being goes on living who has at least a *prima facie* claim to be identical with me, and we are asking whether this being's life contains enough of what I consider central to myself to really *be* me. As in the political case, this question is not and cannot be answered by independent scientific discovery. It is a deep part of evaluative argument itself. There is no neutral fact of the matter concerning whether this purported continuant is or is not me; we can only answer it by looking at our commitments and values. The opponent could reply by insisting that the solitary *eudaimōn* is living a fully human life – that I could imagine myself as myself, continuing on in that life. But what Aristotle's challenge requires, here as in the *Politics*, is that he then go on to describe this life in a coherent and non-evasive way, showing us how it can satisfy our demands. Aristotle has reminded us, in the *Politics*, of myths and stories that express our commitment to regarding anthropomorphic rational solitaries as not properly human; in discussing *philia* he has reminded us of how 'one might see in travels, too, how closely bound (*oikeion*) every human being is to every other, and how dear' (1155a21–2) suggesting that even distant foreigners share our commitment to this value. The opponent would now (as in the *Protagoras*) have to reply with his own story, showing how we could, in fact, see ourselves in a solitary life.

This argument for an intrinsic value, like any argument within the appearances, may seem to stop short of what the opponent requires. For it is crucial to Plato's talk of intrinsic value that species-centered value is not sufficient for real intrinsic value. For a pursuit to have real value, it must be seen to have this from the point of view of a creature who has no needs at all. It is indeed fortunate for us that we are able, by patient work, to assume the standpoint of such creatures, making it our own. But the fact that we can make it our own is no part of what makes the value valuable. *A fortiori*, the fact that the person of practical wisdom (a being who has *not* done this patient Platonic work, but has set himself to live a complex life in the midst of human value) cannot see himself in a solitary life should not count against the claim of that life to be best. Aristotle's argument will seem to such an opponent to stop short of the real true good, establishing only a species-centered value through the use of a much-too-human measure. But the method of appearances reminds us that a good deal of such talk of the real or true good is just talk. The fact that it has the air of going beyond our talk of human goodness does not guarantee that it does this; it may be so weakly rooted in the experience that sets the bounds of discourse that it will be 'mere words, with no understanding of anything'. The use of an anthropocentric standard of judgment and of a humanly experienced judge have been defended as necessary to give the results of ethical inquiry the right sort of connectedness to ourselves and our lives. And even if the opponent should answer this general challenge, the discussion of goodness that we reported in Chapters 10 and 11 has argued that there is no single thing, The True Good (or The Valuable) in relation to which all the goodness and value in all the species can be ranked and ordered. The good of a god is not homogeneous with our good, above it, and normative for it; it is simply a different kind of good, for a different being in a different context. Ours is not lower or lesser on the same scale; it is just ours, with a special tone and quality that would not be present elsewhere. To love people in the ways and with the emphasis that we do seems to be an essential part of that tone and quality.

Aristotle has, then, defended the inclusion in our conception of the good life of a relationship that is highly vulnerable to reversal. But it has sometimes been charged against him that his conception of what love is does not make it vulnerable *enough*.[48] First, that the relationship described is cozy and insular: that by concentrating on the love of people *similar* in character it removes the element of risk and surprise that can be a high value in an encounter with another soul. Second, that Aristotle's emphasis on the superior stability of character-love over other relationships renders his account of love 'bizarre in its determination to reconcile the need for friendship with the aim of self-sufficiency'.[49] To the first charge we can answer by asking the questioner to consider examples of personal love based on a deeply shared conception of human value, and to ask himself whether such a love would be likely to be devoid of discovery. We could ask him to imagine the delight and surprise of finding, in another separate body and soul, your own aspirations: the joy of realizing that you and this other person inhabit the same world of value, in a larger world in which most people are strangers to one another's highest hopes. Aristotle insists, plausibly, that it is in such a love that the best and deepest discoveries about oneself and the other can be made. The lovers depicted in Plato's *Phaedrus* show us that such a love need not be devoid of surprise, passion, exploration, or risk. We are tempted to say that the much vaunted benefits of diversity can be real benefits in love only if this diversity is rooted in a similarity: that you learn from, and learn to love, a foreigner, a member of another race or sex or religion, a person far from you in age or temperament, on the basis of at least some shared human perceptions, values, aspirations, and the mutual acknowledgment of these. It is on such a basis that the learning can mean something to you, be something for you. Otherwise, your curiosity will lead not to loving perception, but to ethnography or natural history.

To the second charge we must concede that Aristotle does stress the superior stability of a love that is based on character. And in other ways, too, he urges the person in search of love not to court disaster – by forming too many close relationships, for example, so that he will be forced to 'parcel himself out', or by choosing to love someone extremely far from him in age, so that the relationship will be vexed more than is necessary by the changes of age. But there is nothing very 'bizarre' in this acknowledgment that we do seek stability and constancy in our lives with one another, that the rich benefits of love themselves require a kind of trustfulness and an accumulation of shared history that could not be found without these. When we consider the full requirements of Aristotelian living-together and the requirements it imposes, the vulnerabilities it creates, we cannot think that Aristotle has courted self-sufficiency to the neglect of richness of value. Indeed we are more likely to be awed and alarmed at the risk such a person runs in valuing so difficult and unlikely a goal. How many people really manage to live through their lives like that, sharing in deep love and excellent activity? How many who live together really *live* together, 'sharing in speech and reason'? (For 'that's what it means for human beings to live together, not just to pasture in the same place like cattle' (*EN* 1170b11–14).) It is, in fact, an extraordinary demand to make on the world; those who make it are likely to be unhappy. But since the goal of the Aristotelian is not so much happiness in the sense of contentment as it is fullness of life and richness of value, it is no solution to omit a value for happiness's sake, to reduce your demands on the world in order to get more pleasing answers from the world. The Aristotelian will simply take on the world and see what can be done with it.

This account of the value of love develops many of the arguments that we have found in the *Phaedrus* (including its connections between value and personal identity): with, however, some crucial differences. The first difference is additive: by his account of the benefits of 'living together' and of the special motivation towards goodness that comes from the thought that something is uniquely your own, Aristotle has gone further than the *Phaedrus* towards explaining why a close lifelong bond is so important, why love is not transferable without loss of value to other similar characters. Both the *Phaedrus* and the *EN* tell us that love has its highest value when the object of love is a good person of similar character and aspirations; both stipulate that the two should, where possible, share a lifetime of activity that also includes pleasure and delight in the association. Aristotle has now added a more detailed account of the importance of this intimacy.

But the second major difference is subtractive. Sexuality and sexual attraction do not play a major role in Aristotle's account of love. Nor does he speak of the benefits of *mania*, of the powerfully erotic transformation of thought and vision that plays a central role in the life of the *Phaedrus* lovers. All elements of an Aristotelian lover's soul will be active and responsive, as they always are in the Aristotelian person of practical wisdom; and Aristotle does insist that love requires taking pleasure in the other person's physical presence. But the specifically erotic pleasure and insight of Platonic lovers is mentioned only as a case of especially intense and exclusive *philia* (1171a11); it is not even clear that the reference is approving.[50] The rhythm of *philia* in its best or highest cases seems to be steadier and less violent than that of Platonic *erōs*; we do not find the element of sudden illumination and dangerous openness that is central to the *Phaedrus* lovers. I have tried to emphasize, as I believe is appropriate, the elements of Aristotelian *philia* that make it real personal *love*, something more vulnerable, more rooted in time and change, than a Kantian 'practical love'. But now it is time to admit that we do not find here, or do not, at least, find emphasized, the structure of tension and release, longing and repletion, that is so important in the *Phaedrus*'s view of true insight. Aristotle says nothing against this sort of *erōs*; but by his silence he indicates that he does not find it of central importance. It seems altogether wrong to charge Aristotle with having a complacent moral personality, insensitive to the goods that come with risk attached to them. What can we then say about his avoidance of *erōs*?

We must, first of all, recall certain historical and cultural facts. Aristotle is a heterosexual male in a culture in which women were more or less uneducated, deprived of the development that would be necessary if they were to become worthy partners in any shared activity connected with most of the major human values. He is, furthermore, a political thinker who has laid great stress upon the family and the household as necessary to the development of any human excellence whatever. It would, then, have been difficult for him to imagine a structure of life that would have maintained the benefits of the family while making available to women an equal measure of education and of opportunity for excellent activity. Plato had denied the ethical value of the household; he was therefore free to accord to women a more equal intellectual place. Aristotle has serious arguments against this loss of intimacy; his possibilities are therefore more constrained. Since this is one of the major unsolved problems of our own way of life, we can perhaps understand how difficult it would have been for a fourth-century Greek to imagine any way around it. But if women remained confined to the household, they could not become *philoi* in the highest sense; and the aspiring male would have to seek for such *philoi* within his own sex. At this point, if he were himself heterosexually inclined, he might well judge that sexuality and aspiration must come apart, that aspiration must be pursued in a different domain, in the context of different relationships. We could say, then, that we find in Aristotle a deep partial agreement with the *Phaedrus* concerning the importance of an intimate personal love that combines strong feeling and shared aspiration; combined with a different set of beliefs about where such relationships are to be sought and about the likelihood that these relationships will be sexual in nature. These beliefs reflect differences in the two philosophers' personal experience of sexuality in its social setting, and also differences in normative political belief about the importance of the family.

Isn't this exactly the sort of cozy defense of the status quo for which the Aristotelian method of appearances has so frequently been maligned? We are at once tempted to say that Aristotle's patient attention to the actual has prevented the bold leap of imagination that would be required in order to imagine a social structure in which the potential of women for excellence could be fully realized. Platonism, because it is less respectful of actual beliefs, is freer to take such leaps.

We have argued, however, that it is an injustice to the appearances method to claim that it makes bold or radical conclusions impossible. Chapter 8 suggested that the method might in fact make use of deep beliefs about the importance of choice to criticize the actual social institutions concerning women. That Aristotle does not do this says less about the possibilities of his approach than about his own defects as a collector of appearances. And if we examine the case before us we will see, I believe, that it is not the method that is at fault, so much as is Aristotle's application of it. For there are at least two areas relevant to this problem in which Aristotle's scrutiny of beliefs is woefully deficient. His investigation of the potential of women for excellence is notoriously crude and hasty. He is able to bypass the problem of developing their capabilities and he is able to deny them a share in the highest *philia*, as a result of bare assertions about their incapacity for full adult moral choice[51] that show no sign of either sensitivity or close attention. Had he devoted to the psychology of women, or even to their physiology (about which he makes many ludicrous and easily corrigible errors) even a fraction of the sustained care that he devoted to the lives and bodies of shellfish, the method would have been better served.

Then too, we find in his writings an almost complete lack of attention to the erotic relationships that Plato defended. The eroticism of male (and female) homosexuality is of so little interest to him, apparently, that he does not even see fit to include these practices and beliefs within the review of opinions concerning *philia*.[52] This avoidance is extremely odd, given the prominence of homosexuality in his culture and in the philosophical tradition of writing about human goodness. And this is not only an injustice to his own method. It is a failure in *philia* as well. For Aristotle's manifest love for Plato and his years of shared activity with him should have made him look to the life of his friend as a source of information concerning the good life. But if he had looked, he would have noticed the ethical importance in that life of the combination of sensuousness and 'mad' passion with respect, awe, and excellent philosophizing. And then, if he did not himself opt for this life through awareness of his difference in sexual inclination, he might at least have set it down among the appearances and given it its due as one human way of aiming at the good.

That none of these things happened, even in this judicious fair-minded man who had, in general, such admirable views about self-correction and self-scrutiny, who laid such stress upon responsiveness of particular perception, shows us the tremendous power of sexual convention and sexual prejudice in shaping a view of the world. It was the one area of life in which he was so deeply immersed that he could not compensate for bias or partiality, he could not even follow his own method, on the way to becoming a person of practical wisdom. The Aristotelian method does not doggedly defend the status quo. It asks for the cultivation of imagination and responsiveness concerning all human alternatives. Aristotle's failure to apply his own method in these cases makes us, as defenders of the method, wish to lay even greater stress upon these elements of practical wisdom than Aristotle himself did, and to defend vigorously the role of reading, and of *philia* itself, in aiding these perceptions.

372   *Aristotle: the fragility of the good human life*

Aristotle has attempted, then, by setting our various beliefs before us, to show us that they contain a conception of human good living that makes it something relatively stable, but still vulnerable, in its search for richness of value, to many sorts of accidents. We pursue and value both stability and the richness that opens us to risk. In a certain sense we value risk itself, as partially constitutive of some kinds of value. In our deliberations we must balance these competing claims. This balance will never be a tension-free harmony. It remains, at best, a tension-laden holding-in-focus, a Heraclitean 'backward-stretching harmony, as of a bow or a lyre'; and its particular judgments frequently have the look of uneasy compromise. We recognize the enormous loss of value that would come with the adoption of an internal-condition conception of the good life; so we decide to stay with the riskier view that the good life requires activity and that even the good condition, in such a life, is not altogether immune from harm. But we do not want to say, either, that *every* deprivation of activity is a loss in goodness; for this would leave us too much, intolerably, open to loss. So we find an uneasy balance; and it is never entirely clear that risk does not threaten too much, or that some genuine value does not escape us. Then again, we want the good life to include, for fullness of value, some relational components that are particularly vulnerable to chance; but, not wanting to be unbearably at the mercy of luck, we opt for a conception of each of these that secures to them a relatively high degree of stability. Again (although we do have independent arguments for the goodness of these conceptions), we can never be certain that we have not made human life too vulnerable, or that in going for stability we have not omitted something. Aristotle shows us by these complex maneuvers the delicate balancing act in which good human deliberation consists: delicate, and never concluded, if the agent is determined, as long as he or she lives, to keep all the recognized human values in play. To some this picture of deliberation will seem mundane, messy, and lacking in elegance. Aristotle would answer (speaking, he will be happy to admit, from the thoroughly anthropocentric standpoint of the person of practical wisdom) that we do well not to aim at a conception that is more elegant, or simpler, than human life is. The person who elevates simplicity to a supreme value is like the architect who uses a straight-edge against a fluted column:[53] his calculations won't build a sound building, and he will leave out much of the beauty and value of what is there before him.[54]

Appendix to Part III: human and divine

Some philosophers (or whatever you like to call them) suffer from what may be called 'loss of problems'. Then everything seems quite simple to them, no deep problems seem to exist any more, the world becomes broad and flat and loses all depth, and what they write becomes immeasurably shallow and trivial...

...quia plus loquitur inquisitio quam inventio...(Augustinus).

Wittgenstein, *Zettel*, 456–7

Up until this point, we have presented a picture of Aristotle that sets him in strong contrast to the Plato of the middle dialogues. This is an Aristotle whom one can find almost throughout the *corpus*, speaking in a consistent and recognizable voice. But we have stressed throughout this book the depth and complexity of these ethical problems, the likelihood that any thinker of depth will not only feel their depth but will also feel the force of both the Platonic and the Aristotelian positions. We have also stressed Aristotle's fundamental commitment to investigate the major accounts of a problem presented him by his philosophical tradition, assessing them sympathetically and responding to their depth. It therefore seems appropriate to pause here and assess the evidence that Aristotle himself was drawn to Platonic intellectualism in ethics. We cannot by any means give a full account of all the passages in question or deal with all the arguments that have been advanced on all sides of these questions. This would be a book in itself. But we will be fairer to our question, and to Aristotle, if we schematically set out the main lines of the issue and sketch a position towards it. We shall deal first with some evidence that lies outside the ethical works, then turn to the notorious problems of *EN* x.6–8.

First, then, there are a number of passages scattered through the corpus that do not, like *EN* x.7, prescribe as best for human beings a Platonic quasi-divine intellect-centered life; but insofar as they rank the available lives in the universe in terms of their value or goodness, placing the divine life at the top, they are at odds with the general anthropocentrism of Aristotle's ethical method (cf. Ch. 10). (1) In *De Caelo* II.12, Aristotle ranks lives in the cosmos, showing how the placement of beings in this cosmic hierarchy explains the types of movements they perform. The best being (the unmoved mover) 'has the good without action'; the next best (the heavenly bodies) get it through a simple and single motion (circular motion); and so on, motion becoming more complex and varied the

373

further the creature is from the true good. (2) In *Parts of Animals* 1.5, Aristotle again, even while defending the study of animals, concedes that the heavenly bodies are higher or superior forms of life, and therefore more lovable to students of nature. (3) In *EN* vi, speaking of the virtue of *sophia*, contemplative wisdom, Aristotle ranks it higher than practical wisdom, defending this ranking by appeal to a ranking of lives or of beings: 'It is odd if one thinks that political excellence and practical wisdom are the best things, if the human being is not the best being in the universe' (1141a20–2). (I translate literally the indicatives, in order to emphasize the ambiguity of the sentence. Ross translates the second 'if' as 'since': this is possible, but by no means necessary.) Aristotle goes on to contrast the context-relativity of practical wisdom unfavorably with *sophia*'s lack of context-relativity. (4) The praises of intellect and its divinity in *Metaphysics* xii and *De Anima* iii.5 are surely part of the same picture. The treatment of the unmoved mover as object of love and worship surely implies a comparative judgment about the value of lives. (By contrast, the use of the unmoved mover in *Physics* viii, as necessary first principle of physical explanation, seems to imply no such ranking.) (5) In *Politics* i, the description of the 'despotic rule' of soul over body and its 'political and kingly rule' over (oddly) *orexis* seems to form part of the same Platonic picture. Surely it is difficult to reconcile with the hylomorphic account of soul and body in *De Anima*, with the account of *orexis* in *De Anima*, *De Motu*, and *EN*, with the *EN*'s account of the relationship between intellect and bodily desire.

These passages (and others like them) do not necessarily imply a view of the *human* good that is incompatible with the one that we have sketched, in which intellectual activity is one of many intrinsic goods. For one might consistently hold that there are many intrinsic goods without which life is less complete, and which, therefore, by the criteria of *EN* i will be parts of, not just means to, *eudaimonia*, while holding at the same time that some of these goods are higher than others. This is plainly the position of *EN* vi, where in one and the same chapter Aristotle claims that *sophia* is one *part* of *eudaimonia* (cf. below) and also that it is in some way the best part. It is, as it were, the biggest and brightest jewel in a crown full of valuable jewels, in which each jewel has intrinsic value in itself, and the whole composition (made by practical wisdom) also adds to the value of each. The passages *are*, however, plainly at odds with the numerous arguments in all the ethical works to the effect that ethics and politics must confine themselves to the question, 'What is the good for a human being?', refusing to attempt a general over-arching account of good, or to produce a universal ranking of lives in terms of their goodness (cf. Ch. 10). The position of these passages seems, then, to be compatible with the position of the *Phaedrus*: the account of the best life for a human being makes room for other areas of intrinsic value; and yet this life can still be compared unfavorably with another life that is exemplified somewhere in the universe. It is not altogether clear to me that this is a coherent position. Once it is granted that there are some general species-independent criteria for ranking across lives, then it becomes very natural to conclude that a life that maximizes these highest elements or activities will also be best for any being who is capable of it. Once one allows the external perspective, it seems hard to see why it should not affect the assessment of the various lives open to members of each species that can be assessed from that perspective.

It is not surprising, then, that this further step towards Platonism is in fact taken somewhere by Aristotle. It is taken, I believe, only once, in a passage that does not fit with its context and that is in flat contradiction with several important positions and arguments of the *EN* taken as a whole. But it cannot be dismissed either: and the best we can do is to set forth its arguments and show clearly how and where they are in contradiction with the *EN*'s overall enterprise. There is a large and helpful literature on this problem.[1] I shall therefore set out briefly the issues that seem to me to be most important.

In *EN* x.6–8, then, Aristotle defends the view that *eudaimonia* is identical with the activity of the best part of a human being, viz., the theoretical intellect. This activity is held to excel all others in continuity (1177a21–2), purity (26), stability (26), and also in self-sufficiency, in that one can contemplate without relying on the contingent satisfaction of external necessary conditions (1177a27–1177b1). Contemplation is explicitly held to be the only activity that is worthy of love or choice for its own sake (1177b1–4). Since the divine intellect is the best part in us, we are urged to identify ourselves with this element and to choose for ourselves the life of this one element. 'We must not follow those who urge us, being human, to reason and choose humanly, and, being mortal, in a mortal way; but insofar as it is possible we must immortalize and do everything in order to live in accordance with the best part of ourselves' (1177b31–4). A life according to 'the rest of excellence' is held to be second-best. (Neither of these two lives, presumably, is the life defended up until this point in the *EN*, since that life will contain both contemplative and non-contemplative components.)

It will be obvious to the reader of this book that this passage has strong affinities with the Platonism of the middle dialogues, and that it is oddly out of step with the view of value that we have been finding in the ethical works. We can now summarize the most important reasons for judging that there is incompatibility here, not just difference of emphasis. (1) In the *EE* and the *MM*, Aristotle explicitly argues that *eudaimonia* is a composite of several parts and that activities according to the excellences of character are 'parts' or constituents of *eudaimonia*, along with *philia* and contemplative activity. (2) This claim is underlined in *EN* VI (= *EE* IV): *sophia* is a 'part of excellence as a whole', and, as such a part, it contributes to *eudaimonia* through its activities (1144a3ff.). The point underlined here is that *sophia* is not merely a productive means towards *eudaimonia*, but an actual part of it; but Aristotle also makes it clear that it is a part and not the whole. (3) In the other books of the *EN*, activities according to the excellences of character are explicitly said to be valuable or choiceworthy for their own sake. It is part of the definition of excellent activity, indeed, that it be chosen for its own sake (1105a31–2). *Philia*, too, is held to be an intrinsic good (cf. Ch. 12).

What is most surprising, even *EN* x.6 cites activity according to excellence of character as an example of something that is good and choiceworthy in and of itself (1176b7–9). Book IX (cf. Ch. 12) expressly rules out a solitary *eudaimonia* as lacking in an important intrinsic value; the conclusion is that, lacking *philia*, it is not really *eudaimonia* at all, since it is not complete. Book I has already made it clear that *eudaimonia* must be inclusive of everything that has intrinsic value (1097b14ff.). So any evidence that some other item has intrinsic value not only clashes directly with the claim of x.7 that only contemplation does, it also clashes indirectly with the claims there identifying *eudaimonia* with contemplation alone. (4) Nothing in Book I implies that *eudaimonia* is a single activity; the sufficiency criterion, as we have said, implies that it will be a composite, unless there is only one thing with intrinsic value. The claim of 1.5, that 'the good for a human being is activity of soul in accordance with excellence, and if the excellences are more than one, according to the best and most complete' does not undermine this: for, given what has already been said about 'completeness', this will require the inclusion of everything with intrinsic value; and it is plainly compatible with the finding that there are many such things. Book x, by contrast, stresses the idea that what we want is the single best activity, the activity of the single best part. (5) The initial statement of the self-sufficiency (*autarkeia*) criterion in Book I is oddly out of step with x's claim that contemplation is *autarkestaton*: for Aristotle there immediately said that we are not looking for a solitary self-sufficiency, but for a life that is self-sufficient along with friends and family and community (cf. Ch. 12). The life of x.7 would, like the solitary life attacked in IX.12, fail to meet the criterion, thus stated. (6) The proper reading of the 'human function' argument in 1.5 is compatible with a non-intellectualistic conclusion. For what it says, properly understood, is that *eudaimonia* is good activity *according to, shaped by*, the work of reason, in which the shared elements are not excluded, but included in a way infused by and organized by practical reason.[2] In the rest of the work, especially in Book VI, Aristotle shows us how practical reason shapes and arranges a life that includes both contemplative and ethical elements. (7) Book x defended the selection of contemplation by saying that each of us should identify ourselves with our theoretical intellect; similar material in IX spoke of practical reason instead (1166a16–17). (8) Book IX twice indicates that it is actually incoherent to aspire to the good life of the god: for this involves wishing for a life that cannot be lived by a being of the same sort as we are, therefore not by someone identical with us. Wishing for the good, both for ourselves and for another, must remain within the confines of our species identity (1159a10–11, 1166a18–23). The insistence throughout the *EN* that our subject matter is not the good life *simpliciter*, but the good human life (cf. Ch. 10), makes the same point.

To these considerations we may add one more that has not, to my knowledge, been sufficiently underlined. This is that the text of *EN* x seems to be oddly composed, giving rise to suspicion that Chapters 6–8 are not originally parts of the same whole. Chapter 9, which begins Aristotle's transition from ethics to politics by a discussion of moral education, begins with a summary of what has preceded. This summary makes no mention of the chapters on contemplation, but gives an orderly summary of the *EN* up to x.5, mentioning excellences, *philia*, and pleasure; having discussed all these things, the summary says, we might think that we have finished our job; but in fact we must go on to consider the practical application of what we have done. (The only possible reference to x.6–8 is in the *toutōn* 'these things' of 1179a33; but that would be a thin allusion indeed to the climax of the whole work.) The beginning of x.6 is peculiar as well: 'Now that we have spoken about the excellences and *philia* and pleasure, it remains to give a sketch of *eudaimonia*.' But a 'sketch' of *eudaimonia* is what 1.7 already claimed to give; and according to the views of I–IX, we have been talking about *eudaimonia* all along, filling in the sketch by talking in detail of its constituents.

What are we to make of all this? There is no strong reason to believe that these chapters were not composed by Aristotle – though questions of authenticity are very difficult to settle and there is also no reason to rule out forgery. What we can say with confidence is that these chapters do not fit into the argument of the *EN*; indeed, that they represent a line of ethical thought that Aristotle elsewhere vigorously attacks. With only slightly less confidence, we can also assert that they do not fit well in their context, and were probably composed separately, perhaps in the context of a different project. We cannot rule out the possibility that Aristotle himself inserted them here, in preparing a course of lectures; but the clashes are more numerous and blatant than in other parallel cases, and a more likely explanation seems to be that they were inserted in their present position by someone else (a not unusual phenomenon in the corpus).

But the passages discussed previously do give evidence, from a wide variety of authentic contexts, that ethical Platonism of some sort exercised a hold over Aristotle's imagination in one or more periods of his career. We should, then, view the fragment x.6–8 as a serious working-out of elements of a position to which Aristotle is in some ways deeply attracted, though he rejects it in the bulk of his mature ethical and political writing. Surely this is not disappointing. Frequently Aristotle is rather quick and dismissive with Platonist positions. It seems far more worthy of him, and of his method, that he should seriously feel the force of this position and try to articulate the arguments for it. Perhaps we can say that, like anyone who has been seriously devoted to the scholarly or contemplative life, Aristotle wonders whether, thoroughly and properly followed, its demands are not such as to eclipse all other pursuits. Although for the most part he articulates a conception of a life complexly devoted to politics, love, and reflection, he also feels (whether at different periods or in different moods at the same period) that really fine reflection may not be able to stand side by side with anything else; we cannot have a harmonious fusion of the human and the divine. So he articulates the Platonist view, not attempting to harmonize it with the other view, but setting it side by side with that one, as the *Symposium* stands side by side with the *Phaedrus*. In a sense there is a decision for the mixed view; but the other view remains, not fully dismissed, exerting its claim as a possibility.

This seems to me to be a worthy way for a great philosopher to think about these hard questions; and therefore worthy of Aristotle.[3]

Interlude 2: luck and the tragic emotions

Aristotle has a high regard for tragedy. Both in the *Poetics* itself and in the *Politics* discussion of the education of young citizens, he gives it a place of honor, attributing to it both motivational and cognitive value.[1] Our discussion of his ethical views has brought us into contact with several features of his thought that help to explain this. The general anthropocentrism of his ethics and his rejection of the Platonic external 'god's eye' standpoint (Ch. 8) leads him to turn, for moral improvement, not to representations of divine non-limited beings (cf. Ch. 5), but to stories of good *human* activity. The value he attributes to emotions and feelings, both as parts of a virtuous character and as sources of information about right actions (Chs. 9, 10), naturally leads him to give another hearing to texts that Plato had banished on account of their representation of and appeal to the emotions. Then, too, since, in our aspiration to grasp ethical truth, the perception of concrete particulars is, for Aristotle, prior in authority to the general rules and definitions that summarize those particulars, since a detailed account of a complex particular case will have more of ethical truth in it than a general formula (Ch. 10), it will be natural for him to suppose that the concrete and complex stories that are the material of tragic drama could play a valuable role in refining our perceptions of the complex 'material' of human life.

In all of these ways Aristotle's ethical writing further develops lines of thought that led to Plato's (partial) rehabilitation of poetry (Ch. 7). Each of these points deserves elaboration. But here, before concluding this book with a return to tragedy, I want to focus on two specific pieces of Aristotle's account of tragedy. These pieces can be clarified by connecting them with the views about the ethical importance of luck that we set out in Chapters 11 and 12. They are: the relationship between tragic action and tragic character, and the nature and value of the tragic emotions.

We can begin with a famous and controversial passage in the *Poetics*, which both points towards the ethical issues we have discussed and is illuminated by them. There are several promising ways of resolving its troublesome textual problems; I translate the version which I consider most defensible, and which seems to bring out most adequately the sequence of Aristotle's thought:[2]

The most important element is the arrangement of the events. For tragedy is a representation not of human beings but of action and a course of life.[3] And *eudaimonia* and its opposite consist in action, and the end is a certain sort of action, not a characteristic (*poiotēs*). According to their characters (*ta ēthē*) people are of such and such characteristics (*poioi tines*). But it is according to their actions that they live well (are *eudaimones*) or the reverse. (1450a15–20)

Aristotle here defends the central importance of tragic action, claiming that a work that merely displayed characters of a certain sort, without showing them in action, would be deficient in the values proper to tragedy. He defends his claim by indicating that action has an intimate connection with human *eudaimonia* that merely *being* a certain sort of person, all by itself, does not. A work that simply displayed the characteristics of the figures involved, without showing them engaged in some sort of significant activity, would fail, therefore, to show us something about *eudaimonia* that is shown us in the plots of the great tragedies. What is this something?

The point of these remarks about *eudaimonia* in a discussion of tragic action has been difficult for interpreters to see. D. W. Lucas, for example, excises them as irrelevant to the issue at hand:

Aristotle's particular views on the end of action are not very relevant to the importance of action in drama, but they are the sort of thing that a commentator might be tempted to explain. The desire for happiness might well be the cause which led to the initiation of the action which was the subject of a play, but this action is just as much an action whether the happiness which is its end is regarded as an action or a state.[4]

John Jones[5] is more sympathetic to Aristotle's remarks; but he takes them in a strange and, ultimately, an unilluminating way. The remark indicates, he says, that Aristotle, unlike modern thinkers, has a preference for exuberant and outgoing characters who are only fully themselves when they are *acting*, not just *reflecting*. Even if this were correct as a description of Aristotle's ethical preferences, which it is not, it would seem dubious that this could be the point of the remark in question. For Aristotle's contrast here is not between one type of character and another, but between a state of character, of whatever kind, and activity, of whatever kind – including, presumably, contemplative activity. His point is that no state of character is by itself sufficient for *eudaimonia*.

Before we can begin to assess these criticisms and develop our own account of the passage, we had better be clear about what Aristotle is and is not saying. He is not expressing indifference to the element of character in drama: indeed, he goes on to say that the depiction of action reveals character at the same time (1450a21–2) – just as, in the ethical works, he repeatedly insists that our best evidence of character is the actual choices a person makes.[6] Nor does he seem to be expressing a preference for works with lots of action over works with well-developed characters. He says that there might be a tragedy without full character-development; but this is clearly not what he himself prefers. What he does say is that plot and action are centrally important and that there could not be a tragedy without them. Tragedy cannot simply represent character types, it must show its characters in action. The implicit contrast, then, is not a contrast between active drama and a more reflective drama; it is a contrast between tragic drama and another literary genre known to Aristotle, the character portrait. The *Characters* of Aristotle's pupil Theophrastus, for example, represent people of a certain sort, without showing them involved in action. Plato's *Republic* recommends speeches describing and praising the goodness of good people. Tragedy, by contrast, 'includes character along with' the representation of action: we see the characters by seeing them choosing and doing.

Aristotle's remarks, I shall now argue, are neither irrelevant nor obscure. As a result of our work in the last two chapters, we are in a position to see in them a serious point about the connection between our ethical values (our conception of *eudaimonia*) and our poetic values, our assessment of whether tragedy is important and what is important about it. His point, as we shall see, is that the value of tragic action is a practical value: it shows us certain things about human life. And these will be things worth learning only on a certain conception of *eudaimonia*, namely one according to which having a good character or being in a good condition is not sufficient for the fullness of good living.

We can focus the issue by pointing out that the puzzling sentences make a claim about the human good that was denied by a number of Aristotle's philosophical contemporaries. In Chapter 11 we saw Aristotle arguing against an opponent who *did* maintain that being a person of a certain sort (being in a certain good condition) was sufficient for living well. Plato's related view identified *eudaimonia* with the most invulnerable activities of the rational soul. Aristotle replied to both of these opponents by pointing to several ways in which a good person could fall short of full *eudaimonia* because of events not under that person's control. First, the person could be impeded from acting well – either altogether, or during a portion of his or her life. Aristotle showed a special interest in reversals that lead to impeded activity in a part of a life that was previously going well; his central example was the case of Priam. In this case the *eudaimonia* of the person of good character is diminished through the frustration of good activity; and Aristotle suggests that in the extreme case the frustration may even eat into or defile the goodness of character itself. We saw next, that his views about impediment could be extended to accommodate two other cases with which tragedy prominently deals: we called them the case of Oedipus and the case of Agamemnon. In Oedipus's case, the world creates an impediment to the blameless or just activity that he intentionally did, by making it the case that, unknown to him and through no fault of his own, the real or most ethically pertinent description of his action made it a hideous rather than a blameless one.[7] There is, as in Priam's case, a gap between being good and living well. Only here there is the added complication that there is also on the scene an action which is the natural expression of the intentions of good character; and as we witness the gap it is a gap between character so expressed and the action that is actually performed (under its truest or most relevant description). In Agamemnon's case, again, there is a gap between what appears to be an antecedently good character and the fullness of good activity. The impediment here is produced by the situation of conflict, which prevents blameless response, making it inevitable that the choices that naturally express his commitment to piety or to filial love should coincide with (intentional) acts of murder or impiety. The world makes it the case that a person who was good, who was 'sailing straight', falls short of *eudaimonia* – indeed, in this case, falls into the commission of a bad action that we find horrible, even while we pity. Finally, in Chapter 12, we saw Aristotle argue that through the important relational values of political activity and personal love, our aspiration to live well becomes especially vulnerable to uncontrolled happenings. For in these cases the world does not simply provide the agent with instrumental means to an activity that can be identified and specified apart from the external; it provides a constituent part of the good activity itself. There is no loving action without someone to receive and return it; there is no being a good citizen without a city that accepts your claims to membership. In these cases *hexis* and *praxis*, character and activity, are so intimately connected that it would not even be possible to represent the appropriate character-states without representing action and communication – and, therefore, vulnerability. This means that interference from the world leaves no self-sufficient kernel of the person safely intact. It strikes directly at the root of goodness itself.

The *Poetics* remark is, then, a summary of some important Aristotelian ethical views about the ways in which goodness of character or soul can prove insufficient for full *eudaimonia*. What we can now observe is that these views are indeed highly relevant to the valuation of tragedy and tragic action. Consider Aristotle's good-condition opponent. This person says that *action*, depending as it does for its completion on happenings in the world, is strictly irrelevant to the *eudaimonia* of the agent – therefore, presumably, to all serious questions about praise and blame, about how valuable a life he is having. Such a thinker would have to say that if we want texts that will show us what is supremely valuable about human life (and all ancient literary theory assumes that this is what we are looking for when we turn to tragedy), these texts will not need to show their good characters engaged in any actual action. They will only need to show them as being of a certain sort. To show this is to show everything of serious practical importance. And texts that indicated that anything else was important would be misleading.

Or consider Aristotle's primary opponent in the *Poetics*, Plato. Plato's middle-dialogue defense of a certain type of rational self-sufficiency is intimately bound up with his repudiation of poetic action as a source of practical insight, his restriction of the poetic task to the construction of praises of the goodness of character of good people. For if the good person is, as *Republic* III (388) insists, altogether self-sufficient,[8] that is, in need of nothing from without to complete the value and goodness of his life (cf. Ch. 7 §IV, Ch. 5 §IV), then, first of all, tragic action becomes *irrelevant* to our search for human good living. If internal goodness of character or soul, or the performance of altogether self-sufficient contemplative activities, is sufficient for full goodness of life, then a praise of that goodness, of those activities, will show an audience all that is ethically important about a good person.* And, second, many of the most common patterns of tragic action will be ethically inappropriate and corrupting: for these plots display their heroic

---

* To bring out the contrast with Plato (unlike the good-condition opponent) we do need to suppose that Aristotle's demand for *action* in drama would not be satisfied by the performance of the most self-sufficient theoretical activities, such as the contemplation of truths of mathematics – except, perhaps, insofar as these interact (as for Aristotle they do) with contingent worldly conditions. Thus far Jones has a point; but inward-looking and reflective agents are in no way ruled out. And I know of no drama that *simply* represents mathematical reasoning as its central action.

figures attaching to chance events, for example the death of a loved one or a reversal in fortunes, an importance *vis-à-vis* human *eudaimonia* that they do not, in fact, possess. Plato informs us in no uncertain terms that the poets 'speak wrongly about human beings in matters of the greatest importance' when they show the lives of good and just people being seriously affected by adverse circumstances (*Republic* 392A–B). Poets are to be forbidden to tell this sort of story and commanded to tell the opposite.

The great tragic plots explore the gap between our goodness and our good living, between what we are (our character, intentions, aspirations, values) and how humanly well we manage to live. They show us reversals happening to good-charactered but not divine or invulnerable people, exploring the many ways in which being of a certain good human character falls short of sufficiency for *eudaimonia*. (In the extreme case, some of these ways may include damage or corruption to the originally good character itself. In such cases, however, it is important that the change should come not from deliberate wickedness, but from the pressure of external circumstances over which they have no control. Thus the damage will still display the gap between being good in deliberately formed intentions or values, and managing to live out a fully good life.) If you think that there is no such gap or that it is trivial, you will naturally judge that tragedy is either false or trivial; and you will not want to give it a place of honor in a scheme of public instruction. Aristotle's belief that the gap is both real and important illuminates his anti-Platonic claim that tragic action is important and a source of genuine learning.

There are many areas in which we could use these insights to press *Poetics* interpretation further. They can provide the basis for a more ethically sensitive account of Aristotle's notions of *peripeteia* and *anagnōrisis*, reversal and recognition, showing us why these notions are of such central importance in Aristotle's estimation of tragedies and helping us to classify the different varieties of reversal in an ethically perspicuous way. They can also be used to increase our understanding of tragic *hamartia*, or missing-the-mark. For despite the thousands of pages that have been written on this notion, we still need an account that is fully responsive to the ways in which, for Aristotle, practical error can come about through some causes other than viciousness of character and still matter to the value of a life. Tragedy concerns good people who come to grief 'not through defect of character and wickedness, but through some *hamartia*' (1453a9–10). *Hamartia* and *hamartēma** are sharply distinguished from flaw or defect of character, both here and elsewhere (*EN* v.8, 1137b11ff., cf. *Rhet.* 1374b6ff.). They are also distinguished from *atuchēma*, or a mischance that has a purely arbitrary and external origin. (An example of the latter is probably Aristotle's case in which someone is killed when a statue happens to fall down on him.) To come to grief through *hamartia* is, then,

---

* Attempts to find a significant systematic distinction between these two words have not been successful. If there is one, the analogy with *phantasia*/*phantasma* indicates that *hamartia* would be the activity, the making of the mistake, *hamartēma* the mistake that gets made. But the similar pair *atuchia*/*atuchēma* do not seem to be systematically distinguished.

to fall through some sort of mistake in action that is causally intelligible, not simply fortuitous, done in some sense by oneself; and yet not the outgrowth of a settled defective disposition of character. Further examination indicates that *hamartia* can include both blameworthy and non-blameworthy missings-of-the-mark: the innocent ignorance of Oedipus, the intentional but highly constrained act of Agamemnon, the passionate deviations of akratic persons inspired to act against settled character by *erōs* or anger. It can, presumably, even include the more deliberate mistakes that result from a momentary or temporary departure from character – for example, the simplifications of Creon (who later regrets his errors, showing that they did not really express his underlying settled character – cf. below, pp. 387–8), the lies of Neoptolemus (who says explicitly that he has departed from his ongoing *phusis* or character). In short, the notion of *hamartia* takes in a variety of important goings-wrong that do not result from settled badness; and thus it is a concept well fitted to discourse about the gap between being good and living well. For what we notice in each of these cases in which good character is not effective in action is an element of constraint or *tuchē*: circumstantial in some cases; working through the agent's system of beliefs in others; in still others through the internal ungoverned *tuchē* of the passions. To pursue these leads in more detail, with reference to all the relevant texts, would be an important clarificatory task.[9]

But now, instead, I want to pursue in detail the connection between Aristotle's ethical views about the gap and his views of the role of the two tragic emotions, pity and fear. Aristotle, like Plato, believes that emotions are individuated not simply by the way they feel, but, more importantly, by the kinds of judgments or beliefs that are internal to each.[10] A typical Aristotelian emotion is defined as a composite of a feeling of either pleasure or pain and a particular type of belief about the world. Anger, for example, is a composite of painful feeling with the belief that one has been wronged.[11] The feeling and the belief are not just incidentally linked: the belief is the ground of the feeling. If it were found by the agent to be false, the feeling would not persist; or, if it did, it would no longer persist as a constituent in that emotion. If I discover that an imagined slight did not really take place, I can expect my painful angry feelings to go away; if some irritation remains, I will think of it as residual irrational *irritation* or excitation, not as *anger*. It is part of this same view that emotions may be assessed as either rational or irrational, 'true' or 'false', depending upon the nature of their grounding beliefs. If my anger is based upon a hastily adopted false belief concerning a wrong done me, it may be criticized as both irrational and 'false'.[12] What I now want to do is to establish that the belief-structure internal to both pity and fear stands or falls with views about the importance of luck in human life that would be accepted by Aristotle and by most ordinary people, but rejected by his philosophical opponents, including Plato.

Pity, Aristotle tells us in the *Rhetoric*, is a painful emotion directed towards another person's pain or suffering (1385b13ff.). It requires, then, the belief that the other person is really suffering, and, furthermore, that this suffering is not trivial, but something of real importance. (He stresses that it must have 'size' (*megethos*, 1386a6–7).) These sufferings he then divides into two groups: painful and injurious things, and substantial damages caused by luck. Representative examples of the former include: death, bodily assault, bodily ill-treatment, old age, illness, lack of food. Examples of the latter include: lack of *philoi*; having few *philoi*; being separated from your *philoi*; ugliness, weakness, being crippled, having your good expectations disppointed, having good things come too late, having no good things happen to you, or having them but being unable to enjoy them (1386a7–13). The rationale for the division into two groups is not altogether clear, since the first are caused by *tuchē* as much as the second, and the second contains examples of bodily harm that seem to belong with the first. It probably is not intended as an important theoretical distinction. In any case, both groups fall under the inclusive notion of injuries caused by luck that we have been working with so far in this book – though the second group contains the examples that have been of the greatest interest to us. In the *EN* examples from the two groups were brought together in the discussion of *tuchē* and external goods. We can see that there is a close connection between the listed occasions for pity and Aristotle's reflections about our vulnerability to the external in the ethical works; these happenings are prominent among the ways in which a good person can fall short of full *eudaimonia*.

Aristotle adds a further condition for pity, which he repeats and stresses in the *Poetics*. Pity, as response, is distinct from moral censure or blame: it requires the belief that the person did not deserve the suffering (*Po.* 1453a3–5, *Rhet.* 1385a13ff.). He claims, and I think correctly, that where we judge that the suffering is brought on by the agent's own bad choices, we (logically) do not pity: the structure of that emotion requires the opposing belief. In the *Rhetoric* he makes the interesting observation that the person who is too pessimistic about human nature will not feel pity at all – for he will believe that everyone deserves the bad things that happen to them (a remark pregnant with implications for the question of Christian tragedy). A dramatic story of such a *deserved* reversal, he tells us in the *Poetics*, will be benevolent and uplifting (*philanthrōpon*), but not tragic (1453a1ff.).

Finally, he points out that pity is closely connected with the belief that you yourself are vulnerable in similar ways. If you believe that you are so badly off that nothing further could happen to you to make things worse, you will not be likely to be capable of pity for others because you will be looking at their plight from the very bottom, from the point of view of one whose sufferings are complete. On the other hand, if you believe yourself self-sufficient *vis-à-vis eudaimonia*, secure in your possession of the good life, you will suppose that what happens to others cannot possibly happen to you. This will put you in a state of bold assertiveness (*hubristikē diathesis*), in which the sufferings of others do not arouse pity (1385b19–24, 31–2). Pity then, evidently requires fellow feeling, the judgment that your possibilities are similar to those of the suffering object.

It is evident that this central tragic emotion depends on some controversial beliefs about the situation of human goodness in the world: that luck is seriously powerful, that it is possible for a good person to suffer serious and undeserved harm, that this possibility extends to human beings generally. Aristotle's philosophical opponents, however, insist that if a person's character is good, the person cannot be harmed in any serious way. So there is within their view no room, conceptually, for pity. It must be considered a thoroughly irrational and useless emotion, based upon false beliefs that ought to be rejected. We rationally must choose between the response of blame, if we judge that what has happened is the fault of the agent, and equanimity or dismissiveness about what has happened, if we judge that it is the fault of the world. Accordingly, Plato does, in fact, repudiate pity in the strongest terms. In the *Phaedo*, which is a clear case of Platonic anti-tragedy, there is repeated stress on the fact that Socrates' predicament is not an occasion for pity (cf. Int. 1). The bad things are trivial, because they are happening only to his body; his soul is secure and self-sufficient. Accordingly, the dialogue's end replaces tragic pity with a praise of this good man's goodness. In *Republic* x, pity is again singled out for special abuse, in connection with the attack upon tragedy. Tragic poetry, Socrates says, does harm to practical rationality, in that 'after feeding fat the emotion of pity there, it is not easy to restrain it in our own experiences' (606B).[13]

But if we should believe, with Aristotle, that being good is not sufficient for *eudaimonia*, for good and praiseworthy living, then pity will be an important and valuable human response. Through pity we recognize and acknowledge the importance of what has been inflicted on another human being similar to us, through no fault of his own. We pity Philoctetes, abandoned friendless and in pain on a desert island. We pity Oedipus, because the appropriate action to which his character led him was not the terrible crime that he, out of ignorance, committed. We pity Agamemnon because circumstances forced him to kill his own child, something deeply repugnant to his own and our ethical commitments. We pity Hecuba because circumstances deprived her of all the human relationships that had given meaning and value to her life. Through attending to our responses of pity, we can hope to learn more about our own implicit view of what matters in human life, about the vulnerability of our own deepest commitments.

We can say something similar about fear. The belief structure of fear is intimately connected with that of pity. Aristotle stresses repeatedly that what we pity when it happens to another we fear in case it might happen to ourselves (*Po.* 1453a4–5, *Rhet.* 1386a22–8). And since pity already, in his view, requires the perception of one's own vulnerability, one's similarity to the sufferer, then pity and fear will almost always occur together. Fear is defined as a painful emotion connected with the expectation of future harm or pain (1382a21ff.). Aristotle adds that fear implies that these bad things are big or serious (1382a28–30), and that it is not in our power to prevent them. Thus we do not, he observes, in general fear that we will become unjust or slow-moving, presumably because we believe that that sort of change usually lies with us to control. Fear is above all connected with a sense of our passivity before events in the world – with 'the expectation of passively-suffering (*peisesthai*) some destructive affect' (*phthartikon pathos*,

1382b30–2); thus, those who believe they cannot passively-suffer anything will have no fears (1382b32–3).

For Aristotle's philosophical opponents, there will be little to fear. The good-condition theorist need not tremble in the face of the power of nature, for the only thing that is of serious importance is within him, as secure as can be. The *Republic*, for similar reasons, spends a long time criticizing and rejecting literary works that inspire fear. Plato's argument, repeatedly, is that correct beliefs about what is and is not important in human life remove our reasons for fear. The good person attaches no importance to any external loss, to any loss, that is, in a sphere of life that is beyond the control of the rational soul. But this means that he or she is in no way passive before nature, has nothing at all to fear. (We can see that the same would be true for Kant.) When we watch a tragic hero's downfall in the spirit of these philosophers, we will feel no fear for ourselves. For either our character and the hero's character are both good, in which case his difficulties give us nothing, really, to fear; or both characters need more work, in which case we had better get to work perfecting ours; or the hero's character is, after all, not similar to ours, in which case we will not be deeply moved in any way by his downfall. Nowhere is there the sense of vulnerability and passivity that gives rise to true fear. But in Aristotle's ethical universe there *are* serious things to fear, things of importance to *eudaimonia* itself. If, as Aristotle urges, we acknowledge the tragic characters as similar to us in their general goodness and their human possibilities, the tragedy as showing 'the sort of thing that might happen' to an aspiring person in human life generally, we will, with and in our fear, acknowledge their tragedy as a possibility for ourselves. And such a response will itself be a piece of learning concerning our human situation and our values.

Aristotle stresses, then, that central to our response to tragedy is a kind of identification with the suffering figure or figures depicted. They must, clearly, be good people, or we will not pity them. But the importance of identification imposes conditions on the ways in which they can be good. First of all, they must be good in a representative and not an idiosyncratic way. We can connect his demand for similarity between ourselves and the hero with his ranking of poetry above history as a source of wisdom. History, he points out, tells us what in fact happened; poetry 'the sort of thing that might happen' (1451b4–5). History tells us 'the particular, such as what Alcibiades did or suffered'; poetry 'the general, the sort of thing that happens to certain sorts of people' (1451b8–11). What he means here, I believe, is that often the events narrated by history are so idiosyncratic that they prevent identification. Because Alcibiades is such a unique and unusual figure, we do not regard what happens to him as showing a possibility for ourselves. (The difference between historical narration concerning Alcibiades and Plato's use of Alcibiades as a (representative) character would correspond to Aristotle's distinction between history and poetry.)* The tragic hero is not

---

* This denigration of history strikes us as odd, given that the greatest Greek historians, especially Thucydides, are plainly philosophical in Aristotle's sense. It is not evident, however, that Aristotle is familiar with Thucydides' work. If we think of Xenophon as the historian he has in mind, the remarks are more intelligible.

similarly idiosyncratic. He or she is seen by us to be a certain sort of good person, roughly similar to ourselves; for this reason we experience both pity and fear at his or her downfall.

Then again, if we are to see the hero as similar, he cannot be *too* perfectly good. Aristotle stresses that the tragic character, while he must indeed be good and while he must fall not through badness of character, must still not be 'one surpassing [perfect]¹⁴ in excellence and justice' (1453a8ff.).¹⁵ He must be 'better rather than worse', and even 'better than us' (1453b16–17, 1454b8–9); but he must not be perfect. There are several points that Aristotle could be making here. First, he could be ruling out the portrayal of the sort of invulnerably secure person mentioned in the *Rhetoric* chapters on pity – for with such a hero no tragic plot will make sense; and if we identify ourselves with the possibilities of such a person, neither pity nor fear will be possible. It seems likely, however, that Aristotle does not believe there *are* any really invulnerable people; and the person who *believes* he is invulnerable would not be an especially good person, as the mention of *hubris* in the *Rhetoric* strongly suggests. So it is unlikely that his 'good, but not perfectly good' is meant to rule out this person. Second, with 'surpassing in excellence' he could be ruling out a degree of perfection with respect to practical wisdom and intellectual excellence that would make mistakes like the ignorant mistake of Oedipus impossible. This is more promising, and is no doubt partly right; but it does not explain the presence of 'justice'. I believe, therefore, that he is making a third and more general point. This is that imperfections in a hero enhance our identification. There is a kind of excellence that is so far beyond our grasp that we regard its possessor as being above and beyond our kind, not among us. This sort of excellence is discussed at the opening of *Nicomachean Ethics* VII under the name 'heroic' or 'divine' excellence, or 'the excellence that is above us' (1145a19–20). It is exemplified by a Homeric quotation telling us that a certain hero is 'not like the child of a mortal man but like the child of a god'. Aristotle is even inclined to say of such a divine figure that he is 'more honorable than human excellence' – i.e., he is not the kind of being to whom it makes sense to ascribe the ordinary virtues at all, his goodness is in an altogether different category from ours. I think that Aristotle's point in the *Poetics* is that if tragedy shows us heroes who are in this way divine, lacking the limitations of patience, vision, reflection, and courage that characterize even the best of human subjects, the sense of similarity that is crucial to tragic response will not develop. The tragic hero should not fall through wickedness; but his being less than perfectly good is important to our pity and fear. Thus Oedipus's shortness of temper is not the *cause* of his decline; but it is one thing about Oedipus that makes him a character with whom we can identify. It is not a 'tragic flaw'; but it is instrumental to the tragic response. So, indeed, are Philoctetes' self-pity, Creon's self-ignorance and his mistaken ambition, Antigone's relentless denial of the civic, Agamemnon's excessive boldness. So, above all, might be the attempts of so many tragic good characters to deny their own vulnerability to chance happenings, those avoidances of their own condition which we, so much of the time, share with them. Aristotle's claim is that none of these defects is sufficient to make the person a wicked person in underlying character: even Creon preserves, beneath his (blameworthy) ambition, a rich and basically balanced set of values and attachments, and the fact is extremely important in determining our response to him. He can claim with some justice that he is a victim of his self-ignorance, not a deliberate perpetrator of evil deeds (cf. *ouch hekōn*, 1340). Such people fall, therefore, not *from* wickedness, but from something more like a mistake or error, blameworthy or not. But the presence of imperfections (some, perhaps, somehow involved in the decline and some not) means that we will see and acknowledge them as like us in kind, though good and, perhaps, better.

We find, then, that for Aristotle the viewing of pitiable and fearful things, *and* our responses of pity and fear themselves, can serve to show us something of importance about the human good. For the Platonist or the good-condition theorist, they cannot. For Aristotle, pity and fear will be sources of illumination or clarification, as the agent, responding and attending to his or her responses, develops a richer self-understanding concerning the attachments and values that support the responses. For Aristotle's opponents, pity and fear can never be better than sources of delusion and obfuscation.

It has been observed by Leon Golden in his excellent articles on the *Poetics* that every element in the *Poetics* definition of tragedy refers back to and summarizes the results of a discussion earlier in the work.[16] Aristotle explicitly announces that this is his plan, prefacing the definition with the remark, 'Let us speak about tragedy, taking up from what has been said the definition of its nature that has come into being' (1449b22–4). It is evident how every element of the definition offered fulfills this aim – with a single exception. The famous claim that the function of tragedy is 'through pity and fear to accomplish the *katharsis* of experiences of that kind' does not appear to pick up on anything that has gone before. It does not if, that is, we interpret *katharsis* in either of the two most common ways, as either moral purification or medical purgation. It is a strong *prima facie* advantage for an interpretation of *katharsis* if we can show that it, unlike the others, offers the desired retrospective link. Aristotle argued in Chapter 4 that our interest in *mimēsis* is a cognitive interest, an interest in learning (1448b13): human beings take pleasure in seeing representations 'because it happens that as they contemplate these they learn, and draw conclusions about what each thing is, for example, that this is that' (1448b15–17; cf. *Rhet.* 1371b5ff.). (If this account of our learning sounds too flat to support any sophisticated account of tragic pleasure, it should be remembered that Aristotle is here speaking very generally of human delight, at all ages, in works of art of many types. Some conclusions may be very simple: 'That's a horse'. Others will be much more complex: 'That's a cowardly action'; 'That's a case in which deprivation of loved ones has dislodged someone from *eudaimonia*'.) Golden points out that if we look to Plato's epistemological vocabulary (a reasonable place to look in interpreting this consciously anti-Platonic text), we find, in fact, that *katharsis* and related words, especially in the middle dialogues, have a strong connection with learning: namely, they occur in connection with the unimpeded or 'clear' rational state of the soul when it is freed from the troubling influences of sense and emotion. The intellect achieves 'purification' – or, better, 'clarification', since the word obviously has a cognitive force – only when it goes off 'itself by itself'.

We can, however, press this point much harder than Golden did if we look briefly at the whole history of *katharsis* and related words (*kathairō, katharos,* etc.). These facts are straightforward and easily accessible; they need to be stated, however, since they have been too often forgotten in discussions of this topic. When we examine the whole range of use and the development of this word-family, it becomes quite evident that the primary, ongoing, central meaning is roughly one of 'clearing up' or 'clarification', i.e. of the removal of some obstacle (dirt, or blot, or obscurity, or admixture) that makes the item in question less *clear* than it is in its proper state. In pre-Platonic texts these words are frequently used of water that is clear and open, free of mud or weeds; of a space cleared of objects; of grain that is winnowed, and so clear of chaff; of the part of an army that is not functionally disabled or impeded; and, significantly and often, of speech that is not marred by some obscurity or ambiguity (e.g. Aristoph. *Wasps* 631, 1046, ?Eur. *Rhes.* 35). The medical use to designate purgation is a special application of this general sense: purgation rids the body of internal impediments and obstacles, clearing it up. And the connection with spiritual purification and ritual purity appears to be another specialized development, given the strong link between such purity and physical freedom from blemish or dirt.

If we now return to Plato's usage, we find that he preserves this general picture. The central sense is that of freedom from admixture, clarity, absence of impediment. In the case of the soul and its cognition, the application of the word-group is mediated by the dominant metaphors of mud and clean light: the eye of the soul can be sunk in mud (*Rep.* 533D1, *Phd.* 69C), or it can be seeing cleanly and clearly. *Katharos* cognition is what we have when the soul is not impeded by bodily obstacles (esp. *Rep.* 508C, *Phd.* 69C). *Katharsis* is the clearing up of the vision of the soul by the removal of these obstacles; thus the *katharon* becomes associated with the true or truly knowable, the being who has achieved *katharsis* with the truly or correctly knowing (esp. *Phd.* 65ff., 110ff.). Thus we even find expressions such as *katharōs apodeixai,* meaning 'demonstrate clearly' (*Crat.* 426B).

We can now add that by Aristotle's time and shortly thereafter – whether through Platonic influence or through an independent development of the applications to speech – this epistemological use of *katharsis* and *katharos* becomes easy and natural, and does not even require a context of metaphor. Xenophon speaks of a *katharos nous,* meaning one that cognizes clearly and truly (*Cyr.* 8.7.30). Epicurus speaks of his epitome written to Pythocles as a *katharsis phusikōn problematōn,* a 'clarification of the difficult issues of natural philosophy' (D.L. x.86; cf. Phld. *Lib.* p. 220 O; *kathairō* means 'explain' in fragments of the *Peri Phuseōs*). Aristotle's *Prior Analytics* speaks of a need to 'examine and indicate each of these things with clarity (*katharōs*)' (50a40); it goes without saying that these uses have nothing to do either with purification or with purgation. And in rhetorical theory above all, the word-family becomes entrenched, indicating the desired quality of clarity and freedom from obscurity in diction (e.g. Isoc. 5.4, Ar. *Rhet.* 1356b26, 1414a13); in Hellenistic Rhetoric it is a technical term (for only one example, see Menander, *Rhet.* 340.24). In none of this development does the process-word *katharsis* get semantically separated from the family; it designates simply the process that yields a *katharos* result, the removal of obstacles whose absence gives that result.

We can, then, say without hesitation that all along the meaning 'clearing up' and 'clarification' will be appropriate and central ones for *katharsis*, even in medical and ritual contexts. In the context of rhetoric and poetry, especially in a work written in reaction to Platonic criticisms of the cognitive value of rhetoric and poetry, we would have strong reason not only to translate the word this way but also to think of the 'clearing up' in question as psychological, epistemological, and cognitive, rather than as literally physical. (Aristotle's general strong opposition to physiological reductionism gives us a great deal of support here.)[17] We can now add that to a middle-period Platonist it would be profoundly shocking to read of cognitive clarification produced by the influence of pity and fear: first, because the Platonic soul gets to clarity only when no emotions disturb it; second, because these emotions are especially irrational. Aristotle is fond of delivering such shocks. I have argued that, in his view, tragedy contributes to human self-understanding precisely through its exploration of the pitiable and the fearful. The way it carries out this exploratory task is by moving us to respond with these very emotions. For these emotional responses are themselves pieces of recognition or acknowledgment of the worldly conditions upon our aspirations to goodness. Golden's view of clarification is that it is a purely intellectual matter.[18] This interpretation (which requires translating Aristotle's 'through pity and fear' by the periphrasis 'through the representation of pitiable and fearful events') is unnecessarily Platonic. *Katharsis* does not *mean* 'intellectual clarification'. It means 'clarification' – and it happens to be Plato's view that all clarification is an intellectual matter. We can ascribe to Aristotle a more generous view of the ways in which we come to know ourselves. First of all, clarification, for him, can certainly take place *through* emotional responses, as the definition states. Just as, inside the *Antigone*, Creon's learning came by way of the grief he felt for his son's death, so, as we watch a tragic character, it is frequently not thought but the emotional response itself that leads us to understand what our values are. Emotions can sometimes mislead and distort judgment; Aristotle is aware of this. But they can also, as was true in Creon's case, give us access to a truer and deeper level of ourselves, to values and commitments that have been concealed beneath defensive ambition or rationalization.

But even this is, so far, too Platonic a line to take: for it suggests that emotion is valuable only as an instrumental means to a purely intellectual state. We know, however, that for Aristotle appropriate responses are intrinsically valuable parts of good character and can, like good intellectual responses, help to constitute the refined 'perception' which is the best sort of human judgment. We could say, then, that the pity and fear are not just tools of a clarification that is in and of the intellect alone; to respond in these ways is itself valuable, and a piece of clarification concerning who we are. It is a recognition of practical values, and therefore of ourselves, that is no less important than the recognitions and perceptions of intellect. Pity and fear are themselves elements in an appropriate practical perception of our situation. Aristotle differs with Plato not only about the mechanisms of clarification, but also about what, in the good person, clarification *is*.[19]

With these observations in place, we might try to summarize our results by saying on Aristotle's behalf that the function of a tragedy is to accomplish, through pity and fear, a clarification (or illumination) concerning experiences of the pitiable and fearful kind. But that is, by a surprising piece of good luck, exactly what Aristotle has already said.

We can represent what has gone on by using the ending of a tragedy as our image. Sophocles' Philoctetes, saying farewell to his island home, tells us that the good outcome, productive of his *eudaimonia*, has been determined by three things: 'great destiny', 'the judgment of friends', and 'the all-subduing *daimōn*, who brought these things to fulfillment'. The significant ordering of these items suggests to us that the practical judgment of these characters is, like Lemnos, an island: something firm in itself, but surrounded by the sometimes enabling and sometimes impeding forces of luck and natural happening.[20] Aristotle's opponents, the Platonist and the good-condition theorist, could not accept this image of human moral life. They would have to represent the island as a vast continent, the surrounding waters as shallow and innocuous. And even the island itself would have to have a different character: for 'the judgment of friends' is itself too unreliable an ethical item. It would have to be replaced by the goodness of the solitary good person. Our investigation of Aristotle's views about goodness and luck might be summarized by pointing out that he, unlike his opponents, can accept this image as true. That is why he can accept tragedy.

Any reader who has followed this book's reflections concerning philosophy and its style this far will, at this point, have a troublesome question. What is Aristotle's own style, and what view of the world does it express? I have argued that Aristotle's ethical views make him hospitable to tragedy and its style as sources of illumination; I argued earlier that the adoption of a related ethical position caused Plato, in the *Phaedrus*, to modify his own philosophical style so as to include emotive and rhetorical elements associated with poetry. Aristotle, plainly, does not do this. He embraces poetic works without altering in any way his own style, which seems to most readers spare and unemotive in the extreme. Does this cast doubt on our reading of his ethical arguments, branding him, after all, as a thinker insensitive to the value of the vulnerable goods? Or, perhaps more disturbing still, does it convict Aristotle of a kind of superficiality about style that we have been eager to criticize throughout this book: of the view, that is, that there is a neutral philosophical style in which all claimants to ethical truth can be equally and impartially assessed?

We hardly have a right to press these questions, since we know far too little about the status of these works as written texts. Aristotle's externally published works, including numerous dialogues, were famous in antiquity for their copious, delightful, and flowing style. Cicero speaks of a 'golden river', a later writer of discourse 'overflowing with controlled eroticism'.[21] These works, which would have shown us how Aristotle interrelated the 'philosophical' and the 'literary', are for ever out of reach; only meager fragments survive. The works we read are, most probably, the texts of written lectures for delivery to an audience of serious and specialized students. The arranging and editing was done by a later hand; and even the internal content of the chapters themselves is likely to be, in many places, only a sketch of the delivered lecture, which would have been fleshed out, like any set of lecture notes, with examples, jokes, dramatic material – in short, with the oral analogue of some of the 'literary' elements we miss. Anyone who gives lecture courses from a written text knows how far such a text can be from the sort of writing one chooses to cultivate in a deliberately composed and finished work; even from the oral style of the delivered lecture.

And even about the style of these lecture notes there is great disagreement. Most students, and many more experienced readers, find it austere, forbidding, even drab. Eminent philosophers have concluded that the writer of so flat and dull a style could not have felt as acutely as Plato did the force of our deepest ethical problems.[22] I myself now find in this style a courageous straightforwardness and directness *vis-à-vis* 'the matter of the practical'; a serene restraint that expresses the determination to acknowledge these difficulties, to let them be there, and not to despair of human life because of them. In my interpretative writing here I have tried to convey this response.

But if we do decide for the moment to consider these works seriously as pieces of deliberately styled writing, we have, even if we respond to their style as I do, some difficult questions to face. In Plato's *Phaedrus* and in Aristotle's ethical thought, we have an agreement that the pursuit of practical wisdom is fostered by works that contain poetic elements and address themselves to the emotional 'part' of the soul. In both there is also, implicitly, agreement that the pursuit of wisdom requires another more reflective and explanatory sort of style, one that seeks understanding by calmly asking for an account of our ethical commitments and their interrelationships. But here the resemblance ends. For Plato's choice is to blend these two styles together into a subtly interwoven whole. His prose moves seamlessly from the spare and formally explanatory to the lyrical and emotive, and back again, breaking down traditional genre distinctions. Aristotle's choice is to commend and venerate the works of actual poets, and to confine his own writing to the reflective and explanatory function. The two styles are kept apart, although they call upon and honor one another. What is the meaning of this difference?[23]

We might first say that it may be less a philosophical difference than a difference of personality and talent. For if one really honors the claim of great literature to explore the truth, one will not lightly attempt to *produce* literature. One will know that the ethically valuable elements of such a work are inseparable from the poetic genius of their production; that a mediocre literary work will not be able to convey tragic learning. Plato was a literary artist of genius, whose talents enabled him to take up the poetic task into his own style. Aristotle was not such an artist; or, if he was, we are not aware of it. Aristotle would then be showing his respect, rather than his disregard, for the literary when he confines his own prose to a more conventional style and turns, for poetic learning, to the dramas of Sophocles and Euripides.

There may, however, be a deeper point here as well. For Plato, despite his partial rehabilitation of poetic art, lacks respect for actual poets. He will perform part of their job himself: what he does not do, even in the *Phaedrus*, is to commend their actual works as sources of insight. The *Phaedrus* does indeed incorporate poetic elements: but it keeps a close watch on them, never allowing them to get very far away from philosophical explanations. Poems, it argues, cannot be sources of insight if they do not engage in dialectic, answering questions about themselves. The good student of Plato would not be reading poetic writing, then, except in close conjunction with the other, more analytical, elements of Plato's philosophical prose. Aristotle, by allowing these works to exist apart as sources of insight in their own right, shows himself to be not less, but more responsive than Plato to their claim to tell the truth to human souls.

This does not in any way imply that Aristotle denies the importance of interpretation and explanation. A commitment to explanation is fundamental in all of his philosophical work. If he respects the autonomous cognitive value of tragic poetry, he thinks, too, that the highest or most comprehensive understanding of their ethical content, the understanding that he calls 'understanding the why',[24] requires a philosophical reflection that will render the salient features of our ethical experience more perspicuous, that speaks to our sense of wonder and perplexity, striving to answer our 'why' questions. His patient and lucid prose is an excellent expression of this commitment. We might think of the ethical works as works of interpretation, orderings of the 'appearances' found in ordinary life and in tragic poetry. They do not replace tragedy: for only tragedy can give us illumination through and in pity and fear. But they supply an essential part of tragic learning, a part that Aristotle might fear losing were he to run together criticism and madness, explanation and passion.

We might remind ourselves at this point of a conclusion of our Chapter 8: that once philosophy exists, responding to and further nourishing the natural human demand for order in confusion, the simplifications of bad philosophy cannot be answered by a simple return to the status quo ante. The powerful appeal of philosophical system and argument cannot be undone by simply putting forward a poem or story; or cannot, at least, for people on whom philosophy has deeply left its mark. The traditional and the ordinary require the patient return of appearance-saving philosophy for their defense. After Plato, tragedy needs Aristotle.

We can now add that these facts are evident in our own style as well. A tragic poem, no less than the complex 'appearances' recorded by Aristotle, stands in need of careful interpretation. Our own attempt to look for insight in these poems and to defend them against Kantian and Platonic objections has required us to give explanations of them that make evident much that was previously concealed or likely to escape notice. The style of our chapters on tragedy attempted to be responsive to the poetic features of the texts; thus it showed a responsiveness to metaphorical and emotive language that is not usually present in recent Anglo-American philosophical writing. But these chapters were still far from being poems in their own right. We did diverge from Aristotle insofar as we indicated that the aims of interpretation will sometimes best be served by a 'mixed' more *Phaedrus*-like sort of writing that incorporates certain literary elements. For to display the function of the tragic emotions we must, evidently, allow ourselves to respond, as an audience or as readers, to what is pitiable and fearful in the play before us, acknowledging in our writing and reading the emotions that it is its function to summon. (If we had Aristotle's published work we might find out that he himself made similar choices.) But our style expresses, too, an Aristotelian commitment to explanation, to reading a poetic work so as to ask of it what it is doing and why.* It seems appropriate to end this book with one more example of this mixed activity, which we might call philosophical criticism.[25]

* The contrast between poetry and philosophy in this respect should not, however, be overpressed. Clearly philosophical texts also stand in need of interpretation and explanation; and such interpretations may also bring forward much that was inexplicit or dark in the original.

Epilogue: tragedy

I see now there's nothing sure in mortality but mortality.
Well, no more words – 't shall be revenged i' faith.

Ambitioso, in Tourneur, The Revenger's Tragedy

Now the dog – the animal upon which, by way of example, we have decided to base our argument – exercises choice of the congenial and avoidance of the harmful, in that it hunts after food and slinks away from a raised whip. Moreover, it possesses an art which supplies what is congenial, namely hunting. Nor is it devoid even of virtue; for certainly if justice consists in rendering to each his due, the dog, that welcomes and guards its friends and benefactors but drives off strangers and evil-doers, cannot be lacking in justice.

Sextus Empiricus, Outlines of Pyrrhonism, 1.66–7
(trans. Bury)

I enjoyed perfect health of body and tranquillity of mind; I did not feel the treachery or inconstancy of a friend, nor the injuries of a secret or open enemy...I wanted no fence against fraud or oppression.

Jonathan Swift, Gulliver's Travels, Part IV, Ch. 10

13   The betrayal of convention: a reading of
Euripides' *Hecuba*

We see a child approaching, floating above the ground as if carried by the wind.[1] A child royally dressed, his face shining with simple dignity. Perhaps it is a young god; or some human child divinized for his beauty or his swiftness. 'Here I am', the child begins, in a voice that seems to express trust and openness. The unaccustomed sight of a child on the tragic stage, opening a play, elicits from us, in turn, a simple directness of response. We think, briefly, of potentiality and hope; of the beginnings of noble character; of the connection between noble character and this childish trustfulness. We feel, perhaps, in this moment, our love for our own children. Then we hear it. 'Here I am. Back from the hiding-place of the dead and the gates of darkness. Polydorus, child of Hecuba and Priam.' We are watching, then, not a child, but a dead child.[2] A child-ghost. A shade without hope, its possibilities frozen. And there is more. This child, as he soon tells us, has been brutally murdered by his parents' best friend, to whom they had entrusted him for safe-keeping in wartime. Killed for his money, he has been tossed, unburied, into the waves that break on this Thracian shore.

Euripides has chosen to begin this play in a very unusual manner. No other extant Greek tragedy has a prologue spoken either by a ghost or by a child; the combination occurs nowhere in any extant play. He thus deliberately, strikingly, evokes in us, however briefly, the hopes and deep feelings that we connect with the life and growth of children – only to shock us with the news that this is a child whose future does not exist. From the beginning, this is an assault upon our fondest thoughts about human safety and human beneficence.

A little later in his speech, this child takes us further into the play's central issues with a revealing description of his life in the home of the killer Polymestor:

As long as the boundary markers of this country stood straight and the towers of the Trojan land were intact, as long as my brother Hector had good fortune with his spear – so long I lived with the Thracian, my parents' guest-friend. I grew like a young shoot under his nurture. (16–20)

A young child, he suggests (in an image well known to us), is like a green plant: its very growth to maturity and good character depends on the provision of nourishment from without. Put in the mouth of a murdered child, this image makes us recall that our possibilities for goodness depend on the good faith of others, who are not always faithful. And even when a plant comes to maturity and flourishes, it is still, after all, nothing harder or tougher than a plant. Even healthy plants can be blasted from without by storms, disease, betrayal.

So Euripides starts us thinking about the central concerns of this disturbing play: the nature of good character, its connection with a child's trusting simplicity, its vulnerability to disease when trust is violated. This play contains a famous speech about the incorruptibility of noble character based on nurture and shared conventions. It is the speech of a proud mother. And in the character of her daughter Polyxena the play shows us a deeply moving evidence of Hecuba's claim, the calm unswerving goodness of a well-raised child now entering adulthood, a goodness whose generosity elicits awe even from the most brutal. But before the end of the play we witness the transformation of two of its central personages, both respected adult characters, into beasts. One of these beasts is Hecuba: the mother who made the claim herself refutes it.

The story can be briefly told. Troy has fallen. Hecuba, formerly its queen, now a Greek slave, arrives on the coast of Thrace with her captors and fellow slave-women. Despite her sorrow at the destruction of her city, her loss of power, the death of her husband and most of her children, she is consoled by the thought that her two youngest children remain: Polyxena, who travels with her as a slave, and Polydorus, her youngest, who has been entrusted to the care of the local Thracian king, a man who is 'first among my loved ones in the rank of guest-friendship'. In the play's first episode, Polyxena is taken from her. Odysseus appears, demanding that she be turned over to the Greek army as a human sacrifice to appease the angry ghost of Achilles, who has appeared demanding an underworld bride. Hecuba's pleas fail to move him. Polyxena herself responds with remarkable dignity and courage. She goes off to meet death willingly, saying that death is better for a free and noble person than a slave's life. Her splendid demeanor during the offstage execution, described by a herald, so moves the Greek soldiers that they decide to give her an honorable burial. Hecuba declares that her grief is mitigated by knowledge of the firmness of her daughter's noble character. This leads to a more general statement about the stability of good character in adversity.

Then a servant enters from the beach, holding the mutilated corpse of Polydorus. Hecuba at first takes it for Polyxena's body. When she recognizes her son, she guesses immediately the treachery of Polymestor, and is shattered. She decides to devote herself from now on to revenge. Failing to obtain the help of Agamemnon, the Greek commander, she concocts a private plan. Inviting Polymestor and his two children to the private women's quarters of the camp, ostensibly to give them information about a hidden treasure, she murders the children and puts out Polymestor's eyes. He crawls onstage on all fours, hunting for his enemy. The corpses of his children are brought on, but he neglects them in favor of pursuing his revenge. Finding Hecuba at last, he prophesies that she will end her life in the shape of a dog with fiery eyes; when she dies in this form, the promontory Cynossema, 'Memorial of the Bitch', will be named after her and will serve as a mark for sailors. Agamemnon, finding the anger of these enemies distasteful, and fearing Polymestor's prophecy of his own death, has Polymestor gagged and taken off to a desert island. Hecuba goes to bury her two children, then on to her predicted end.

This alarming story of metamorphosis arouses and explores some of our deepest fears about the fragility of humanness, and especially of character, which might seem to be the firmest part of humanness. The story of its reception is mixed. For many centuries it ranked very high within the tragic corpus. Ovid recasts it in the *Metamorphoses*. In Byzantine times it was a central school text. Dante gives it a place of importance in the *Inferno*, using it to show degeneration of character resulting from chance events.[3] But for the nineteenth century and on into this one, it is usually counted as one of the weakest of the extant tragedies. Its violence and its spectacle of decline are found crudely shocking and repellent.[4] Hecuba's speech about nurture is frequently excerpted and studied as a part of the history of Greek ethical thought; the play that undercuts the speech is avoided.[5] Not surprisingly, this metamorphosis in critical opinion coincides in time with the dominance of a moral philosophy that speaks of the incorruptibility of the good will, sharply distinguishing the sphere of contingent happenings from the domain of the moral personality, itself purely safe against the 'accidents of step-motherly nature'.[6] For in terms of that view (or, we can now say, in terms of Platonist and 'good-condition' views about value and damage) this play tells dangerous lies.[7] To confront it will, then, teach us more about these views, both ancient and modern: namely, what possibility they regard as so repugnant that it must be ruled out ahead of time, by definition. It will also test our reading of Aristotle: for by showing us the worst possibility for damage to goodness left open in an Aristotelian ethical universe, it will show us the extent and depth of Aristotle's return to the appearances of his cultural tradition. We will then be forced to ask ourselves whether we really think we live, and whether we really wish to live, in this Aristotelian world.*

I

At first, Hecuba is merely unhappy. Citiless, widowed, enslaved, she experiences a still crueler loss when Polyxena is taken from her. But she herself, in the face of these arbitrary events, remains loyal and loving. Furthermore, the example of Polyxena's nobility convinces her that, in general, human good character is a firm and stable thing, capable of surviving catastrophe undefiled. The herald tells her of her daughter's moderate, courageous, and generous behavior before and during the execution. She responds with a mixture of grief and pride:

...And yet, the grief is not excessive, since I have heard that you were noble (*gennaios*). Isn't it remarkable (*deinon*), the way that bad soil, receiving opportunity from god, bears a good crop, and good soil, if it fails to get what it needs, will give a bad crop; but among human beings the wicked is never anything but bad, and the noble anything but noble,

---

* This reading of the *Hecuba* does not, of course, rely on Aristotle. It could stand at an earlier point in the book. We shall interpret the play in the light of its own historical context. But the juxtaposition of this reading with our discussion of Aristotle will help us to assess Aristotle's attitude towards tragic events; and also to understand why he singles out Euripides as 'the most tragic of all', therefore the most suited for the educational function that he ascribes to tragedy.

and is not corrupted (*diephtheir'*) in its nature by contingency, but stays good straight through to the end?...To be nurtured well does offer instruction in nobility. If once one learns this well, one also knows the shameful, learning it by the measuring-stick of the fine.

Polydorus had compared the development of a human being to the growth of a plant. Hecuba both accepts and attacks the comparison. A human being does, like a plant, stand in need of nurture from without. This nurture is a crucial factor in becoming noble. But once good character is formed through instruction, the human being ceases to resemble a plant. The adult product is something far firmer, something that will keep its nature or character, and be true to it, regardless of circumstances. A good person will be stably disposed to choose noble actions and to avoid shameful ones. No matter what happens in the world, this character will escape defilement or corruption.[8]

This speech will be crucial for our study of Hecuba's decline: for even as it presents an argument for the stability of good character under adversity, it reveals features of Hecuba's conception of excellence that will help to explain her later instability. First, the social and relational nature of her central value commitments, her reliance upon fragile things; second, her anthropocentricity: her belief that ethical commitments are human things, backed by nothing harder or more stable. The second point is already implicit in her contrast, here, between what happens in nature and what happens 'among human beings'. Ethical standards exist, apparently, entirely within the human world. This becomes even clearer later, when Hecuba denies explicitly that moral bonds are secured by anything more stable than our agreements:

The gods are strong, and so is convention (*nomos*)* which rules over them. For it is by *nomos* that we recognize the gods and live our lives, making our distinctions between injustice and justice. If *nomos* is destroyed [or: corrupted]...there is nothing else like it† in human life. (799–805)

Deep human agreements (or practices) concerning value are the ultimate authority for moral norms. If 'convention' is wiped out, there is no higher tribunal to which we can appeal. Even the gods exist only within this human world.[9]

In both of these speeches we see, too, clear evidence of our first point: the importance within this anthropocentric conception of the relational values. In the earlier speech, values are said to be imparted through nurture in a community; the later speech explicitly tells us that one of the central values imparted by this

---

* Arrowsmith translates *nomos* here as 'some absolute, some moral order'. (He tells me that he now agrees with my translation.) There are, however, strong reasons for taking it to be a human and not an eternal *nomos*. The next sentence, introduced by 'for' (*gar*) must give the reason for believing that *nomos* is over the gods. But this sentence refers to human practices according to which we believe in the existence of gods and *make* (not: *find*) basic ethical distinctions. Cf. also 866, where the phrase *nomōn graphai*, 'writings of *nomoi*' again reminds us that we are speaking of a human artifact.

† *Ouden...ison*, 'nothing...equal', conveys in fact a double sense: (a) nothing equal to or like *nomos*; and also (b) nothing fair or impartial. The second, less obvious meaning brings out the extent to which all of social justice or equity stands or falls with *nomos*.

nurture is a social value, justice. We will shortly see that another social value, friendship or love, is equally deeply rooted in Hecuba's conception of the good.

We can begin to see several points of resemblance between Hecuba's conception and Aristotle's. Both insist on the importance of relational goods; both emphasize the role of community in teaching values; both deny that there is, behind human practices, some higher tribunal to which we could have recourse. This should not be surprising, since Hecuba's view, if it is one pervasively held in fifth-century culture, would be a prominent part of the 'appearances' to which Aristotle's ethical theory is committed. More concretely, her speech has a good deal in common with the views expressed by Plato's Protagoras, who explicitly claims to express a widely-held view and whose position we have already compared to Aristotle's. But in order to advance further we need to ground our reading of Hecuba's claims in a more solid grasp of the force of her distinctions within her own time, asking what, exactly, is the relationship of her speeches to the famous contemporary debate about *nomos* and the status of ethical value. If we digress briefly to explore these connections, we will have a richer background from which to explore the rest of the play.

Long before Plato, a well-entrenched tradition in Greek ethical thought was claiming that ethical agreements and practices are based upon standards fixed eternally in the nature of things. This is frequently (though not always) what is meant by the claim that ethical values exist 'by nature': they are out there, independently of us and our ways of life. This story of the extra-human status of value (often associated with a story of extra-human origins) provided a justification for the hardness and inviolability that people wished to associate with the deepest ethical requirements.[10] The view implied, among other things, that these requirements could never be set aside or annulled by human action. It also meant that our most fundamental ethical relationship is not to unstable entities such as persons and city, but to something firmer than any of us. If humans violate a law of hospitality, they can rely on the continued concern of Zeus Xenios; if humans care little for oaths, Zeus Horkios never deviates or alters. All this gives a sense of deep structure and security to the ethical universe; it imparts stability to human lives within it.* We have seen, of course, how Plato draws upon this tradition and develops it; and how Aristotle criticizes the tradition as a whole. But if we wish to think of the tradition as it confronted Hecuba, we would do well to think of the moral security of the elders in Sophocles' *Oedipus*, who are able to sing of:

---

* We should, however, remind ourselves here of a fact by now familiar from our second and third chapters: that the Greek gods are capable of change, of double or contradictory action, of disagreement, and of a justice that can appear quite unjust by mortal standards. Zeus presides over and engineers the breaking of oaths, as well as their sanctity (e.g. *Iliad* IV.68ff.) – just as Artemis both protects and destroys young animals (Ch. 2). Thus when a mortal relies on a god there is, along with the basic security, an element of uncertainty and vulnerability that makes this ethical posture nearer to that of the 'plant' tradition that some texts taken in isolation might suggest.

...laws with a lofty basis, born in the airy heavens. Their only father is Olympus, nor did any mortal nature of human beings give birth to them, nor will forgetfulness lull them to sleep. There is a great god in them; he does not grow old. (865–72)

On the other side, we have a strain in traditional thought about ethics (coexisting, early on, with the first, though potentially in tension with it) that speaks of ethical value as something growing, flowing, and mutable, existing within the human community and its long traditions of praise and blame.[11] This way of thinking finds forceful expression in late fifth-century talk about *nomos*; but it is, in fact, far older, as our discussion of Pindar's image and its epic background has indicated (cf. Ch. 1 n. 3). The plant imagery of this tradition is echoed by both Polydorus and Hecuba; she, in addition, uses as her central word for excellence the word '*gennaios*', closely linked to this imagery through the idea of true or appropriate growth. This imagery implies both anthropocentricity (rootedness in the world of change and history) and the central importance of the social; it also displays the neediness of the good person through her dependence on the social.[12] These features of plant talk are in principle separable. One could characterize the individual as needy and fragile while believing that immutable norms exist; indeed, this situation prevailed through much of the archaic period. One might also try to depict the individual as rock-hard, despite the human nature of value. But in the former case the existence of immutable standards limits the individual's vulnerability: if a human requirement is violated, a divine law will effect, in the long run, a righting of the balance. And the latter type of separation is difficult to sustain, as Hecuba will discover: for if there is no external appeal, no incorruptible standing structure, this fact will be likely to affect the stability of the individual in both activity and internal goodness.[13] As Aristotle expresses this point: since 'the law has no power towards obedience but that of habit', enforced changes in these habits may lead to a climate of rootlessness and upheaval (*Pol.* 1268b22ff., cf. Ch. 10, pp. 304–5).

In the years immediately preceding the writing of this play, these questions about the origin and status of ethical value were the subject of intense controversy. Disturbed by the perception of ethical differences brought about by travel and comparative ethnographical work,[14] many of Hecuba's 'contemporaries' were asking whether in fact ethical practices were not of merely human origin (existed merely by *nomos*),[15] and, if they were, whether this implied that they were superficial, arbitrary, even replaceable at will.[16]* Once again, as earlier, the

---

* We cannot recapitulate the details of this fifth-century controversy here. Briefly, however: thinkers divided on the question whether ethical norms and practices are human artifacts. This, in turn, gave rise to some further questions: if they are contingent and human, does this imply that they are merely arbitrary and/or replaceable at will? The claim that ethical norms exist by *nomos* does not in general directly imply relativism about value, though some Greek thinkers take it to do so; it merely makes the relativity of values a live option. (Protagoras, for example, seems to make the human species his ethical measure without embracing any narrower societal form of relativism.) Finally, once a thinker has taken a position on these questions about the status of our ethical norms, he must go on to say whether, so situated, they are good things to follow, or whether some sort of return from them to a standard of nature might not be preferable, for some people or for all. (For some further details and references, see notes.)

anthropocentric view was linked with an emphasis on social and relational excellences, the ones that evidently came into being with the city. A praise of *nomos* is almost always a praise of these values.[17] The etymology of our 'convention' implies the relational; even so, Greek '*nomos*' is etymologically connected with ideas of distribution, apportionment, and boundary, hence, of interpersonal agreement.[18] (Some thinkers saw this as a logical connection: the relational excellences more than others have their point only within the context of human life, with its needs and limitations.)[19]

In the debate about *nomos* and its value, Hecuba's speeches take up an interesting and constructive position. She clearly holds that our ethical values (prominent among which are social values) exist 'by *nomos*' in the sense that they are just human; but this fact does not, she seems to argue, license us to regard them lightly. Nor does it seem that we can replace or alter them at will. We are raised inside these distinctions; they structure everything that we do; we cannot so easily depart from the world that they constitute.[20] And, finally, once we have been brought up in them, they are in us: they form the internal structure of our 'nature', making us psychologically stable against any events that the world can devise. Human virtue is incorruptible, more stable by far than a plant.

But Hecuba's admission that our central values are simply human and, within the human world, social, leaves her still in a vulnerable position. We wonder whether the internal fragility of a plant can really be separated off from the other features of the plant image. She has given pride of place to values that depend on a changeable context for their exercise. The agent she describes can be firmer than a plant only if her social environment is more dependable than the world of nature; this may fail to be so. Furthermore, the process of moral development, as she describes it, seems to presuppose, on the part of both parent and child, an unsuspicious trust in the authority and efficacy of *nomos*.[21] For a child will not learn the distinctions that are the *nomoi* of her society if either parent or child is always doubting whether this is, in fact, the ethical language we speak, or asking skeptically whether these agreements are, in fact, in force. Nor can a loving parent encourage a child to want the things that the *nomoi* commend unless she can herself believe in their effectiveness. All this suggests that our ethical practices, and adult ethical goodness itself, may be more vulnerable, in times of general upheaval, than Hecuba has acknowledged.

These questions are made the more acute by her combination of an external-related conception with ethical anthropocentricity. For if moral distinctions are agreements in ways of living and talking, if morality is a system of human practices, then there is a distinct possibility that circumstances or human acts can change or defile *nomos* itself. The requirements of Zeus could be violated; Zeus himself remained watchful, undefiled, a suitable object of human trust. If many things are unreliable, there is something that is perfectly reliable; the trust that seems to be a necessary part of a good ethical life has somewhere to go. But Hecuba's human *nomos* can, she concedes, itself suffer 'destruction' or 'corruption'. If one party acts against the common understanding, the agreement that made the convention firm is itself weakened; no rock-hard underlying nature shores it up. If you and I agree to call certain acts unjust, and you suddenly change your use of the moral term, no eternal law will bring you to book or justify me against you. If I promise to care for your child and I murder him, that promise does not sit unblemished in some holy realm, witnessing against me. It is defiled; nothing replaces it.

In general, such unsettling facts will escape notice, since the injured party can call upon standing cultural agreements and laws to bring the offender to justice. Only a single agreement is defiled; and *nomos* in the deeper sense will come to the rescue. Such deeply shared agreements can themselves, however, shift and degenerate. If the individual failure occurs at a time when the social fabric of use is not whole, then we will see very clearly what it means to concede that *nomos* is in the world and not 'out there'. There is, simply, nowhere to turn. The foundation has undergone corruption. And then, adds Hecuba, there is no substitute. 'There is nothing like it in human life.'

Such anxieties would have burdened any audience at this time. Euripides could expect to tap and work with our already active reflections on precisely this issue. The play was produced in 425 or 424.[22] In 424, the three-year civil war in Corcyra came to its ugly and violent conclusion. Thucydides tells us that this conflict attracted attention because of its horrifying evidence of moral degradation in time of stress; it served as a sign of the fragility of *nomos*, of the possibilities in our nature for betrayal, heedlessness, vengefulness:[23]

...Many were the calamities that befell the Greek cities through this civil strife... The customary verbal evaluations of deeds were exchanged for new ones when ethical assessments were made: an unreasoning daring was called courage and loyalty to party, a prudent delay specious cowardice; moderation and self-control came to be reckoned but the cloak of timidity, to have an understanding of the whole to be everywhere unwilling to act... If a man plotted and succeeded, he was intelligent; if he suspected a plot he was even cleverer; and one who took care so that neither a plot nor suspicion be needed was a subverter of his party... Good faith between the members of a party was secured not by the sanction of divine *nomos* so much as by the partnership in crime; and as for fair offers from opponents, they were received only with precautionary action by the stronger party, not with noble candor (*gennaiotēti*). A man thought more of avenging an injury than of having no injury to avenge.

Thus did every type of bad practice take root in Greece, fed by these civil wars. Openness (*to euēthes*), which is the largest part of noble character (*to gennaion*), was laughed down; it vanished. Mistrustful opposition of spirit carried the day, destroying all trust. To reconcile them no speech was strong enough, no oath fearful enough. All of them alike, when they got the upper hand, calculating that security was not to be hoped for, became more intent on self-protection than they were capable of trust.[24]

We are confronted here with the total disintegration of a moral community, the slippage and corruption of an entire moral language. The ethical community changes its character. It functions as function the agents within it; no external law intervenes to halt or correct this organic process of change. (Divine *nomos* is mentioned only as that which is disregarded or no longer believed in.) Worst of all, even formerly good agents are blighted when betrayal and violation take root. Nothing protects them.

There is much that can be said about the fate of good characters in such times. First, they are treated differently – mocked and abused. Then, too, they lose, from without, the ability to exercise inherently relational virtues. But it is in the area of confidence and trust that the lesson of Corcyra most plainly threatens Hecuba. Thucydides stresses that virtuous character rests on a foundation of confidence in conditions that exist outside the self. The 'greatest part' of noble character is *to euēthes*, which can be rendered as 'guilelessness', 'openness', 'simplicity', and which is here contrasted with suspiciousness and the inability to trust.[25] The noble person is not constantly suspicious, skeptical. He or she receives the actions of others with generosity, not with 'precautionary action', confident that the conventions are in force, the structures of the world in place. Trust, however, can be destroyed from without, by the actions of others. In certain externally caused conditions any normal, reasonable person will come to be skeptical and suspicious; this 'openness' will be 'laughed down'. But with the departure of openness comes a loss of goodness. If speeches and oaths no longer look reliable, if I question everything and look for betrayal behind every expression of love, I am, quite simply, no longer a noble person; perhaps no longer a person at all. This, as we shall see, is Euripides' central interest in Hecuba's fate.

We must now return to Polyxena, the play's example of uncorrupted nobility. As we do so, we see that what moves us to awe in her is precisely this Thucydidean openness or generous trust.[26] Here is a woman, we see immediately, who has been taught to have a high sense of her own personal worth and of that of others. She firmly expects that she will be treated according to her worth, and she assumes, without suspicious reflection, that this is how she will treat others. She has no fear that the deepest conventions in which she was raised will vanish. She tells Odysseus that she understands his reluctance to receive her in the posture of a suppliant; she will respect that reluctance by refusing to make the demand. In this entire lengthy speech, she relies on the fact that this wily Greek will respect the religious requirements of the suppliant convention, if once he should enter into such a relationship. 'I have been nurtured in noble hopes' (351), she tells us; we see the nobility of her hope throughout, in her unsuspicious responses. Most touching of all, perhaps, is her final display of maidenly modesty. As she fell in death, reports the incredulous herald, even at that ultimate moment she took thought to arrange her skirts so that her body would not be revealed in an immodest way. This displays, of course, astonishing presence of mind. But it is even more astonishing for its display of trust. Dying, she does not think to doubt that a group of Greek soldiers will respect, after her death, the chastity of her skirt. If she acts well, her act will stand, and be received. Indeed she is, as she herself tells us, 'not accustomed to taste of bad things' (375). Appropriately, she is named a name that can mean either 'giver' or 'receiver' 'of much hospitality'.

The simple splendor of this girl is, as Thucydides' account of nobility suggested, largely constituted by this trusting openness concerning the conventions that structure her life. Euripides presents this not as childish *naïveté* but as a mature commitment to social values, based upon the trust that these values require. But if we see what they require we also begin to see what Polyxena dimly divines: that her nobility may be in jeopardy in this world. To her honored enemy, she candidly concludes: 'I send out this light from free and generous eyes, turning my body over to Hades' (367–8). Eyes, for her, are the seat of trust, both given and received.[27] Their open light expresses her confidence in *nomos*; and what she trusts, in the world of *nomos*, is the expression, through the eyes of others, of friendship, honesty, compassion. By contact of eyes, these characters join each other in, and acknowledge, a shared moral universe. But as Polyxena vaguely senses, and as Hecuba will shortly be shown, eyes can simulate non-existent trust, feign tears, falsely assume honest looks. Polyxena's self-affirmed journey to Hades, whose name means 'the sightless place', may prove necessary in order to preserve the free and generous looks of her spirit from a more horrible blinding. Vaguely aware of a danger, she appeals, 'Help me plan how to die before I encounter shameful things that I do not deserve.' Unlike her mother, she finds the right time.[28]

II

Many commentators have condemned this play for its lack of unity, charging that the Polyxena story and the Polymestor story are separate episodes joined, at most, by being chapters in the suffering life of the heroine.[29] I hope that it is emerging, by now, that a deeper connection can be found. If we focus on the question of good character and its stability, we will see that the first episode sets forth a view on this issue which the second episode will give us reason to question. At the same time it reveals to us, in the person of Polyxena, features of nobility on account of which it cannot possibly be as stable as Hecuba thinks, features whose violent removal will be the source of Hecuba's degeneration in the play's second half.

Hecuba is capable of remaining firm in adversity. Among her evident virtues are civic concern and loyalty, generosity towards the needy and the suppliant, moderation, fairness, and an unwavering, loving concern for her children. And even the death of her daughter, with its arbitrary cruelty, does not shake her from these virtues. But the knowledge of Polydorus's murder brings about a reversal astonishing in its abruptness. The climate of wartime, together with her other previous losses, certainly help to explain why she proves so vulnerable to this shock. But we are invited to look closely at the particular meaning of this relationship and this crime, in order to understand why they should have this singular power.

Polymestor is a *xenos*, or guest-friend, of Hecuba and Priam. This relationship receives enormous emphasis in the play: it is mentioned fifteen times.[30] He is also a loved one, or *philos*.[31] To be precise, he held, she tells us, 'the first place among my loved ones in the rank of guest-friendship'. The relationship of *xenia* is the deepest and most sacred conventional relationship in which one inhabitant of this world can stand to another. The giving and receiving of hospitality imposes obligations of care and protection whose inviolability is fundamental to all interpersonal relationships, all morality. Even when *xenoi* encounter one another on the battlefield, if they recognize each other as such they will suspend hostilities.[32] Polymestor and Hecuba are bound, then, by the most binding tie that exists by *nomos*, the tie that most fundamentally indicates one human's openness to another, his willingness to join with that other in a common moral world. And they combine this deep obligation with personal affection. In their later scene of simulated friendship we see, through their ghastly mutual parody of affection, the depth of sympathy that once joined them. He was both *xenos* and friend; he was the one person to whom she and Priam saw fit to entrust, in secrecy, their child, whose name means 'giver of many things', this giver of hope for their future and the future of their city. He was, above all others, the one towards whom they looked their free and generous looks. This tie is a better or stronger case of love or friendship, in the play's terms, than an erotic tie would be: for those bonds are *conventionally* unreliable and unstable, weakest or worst cases of promising.[33] If the relationship lacks some of the emphasis on shared pursuits and continuous living-together that characterizes Aristotelian *philia*, it still plays a similarly deep role in this world, is similarly based upon trust, and is similarly fundamental to all interpersonal morality.

Polymestor's crime of child-murder is especially horrible, is itself a 'worst case' of crime, in several ways. First, we think of the fact that this child had not fully received the nurture that was Polymestor's charge; he has not, in consequence, had the chance to lead an actively good human life. Furthermore, we know how Hecuba staked her hope for herself and her city on this last remaining boy; this hope, known to Polymestor, ought to have imposed an especially strong obligation to protect and defend. This obligation was explicitly undertaken by him, over and above the usual obligations imposed by *xenia*. But worst of all for us, perhaps, is our thought of the child's defenseless simplicity. Polydorus's story of growth 'like a green plant' gives us a vision of happy guileless childhood suddenly cut off. 'I grew well by his nurture. Poor me.' Openness imposes its own obligations. Polyxena's virtue elicited respect and care even from a group of soldiers described as especially unruly. Their eyes and hands kept the trust which she demanded by her modest fall: they vie to cover her, strewing her body with leaves, adorning her with robes. To defile a guileless child is altogether different from counter-plotting against a plotter. The horror of it is summarized in Hecuba's dream of the young deer being torn by the wolf who (humanly) snatches it 'without pity' (90–1). For, worst of all, Polymestor committed this worst crime carelessly, without a strong need, and without guilt or care, taking no thought even for the burial of his victim's corpse.[34]

We have all the materials of Hecuba's downfall in place. On the one hand, she herself is a very strong case of firm adult good character: if she can be corrupted, this creates a persuasive argument that this is a possibility for adult excellence in general. On the other side, we are presented with circumstances of unusual extremity: in a time of general social upheaval, her deepest and most trusted friend has committed, heedlessly, the worst crime. Extreme in fact these circumstances are; but they are in no way implausible, idiosyncratic, or even – especially in wartime – rare.

What, then, for Hecuba, is the experience of that moment in which she finally recognizes that the faceless, mangled corpse before her is her Polydorus?[35] It is a sight the violent intimacy of whose horror we can scarcely begin to understand. The servant woman who retrieved the body knows that she brings a knowledge that will defile; for, otherwise strangely, she remarks that it is not easy to avoid speaking *blasphemously* when one is in the presence of such misfortune. This news is, in the mind of this simple woman, a blasphemy against everything. She represents it to us as a horrible tangible object, something that Hecuba must *touch* or *grasp* and take to herself; and, when she does, she will be 'no longer looking at the light' (668). It will cover her round, take away the light from her eyes. But finally the woman brings it out. 'Look', she reluctantly bids. 'Look at the naked body of this dead person. Look and see whether it seems to you a wonder beyond all expectation' (679–81).

'I see indeed. I see my dead child, Polydorus. The Thracian was protecting him for me' (681–2). In that instant of recognition, Hecuba has grasped it all. The woman asks her, 'Have you known the ruin of your child, you unhappy woman?' (688). Her answer, language nearly failing, is, 'Untrustworthy, untrustworthy, new, new, are the things I see' (689).[36] What she sees is that the deepest trust was not trustworthy. What is firmest is, can be, heedlessly set aside. And in that heedlessness she reads another piece of knowledge: that the *nomoi* that structured her world never were, for this beloved other party, binding *nomoi*. He never really saw them or responded to them. 'Where is the binding claim of guest-friendship (*dika xenōn*)?' she cries out. 'O cursed man, how you cut his flesh into sections, how you cut the limbs of this child with a sword and had no pity' (718–20). What this fact shows her is that nothing is beyond defilement. If this best and deepest case of human social value has proven *apiston*, 'untrustworthy', then nothing is ever entirely deserving of my trust.

It is a dislocation, a rending of the world. Even language and its distinctions cannot grasp it. 'Unspeakable, unnameable, beyond wonder' (714), she cries. 'Impious. Unbearable.' We make distinctions, Hecuba had said, we cut up the world, by *nomos*. Language is based on and embodies these *nomoi*. The cutting of this child now seems to Hecuba to reveal the groundlessness, the superficiality of these cuttings. It cuts beneath them. Later on, when Agamemnon asks, 'What woman was ever so unfortunate?' Hecuba answers, 'None, unless you mean Luck (*Tuchē*) herself' (786).[37] This strikes us as an odd response, if we take her to be thinking of *Tuchē* as a commanding goddess who controls the luck of mortals. But it should not be read this way. What she expresses, I believe, is a feeling of complete disorder, lack of structure. *Tuchē*, luck or the absence of human rational control, is contrasted implicitly with the rational and intelligible order of *nomos*. What she means to say is that nobody is more in disorder, more dislocated than she, unless you think of Uncontrol or Disorder herself.

But now we begin to see what is even more truly 'beyond expectation': that this disordering knowledge of the possibility of betrayal, which comes to this woman from outside, is itself a defilement of her and a poison against her character.[38] Polyxena's nobility rested on unquestioning, generous-hearted trust. Hecuba's love of her friend was once like this too. Now, confronted with the failure of *nomos*, she seems to have two choices only. She can blind herself to these events, finding some way to distance the knowledge or to confine it. (Taking this path of self-deception, Agamemnon later declares that violations of deep *nomoi* are easy only for barbarians; Greeks, of course, behave differently.) Or she can accept the knowledge, touch it, take it in as something true of *nomos*, of social bonds in general. But then it seems impossible, in these rending circumstances, to escape the corrosion of that openness on which good character rests. She cannot escape becoming caught up in a questioning and suspicion, 'more intent on self-protection than capable of trust'. Either she blinds herself, in which case she is a fool and corrupt, or else she allows herself to see, in which case she becomes contaminated. Once this 'wonder' touches her it seems that she must go one way or the other.

And from now on the *nomos* of trust, and Hecuba's trust in *nomos*, will be replaced by something new from these new events:

> O child, child
> now I begin my mourning,
> the wild newly-learned melody (*nomos*)
> from the spirit of revenge. (684–7)

Hecuba's revenge song is a newly-learned 'melody' (*nomos*): it is also a new convention (*nomos*) and a new way of ordering the world. The root meaning linking these two senses is that of an ordering, distributing, or bounding:[39] the melody is an ordering of the continuum of sound, law or convention an ordering of social life. By the untranslatable pun Euripides indicates what the rest of the play will explore: that the destruction of convention effects not simply an unstructuring, but also a restructuring: that the void left by Hecuba's discovery will be filled by a new trust and a new law.

III

Revenge, for Hecuba, is the *nomos* that fills the place left by the collapse of the old. We do not know that it is the only possible replacement; but it is, clearly, her replacement. 'I shall place everything in good order', she tells Agamemnon, as she inaugurates her scheme. Concerning convention she had said, 'If *nomos* is destroyed, there is nothing like it among human beings.' And in fact this new song, substituting for *nomos*, proves unlike it. Like *nomos* it is a way of placing the world in order, making things habitable. But unlike *nomos* it will not require a trust in anything outside the thoughts and plans of the avenger. The old *nomos* was a network of ties linking one person with another. The new one will prove a solitary song, for which no confidence in untrustworthy human things is required.

This quick move from the bankruptcy of trust to the value of solitary, power-seeking vengefulness – encouraged, though clearly not inaugurated, by Agamemnon's cowardly refusal of aid – takes place because the helplessness of complete dislocation is intolerable and because return to the old ways now seems equally intolerable. She cannot live and plan feeling like uncontrol itself; nor (she feels) can a person of sense in her position embrace again the old deceptive trust. Revenge attracts because it offers structure and plan without vulnerability. (We saw a similar shift in Thucydides' Corcyreans who, despairing of good faith, come to delight in the clever revenge that gives them power over an unguarded enemy.)

We must now examine in more detail the connection, in Hecuba's revenge, between this aim of self-sufficiency and closure and the particular forms of her vengeful planning. As an order-bringing project, Hecuba's revenge plan, we notice, has two distinct aspects: the retributive and the mimetic. First of all, she seeks to right the imbalance in her world by bringing the defilement back to its source, by giving the giver the same pain and horror that he has originated for her. The child-killer must suffer child-killing; the person who abused *xenia* must suffer an equally ghastly abuse of *xenia*; the person who maimed her must be maimed. This retributive aspect comes out most clearly in the role played by hospitality conventions in the plan. Polymestor is assaulted while being entertained with every customary form; each element of the plot to secure control over his person and his children involves a false use of some feature of the old *nomos*.

But there is another equally important part to the logic of this plan. This is the claim it implicitly makes to imitate and reveal the world as it always was, beneath the attractive trappings of *nomos*. *Xenia* is abused because *xenia* was false all along. The most apparently trustworthy prove untrustworthy here because the most trustworthy always *were* untrustworthy. Children can be murdered here without pity because that's the way it always was: no *nomos* ever effectively stood before a child to protect it. Language is abused because the conventions of truth-telling never held firm, and mere persuasion, without regard to veracity, always was 'the tyrant of human beings'.

This double structure emerges with greatest clarity when we examine the role of eyes and seeing in Hecuba's plan. We saw that for these people eyes are the most intimate places of connection between one human being and another, the place where a human being most clearly expresses his or her trust in another human being and in the world of convention that joins them.[40] The 'light of free and generous eyes' was what Polyxena cherished, and preserved in virtue of her early death. Hecuba's revenge plan is, centrally, a plan to blind Polymestor. At the moment of knowledge, her deepest wish is not to kill him; not to mutilate his limbs, his ears, his chest, his sexual organs. It is, specifically, a wish to mutilate his vision.

We see what this means for her very clearly when Polymestor enters, unaware of her discovery. What we are made to see about him immediately is that this is a man who makes a great deal of eyes and their abilities. He uses them to express, with direct looks, a binding trustfulness, and, with tears, a sympathetic responsiveness. It is of the greatest importance for the audience's experience here that this man, when he enters, should look anything but evil or untrustworthy. He should be direct, deliberate, a 'giver of much counsel', as his name implies. He must be in every sense a 'confidence man', with all the power and allure, as well as the hidden corruption, that this name implies. A good confidence man is trustworthy. This one says, 'O you most beloved Hecuba, I weep, seeing your city and this child of yours, who has just died. Alas. Nothing is trustworthy, not good reputation, not prosperity' (953–5). The only thing that disturbs him here is, as he remarks, her failure to look him in the eyes, establishing the old directness of connection. On these looks he thrives; in their absence he begins to be ill at ease. So, unanswered, he looks his trust at her, weeping false tears for a corpse which he has made and, heedlessly, does not even recognize. (For he takes his victim's body for Polyxena's, not even noticing the difference between male and female, between a newly dead corpse and a corpse mangled by the fish.)

In one way, the blinding is clearly retributive. He abused the looks of her eyes, so his will be defiled in return. He put out, by his act, the light of her eyes, making her one who 'no longer looks at the light'; so he too must cry (as he later does), 'I am blinded. Gone, the light of my eyes' (1035). But in another way, we see that Hecuba is simply bringing to light what has always been between them. She blinds him because blind is what he always was. He never really sealed a promise with a truthful look, never truly wept, never *saw* her boy. Nothing ever was trustworthy: not his good reputation, not his prosperity. The logic of revenge sets the world to rights, most of all by making it reveal the hidden nature of its former crimes.

We can say the same about the way in which Hecuba, in this splendid and terrible scene, refuses him the look of her eyes. As Polymestor weeps his false tears, we watch Hecuba, who is turned away from him and towards us. We have a sense of the mixture of disgust and visceral exultation with which she must hear this man so thoroughly condemning himself. All this time, even when he begins to wonder what is wrong, she refuses to 'look straight across' (965) at him. She says, 'I am not able to look at you with direct pupils (*orthais korais*). Don't think that it is bad feeling about you, Polymestor. Besides, *nomos* is the reason.' Then, almost as an afterthought, she adds, '– the *nomos* that women should not look directly at men' (974–5). This is unconvincing, and he knows it; they are obviously accustomed to a different *nomos*. What, then, are her real reasons?

We take Hecuba's refusal, first, as a retributive denial: you abused my offers of love, so I shall abuse yours in return. But this will not explain it, since looking falsely would be a more commensurate abuse than not looking. We then see, beyond this, that she is also representing their love as it has always really been. There never was any genuine mutuality or connectedness. To look at him 'with direct pupils' means, for her, to let her image shine, reflected, in his eyes. The word for pupil, '*korē*', is also the Greek word for girl or woman, metaphorically transferred. The popular idea behind this transferral is, evidently, that the pupil is the place where the image of the looker is reflected in the eyes of the person seen. It is an image of the reality of the connection between me and you, of knowledge and its mutuality. I come to be *in you*, I make my appearance inside your eyes.[41] (Euripides' intention of playing on this doubleness emerges clearly later, when Polymestor uses the word in both of these senses in close proximity, as he tells the story of the blinding.) Hecuba will not let her image shine in his eyes, not merely to punish, but because her image never stood in those eyes. She makes his pupils empty of images even before she blinds him, because that's the way he always saw.

But even this is not enough; for it ignores the fact that her refusal is more a refusal to *see* than a refusal to *be seen*. He still looks at her; what she refuses to do is, herself, to act, to look. If we think about this, we see that what we have ignored so far is the depth of Hecuba's friendly feeling for this man. We must understand that he was the one she loved and trusted most. When he looked those looks and she returned them, she was, habitually, aware of a rare intimacy, so much so that she called him 'first' and was willing to give him her future. In his eyes she saw her own image; this image was an image of herself looking at him, looking for her own image in those eyes. She was not simply Hecuba, but Hecuba in Polymestor, gazing, again, at Polymestor with Hecuba contained there. So much, she assumed, was true of him. She saw even her own identity, then, as something relational; she was, as a social being, a creation of his vision and his care.

When he enters now and says what he says, she does feel furious anger; she does want to rip his eyes. But it is inconceivable that she does not feel, at the same time, the old customary impulse of trust and confidence, the loving desire to see him and to see herself as in him. What we must realize is that Polymestor does not make a changed appearance; he does not raven like a wolf. The most horrible thing about betrayal is that the person does look the same. He is identical with the person she has loved. She cannot help being moved; but she knows that she must not be moved. If once she looks at those eyes that open to contain her, then her hope of safety is gone. She is his *relatum*, his eyes' creature. She is, above all, what he sees when he sees her. Given the nature of his vision, that would make her nothing.

If, then, she refuses to look at him, it is, in fact, *nomos* that is the reason: the old *nomos* of their love. That is the power that she must resist in order to have *her* power and her secure new *nomos*. 'Don't think it's bad feeling about you, Polymestor', she tells him. She knows, we see, that she is telling him the truth, as well as lying.

And what are we to make of the reason she actually offers him, that women should not look men in the eye? What, more generally, are we to make of the fact that this revenge play has as its central figure a woman, and stresses the fact that what we are witnessing is the transformation of a human being into a female animal, a bitch?[42] Women, in this play and in other plays of Euripides, are the creatures who, by their social position, stand most vulnerable to chance. Euripides' famous interest in women[43] is an interest in this condition of exposure, this powerlessness before the affronts of war, death, betrayal. It is women who are raped and enslaved in wartime, while their men at least have the chance to die bravely. It is women whose bodies, as Euripides repeatedly and graphically stresses, are regarded as part of the spoils of war, to be possessed as one might possess an ox or a tripod. If we are looking for a situation in which good character is corrupted by extreme circumstances, then we do well to look at human beings who, on the one hand, can grow up just as good as any – and this Euripides really seems to think, and often stresses – but who, on the other hand, are exposed more clearly than others to the extreme in fortune. Through the not uncommon social reality of a woman's life (for when women are not queens such adversity does not even require extremity) we come to see a possibility for all human life.

Without surrendering her claim and the claim of women to be best cases of human excellence, Hecuba, then, stresses the degree to which daily inequalities in power expose women to a higher degree of risk. And when she says that women *should* not look men in the eye, we can read it, in addition, in the light of her new *nomos*, as a claim that women *ought* to be revengers, trusting in no eyes. The two readings are obviously connected: for if women are subjected to an unusual measure of exploitation and abuse, they may have an unusual need for, or inclination towards, revenge and doggishness. Earlier Agamemnon expressed doubt as to whether women are capable of planning on their own and executing their plans. Hecuba's reply cites cases of successful female plotting. Both are crimes of vengeance: 'Didn't women get Aegyptus's sons, and make Lemnos empty of men? Let it happen that way here.'[44]

So Hecuba makes the world over in the image of the possibility of non-relation, the possibility knowledge of which destroyed her trust. It is a world of splendid security and splendid isolation. It is thoroughly self-contained, looking directly at nobody, risking the light of no eyes. It is buried, private, dark. She persuades Polymestor to come to hear 'a private message of my own' (978) about a fortune in gold that lies buried beneath 'a black rock towering above the land' (1010). So many images of darkness and hiddenness now inhabit her imagination. She takes her old friend to the 'private quarters' (1016) of the slave-women, a place that is 'trustworthy and empty of men' (1017). In this covered place the women entertain him, remove his outer clothing. Once he is defenseless, they hold him, attack and murder his children, and then stab, these *korai* with their brooch-pins, his own 'wretched *korai*', making them pools of blood. Each woman who stabs eclipses by her act the light of her image in those eyes.[45] This leaves the world, in a sense, as it always was, since Polymestor never saw or loved. But at the same time it makes Hecuba different, since she did love. When she stabs her image in another she destroys something deep about herself, namely her tie to the other and to otherness. She makes herself as secret and unrelated as Polymestor always was. In making his world like the world of a 'four-footed mountain beast', without clear images of others, Hecuba changes her own image to a pool of blood. But then, as she gazes on her own handiwork, her own eyes are bound to take on a blurred, blood-red glow. And in fact her eyes are said hereafter to shine with the 'fiery glances' (*pursa dergmata*) of a dog, also a four-footed beast.

The dog is in no sense, for the Greeks, a high or quasi-human animal. Unlike the lion and the eagle, it ranks very low on the scale of animal nobility. Its salient characteristics are its keenness in tracking its prey, its tenaciousness in warding off its enemies, and its snarling protectiveness of its own territory. Above all, it is despised and feared as the animal that devours the flesh of human corpses, indifferent to the most sacred law of human society. No bond of trust or fellowship will hold it back: Priam knows well that if he falls his corpse will 'be torn apart / on my own doorstep by the hounds / I trained as watchdogs, fed from my own table. / These will lap my blood with ravenous hearts...' (*Il.* XXII.66–70, trans. Fitzgerald). This animal represents, then, for the Greeks, a thorough absence of concern for *nomos*, a complete imperviousness to social or relational values. To call someone 'dog' or 'dog-eyes' is, from the *Iliad* on, to deliver a very serious insult, one that lays particular stress on the insulted person's selfishness and lack of regard for the community.[46] When Achilles wishes to insult Agamemnon for his self-regarding behavior, he calls him 'dog-eyes' (1.225) and follows this up with the charge that he is a *dēmoboros basileus*, a king who feeds on the flesh of his own people (1.231). When Helen wants to insult herself for having caused, heedlessly, untold pain to others, she does so by calling herself 'bitch' (VI.344). Centuries later, the associations are still in place: Sextus Empiricus offers a *reductio* of a prominent ethical view by showing that even a dog could fulfill its requirements for justice and social excellence (*PH* 1.66–7, cited as epigraph). When, then, we hear of a transformation from woman to dog, we are not to think of bestiality in vague or indefinite terms. We are to think of the absence of regard for community and relationship and the specific form of animality that this entails.

In the *nomos* of revenge, the traditional virtues of character still exist, but each in altered form. All, first, become instrumental to the personal ends of power and safety. No prudence, no thought of justice, no piety holds her, once she enters that private room. Even her love of her one surviving child, the mad prophetess Cassandra, is used as a tool of her plan. Cassandra is now the mistress of the Greek commander Agamemnon. Instead of seeking, out of love, to mitigate the girl's unwilling suffering (which, as Polymestor predicts, will later bring her death), Hecuba seeks instead to use the relationship for her own ends, attempting through it to gain influence over Agamemnon so that he will help her in revenge. In what even Hecuba's sympathizers find the low point of her moral reasoning,[47] she appeals to him for aid, using her daughter's body as an argument:

My child the priestess sleeps close to your ribs, the one named Cassandra. What will you give for those pleasant nights, lord? What thanks will my child have for her pleasant embraces in bed? What thanks will I receive, in turn, from her? (825–30)

Mother-love, formerly the central prop of this woman's thought and character, has been transformed in the change to revenge. Now, like everything else, it takes on a purely instrumental relation to her good, which cannot include as a component part the good of any other person. Revenge takes over the entire world of value, making its end the one end.

We see, too, how each virtue subtly shifts its nature when it is no longer based on trust and association. Polyxena showed us a courage based on confidence in the nobility of her country and its shared ways of life; a modesty based on trust in the decency of others; a fairness based on reliance upon the goodness of others' deliberations. In Hecuba's new scheme courage, now based on no communal commitments, serving only a solitary goal, becomes a kind of brazen daring that yells, 'Rip! Spare nothing!' (1044). Prudence or moderation becomes a solitary cunning which has no respect for any decency and trusts no man's respect for hers. Justice becomes an instrument of personal punishment and personal safety; in this sense, even a dog *can* be just, as Sextus handily demonstrated. Wisdom is simply the clever plotting that 'will put everything in good order'. Aristotle told us that justice, broadly construed, is like the entirety of excellence – meaning by that that every virtue has an other-regarding and communal aspect that cannot be severed from it without destroying its character as virtue (cf. above, pp. 351–2). Hecuba's transformation shows us the deep truth of this by showing us the virtues stripped bare of communality. There is still something that we can recognize as the shell of character, but we miss the nobility that was supposed to be so immutable.

Language, too, changes. The revenger, being without trust, cannot rely on the 'accustomed usage' of words. As Thucydides also saw, he or she must recognize that words can undergo a change in their relation to actions and objects, if the agents decide that this is in their interest. This means that words will become not bonds of trust, but instruments of ends; communication is replaced by persuasive rhetoric, and speech becomes a matter of taking advantage of the other party's susceptibility. Hecuba now exclaims angrily that her education in conventional discourse has been a waste of effort:

Why on earth do we mortals take so much trouble to learn all sorts of things, as is customary? Why do we waste our time, while Persuasion, the only tyrant of human beings, is not the object of our eagerness? Why do we not pay any price to be able to persuade others, and so to get what we want? (814–19)

If language is human and customary, it is not trustworthy. But then the clever way to use language is as a persuasive force inside the game of revenge. In a ghastly moment she wishes her entire body turned to forms of persuasive rhetoric: 'Voices in my arms, my hands, my hair, in the stepping of my feet, all crying out together..."O master, O great light of Hellas, be persuaded, provide an avenging hand to this old woman'" (836–43).[48] Like Cassandra's body, her own is now a mere tool of the new plan. Her doggishness is increasingly evident, except that no non-human bitch could use argument so well.

In the *Oresteia*, Aeschylus showed us the creation of the city and the political virtues as a process which centrally involves the replacement of revenge structures by structures of civic trust and civic friendship. The Erinyes begin the final play of the trilogy as bestial, more specifically as dog-like creatures, who sniff after their prey with dripping eyes, thrilled by the scent of blood.[49] At the end, robed in human clothing, a gift from the citizens of Athens, they stand before us transformed into human women. As they look to the men of Athens and pronounce a blessing on the land and its people, they cease to growl, to crouch, to sniff for blood. They stand erect, they 'depart according to *nomos*' (*Eum.* 1033), they show that they have 'thought how to find the road of good speech' (987–8). The crucial moment of transition is a moment of reception and trust: they put aside their suspiciousness and allow themselves to be persuaded (794, cf. 885), accepting Athena's promise (804) and her offer of a place in the city. With the words, 'I receive a fellow dwelling-place (*sunoikia*) from Pallas' (916), they yield to the 'holy honor of persuasion' (885) and become political creatures like the citizens they will protect. (At this point, appropriately, Athena compares herself, in her function of caring and nurturing, to a gardener who loves his plants (911).) The dog-like Erinyes looked only after their prey and with vengeful loathing; these Eumenides (so renamed for their kindly intentions)[50] join Athena in her love of the eyes of Persuasion (970), who dispelled their anger and brought them into community.

Euripides here inverts this process, alluding, as he does so, to many of the play's most famous images. There dog-like revenge goddesses become women with kindly intentions; here a woman with kindly intentions becomes a dog with fiery eyes, thirsty for blood. There Persuasion provides a basis for acceptance and civic trust; here Persuasion becomes a 'tyrant' inside the solitary game of revenge. There speech creates bonds of fellowship; here, set free of social constraint, it serves the ends of each revenger. There unresponsive dogs became the receptive friends of the plantlike; here plantlike excellence becomes invulnerable bestiality. There the gift of robes sealed a bond of trust and hospitality; here the women, removing the robes of a guest whom they intend to maim, cut themselves off from all trust. Euripides shows us that our self-creation as political beings is not irreversible. The political, existing by and in *nomos*, can also cease to hold us. The human being, as a social being, lives suspended between beast and god, defined against both of these self-sufficient creatures by its open and vulnerable nature, the relational character of its most basic concerns. But if being human is a matter of the character of one's trust and commitment, rather than an immutable matter of natural fact (if, as tradition suggests, the Cyclopes were non-human just *because* of their disregard of *nomos* and hospitality, their *apaideusia*, as both Euripides and

Aristotle say),[51] then the human being is also the being that can most easily cease to be itself – either by moving (Platonically) upwards towards the self-sufficiency of the divine, or by slipping downward towards the self-sufficiency of doggishness. And the difference between the two movements is not altogether obvious, since both involve a similar closing-off of important human things. We can become dogs or gods, existing without trust – sometimes through a lifetime of solitary contemplation, and sometimes through a series of accidents, without even desiring the transformation.

Hecuba had argued that *nomos*, though human and contingent, is stable, and that through *nomos* humans can make themselves stable. The events of this play show us that the annihilation of convention by another's act can destroy the stable character who receives it. It can, quite simply, produce bestiality, the utter loss of human relatedness and human language. Bestiality, in the final scene, is shown us most clearly in the person of Polymestor, who, after the blinding, enters half-naked, on all fours, 'a mountain beast' (1058) wild for the blood of his injurers. This scene, which parodies the dignities of the ending of Sophocles' *Oedipus* (a protagonist blinded with a brooch-pin, mourning his loss of light),[52] is designed to shock and revolt. The sight of this former human screaming for his enemy 'so that I can snatch her in these hands and rip her apart, tear her flesh to bloody shreds' (1125–6), the hint even of cannibalistic desires (1071–2) – all this is meant to be, as it is, almost unendurably foul. But fouler even than the degradation of this criminal is the equal fury of his pursuer. His end serves the more horribly to underline the extent of her crime. He is made a beast by her act, as she by his. She will become, because she has been and is, what he prophesies. Openness, which is the largest part of good character, has been laughed down; it vanishes. The death of *nomos* leaves behind nothing like it for human life. Neither of them could endure to be human, with the openness to risk that that condition requires. Doggishness arrives as a welcome gift, a release. They embrace it. If *we* find it foul, we are forced to ask what human life could be happier.[53]

Nietzsche, whose discussion of revenge is the most sustained and remarkable one I know in the philosophical tradition, saw, in his lifelong reflection on Greek culture,[54] many of the features of revenge which this play explores: its ability to make or structure the world, revaluing all values; its connection with the desire of the wounded for safety and power; its capacity for disguising itself as love or justice. But Nietzsche speaks of revenge as the project of an abased or deprived people; he does not show us cases in which a noble character is driven to it. Indeed, he speaks as though revenge is always the reflex only of the base or weak. This play shows us that the person of noble character is, if anything, more open to this corrosion than the base person, because it is the noble person, not the base, who has unsuspiciously staked a world on the faith and care of others. It was Hecuba's very strength, in terms of the traditional virtues, that contributed most to unseat her. It was her love for this friend, her faith in promises, her unsuspicious fairness. Now, in the wake of this friend's act, she must have revenge not against some personal or sectarian weakness (as is the case with Nietzsche's Christians), but against human life itself and the very conditions of virtue in the world.

IV

We must now pause to ask what Aristotle would make of all this: first, whether these are possibilities for degeneration that his ethical view in fact allows to exist, and, second, what he explicitly says about the existence of these possibilities. The answer to the first question seems clear. Insofar as Aristotle bases human excellence on the social nature of the human being; insofar as he stresses that all of excellence has an other-related aspect; insofar as he holds that personal love and political association are not only important components of the good human life but also necessary for the continued flourishing of good character generally; and insofar as he mentions explicitly that trust is required to reap the benefits of these associations – he cannot consistently close off the possibility of these events, although he can insist upon their rarity. Furthermore, there is explicit recognition of these dangers in his text: most clearly in the *Rhetoric*, but also in the ethical works themselves. The resemblance between this Euripidean account of the central role of trust in the virtues and the *Rhetoric* discussion of the virtues of youth and age is particularly striking. Euripides, Aristotle, and Thucydides concur in the view that openness is an essential condition of good character and that a mistrustful suspiciousness, which can come to an agent through no moral failing, but only through experience of the bad things in life, can be a poison that corrodes all of the excellences, turning them to forms of vindictive defensiveness. This agreement is a sign of the fidelity with which Aristotle mines the traditions of his culture, preserving what is deepest. Finally, both Aristotle's account of the appearances and his remarks about the origins of the binding force of *nomos* (*Pol.* II.8, cf. above pp. 304–5) state explicitly the views about the fragility of convention on which Euripides' account of Hecuba's decline relies.

Aristotle's discussion of Priam's case in *Nicomachean Ethics* I might seem to tell a different story, placing a higher floor than the *Hecuba* does beneath the good person's degeneration. For although Aristotle there allows, as we argued, that character itself can be corrupted in some measure by these events, he still insists that the good person will never be brought to do what is truly 'hateful and base'. He will go down, but not all the way down. It is difficult to say whether Hecuba's actions here are vicious in the sense in which Aristotle denies viciousness to Priam. There are such extraordinary extenuating circumstances that pity and horror indeed seem more appropriate responses than blame. Her actions do not express an antecedent vicious disposition; indeed, in a ghastly way they could even be seen as examples of the Aristotelian 'doing the best with the material at hand', in that they show what each of the virtues is like when their social fabric, their aspect of *dikaiosunē*, is no longer available. Surely it is important that we see Hecuba's actions as in some sense justified, at the very least extenuated, by the circumstances, not as simply expressing a murderous character.[55] (Agamemnon decides that she is in the right.) But it remains unclear whether Aristotle's explicit statements in the Priam passage coincide with our judgments about this play's vision of decline.

We can conclude, however, that most of Aristotle's other explicit material on the issue does strikingly match our reading, and that the general view of excellence developed in the *EN* leaves open the same areas of risk and vulnerability. We therefore have strong warrant for exploring this play as a source of Aristotelian practical knowledge.

V

I have said that this tragedy shows us a case of solid character and shows us that, under certain circumstances, even this cannot escape defilement. It also has shown us that even the good character who has not suffered any actual damage or betrayal lives always with the risk of these events: for it is in the nature of political structures to change, and in the nature of personal friendship that the confidence man should be indistinguishable from the trustworthy man – sometimes even to himself. In this sense, nothing human is ever *worthy* of my trust: there are no guarantees at all, short of revenge or death. Agamemnon's assertion that this risk belongs only to barbarians (1247–8)[56] must be seen as a way of avoiding the knowledge of the possibilities for all human beings which these tragic events display. The risk of bestiality is not far from Agamemnon, who will shortly be hunted down and netted by his wife, even as he has himself hunted his child. Unable to endure the prophecy of this end, he has Polymestor gagged, saying, 'Won't you take him away by force, men?... Won't you shut his mouth?... Won't you take him as quickly as you can and throw him out somewhere on a desert island, since he speaks this way, so rashly?' (1282–6). But, as Polymestor says, 'Shut me up. I've spoken' (1284). The threat displayed in these revengers lies exposed in the structure of this conception of excellence itself, since its deepest commitments to value take them to a world of objects both unstable and uncontrolled.

We are, then, brought back to the children. Polydorus dies too young, before he has had a chance to become good and to act well. Hecuba dies too old, in the grip of revenge. Only Polyxena, through good luck, finds a time between nurture and disillusionment and dies a noble character. In the tragedies of Euripides it frequently seems that the good die young. This, however, is not the result of special divine malevolence. It is because if they had not died young they would in all likelihood not have remained good. To live on is to make contact in some way at some time with the possibility of betrayal; to live on in times of extremity like those to which Euripides is repeatedly drawn is, very likely, to make contact with betrayal itself. But the encounter with betrayal brings a risk of defilement: the risk of ceasing to look at the world with the child's free and generous looks; of ceasing, in the Euripidean way, to be good.

Such reflections show us, once again, the great attractiveness of closing off these risks. Inside the Aristotelian or tragic conceptions, they cannot be closed off. But if we were able to live an entire life inside the Platonic view that the best and most valuable things in life are all invulnerable, we would effectively get revenge, ourselves, upon our worldly situation. We would put the world in good order by sealing off certain risks, closing ourselves to certain happenings. And this world could remain relatively rich in value, since it would still contain the beauty of the Platonic contemplative life. If this is revenge, it may strike us that this is a very attractive and fruitful type of revenge: we effectively get the better of our humanity and keep for ourselves the joys of godlike activity.

What this play has shown us, however, as it explores the possibilities of an ideal similar to Aristotle's – what Aristotle himself has shown us, and the *Antigone*, and Protagoras's speech, and Plato's *Symposium* and *Phaedrus* – is that there is in fact a loss in value whenever the risks involved in specifically human virtue are closed off. There is a beauty in the willingness to love someone in the face of love's instability and worldliness that is absent from a completely trustworthy love. There is a certain valuable quality in social virtue that is lost when social virtue is removed from the domain of uncontrolled happenings. And in general each salient Aristotelian virtue seems inseparable from a risk of harm. There is no courage without the risk of death or of serious damage; no true love of city that says (with Alcibiades), 'Love of city is what I do not feel when I am wronged'; no true commitment to justice that exempts its own privileges from scrutiny. This willingness to embrace something that *is* in the world and subject to its risks is, in fact, the virtue of the Euripidean child, whose love is directed at the world itself, including its dangers. The generous looks of such a child go straight to the world with love and openness; they do not focus upon the safe and the eternal, or demand these as conditions of their love. It is this quality of loving affirmation that both Euripides and Aristotle (along with the parts of Plato who speak as Protagoras and the interlocutors of the *Phaedrus*), wish, in their different ways, to hold before us as an adult way of being excellent. They would insist that the stabler values of the intellectual life are best nourished and promoted in a life that includes these riskier commitments; and that, even were such nourishment not in all cases strictly necessary, still any life that devoted itself entirely to safe activities would be, for a human being, impoverished. The *Hecuba* does not conceal from us the seductive danger of romanticizing risk itself: for it displays the special and unequal risks of a woman's social life as unjust dangers, in no way constitutive of any important virtues. But it asks us to consider that not all devotion to the uncertain is foolish romanticism; or, rather, that something that might be called foolish romanticism, that is to say the daring and exposed pursuit of transient value, may actually be an essential ingredient in the best life for the human being, as our best account, arrived at by the best method we know, presents it. There are certain risks – including, here, the risk of becoming unable to risk – that we cannot close off without a loss in human value, suspended as we are between beast and god, with a kind of beauty available to neither.

The play leaves us, as it ends, with the image of the promontory Cynossema, 'The Bitch's Gravestone', which is to be 'a sign (*tekmar*) for sailors'. The word '*tekmar*' indicates to us that Cynossema is not just any ordinary landmark, but a solemn mark, perhaps even a pledge or solemn guarantee. So, too, the possibilities of this play stand in nature: as markers of the boundary of social discourse and as warnings against catastrophe – but also as the pledges or guarantors of a specifically human excellence. If that rock did not stand, we would not stand as we humanly do. If we could not be turned into dogs, we would no longer be humans. And a question linking tragedy and philosophy in this culture, as all these works have in their different ways seen, is whether, and how, that dog's rock is to be allowed to stand in our world. Whether we want an ethical conception that puts an end to these problems, or whether we wish to be left where we began, as characters in a tragedy. Whether we want an art of thought, and also of writing, that engenders, and embodies, fixity and stability, or an art that encourages our souls to remain plantlike and fragile, places of glancing light and flowing water.

These alternatives are not exhaustive, either for ethical judgment or for speech and writing. For the Aristotelian will argue that plantlike flexibility, far from being at odds with stability, provides the best sort of stability for a human life. And Hecuba's view of language has shown us that there is, on the other hand, a false sort of flexibility or rootlessness of ethical judgment that issues precisely from the revenger's attempts to fix or seal off the risks involved in planning a life. Similarly, the looseness of a certain sort of persuasive rhetoric, spoken or written, expresses a refusal of true responsiveness. The Aristotelian view does not, then, repudiate every sort of fixity and stability; nor does it advocate any and every form of openness and pliability. It insists on fidelity to standing commitments, both individual and social, as the basis for true flexible perception. Aristotelian writing, in a similar way, must strive for a balance between structure and fine nuance, neglecting neither.

We have discovered that we do live in the world that Aristotle describes; that we share, at the same time, a deep longing for another simpler or purer world. But the Aristotelian argument, which continues and refines the insights of tragedy, reminds us that we do not achieve purity or simplicity without a loss in richness and fullness of life – a loss, it is claimed, in intrinsic value. Our own Aristotelian inquiry cannot claim to have answered our original questions once for all in favor of an Aristotelian ethical conception, since, as we said in the beginning, it represents only a preliminary part of the work that a full inquiry of this sort would eventually require. And even against Plato the Aristotelian argument may not appear directly conclusive, since it arrives at its results by procedures that the Platonist would consider untrustworthy. But the alternatives and the arguments for and against them have emerged from these works with a vividness and power that ought to help us in our future work on the problems. The *Hecuba* leaves us with an appropriate image for that further work. In place of the story of salvation through new arts, in place of the stratagems of the hunter and the solitary joy of the godlike philosopher, we are left with a new (but also very old)[57] picture of deliberation and of writing. We see a group of sailors, voyaging unsafely. They consult with one another and take their bearings from that rock, which casts (under the liquid sky) its shadow on the sea.[58]

Notes

1 Luck and ethics

1. Pindar, *Nemean* VIII.40–2; the following citations are from lines 39 and 42–4. 'Vine tree' results from an emendation by Bury, now widely, though not universally, accepted; the unemended text would read 'as a tree shoots upward'. This issue makes no difference to my argument. On *aretē*, 'excellence', see below, p. 6.

2. The conventions of the epinician genre received penetrating study in the now classic work of the late Elroy Bundy (*Studia Pindarica* (Berkeley 1962)), which transformed Pindar criticism by showing the extent to which shared convention, and not idiosyncratic autobiographical fact, shapes the poet's self-presentation and other features of his practice. On these developments in criticism, see H. Lloyd-Jones, 'Modern interpretation of Pindar', *JHS* 93 (1973) 109–37; for a penetrating introduction to the poet and the criticism about him, see H. Lloyd-Jones, 'Pindar', Lecture on a Master Mind, *PBA* (1982), 139–63. Two recent studies of the epinician tradition and Pindar's place in it are M. R. Lefkowitz, *The Victory Ode* (Park Ridge, NJ 1976) and K. Crotty, *Song and Action* (Baltimore 1982).

3. The plant imagery is deeply traditional: see, for example, the *Homeric Hymn to Demeter* 237–41, *Iliad* XVIII.54–60, 437–41, of the growth of the hero. Other later occurrences will be discussed in Chs. 3, 4, 6, 7, and 13. For a very interesting discussion of the connection between plant imagery and lamentation, which supports our idea that the plant image expresses a picture of specifically mortal and vulnerable excellence, see G. Nagy, *The Best of the Achaeans* (Baltimore 1979) 181ff. Nagy offers a perceptive account of the development, in the early poetic tradition, of a picture of human excellence that is unavailable in, and contrasted with, the condition of a self-sufficient or needless being. (I have discussed earlier work of Nagy on this subject in my '*Psuchē* in Heraclitus, II', *Phronesis* 17 (1972) 153–70, where I ascribe to Heraclitus a contrast between the self-sufficient excellence of gods and the needy excellence of vulnerable humans.) For other related material concerning traditional conceptions of the 'human situation' in early Greek poetry, see J. Redfield's *Nature and Culture in the Iliad* (Chicago 1975), esp. 60–6, 85–8. Aristotle's more pejorative use of the plant image will be discussed below, Chs. 8 and 11. See also Plato, *Timaeus* 90A, which insists that we are not earthly but heavenly plants. Some relevant Platonic and Aristotelian material is discussed in E. N. Lee, 'Hoist with his own petard', in Lee, *Exegesis*. For other use of plant imagery in the poem, see *eblasten* line 12 (the child 'sprouts forth'), *phututheis* line 28 (wealth can be 'planted and tended' with a god's help).

4. This seems to be the implication of the verb *masteuei* here: compare Aes. *Ag.* 1093–4, and the commentary on the passage by E. Fraenkel, *Aeschylus: Agamemnon* (Oxford 1950) *ad loc.* The word seems to mean, in general, 'seek out', 'search after', 'pursue the track of'. In the Aeschylus passage, Clytemnestra is explicitly compared to a hunting dog sniffing out the trail of blood; the subsequent sentence *mateuei d' hōn aneurēsei phonon*

is translated by Fraenkel, 'she is on the track of the murder...'; similar versions are offered by others. It is a little difficult, given the relative rarity of the word, to know whether its presence alone implies the idea of hunting or tracking. We can at least infer from the Aeschylus passage that it was felt to be particularly appropriate for the sort of eager, intense searching that a hunting dog performs. The phrase *en ommasi thesthai piston*, which follows the verb, is difficult and multiply ambiguous. Literally, it can be rendered, 'to place for oneself the trustworthy in eyes'. This can, in turn, be taken at least four ways: (1) to repose trust (locate the trustworthy for oneself) in someone's (the friend's) eyes; (2) to place something or someone trustworthy (viz., the friend) before one's eyes; (3) to make visible (place before eyes) a sure or trustworthy item (viz., perhaps, the poem?); (4) to make a trustworthy bond or pledge before people's eyes. In short – we cannot determine whether the eyes in question are those of the person, of the friend, or of the group; and we also do not know whether *to piston* is the friend, the poem, a specific pledge, or the trustworthy in the abstract. I have chosen and translated the reading (1), also favored and well defended by Farnell (*The Works of Pindar* (London 1932)); each of the other versions has had its influential defenders. I am not eager to disambiguate in an arbitrary way a suggestive phrase some of whose ambiguity is doubtless deliberate. But it seems to me that (1) and (2) fit the context in some ways better than (3) and (4). The whole passage before and after is concerned with personal friendship, the bond of trust and reliance linking one friend with another. The overall sense must, in general, be: 'We have all sorts of needs for beloved friends, especially in difficulty (or labor); but we need to be able to rely on them in joyful times too (or to share with them our joy in victory, as with someone whom we trust). This I cannot do in this present case, since Megas is dead and I cannot bring him back. My desire to share this joy with him is empty and vain. But I can at least write this poem...' Either (1) or (2) suits this overall meaning; (1) seems slightly easier because *en ommasi* more easily means 'within' than 'before' the eyes; but there are a few precedents for the latter, so we cannot decide firmly. (The scholiast compares Euripides' *Ion* 732, *es ommat' eunou phōtos emblepein gluku*, 'to look at sweetness in the eyes of a well-disposed person', showing that he understands the passage in sense (1).) (3), which (at least as articulated to me informally by Professor Lloyd-Jones) has these lines already making reference to the poem as a token of friendship, does not seem to me to work well, since we do not then expect the poet to say that his hopes have been frustrated by Megas's death. If the hope *en ommasi thesthai piston* is frustrated, it cannot be the hope to write the poem. The poem is presented not as the fulfillment of this hope – this, I think, is quite important for Pindar's view of the magnitude and ethical importance of the loss of friendship – but as a substitute or consolation, after the termination of friendship and its exchange of trust by death. As for (4), it is not altogether clear to me what pledge its defenders have in mind; nor have I seen convincing parallels for *thesthai piston* in this sense. One final reason for preferring (1) lies in the idea it conveys, that eyes are the seat of trust between one friend and another. This deeply rooted and pervasive Greek idea, which will be further exemplified and discussed in Chs. 3 and 13, is a most appropriate one for Pindar to allude to in this context; it enriches the poem's meaning.

5. Euripides, *Trojan Women* 820ff. Ganymede will reappear, as an example of specifically human and vulnerable excellence, in Plato's *Phaedrus* – cf. Ch. 7.
6. *Odyssey* v.214–20.
7. Plato, *Ph.* 80B.

8. For further discussion of the notion of *tuchē* in pre-Platonic thought, and of the antithesis between *tuchē* and rational *technē*, see Ch. 4 and references.

9. As, for example, in the influential work of A. W. H. Adkins, especially Adkins, *Merit*, which begins with the claim (p. 2) that 'We are all Kantians now', and makes use of Kantian assumptions throughout in both exegesis and assessment. I have criticized Adkins's methodology in Nussbaum, 'Consequences' 25–53. For other valuable criticisms, see Lloyd-Jones, *JZ*; A. A. Long, 'Morals and values in Homer', *JHS* 90 (1970) 121–39; K. J. Dover, 'The portrayal of moral evaluation in Greek poetry', *JHS* 103 (1983) 35–48.

10. Two recent articles that, in different ways, challenge Kantian views about luck are B. A. O. Williams, 'Moral luck', *PASS* 50 (1976), reprinted in Williams, *ML* 20–39, and Thomas Nagel, 'Moral luck', *PASS* 50 (1976) reprinted in *Mortal Questions* (Cambridge 1979) 24–38. Williams's views about Greek ethical thought on these issues are discussed in this chapter, pp. 18–21, and in Ch. 2, p. 29.

11. *Rep.* 612A.

12. On *kalon*, see further in Ch. 6, p. 178.

13. This is terminology used by Williams, *ML*. Although I have been using these expressions 'internal' and 'external contingency' for a long time and find them natural, it is likely that I first heard them in a seminar of Williams's at Harvard in 1973.

14. On madness (*mania*) and Plato's view of its role in the good life, see Ch. 7.

15. I have not extended the inquiry to include the Hellenistic period, in which issues of self-sufficiency and immunity to luck are extremely prominent, and in which the related question or questions of free will take on something more like their familiar modern form. First, the earlier texts, unlike most of the Hellenistic material, are preserved as whole pieces of writing; this permits us to raise related questions about the relationship between content and style that we could not easily raise using fragmentary sources. Second, it is a striking feature of much of Hellenistic ethical writing that individual immunity from luck is taken for granted as a valuable ethical end, even as *the* end. This means that the sort of debate in which I am here most interested – debate about the value of self-sufficiency (either individual or communal) as an end and about its relation to other valued ends – is less frequent. I intend, however, to discuss the Hellenistic material in the Martin Classical Lectures at Oberlin College, 1986.

16. It has more recently been defended and used, with reference to Aristotle, by both Sidgwick (*Methods of Ethics* (7th ed. London 1907), see especially pref. to 6th edition) and J. Rawls (*A Theory of Justice* (Cambridge, MA 1971) 46–53). Sidgwick's views about the relationship between ethical theory and ordinary belief, which seem importantly different from Aristotle's, are discussed in Ch. 4.

17. *EN* 1095a3ff., 1095b3ff.

18. See, for one interesting example, I. Murdoch, in 'Philosophy and literature: dialogue with Iris Murdoch', in *Men of Ideas*, ed. B. Magee (New York 1978): 'These two branches of thought have such different aims and such different styles, and I feel that one should keep them apart from each other.'

19. See Interlude 1; also Chs. 6 and 7, Interlude 2; for other related writing of mine, see Nussbaum, 'Crystals', in an issue of *NLH* devoted to investigating the relationship between literature and moral philosophy; and Nussbaum, 'Fictions' (with the proceedings of a conference on style held at Harvard, March 1982).

20. Some studies of 'popular morality' begin with the assumption that it can straightforwardly be used as evidence for ordinary belief. The most methodologically naïve of

these writers is Adkins, who treats single lines in a dramatic work as evidence for ordinary belief, in complete isolation from dramatic context. L. Pearson (*Popular Ethics in Ancient Greece* (Stanford 1962)) does at least believe it worthwhile to examine the entire action of a drama, asking how the positions expressed by its characters stand to one another. A more cautious use of tragic evidence is in Dover, *GPM*. Lloyd-Jones, *JZ*, contains an excellent criticism of writers who fail to work through the complex literary structure of a work in asking what moral view or views it expresses; and also many examples of readings of texts that do not in this way do violence to their internal integrity. One result of his procedure (which will be supported by our study of tragedy and of Aristotle here) is to show that there is far more continuity and constancy in Greek ethical thought than the procedures of Adkins were able to bring out.

21. A fine and illuminating study of the way in which Greek tragedy, against the background of ritual, works out problems connected with human vulnerability and mortality is W. Burkert, 'Greek tragedy and sacrificial ritual', *GRBS* 7 (1966) 87–121; we shall discuss some of the details of his position in Ch. 2. The final sentence of the article summarizes Burkert's position concerning the significance of the background connection with ritual sacrifice: 'Human existence face to face with death – that is the kernel of *tragoidia*' (121).

22. Though not even this would be so if an adequate confrontation with these elements in our nature required, as Burkert argues, the enactment before us of an elaborate ritual-dramatic structure.

23. On Plato, see Chs. 5–7 and Interlude 1; also Nussbaum, 'Fictions'.

24. See Chs. 2, 3, 10, and Interlude 2. On the connection between this claim and Aristotle's view of *katharsis*, see Interlude 2.

25. Murdoch, 'Philosophy and literature' 265; Locke, *An Essay Concerning Human Understanding*, ed. P. H. Nidditch (Oxford 1975) Bk 3 Ch. 10. On both passages, see Nussbaum, 'Fictions'.

26. Bernard Williams, 'Philosophy', in *The Legacy of Greece: a New Appraisal*, ed. M. I. Finley (Oxford 1981) 202–55. Now, however, the reader should compare his important *Ethics and the Limits of Philosophy* (Cambridge, MA 1985), which gives a fascinating and sympathetic account of Greek philosophical ethics that modifies some of the views with which I take issue here.

27. Williams, 'Philosophy' 253.

28. Paris 1974. The views of Detienne and Vernant are further discussed in Ch. 7 n. 36 and in Ch. 10.

29. For one connection among these images not to be discussed below, see Plato, *Laws* 789E, on the 'liquid' nature of the child.

30. For valuable suggestions towards the revision of this chapter, I am grateful to Sissela Bok, E. D. Hirsch, Jr, Barry Mazur, Hilary Putnam, Charles Segal, Nancy Sherman, and Harvey Yunis.

2 Aeschylus and practical conflict

1. On this case and the problems it raises for an account of action, see Ch. 9.

2. See further discussion of his case below, p. 30.

3. Cf. also Ch. 3. The moral implications of this feature of Greek religion are strikingly discussed by Lloyd-Jones, *JZ* 160. He concludes, 'It follows that it is often difficult to determine whether a particular desire is wrong, a proposition which is suggested

to most human beings by one or another of the experiences of life, but to which dogmatic monotheism does not always lend a hearing.' (I shall argue here that the difficulty goes beyond a difficulty of deciding what is better, and infects cases in which the decision itself is not in doubt.) We should perhaps not suggest that the Greek view of moral conflict *resulted from* these theological beliefs; rather the theology and the moral view coherently express, together, a certain characteristic response to the problem of human choice. Compare the incisive statement of the problem in J.-P. Vernant, 'Tensions et ambiguités dans la tragédie', in Vernant and Vidal-Naquet, *MT* 33.

Since I shall be speaking in this and the next chapter of conflicts generated by obligations that are religious in origin, it is important to point out that the relationship between the sphere of religion and the moral/practical sphere was not the same in Greek Olympian religion as in the Judaeo-Christian tradition. The two spheres are, in the Greek case, far more difficult to distinguish. Though I can by no means go into this fully, I can point out that Olympian religion lacked the idea that divine authority is an intrinsically inscrutable item towards which the proper attitude is irrational faith and the withholding of rational assessment. Religion is above all a system of practices, continuous with other conventional social practices, and arranged so as to stress the importance of the areas of moral and social life that are felt to be the most important. Such is the continuity with thought about value in other areas that it is taken to be perfectly reasonable to discuss the gods' reasons for valuing what they value. Gods are anthropomorphic beings who act for reasons; it is appropriate and not impious to seek to grasp those reasons. A Judaeo-Christian faith in the unknown and rationally incomprehensible has little place in any aspect of the Olympian religion. We can also observe that for every area of human life that human beings take to be of deep importance there is a divinity protecting it; it will frequently be unclear (as it would not be in the Judaeo-Christian tradition) whether the divine backing adds anything further to the human sense of deep ethical requirement, or simply underlines the importance, permanence, and binding nature of that requirement. (Thus the absence of a more than passing acknowledgment of Olympian divinities in Aristotle does little to change the shape of the ethical picture presented.) We might say, then, that the shape of Greek religious institutions is in harmony with the intuitive ethical beliefs of the Greeks; they shape and inform one another. See, however, ch. 13, pp. 401–4.

4. M. Gagarin, *Aeschylean Drama* (Berkeley 1976) 13. Similar observations are made by Vernant in 'Le moment historique de la tragédie', in *MT* 13–17, and in 'Tensions et ambiguités' 31. Although Vernant does elsewhere describe vividly and not condescendingly the tragic view that valid requirements can collide (above n. 3), here he seems to conflate three distinct claims: (1) that requirements of *dikē* can conflict; (2) that the requirements of *dikē* are ambiguous; (3) that the requirements of *dikē* are in process of change, and can transform themselves into their contrary. It appears to me that his arguments support only (1).

5. A. Lesky, 'Decision and responsibility in the tragedy of Aeschylus', *JHS* 86 (1966) 78–85, at pp. 82–3. Similar views are expressed (among others) by John Jones, Denys Page, and John Peradotto – for full references see n. 22 below.

6. For contemporary philosophical discussion of these issues, see: I. Berlin, *Concepts and Categories* (New York 1978) *passim*; P. Foot, 'Moral realism and moral dilemma', *JP* 80 (1983) 379–98; B. van Fraassen, 'Values and the heart's command', *JP* 70 (1973) 15–19; R. M. Hare, *The Language of Morals* (Oxford 1952) esp. pp. 50ff., and *Moral Thinking* (Oxford 1981) esp. pp. 25–64; J. Hintikka, 'Deontic logic and its philosophical

morals', *Models for Modalities* (Dordrecht 1969) 184–214; E. J. Lemmon, 'Moral dilemmas', *PR* 71 (1962) 139–58; R. B. Marcus, 'Moral dilemmas and consistency', *JP* 77 (1980) 121–35; T. Nagel, 'War and massacre', *PPA* 1 (1972) reprinted in *Mortal Questions* (Cambridge 1979) 53–74; W. D. Ross, *The Right and the Good* (Oxford 1930); J. Searle, '*Prima facie* obligations', in *Philosophical Subjects: Essays Presented to P. F. Strawson* (Oxford 1980) 238–59; M. Walzer, 'Political action: the problem of dirty hands', *PPA* 2 (1973) 160–80; Bernard Williams, 'Ethical consistency', *PASS* 39 (1965) repr. in *Problems of the Self* (Cambridge 1973), 166–86, and 'Conflicts of values', in *ML* 71–82. I shall discuss some of Williams's points further below. The Marcus and Searle papers, published only after this chapter was already in draft and had been publicly read, did not influence the development of my views; I shall discuss Searle's criticisms of the idea of *prima facie* obligation in n. 20 below. Ch. 3 criticizes what is the conclusion of Marcus's discussion: that the possibility of irreconcilable conflicts is a sign of irrationality in a moral or political conception and gives us a reason to revise it.

7. *EN* III.1, 1110a4ff. Aristotle is here attempting to distinguish these cases from cases of action that is straightforwardly involuntary, *akousion*, because of physical compulsion or excusable ignorance. In these cases, he stresses, the origin of the action is in the agent and he is fully aware of what he is doing. His other case is that of a tyrant who demands of the agent a shameful action, threatening death to his family if he does not obey. See the further discussion of these examples in Ch. 11.

8. Aristotle expresses this contrast by saying that in the circumstances the action is voluntary, but in itself (*haplōs*) it is not – for the person would never have chosen such an action but for the presence of situational constraint.

9. Aristotle's own view about assessment is like this: in some such cases we will ascribe blame; in some we will pity, or blame in a reduced way; in still other cases, we may even praise the agent for enduring 'something base and painful in return for great and noble objects gained'. He does say that there are some actions which no circumstances should be able to force the agent to perform: for example matricide. But by describing the case as one in which there is an innocent alternative (the agent could choose to die himself, without harming anyone else, rather than to commit the bad action) Aristotle avoids some of the most difficult problems that will be raised by our cases. See Ch. 11, however, for argument that his ethical view is hospitable to the tragic portrayal of conflict.

10. 'Ethical consistency', see n. 6 above.

11. In *ML* 20–39, Williams seriously questions the view that moral claims are the only ones to which an agent can, and should, attach the most serious practical value. If this is so, we must then wonder what characterization of the moral he is there using; from the examples, it appears to be a characterization by subject matter: moral claims are those involving benefit and harm to other persons.

12. One advantage, for Williams, of separating out conflicts of 'oughts', from other related cases is that this permits him to focus attention on the alleged problem of their logical structure. The logical analysis of these cases poses problems, particularly if we want the analysis to point to the real nature of the conflict. (Searle, '*Prima facie* obligations' shows how easy it is for philosophers to preserve a certain picture of deontic logic by denying the real nature of the cases.) Looking at those cases where we feel that the agent ought to do *a* and ought to do *b*, but cannot do both, we seem, Williams argues, to have two alternatives if we wish to avoid making this look like

direct logical contradiction: (1) We can deny that *ought* implies *can*; (2) We can deny that from 'I ought to do *a*' and 'I ought to do *b*' it follows that 'I ought to do *a* and *b*': in other words, 'ought' is not 'agglomerative'. Williams defends the second alternative; the first is chosen by Lemmon, 'Moral dilemmas'.

In *Ethics and the Limits of Philosophy* (1985), Williams explicitly abandons the moral/non-moral distinction as a basis for ethical inquiry, arguing that the moral (understood as centered around notions of duty and obligation) should be regarded as a deviant and mistaken sub-class of the ethical, which he treats as a broad, inclusive, and not rigidly demarcated category. He argues that the Greek question, 'How should one live?' is the most promising starting-point for ethical inquiry, and that good pursuit of this question does not lead to a rigid separation of moral requirements from other concerns that arise in response to that question, or to a ranking of these requirements above other concerns. I am grateful to Williams for allowing me to read and refer to this important discussion, which satisfies the criticisms I have made here.

13. Searle's article (*op. cit.*) shows the power of this view in contemporary deontic logic, arguing that strategies for eliminating conflict here rest upon a weakly described intuitive basis and some serious conceptual confusions. He shows that once these confusions are removed there is no obstacle to a perfectly consistent formalization of the conflict situation. See n. 20 below.

14. It is not clear, in fact, that there would be general agreement that Euthyphro has an obligation to prosecute his father because of the servant's death; but the situation does seem to call for a prosecution, and one of the serious gaps in Greek homicide law is that no specific provision is made for a case in which the deceased is a foreigner and therefore has no relations present to assume the duty. Euthyphro could appropriately feel that if someone ought to prosecute, the obligation fell naturally to him as the citizen most closely associated with the interests of the deceased.

15. J.-P. Sartre, '*L'Existentialisme est un humanisme*' (Paris 1946). The view of *L'Être et le Néant* may be more complex; but the same simple view is found again in *Les Mouches*.

16. The point is that even though the obligations of patriotism and the duty to care for his mother have coexisted harmoniously until this time, their contingent conflict at this time should show the agent that they were bad guides all along. On this view see further this ch. pp. 47–8.

17. Hare, *Language of Morals*, 5off.

18. In his new *Moral Thinking*, Hare has a more complicated position. He contrasts the intuitive perception of moral conflict with a 'higher' type of critical thinking that removes the conflict; the former he associates with a thinker whom he calls 'the prole', the latter with a more exemplary figure whom he calls 'the archangel'. He admits, then, how major a revision in ordinary ways of thinking it would require to make the conflict go away.

19. I. Kant, *Introduction to the Metaphysics of Morals* (1797), Akad. p. 223. For the most part I am following the translation of J. Ladd, in *The Metaphysical Elements of Justice* (Indianapolis 1965). But in the last sentence I adopt the version proposed by A. Donagan, in 'Consistency in rationalist moral systems', *JP* 81 (1984) 291–309, on p. 294. Donagan points out that the German makes a distinction between merely winning out ('die Oberhand behalte') and holding the field ('behält den Platz'): the point being that, in Kant's view, the losing 'ground' is not merely defeated, it ceases altogether to be on the scene, it vacates the field.

20. Some philosophers, following the lead of W. D. Ross (*The Right and the Good*, 19ff.),

modify the Kantian picture by importing a distinction between *prima facie* duties and absolute duties. Like Kant, Ross insists that the conflicting duties cannot both be genuine binding duties; one, at least, is merely a *prima facie* duty which, when the real duty is discovered, ceases to bind. But, unlike Kant, Ross insists that the losing duty may still bring with it an obligation to make reparations and perhaps even the need to feel 'not indeed shame or repentance, but certainly compunction'. Searle correctly points out that the notion of *prima facie* duty, in Ross and his followers, has had a bad influence on the description and assessment of cases. A technical non-ordinary notion, it has served to conflate several ordinary distinctions that ought to be kept clearly apart:

(1) The distinction between merely apparent obligation and real or genuine obligation

(2) The distinction between a lower-grade obligation and a higher-grade obligation

(3) The distinction between what one ought to do all things considered and what one has an obligation to do.

Only the first distinction really entails that the losing alternative ceases to exert any claim. But this distinction does not capture what is going on in many conflict situations. The second distinction is more promising, showing us how the second obligation might lose out and still exert its claim; but it seems to be false that in all conflict situations one of the obligations is going to be of a lower grade or type. Only the third distinction, Searle argues, allows us to describe the cases in which one obligation is clearly the one that ought to be fulfilled all things considered, and yet both are serious high-grade obligations that continue to exert a claim. Our cases of tragic conflict will support his criticism: for they show two real and extremely serious high-grade obligations conflicting in a situation in which one course is definitely the one that ought to be pursued all things considered; nonetheless, there is no temptation to suppose that this makes the other obligation unreal or non-serious.

21. This is particularly clear in *Les Mouches* and in Hare's *Moral Thinking* (see n. 18 above).
22. The literature on the *Agamemnon* is far too vast for me to aim at anything like completeness of reference. The works that I have most centrally consulted, and to which I shall refer below, are: J. D. Denniston and D. Page, eds., *Aeschylus, Agamemnon* (Oxford 1957); E. R. Dodds, 'Morals and politics in the *Oresteia*', *PCPS* 186 NS 6 (1960) 19ff.; K. J. Dover, 'Some neglected aspects of Agamemnon's dilemma', *JHS* 93 (1973) 58–69; M. Edwards, 'Agamemnon's decision: freedom and folly in Aeschylus', *California Studies in Classical Antiquity* 10 (1977) 17–38; E. Fraenkel, ed., *Aeschylus, Agamemnon*, 3 vols. (Oxford 1950); Gagarin, *Aeschylean Drama*; N. G. L. Hammond, 'Personal freedom and its limitations in the *Oresteia*', *JHS* 85 (1965) 42–55; J. Jones, *On Aristotle and Greek Tragedy* (London 1962); R. Kuhns, *The House, the City, and the Judge: the Growth of Moral Awareness in the Oresteia* (Indianapolis 1962); A. Lebeck, *The Oresteia* (Cambridge, MA 1971); A. Lesky, 'Decision and responsibility'; Lloyd-Jones, 'Guilt' 187–99, and *JZ*; Colin MacLeod, 'Politics and the *Oresteia*', *JHS* 102 (1982) 124–44; J. J. Peradotto, 'The omen of the eagles and the *ēthos* of Agamemnon', *Phoenix* 23 (1968) 237–63; W. Whallon, 'Why is Artemis angry', *AJP* 82 (1961) 78–88.
23. On the strangeness of this interpretation, see also Lloyd-Jones, 'Guilt' 189, Fraenkel, *Agamemnon*, Peradotto, 'The omen'. Lloyd-Jones, finding Calchas's explanation, as

usually rendered, 'incredible', argues that we should understand 'the abundant herds of the people' to mean 'the abundant herds that *are* the people'. Though I am happy to see this as *one* reading of the ambiguous language, keeping the more natural translation also in view gives us, I would argue, a richer understanding of Agamemnon's crime.

24. See the shrewd observations on this passage, and on the motif of sacrifice in this play generally, in W. Burkert, 'Greek tragedy and sacrificial ritual', *GRBS* 7 (1966) 87–121, at 112ff.

25. Denniston and Page, *Agamemnon* (xxvii–xxviii) correctly stress the necessity of obedience to Zeus and the fact that no background guilt of Agamemnon's led to his being in the tragic situation. But they are moved for this reason to exonerate Agamemnon altogether. E. Fraenkel (Vol. II *ad loc.*) stresses the element of choice, but then distorts the picture by explaining away the evidence of constraint. Dodds, 'Morals and politics' 27–8 stresses the clear evidence that Agamemnon's act is a crime. Lesky, 'Decision and responsibility' says that the action is determined by divine necessity and also chosen by Agamemnon; he believes that this is a primitive pattern of explanation and does not try to make it reasonable. He assumes, further, that the necessity and the blame attach to the same aspects of Agamemnon's situation. Lloyd-Jones, 'Guilt' seems virtually alone in insisting, correctly, that the necessity and the blame are both there: Zeus has forced Agamemnon to choose between two crimes (191).

26. See Denniston and Page, *Agamemnon* 214ff., Lloyd-Jones, 'Guilt' 188–91.

27. On Calchas's interpretation, compare Dover, 'Some neglected aspects' 61ff., Peradotto, 'The omen' 247–8, Fraenkel, *Agamemnon ad loc.* On Artemis's role as protector of the young, see Peradotto, 'The omen' 242–5, A. Henrichs, 'Human sacrifice in Greek religion: three case studies', in *Le Sacrifice dans l'antiquité*, Fondation Hardt *Entretiens* 27 (1981) 195–235.

28. The omission of the reasons for Artemis's anger, and the differences between this and other known versions of the story, are discussed by Fraenkel, *Agamemnon II*, 99, Lloyd-Jones, 'Guilt' 189, Peradotto, 'The omen' 242, Hammond, 'Personal freedom' 48, Whallon, 'Why?'. Fraenkel's claim that the suppression of these well-known stories of a personal offense by Agamemnon against the goddess enhances 'the element of voluntary choice' is unconvincing. Instead, it acquits Agamemnon of guilt with respect to the genesis of his predicament, forcing us to see that the necessity to choose to commit a crime is one that comes upon him from without. As for the real reasons for the anger, Lloyd-Jones alleges her general pro-Trojan sympathies; others the future offenses against the innocents at Troy. Page's suggestion that it is simply the killing of the hare that enrages her is unconvincing in its conflation of omen and the thing symbolized (see Lloyd-Jones, 'Guilt' 189). See also Lloyd-Jones's recent 'Artemis and Iphigeneia', *JHS* 103 (1983) 87–102, a penetrating study of Artemis's double nature as both protector and destroyer of young things.

29. See Lloyd-Jones, 'Guilt' 191–2. Several critics of Lloyd-Jones's article have not understood this point. Hammond, for example, says that Lloyd-Jones has made Agamemnon a mere 'puppet' with 'no freedom of choice or action' (*op. cit.* 44). This is plainly not the case.

30. On the strongly pejorative connotations of this word, see Fraenkel, who compares *lipotaxis*, a current term for deserter.

31. Here I am in agreement with Lloyd-Jones, 'Guilt' 191, Whallon, 'Why?' 51,

Hammond, 'Personal freedom' 47; Fraenkel's concluding remark at *Agamemnon* III, 276 seems to express a similar view; Lesky, 'Decision and responsibility', persistently conflates the question, 'Was there a *better* choice available?' with the question 'Was there a guilt-free choice available?' – in much the same way that Agamemnon himself later does. Dover, 'Some neglected aspects' similarly, suggests that the difficulty is one of uncertainty and of the limits of knowledge. See also the admirable discussion of related issues in P. M. Smith, *On the Hymn to Zeus in Aeschylus' Agamemnon*, American Classical Studies 5 (Ann Arbor 1980).

32. Compare Hammond, *op. cit.* 47, 55. This is the interaction of choice and necessity that is articulated in the structure of the Aristotelian practical syllogism – cf. Ch. 10, and Nussbaum, *De Motu* Essay 4.

33. On the two questions, see Denniston and Page *ad loc.*, Hammond, *op. cit.* Hammond gives a good account of the speech, arguing that it shows a deep insight into the problems of war and command.

34. On this parallel, see Henrichs, 'Human sacrifice' 206.

35. This change is also noted by Hammond, 'Personal freedom' 47.

36. I translate the text of the MSS, convincingly defended by Fraenkel, whose sense of Aeschylean language is, here as elsewhere, unsurpassed. He finds the most convincing defense of the phrase to lie in its excellence as an example of Aeschylean poetic expression. I agree. Objections to the phrase are weakly based. Some critics call it a 'tautology'; but Fraenkel rightly says that the repetition (literally: 'in passion most passionately') gives emphasis to the unnatural character of Agamemnon's desire. He produces numerous examples of intensification produced by the juxtaposition of two related words, both in Aeschylus and in other related authors. Although none is precisely parallel to this one in having two adverbial elements (one being the noun used adverbially), that is not the point (*pace* Denniston and Page): nobody has ever alleged that the phrase is actually ungrammatical. The parallels suffice to show that intensification by redoubling is a feature of archaic poetic practice in general, and a characteristic Aeschylean device in particular. Attempted emendations are well criticized by Fraenkel. Some scholars substitute *audai* ('he says'), a marginal variant in one MS and in Triclinius, for *orgai*, and then introduce Calchas as the subject, making the whole utterance a report of what the prophet says. This is highly implausible; Calchas is nowhere mentioned in the context, nor did he say any such thing. The emendation *orgai periorgōi sph' epithumein themis* (preferred by Denniston and Page) allows the soldiers and not Agamemnon to do the desiring: 'it is right that they should desire...' This solution accords well with their interpretation, according to which Agamemnon is simply a guiltless victim of necessity. But there is ample evidence in the context that Agamemnon takes the situational constraint to license eager and even callous performance of the sacrifice; whereas there is no other reference to a complaint from the soldiers. *Sph'* might also be construed as singular and taken to refer to Artemis. This attempt is brusquely (and appropriately) dismissed by Fraenkel, who notes that it came into the picture only as a result of Casaubon's ill-fated attempt to emend *themis* to *Artemis*. We may add that it would be most odd for a mortal in such a situation to say, it is *themis* for a god to desire thus and so. Once one knows that a god has commanded, one certainly may ask whether the command is just; it is not clear that one can ask whether it is according to *themis*; if this is true of the command, it is even more true of the desires accompanying or motivating the command. But the

single biggest defense of the traditional reading is that it is there, excellent and appropriately difficult (though in no way ungrammatical or unmetrical), a fine example of Aeschylean poetry and thought.

37. On the force of transitive *edu*, see Peradotto, 'The omen' 253, who correctly argues that it must mean 'put on', and cannot support a weaker meaning like 'fell into'. Dover, 'Some neglected aspects' attempts to argue that *dunai* can be used of both deliberate and involuntary movement; the alleged parallel of *Ag.* 1011 is not helpful, since *dunai* there is intransitive.

38. Lesky, 'Decision and responsibility' (82) finds this simply unintelligible: for blame surely cannot concern 'the irrational sphere only, which has nothing to do with the will that springs from rational considerations'. This is as clear an example as any of the bad influence of Kant on the understanding of Greek tragedy. Contrast Dover, *op. cit.* 66: 'They react in this way because the cutting of a girl's throat as if she were a sheep constitutes a pitiable and repulsive event; whether it is necessary or unnecessary, commanded by a god or the product of human malice and perversity.'

39. Burkert, 'Greek tragedy' (cf. also his *Homo Necans* (Berlin 1972)).

40. This name is taken over by Burkert from Karl Meuli, 'Griechische Opferbräuche', in *Phyllobolia, Festschrift P. von der Mühll* (Basel 1960). Meuli stresses, as does Burkert, the way in which the sacrificer's ritual act expresses (in Burkert's words) 'a deep-rooted human respect for life as such, which prevents man from utterly destroying other beings in an autocratic way' (106).

41. Burkert, 'Greek tragedy' 111.

42. On these substitutions (and other related cases), see Burkert, 'Greek tragedy' 112–13 and n. 58; also Freud, *Totem and Taboo* (1912–13), trans. J. Strachey (New York 1950), on the psychological impulses underlying sacrifice.

43. On these aspects of the *Seven*, and especially its ending, see: S. G. Bernardete, 'Two notes on Aeschylus' *Septem*', *Wiener Studien* 1 (1967) 29ff., 2 (1968) 5–17; R. D. Dawe, 'The end of the *Seven Against Thebes*', *CQ* NS 17 (1967) 16–28; H. Erbse, 'Zur Exodos der *Sieben*', *Serta Turyniana* (Urbana 1974) 169–98; E. Fraenkel, 'Schluss des *Sieben gegen Theben*', *Mus Helv* 21 (1964) 58–64; H. Lloyd-Jones, 'The end of the *Seven Against Thebes*', *CQ* NS 9 (1959) 80–115; A. A. Long, 'Pro and contra fratricide: Aeschylus' *Septem* 653–719', in volume in honor of T. B. L. Webster, ed. J. H. Betts (Bristol, forthcoming); C. Orwin, 'Feminine justice: the end of the *Seven Against Thebes*', *CP* 75 (1980) 187–96; A. J. Podlecki, 'The character of Eteocles in Aeschylus' *Septem*', *TAPA* 95 (1964); F. Solmsen, 'The Erinys in Aischylos' *Septem*', *TAPA* 68 (1937) 197–211; R. P. Winnington-Ingram, '*Septem Contra Thebas*', *YCS* 25 (1977) 1–45; F. Zeitlin, *Under the Sign of the Shield: Semiotics and Aeschylus' Seven Against Thebes* (Rome 1982).

44. See also Orwin, *op. cit.* 188; Benardete, *op. cit.* Long's article provides a subtle and thorough analysis of Eteocles' arguments and reactions in the speech as a whole.

45. In fact this is not clearly established within the play, since we have no independent evidence that Eteocles is the only champion who could have saved the city.

46. Lesky, 'Decision and responsibility' 83, notices this point and also stresses the parallel with Agamemnon's response; see also Solmsen, 'The Erinys'. Long, 'Pro and contra', stresses Eteocles' reply: the desire itself is blamed on the workings of his father's 'dark curse', which 'sits on my dry unclosed eyes' (695–6). The Chorus, however, do not accept this as exonerating Eteocles himself from responsibility for the desire. For they immediately reply, 'But still, don't *you* stir yourself up' (697). Long portrays Eteocles

as admirably lucid concerning all the unfortunate aspects of his tragic predicament; I would point to this use of divine causality as putative excuse as a sign that he is not altogether lucid.

47. This remains unclear, since it is never altogether clear whose claim to rule is to be regarded as just. The presence of Dike on Polynices' shield does not seem to be the decisive 'theophany' claimed by Orwin, 'Feminine justice' (191–3), following Benardete, 'Two notes' (16). Long, *op. cit.* correctly emphasizes the arguments in which Eteocles rebuts that claim (lines 667–71).

48. Cf. Orwin, *op. cit.* 190ff.; and for a somewhat different account of Eteocles' misogyny, see Zeitlin, *Under the Sign*.

49. An excellent analysis of this mythology and its civic function is provided in N. Loraux, *Les Enfants d'Athéna: idées athéniennes sur la citoyenneté et la division des sexes* (Paris 1981). For Creon's attitude towards the female, see Ch. 3; and on Plato's use of the mythology of autochthony and the denial of the family, see Ch. 5.

50. For the debate, see the articles mentioned above n. 43. The philological issues are not decisive, and the decision rests with our appraisal of the content: does it have the requisite thematic unity with what has preceded? Orwin, 'Feminine justice' argues persuasively that it does, if we have all along been sufficiently attentive to questions about the character of Eteocles and his view of justice.

51. This point has been appropriately stressed by a number of recent writers on Aeschylus, especially by Lloyd-Jones, 'Guilt', *JZ*. See also n. 3.

52. *Eum.* 517–25.

53. I have taken no stand on the larger question of Agamemnon's character. Peradotto, 'The omen', for example, argues that his response is intelligible only as the outgrowth of an antecedently bad and murderous *ēthos*. I believe that the initial accuracy of his response tells against this; his shift may be inspired by horror at the situation confronting him, which he can endure in no other way than to deny that it exists.

54. With Fraenkel, I have changed *thrasos*, which does not scan, to *tharsos*. But Fraenkel has shown convincingly that the distinction between the two is secondary and probably did not exist in the time of Aeschylus. There seems to be no obstacle to understanding *tharsos* in a derogatory sense (11, 364).

55. On *hekousion* and *akousion*, see further in Ch. 9; and for related uses, see ?Aes. *Prom.* 19, 266, 671, 771, 854; cf. also Soph. *Oed. Col.* 827, 935, 965, 985–7.

56. For this objection, see Fraenkel, Denniston, and Page *ad loc.* Another line of objection to the text involves assuming that *komizō* must mean 'restore' and that the entire phrase should be translated 'restoring confidence to dying men'. G. Hermann, *Euripidis Opera* (Leipzig, 1st ed. 1800; 2nd ed. 1831) has objected that *komizō* cannot, like *pherō*, be used to mean restoring something with the result that the thing restored is put *into* the person; rather it must mean that the thing is set *by* the person. To this we might fairly object that the passions in Aeschylus are often described as taking up their stance beside the person (e.g., *Ag.* 13, 14, 976, 982–3). If we reject this objection and keep *tharsos...komizōn*, but still object to *hekousion*, we might then accept Ahrens's *ek thusiōn*, 'from sacrifices'. But this expedient seems unnecessary.

57. E. G. Weil: 'feminae audaciam voluntariam, h.e. feminam perfidam, virorum morte recuperare conans'. Or Verrall, 'that thou for a willing wanton wouldst spend the lives of men'. (Cf. Peradotto, 'The omen' 255, Hammond, 'Personal freedom' 46.)

58. It offers an odd reading of *andrasi thnēiskousi*: the context, which all has to do with Aulis, makes it natural to think of men who were dying *there*, rather than of the war's future

cost in human lives. Furthermore, the dative of disadvantage is harsh. Third, the present participles *nōmōn* and *komizōn* should be read as parallel; but it is at Aulis that Agamemnon is not wielding the helm of sense; and it is only in the future that he will restore Helen at such a cost. Finally the periphrasis seems difficult to understand – for it is far more difficult to see how a *person* could be 'voluntary' than to see how the passions of that person could be. As for *komizō* in the sense 'protect', 'nourish', 'cherish', this is a very common meaning in Homer, and appears elsewhere in Aes., e.g., *Cho.* 262, possibly 344. (Cf. Stephanus, *Thesaurus*, 1778D–1779A.)

59. See Nussbaum, 'Consequences'.
60. Cf. Chs. 9, 10.
61. On the cultivation of appropriate feeling, see further remarks in Interlude 1 and Chs. 7, 9, and 10, with references. On this and other issues discussed in this section, see I. Murdoch, *The Sovereignty of Good* (London 1970).
62. See H. Putnam, 'Literature, science, and reflection', in *Meaning and the Moral Sciences* (London 1979) 83–96.
63. I am thoroughly in agreement, on this point, with Foot (above n. 6), who argues that the existence and indefeasibility of these dilemmas does not in any way tend to undermine moral realism. We shall see in Chs. 8–12 how a certain form of realism can in fact be built around the recognition of an irreducible plurality of values, and therefore around the permanent possibility of conflict.
64. Kant would in fact have a way of defusing this particular conflict: for alleged divine orders to commit immoral acts are not binding (*Religion Within the Limits of Reason Alone* IV.4). This, however, in no way affects the general point; for he cannot extricate himself from all conflicts this way; and yet he has an antecedent commitment to acknowledge at most one claim as binding. We might even argue that by refusing to God the recognition of human conflict situations he adopts a conception of divinity that is less rich than the Greek conception in just the way that his moral conception is less rich than theirs. One further remark on the religious dimensions of these conflicts. Donagan observes (p. 298) that St Gregory the Great recognized the existence of genuine moral dilemmas, but ascribed them to the work of the devil, who could trap human beings into situations in which they were forced to violate some divine commandment. The difference between this view and the Greek view is that the causal role played by the devil in the one is played in the other by the world; and furthermore, as we shall see in Ch. 3, the Greeks connect the ongoing possibility of such conflicts with good and even divine things, such as richness of life and recognition of the diversity of value that is there to be seen.
65. Something like this seems to be the view towards moral dilemma expressed by Wittgenstein in a 1947 conversation with Rush Rhees, reported in 'Wittgenstein's lecture on ethics', *PR* 74 (1965) 3–26. After insisting that in order to talk about the problem it is necessary to have a case described in detail, so that we can really imagine and feel what it comes to (here he makes some disparaging remarks about textbooks in ethics), Wittgenstein goes to work on a sample case of dilemma that is very similar in structure to ours. After describing the tragic choice faced by the agent, in which there is no guilt-free way out and we feel we can only say, 'God help him', Wittgenstein surprises Rhees by remarking, 'I want to say that this is the solution to an ethical problem.' He indicates then, our point: that the perspicuous description of the case, the unswerving recognition of the values it contains and of the way in which, for the

agent, there is no way out, is all there is by way of solution here; so-called philosophical solutions only succeed in being misdescriptions of the problem.

66. I have read drafts of this chapter at Brandeis University, Vassar College, the University of Massachusetts at Boston, the University of Maryland, the University of Pittsburgh, and Stanford University. I am grateful to those present, and also to A. Lowell Edmunds, A. A. Long, and Nick Pappas, for their helpful comments.

3 Sophocles' *Antigone*: conflict, vision, and simplification

1. I have chosen to discuss the emergence of this view by discussing one example in depth. But it is generally admitted that the strategies I ascribe to Creon link him with certain aspects of sophistic rationalism – see n. 10 below. I discuss a closely related view in 'Consequences' 25–53; on connections between this play and the sophists, see P. Rose, 'Sophocles' *Philoctetes* and the teachings of the Sophists', *HSCP* 80 (1976) 49–105. Relevant background material can also be found in M. O'Brien, *The Socratic Paradoxes and the Greek Mind* (Chapel Hill 1967), and in Guthrie, *History* III. Ch. 4 contains a full discussion of some aspects of these issues, as they provide a background for Plato's idea of *technē* – and many more references.

2. Naturally thinkers who take an 'anti-tragic' view of the individual case (cf. Ch. 2) will hold the related view about the larger picture. But some defenders of the tragic view for individual cases have endorsed the elimination of conflict as an end, or even a criterion, of political rationality. Consider, for example, R. B. Marcus, 'Moral dilemmas and consistency', *JP* 77 (1980) 121–35, and M. Gibson, 'Rationality', *PPA* 6 (1977) 193–225. Although these views are probably not indebted to Hegel, they are distinctly Hegelian in spirit. The opposing view is most vividly defended, in recent philosophical writing, by Sir Isaiah Berlin (see *Concepts and Categories* (New York 1978) *passim*), and Bernard Williams (see references in Ch. 2).

3. For its effect on Aeschylus criticism, see Ch. 2; for its influence on discussion of the *Antigone*, see below n. 7 and 8.

4. Compare Aristotle's claim that tragedy presents a *bios*, a whole course or pattern of life and choice – see Interlude 2 for references and discussion.

5. The literature on the *Antigone* is vast; I have not attempted anything like full coverage. The main works which I have consulted are: S. Benardete, 'A reading of Sophocles' *Antigone*', *Interpretation* 4 (1975) 148–96, 5 (1975) 1–55, 148–84; R. F. Goheen, *The Imagery of Sophocles' Antigone* (Princeton 1951); R. Bultmann, 'Polis und Hades in der *Antigone* des Sophokles', in H. Diller, ed., *Sophokles* (Darmstadt 1967) 311–24; R. C. Jebb, *Sophocles: the Antigone* (Cambridge 1900); J. C. Kamerbeek, *Sophocles' Antigone* (Leiden 1945); Bernard Knox, *The Heroic Temper: Studies in Sophoclean Tragedy* (Berkeley 1964); I. M. Linforth, 'Antigone and Creon', *University of California Publications in Classical Philology* 15 (1961) 183–260; Lloyd-Jones, *JZ*; G. Müller, *Sophokles, Antigone* (Heidelberg 1967); G. Perrotta, *Sofocle* (Messina–Florence 1935); G. Ronnet, *Sophocle: poète tragique* (Paris 1969); M. Santirocco, 'Justice in Sophocles' *Antigone*', *Phil Lit* 4 (1980) 180–98; W. Schmid, 'Probleme aus der sophokleischen Antigone', *Philologus* 62 (1903) 1–34; C. Segal, 'Sophocles' praise of man and the conflicts of the *Antigone*', *Arion* 3 (1964) 46–66, repr. in T. Woodard, ed., *Sophocles: A Collection of Critical Essays* (Englewood Cliffs, NJ 1966) 62–85; C. Segal, *Tragedy and Civilization: an Interpretation of Sophocles* (Cambridge, MA 1981); J. P. Vernant, 'Le moment historique

de la tragédie', 'Tensions et ambiguités dans la tragédie grecque', in Vernant and Vidal-Naquet, *MT* 13–17, 21–40; J. P. Vernant, 'Greek Tragedy: Problems and Interpretation', in E. Donato and R. Macksey, eds., *The Languages of Criticism and the Sciences of Man* (Baltimore 1970) 273–89; C. Whitman, *Sophocles: a Study of Heroic Humanism* (Cambridge, MA 1951); R. P. Winnington-Ingram, *Sophocles: an Interpretation* (Cambridge 1980). Except where otherwise indicated, I am using the Oxford Classical Text of A. C. Pearson (Oxford 1924).

6. Eleven words connected with practical deliberation, occurring a total of 180 times in the seven plays of Sophocles, occur a total of 50 times in the *Antigone*. (The words in question are: *boulē, bouleuma, bouleuō, euboulos, euboulia, dusboulia, phronēma, phronein, phrēn, dusphrōn, dusnous*; my count is based upon Ellendt's *Lexicon Sophocleum*, and does not include the fragments.) The word *phronēma* occurs six times in the *Antigone* and in no other play; *dusboulia* and *euboulia* occur twice each in the *Antigone* and nowhere else; *phrēn* has 17 of its 58 occurrences in the *Antigone*.

7. We must avoid from the beginning a confusion between the assessment of the decision and the assessment of the deliberations that led to the decision. It is perfectly possible for a person to have reached the better overall decision through a deliberative process that neglects certain valid claims; the decision will still, then, be correct – but not for the right reasons, and almost, as it were, by accident. The view of conflict criticized in Ch. 2 has influenced a number of critics to hold that if Antigone's *decision* is better she cannot be criticized for her neglect of the conflicting claims of the city: all we have to ask is, who is right. Thus Jebb, Bultmann, 'Polis', and Perrotta, *Sofocle*; Perrotta holds that if Antigone's decision is correct overall, the Chorus's blame of her must be 'senza logica e senza coerenza' (85). The relevant distinction is well grasped by Knox, *Heroic Temper* (114–16), Segal, *Tragedy* (170), Benardete, 'A reading' (*passim*, esp. 1.1, 2.4, 4.1), Vernant, 'Tensions et ambiguités' (see n. 8 below), Linforth, 'Antigone and Creon' (191, 257–8), Santirocco, 'Justice' (*passim*), Winnington-Ingram, *Sophocles* (128).

8. This idea is endorsed by a number of critics who view the conflicting claims as both valid and ineliminable, within the play's terms. Thus, for example, Linforth, 'Antigone and Creon' 257: 'For all Athenians, the play offers a powerful warning to see to it that the laws they enact are not in conflict with the laws of the gods.' Cf. also Santirocco, 'Justice' 182, 194. Segal's concluding remarks may suggest a similar view: 'Through its choral song, the *polis* arrives at self-awareness of the tensions between which it exists. Embodying these tensions in art, it can confront them and work towards their mediation, even though mediation is not permitted to the tragic heroes within the spectacle itself. The play in its social and ritual contexts achieves for society what it refuses to the actors within its fiction. Its context affirms what its content denies' (*Tragedy* 205). It is, however, not altogether clear to me to what extent Segal and I really disagree here; this would depend on what, more precisely, is involved in 'mediation', and how this is related to the picture of practical wisdom that I shall develop below.

Vernant's position is, once again (see Ch 2 n. 3–4) complex. Although he gives a most vivid characterization of the irreconcilable nature of the tension that tragedy depicts (cf. esp. 'Tensions et ambiguités' 30–1, 35), he tends to suggest three further things that do not appear to follow from this observation: first, that the tragic conception of justice is therefore *ambiguous*; second, that it is continually *moving around*, transforming itself into its contrary (cf. 'Le moment historique' 15); third, that these conflicts would disappear with the development of a *clear* conception of the will and of the distinction between voluntary and involuntary action ('Greek tragedy' 288). The first and second are criticisms that Plato will certainly make against the tragic view; however, it seems important for *us* not to think of the contingent conflict of two valid requirements as a confusion or ambiguity in the conception of justice, a problem to be solved by intellectual clarification (cf. Ch. 2). To the third (where his position is strikingly similar to that of Lesky – cf. Ch. 2, n. 5) one can only point out that these situations seem to arise every day, and the concept of the will – unless we combine it with a particular set of controversial views about consistency – does nothing to make them go away.

9. For Creon, see n. 12 below; for Antigone, lines 2, 18, 448.

10. For general discussion of this speech and its cultural background, its connections with sophistic rationalism, see esp. Schmid, 'Probleme', Knox, *Heroic Temper* 84, Winnington-Ingram, *Sophocles* 123, Goheen, *Imagery* 152 and n. 28.

11. For an excellent discussion of the play's imagery of health and disease, see Goheen, *op. cit.* 41–4.

12. At 176–7, Creon tells us: 'It is impossible to get a thorough understanding (*ekmathein*) of the soul, the reasoning, and the judgment of any man, until he shows himself in experience of government or law' (176–7). Accordingly he claims knowledge of other people only in connection with their relation to civic safety (cf. 293–4). He claims to know only three general truths, all closely connected with the primacy of the civic good: the ease with which a rigid opponent can be subdued (477–8), the unpleasantness of living with a woman who is not city-centered in spirit (649–51), and the fundamental role of the city itself in preserving human lives and goods (188ff.).

13. Cf. Linforth, 'Antigone and Creon' 191.

14. These issues receive full and illuminating discussion especially in Perrotta, *Sofocle* 60–1, Linforth, 'Antigone and Creon' 191ff., 255ff.; see also Winnington-Ingram, *Sophocles* 120, Segal, *Tragedy* §11. The ancient evidence is gathered in D. A. Hester, 'Sophocles the unphilosophical: a study in the *Antigone*', *Mnemosyne* 4th ser. 24 (1971) 54–5, Appendix C. The tremendous importance of the obligation to bury is conceded by all interpreters; see also H. Bolkestein, *Wohltätigkeit und Armenpflege* (Utrecht 1939) 69–71, who reconstructs the *arai bouzugioi*, the famous list of traditional duties held to have been given by the founder of civilization, the one who first put oxen before the plow. This list includes, Bolkestein argues, the injunction, 'Do not allow a corpse to remain unburied', *ataphon sōma mē perioran*. In Aeschines 1.14 (cf. Benardete, 'A reading' 4.3, n. 11), it is clear that even a son who was sold into prostitution by his father still has a legal and moral obligation to bury him.

On the other hand, it is important to realize the extent to which a traitor was an exception to the general rule. Critics of Creon frequently allude to customs concerning the return of the corpse of an *enemy*, not recognizing the great difference between a mere enemy and a traitor under Athenian law (so, oddly, Jebb, xx ff.). Winnington-Ingram, referring to O. Taplin, *CR* 26 (1976) 119 and W. R. Connor, *The New Politicians of Fifth-Century Athens* (Princeton 1971) 51, argues that Creon's action would be perfectly acceptable, did it not show a neglect of Polynices' status as his own kin. Linforth, 'Antigone and Creon' and Perrotta, *Sofocle* carefully distinguish between enemy and traitor, referring to Thuc. 1.138 (where Themistocles is not allowed burial in Attica), Xen. *Hell.* 1.7.22, Eur. *Phoen.* 1629. Perrotta points out that Athenian traitors, though forbidden burial in Attic territory, were frequently buried by their kin in Megara. Even the harshest treatment mentioned, the casting of the corpse into a pit or *barathron*, still does not permit the corpse to be devoured by dogs.

We can conclude that Creon is within custom and justified (ignoring for the moment his family tie) insofar as he shows dishonor to the corpse and forbids it burial in or near the city; he is outside of custom in his attempt to obstruct *all* efforts at burial (though the issues are blurred here, since the attempt he obstructs involved burial near the city and would thus be illegal under Athenian law). He is, of course, outside custom in his complete neglect, as kinsman, of his own family duties.

15. Cf. also 299, 313, 731.

16. On Creon's view of justice, see Segal, *Tragedy* 169–70, Santirocco, 'Justice' 185–6, Bultmann, 'Polis' 312.

17. In one startling passage, 'justly' is even used of the submissive obedience of citizens to civic power: 'They were not keeping their necks justly under the yoke and obeying my authority' (291–2).

18. By this I mean to include both *erōs* or (primarily sexual) passion and *philia*, which includes family ties (with or without felt affection) and the love of friends (cf. Ch. 12). It is worth noticing that in the terms of the play (as in the historical context) *philia* imposes valid obligations even in the absence of felt affection.

19. On the oddness of Creon's view of *philia*, see Schmid, 'Probleme', Knox, *Heroic Temper* 80, 87, Segal, *Tragedy* 188, Winnington-Ingram, *Sophocles* 123, 129, 98ff., 148, Benardete, 'A reading' 12.6. The 'brother' decree is stressed by Segal, *Tragedy* 188 and Knox, *Heroic Temper* 87; the making of *philoi* by Winnington-Ingram, *op. cit.* 123, Knox, *op. cit.* 87, Benardete, *op. cit.* 12.6.

20. On Creon's denial of *erōs*, see Schmid, 'Probleme' 10ff., Vernant, 'Tensions' 34–5, Segal, *Tragedy* 166, 198, Winnington-Ingram, *Sophocles* 97ff.

21. Compare the *Euthyphro*, on which cf. Ch. 2, pp. 25, 30. On Creon's religious conception, see Schmid, *op. cit.* 7ff., Segal, *op. cit.* 174–5, 164, Linforth, 'Antigone and Creon' 80, 101, Knox, *Heroic Temper* 216, Benardete, 'A reading' 19.3, and especially Vernant, 'Tensions' 34: 'Des deux attitudes religieuses que l'*Antigone* met en conflit, aucune ne saurait en elle-même être la bonne sans faire à l'autre sa place, sans reconnaître cela même qui la borne et la conteste.'

It should be noted once again (cf. Ch. 2, p. 34 and n. 29) that none of this requires us to neglect the importance of the curse upon the house, stressed by Lloyd-Jones, *JZ*, Perrotta, *Sofocle*, and also Segal, *Tragedy* (190). For, as Lloyd-Jones correctly argues 'Guilt' (cf. Ch. 2 n. 29), the curse works itself out through humanly assessible actions. Segal makes the interesting observation (166) that one of Creon's failings is his neglect of the past: 'life centers upon a static gnomically comprehensible present or a future rationally calculable in terms of gain (*kerdos*)'.

22. On eyes and seeing, cf. this Ch. pp. 70–72, and 76–7, 79; cf. also Chs. 7, 13.

23. Cf. Segal, *Tragedy* 179 and n. 85 p. 447.

24. Cf. Segal, *Tragedy* 145, 166, Goheen, *Imagery* 14–19. For Creon's use of money imagery, see lines 175–7, 220–2, 295–303, 310–12, 322, 325–6, 1033–9, 1045–7, 1055, 1061, 1063. Cf. Goheen, *op. cit.* 14–19.

25. For use of the image prior to the date of this play (441 B.C.), see Alcaeus 6, Theognis 670–85, Aes. *Septem* 1ff., 62, 109, 192, 780, 1068; *Eum.* 16. For subsequent uses, see for example Aristoph. *Peace* 699, Plato, *Rep.* 389D, 488A–89A, *Euthyd.* 291D, *Sts.* 302Aff., 299B, *Laws* 641A, 758A–B, 831D, 945C. There are many others. See discussion in Jebb and Kamerbeek *ad loc.*, Goheen, *op. cit.* 44–51, P. Shorey, 'Note on Plato *Republic* 488D',

CR 20 (1906) 247–8, and Tucker's commentary on Aes. *Septem*. The scholiast to Aristoph. *Wasps* 29 remarks that the image is a poetic commonplace.

26. For the general argument, compare Thuc. 11.60 (cf. *orthoumenon*), Democritus fr. 252.

27. *De Falsa Legatione* 246–50. It is worth noting that Aeschines was apparently the *tritagonistēs*; this implies that the view that Creon is the 'hero' of the tragedy was not supported by ancient performance practice.

28. So too Thuc. 11.60, where the ends of the 'city as a whole' (*polin xumpasan*) are contrasted implicitly with the individual ends of private citizens (*kath' hekaston tōn politōn*). Demosthenes' account of how Aeschines opposed *to kath' heauton* to the good of the whole brings out the possibilities of conflict that were always latent in the image.

29. Cf. Ar. *De An.* 413a9, where to ask whether the soul is the actuality of the body the way the sailor is of a ship is, apparently, to ask a question about separability; compare also 406a6, where the sailor in the ship is used as an example of something that is transported as in a conveyance.

30. The idea of *sōzein*, of life-saving, and the idea of shutting out external dangers, are present in the image from the beginning. See the good discussion in Jebb *ad loc.*, and the passage cited in n. 25.

31. On male and female in the play, see esp. Segal, *Tragedy* §x.

32. Creon is probably assimilating Polynices to an animal at 201–2; at 775–6, he speaks of leaving *fodder* for Antigone. On his assimilations of the human to the animal, see Segal, *Tragedy* §11, and Goheen, *Imagery* 26ff., who points out that Creon is almost alone in the play in using animal imagery for human things.

33. Cf. also Creon's implicit comparison of Haemon to a domestic animal: *Paidos me sainei phthoggos*, 'My son's voice fawningly-barks me greeting' (1214). See Goheen's perceptive comments on this line, 34–5. (Note that this line, although quoted late in the play, is a report from a time prior to the changes in Creon that we shall describe below.)

34. At 1175 the Messenger says, 'Haemon is dead; he is bloodied (*haimassetai*) with his own hand.' Cf. also 794; and Knox, *Heroic Temper* 88 and n. 54, Santirocco, 'Justice' 184.

35. For *phrenes* in Sophocles as connected primarily with judgment and practical reason, see Ellendt, *Lexicon Sophocleum*, s.v. For only a few examples, see *Ai.* 445, *Phil.* 1113, 1281, *Oed. T.* 528; this play 298, 492, 603, 792, esp. 1015.

36. On the reversal of the imagery of animal-taming in this passage, see Goheen, *Imagery* 31–2, Segal, *Tragedy* 159. On Eurydice, see Santirocco, 'Justice' 194.

37. Cf. n. 7 above.

38. Cf. Benardete, 'A reading' 1.1, Knox, *Heroic Temper* 79. The emphatic word *autadelphon*, 'own-sibling', is used twice again in the play, both times of Polynices: once by Antigone (502–4), once by Haemon, reporting her argument (694–9).

39. Cf. Benardete, 'A reading' 2.4.

40. See lines 10, 11, 73, 99, 847, 882, 893, 898–9. Cf. Benardete, *op. cit.* 8.6, 9.5, Segal, *Tragedy* 189, Winnington-Ingram, *Sophocles* 129ff., Knox, *Heroic Temper* 79–80.

41. A number of scholars have claimed that Antigone is motivated by deep personal love for Polynices: for example, Santirocco, 'Justice' 188, Knox, *Heroic Temper* 107ff., Winnington-Ingram, *op. cit.* 130. Contrast the effective negative arguments of Perrotta, *Sofocle* 112–14, Lloyd-Jones, *JZ* 116, Linforth, 'Antigone and Creon' 250. Perrotta correctly observes that she loves Polynices not *qua* Polynices, but *qua* falling under a family duty. She is exclusively animated by her passion for the duties of family religion,

and she has no tenderness for individuals: 'Questa terribile eroina non e la donna d'amore che molti hanno voluto vedere in lei.' With her abstract and cold remarks of mourning we might contrast, for example, the agonized mourning of Hecuba (in Euripides' *Trojan Women*, cf. Ch. 10, pp. 313ff.) over the corpse of her grandchild, where each part of the loved body conjures up a new memory of shared affection. There are many similar cases.

42. Cf. Perrotta, *op. cit.* 112. We must ascribe 'O dearest Haemon, how your father dishonors you', to Ismene as in all the manuscripts. Pearson and other editors have assigned it to Antigone, out of their desire to have Antigone say something affectionate about Haemon. But *philtate*, 'dearest', is not unusually strong inside a close family relationship, and it is perfectly appropriate to the affectionate Ismene; it need not, in fact, even designate close affection. Creon's reply that the speaker's continued harping on marriage 'irritates' him is appropriate to his relationship with Ismene (who is, in any case, the one who has been 'harping' on marriage), but is far too mild to express his deep hatred for and anger against Antigone. See the arguments of Linforth, *op. cit.* 209, Benardete *ad loc.*

43. On Antigone's refusal of *erōs*, see Vernant, 'Tensions' 34–5, Benardete, 'A reading' 8.6; compare Segal, *Tragedy* §VIII. Vernant correctly writes, 'Mais les deux divinités [sc. Eros and Dionysos] se retournent aussi contre Antigone, enfermée dans sa *philia* familiale, vouée volontairement à Hadès, car jusque dans leur lien avec la mort, Dionysos et Eros expriment les puissances de vie et de renouveau. Antigone n'a pas su entendre l'appel à se detacher des "siens" et de la *philia* familiale pour s'ouvrir a l'autre, accueillir Eros, et dans l'union avec un étranger, transmettre à son tour la vie.'

44. This speech is notoriously controversial. It would surely have been branded spurious had it not been quoted as genuine by Aristotle in the *Rhetoric*; this dates it so early that, if spurious, it could only be an actor's interpolation. And it is difficult to imagine an actor giving himself such an oddly legalistic and unemotional speech at a climactic moment in the dramatic action. It is, then, (despite the wishes expressed by Goethe) almost certainly genuine; and it is very difficult to explain as a confused and incoherent outpouring of passionate love – though this approach has indeed been tried (e.g. by Winnington-Ingram, *Sophocles* 145ff., Knox, *Heroic Temper* 144ff.). The best explanation for this coldly determined priority-ordering of duties is that Antigone is not animated by personal love at all, but by a stern determination to have a fixed set of ordered requirements that will dictate her actions without engendering conflict; her refusal of the erotic (cf. n. 43 above) is then sufficient to explain her choice of the brother. For review of the controversy about authenticity and about the relation of the passage to Herodotus III.119, see Hester, 'Sophocles the unphilosophical' 55–80, Jebb, Appendix, 258–63, Müller, *Sophokles, Antigone* 198ff., 106ff., Knox, *op. cit.* 103–6, Winnington-Ingram, *op. cit.* 145ff. See also D. Page, *Actors' Interpolations in Greek Tragedy* (Oxford 1934).

45. See Benardete, 'A reading' 9.3.

46. See Knox, *Heroic Temper* 94ff., Segal, *Tragedy* §VIII. Winnington-Ingram calls the way in which she denies the hatred of brothers for one another after death a 'heroic fiat', 'a supreme effort to impose heroic will upon a recalcitrant world' (*Sophocles* 132).

47. On Antigone's conception of *dikē* and its novelty, see R. Hirzel, *Themis, Dike, und Verwandtes* (Leipzig 1907) 147ff.; also Santirocco, 'Justice' 186, Segal, *op. cit.* 170.

48. Segal, *op. cit.* provides an excellent discussion of this aspect of Antigone in several places – esp. 156ff., §VIII, §IV, 196.

49. See esp. 810–16, 867, 876–80, 891, 916–18.
50. Cf. 842–9, 876–7, 881–2.
51. Cf. above pp. 54–5 and n. 14.
52. The importance of this link with the yielding world of nature is seen by Segal, *Tragedy* 154ff., who compares 423–5, 433.
53. Cf. A. C. Bradley, 'Hegel's Theory of Tragedy', *Oxford Lectures on Poetry* (London 1950) 69–95, reprinted in *Hegel on Tragedy*, ed. A. and H. Paolucci (New York 1975) 367ff.
54. G. W. F. Hegel, *The Philosophy of Fine Art*, tr. P. B. Osmaston (London 1920) Vol. IV, reprinted in *Hegel on Tragedy* (above n. 53) pp. 68, 71.
55. Cf. above n. 8.
56. For a related development of this same idea, see Nussbaum, 'Crystals'.
57. What I shall say about the lyrics is closely related to observations in Goheen, Linforth, and Segal. A related study from which I have learned is A. Lebeck, *The Oresteia* (Cambridge, MA 1971).
58. This illuminating comparison was first made by Nietzsche in *The Birth of Tragedy* (1872), trans. W. Kaufmann (New York 1976). (It should be remembered that ancient dreams are taken to be prospective as well as retrospective.)
59. The terms 'density' and 'resonance' are discussed and further developed in the excellent analysis of the style of Heraclitus that forms part of C. Kahn's *The Art and Thought of Heraclitus* (Cambridge 1979), esp. pp. 87–95.
60. Fr. DK B67a. See the interpretation of this fragment and the defense of its authenticity in my '*Psuchē* in Heraclitus, 1', *Phronesis* 17 (1972) 1–17.
61. Cf. Ch. 12 and Interlude 2.
62. On the Parodos see especially Linforth, 'Antigone and Creon' 188, Benardete, 'A reading' 11.4, Winnington-Ingram, *Sophocles* 112ff., Segal, *Tragedy* §xiv. On the text, see H. Lloyd-Jones, 'Notes on Sophocles' *Antigone*', *CQ* NS 7 (1957) 12–27; he defends the *oxutoroi* of the MSS at 108 and interprets the bit metaphorically, as the bit of necessity, or Zeus.
63. This idea is further developed in Ch. 6, where we examine Diotima's claim that the 'sight of the body' and the 'sight of the soul' are mutually exclusive; in Ch. 13, where we discuss connections between vision and *philia*; and in Ch. 10, where we examine Aristotle's claim that 'the decision rests with perception'. On symbolic associations of eyes and vision in Greek and related cultures, see W. Deonna, *Le Symbolisme de l'oeil* (Paris 1965); for other ancient references, Ch. 13 n. 27.
64. Cf. also 215, 314, 325, 406, 562, 581.
65. My reading of this ode owes a considerable debt to Segal, 'Sophocles' praise', which contributed to the early formation of these thoughts – though I shall be emphasizing somewhat different aspects of the ode's self-undercutting. More recently I have profited from the discussion of its imagery that pervades Segal's longer discussion, and I have also learned from Goheen's sensitive account. See also Ronnet, *Sophocle* 151ff., Linforth, 'Antigone and Creon' 196–9, Benardete *ad loc.*
66. On progress through arts or *technai*, and on other related stories of the discovery of arts, see Ch. 4.
67. The ode on *erōs* is well discussed by Winnington-Ingram, *Sophocles* 92–8; cf. also Benardete, 'A reading' 44.6, Santirocco, 'Justice' 191, Linforth, 'Antigone and Creon' 221.
68. Contrast the *orgas eumeneis* of the gods at 1260, when Creon performs the burial.

69. On anger and revenge, see further in Ch. 13.

70. See Winnington-Ingram, *Sophocles* 98–109, Linforth, *op. cit.* 231–3, Goheen, *Imagery* 64–74, and especially Segal, *Tragedy* 182ff., who remarks that the cave could be seen to symbolize the sort of lonely mystery that Creon has refused. On the second antistrophe, see Lloyd-Jones, *CQ* NS 7 (1957) 24–7.

71. A. Schopenhauer, *The World as Will and Representation*, trans. E. J. Payne (New York 1969) Vol. I, pp. 252–3.

72. Cf. Segal, *Tragedy* 154ff.

73. Cf. Ch. 10.

74. Compare Segal, *Tragedy* 201.

75. Cf. Segal, *op. cit. passim.*

76. Cf. Ch. 13 on *nomos* (with references).

77. On this ode see esp. Segal, *Tragedy* 202ff., to a number of whose observations I am indebted; also Linforth, 'Antigone and Creon' 238, Santirocco, 'Justice' 192.

78. In my work on this chapter I am indebted to several generations of students and teaching assistants: especially to Janet Hook, Nick Pappas, Gail Rickert, and Nancy Sherman. I am also grateful to Stanley Cavell, with whom I taught this material, and to Barry Mazur, who first listened to some of the ideas that became its concluding section. I am also grateful to Mary Whitlock Blundell and to Lowell Edmunds for their comments.

4   The *Protagoras*: a science of practical reason

1. For relevant general accounts of the intellectual life of Athens in this period, see G. Grote, *A History of Greece*, vol. VII (London 1888); W. K. C. Guthrie, *The Sophists* (= *History* III, Pt I) (Cambridge 1971); G. Kerferd, *The Sophistic Movement* (Cambridge 1981); see also N. Loraux's stimulating *L'Invention d'Athènes* (Paris 1981). On progress, see L. Edelstein, *The Idea of Progress in Classical Antiquity* (Baltimore 1967), with many references to the literature on particular texts; Dodds, *ACP* 1–25.

2. On the *technē–tuchē* antithesis, see especially A. L. Edmunds, *Chance and Intelligence in Thucydides* (Cambridge, MA 1975). On *technē* and related notions, the most comprehensive review of the evidence is in R. Schaerer, *Epistēmē et Technē: études sur les notions de connaissance et d'art d'Homère à Platon* (Lausanne 1930); an excellent related study is D. Kurz, *Akribeia: Das Ideal der Exaktheit bei den Griechen bis Aristoteles* (Göppingen 1970); see also L. Camerer, *Praktische Klugheit bei Herodot: Untersuchungen zu den Begriffen Mechane, Techne, Sophie* (Tübingen 1965) and M. Isnardi Parente, *Technē* (Florence 1966), which covers the period Plato–Epicurus. Two related studies of scientific and practical intelligence of considerable interest are: M. Detienne and J.-P. Vernant, *Les Ruses de l'intelligence: la Mètis des grecs* (Paris 1974) and G. E. R. Lloyd, *Magic, reason, and experience* (Cambridge 1981); see also Vernant's *Les Origines de la pensée grecque* (Paris 1981) and his briefer papers, 'Le travail et la pensée technique' and 'Remarques sur les formes et les limites de la pensée technique chez les Grecs', in *Mythe et pensée chez les Grecs*, II (Paris 1965) 5–15, 44–64. For general studies of *tuchē*, see A. A. Buriks, *Peri Tuches: De ontwikkeling van het begrip tyche tot aan de Romeinse tijd, hoofdzakelijk in de philosophie* (Leiden 1955); H. Meuss, *Tuche bei den attischen Tragikern* (Hirschberg 1899); H. Strohm, *Tyche: zur Schicksalsauffassung bei Pindar und den frühgriechischen Dichtern* (Stuttgart 1944). See also Lloyd-Jones, *JZ*, esp. 142, 162.

3. For an account of the most important elements of continuity and discontinuity, see Interlude 2.

4. My version of the story is largely taken from Prometheus's speech in the *Prometheus Bound* (whose disputed authorship makes no difference to our reflections here). See Edelstein, *Idea of Progress* and Guthrie, *History* (above, n. 1) for a full account of other related texts. The once widespread view that the anthropology reported in Diodorus Siculus (60–30 B.C.) derives from Democritus (see, for example, T. Cole, *Democritus and the Sources of Greek Anthropology* (New Haven 1967)) is rejected by Dodds, who argues that it derives from a much later doxographic tradition. For other influential versions of the story, see Solon 13 (West), 43ff.; Gorgias, *Apology of Palamedes*; and of course the chorus on the human being in the *Antigone* – cf. Ch. 3. The *PV* story does not include mastery of internal passions.

5. On the problem of the dramatic date, see A. E. Taylor, *Plato* (London 1926) 236, Guthrie, *History*, IV 214, C. C. W. Taylor, *Plato: Protagoras* (Oxford 1976) 64, all of whom concur on a date of approximately 433. The reference at 327D to a play produced in 420 is an anachronism. As for the date of composition, this dialogue has sometimes been taken to be among the very earliest; but a majority of recent scholars have argued that it is a transitional work, later than the briefer aporetic dialogues and earlier than *Meno* and *Gorgias*.

6. It is worthy of note that the four dialogues that we shall consider in this section form a chronological continuum in dramatic dates as well as in dates of composition. This does not hold true in general; but it may be significant that dialogues which I have singled out for their thematic continuity (all deal in some way with the relationship between philosophical expertise and our problems of *tuchē*, all are centrally concerned with 'madness' or control by the passions, all are concerned with the commensurability or harmony of different values) should also illustrate a dramatic development in the character of Socrates, in his relationship to these issues. The significance of the changing dramatic portrait is discussed in each of the four chapters of Part II, most extensively in Chs. 6–7. We also notice that in three of the four dialogues Alcibiades plays a central role (for the relationship between Phaedrus and Alcibiades, cf. Ch. 7, pp. 212–13); in the *Republic*, the tyrannical soul plays a similar role.

7. On the metaphor of hunting as expression of a pervasive picture of practical intelligence setting itself against contingency, see Detienne and Vernant, *Les Ruses*; cf. Ch. 1, where I criticize their sharp opposition between the 'hunter' and the philosopher and examine some related aspects of Plato's imagery. In this dialogue the continuity between ordinary *erōs* and the philosophical ascent is forcefully stressed, as Socrates the hunter of Alcibiades becomes Socrates the wily new Odysseus, saving lives through the philosophical art. For a related discussion of hunting as an ethical image, see Nussbaum, 'Consequences' 25–53. On Socrates as *erastēs*, later *erōmenos*, see Ch. 6; on this erotic relationship in general, see Dover, *GH*.

8. The *Charmides* is probably close in date of composition as well, coming late in the group of 'aporetic' early dialogues. For a fuller discussion of the history of the analogy between philosophy and medicine, see Nussbaum, 'Therapeutic arguments; Epicurus and Aristotle', in *The Norms of Nature*, ed. M. Schofield and G. Striker (Cambridge 1985) 31–74.

9. For Protagoras's claim, see 316D, and esp. 318E–319A.

10. See for example Isnardi Parente, *Technē* 1, Schaerer, *Epistēmē passim* (who notes,

however, that '*epistēmē*' is used more often than '*technē*' to designate the cognitive condition of the agent. Dodds concludes that the concept of *technē*, in the late fifth century, is the concept of 'the systematic application of intelligence to any field of human activity' (11); cf. Guthrie, *History* III, Pt 1, 115 n. 3: 'It [sc. *technē*] includes every branch of human or divine skill, or applied intelligence, as opposed to the unaided work of nature.' These informal results are confirmed and supplemented by the rigorous and extensive linguistic analysis of the entire semantic field of the Greek verbs *epistasthai, gignōskein, eidenai*, and their related nouns *epistēmē, technē*, and *gnōsis* in J. Lyons, *Structural Semantics: an Analysis of Part of the Vocabulary of Plato* (Oxford 1963). Lyons shows that *technē* and names of specific *technai* function semantically as the most common direct object of the verb *epistasthai*; he observes that '*epistēmē* and *technē* are very frequently, if not always, synonymous in the contexts in which they occur in colligation with adjectives of class At', that is to say, with -*ikē* adjectives naming some art or science (187). He shows how productive this class is, how easily a Greek writer could thus give the name *technē* to any sort of organized know-how, anything which might be the object of *epistasthai*. His examples show the breadth and the heterogeneity of this class. He does observe that *epistēmē* is broader than *technē* in one way: it can sometimes be used interchangeably with *gnōsis*, where *technē* cannot. Lyons's argument concerning *gignōskein* and *gnōsis* is that they cover the area of personal acquaintance and familiarity, an area in which we do not find the verb *epistasthai*. So the point is that *technē* goes everywhere *epistasthai* does; it stops short of the area of personal familiarity, an area into which the noun *epistēmē* can enter. Although Lyons's analysis deals only with the Platonic corpus, it seems to me likely that his results in this respect would also describe the use of *technē* and *epistēmē* in the late fifth century and in other writers contemporary with Plato.

11. The passage of *Metaph.* 1 with which we shall be concerned is a salient case of this. In one passage (*EN* 1140b2ff.), Aristotle does explicitly distinguish *epistēmē* and *technē*, associating the latter entirely with productive art. (Cf. also 1112b7.) The same distinction is made in *Magna Moralia* 1197a33, which may not be genuine; this passage, however, says explicitly that in some of the arts that we shall see Plato calling *technai*, e.g., lyre-playing, the activity itself is the end. Aristotle's verbal distinctions are not dogmatically or even consistently maintained in this area: the distinction between *praxis* and *poiēsis* is one clear example of this. It is also not uncommon for him to use a word in both a wide and a narrow sense – both for the genus and for one of its sub-species: he does this explicitly with '*phronēsis*' and '*dikaiosunē*', implicitly, as I argue, with '*aisthēsis*' (cf. Nussbaum, *De Motu* Essay 5). It is clearly impossible to make the narrow *EN* sense of '*technē*' fit the rest of his usage, above all in *Metaphysics* 1; the fact that this book is devoted to the views of predecessors helps to explain why his usage here remains close to the traditional usage.

12. Cf. esp. 356Dff., where there are repeated verbal shifts back and forth between the two, so that it is frequently difficult to tell to which noun the adjective '*metrētikē*' refers. In an earlier passage, Protagoras refers to his *technē* and to a *mathēma*, apparently interchangeably (316D, 318E, 319A).

13. For the background, cf. esp. Schaerer, *Epistēmē*, Edmunds, *Chance* (with refs.).

14. For the antithesis in Hippocrates' epitaph, see G. Pfohl, ed., *Greek Poems on Stone* 1 (Epitaphs) (Leiden 1967) 144 (= Anth. Pal. VII.135); cf. Edmunds, *op. cit.* 2 and n. 3. The dating of the various Hippocratic treatises is controversial. I concentrate on those that are generally dated to the fifth century. G. E. R. Lloyd has questioned this

received view for *Vet. Med.*: see his 'Who is attacked in *On Ancient Medicine?*', *Phronesis* 8 (1963) 108–26; but he does not date it after Plato.

15. Xen. *Mem.* III.10; for other examples, see Schaerer, *op. cit.*, Kurz, *Akribeia*. The *Gorgias* denies the title of *technē* to anything that cannot give a general *logos* of its procedures; its distinction between *empeiria* (experience, an empirical knack) and *technē* corresponds closely to the distinction of *Metaph.* I. The question of how we make the transition from an accumulation of experience to a general account remained a central problem in Greek medical theory. Galen's *On Medical Experience* records a debate that uses a form of the Sorites paradox: if *n* medical observations are not sufficient for *technē*, surely *n* + 1 will not be sufficient; one observation is clearly not sufficient. From these premises we can show that no number, however large, will be sufficient, and so medicine, so grounded, cannot be a *technē*. The empirical doctor replies in an interesting way: he points to the success of his practice and of his empirically based generalizations in curing disease. The point seems to be that if it works well against *tuchē*, it is *technē* enough.

16. On some early passages, see Schaerer, *Epistēmē* 2ff.; he, however, seems to me to make some unwarranted inferences from them. The related sections of Kurz's discussion (*op. cit.*) of *akribeia* are helpful.

17. Cf. also Eur. *El.* 367ff., where the absence of *akribeia* in human judgment is associated with the absence of a sure standard of judgment; and this, in turn, is traced to inner upheavals caused by elements of human nature.

18. Irwin, *PMT passim*, esp. III.9–11. Section III.9 contains a good discussion of some of the Platonic associations between craft and knowledge, and between both of these and the ability to give accounts. The crucial claim about *technē* is made on pp. 73–4: every person of *technē* 'produces a product which can be identified without reference to his particular movements'. Here Irwin must clearly be talking about the ordinary conception rather than about some divergent Socratic use, since he uses this account as a basis to interpret the force of analogies to the *technai* in the dialogues, even when Socrates is not using the word '*technē*'. His point is that any craft analogy will evoke in the mind of the reader a certain picture.

19. It is very important that Irwin be correct about what is implied by the word '*technē*' and by the presence of *technē* examples. His explicit evidence for an instrumental conception of excellence in the early dialogues is slight: one premise from an argument in the *Lysis*, a dialogue of a highly aporetic character: and then, as we shall see, the evidence of the latter half of the *Protagoras* – which, however, does not provide, by itself, any evidence for an instrumental reading of other early dialogues. Forceful objections to this reading have been brought forward by G. Vlastos, both in a review of Irwin, *PMT* in the *Times Literary Supplement* ('The virtuous and the happy', *TLS* 24 Feb. 1978, pp. 230–1) and in 'Happiness and virtue in Socrates' moral theory', *PCPS* 210, NS 30 (1984) 181–213.

20. See n. 10 above and refs. in n. 2.

21. Xen. *Oec.* 1; cf. Schaerer, *Epistēmē* on Xenophon's use of '*technē*' and '*epistēmē*'.

22. *EE* 1219a12ff., *MM* 1211b28, 1197a9–11 (on which see above n. 11). For the Hellenistic view, see esp. Cicero, *Fin.* III.24; and Striker, 'Antipater', in *The Norms*.

23. At *EE* 1219a12ff., Aristotle contrasts medical science with mathematical science: in the former there is an end, health, that is not identical to the activity of healing; in the latter the activity of *theōria* is an end in itself. But in *Metaph.* VII.7 he clearly states that the activity of the doctor involves producing a further specification of the 'parts' or elements of the end itself.

24. Irwin is troubled by the prominence of these examples in Plato. He never disputes that they are, for Plato, central cases of *technē*. He produces an odd solution: the flute-player 'still produces a product which can be identified without reference to his particular movements. When we can recognize a tuneful sound in music . . . we can decide if certain movements are good flute-playing . . . ; a tuneful sound is not a good product *because* it is the result of good production, but the production is good because of the product' (73–4). This seems to be a desperate stratagem; even if this position has occasionally been defended in aesthetics, it seems plainly false. (Is Horowitz a great artist because he is efficient at fulfilling the instrumental conditions to the production of a 'tuneful sound' that we would desire and value as much if it were made by a machine? Could we adequately characterize the ends of piano-playing without mentioning hands, fingers, feet, imagination, and the piano?) Furthermore, such a position is completely unparalleled in this historical period: Aristotle regards it as entirely uncontroversial and self-evident that in the musical arts the performer's activities are ends in themselves. Irwin makes no attempt to argue that his conception is one that could have been held by a Greek thinker at this time; nor does he defend it as a plausible one for ours.

25. This element of music and other *technai* is explored in the *Philebus*.

26. Taylor, *Plato: Protagoras* (83) ascribes to Protagoras the assumption that an art that is *not* productive, i.e. one in which the ends of the art are up for debate within the art, cannot avoid collapsing into subjectivism. Though I do not believe, as Taylor does, that we need to attribute this assumption to Protagoras, and though as a claim it seems false, it is illustrative of the sort of worry that motivates the push towards an external-end *technē*, in modern as well as in ancient moral philosophy.

27. Discussion of Protagoras's speech can be found in: A. W. H. Adkins, '*Arete, Techne,* democracy and Sophists: *Protagoras* 316B–328D', *JHS* 93 (1973) 3–12; A. T. Cole, 'The relativism of Protagoras', *YCS* 22 (1972) 19–46; Dodds, *ACP* 1–25; Guthrie, *History* III, 63–8, 255ff.; E. Havelock, *The Liberal Temper in Greek Politics* (London 1957) 407–9; F. Heinimann, *Nomos und Phusis* (Basel 1945) 115–16; G. B. Kerferd, 'Plato's account of the relativism of Protagoras', *Durham University Journal* 42, NS 11 (1949–50) 20–6, and 'Protagoras' doctrine of justice and virtue in the *Protagoras* of Plato', *JHS* 73 (1953) 42–5; A. Levi, 'The ethical and social thought of Protagoras', *Mind* 49 (1940) 284–302; D. Loenen, *Protagoras and the Greek Community* (Amsterdam 1940); S. Moser and G. Kustas, 'A comment on the 'relativism' of Protagoras', *Phoenix* (1966) 111–15; A. E. Taylor, *Plato*, 241–7; C. C. W. Taylor, *Plato: Protagoras, ad loc.*; G. Vlastos, ed., *Plato's Protagoras* (Indianapolis 1956). Much of the literature focuses on the question of Protagoras's alleged relativism (cf. below n. 39) and on the evidence here for views of the historical Protagoras; none of it focuses directly on the issue that will most concern me.

28. Protagoras divides his speech into the 'story' (*muthos*) and the 'argument' or 'account' (*logos*); but it is by no means clear how he understands this division. The *logos* begins only at 324D – and yet the immediately preceding section (323A–324D) seems to belong, stylistically, with what follows rather than with the preceding story. Kerferd, 'Protagoras' doctrine' concludes that 323Aff. is a summary of the *muthos*. We might also suspect that Protagoras does not have a firm or careful grasp of the categories of his own discourse.

It was at one time customary to read this speech as derived from the historical Protagoras's 'On the way things were in the beginning'. It is even printed in

Diels–Kranz, though under the section 'Imitation'. I shall here treat the speech simply as the speech of a Platonic character; though we should not ignore the possibility that Plato is showing us how the issues of the dialogue grow out of the intellectual currents of his own day.

29. I use scare quotes because these powers are clearly not *technai* in the sense specified above; nor are they called this by Protagoras. They have in common with *technē* that they are resources with which a living creature is enabled to make its way in the world, defending itself against its dangers.

30. It is hardly necessary to mention that the 'What is it?' question is a, if not the, central question of the early tradition of Greek natural science. Asked about a changing thing, this question is often phrased as a question about its *phusis*: what is the thing's essential nature, as this is revealed in its characteristic mode of life and growth? Cf. E. Benveniste, *Noms d'agent et noms d'action en indo-européen* (Paris, 1948) 78; D. Holwerda, *Commentatio de vocis quae est* φύσις *vi atque usu* (Groningen 1955); Heinimann, *Nomos und Phusis*, esp. 89ff.; C. Kahn, *Anaximander and the Origins of Greek Cosmology* (New York 1960) 200–3. Aristotle tells us that the 'What is it?' question (to which he himself gives an answer that stresses capabilities to function in certain characteristic ways) is *the* question that has been 'a perpetual subject of inquiry and perplexity' for his entire tradition (*Metaph.* VII 1028b2ff.). So it is not surprising – though it has rarely been noticed – that Protagoras should draw upon and illuminate this tradition of speculation. On the importance of kinds and kind-terms in answering the 'What is it?' question, see D. Wiggins, *Sameness and Substance* (Oxford 1980), esp. Chs. 2 and 3 – with reference to the Aristotelian view and its antecedents.

31. D. Hume, *A Treatise of Human Nature*, Bk III, Pt II, Sections 1–2.

32. Furthermore, it seems to follow from the Humean account that we have reason to be just and law-abiding only when we are convinced that it is advantageous, in terms of other, more fundamental ends, to be so. Such an account seems unable to offer any reason why I should not act unjustly in my own interest in a particular case where (a) it is to my advantage to be unjust, (b) I am convinced that I will not be found out and punished, and (c) I believe with good reason that my unjust action will not undermine the generally useful practice of justice.

33. For Aristotle's criticism of such an account of human ends, see Ch. 12. A number of similarities between Protagoras and Aristotle will emerge in what follows: the general anthropocentrism about ethics; the view that social excellence is a combination of shared natural sociability and social training; the view that *philia* is an important civic value, holding cities together; the view that all adults in a city are in some sense teachers of excellence, but that there is still room for a teacher to advance our reflective awareness of our practices; the view that what it is to be a certain sort of creature is to have certain functional capabilities. Some of these similarities have frequently been noticed: see, for example, Guthrie, *History* III, 67; Loenen, *Protagoras* 103–26 with references.

34. Adkins, '*Arete, Technē*' charges that Protagoras equivocates, speaking of *aretē* sometimes as 'cooperative excellence' and sometimes as individual competitive skill. His analysis of 318 and 328 does not convince me that there is incoherence here. If anything, it is Adkins who equivocates: having argued that '*technē*' has at this period an extremely broad range, he then reads later *technē*-analogies as suggesting, by themselves, that skill of a competitive sort is in question.

35. This agrees with the view expressed by the historical Protagoras (DK B3): 'Teaching

needs nature and practice.' That this is the way of reconciling Protagoras's account of the gifts of Zeus with his claim that excellence is taught is widely agreed: see, for example, Guthrie, *History* III, 67; Loenen, *Protagoras*; and the good account in Levi, 'Ethical and social thought' 294; cf. Heinimann, *Nomos und Phusis* 115–16. Kerferd's ('Protagoras' doctrine') objections to this position seem unconvincing: in particular, he appears to ignore 328B8, C1. We can concede to him, however, that Protagoras does not express his meaning with clarity.

36. These 'must's are said, it is true, partly with a view to the city's survival; but this is not enough to make the point a Humean one. Survival is not an external end in the Humean sense; even here, the *city* is the entity whose survival is desired.

37. In the same way, the traveler set down among apolitical savages is said by P. to feel not *fear* (as he would among less restrained fellow humans), but *loneliness* and *homesickness*, appropriate to one who does not see around him beings of his own kind. It is not altogether clear, in these two cases, whether the people described lack the (innate) *sense* of justice, or only its effective development. Even in the latter case they might be so hopelessly 'gnarled' and 'crooked' as to be unrecognizable.

38. Some critics stress the difficulty that Protagoras faces, as a self-proclaimed expert trying to win pupils in a democratic culture; see Kerferd, 'Protagoras' doctrine'; J. S. Morrison, 'The place of Protagoras in Athenian public life', *CQ* 35 (1941) 1–16; Adkins, '*Arete, Techne*' goes so far as to suggest that the entire speech is a *captatio benevolentiae*, with 'something for everyone', therefore full of ambiguity and inconsistency. But the position seems perfectly consistent; Aristotle too will combine reverence for civic acculturation with a defense of the usefulness of the expert. The problem arises for anyone who claims to teach ethics in a democratic society; the existence of this book is evidence that I believe there to be some non-incoherent solution to it.

39. The assimilation of this speech to relativism or subjectivism has come about in three ways: (1) by an unjustified assimilation of this dialogue to the 'Protagorean' doctrine of the *Theaetetus*; (2) by mistaking Protagoras's defense of law for a defense of each particular system of laws (whereas the speech plainly implies that a system of laws could be criticized for failure to perform the general function of law); (3) by the assumption (see n. 26 above) that any *technē* in which ultimate ends are up for debate must be hopelessly relativistic. In favor of a relativistic reading are, for example, Vlastos, Cole, A. E. Taylor; against are Loenen, Kerferd, Levi, Moser and Kustas. (The last two papers are especially forceful in their criticisms of the relativistic reading.)

40. By this point Protagoras somewhat passively joins Socrates in attacking the 'many'; but his own earlier view of education gave a central place to correct shaping of the passions (356A–B), and his explanation of residual error, though sketchy, seems to invoke the incomplete training of these elements – since it is to these, more than to the intellect, that punishment as teaching is addressed.

41. Cf. 315B, where a Homeric quotation links Socrates to Odysseus, Hippias to the shade of Heracles; 315C, where Prodicus is, similarly, compared to Tantalus. The comparisons are unlikely to indicate particular similarites of character or achievement – for Prodicus is portrayed as a dignified and morally concerned person; the central point is that there is only one daring, resourceful, living man here, among the resourceless, artless dead. On some implications of this comparison for Socrates' view of *technē* and of the continuity between philosophical *technē* and ordinary artfulness, see also Ch. 7 n. 36. On the popular conception of resourceful intelligence that is being skillfully used here, see Detienne and Vernant, *Les Ruses*, discussed in Ch. 1 and Ch. 7 n. 36.

42. On this see Nussbaum, 'Eleatic conventionalism and Philolaus on the conditions of

thought', *HSCP* 83 (1979) 63–108, esp. 89–91, with references both textual and secondary. Valuable studies of early Greek thought about *arithmos* and its importance include O. Becker, *Zwei Untersuchungen zur antiken Logik*, *Klassisch-Philologische Studien* 17 (1957) 20ff.; J.Stenzel, *Zahl und Gestalt* (Leipzig 1933) 25ff.; J. Annas, *Aristotle's Metaphysics M and N* (Oxford 1976).

43. *Iliad* II.488, XXIV.776; for other texts, see Nussbaum, 'Eleatic conventionalism' 90–1.

44. Cf. Nussbaum, 'Eleatic conventionalism' on the interpretation of Philolaus's epistemology. Compare Ar. *Metaph.* 1052b20, *Rhet.* 1408b27, *Metaph.* 1053a18. For an excellent discussion of quantitative measurement in Greek science, see G. E. R. Lloyd, 'Measurement and mystification', forthcoming. Lloyd criticizes Koyre's well-known claim that Greek science lacked interest in the quantitative by examining the different sciences one by one and showing the enormous variety of positions and practices on this issue. There was, clearly, widespread awareness of the importance of quantitative measurement, even though this awareness was not uniform.

45. See, for example, *ametrētos* at *Od.* XIX.512, XXIII.249, etc.; Eur. *El.* 236, 433; *ametria* and *ametros*, Democ. DK B70, C3; *summetron* as 'appropriate', 'suitable', Aes. *Eum.* 532, Isoc. 4.83, etc.' *summetria* as 'due proportion' at Democ. B191, cf. Pythag. DK D4, Crit. B6. In Plato these ethically charged uses are extremely common: cf. for example *Gorg.* 525A, *Tim.* 86C, 87D; *Rep.* 486D; *Soph.* 228C; *Laws* 690E, 820C, 918B. On the *Philebus* see Ch. 5. The central importance of '*metrios*' as an ethical term requires no exemplification.

46. See K. von Fritz, 'The discovery of incommensurability by Hippasus of Metapontum', in D. Furley and R. E. Allen, eds., *Studies in Presocratic Philosophy* (London 1970) 382–442; T. Heath, *A History of Greek Mathematics* (Oxford 1921) I, 154ff. These stories probably do not indicate real worries on the part of practicing mathematicians, who continued busily with their work. They are nonetheless good evidence of popular conceptions of cognition.

47. The sentiment is close to one expressed in Gorgias's apology of Palamedes (30): 'Who was it who made human life resourceful from resourcelessness, and ordered from disorder...discovering..., and measures and weights, resourceful adjudications of our dealings...?'

48. 522Bff.; the words '*technē*' and '*epistēmē*' are used without differentiation.

49. 987Cff. Even if this is not a genuine work of Plato (as I believe it is) it develops a recognizably Platonic position. Here again, the author switches back and forth between '*technē*' and '*epistēmē*' without distinction, so that it is not possible to tell to which noun the adjectives in -*ikē* refer. Cf. also *Laws* 819–20, where lack of knowledge of the commensurable and incommensurable is called 'a condition not human but more appropriate to certain swinish creatures', concerning which the Stranger declares himself 'ashamed not only on my own behalf but also on behalf of all Greeks' (819D). It should be observed, however, that the greatest problem, according to the Stranger, is that people believe things to be commensurable when really they are *not*. This, together with the fact that he acknowledges shame on his own behalf, may indicate a later criticism of the single science of measurement, in keeping with shifts in Plato's thought that we shall discuss in Ch. 7. See Nussbaum, 'Plato on commensurability and desire', *PASS* 58 (1984), 55–80.

50. Below, this point is explicitly applied to the question of measuring by pleasure as the coin of ethical value.

51. The literature on this issue is large. Much of it deals with questions about the

relationship between this dialogue and other early dialogues, and between both and the views of the historical Socrates. I shall not take up either of these large questions here; for the present I shall regard this dialogue as a self-contained work of Plato, continuous in its problems and concerns with other Platonic works. The accounts of hedonism in the dialogue that I have found most impressive are those that treat it as a seriously held position of the character Socrates, an essential part both of this immediate argument and of the entire discussion of the unity of the virtues. Taylor, *Plato: Protagoras* and Irwin, *PMT* convincingly show that the discussion of the unity of the virtues is concluded only at 356, with the proposal for the science of measurement; both provide excellent discussions of the art of measurement, stressing the importance of the superior precision and objectivity it offers. Cf. also I. M. Crombie, *An Examination of Plato's Doctrines*, esp. 1, 232–45, who gives an excellent summary of the issues, and R. Hackforth, 'Hedonism in Plato's *Protagoras*', *CQ* 22 (1928) 39–42. Among those who deny that Socrates seriously holds the hedonistic premise, some claim that hedonism in its ordinary form is not really present in the dialogue at all, and some argue that it is an *ad hominem* position. Versions of the former position are found in Vlastos, *Plato's Protagoras* xi ff. (who stresses the seriousness with which Socrates holds the premise, but argues that it does not amount to ordinary hedonism), W. K. C. Guthrie, *Plato, Protagoras and Meno* (London 1956) 22, A. E. Taylor, *Plato* 260; versions of the latter are in J. P. Sullivan, 'The hedonism in Plato's *Protagoras*', *Phronesis* 6 (1967) 10–28; D. J. Zeyl, 'Socrates and hedonism: *Protagoras* 351B–358D', *Phronesis* 25 (1980) 250–69, with full bibliography. Now see also Gosling and Taylor, *The Greeks on pleasure* (Oxford 1982) 45–68. The dispute is motivated in part by the belief that hedonism is a base moral position. Thus Guthrie: 'The doctrine...is indeed consistent with a morality as high as most people would aspire to....This is hardly hedonism in any accepted sense.' This is short-sighted; it is also surprising that someone who was raised in a culture pervaded by the influence of the British Utilitarian tradition should say this.

52 Irwin's (*PMT*) complicated argument makes the *Protagoras* the natural culmination of the entire group of early dialogues, the *Gorgias* a transition to the middle group. While I take issue with his use of the craft analogy and with some aspects of his interpretation of other dialogues, I can agree with him that this dialogue shows us one logical outcome of pervasive concerns about deliberation and knowledge. Vlastos is too extreme in his claim that 'hedonism is not in keeping with the general temper or method of Socratic ethics' (*Plato's Protagoras* xl–xli).

53. Thus my position is similar to those of Crombie, *An Examination* and Hackforth, 'Hedonism', both of whom see Plato as 'trying out' hedonism out of certain background concerns with practical knowledge. Zeyl, 'Socrates and hedonism', though he describes his position as 'anti-hedonist' and claims that the choice of pleasure as end is *ad hominem*, comes close to my position when he points out that to establish his conclusion Socrates needs not hedonism as such, but some premise that ensures singleness and commensurability (260).

54. Creon spoke of commensurability (387) – though without any precise quantitative account of the end in question: Cf. Ch. 3. Cf. also the *Philoctetes* of Sophocles, where the Chorus's anxious demand to be shown a practical *technē* leads them ultimately to sympathize with the consequentialist view of Odysseus, which judges actions right insofar as they contribute to a single final good (see Ch. 3 and Nussbaum, 'Consequences'. This is clearly, in the plays' terms, a modern progressive view, associated

with Odyssean artfulness and resourcefulness. It challenges a traditional view which is similar to Protagoras's in its emphasis on action as a value in itself and on the importance of a plurality of intrinsic ends. The play testifies to the contemporary interest in a revisionary ethical science; Neoptolemus's conservatism, like Protagoras's here, is attacked as retrograde.

55. Vlastos, *Plato's Protagoras* adds an important methodological point; it is uncharacteristic of Socrates to argue to an important conclusion of his own using a premise that he himself regards as unreliable (xl, n. 50).

56. This could also be translated 'what I mean' – though I find this translation less plausible, especially when the phrase is repeated at 351E1–2. So the 'I say' does not settle the issue on its own; but the *egō* of c4 is very emphatic, and seems to tell against an *ad hominem* reading.

57. Cf. also 360A. Zeyl, 'Socrates and hedonism' argues for his *ad hominem* reading by pointing out that it is possible to see Socrates as playing an *ad hominem* role straight through to the end. Since this involves ascribing to him non-sincere statements about several important matters, it appears to raise more interpretative problems than it solves (cf. above n. 55).

58. For Bentham's preoccupation with the elimination of contingency and connections between this and his obsessive concern with number and measure, see C. Bahmueller, *The National Charity Company* (California 1981), which contains many fascinating citations from the unpublished MSS. For the epigraph to this chapter, see p. 83. For discussion of Sidgwick's views about the relationship between Utilitarian morality and common sense, see J. B. Schneewind, *Sidgwick and Victorian Morality* (Oxford 1977).

59. *Methods of Ethics*, 7th edn (London 1907) 401. Sidgwick writes that an argument deriving a Utilitarian account of ultimate good from common sense 'obviously cannot be made completely cogent, since ... several cultivated persons do habitually judge that knowledge, art, etc. – not to speak of Virtue – are ends independently of the pleasure derived from them'. Cf. also the section 'Hedonism as a method of choice' in J. Rawls, *A Theory of Justice* (Cambridge, MA 1971) 554–60.

60. Sidgwick, *op. cit.* 406; cf. 478–9.

61. Rawls, *op. cit.* 425. Crombie's (*An Examination*) interpretation of the *Protagoras* makes a similar point: Socrates' thesis 'implies that moral categories are crude and provisional and that we ought to substitute for them judgments of relative pleasurableness'. Zeyl, 'Socrates and hedonism' makes valuable observations about the way in which Socratic hedonism is a natural extension of the interlocutor's position.

62. On the argument, see especially Irwin, *PMT* Ch. 4, to whose account I am indebted; see also Zeyl, *op. cit.*, C. C. W. Taylor, *Plato: Protagoras*. A somewhat different account is in G. Santas, 'Plato's *Protagoras* and explanations of weakness', *PR* 75 (1966) 3–33, repr. in Vlastos, *Socrates*.

63. This condition is mentioned at 352D7. D. Davidson has argued that, strictly speaking, we need only mention that the agent *believes* both courses to be open ('How is weakness of will possible?', in *Moral Concepts*, ed. J. Feinberg (Oxford 1969) 93–113). But this seems insufficient to rule out cases of psychological compulsion, which Plato may have in mind here. For an interesting account of Plato's difficulty distinguishing *akrasia* from compulsion, see G. Watson, 'Skepticism about weakness of will', *PR* 86 (1977) 316–39.

64. Cf. also Zeyl, 'Socrates and hedonism' 260.

65. Cf. 358D, where this principle is stated. My formulation here is indebted to Irwin, *PMT*.

66. For further discussion of this issue, see Nussbaum, 'Plato on commensurability and

desire', *PASS* 58 (1984). A similar connection between incommensurability and weakness is developed in D. Wiggins, 'Weakness of will, commensurability and the objects of deliberation and desire', in *PAS* 79 (1978–9) 251–77, repr. in Rorty, *Essays* 241–65. I read this article in 1975 before starting work on this manuscript, and discovered its relationship to my point in 1982, while making this most recent revision. Thus my impression that I made an independent discovery of this point probably should be qualified.

67. For further discussion of these connections, see Chs. 5, 6, 11.

68. The children would learn these things most readily if, like children in the Ideal City, they were raised not by parents but by (interchangeable) public functionaries, and if, furthermore, they lived in a society that mandated full communism of property and did away with the exclusivity of sexual relations. Plato correctly sees that psychological changes this profound cannot be effected by lectures; they require a thorough restructuring of human experience. See Nussbaum, 'Plato on commensurability' for further discussion of these points. I ignore here the possibility raised there, that a thoroughgoing belief in commensurability would deprive people of the logical/metaphysical basis for individuating objects.

69. On issues of chronology, see Ch. 4 n. 5, Ch. 5 n. 21, Ch. 7 n. 5.

70. See the good discussion in Crombie, *An Examination* I, 243; he argues that the *Republic* and *Phaedo* are a natural development of the *Protagoras*'s proposal for a measuring science. Although I do not think he devotes enough emphasis to Plato's later criticisms of the singleness and externality of pleasure, he is surely right to emphasize this continuity.

71. These questions are very well discussed by C. C. W. Taylor, *Plato: Protagoras*, 195–200 and in Irwin, *PMT* 108–9. See also the good general discussion of varieties of hedonism in J. C. B. Gosling, *Pleasure and Desire* (Oxford 1969) esp. Ch. 3.

72. See Ch. 5, esp. n. 19; and *Philebus* 12D–E.

73. In this chapter I am indebted to the questions and criticism of several groups of students; I do not mean to slight others by singling out Robin Avery, John Carriero, Arnold Davidson, and Nancy Sherman. I am grateful, too, to Stanley Cavell, with whom I taught and often discussed this material. To Geoffrey Lloyd I am grateful not only for his comments, but also for allowing me, in the last stages of revision, to read and refer to his 'Measurement and mystification' (cf. n. 44), a fundamental study whose range and richness cannot be indicated in brief references.

Interlude 1   Plato's anti-tragic theater

1. I have discussed these issues further, contrasting Plato's views about writing with Proust's defense of narrative teaching, in Nussbaum 'Fictions'.

2. These issues have not been very frequently discussed by Anglo-American philosophers in recent years; most recent work on them comes either from classicists who are not closely affiliated with philosophy or from philosophers working in other traditions. For example, J. Derrida, 'La pharmacie de Platon', *Tel Quel* 32, 33 (1968), repr. in *La Dissémination* (Paris 1972); R. Schaerer, *La Question Platonicienne* (Neuchâtel 1938, 2nd ed. 1969); H. Gundert, *Der platonische Dialog* (Heidelberg 1968); H. G. Gadamer, *Platons dialektische Ethik* (Hamburg 1968); W. Wieland, *Platon und die Formen des Wissens* (Göttingen 1982) 13–94; V. Goldschmidt, *Les dialogues de Platon* (Paris 1947); Guthrie, *History* IV; H. Kuhn, 'The true tragedy: on the relationship between Greek tragedy

and Plato', *HSCP* 52 (1941) 1–40 and 53 (1942) 37–88. An exception from the 'analytic' tradition is J. Hartland-Swann, 'Plato as poet: a critical interpretation', *Philosophy* 26 (1951) 3–18, 131–41. A very helpful article is A. A. Krentz, 'Dramatic form and philosophical content in Plato's dialogues', *Phil Lit* 7 (1983). Writers about Plato influenced by the work of Leo Strauss pay attention to questions of dialogue form, but frequently in an idiosyncratic way that imports principles of reading alien to the Platonic text. The most helpful general accounts of the dialogue from this background are C. Griswold's 'Style and philosophy: the case of Plato's dialogues', *The Monist* 63 (1980) 530–46, and D. Hyland's 'Why Plato wrote dialogues', *Philosophy and Rhetoric* 1 (1968).

3. Strictly speaking, there probably were a few pre-Platonic examples of dialogic writing. Diogenes Laertius (3.48) mentions a report concerning Zeno of Elea; this is untrustworthy, and Zenonian dialogues, if they existed, would not have been concerned with ethical subjects. Both Diogenes and Athenaeus (505B) mention one Alexamenus of Teos or Styria. Diogenes cites as his authority Aristotle's (lost) *On the Poets*; Athenaeus (citing two historians) calls Alexamenus the founder of the dialogue genre. But it is very unlikely that this otherwise completely unknown and unmentioned figure had any substantial influence on Plato; nor is his work likely to have been concerned with similar issues. As for the Socratic writings of Xenophon, his career overlaps to such an extent with that of Plato (and his productions are so generally inferior both in style and in philosophical content) that we should not consider him as a formative influence; he may, of course, have influenced Plato as a rival. But, all in all, we can agree with Diogenes' concluding judgment: 'My view is that, since it was Plato who developed this form in a definite way (*akribōsas to eidos*), he deserves to carry off the first prize for inventing it, as he also does for doing it well.'

4. Ar. *Poetics* 1447b9–11; cf. also *On the Poets*, fr. 4 Ross (where Aristotle is reported as saying that Plato's writing occupies a middle ground between poetic and prose works). It is unfortunate that next to nothing is known about the mimes in question. Probably they were briefer and sketchier than even the briefest Platonic dialogues; and they were not similarly serious in their concern with the pursuit of an argument. They were 'realistic' in the sense that they showed scenes from contemporary life, not in the sense that they purported to be transcriptions of actual conversations – a point wrongly urged by Burnet and others to support the implausible thesis that Plato transcribes actual conversations held by the historical Socrates.

5. For critical discussion of the biographical tradition concerning Plato, see A. Riginos, *Platonica* (Leiden 1976); cf. also I. Düring, *Aristotle in the Ancient Biographical Tradition* (Göteborg 1957). On the signs in Plato's work of his earlier career, see D. Tarrant, 'Plato as dramatist', *JHS* 75 (1955) 82–9. Riginos is skeptical about this story; but even if it were not literally true, it truly expresses a real tension that is evident in Plato's writing, and correctly describes Plato's mixed abilities.

6. Discussion of these issues in the recent Anglo-American literature on Greek philosophy has been slight, since the tradition itself has taken for granted a sharp division between philosophical and non-philosophical ways of writing about ethics (and between philosophical and non-philosophical works of the philosophers). Thus most books on pre-Socratic philosophy, even if they include material on ethics, include Heraclitus and Xenophanes and Democritus, but not the poets and historians; and these included writers are usually studied without much attention to the literary dimensions of their work. An impressive exception is C. H. Kahn's *The Art and Thought of Heraclitus*

(Cambridge 1979). The poets are usually treated, in such works, only as evidence for a background of 'popular morality' underlying philosophical speculation (see further remarks and references in Ch. 1). Two excellent exceptions, which have stressed the continuity between 'literary' and 'philosophical' treatments of fundamental problems, are: Dodds, *GI*, and Lloyd-Jones, *JZ*. Continental intellectual historians have remained sensitive to the close interconnections between poetry and moral philosophy: for example, J.-P. Vernant, *Les Origines de la pensée grecque* (Paris 1981), M. Detienne, *Les Maîtres de vérité en grèce ancienne* (Paris 1967); see also G. Nagy, *The Best of the Achaeans* (Baltimore 1979).

7. On the problems involved in assessing the ethical fragments transmitted under the name of Democritus, see Z. Stewart, 'Democritus and the Cynics', *HSCP* 63 (1958) 179–91. Even if they are authentic, they do not seem to form a continuous argument. The writings of Anaxagoras and Anaximenes, even if they were available to Plato, probably did not deal with ethics. Heraclitus's aphorisms were quite possibly known to Plato; but, concerned as he is with explanation and the avoidance of ambiguity, he probably did not find them congenial.

8. On the importance of the tragic poets in education, see esp. *Frogs* 1063–6, where 'Aeschylus' says: 'Little boys have a teacher who tells them what to do; young men have the poets. We must by all means tell them what is right.' On the relationship between this tradition and Socratic educational practice, see also Nussbaum, 'Aristophanes'.

9. I do not mean here to neglect the enormous influence of sophists and rhetoricians at this period: it is important as well to assess Plato's stylistic choices against the background of their dazzling and specious use of argument, their use of the resources of language to bewitch and work on the hearer. (Gorgias's *Helen*, for example, describes *logos* as a 'great power' that works like a drug to elicit certain emotional responses from the listener (14).)

10. References to writing about the tragic poets can be found in the chapters devoted to each, to some of the pertinent Pindar literature in Ch. 1. On the Homeric tradition of praise and blame, see Lloyd-Jones, *JZ*; J. Redfield, *Nature and Culture in the Iliad* (Chicago 1975); Nagy, *The Best;* Adkins, *Merit*. Adkins's simplistic account is well criticized by Lloyd-Jones, and by A. A. Long, 'Morals and values in Homer', *JHS* 90 (1970) 121–39.

11. On *elenchos*, see Nussbaum, 'Aristophanes', with references. The best account of *elenchos* I know is in an unpublished manuscript by Gregory Vlastos; but cf. also R. Robinson, *Plato's Earlier Dialectic* (Oxford 1953). Important descriptions of Socrates' effect on the interlocutor are at *Meno* 84A–C and *Sophist* 229E–230E.

12. On the criticism of writing, see also Ch. 7, with reference to the ample modern literature. Cf. esp. Hyland, 'Why Plato wrote', Burger, *Plato's Phaedrus*, Wieland, *Platon und die Formen*, Derrida, 'La pharmacie'.

13. Eristic is contentious argument aimed only at *ad hominem* victory, not at truth: see G. E. L. Owen, 'Dialectic and eristic in the treatment of the forms', in *Aristotle on Dialectic: the Topics*, ed. G. E. L. Owen (Oxford 1968) 103–25.

14. Cf. above n. 5.

15. One way of understanding this relationship is developed in R. Patterson, 'The Platonic art of comedy and tragedy', *Phil Lit* 6 (1982) 76–93; see Chs. 6 and 7 for other references.

16. The account that follows is intended to apply above all to the 'early' and 'middle' dialogues, that is, to dialogues up through and including the *Republic*, but not the *Symposium* and *Phaedrus* (on which see below).

17. Of course there is a strong dramatic element in Homeric and Hesiodic poetry; but for Plato in the *Republic* the distinction between a form in which the poet, speaking in his own voice, also reports speeches, and a form in which the maker appears nowhere inside the work, is fundamental; even though some of his dialogues have Socrates reporting all the speeches, they are nonetheless all, in the *Republic* sense, dramatic representations through and through.

18. Cf. above n. 9.

19. Cf. esp. *Sophist* 229E–230E; also *Meno* 84A–C, *Apology* 30E.

20. 230B–D.

21. Although it is not safe to rely on the titles of ancient works as the choice of the author (in the case of Aristotle, all titles are the work of later generations), the tradition of the Platonic titles goes back far enough and is securely enough established for us probably to be able to rely on it.

22. The only exception that I can think of is Aristophanes' *Lysistrata*, where the name of the leading character is also semantically significant (it means 'Disbander of the Army'); and there may also be an intended reference to a contemporary historical figure – see D. M. Lewis, 'Who was Lysistrata?', *Annual of the British School of Athens* (1955) 1–12, and K. J. Dover, *Aristophanic Comedy* (London 1972) 152 n. 3.

23. We do not, of course, know much about how the dialogues were first presented to the public; Ryle's story of public readings (*Plato's Progress* (Cambridge 1966), cf. Ch. 7) has not found many supporters in the form in which he argues it. But some form of public oral performance may have taken place. Even so, the ordinariness of the dialogue would have been very striking; if the dialogue in Euripidean drama is so mercilessly parodied by Aristophanes for its flatness and everyday character (*Acharnians, Thesmophoriazusae, Frogs*), how much more surprising must this speech have been.

24. R. W. Livingstone, ed., *Portrait of Socrates* (Oxford 1938) viii; see D. D. Raphael, 'Can literature be moral philosophy?', *NLH* 15 (1983) 1–12. On the Socratic/Platonic opposition to lamentation, see Ch. 7, Interlude 2; on the ways of seeing individual persons that are proper to tragedy and to inquiry, see Ch. 6.

25. See C. Segal's excellent article, '"The myth was saved": reflection on Homer and the mythology of Plato's *Republic*', *Hermes* 106 (1978) 315–36.

26. This is not, of course, to deny that considerable art has been used in its construction. For one account of the relationship of the *Apology* to sophistic rhetoric (with references to others), see K. Seeskin, 'Is the *Apology* of Socrates a parody?', *Phil Lit* 6 (1982) 94–105.

27. On these emotions, and tragedy's relation to them, see also Interlude 2.

28. On the emotions and their value, see Chs. 5 and 7. On *erōs* in particular, Ch. 6.

29. See the account of the ascent of love in Ch. 6.

30. Compare the discussion of Haemon in Ch. 3, and the account of Aristotelian deliberation and *nous* in Ch. 10, and Interlude 2; also my 'Practical syllogisms and practical science', in Nussbaum, *De Motu* Essay 4.

31. A version of some of this material was read to a conference on Theory of the Theater at the University of Michigan in 1980: I would like to thank those present, and especially Jeffrey Henderson, for their helpful comments. I also owe thanks to the

members of my Philosophy and Literature Pro-Seminar at Harvard that same year, especially to Daniel Brudney and John Carriero, and to Arnold Davidson, who read and discussed with me a draft of this material.

5   The *Republic*: true value and the standpoint of perfection

1. On the historical background, see Lysias, Oration 12; Guthrie, *History* IV, 437–9; F. E. Sparshott, 'Plato and Thrasymachus', *University of Toronto Quarterly* (1957) 54–61. The problems of settling the dramatic date are well discussed by Guthrie. Cf. also Dodds, *GI* 208–16.

2. Cf. also 561C–D, where Socrates describes the life based on such egalitarian evaluations: 'Does he not...also live out his life in this fashion, day by day indulging the appetite of the day, now getting drunk and abandoning himself to the pleasure of the flute, now drinking only water and dieting; now exercising, now taking it easy and neglecting all that, now giving the appearance of doing philosophy? And frequently he goes in for politics, and bounces up and says and does whatever enters his head...And there is no order and no compulsion in his existence, but he calls this a pleasant life, and free and happy, and clings to it till the end.' See the discussion of this passage in my 'Shame, separateness, and political unity', in Rorty, *Essays* 395–435.

3. Since the appetites are now seen not to be directly responsive to teaching or judgment, the training that effects this liberation from 'madness' must include habituation as well as teaching; see n. 5 below, Interlude 2, and Ch. 7.

4. *Rep.* 441E. For an account of the preceding argument and of the distinction between motivation and valuation which it develops, see G. Watson, 'Free agency', *JP* 72 (1975) 205–20; a related account is in Irwin, *PMT*. On the translation of '*logistikon*', see Ch. 7, n. 5.

5. This is the point made in the rather obscure discussion of 'qualified' and 'unqualified' desires at *Rep.* 438–9: the object of thirst is not *good* drink, but simply drink. On this argument see Irwin, *PMT* 123–4, 191–5, and T. Penner, 'Thought and desire in Plato', in Vlastos, *Plato* II, 96–118. On the third part of the soul, in which Plato places the emotions, see Ch. 7 and Irwin, *PMT* 193–5. Plato nowhere gives a systematic story about the differences between this part and the appetitive part; but his point seems to be that the members of the third part have an intimate relationship to beliefs about their objects (and therefore potentially to teaching) that appetites do not. Anger involves the belief that I have been wronged; grief involves the belief that I have suffered an important loss; hunger and thirst have no such complex cognitive structure, and cannot, therefore, be modified in the same way.

6. Cf. Watson, 'Free agency' 212: '...the value placed upon certain activities depends upon their being the fulfillment of desires that arise and persist independently of what we value...Here an essential part of the *content* of our evaluation is that the activity in question be motivated by certain appetites. These activities may have value for us only insofar as they are appetitively motivated, even though to have these appetites is not *ipso facto* to value their objects.' Cf. also Richard Kraut, 'Reason and justice in Plato's *Republic*', in Lee, *Exegesis* 207–24, on the two kinds of rational 'rule' in the *Republic*.

7. *Republic* 587E; I do not claim to understand the meaning of the emphasis on the numerical calculation here. The tyrant is further discussed in Nussbaum, 'Shame, separateness'.

8. *Rep.* 504A–D. This passage, and Aristotle's criticism of it, are further discussed in Ch. 8.

9. *Phd.* 64Aff. The similarities – and some differences – between *Republic* and *Phaedo* on these issues will be further discussed below.

10. Watson, 'Free agency', cf. n. 4; he does not, however, clearly commit himself to any particular account of the good. He is anxious only to stress that motivation and valuation can overlap in this way, and most often will.

11. Irwin, *PMT*; on these aspects of his view, see also the review by M. F. Burnyeat, *NYRB* 26 (1979) 56–60.

12. On this point see Burnyeat's review, and the further discussion in an exchange of letters between Burnyeat and Thomas Nagel, *NYRB*. Burnyeat is clearly right in saying that Irwin's 'QR' ('quasi-recollection') is crucially different in several ways from Plato's own conception of recollection, and that the attempt to sever recollection from its metaphysical commitments has importantly altered the character of the ethical theory presented.

13. Irwin's argument is at this point more complicated than Watson's. It is not enough, in his view, that the agent should have an orderly plan; and he acknowledges (*PMT* 226ff.) that such a simple account of rational rule would not suffice to rule out any of Plato's defective types. What is required in addition, he argues, is that the ordered ends be chosen in accordance with certain deliberative procedures: the 'deviant' people are ruled out because 'though their rational part decides which of the first-order ends will be, they acquire first-order ends, not by deliberation about overall good, but by emotion or appetite' (232). Irwin now, however, concedes that this additional requirement (which is, in any case, found in Plato by a controversial conflation of highly modified doctrines from the *Phaedo* with a reading of parts of Diotima's speech from the *Symposium*) will not itself clearly suffice to get Plato to the conclusions he wants. 'Unfortunately and inexcusably, Plato has no direct or detailed answer to these questions' (233). The most we can conclude, then, is that Plato's 'overall position has not been shown to be worthless' (248).

14. Irwin, *PMT* 247, 248.

15. On various Platonic reflections about the relationship between argument and interest, see: the end of Ch. 4; Interlude 1; the end of this chapter; and especially Chs. 6 and 7.

16. Cf. also Irwin, *PMT* 246, where the basis for this view is called 'shadowy metaphysic[s]'.

17. The structure of the end of Book IX is complex; for various accounts of it, see: J. Annas, *An Introduction to Plato's Republic* (Oxford 1981) *ad loc.*; I. M. Crombie, *An Examination of Plato's Doctrines* (London 1962) I, 136ff.; R. C. Cross and A. D. Woozley, *Plato's Republic: a Philosophical Commentary* (London 1964) 263ff.; N. R. Murphy, *The Interpretation of Plato's Republic* (Oxford 1951) 92ff.; N. P. White, *A Companion to Plato's Republic* (Indianapolis 1979) *ad loc.* This represents, of course, only a fraction of the enormous literature, which I shall not attempt to cite in full; other references can be found in these authors, particularly in White and in Guthrie, *History* IV. See now also J. C. B. Gosling and C. C. W. Taylor, *The Greeks on Pleasure* (Oxford 1982) 97–128, esp. 128.

18. On the meaning of '*eudaimōn*' and '*eudaimonia*', see Ch. 1 p. 6.

19. It is worth detailing some textual considerations supporting my reading: (1) this argument is a 'demonstration' that is supposed to establish a conclusion about the best

(most *eudaimōn*) life. At 588A, Socrates explicitly draws, from his conclusion about pleasure, further conclusions about 'fitting form' (*euschēmosunē*), nobility or fineness (*kallos*), and excellence (*aretē*); but if the ranking had been a ranking in terms of intensity of pleasant feeling, it is obvious that no such conclusion would follow. Plato repeatedly insists on the felt intensity of the very worst pleasures (e.g. *Rep.* 560B, 573A–576C, 586B, *Phlb.* 63D); the *Philebus* calls them the 'greatest and most intense' (63D); the description of the life of the tyrannical man in *Rep.* IX gives us a similar picture of their power. (2) The logic of Greek pleasure words, extensively studied in recent years, makes it very easy for an author to speak of '*hēdesthai*' (to enjoy) and '*hēdonē*' (pleasure) interchangeably: thus to speak of my 'pleasures' is, frequently, not to speak of feelings at all, but of the things I enjoy doing, the activities into which I enter with alacrity. Thus a list of my 'pleasures' would be most likely to be a list, not of sensations, but of pursuits, e.g. eating, doing geometry, watching Euripides. See esp. G. E. L. Owen, 'Aristotelian pleasures', *PAS* 72 (1971–2) 135–52; on related material in the *Philebus*, see B. A. O. Williams, 'Pleasure and belief', *PASS* 33 (1959). Plato in this passage speaks sometimes of 'enjoying', more often of 'the pleasure of *A*-ing', where '*A*-ing' is the name of an activity. 581D1, where 'the pleasure of earning' is replaced by, simply, 'earning', indicates to us that the correct way to understand all these expressions (in any case the most natural construal of the Greek) is as 'the pleasure that consists in *A*-ing', not, 'the pleasure that is yielded by (derived from) *A*-ing'. The *Philebus* shows Socrates explicitly distinguishing these two and opting for the former, in a context where components of lives are being ranked. (3) The passage considers all major activities that are prospective candidates for inclusion in the good life – everything, that is, that *someone* goes for with alacrity. It is agreed early on that each pursuit has its intensely ardent defenders, that from the intensity of their enthusiasm alone no decision would be forthcoming (581C–D). We must go on to ask the further question, which objects of enthusiastic choice are *worth* being enthusiastic about – or, the closely related question, who is the correct or 'authoritative' praiser or enthusiast (*kurios epainetēs*, 583A4; on worth, cf. 581D1, 6). The passage goes on to divide activities as *true* and *false* pleasures: where to call a pleasure *false* means not that it is not really enjoyed, but that it is enjoyed only relatively to some contingent deficiency, not from the standpoint of correct judgment. 586B shows us that the false pleasures give rise to very intense feelings of pleasure in those who lack knowledge of the truth (cf. (1) above). *Philebus* 37A–B makes the point clearly: just as to call a belief *false* does not imply that it is not really *believed*, so to call a pleasure false does not imply that it is not really enjoyed. Throughout the *Rep.* IX passage, considerations of the *real* or *natural truth*, and of *health*, are prominent (e.g. 584D, E; cf. 561C). (4) There is no hint that the pleasures are being compared by a single standard for quantitative intensity of feeling. 586B, 581C–D, and other passages tell strongly against this way of reading Socrates' competition; and there is no hint in the dialogue of a view of pleasure that would support it.

We can conclude, I think, that here, as in *Philebus* 37ff., Socrates is concerned with ranking activities chosen with enthusiasm. The emphasis on enthusiasm contributes only the point that all the lives being considered are lives that *someone* really *likes* and *praises*. (This is not insignificant – cf. p. 162 below.) As for the distinction at 581E, it is probably best to understand Socrates as saying that we are now going to consider any and all proposed candidates for the *eudaimōn* life, asking *not* which is most profitable (*agathon*), *not* which is most uprightly respectable (*kalon*), but, simply, which is the most worth going for *überhaupt*. '*Agathon*' has been associated with rewards early in the dialogue; '*kalon*' is closely linked in some interlocutors' minds with a notion of honorableness or respectability (most clearly in the interchange with Polus in the *Gorgias*); we will have answered Glaucon's original question only if we can defend the life we choose *apart from* honorableness and rewards, showing that the tyrant loses not by a standard that he would himself reject, but by a looser standard that we share with him. This is the most elusive and demanding task, but it is the only one whose successful completion would be the answer Glaucon requires, and the fitting conclusion of the main argument of the *Republic*. Within the literature on this difficult passage, I have been most helped on these issues by Crombie, *An Examination* 140–2; see also White, *A Companion* 229–30, 233, 256; Murphy, *The Interpretation* 212–17.

20. Some commentators are brusquely dismissive of these arguments: see for example, Cross and Woozley, *Plato's Republic* Ch. 11; a fairer estimate of their value is in the commentaries of Annas and White, and in the briefer accounts by Crombie, *op. cit.* and Murphy, *op. cit.*; see also Gosling and Taylor, *The Greeks*, esp. 'A note on "truth"', p. 128.

21. In this chapter, unlike the other three chapters on Plato, I allow myself to draw together material from more than one dialogue. I do so having reached the conclusion that this does not do violence to the internal argument of the *Republic* as I understand it, and is, in fact, necessary in order to clarify that argument. I believe that there is a fundamental methodological difference between my method and Irwin's here. I use cross-reference not in order to fill up what I take to be a culpable omission or gap, but only in order to expand or clarify what I have found to be present in the text of the *Republic* itself. It is clear that the value-distinctions which I shall discuss are not only present in the *Republic*, but are alleged by Socrates to be a central part of his argument. Nothing like this can be said concerning the theory of recollection, or about the *Symposium* account of the ascent of desire. In fact, these two importations appear to be incompatible with one another, since denial of individual immortality is central to the *Symposium*'s argument, while the *Phaedo* recollection material is part of an argument that establishes the individual immortality of the soul. I do not believe that my appeals to other dialogues give rise to this sort of problem.

As for questions of chronology: I assume that there is general agreement that the *Phaedo* and *Republic* come from the same period of Plato's work; they are very close in many ways, and are frequently used to illuminate one another. The *Gorgias* is generally considered to be an earlier work; most scholars would put it in a period of transition between early 'Socratic' dialogues and 'middle' dialogues. It is one of the important achievements of Irwin's book (*PMT*), together with his Clarendon Plato Series commentary on the *Gorgias* (1979) to have convincingly established the close relationship between *Gorgias* and *Republic* concerning the structure of the soul and the nature of irrational desire. The most likely story seems to be that the *Gorgias* opens up questions and sketches arguments which the *Republic* frequently develops at much more considerable length. The *Philebus* is generally agreed to be a later dialogue – partly on stylistic grounds, and partly because it uses the 'Method of division', a dialectical method also present in *Phaedrus*, *Statesman*, and *Sophist*. And yet in some respects (e.g. its lengthy treatment of pleasures of anticipation and of the emotions) it appears to be fulfilling a critical program inaugurated in *Republic* IX. Recently R. A. H. Waterfield has attempted to challenge the orthodox picture, suggesting a middle-period date ('The place of the *Philebus* in Plato's dialogues', *Phronesis* 25 (1980) 270–305). While I do not find all of his arguments convincing, he does, I think, succeed in showing that the orthodoxy rests on a weaker foundation than we usually realize. My own procedure in this chapter does not presuppose anything about the precise solution to this problem, although Ch. 7 will make it of obvious relevance to ask about the chronological relationship between *Philebus* and *Phaedrus*. I claim here only that there is certain material in the *Philebus* that helps us to understand and flesh out the distinctions present in the *Republic*. In fact, I believe that the *use* finally made of these distinctions is significantly different in the two cases. (And I do not rule out the view long pressed by G. E. L. Owen, according to which the *Philebus* is a patchwork of earlier and later pieces, put together hastily for a particular historical occasion.)

22. Notice the frequency of words connected with replenishment (*apopimplanai, plērōsis, ekporizesthai*) in this section of the dialogue.

23. This quantitative point is not strictly relevant to Callicles' general argument: he could defend the superior value of these pleasures as episodes in the good life without claiming that *more* of them was always *better*. We should notice that the question to which Callicles is responding is '*pōs biōteon*', 'how should one live'? Thus the talk of *eudaimonia* is naturally construed as talk about *living well*, not about *feeling content* (cf. Ch. 1, p. 6): Callicles is making a claim about the content of the good human life. In fact, he shifts from talk of 'living well' to talk of 'living pleasantly' only at 494, in order to lay stress on awareness, in objection to the idea that a stone might be thought to live well. The hedonism that is the target of Socrates' later argument is not fairly attributable to Callicles in this earlier section. For a penetrating discussion of Callicles' character and of the way the argument exploits a tension in his ethical views, see C. Kahn, 'Drama and dialectic in Plato's *Gorgias*', *OSAP* (1983), 75–121.

24. At this point, Socrates turns to the examination of the hedonistic thesis which he ascribes to Callicles; since this thesis does not seem to be the same as his original thesis, we shall pursue this argument no further here. (See Irwin, *Plato: Gorgias ad loc.*)

25. Note that scratching is being considered as if it were a prominent constituent of a life, not an isolated episode: the parallel with eating is stressed. For further discussion of the passage, see Irwin, *Gorgias, ad loc.* and E. R. Dodds, *Plato: Gorgias* (Oxford 1959) *ad loc.*

26. Again, the quantitative point here is not strictly relevant.

27. We should notice that this example, which is supposed to be the most extreme case of a non-valuable need-relative pleasure and the one that puts an end to the argument (at 496E it is called the *kephalaion*, 'summary' or 'end-point', of what has preceded), is an example in which Plato shows a keen interest, and which he uses as emblematic of a more general passivity or vulnerability in more than one dialogue – cf. Chs. 6, 7. Some important developments in his ethical view are revealed in his shifting attitudes towards this case (see Ch. 7). I would like to leave no doubt here that I dissociate myself from the social prejudices shown in the interlocutors' treatment of the example.

28. On these views, see Dover, *GH*, and J. J. Henderson, *The Maculate Muse* (New Haven 1975) 209–15. Henderson's investigation of bodily humor in Greek comedy provides a rich source of further material about the Greek attitude towards the 'need-relative' pleasures. He argues that most scatological humor in Old Comedy, for example, rests on our perception of the baseness and silliness of acting in a way that looks worthwhile only because it brings relief from a painful tension. Of jokes about impending defecation, Henderson writes: 'No spectator can feel anything but merry superiority to the plight of such a character, whose rising desperation serves merely to degrade

him further and thus increase our amusement.' It is Plato's aim to get us to view all of our merely bodily activities from the point of view of this comic spectator. (Cf. the section on the speech of Aristophanes in Ch. 6.) On this example, see in particular the insults on the topic directed to the comic audience itself in Aristophanes' *Clouds*, a play whose criticisms of the body deserve, as I have argued, serious comparison with Plato's (Nussbaum, 'Aristophanes').

29. *Gorgias* 493A. On the 'torrent-bird', see Irwin and Dodds *ad loc.*

30. Health might appear an exception – but I believe that this is to be understood as a short way of referring to the healthy functioning or flourishing of the organism, what Aristotle calls 'the unimpeded activity of the natural disposition'.

31. One example of such a pursuit would be activity according to justice, as understood in Protagoras's speech as I have interpreted it in Ch. 4.

32. Plato here uses '*boulesthai*' apparently to contrast true wants with occurrent desires: if someone does something as a result of error or false belief, he or she does not do what he *bouletai*, i.e., presumably, what he would desire if he were not in this deficient condition. The contrast between mere desiring and *boulesthai* is, plainly, closely related to our contrast between deficiency-relative and true value: truly valuable activities are the objects of *boulēsis*.

33. In the *Republic*, unlike the *Philebus* (cf. below), Plato does not explicitly make this point about the intellectual pleasures. He speaks of ignorance as an emptiness of the soul (585B), without making the *Philebus*'s point that it is a non-painful emptiness; intellectual activity is, however, said to be a 'true' filling, in contrast with eating and drinking, in that it is a filling with the true and stable (585C); Plato's color analogy (584E–585A) stresses that, unlike the bodily replenishments, they are not pleasant *only* by contrast to some preceding need or pain.

34. *Phaedo* 64Cff.

35. I am very grateful to John Ackrill for helpful comments on this point.

36. On these form-properties, see especially G. Santas, 'The form of the good in Plato's *Republic*', *Philosophical Inquiry* 2 (1980) 374–403; see also White, *A Companion* 229–30.

37. On the context-relativity of emotions, see White, *op. cit.* 256. The connection between hope (*elpis*) and human deficiency is a traditional motif in Greek reflection about the human condition. Cf. for example *Prometheus Bound* 248–50, where Prometheus claims that he replaced foreknowledge of death with 'blind hopes'; cf. also Hes. *Erga* 96–8. A very interesting discussion of these texts and related issues is J.-P. Vernant, 'À la table des hommes', in Detienne and Vernant, eds., *La Cuisine du sacrifice en pays grec* (Paris 1979) 37–132. Vernant concludes, 'Pour qui est immortel, comme les dieux, nul besoin d'*Elpis*. Pas d'*Elpis* non plus pour qui, comme les bêtes, ignore qu'il est mortel' (132). Hope and its pleasures are a characteristic mark of this one limited rational being. (For an excellent related discussion of hope in the Christian tradition, I am indebted to A. Davidson's Harvard Ph.D. thesis (1982), *Religion and the Fanaticism of Reason*, and to discussion with him.) These considerations should help us to see why the *Republic* rules out all pleasures of hope and anticipation, not only those associated with false beliefs. A perfect being could, of course, anticipate; but it would not have the same *pleasure* in doing so that a human does, since it can at any time effortlessly procure whatever it wants.

38. In this later section, Plato shifts from ranking 'pleasures' to ranking activities *simpliciter*. I do not claim to understand this shift, since the 'pleasures' previously ranked were in any case activities, and the dialogue had from the start denied that

pleasure was a single thing yielded by all different sorts of activities. Since the internal unity of the *Philebus*'s argument is notoriously problematic, and since leading scholars have even supposed it to be a patchwork, I hope that my selective use of its material will be excused. (See n. 21 above. The 'patchwork' view was forcefully defended by the late G. E. L. Owen, in unpublished material.) The 'mixed' life constructed out of the elements thus analyzed is not the ascetic life of the *Phaedo*; but its relation to the moral psychology of *Phaedrus, Laws,* and *Statesman* is obscure; perhaps, not consistent. At 53B–C, Socrates declares once again that pleasures cannot be ranked by a quantitative standard. In the next section of the argument, at 53E, it is worth noting that self-sufficiency emerges as a separate mark of value.

39. This sort of argument is probably to be traced to Eudoxus; note that it is the sort of argument for hedonism that I contrasted with Socrates' *Protagoras* argument in Ch. 4.

40. For this I combine the denunciation of the senses as inaccurate and unclear perceivers of health and strength with the claim that following the body's perceptions compels people to enter into various harmful and unnecessary activities.

41. The *Republic* is less clearly ascetic, stressing the need to nourish the body up to the point of health and well-being (558Dff.), and apparently even allowing a healthy amount of sexual activity (559C). (On this see White, *A Companion* 219). One reason for this difference is that the *Republic* (like the first two speeches in the *Phaedrus* – cf. Ch. 7) is more aware than the *Phaedo* of the distraction to work that can be caused by emptiness and need (571E). But another reason clearly comes from the political need of the city. Its demand for the reproduction of a guardian class requires the devotion of some time to sexual activity. Here the philosopher-ruler runs up against the difficulty that sexual function will become a problem for a human being who has the proper Platonic attitude towards this functioning. For its full success, the ideal city needs the state of affairs movingly described by Augustine (*City of God* XIV) as the situation of Eden, where every part of the body functions in direct obedience to the rational will.

42. See above, n. 5; for criticisms of this picture, see Ch. 7. The Book IX image of appetite as 'many-headed beast' and emotion as lion makes these points again.

43. E. Hanslick, *The Beautiful in Music* (7th ed., Leipzig 1885), tr. G. Cohen (Indianapolis 1957) 47; also 7ff. The meaning of *melos* in the *Phlb.* passage is unclear; it might also mean 'tune' – though one suspects that Plato also wishes to omit temporal motion.

44. This appeal to what befits the god probably had its origin in Xenophanes' arguments for a de-anthropomorphized theology: see especially DK B11–16, 26–8; and see the further remarks about Xenophanean allusions in Plato in Ch. 6.

45. It is now time to begin to summarize my difference from Irwin, *PMT*. The central point is that on his account lives are ruled out only on formal and procedural grounds; on mine the *internal* structure and nature of the constituents is also, and centrally, taken into account. For him, order and stability are important characteristics of the plan as a whole, but not of each individual component; for me, each component end must possess the marks of value. It is clear that, using our two very different accounts of Plato's argument, each of us can get Plato to many of his actual conclusions. But I would now claim two advantages for my version: (1) It is the argument that Plato actually offers for his conclusions in the *Republic* and *Phaedo*. Irwin understands himself to be reconstructing an argument to fill what he believes to be an absence of serious argument. (A sign of this difference: Irwin concludes (p. 237) that the philosopher's desire for contemplation 'will not be rational because it is a desire *for* theoretical

reasoning, but because it is a desire arising *from* practical reasoning'. But Plato's text clearly and repeatedly speaks of the intrinsic value of theoretical reasoning, defending its selection by pointing to its characteristics and those of its objects. (2) As Irwin emphasizes, his reconstructed argument does not support Plato's choice of the contemplative life over certain other available lives; Irwin speaks of an 'interest in contemplative rather than practical wisdom' that leads Plato to present what Irwin considers a defective and 'unforgivable' argument here. My interpretation supports Plato's actual conclusions.

46. The point is similar to the point made by Socrates against Euthyphro's definition of piety: if the pious is simply defined as that which the gods love, and there is nothing about the nature of the pious that can explain their love, then they look like arbitrary authorities.

47. Aristotle will be highly critical of this stratagem – see Ch. 12. Plato makes one salient exception to his overall policy of generalizing love: to avoid incest, citizens do single out an entire generation as parents.

48. The context makes it very clear that nothing in the realm of mere human opinion will satisfy this desire and complete this inquiry (505D).

49. *The Will to Power*, trans. W. Kaufmann and R. J. Hollingdale (New York 1967) 519; cf. 576. Contrast Nietzsche's own account of value, which makes it relative to 'the preservation and enhancement of the power of a certain species of animal' (567). Nietzsche's point is not only that intrinsic values can, and must, be found within and through the anthropocentric perspective. It is also that the very things which the negative metaphysician most anxiously tries to eliminate – change, risk, transience – are themselves partly constitutive of the highest human values. (Cf. 576 and *Thus Spoke Zarathustra*, trans. W. Kaufmann (New York 1954) I, prologue.)

50. This sentence may suggest that my view is after all not so far from Irwin's, since he, to, speaks of uncovering our deepest desires or needs. I believe that the views are, however, distinct in a crucial way. For Irwin, the fact that activity *x* answers to the deepest desires of an agent *A* (when these are arrived at by a procedure of rational deliberation about the overall good for *A*) is sufficient to make *x* truly valuable for *A*. The introspective procedures are not just heuristic devices; they are themselves criterial of value. On my interpretation, this is not so. Needs or desires come in only in connection with motivation and education, not as the answer to a question about what value *is*. It is a fortunate fact about human beings that many of them are so constructed that they can be motivated to seek true value. So much, as the *Phaedrus* myth tells us, is not true of any other animal; the theory of recollection, interpreted with its full metaphysical commitment, shows us how it could be true of us. But its relation to human motivational equipment is no part of what *makes* intellectual activity valuable. If humans had never existed, it would still be valuable; and if humans exist for whom Plato's motivational claims are not true, Plato will not conclude (as Irwin must) that they have a different good; he will conclude that they are simply cut off from the only good that there is. Furthermore, even the motivation that we have to pursue the good is, as I have argued, different in character from our other practical motivations: for there is a positive desire for intellectual activity which (as the *Philebus* insists) is not felt as a pain or a distress. On Plato's account, it could not be truly valuable if we were motivated to pursue it only by felt lack or distress; and this distinction does not figure at all in Irwin's account of deepest needs.

51. Plutarch's language here might suggest that he is comparing pleasures for their felt

intensity, using a single quantitative scale. In using this passage, I do not wish to endorse any such way of reading Plato. Plutarch almost certainly does not either, as other passages in the treatise would show.

52. This is all the more true for Irwin, since Irwin's Aristotle has a view much closer to the one he ascribes to Plato than do the Aristotles of most interpreters. See his 'Reason and responsibility in Aristotle', in Rorty, *Essays* 117–56. I discuss his interpretation in Ch. 9.

53. *Thus Spoke Zarathustra* I, 'Zarathustra's Prologue' (tr. Kaufmann).

54. This chapter has benefited more than any other in Pt II from the criticism and discussion of others. Versions have been read (in chronological order) at: Dartmouth College, Yale University, The University of California at Berkeley, Boston University, Oxford University, The Johns Hopkins University, Brown University, MIT, the University of Pennsylvania, Wellesley College (NEH Summer Seminar), The University of Virginia, The University of Maryland, and Emory University. I am grateful to Ruth Anna Putnam, who publicly commented on the paper at Boston University. Among the many members of this and other audiences whose comments and criticisms have helped me, I am particularly aware of responding to points raised by: John Ackrill, Myles Burnyeat, Joshua Cohen, Michael Ferejohn, Charles Kahn, Thomas Ricketts, James Ross, Barry Stroud, Judith Jarvis Thomson, and Susan Wolf.

6   The speech of Alcibiades: a reading of the *Symposium*

1. These stories, though probably not all true, are representative of the popular legends about Alcibiades that form the background for the dialogue. All sources are in general agreement about his character and the main facts of his life. From Thucydides come the account of his career, the spectacle-giving, the military and political abilities, as well as the Olympia story (VI.15) and the remarks about love of country (VI.92.4). On the Herms, see below n. 17. From Plutarch come the stories about the flute (2), the resident alien (5), and the dog (9). Another important source is Xenophon, *Hellenica* I. For analysis of the evidence, see A. W. Gomme, K. J. Dover, and A. Andrewes, *A Historical Commentary on Thucydides* IV (Oxford 1970) especially 49ff., 264ff., 242ff.

2. G. Vlastos, 'The individual as object of love in Plato's dialogues', in Vlastos, *PS* 1–34. Irwin, *PMT* criticizes some aspects of Vlastos's interpretation, but agrees with him in this criticism of Plato.

3. In *La Théorie platonicienne de l'amour* (Paris 1933), L. Robin argues that any element of truth in the preceding speeches is picked up and developed in Diotima's speech, so that an analysis of that speech alone suffices for our understanding of the dialogue's view of love. He does not even speak of Alcibiades' speech, referring to Diotima's as 'ce dernier discours'. Interpreters who insist that the dialogue must be read as a whole, with due attention given to the philosophical contribution of each speech, include S. Rosen, *Plato's Symposium* (New Haven 1968); T. Gould, *Platonic Love* (London 1963); and G. K. Plochmann, 'Supporting themes in the *Symposium*', in J. Anton and G. Kustas, eds., *Essays in Ancient Greek Philosophy* (Albany 1972) 328–44. Plochmann's spirited introductory remarks about philosophy and literature clear the air in a helpful way. (See also V. Goldschmidt, *Les Dialogues de Platon* (Paris 1947, 2nd ed. 1963) 222–35.) Unfortunately, K. J. Dover prefaces his brief commentary (Cambridge 1980) with the 'working hypothesis' that there is no convincing argument in *any* part of the dialogue, which is a piece of literary and forensic advocacy through and through (viii).

One recent interpreter who gives due weight to Alcibiades' speech and its criticisms of Socrates is M. Gagarin, 'Socrates' *hubris* and Alcibiades' failures', *Phoenix* 31 (1977) 22–37.

4. On Apollodorus, cf. also *Phd.* 59A, 117D; *Apol.* 34A.

5. Rosen oddly calls him a 'businessman', contrasting him with the leisured Polemarchus; this would certainly rule out identification with either of the known Glaucons (cf. below n. 14). It is very hard to know what actual Athenian class Rosen has in mind. Clearly a 'leisured' Athenian gentleman is precisely the person most likely to be 'rushing around' busying himself with political affairs; and the disdain of the Athenian political man for philosophical pursuits and the philosopher's abstraction from politics is a recurrent Platonic theme. We need not suppose Glaucon a craftsman or tradesman to understand why he thinks philosophy less important than politics.

6. R. G. Bury, *The Symposium of Plato* (Cambridge 1932, repr. 1966) lxvi; cf. also Guthrie, *History* IV, 366.

7. The date of composition is disputed. There is now widespread agreement that the dialogue is earlier than the *Phaedrus* and roughly contemporary with the *Republic* and *Phaedo*. K. J. Dover convincingly argues for an upper terminus of 385 (on the basis of an anachronistic historical allusion at 183A1–3: 'The date of Plato's *Symposium*', *Phronesis* 10 (1965) 2–20); his tentative argument for a lower terminus of 378 seems less convincing. In any case, indications are that it is to be closely linked with the *Republic*, which was most likely written during the decade 380–370. See Ch. 5 n. 21 and Ch. 7 n. 5.

8. Cf. Plutarch 38; Aristoph. *Frogs* 1422ff. Thucydides obliquely refers to the absence of Alcibiades as a major cause of Athenian difficulties: II.65.12; for this interpretation cf. Dover in Gomme, Dover and Andrewes, *Historical Commentary* IV, 244.

9. A persuasive study of the *Frogs*' portrayal of the connection between the death of tragedy and the demise of comedy is in C. Segal, 'The character of Dionysus and the unity of the *Frogs*', *HSCP* 65 (1961) 207–30. Even though there were major political changes between 405 and 404, the threat of the extinction of literary freedoms is certainly in the air in 405.

10. Plutarch 38; cf. Isocrates XVI.21.

11. The rest of Aeschylus's political advice is also democratic: he urges the Periclean policy of relying on the navy while allowing the enemy to invade (1463–5).

12. Cf. *Frogs* 1491–5.

13. In the *Apology*, Socrates presents himself as an opponent of the unconstitutional extreme measures of the Thirty. There is thus a problem here about determining the relationship between Plato and his character Socrates, and between the character and the historical Socrates. This may be one more reason why the speech that gives a prescription for the removal of disorder and the rejection of Alcibiades is put in the mouth of a character who is not identical with Socrates, though she instructs him.

14. The Glaucon of the *Republic* is Plato's older (half-)brother; the other Glaucon (cf. *Charmides* 154) is the father of Charmides, and so Plato's mother's brother. Since this character is at least fairly young, he cannot be Charmides' father (*pace* Bury, *The Symposium*, who favors this identification, without argument). The identification with the Glaucon of the *Republic* is opposed without argument by Guthrie (*History* IV, 366 n. 2), who favors an otherwise unknown figure, and by Bury, though it has also had distinguished supporters (see references in Bury). The primary difficulty, apart from the failure to call him son of Ariston, is, again age. If the 'we' of Apollodorus's 'when

we were boys' (173A) is taken as inclusive of Glaucon, it cannot be the man who fought with distinction in 424. But Apollodorus might equally mean 'when people of my generation were boys'. For another case of Platonic homonymous characters, note the two Adeimantuses in the *Protagoras*.

15. It will now be asked, why should these events be mentioned so indirectly? Surely if Plato wanted us to think of Alcibiades' death he would have said so openly. This, however, is not so clear: compare the veiled reference to these same events at Thuc. II.65.12, a reference which Dover defends against charges of obscurity by pointing out that Thucydides could assume that his readers would be so acutely aware of the events and their dating that a highly subtle allusion would more than suffice, and explicitness would be heavy-handed. It is easy to construct contemporary parallels.

16. Cf. Athenaeus v.217a.

17. The later tradition (beginning at least with Demosthenes) in most cases takes Alcibiades to be guilty of both the mutilation of the Herms and the profanation of the Mysteries. Thucydides is more guarded about the Herms (cf. VI.53, VI.61), saying only that he was *thought* to be implicated in the attack (VI.28.2). The official accusation seems to have been based on charges relating to the Mysteries alone. (See Dover in Gomme, Dover, Andrewes, *Historical Commentary* IV, 264–88.) But Plato wrote at a time when both crimes were commonly laid at Alcibiades' door; most of his audience could have been expected to believe the charges.

18. *Biazesthai* 'force', was a common term for violent sexual assault: cf. LSJ s.v., and especially Aristoph. *Pl.* 1052. The connection of Hermes with luck is a central theme in the *Cratylus*, where Cratylus argues that if young Hermogenes is not fortunate, he has no right to that name.

19. The hiccups have been extensively discussed. See (with further references) Plochmann, 'Supporting themes', *passim*, Guthrie, *History* IV, 382 n. 2 and Rosen, *Plato's Symposium* 90ff., esp. 120.

20. Xenophanes (DK B23–6) imagines a god 'not similar in shape to mortal men'. Aristotle frequently cites the circle as the most perfect shape and the one most suited for the divine. Also relevant here are the arguments of *Philebus* 51B–C, on which cf. Ch. 5. J. S. Morrison, 'The shape of the earth in Plato's *Phaedo*', *Phronesis* 4 (1959) 101–19, argues that the creatures are wheel-shaped, rather than (as many commentators assume) spherical. This makes no difference to my argument. On Aristophanes' speech in general, see K. J. Dover, 'Aristophanes' speech in Plato's *Symposium*', *JHS* 86 (1966) 41–50.

21. Contrast Milton's extraordinary account of the sexual life of angels, who 'obstacle find none / Of membrane, joint, or limb' (*Paradise Lost* VIII.620ff.). (I am indebted to John Hollander for bringing this passage to my attention.)

22. Soph. *Antigone* 568–70: cf. Ch. 3. Epictetus shrewdly comments on the depth of this view in the stories on which Greek literature is based, saying that if Menelaus had been able to think of Helen as just another woman, and a bad one at that, then 'gone would have been the *Iliad*, and the *Odyssey* as well' (*Diss.* 1.28.13). It seems, therefore, superfluous to multiply examples.

23. R. B. Brandt, 'The morality and rationality of suicide', in J. Rachels ed., *Moral Problems* (N.Y. 1975) 363–87.

24. Even at 207E, the contrast between *psuchē* and *sōma* is not the contrast between the material and the immaterial – or at least not as this contrast is usually drawn by Plato

in other middle-period dialogues. *Psuchē* includes habits, character, opinions, appetites, pleasures, pains, fears, understandings.

25. For possible sexual associations of 'die' and related words in Greek, see, for example, Heraclitus DK B15, 77, 117, perhaps 85; and the elaborately metaphorical ending of Aristophanes' *Acharnians*.

26. Cf. *Odyssey* VIII.266ff. See K. Dorter, 'The significance of the speeches in Plato's *Symposium*', *Philosophy and Rhetoric* 2 (1969) 215–34.

27. Rosen, *Plato's Symposium* 8 notes that Aristophanes is the only speaker who is not involved in an erotic relationship with another person present.

28. 'Timandra' is most likely to mean 'honor the man', while 'Diotima' simply means 'Zeus-honor' and would in all likelihood have been construed by Plato as ambiguous between 'the one who gives honor to Zeus' and 'the one who receives honor from Zeus'. It is barely possible that Timandra was invented by Plutarch (who knew the *Symposium*) to correspond to Diotima, rather than the other way round. Although we cannot rule this out, what we can say is that in this case Plato's invented name will still be significant, though in a more abstract way; and Plutarch will have shown himself to be a very sharp interpreter. W. Kranz, 'Diotima', *Die Antike* 2 (1926) 313–27, argues that Diotima is a real historical character: but only on the grounds that all the other characters in the dialogue are. Since she is not a character in the same sense, this is a weak argument. His description of her revelation to Socrates as inspired by maternal affection of a highly particularized sort (he reminds us that since priestesses could marry there is no reason why she could not have fulfilled 'das Schicksal der Frau'!) seems to me fanciful and sentimental. (Most of the article, however, is a very interesting disicussion of Hölderlin's use of the *Symposium*.)

29. There is an extra step here, in which they agree that the implication holds necessarily (200B2–3).

30. *Endees estin*, 'lacks', 'is in need of', is, throughout, used interchangeably with *ouch echei*, 'does not have'. I omit here the interesting digression in which Socrates concedes that an agent may desire something that he does now have, but argues that what he really desires in such cases is something he does not now have, viz. the continued future possession of the object.

31. It is not at all clear what Plato would say about the well-known Aristotelian problem of the individuation of items in non-substance categories.

32. Two passages are less clearly quantitative: 'more honorable' at 210B7, and 'gold for bronze' at 219A1. But both are compatible with a quantitative reading (gold is *worth more* on a single scale of financial measure; and it is just what is at issue whether differences in honorableness are qualitative or only quantitative). So neither passage cuts against the preponderant evidence for a single quantitative scale. See my 'Plato on commensurability and desire', *PASS* 58 (1984) 55–80.

33. *Rep.* 521cff., cf. Ch. 5.

34. *Biōtos* means 'livable', 'worth the living'. It is most often found negated, frequently in connection with the willing acceptance of death, or even suicide. Joyce's translation, 'and if, my dear Socrates, man's life is ever worth the living', is correct. W. Hamilton's 'the region where a man's life should be spent' is deficient; it misses the force and the nature of the argument.

35. T. H. Irwin, *PMT* and J. M. E. Moravcsik ('Reason and Eros in the Ascent Passage of the *Symposium*', in Anton and Kustas, *Essays* 285–302) also stress the role of need

and dissatisfaction in moving the agent from one level to another. Neither discusses the precise nature of the propelling practical needs or points out the enabling role of questionable judgments of qualitative similarity. But Moravcsik's very interesting discussion of the role of aspiration and discontent in the ascent seems fully compatible with my observation (as the author has now assured me). Another valuable discussion, focusing on the nature of erotic creativity in the ascent, is L. A. Kosman, 'Platonic love', in W. H. Werkmeister, ed., *Facets of Plato's Philosophy* (Assen 1976, *Phronesis* Supplement 11) 53–69.

36. Rosen, *Plato's Symposium* also notes the repetition of '*exaiphnēs*' (pp. 288, 325), though he does not make this point. Cf. also Robin, *Théorie* 183, who compares *Republic* 515C, 516E. R. Hornsby, 'Significant action in the *Symposium*', *CJ* 52 (1956–7) 37–40, makes the interesting observation that between the departure of the flute girl and the entrance of Alcibiades there is no description of bodily movement from place to place – the dinner is in a state of rest, 'as though the earlier portion of the party had achieved a condition similar to that of the Idea of Beauty'.

37. See Ch. 7.

38. Of course this requires that in another way the stories about particulars be general rather than particular: that they be not eccentric or idiosyncratic, but representative (as Aristotle says, 'the sort of thing that might happen'). See Ch. 1 and Ch. 13. For further development of some of these issues, see Nussbaum, 'Crystals'.

39. Cf. Interlude 1 and references there. Although P. Geach seems wrong to say that Socrates altogether rejects a list of examples as a contribution to discourse ('Plato's *Euthyphro*', *The Monist* 50 (1966) 369–82), Socrates clearly believes that inquiry has made real progress only when we have risen above them. Cf. L. Wittgenstein, *The Blue and Brown Books* (Oxford 1958) 19–20, 26–7.

40. Compare the *Phaedo*'s rejection of the testimony of the senses – cf. Ch. 5.

41. Esp. J. Locke, *An Essay Concerning Human Understanding* (1690), ed. P. H. Nidditch (Oxford 1975) Bk 3, Ch. 10, discussed on p. 16 and n. 25.

42. Dover's edition, back jacket blurb. The Clarendon Plato Series, whose charge was to present new commentaries on Platonic works 'of interest to present-day philosophers', had originally no plan to include either *Symposium* or *Phaedrus*. In August 1982 the *Phaedrus* was added; I am currently preparing the translation and commentary.

43. Guthrie claims that Alcibiades *is* fulfilling the Socratic request, since 'Eros is made visible in Socrates' (*History* IV, 395). I hope it is clear by now why I do not think this an adequate account of what is going on.

44. Dover, *GH* esp. II.C.5. See also the reviews by B. Knox, *New York Review of Books* 25 (1979) 5–8 and H. Lloyd-Jones, *New Statesman* (6 October 1978) and *Classical Survivals* (1982) 97ff.

45. Dover, *GH* 96. Dover may not be justified in supposing that these pictures display unvarying cultural *facts*; what is more important is that they clearly depict cultural *norms*.

46. Cf. *Euthyphro* 11A–B.

47. For some interesting remarks about 'lover's knowledge' and its relationship to the analytical, see L. Trilling, 'The Princess Casamassima', in *The Liberal Imagination* (NY 1950) 86ff.

48. See Ch. 10 and my 'Practical syllogisms and practical science', in Nussbaum, *De Motu* Essay 4, and Wiggins, 'Deliberation'.

49. Cf. J. M. E. Moravcsik, 'Understanding and knowledge in Plato's dialogues', *Neue*

Hefte für Philosophie (1979) and M. F. Burnyeat, 'Aristotle on understanding Knowledge', in *Aristotle on Science: the 'Posterior Analytics'*, ed. E. Berti (Padua 1981).

50. For uses of '*dialegesthai*' of sexual relations, see references in J. J. Henderson, *The Maculate Muse* (New Haven 1975) 155.

51. *Republic* 507Aff.

52. Alcibiades later removes the garlands that were attached to the wreath and puts them on the heads of Agathon and Socrates. But the Greek text indicates that the garlands were a separate item (cf. 212E2), and it appears that the violet–ivy wreath is worn throughout his speech. On this point Joyce's translation is correct, Hamilton's misleading.

53. See A. L. Edmunds, *Chance and Intelligence in Thucydides* (Cambridge, MA 1975). On improvisation, see further in Ch. 10.

54. Cf. Rosen, *Plato's Symposium* 287; Gould, *Platonic Love* 39–41; J. Anton, 'Some Dionysian references in the Platonic dialogues', *CJ* 58 (1962–3) 49–55.

55. The remarks on the tragic and comic poets are the subject of a large literature, much of which takes the view that it is Socrates himself (and therefore also Plato) who unites both comedy and tragedy. Two interesting recent defenses of that view are in D. Clay, 'The tragic and comic poet of the *Symposium*', *Arion* NS 2 (1975) 238–61 and R. Patterson, 'The Platonic art of comedy and tragedy', forthcoming in *Phil Lit*. Cf. also H. Bacon, 'Socrates crowned', *Virginia Quarterly Review* 35 (1959) 415–30. I think it important to distinguish Socrates from Plato here: Socrates is the opponent of both tragedy and comedy, while Plato here gives utterance both to the Socratic view and to the view that opposes it. Cf. also Anton, *op. cit.* 51–2, who argues that Plato and *not* Socrates is the tragic/comic poet.

56. *Hubris*, ironically, is also a legal and popular term for sexual assault; see LSJ sv.; Henderson, *Maculate Muse* 154; and Gagarin, 'Socrates and Alcibiades'.

57. See the discussion and illustrations in Dover, *GH* 94–5, and plates. This 'most characteristic configuration of homosexual courtship' (Dover, *GH* 94) was earlier described in Sir John Beazley's important article 'Some Attic vases in the Cyprus Museum', *PBA* 33 (1947) 195–244.

58. Compare Rosen, *Plato's Symposium* 300.

59. Compare the reading of Othello in S. Cavell's *The Claim of Reason: Wittgenstein, Skepticism, Morality, and Tragedy* (New York 1979).

60. I wish here to thank all those who helped me with their generous comments at many stages: especially Myles Burnyeat, John Carriero, Stanley Cavell, Arnold Davidson, John Hollander, Julius Moravcsik, Nick Pappas, Gregory Vlastos, and Susan Wolf.

7 'This story isn't true': madness, reason, and recantation in the *Phaedrus*

1. The epigram is reported in Diogenes Laertius III.30 = Anth. Pal. VII.99. Its authenticity is defended in detail by C. M. Bowra, 'Plato's epigram on Dion's death', *AJP* 59 (1938) 394–404; cf. also W. Wilamowitz, *Platon* 1 (Berlin 1940) 644, who offers an excellent poetic German translation. The only argument seriously advanced against authenticity is that such deep emotion is inappropriate to a man of seventy (A. E. Taylor, *Plato* (London 1926) 544). This seems to me a very weak argument (cf. also n. 5).

2. Cf. 251A–E and this ch. pp. 215–18.

3. R. Hackforth, *Plato's Phaedrus* (Indianapolis 1952) 37.

4. The place is precisely described and can be precisely located – see R. E. Wycherley, 'The scene of Plato's *Phaedrus*', *Phoenix* 17 (1963) 88–98 and D. Clay, 'Socrates' prayer to Pan', in *Arktouros: Hellenic Studies Presented to Bernard M. W. Knox* (Berlin/New York 1979) 345–53. The place has deeply moved many visitors. (Clay quotes some lines from Seferis about the river Ilissos which convey a sense of sudden insight, at once emotional and intellectual, very much in the spirit of the dialogue.) F. M. Cornford (*Principium Sapientiae* (Cambridge 1952) 66–7) says plausibly that we are to feel the strangeness of seeing Socrates 'taken out of the surroundings which he never left. Within the limits of his dramatic art Plato could not have indicated more clearly that this poetic and inspired Socrates was not known to his habitual companions.'

5. On the chronological issues, see also Ch. 5, n. 21. There is now general agreement that the *Phaedrus* is later than both *Republic* and *Symposium* in date of composition and close to the *Theaetetus*, which can be dated to not long after 369 (since it commemorates Theaetetus's death in the battle at Corinth in that year). The issues are summarized (with many additional references) by L. Robin, *La Théorie platonicienne de l'amour* (Paris 1933) 63–109 and Hackforth, *Plato's Phaedrus* 3–7; cf. also Guthrie, *History* IV, 396–7 – who, however, for no very strong reason places it just prior to the *Republic*. One set of arguments for a late dating is stylometric: various criteria used independently converge, consistently placing it just before, but close to, the group *Sophist, Statesman, Philebus, Laws*; (some would include the *Timaeus* – but L. Brandwood's work suggests reasons for doubt in this case). But these criteria, though apparently impressive in their unanimity, cannot be used in isolation, especially when we are dealing with a dialogue in which Plato is playing with a number of different styles. Also suggestive, but finally unreliable, are the historical considerations brought forward by G. Ryle, *Plato's Progress* ((Cambridge 1966) – see below n. 59) which support a post-*Theaetetus* date. Doctrinal considerations are more probative, though difficult for us to use here without suspicion of circularity. Most striking among issues not at the heart of our project is that the method of division, apparently introduced here, is found only in a group of dialogues agreed on other grounds to be late: *Sophist, Statesman, Philebus*. And even if Guthrie should be right in claiming that this method is not altogether new, what *is* new is that this method is said in all these dialogues to be *the* method of dialectic and *the* occupation of the philosopher; it thus replaces (and is incompatible with) the hypothetical method of *Phaedo* and *Republic*. (Cf. J. L. Ackrill, 'In defense of Platonic division', in *Ryle*, ed. O. Wood and G. Pitcher (Garden City 1970) 373–92.) Another impressive argument concerns the view of soul: the *Phaedrus* theory can be shown to have affinities with the *Laws* far more than with *Phaedo, Republic*, and *Timaeus*. Cf. this ch. pp. 222–3. The arguments for incompatibility between *Phaedrus* and *Phaedo/Rep./Tim.* are fully and ably set out by E. Groag, 'Zur Lehre von Wesen der Seele in Platons Phaedros und im X. Buche der Republik', *Wiener Studien* 37 (1915) 189–22; unfortunately, Groag's guiding assumption that the *Timaeus* represents Plato's latest and most mature view of soul makes him take his own arguments to prove that *Phaedrus* antedates this entire group of dialogues; he ignores the issues raised by a comparison with the *Laws* (on which see Robin, *La Théorie*). The main arguments that have been advanced for an early dating of the *Phaedrus* are: (1) its moving poetic language, apparently incompatible with the condemnation of the poet in the *Republic*; and (2) the striking description of sensuous passion, which (allegedly) could not have been written by a man in his fifties (for references see Robin, Guthrie, Hackforth). The first point is well taken; but it supports only a judgment

of incompatibility, not of priority (cf. below, §III). The second is just silly. It seems safe to date the dialogue around 365, either shortly before or shortly after the *Theaetetus*. (See nn. 58 and 59 on the connection with Plato's second visit to Syracuse.)

6. The following remarks are based upon a complete study of '*mania*' and related words in the *corpus*: cf. L. Brandwood, *A Concordance to Plato* (Leeds 1976). For the connection with *erōs*, cf. esp. *Rep.* 329C, 403; *Symp.* 213D, 215C–D, *Crat.* 404A; on the opposition to *sophrosunē*, see esp. *Protag.* 323B5, *Rep.* 573A–B. On madness in Plato and its antecedents, see also Dodds, *GI* Chs. 2 (64–101) and 7 (207–35).

7. This word, which seems to mean 'calculative', 'measuring', 'intellectual', frequently gets translated by 'reason' and 'rational'. I try here to avoid this practice in order to avoid normative implications (about what practical rationality is) that are absent from Plato's text.

8. The situation in the *Symposium* is of course more complex because of the variety of speakers, cf. Ch. 6.

9. On all these points see Ch. 5 and references.

10. I shall assume, in what follows, what more or less all commentators agree: that Lysias is using this speech to seduce Phaedrus, and that he identifies himself with the 'non-lover', Phaedrus with the boy addressee.

11. It should, however, be noticed that Socrates' first speech connects the erotic appetite with beauty, thus anticipating the view of his second speech. This was true of his speech in the *Symposium* as well, and indicates a continuity between *Symposium* and *Phaedrus*. T. Gillespie has argued in an unpublished paper that this and other points of continuity should lead us to the conclusion that the *Symposium* was written after the *Republic* and is, in at least some respects, a transitional work, even with regard to Socrates' speech. Contrast *Republic* 580E, with mentions only intercourse (*aphrodisia*) in connection with *erōs*, and 586A–B, which uses animal language of human intercourse. The *Philebus*, presumably later than the *Phaedrus* (see Ch. 5, n. 21), classifies *erōs* not with the desires for bodily replenishment, but with complex emotions like anger, grief, spite, and envy, which are dependent for their identity upon the nature of the beliefs with which they are associated. Contrast the different use of the verb *eran* at *Rep.* 403A, *Phd.* 68A.

12. Hackforth, *Plato's Phaedrus* 31.

13. Some of the issue that I shall pursue in this section first occurred to me as the result of conversations with Alexander George, to whom I am grateful for a very interesting paper criticizing an earlier draft of this chapter. Our views remain different, but I hope that this answers some of his questions.

14. It is possible that the Puth- in Puthokles is the aorist stem of the verb *punthanomai*, 'seek after', 'inquire after'. The name would then mean 'Son of Seeker after Fame'. But our slightly more likely choice, 'of Pythian fame', i.e. having fame for victory at the Pythian Games, has a similar connotation: in either case the patronymic emphasizes civic prominence and renown.

15. All this paraphrases arguments from the first two speeches; I see no need to list the passage references, since they are obvious.

16. Lysias tells the story of his own life during those years in oration 12 (*Against Eratosthenes*). On his career in general, see K. J. Dover, *Lysias and the Corpus Lysiacum* (Berkeley 1968). On Plato's use of Lysias and his family as characters, see also F. E. Sparshott, 'Plato and Thrasymachus, *University of Toronto Quarterly* 1957, 54–61.

17. Cf. Ch. 5, n. 41.

18. Lucretius (IV.1063ff.) advocates promiscuity as a good way of avoiding the madness of love. The evidence concerning Epicurus's views on this matter is complicated and difficult to interpret. Some fragments suggest that he urged abstaining from sex altogether; but the tone of some of his surviving letters to members of his community suggests a light-hearted and non-passionate sexuality. His condemnation of love is, in any case, vehement and unequivocal.

19. For one contemporary parallel, see Simone de Beauvoir's remarks about the self-possession of young women in America (*The Second Sex*, trans. H. M. Parshley (NY 1974) 436).

20. See the good discussion of superstitions surrounding the noonday hour in D. Clay, 'Socrates' prayer'. The whole system of Greek belief regarding the connection between summer heat and the dangers of unbridled sexuality is given a stimulating discussion in M. Detienne, *Les Jardins d'Adonis* (Paris 1972), with an excellent introduction by J.-P. Vernant. We should notice that in the *Phaedrus* the sun plays the part of an active, moving natural causal force, a part of the human world (contrast Ch. 6, and cf. this ch. pp. 216–17).

21. See *Symp.* 198B–204C.

22. On connections between the Platonic use of *kathairō* and related words and Aristotle's discussion of tragedy, see Interlude 2.

23. '*Pothos*' is used of longing for an absent object, and '*himeros*' can be implicitly contrasted with it. '*Himeros*' is not used of purely intellectual aspiration, but implies the presence of strong emotional or appetitive feeling.

    The two remaining names deserve at least some comment. 'Stesichoros' itself has an etymology: 'the one who stages the performance of the chorus'. Socrates' choice of poet names thus has the added feature of linking reverence towards *erōs* explicitly with a new respect for music and poetry. 'Murrhinousios' is Phaedrus's real deme name, as we know from an inscription; thus in this case, as in other cases where we are dealing with an actual historical name, we need to be cautious. But Plato repeatedly puns on the significance of actual names, both in this dialogue and elsewhere (especially the *Cratylus*). The games he plays in this section, together with the etymological puns that connect Phaedrus with Ganymede (cf. this ch. p. 231) prompt us to record, at least, the following facts. Myrrha was a lady infamous for her incestuous seduction of her father (cf. Ovid, *Metam.* x); as penalty she was turned into the myrrh tree (Greek *murrhis*), which (either because of this story or antecedently) has marked ritual associations in Attic culture as an aphrodisiac (for one example, cf. Aristoph. *Birds* 160–1). Myrrha was also the mother of Adonis, whose sexuality brings him to grief. The myrtle tree (in Attic *murrhinē*) also has marked sexual associations: a colloquial name for the end of the *membrum virile* is *to murrhinon*, 'the myrtle branch' (Aristoph. *Kn.* 964). At least at a later date, *murrhis* became a name for female genitalia. Plato's etymological playfulness is so evident in this dialogue, and so explicitly sexual in the Ganymede example, that we could see this insistence on the deme name (nowhere else mentioned in the dialogues), and the rather uncommon phrase 'a Murrhinousian man' as a reminder that Phaedrus, though he has tried to deny it, is actually a markedly erotic person. If the dual male/female associations do exist by this period, it may also be a prefiguring of all the androgynous active/passive imagery of the second speech and the Ganymede references.

    The story of Myrrha and Adonis, and its cultural/religious associations, is explored in Detienne, *Les Jardins*, esp. 117–38 – though Detienne's arguments are frequently not cautious enough about the different periods from which evidence is drawn.

24. See Hackforth, *Plato's Phaedrus* 8, Guthrie, *History* IV, 297. Lysias returned from Thurii, to Athens in 412–411; Polemarchus, his brother, who was put to death in 404, is spoken of as still alive.

25. Cf. K. J. Dover, 'The date of Plato's *Symposium*', *Phronesis* 10 (1965) 7, n. 15. The relevant inscriptions are *SEG* XIII.13, 188, 17, 110; cf. B. D. Merritt, 'Greek inscriptions (14–27)', *Hesperia* 8 (1939) 69ff., J. Hatzfeld, 'Du nouveau sur Phèdre', *REA* 41 (1939) 311ff. Dover points out that Hackforth ought to have known this information.

26. Cf. L. Robin, *Platon: Phèdre* (Paris 1939), who calls the scene 'en dehors de toute histoire'.

27. Socrates links the Lysias speech and his own first speech very closely together; note the dual forms at 242E–243A.

28. On this view of prophecy and its religious background, see Dodds, *GI* Ch. 2, and Guthrie, *History* IV, 417 and n. 2, who argues that the *Phaedrus* marks an important change in Plato's view.

29. It should be noticed that '*philos*' and '*philia*', not prominent love words in the middle dialogues, here attain new importance, in keeping with the dialogue's Aristotelian emphasis on mutuality and on attachment to character (see Ch. 13). The dialogue begins with '*Ō phile Phaidre*'; its mid-point is marked by '*Ō phile Erōs*' (257A); its final prayer begins, '*Ō phile Pan*'; and its next to last line is the proverbial '*koina ta tōn philōn*' (cf. this ch. p. 233). See Clay, 'Socrates' prayer'.

30. See Ch. 5, with references.

31. See the good discussion by Groag, 'Zur Lehre' 208–9. Guthrie, *History* IV, 422ff. seems wrong to dismiss his arguments.

32. Aristotle makes a related criticism of Plato's ideal state in *Politics* II: by removing the family, it weakens and makes 'watery' all human ties – cf. Ch. 12. In the myth of the cicadas that follows his second speech, Socrates emphasizes the danger that the discovery of an art – including the 'art' of philosophy – might make the artist forgetful of necessary food and drink, even to the point of death (259B–C).

33. These points receive illuminating discussion, with reference to this dialogue, in I. Murdoch's *The Sovereignty of Good* (London 1970) 59–60, 84–6; unfortunately, her more recent *The Fire and the Sun* (Oxford 1977), a book devoted to Plato's views of art and beauty, does not seem to add much to these remarks; see my review in *Phil Lit* 2 (1977–8).

34. The imagery of this passage (including the important imagery of plant growth) is given an excellent discussion in A. Lebeck's 'The central myth of Plato's *Phaedrus*', *Greek, Roman, and Byzantine Studies* 13 (1972) 267–90. The fact that the two most illuminating articles that I newly discovered in the course of my most recent revision (Groag and Lebeck) were both written by people who died before the age of 35 makes their comments on the fragile plant-like nature of intellectual aspiration especially poignant. I should like to record here my sense of loss.

35. Though this is nowhere explicitly stated, it can be inferred by the transitivity of similarity; cf. my remarks in Ch. 6 on Socrates' prayer to the sun at Potidaea.

36. Cf. Lebeck, 'Central myth' 251–2. On the significance of the imagery of hunting and trapping, cf. Detienne and Vernant, *Mètis*, on which cf. Ch. 1, pp. 18–21. Plato returns to the mythology of crafty practical intelligence in the *Sophist*, where he depicts

the struggle between the materialists and the 'Lovers of the Forms' as a Gigantomachia (battle between Titans and Olympians), in which each side struggles to control the universe by denying being to some part of it. The form-lovers, probably Platonists, stand in for the Olympians of the traditional story, who fight against the gross physical force of the giants using the stratagems of *mētis* and *technē*. In this case, their crafty device is to 'force certain intelligible and bodiless forms to be true being'; and 'breaking up the opponents' bodies and the truth as they describe it into little pieces, they call it a moving process of becoming instead of being' (246B–C). The project of getting bodiless forms to be true being involves a violent assault on being, or that part of it that is mutable, fragile, tangible. The Stranger is critical of the stratagems of both sides, in that they force being to be narrower than it is, apparently for reasons of power and control. The materialists deny what they cannot manipulate; the form-lovers take a more clever line, seeing that body can be broken into pieces and that another sort of true being could hide from the enemy's eyes as well as his grasp. Criticizing these repudiations, the Stranger later proposes a new criterion of true being: the power to affect something or to be affected 'in however small a degree, by the most insignificant agent, though it be only once' (247E). This shift has implications, clearly, for the status of unique complex mortal individuals, compounds of soul and body. It is important, however, that the form-lovers' commitment to intelligence and to argument leaves them open to the Stranger's persuasion in a way that the materialists, disdaining argument, are not. The *Republic*'s love of the truth, we might say, leads directly to the *Phaedrus*'s recantation.

37. Plato here rejects the famous dictum of Heraclitus that the wisest and best soul is a dry beam of light, and, with it, the associated condemnation of the 'wetness' of passion. See the excellent discussion of Heraclitus B118 in C. H. Kahn, *The Art and Thought of Heraclitus* (Cambridge 1979) 245–54, who shows that 'this conception is deeply rooted both in the language of early Greek poetry and in the theories of pre-Socratic philosophy' (247).

38. Cf. Lebeck, 'Central myth' 255.

39. Contrast the imagery of trapping in the *Symposium* – cf. 203D and n. 36 above. On separateness and uniqueness and the aspiration to control them, see Ch. 4; cf. also Vernant and Detienne, *Mètis, passim*. I have discussed some of these issues further in Nussbaum, 'Crystals'.

40. See G. E. L. Owen, 'The place of the *Timaeus* in Plato's dialogues' in *Studies in Plato's Metaphysics*, ed. R. E. Allen (London 1965) 329–36. This is not Owen's only piece of evidence for a rejection, in the *Sts.*, of major tenets of the *Rep.–Tim.* view.

41. This point is recognized by T. Gould, *Platonic Love* (London 1963) 120. See also Vlastos, 'Sex in Platonic love', Appendix II to 'The individual as object of love in Plato', in Vlastos, *PS* 38–44.

42. Cf. my earlier essay on this dialogue in *Plato on Beauty, Wisdom and the Arts*, ed. J. M. E. Moravcsik and P. Temko, APQ Library of Philosophy (Totowa, N.J. 1982) 79–124. The issues are well discussed in Groag's article, which I did not know when I published my earlier discussion. I disagree with him, however, as will be seen, on some important points. The essay includes discussion of relevant parallels in *Parmenides* and *Philebus* and a general discussion of the anthropocentrism of the Method of Division.

43. Cf. Groag, 'Zur Lehre' 209, who argues well that this remains an ongoing possibility even for the best human souls.

44. In the *Phaedo*, the soul seems to be identical with the intellectual element. Desires and

appetites are part of body. Only the non-composite is stable and enduring (78c). Although *Republic* IV speaks of a tripartite soul, including desires and emotions as parts of soul, *Rep.* IX indicates that the three parts are an artificial 'composite' only contingently held together by the bodily 'envelope'; in reality, the really human part is only one element, the intellectual (58Dff.); so it is not clear that all three will be equally parts of the soul as distinct from body. *Rep.* x, by denying immortality to the composite (611B), seems to indicate that the whole soul, construed as a composite, is not immortal. The 'soul in its truest nature', the immortal soul, may be only the 'little human being' of Book IX, i.e. the intellectual element. These obscurities are clarified if we turn to the *Timaeus*, where we are explicitly told that the 'mortal form of soul' – that is, whatever is not intellect – gets 'built on' to the intellect at the time of incarnation (69c). This picture, consistent with everything that is said in the *Republic*, brings the two dialogues very close to the *Phaedo*; the remaining differences are trivial and verbal. On all these points, see W. K. C. Guthrie, 'Plato's views on the nature of the soul', in Vlastos, *Plato* II, 230–43, and Guthrie, *History* IV, 422ff. Although Guthrie convincingly argues for the essential sameness of *Rep.–Tim.–Phd.* on this issue, he is unconvincing when he dismisses the conflict between all of these and the *Phaedrus*, cf. Groag, *op. cit.* These points are recognized by I. M. Crombie, *An Examination of Plato's Doctrines* I (London 1962) 371ff., who, however, too quickly says that the differences don't really make much difference.

45. Cf. esp. *Laws* x.896c–D.
46. Cf. Guthrie, 'Plato's views'. Similarities to later dialogues are well discussed in Robin, *La Théorie, loc. cit.*
47. On questions of self-knowledge in the dialogue, see C. Griswold, 'Self-knowledge and the "*idea*" of the soul in Plato's *Phaedrus*', *Revue de Métaphysique et de Morale* 26 (1981) 472–94. Lebeck, 'Central myth' 281 points out that Socrates, who says he has leisure only for self-inquiry, still says he has leisure for conversation with Phaedrus (229B, 228A); this indicates that he views his conversation as a contribution to his self-understanding.
48. See also Lebeck, *op. cit.* 280–3.
49. As Lebeck, *op. cit.* notes, Socrates' description of his own transport at 234D5 has precise verbal parallels with his later account of the lovers' experience: *sunebakcheusa* 234D5 ‖ 253A6–7; *ekplagēnai* D1–2 ‖ 250A6; *epathon* D2 ‖ 250A7. Note that the parallels stress the receptive aspects of the experience. The new emphasis on mutuality is prefigured in Phaedrus's 'equal' teasing of Socrates, and in the wrestling metaphor of 236B.
50. On chronology, see above n. 5 and Ch. 5 n. 21. The criticisms of poetry in Book x have frequently been studied – most recently in the collection, ed. Moravcsik and Temko, *Plato on Beauty, Wisdom, and the Arts*, where an earlier version of this chapter first appeared. The arguments of *Republic* x are treated in the papers there by Annas, Moravcsik, Nehamas, Urmson, and Woodruff; see these also for further references. (I am indebted to all of these people for their questions and discussion at the original conference.) The Book x criticism of the poets has been connected with peculiarities in that book's treatment of the theory of forms by C. Griswold in an ingenious and stimulating article, 'The Ideas and the criticism of poetry in Plato's *Republic*, Book 10', *JHP* 19 (1981) 135–50.
51. A further problem with the representation of certain emotions is, Plato believes, that they are thoroughly based on false belief (cf. this ch. p. 230 on grief, Ch. 5 on grief

and love, Ch. 6 on love). Characters who see the world correctly will not feel them at all; thus a drama filled with good characters would lack them. I have discussed these and related issues (together with an account of Proust's criticism of Plato in Nussbaum, 'Fictions'. On all of this, see Interlude 2.

52. Cf. Interlude 1 and references. The *Phaedrus*'s relation to its own remarks on writing is discussed by many writers, including C. Griswold, 'Style and philosophy: the case of Plato's dialogues', *The Monist* 63 (1980) 530–56. See also R. Burger, *Plato's Phaedrus* (Birmingham 1980); H. Sinaiko, *Love, Knowledge, and Discourse* (Chicago 1965); J. Derrida, 'La pharmacie de Platon', *Tel Quel* 32, 33 (1968), repr. in *La Dissémination* (Paris 1972) 69–197.

53. W. H. Thomson, commentary (1868), *ad loc.* In the margin of the copy that I was reading in the library of the Classics Faculty at Cambridge University, someone had pencilled, 'Is rape harmless?'

54. The *mousikos* may be a poet or a composer of music; usually these occupations would be combined. '*Mousikē*' is the generic term Plato uses for the poetic-musical education received by young citizens (cf. *Rep.* II–III *passim*; 521B, 522A–B). It corresponds, as training for the soul, to *gumnastikē* as training for the body. It is, however, unlikely that we are to understand '*mousikos*' here in a more general sense of 'cultivated', 'trained', and therefore to count as *mousikos* anyone who has received a decent early training. The proper connection between the philosopher and the Muses is explicitly developed and stressed in the rest of the dialogue (cf. this ch., pp. 220–7), where it emerges that the genuine *mousikos* would not be just any well-brought-up person, but only someone whose life is devoted to the new form of philosophical art, which serves Calliope and Urania together. The contrast between the mere *poiētēs* (who is certainly well trained in the ordinary sense) and the *mousikos* seems to depend upon this point. In the *Phaedo* (60E), Socrates' dream that he is being commanded to practice and make *mousikē* never even suggests to him the interpretation that he is being commanded to practice being (as of course he, with his fellow citizens, is) a normally trained and acculturated person. It suggests to him only two possibilities: that he should go on doing philosophy (which, at first, he takes to be the 'greatest *mousikē*'); and, when that interpretation is rejected as insufficient, that he should become a poet and put stories into poetic language (61B). What the *Phaedrus* now shows is that the two interpretations, each properly construed, fall together: to practice philosophy well is indeed the highest form of *mousikē*; but its proper practice involves the use of myths, likenesses, and poetic speech.

55. Compare *Rep.* IX, 581Eff., and *Phd.* 64cff. It is never suggested, in the middle dialogues, that poetry is anything but a very early stage in the future philosopher's education, to be given up for the hypothetical method of dialectic and its pure, non-sensuous deductions (cf. the criticism of the mathematicians for their use of sensible likenesses). The *Phaedo*, like *Rep.* X, expresses uneasiness about this dismissal of the poet. Socrates (n. 54 above) worries that he should after all practice the *mousikē* that he has deposed. His reference to a need to satisfy a religious demand for purification by returning to poetry (*aphosioumenos*, 60) is echoed, probably deliberately, in the *Phaedrus* recantation scene, as is the remark that the fulfillment of the dream's command requires the making of *muthoi*, not just *logoi* (60D–61C). But it seems likely that the Phaedrus's 'mad' poetry is a more satisfactory answer to the dream than the *Phaedo* Socrates' project of putting Aesop's fables into verse.

56. See Lebeck's ('Central myth') last beautiful paragraph (also, I believe, her last published work).

57. See Hackforth, *Plato's Phaedrus* 99 n. 2; Wilamowitz, *Platon* 1, 537 regards the allusion as established beyond reasonable doubt.

58. This highly complex epigram plays both on the fact that the boy's name means 'Star' and also on the fact that morning and evening star are one and the same, but have different names; and all of this in two lines. (Those who are fond of saying that Plato was too naïve to think about the distinction between sense and reference should consider these lines.)

59. On Dion's influence, see Guthrie, *History* IV, 20; on the connection between the *Phaedrus* and the second visit to Syracuse, see Ryle, *Plato's Progress*, Robin, *Phèdre*, and Hackforth, *Plato's Phaedrus*. Ryle's argument is based on the claim that the dialogue contains references to buildings and landmarks that could only be seen at Olympia; we know that Plato stopped at Olympia on his return journey from Syracuse. Ryle argues that the *Phaedrus* was written up for a public 'performance' on that occasion, and that it was actually the young Aristotle who played the role of Phaedrus. I do not find all of this convincing; and I am not in a position to assess the archaeological claims, comparing them with the recent work that has been done on the Athenian setting (cf. n. 4). But there seems to be no reason to deny a close connection with the second visit; and we can see the hand of Aristotle in the dialogue's changed views, whether we think of him as an actor or not. I am not clear about the chronological relationship with the *Theaetetus*; but we should beware of hastily assuming that the latter work was written up *immediately* after Theaetetus's death. If Plato wanted to write a work that would commemorate the career of that great mathematician in a truly fitting way, it might have taken him some time.

60. Cf. Lebeck, 'Central myth' 278–9, 281; and cf. n. 49.

61. I am grateful to Harvey Yunis for discussion on this point and for allowing me to read a paper he wrote about my interpretation of the *Symposium*, which strikingly paralleled some of my conclusions concerning the *Phaedrus*, of which he was ignorant.

62. The prayer has been discussed in Clay, 'Socrates' prayer', and in T. G. Rosenmeyer, 'Plato's prayer to Pan', *Hermes* 90 (1962) 34–44, both of whom stress the connection with the *Cratylus* etymology and with its claim that Pan is the son of Hermes. Both see the prayer as (at least in part) about the nature of speeches.

63. This includes, of course, the question of the truthfulness of speeches – and so this dialogue points forward to the *Sophist*, which probably follows it immediately in the sequence of composition.

64. This chapter, like Ch. 5, has been read in many places and has profited from the suggestions of many people. I am, first of all, indebted to the seriousness and the critical spirit of graduate students in my Plato courses in 1980 and 1982, especially Alexander George, Miriam Solomon, and Douglas Winblad in 1980, Elizabeth Anderson and Thomas Gillespie in 1982 – all of whom wrote impressive papers on this dialogue; I am grateful to Alexander George for written comments on two separate drafts. I have also learned a great deal from audiences at: the Plato conference in Bodega Bay (cf. n. 50), the University of Texas at Austin, Vassar College, the University of California at Berkeley, the University of North Carolina at Chapel Hill, King's College (London), St John's College, Annapolis, Maryland, Mount Holyoke College, Bryn Mawr College, and the Division for Philosophical Approaches to Literature at the

Modern Language Association meetings, 1982. I am especially grateful for the helpful questions and the illuminating conversation of: Richard Bernstein, Eva Brann, Myles Burnyeat, Stanley Cavell, Arnold Davidson, Ray Gaita, Maud Gleason, Charles Griswold, Charles Kahn, Barry C. Mazur, Julius Moravcsik, Michael Nagler, Hilary Putnam, Gail Ann Rickert, Thomas Rosenmeyer, Peter M. Smith, Peter Winch, Paul Woodruff, and Harvey Yunis. To Richard Sorabji and Gregory Vlastos I owe special thanks for their detailed written criticisms of an earlier draft.

8   Saving Aristotle's appearances

1. I follow W. D. Ross's rendering of *epi tois allois*. Although the word 'all' is not explicitly present, I agree with Ross that this is the force of the unqualified *tois allois*; it certainly cannot mean 'in some other cases'. *APr* 46a17–22 makes explicit the crucial role of the *phainomena* (there used interchangeably with *empeiria*, 'experience') in providing the starting-point for 'any art (*technē*) and understanding (*epistēmē*) whatever'. On *endoxa*, cf. *Top.* 100b21.

2. See the account of a related argument in Ch. 4 p. 115. This chapter will argue that Aristotle's reply is not the conservative reaction that we imagined there.

3. W. D. Ross, trans. *Ethica Nicomachea*, *The Works of Aristotle* (Oxford 1915) IX.

4. Owen, '*Tithenai*' 83–103; reprinted in Barnes, *Articles* I, and in J. M. E. Moravcsik, ed., *Aristotle* (Garden City, NY 1967).

5. 'And about all these things we must try to seek conviction through argument, using the appearances as our witnesses and standards (*paradeigmasi*). For it is best that all human beings should be seen to be in agreement (*phainesthai sunomologountas*) with what we shall say, but, if not, that all should in a way. This they will do if they are led to change their ground; for each person has something of his own to contribute towards the truth, and it is starting from these that we must give a sort of proof about them' (*EE* 1216a26–32).

6. See H. Boeder, 'Der frühgriechische Wortgebrauch von *Logos* und *Alētheia*', *Archiv für Begriffsgeschichte* 4 (1959) 82–112; T. Krischer, '*Etymos* und *alēthēs*', *Philologus* 109 (1965) 161–71.

7. On Parmenides' attack on 'convention' and one early answer, see my 'Eleatic conventionalism and Philolaus on the conditions of thought', *HSCP* 83 (1979) 63–108.

8. For only a few representative passages, see *Rep.* 476A, 598B, 602D; '*phainomena*' is significantly replaced by '*nomima*', 'conventional beliefs', at *Rep.* 479D.

9. For a contrast between the Aristotelian and the Platonic notions of the 'unhypothetical', see this ch. p. 255.

10. Owen, '*Tithenai*'; Owen considers and rejects, on the basis of the evidence, the suggestion that we should distinguish senses of '*phainomena*' in a way that corresponds to the distinction between '*phainesthai*' with the infinitive and with the particle (n. 4).

11. Owen, *op. cit.* even claims (86–7) that 'This ambiguity in *phainomena*... carries with it a corresponding distinction in the use of various connected expressions'. These turn out to include '*aporiai*' ('puzzles') and '*epagōgē*' (usually rendered 'induction'), two central terms in Aristotle's epistemology whose ambiguity, on this story, also remains concealed or unnoticed by him. This makes the cost of the interpretation even clearer. Owen does add (89–90) that the different uses or senses have a great deal in common; he even suggests that one common link is that both involve a reliance upon experience. But his conclusion from this is, nonetheless, that it is a mistake to press for any general

account of what *phainomena* are and what role they play. I suggest that we can offer such a univocal general account, and that this will in no way require us to disregard Owen's entirely correct observation that 'the function can vary with the content and the style of inquiry'.

12. For further discussion of the selective nature of Aristotelian perception, see 'The role of *phantasia* in Aristotle's explanation of action', Nussbaum, *De Motu* Essay 5, 221–69.

13. It has often been noted with alarm that the *Historia Animalium*, Aristotle's data-book, mentions beliefs and stories side by side with the records of field-work. Properly understood, this should not alarm us. Cf. also *Cael.* 303a22–3, where Aristotle criticizes a view on the grounds that it 'does away with many common beliefs (*endoxa*) and many perceptual appearances (*phainomena kata tēn aisthēsin*)' – apparently two subdivisions of the *phainomena*, broadly construed.

14. Cf. *Top.* 100b21, 104a8–12.

15. There is still a difference in the way in which ethics is anthropocentric and the way in which the sciences rest upon human experience: for this difference, see Ch. 10.

16. The main purpose of this immediate context is to contrast human beings with other animals; the human being is said to be the only *zōion* with understanding of ethical distinctions. However, divine beings are sometimes recognized as *zōia* in Aristotle's terminology; most certainly they are *empsucha*, living creatures; and the subsequent passage explicitly contrasts human beings with both bestial and divine creatures.

17. Heraclitus B35: 'They would not have known the name of justice if these things [sc. – according to Clement – experiences of injustice] did not exist.'

18. There is a valuable discussion of this and other points concerning the relationship of Aristotle to Hellenistic skepticism in A. A. Long, 'Aristotle and the history of Greek skepticism', in D. J. O'Meara, ed., *Studies in Aristotle* (Washington, D.C. 1981) 79–106.

19. Contrast *Cael.* 270b5, where arguments and *phainomena* are seen to support one another. *Top.* 104a8ff., insists that the views of 'the wise' will be entertained only so long as they do not contradict 'the opinions of most people'. Presumably this would not prevent the scientist from attempting to show that an apparently appearance-violating theory really did 'save' basic appearances better than any other (cf. this ch. p. 258).

20. The fact that both of these passages occur in ethical contexts may be significant. In science we are likely to be forced to revise radically some pre-theoretical beliefs; and yet even here Aristotle would insist that the theory must return to and account for our original experiences. Cf. also *EE* 1216b26–35.

21. The whole context indicates that the issue here is probably not the Cartesian question of distinguishing dream-states from real, but rather the question whether a waking person regards his (previous) dream experiences as having equal weight with his waking experience.

22. The Aristotelian method does not provide for the situation in which there is a deep-rooted disagreement as to who is the expert and what procedures make for expertise. For example, the situation in Greek medicine shortly after Aristotle's time was one in which three competing schools, each with quite different ideas about the relative importance of general theory and observed evidence, competed for the allegiance of the public; here there is no ready answer to Aristotle's demand for the adjudication of competing appearances. But in such a case the Aristotelian has one further move to make. He can produce some specification of the end of the science that will be acceptable to all parties, and then ask us to consider how each of the competing experts delivers the value in question. In this case, he could attempt to

characterize health in a way acceptable to all the competing schools, and to the layman as well – this would of necessity be a thinner and more general characterization of health than the ones operative within each of the different schools – and then ask the prospective patient to trust the expert that seemed to have the most felicitous relationship to that goal.

23. Some related points receive an interesting discussion in R. Bolton, 'Essentialism and semantic theory in Aristotle', *PR* 85 (1976) 514–55; Bolton's account of this passage is convincingly criticized by T. H. Irwin, in 'Aristotle's concept of signification', in M. Schofield and M. Nussbaum, eds., *Language and Logos* (Cambridge 1982) Ch. 12. The passage is discussed in connection with the Putnam/Kripke account of the meaning of natural-kind terms by D. Wiggins, *Sameness and Substance* (Oxford 1980) Ch. 3.

24. On this point, see Wiggins, *op. cit.*, Ch. 3.

25. It is yet another problem, of course, to relate this norm to the practice of Aristotle's scientific treatises, where deductions of this sort are very rarely present. This discrepancy may indicate only that Aristotle does not believe he is ready to claim full *epistēmē*; on the other hand, it is plausible, as I argue in Nussbaum, *De Motu*, Essay 2, that the evidence uncovered in actual scientific work led Aristotle to make some revisions in his methodological norms, especially with regard to the autonomy of the sciences.

26. On differences between science and ethics, see further this ch. pp. 257–8, and Ch. 10.

27. A. Kosman, 'Explanation and understanding in Aristotle's *Posterior Analytics*', in Lee, *Exegesis* 374–92; J. Lesher, 'The role of *nous* in Aristotle's *Posterior Analytics*', *Phronesis* 18 (1973) 44–68; M. F. Burnyeat, 'Aristotle on understanding knowledge', in E. Berti, ed., *Aristotle on Science: the 'Posterior Analytics'* (Padua 1981). The standard interpretation is defended by T. H. Irwin, 'Aristotle's discovery of metaphysics', *RM* 31 (1977) 210–29; Irwin's position has been ably criticized in an unpublished paper by Thomas Upton, read to the Western Division of the American Philosophical Association, April 1983. See also the helpful related account of Aristotelian *epagōgē* in T. Engberg-Pederson, 'More on Aristotelian epagoge', *Phronesis* 24 (1979) 301–19.

28. Burnyeat, *op. cit.*

29. Burnyeat, *op. cit.*, argues this convincingly; this forms part of his case that *epistēmē* is understanding, rather than knowledge.

30. *Apaideusia* is straightforwardly associated with *paideia* (as its privative) in both pre-Aristotelian and other Aristotelian passages. It usually designates the absence of some sort of social and interpersonal awareness; sometimes the word is interchangeable with words meaning 'simple' or 'naive'; but sometimes, in association with words meaning 'boorish' or 'rude', it denotes a more active refusal of custom. Democritus, in what may be the earliest attestation of the word, says that people who sleep excessively in the daytime give evidence either of bodily illness 'or of either torment or idleness or *apaideusia* of soul' (B212); here *apaideusia* is presumably some sort of refusal of ordinary social usage. In Thucydides (III.42), Diodotus cites *apaideusia* as a cause of over-hasty deliberation; it is the state of character that leads to an avoidance of careful moral thought. In Plato, *apaideusia* is most frequently associated with failings of moral character, especially with the presence of untrained appetites; but the word is also used in connection with other failures of agreement (e.g. *Gorg.* 523E), deficiency in civic training (e.g. *Alc.* I, 123D7), with a childishly fearful attitude to death (*Phd.* 90E–91A). Perhaps most interesting for our purposes is the *Theaetetus*'s contrast

between the true philosopher and the person who is lacking in self-awareness and in reflective grasp of his community's conceptions of value. This person, charged with *apaideusia* at 175A, will, when subjected to elenctic questioning, appear laughable in his combination of boastfulness and confusion – not to other *apaideutoi* (175D), 'for they don't notice, but to all those who were raised in the opposite manner from slaves'. Being *apaideutos* is, then, associated with being underdeveloped, crude, slavish, lacking in a finely tuned sense of the important things. Socrates' final description of this person is worth quoting for the light it sheds on what I claim to be the anthropocentric and communal nature of Aristotle's argument. The *apaideutos*, clever though he may be in certain ways, is someone who 'doesn't know how to strike up a song skillfully, in the manner of a free-born man, or how to take up the harmony of discourse and rightly sing the praises of the lives of gods and of men who live well' (175E–176A). The same could be said of Aristotle's opponent.

Aristotle's own usage bears out the idea that *apaideusia* is a lack of some sort of human experience and acculturation. For example: the newly wealthy person is called '*apaideutos*' because of his deficient personal experience (*Rhet.* 1391a17); for a young man to make generalizations about matters concerning which he has no personal experience is 'simple and *apaideutos*', something done by 'rustics' (*Rhet.* 1395a6); in the *EN*, the *apaideutoi* are the people who laugh at crude, dirty jokes in the theater, whereas people with *paideia* are said to prefer subtle suggestion (1128a20ff.); the tendency of some speech-writers to claim for their skill the status of political *technē* is explained by saying, 'Sometimes this happens through *apaideusia*, sometimes through boastfulness, sometimes through other human failings' (*Rhet.* 1356a29; cf. *EE* 1217a8, to be discussed later); cf. also *PA* 636a1ff. At *Metaph.* 1005b3 Aristotle does indeed speak of logical *apaideusia: apaidusia tōn analutikōn*. But this in no way tends to undermine our claim that *apaideusia* means 'lack of training through experience', 'lack of acculturation'. As we have remarked, it appears that *nous* or understanding is gained, concerning basic principles, precisely through experience and habituation. In fact, we could say that that interpretation of *nous* is further supported by Aristotle's use, in this connection, of a word that everywhere else refers to experiential, and not *a priori*, knowledge.

31. In fact, Aristotle claims that he can handle the opponent even if he says just a single word, so long as he gives it some definite sense; the argument is complex, and it would take a detailed analysis to show whether he succeeds in this enterprise. I therefore confine myself to a more cautious statement of what is to be shown.

32. Cf. J. Annas, 'Truth and knowledge', in M. Schofield *et al.*, eds., *Doubt and Dogmatism* (Oxford 1980) 84–104. Long, 'Aristotle and the history', assimilates Aristotle's reply to that of the Stoics, claiming (wrongly, in my view) that he means to provide the demanded certainty by developing a foundationalist theory of knowledge based on perception. (Long has told me in correspondence that he no longer maintains this.) Irwin ('Aristotle's discovery') advances very briefly an account of elenctic demonstration that seems to be somewhat closer to the one being developed here, although there would, I believe, be important differences; and Irwin links it in quite different ways with other features of Aristotle's scientific method.

33. Cf. M. Burnyeat, 'Can the skeptic live his skepticism?', in Schofield *et al.*, *Doubt and Dogmatism* 20–53. Aristotle would need to say more in order for his reply to be successful against later Greek skepticism: and this for two reasons. First, the Greek skeptic does not present himself as seeking an external justification for beliefs. He is

seeking freedom from disturbance; and he wishes to attain this happy condition by suspending belief. The equal force of opposing beliefs achieves, for him, this effect. He never moves outside the 'circle' of belief; but by allowing the opposing beliefs to knock one another out he achieves security within this circle; he is in it and not of it. In this way he appears to be different from most modern skeptics; and also from the opponent whom Aristotle has in view. Secondly, Aristotle's argument about action was anticipated in later Greek skepticism, and an answer was made: we *can* act without belief, because (like animals) we follow along with the way things appear, without committing ourselves in any way to the *truth* of appearances. In other words, we might say: there is something between the vegetable and the typical human, namely the animal. Aristotle could, I think, successfully reply to the skeptic on both of these points, showing that a life without belief is insufficient to sustain the skeptic's own practices of searching and arguing (see Burnyeat, *op. cit.*). That he does not do so is explained by the nature of his (earlier and less developed) opposition.

34. A valuable discussion of the different varieties of the *a priori*, and a defense of a position closely related to Aristotle's, is in H. Putnam, 'There is at least one a priori truth', *Erkenntnis* 13 (1978) 153–70.

35. Aristotle's actual example is not entirely appropriate, since the blind man would, presumably, be able to refer to colors because color-words are part of his language, even if they enter the language on the basis of others' experience, and not his own.

36. At *Metaph.* 1040b34–1041a3, Aristotle may be conceding to the skeptic the possibility that there might be something 'out there' to which our language has no access. He concludes his attack on the Platonic separated forms with the following qualification: 'And yet, even if we had not seen the stars, nonetheless, I think, there would have been eternal substances over and above the ones of which we were aware.' We are aware of ourselves as finite, of our understanding as limited. Thus within the appearances resides the view that the appearances are imperfect. So in this way we cannot get rid altogether of the possibility that there *are* some entities out there that do not figure in our experience. But Aristotle firmly insists that this does not make the Platonic view *true* or Platonic referring successful. What is outside of our limits cannot enter our discourse.

37. On some of these points, see Nussbaum, *De Motu*, Essay 2, esp. 133–8. The idea of an 'internal realism' has been most perspicuously developed, in recent philosophical writing, in the work of H. Putnam: especially in *Reason, Truth, and History* (Cambridge 1981).

38. We should remember that Aristotle's final answer to the problem of *akrasia* is not simply a list of popular truisms, but a complex and controversial account that is *argued* to be the best way of preserving the most important appearances on the subject.

39. Cf. also B2: 'Although the discourse is shared, most people live as if they had a private understanding.' A position similar to Aristotle's concerning the connection of language with species-experience is suggested in B35 and 102.

40. I discuss this passage in Nussbaum, *De Motu*, Essay 1, 98–9, and in 'Aristotle', in *Ancient Writers*, ed. T. J. Luce (New York 1982) 377–8; but it seems worth mentioning again.

41. *EN* 1109a24–6: though the context is ethical, the remark is explicitly extended to the difficulty of ascertaining the 'mean' in all inquiries.

42. *On the Good*, fr. 1 Ross, from *Vita Aristotelis Marciana*, p. 433, 10–15 (Rose).

43. I would like to thank audiences at Stanford University, the University of Massachusetts at Amherst, the University of Wisconsin, and the University of Vermont for discussion

that contributed to the revisions of this chapter. I am also grateful to the many people who have generously helped me with comments on earlier versions: especially Julia Annas, Myles Burnyeat, John Carriero, Roderick Firth, Randall Havas, Geoffrey Lloyd, Julius Moravcsik, Edward Minar, Hilary Putnam, Israel Scheffler, Malcolm Schofield, Gregory Vlastos, and David Wiggins. My gratitude to the late G. E. L. Owen is fundamental. Concerning the delicate and difficult philosophical enterprise I have described here, Aristotle once remarked, 'To do it well is something rare and praised and noble'. We see this in Gwil Owen's work. I dedicated this chapter to him when *Language and Logos* was presented to him on the occasion of his sixtieth birthday. Less than two months later he died of a heart attack. During our last philosophical conversation, a month before his death, we discussed this chapter and he made suggestions for which I am grateful. I would like to dedicate this chapter to his memory.

9   Rational animals and the explanation of action

1. This chapter is closely related to my paper, 'The "common explanation" of animal movement', published in the Proceedings of the Ninth Symposium Aristotelicum, ed. P. Moraux (Berlin 1983). It differs from that paper in several ways: (1) the published paper contains lengthier discussions of the *De Motu* account of 'involuntary' and 'non-voluntary' motions in Ch. 11; and of the issues involved in individuating voluntary and involuntary actions. (2) The published paper was part of a Symposium addressing the issue of the authenticity of dubious Aristotelian works; it therefore contained a brief discussion of the current state of opinion on the authenticity of *De Motu*. (3) This chapter contains a lengthier discussion of the ethical implications of the account of action.

2. Cf. Ch. 11 for comment on this issue.

3. See also Nussbaum, *De Motu*. I now believe that it would be best to translate '*aitia*' as 'explanation' rather than as 'reason' here, for the obvious reason that reason-giving *aitiai* are only one species of *aitia*. The whole issue of the translation of *aitia* and *aition* has been well discussed by M. Frede, 'The original notion of cause', in *Doubt and Dogmatism*, ed. M. Schofield *et al.* (Oxford 1980) 217–49. In discussion at the Symposium, M. Burnyeat pointed out that the *De Motu*'s initial question can have two different interpretations. It could be, as I read it, a request for a general account that will explain any particular occurrence of animal movement, no matter of what sort; or it could be a request for an account of why animals are moving creatures at all, what the point of self-movement is in an animal's life. I think it is clear that *De Motu*, Chs. 6–10, with which we shall be concerned here, focus on the first question; this is particularly evident from the opening of Ch. 7. Since self-movement is, for Aristotle, an essential attribute of most animal kinds and has eternally been so, the second question cannot be a request for an efficient causal account of how that capacity came to be in the animal; if it is a legitimate question, it must be construed as a request for a functional account of the way movement fits with other aspects of the animal's characteristic life. (Compare the functional account of perception in *De Anima* III.12.) So construed, its answer would have much in common with the answer to the first question: we would mention the need of the animal for objects that lie at a distance, its perception of those objects through senses that work at a distance, etc.

4. *DA* II.3, 414b25–8. The translation is controversial, but I believe that it can be shown to be the best.

5. Anthony Kenny, in his essay on the style of the disputed works discussed at the

Symposium (above n. 1, in the volume of Proceedings), notes only one statistical peculiarity of the language of the *De Motu: alla*, 'but', occurs unusually rarely. This gives me another way of putting my question about Aristotle's procedure: why does he choose to write here in such a way as to say 'but' (draw contrasts) so rarely? (This sort of question makes us begin to realize how few words used by a thinker are truly content-neutral.)

6. It used to be possible to avoid these questions by denying the authenticity of the *De Motu*. On this debate, see Nussbaum, *De Motu* 3–12. The authenticity of the treatise is now generally accepted; indeed, it was the absence of anyone wishing to impugn it that gave me the opportunity to address the Symposium on this philosophical topic rather than on the topic of authenticity. And even if someone were to reopen the debate, the same difficulties arise, as well, for the interpreter of *De Anima* III.9–11. The *De Anima* discussion refers to the related material in *De Motu* at 433b21–30; see the discussion in my book, p. 9, with cross-references and bibliography.

7. Homer, *Iliad* XII.299–306 (trans. Nussbaum); Sophocles, *Philoctetes* 161–8 (trans. Nussbaum); Thuc. II.42.3–4 (trans. Crawley, with the adoption of a suggestion by A. L. Edmunds, *Chance and Intelligence in Thucydides* (Cambridge, MA 1975) 217–35).

8. It is also worth noting that in each case the explanation has, at least implicitly, the structure that (in Essay 4 of my book) I called 'anankastic': it presents the desired goal, and cites beliefs about not just what *can* be done to realize it, but what (given the possibilities) *must* be done in order to realize it. The lion's determination is explained by the fact that failure here would mean 'turning back empty'. Philoctetes' painful journey is (given the absence of human helpers) the only available means to the satisfaction of hunger. The soldiers' deliberation comes down to the conclusion that standing and fighting is what *must* be done if the goal (revenge) which they have already preferred to another goal (safety) is to be attained. On the connection between ordinary paradigms of explanation and a good philosophical account of explanation, see H. P. Grice, 'Method in philosophical psychology', *PAPA* 48 (1974–5) 23–53. This important paper is of interest in connection with many of the issues that I shall discuss here.

9. This material is presented in slightly fuller form in my Symposium paper (above n. 1).

10. *De Anima* 403b26–7, 403b29ff., 405b11, 31ff., 413a22–5, 413b12–13, 432a15ff.

11. Diogenes, DK 64 B4, 5; cf. also Archelaus, DK 60 A1, 4, cf. A17.

12. *DA* 405b21–5; cf. also, on Heraclitus's views, 405a5–7, 405b25–9.

13. *DA* 405a8–13, 406b15–22, 403b31–404a16.

14. Diogenes DK 64 B4; cf. also B5, A19, 20, 29.

15. Cf. Democritus DK 68 B9; Diogenes is said to have a similar view in 64 A27. In his ethical fragments (if, indeed, they are his – cf. n. 26 below), Democritus does use the ordinary language of belief and desire. But if his ethical thought is consistent with his atomism and his conventionalism about appearances, he would have to say that the real underlying explanation of movement is the one that speaks of the interactions of spherical atoms.

16. For example, *PA* 640b5ff., *Metaph.* 983b6ff.; cf. *Ph.* 193a9ff., 198a21ff.; *DA* 403a29ff., *Metaph.* 1035a7–9.

17. G. E. R. Lloyd has pointed out to me that Aristotle may have been aware of a more subtle and non-reductionistic form of materialism in the work of Hippocratic writers; if this were so, it could then seem odd that his objections to materialism do not take

account of these positions. I can agree with Lloyd that Aristotle shows knowledge of quite a few Hippocratic texts; this has been carefully and, for the most part, cogently argued in F. Poschenrieder, *Die naturwissenschaftlichen Schriften des Aristoteles in ihrem Verhältnis zu der hippocratischen Sammlung* (Bamberg 1887). But the demonstrated connections are all in anatomical and physiological contexts, not in contexts concerned with the explanation of action or goal-directed motion. They do not seem to be passages that show the Hippocratic authors' attitude towards the project of giving a material account of perception, thought, and desire. I would therefore be unwilling to infer that Aristotle was aware of their thought on those issues; thus it seems to me that we can still regard him as giving a fair account of the most prominent philosophical positions on animal motion known to him.

18. Diogenes DK 64 A29.
19. Grice, 'Method' provides a graphic illustration of the radical consequences of a materialist elimination of ordinary action-concepts for practice:

> Let me illustrate with a little fable. The very eminent and very dedicated neuro-physiologist speaks to his wife. 'My (for at least a little while longer) dear', he says, 'I have long thought of myself as an acute and well-informed interpreter of your actions and behaviour. I think I have been able to identify nearly every thought that has made you smile and nearly every desire that has moved you to act. My researches, however, have made such progress that I shall no longer need to understand you in this way. Instead I shall be in a position, with the aid of instruments which I shall attach to you, to assign to each bodily movement which you make in acting a specific antecedent condition in your cortex. No longer shall I need to concern myself with your so-called thoughts and feelings. In the meantime, perhaps you would have dinner with me tonight. I trust that you will not resist if I bring along some apparatus to help me to determine, as quickly as possible, the physiological idiosyncrasies which obtain in your system.'
>
> I have a feeling that the lady might refuse the proffered invitation. (p. 52, n. 4)

Grice uses this 'fable' to argue that a psychological theory that retains the ordinary notions of belief and desire 'contains the materials to justify its own entrenchment' (52). If I am right, this is a very Aristotelian thought.

20. Plato, *Phd.* 99B2–3.
21. Frede, 'Original notion' has pointed out that the *aition* is frequently that of which the *aitia* is the account. This passage does not always maintain this distinction with clarity. (For example, it is difficult to distinguish the function of '*aitia*' in 99A4 from that of '*aition*' in B3–4.) But in general Frede's is a helpful way of understanding the original motivation for keeping these two words in play.
22. It is actually not clear that Socrates should concede this much to the materialist. First, given the view of soul which he has been developing, it is not really true that correct judgment and virtuous action require a certain disposition of bodily parts (cf. esp. 115C6ff.). Secondly, even without a dualist view of soul, one might still wish to distinguish between the claim that *some* suitable matter must be present in order for these functions to take place, and the claim that these particular materials must be there. It is not entirely clear which of these Socrates actually concedes to the materialist here, but the latter thesis would be a bigger concession than even Aristotle would be willing to make, I believe.
23. In connection with assessing the changes that this view undergoes in the *Phaedrus*, it

would also be important to clarify the status of psychological explanation in *Laws* x, where many items that have no connection with intellect are included as 'motions of soul' and intellect is not given separate status as it is in middle-period works.

24. Cf. *EN* 1111b1–3. It is plain that in the *Phaedo* and *Republic* the 'real human being', the only part whose immortality is established, is the intellectual soul – cf. Chs. 5, 7.

25. Cf. Ch. 8. On '*phantasia*' as a similar case, see Essay 5 of Nussbaum, *De Motu*.

26. Democritus DK 68 B27, 219, 284. For a strong argument in favor of a post-Aristotelian redaction, see Z. Stewart, 'Democritus and the Cynics', *HSCP* 63 (1958) 179–91.

27. Plato, *Laws* 629C3, 661A1, 714A4, 757C7, 807C6; *Protag.* 326A3; *Rep.* 439B1, 485D4, 572A2; *Phd.* 65C9, 75A2, B1. (This transitive use occurs at *Phd.* 117B2.)

28. A good example of this is Plato, *Charmides* 16D–E, where *boulēsis* is directed at the good, *epithumia* at the pleasant.

29. Cf. LSJ s.v.; I have carefully examined each use of the word in Homer, Aeschylus, Sophocles, Euripides, Aristophanes, Herodotus, Thucydides, and Plato. There is an interesting discussion of the etymology of the word and its connection with an important group of Indo-European words in E. Benveniste, *Le Vocabulaire des institutions indo-européennes* II (Paris 1969); for our purposes, the most interesting of his conclusions is that the original semantic content of the word has to do with going forward or reaching forward in a straight line (as opposed to aslant, or by some indirect path).

30. Cf. for example, Thuc. II.61.1, III.42.6, IV.17.4, IV.21.2; Eur. *HF* 16, *Hel.* 1238, *Ion* 842, *Or.* 328; Plato, *Rep.* 439B1, 485D4, 572A2 (of which J. Adam, ed. *The Republic of Plato* (Cambridge 1902, repr. 1969) writes, '*Oregesthai* expresses the instinctive and unconscious turning of the soul towards the fountain of her being').

31. In Empedocles DK B129.4 no particular object is expressed; but 'the truth' or 'knowledge' is surely implicit.

32. *DA* 433a21–3, b1–4. On these three desire-words in Aristotle, see Nussbaum, *De Motu*, commentary on Ch. 6. *Boulēsis* seems to be desire for an object specified as the result of some sort of deliberation.

33. Cf. Ch. 5. Plants – the other non-self-sufficient members of Aristotle's universe – are not characterized as orectic. But this is presumably because for Aristotle the notion of *orexis* is conceptually bound up not only with need or lack, but also with awareness of that lack. The awareness of pleasure and pain is a sufficient condition of the ascription of *orexis* in *DA* III.11, 434a2–3; we suspect that it is also a necessary condition. Feeling a lack, wanting, perceiving objects in the world, moving from place to place – all these characteristics of the animal are so closely connected with one another, both causally or functionally and, as it seems, conceptually and logically, that Aristotle believes that the very presence of one of them cannot (except in the case of the 'stationary animals' who have touch alone) be understood or characterized without ascribing to the creature the others as well.

34. On the activity and selectivity of *phantasia* and its importance for Aristotle's account of action, see Essay 5 in my book. D. Todd, in his review of the book for *Phoenix* 34 (1980) 350–5, does additional work to show that Aristotelian *aisthēsis* is active and selective. I am not sure why he believes that this evidence tells against my reading of *phantasia*, since I go to some trouble to interpret Aristotle's remarks that *aisthēsis* and *phantasia* are 'one in number', arguing that *phantasia* is one function or aspect of the faculty of *aisthēsis*.

35. As I point out at greater length in the Symposium paper (above n. 1), there are a number

of deficiencies in the *De Anima* account. (1) Aristotle sometimes suggests that some *orexis* is involved in every movement, but sometimes speaks as if there are actions produced by reason winning out over *orexis*. (2) No real attempt is made to describe the way in which cognition and desire must interact to produce action. (3) We are told nothing about the relationship between the desire/cognition explanation and the physiological explanation. (4) We are not told *which* movements of the animal are explained with reference to desire and cognition: questions raised in *Physics* VIII remain unanswered. Cf. *Ph.* 253a7–19, 259b1–16. Both W. D. Ross, *Aristotle's Physics* (Oxford 1936) *ad loc.* and D. Furley, 'Self movers', in *Aristotle on Mind and the Senses*, ed. G. E. R. Lloyd and G. E. L. Owen (Cambridge 1978) 165–80 read these passages as implying a mechanical view of all animal motion, at least at the time when these passages were composed. In Essay 2 of my book I argued that Aristotle leaves it unclear here what his final view of movement from place to place will be; he says only that, at any rate, it is not a case of completely spontaneous self-movement. This is completely compatible with the *DA* and *MA* material, which emphasizes the moving role of the external object of desire. It is not necessary to understand the stronger claims about environmental influence as meant to apply to all cases of movement: the examples cited are all cases which Aristotle will go on, in *MA* 11, to treat as 'not *hekousioi*'.

36. For textual problems in this list, see my commentary *ad loc.*, and also my 'The text of Aristotle's *De Motu Animalium*', *HSCP* 80 (1976) 143–4. J. Barnes argues in favor of printing the full list of 'movers' (found in one manuscript sub-family) in his review in *CR* NS 30 1980, 222–6. I agree with Barnes that the full list is eventually required for the argument; but since the other members of the *b* family agree with the *a* family in having the shorter list, it is better to suppose that the shorter list is the original, and that a scribe made the additions, noting that they are required for the argument.

37. For a much more detailed discussion of each sentence of the text and of parallel passages, see my *De Motu* commentary.

38. On the use of '*noēsis*' here, see my commentary on 700b17 and 701a7, with references.

39. On the meaning of '*kritikon*', see my commentary on 700b20–1, with references; the most important parallel is *DA* 432a15ff., which uses the word as a generic term for thinking and perceiving, or rather for the common discriminatory function which these perform.

40. On these two functions of cognition, see my commentary on 701a7.

41. On the difficulty of determining whether *pathē* here are psychological or physiological, see my Essay 3 and commentary *ad loc.*

42. Cf. Frede, 'Original notion'. It is interesting to note that Aristotle uses the strongly causal *dia* + accusative at 701a37–b1, of the role of the desires in producing action; on the other hand, at 701a36 he uses *dia* + genitive (which frequently introduces an occasion or condition that is not a cause) of the relationship between perception and desire. This may suggest that perception is the *occasion* for the activation of desire (which is possibly ongoing). But Bonitz's examples of interchangeable genitive and accusative with *dia* warn against too heavy an emphasis on this distinction (*Index Aristotelicus*, Berlin 1870, s.v.).

43. Unfortunately, Aristotle does not tell us what sorts of impediments he has in mind – see Nussbaum, *De Motu* Essay 4, 191–3, for one worry about this. R. Sorabji, in *Necessity, Cause, and Blame* (London 1980) 239–40, has raised the important question whether this phrase is meant to include the possibility of rival desires.

44. It seems likely that the force of '*kuriōs*' is to indicate the victory of this desire over

all its rivals. Aristotle would then be saying that when one desire has decisively won out, and other conditions are met, then action is necessitated. This could be compatible with Sorabji's insistence that there can be other cases in which the action is caused but not necessitated. However, Aristotle, in that case, would be offering here not a general account of actions caused by rational powers, but only an account of a special sub-group in which rival desires are eliminable. This is not what the text suggests.

45. Cf. Nussbaum, *De Motu* 87–8, 188.

46. On the alleged incompatibility between logical and causal connection, see, for example, A. Melden, *Free Action* (London 1961) 53; G. H. von Wright has sometimes argued for a similar view (see references and discussion in Nussbaum, *De Motu* Essay 4). For one forceful criticism of the incompatibility view, see J. L. Mackie, *The Cement of the Universe* (Oxford 1974) 287ff. After I began working on these self-criticisms of my earlier position, I discovered that some of them were also advanced by W. F. R. Hardie in his Appendix to the second edition of *Aristotle's Ethical Theory* (Oxford 1981).

47. On the 'premises', see Nussbaum, *De Motu* Essay 4. There is a challenging discussion of this essay in the review by M. F. Burnyeat, *AGP* 63 (1981) 184–9.

48. For references and discussion, see Nussbaum, *De Motu* Essay 3, esp. 146ff.; I have, however, modified the view expressed there, as will be evident. For my current view, see my review of E. Hartman, *Substance, Body, and Soul*, in *JP* 77 (1980), and my 'Aristotle', in *Ancient Writers*, ed. T. J. Luce (New York 1982) 377–416. On constitution and identity, with reference to Aristotle, see D. Wiggins, *Sameness and Substance* (Oxford 1980).

49. There is some evidence that Aristotle had an interest in such theories: see my account of the role of *pneuma* in Essay 3; but to establish that *pneuma* is the only sort of matter suitable to be associated with the movements of *orexis* is not to say much with empirical content, especially since the *pneuma* is itself a constituent introduced for its explanatory value, not discovered by observation.

50. Cf. Ch. 8 on *epistēmē*, with references.

51. Richard Sorabji (above n. 43) has given an impressive treatment of these issues, arguing that human action, in Aristotle's view, is caused but not necessitated. He admits that the *De Motu* provides strong evidence for a close connection between cause and necessity, but argues that that treatise carelessly extends to many cases an account that does not fit all of them. I believe that the *De Motu* offers a 'common account' by design and not by carelessness; *Metaphysics* IX provides confirming evidence from a different (explicitly human) set of cases. Nor am I convinced, as Sorabji is, that human action could not be ethically assessible if it is necessitated. Nonetheless, to argue against his case would require treating each of the passages on which it is built; and this cannot be attempted here.

52. Cf. Sorabji, *Necessity* 241–2.

53. Compare my remarks on hypothetical necessity in Essay 1 of my book. See now also J. Cooper, 'Hypothetical necessity', forthcoming.

54. *MA* 703a4–6; cf. my *De Motu* commentary *ad loc.*, and Essay 3. I still believe the argument about the motivations for the introduction of *pneuma*, but would now be more careful to avoid the implication that Aristotle intends two parallel explanations, each of which might be sufficient, in isolation, to explain the movement.

55. The most puzzling passage is 702a17–20, which suggests, against the clear meaning of Chs. 6–7, that there is a single causal account involving some sort of movement from the psychological to the physiological. And certainly Aristotle nowhere elaborates

on the relationship between the two parts of his account in a way that would decisively answer all of our questions. I try to answer some of them in Essay 3 – but cf. n. 54 above. Geoffrey Lloyd has brought to my attention several other passages in which Aristotle conflates the two sorts of explanation in a puzzling way: *PA* 650b27, 651a3, 667a20, 675b25, 676b23, 692a22ff.

56. *De Motu* Ch. 11 introduces a distinction between all the movements heretofore discussed – now called *hekousioi* or 'voluntary' – and two other sorts of non-constrained or natural movements. Examples of the first of these, the so-called *akousioi*, 'involuntary', are reflex responses of certain bodily parts; examples of the second sort, called *ouch hekousioi*, 'not voluntary', are systemic movements such as going to sleep, waking, and respiration: precisely the movements which in *Physics* VIII (n. 35 above) had been treated as sufficiently explained by the action of the environment upon the animal. Of the reflex motions he says that the animal's own thought or *phantasia* of the object does enter into the explanation of what happens; but there is lacking any *orexis* to perform the action. In the second group of cases, he asserts that neither *orexis* nor *phantasia* is *kurios* over, 'in control of', any of them; the explanation to be given is simply one that refers to physiological necessity.

57. In the *EN*, an action will be *akousios* if either (1) its origin or *archē* is not in the agent (i.e. is external to the agent), or (2) it is done from excusable ignorance. In the *EE*, although Aristotle initially searches for a positive criterion of the *hekousion* in terms of the action's relation to desire, choice, or thought, he ends by offering an account similar to that of the *EN* in its mixture of positive and negative criteria; an action is *hekousios* if and only if it is done 'through the creature itself' and not out of ignorance. Cf. A. Kenny, *Aristotle's Theory of the Will* (London 1979) Pt 1.

58. On Oedipus, see the explicit discussion at *MM* 1195a15ff.

59. This helps us, too, to understand the *EN*'s emphasis on *ex post facto* regret as a necessary criterion of the *akousion* from ignorance: regret is what really shows us that the agent's desires were not such as to have caused the action. But the *De Motu* helps us, as well, to see a problem with this insistence on regret. For Oedipus might well have desired his father's death, even to the point of rejoicing at it, without being guilty of murder. The presence of a motive is not enough to convict the criminal, however hard it is to get at the real causal connections in a particular case.

   On the difficulty of knowing how to individuate and count the actions in question, see J. L. Ackrill, 'Aristotle on action', *Mind* 87 (1978) 595–601, repr. in Rorty, *Essays* 93–103.

60. T. H. Irwin, 'Reason and responsibility in Aristotle', in Rorty, *Essays* 117–56.

61. Irwin, *op. cit.* rules out the sort of capability that children have for eventually developing choice and deliberation.

62. The *hekousion* is connected with praise and blame at (for example) *EN* 1135a19, 1109b30, *EE* 1223a11. *Prohairesis* is said to be 'most intimately bound up with' character and to be the ground for our judgments of character at *EN* 1111b5–6, 1112a1–2. At *EN* 1112a14–15, Aristotle claims that the *hekousion* is extensionally wider than the *prohaireton*, and offers in evidence the fact that the *hekousion* belongs to children and animals, while the *prohaireton* does not. The *hekousion* is again ascribed to animals and children at 1111a24–6; animals are denied *prohairesis* at *MM* 1189a1–4, *EE* 1225b26–8. For some other passages distinguishing adult humans from other animals and/or human children, see *EN* 1099b32–1100a5, 1147b3, *Metaph.* 980b25–8, *DA* 434a5–9.

63. Irwin, 'Reason and responsibility', 124.
64. Irwin, *op. cit.* esp. 134.
65. Aristotle's account also permits us to regard akratic action as a kind of moral immaturity and to blame it in a different way from the way in which we blame vicious action; whereas Irwin's account appears to assimilate the two.
66. See N. Sherman, *Aristotle's Theory of Moral Education*, Ph.D. thesis, Harvard, 1982, for a good account of much of the relevant material.
67. This is, of course, a splicing together of Thuc. II.43 (trans. Crawley) with *De Motu* 701a33–701b1.
68. I would especially like to thank the participants in the Ninth Symposium Aristotelicum in Berlin for their illuminating comments: and especially, Jacques Brunschwig, Myles Burnyeat, Anthony Kenny, G. E. R. Lloyd, G. E. L. Owen, D. Rees, R. Sorabji, and M. Woods. For helpful comments at a later date, I am grateful to members of my seminar at Harvard in the fall of 1982, to audiences at the Boston University Colloquium for the Philosophy of Science, the University of Connecticut, Brown University, and The Johns Hopkins University: especially to Peter Achinstein, Margery Grene, Hilary Putnam, David Sachs, Ernest Sosa, and Steven Strange.

10 Non-scientific deliberation

1. Some of the material in this chapter is closely connected to my 'Practical syllogisms and practical science', Essay 4 of Nussbaum, *De Motu*; also see my 'Aristotle', in T. J. Luce, ed., *Ancient Writers* (New York 1982) 377–416, esp. 397–404. A study of Aristotelian practical reason to which I am indebted throughout is D. Wiggins, 'Deliberation'. Many of these arguments are developed further, with reference to contemporary models of choice, in 'The discernment of perception', in J. Cleary, ed., *Proceedings of the Boston Area Colloquium* (New York 1985) 151–201.
2. On Aristotle's usually interchangeable use of '*technē*' and '*epistēmē*', and on the distinction he does rarely make between them, see Ch. 4 n. 11.
3. There is also a single *measure* of time selected, in the movements of the heavenly bodies; although here it is not obvious that we could not have different measures for different purposes.
4. On this argument, see J. L. Ackrill, 'Aristotle on "Good" and the Categories', in *Islamic Philosophy and the Classical Tradition: Essays Presented to Richard Walzer*, ed. S. M. Stern, *et al.* (Oxford 1972), repr. in Barnes, *Articles* II, 17–24. Also H. Flashar, 'The critique of Plato's ideas in Aristotle's Ethics', trans. in Barnes, *Articles* II, 1–16; L. A. Kosman, 'Predicating the good', *Phronesis* 13 (1968) 171–4. On the general problem of whether there can be a single science of good or of being, and Aristotle's shifting attitudes to that question, see G. E. L. Owen, 'Logic and metaphysics in some earlier works of Aristotle', in *Aristotle and Plato in the Mid-Fourth Century*, ed. I. Düring and G. E. L. Owen (Göteborg 1960), repr. in Barnes, *Articles* III.
5. There has been a dispute about whether, in this passage, Aristotle invites us to focus on *all* the characteristic functions of the creature in question, or only on those that are non-shared. I argue in detail for the former interpretation (with bibliography) in 'Aristotle on human nature and the foundations of ethics', forthcoming.
6. Cf. *EN* 1095a16, 1096b32–5, *MM* 1182b3ff., 1183a7, 33–5, *EE* 1217a30–40.
7. This is Aristotle's position throughout the *MM* and *EE*, and also in Books I–IX of the *EN*. On the difficulties of reconciling *EN* x.6–8 with everything else, see Appendix to Pt. III. On the authenticity and value of the *MM*, see Ch. 11 n. 1.

8. This interpretation is defended at length, with historical parallels and bibliography, in my 'Aristotle on human nature'. See also Ch. 12, where I examine Aristotle's use of this sort of argument in the specific case of social excellence, claiming that the considerations involved bring him into close relation with the position of Protagoras discussed in Ch. 4.

9. See also Ch. 5 on objections to Plato's attack on context-relativity.

10. See Ch. 4 for historical evidence and bibliography. For the complexity of debate on this issue in the different sciences, see G. E. R. Lloyd, 'Measurement and mystification', forthcoming.

11. Compare the good discussion of the evidence in D. Wiggins, 'Weakness of will, commensurability, and the objects of deliberation and desire', in Rorty, *Essays* 241–65, esp. 255–6.

12. There is a large literature on this difficult issue. For just some of it, see: A. J. Festugière, *Aristote: le plaisir* (Paris 1946); G. Lieberg, *Die Lehre von der Lust in den Ethiken des Aristoteles* (Munich 1958); F. Ricken, *Der Lustbegriff in der Nikomachischen Ethik* (Göttingen 1976); G. E. L. Owen, 'Aristotelian pleasures', *PAS* 72 (1971–2) 135–52, repr. in Barnes, *Articles* II; J. C. B. Gosling, 'More Aristotelian pleasures', *PAS* 74 (1973–4) 15–34; most recently, J. C. B. Gosling and C. C. W. Taylor, *The Greeks on Pleasure* (Oxford 1982) 204–24. Gosling and Taylor argue for a different interpretation of Book x: pleasure is just the completion or perfection of the *energeia* itself. This cannot be debated here; but it does not affect the ethical issues with which we are concerned.

13. *EN* 1153b9–12.

14. *EN* x.4, 1174b23ff.

15. On this passage and other related material, see Ch. 11.

16. A scrutiny of Aristotle's use of the notion of the *sumpheron*, 'useful' or 'advantageous', shows clearly that he has no tendency to make this into a single measure.

17. Cf. Ch. 4, especially the discussion of Sidgwick on pp. 112–113.

18. Again, *EN* x creates a problem for this interpretation – cf. Appendix to Pt. III, and Ch. 11 n. 37; but the bulk of the *EN*, especially the discussions of the excellences and of *philia* (cf. Ch. 12) clearly has the inclusive picture.

19. Places where Aristotle allegedly says this include: *EN* 1111b26, 1112b11–12, 1113a14–15, 1113b3–4; *EE* 1226a7, 1226b10, 1227a12.

20. See for example H. A. Prichard, 'The meaning of *agathon* in the ethics of Aristotle', *Philosophy* 27 (1935), repr. in J. M. E. Moravcsik, ed., *Aristotle* (Garden City 1967); and the devastating reply by J. L. Austin, '*Agathon* and *eudaimonia* in the ethics of Aristotle', in Moravcsik, *op. cit.* and in Austin, *Philosophical Papers* (Oxford 1970) 1–31.

21. This point was made first, in the modern literature, by Wiggins, in 'Deliberation' (which has circulated in typescript since 1962). It is further argued in J. Cooper, *Reason and Human Good in Aristotle* (Cambridge, MA 1975). I discuss Wiggins's view in Nussbaum, *De Motu* Essay 4 (a draft of which is also discussed by Wiggins in the published version of his paper).

22. See for example *Metaph.* 1032b27, *Pol.* 1325b16, 1338b2–4, *EN* 1144a3ff.

23. On specifying the end, see Wiggins, 'Deliberation', especially his account of 1112b11ff.; and my 'Aristotle' and *De Motu* Essay 4.

24. *EN* 1097b14ff. See the excellent account of this passage in J. L. Ackrill, 'Aristotle on *eudaimonia*', *PBA* 60 (1974) 339–59, repr. in Rorty, *Essays*, 15–33. Cf. also *MM* 1184a15ff.

25. This, however, does not preclude all attempts to adjust and harmonize ends; frequently

the determination of what is appropriate with respect to the subject matter of one of the virtues will involve taking account of the relationship of this action to other concerns of and claims upon the agent.

26. On Aristotelian understanding and its connection with general accounts, see Ch. 8 with references and bibliography.

27. Cf. 1103b32–3, 1119a20, 1114b29, 1138a10, 1138b25, 34, 1144b23–8, 1147b3, 31, 1151a12, 21.

28. See my Essay 4, and, on *epistēmē*, Ch. 8.

29. For the claim that action is concerned with ultimate particulars, see 1109b23, 1110b6, 1126b4, 1142a22, 1143a29, 32, b4, 1147a3, 26, b5.

30. My discussion here closely follows Essay 4, pp. 210ff., though there are many changes and corrections.

31. Cf. Ch. 6.

32. Again, compare the account of *technē* in Ch. 4; Aristotle's view is compared to the view of Protagoras, as interpreted in that chapter.

33. For the connection between particulars and *aisthēsis*, see 1113a1, 1109b23, 1126b4, 1147a26.

34. It is very difficult to translate '*logos*' in these contexts; frequently I have rendered it 'statement'; but in other cases, as here, it must refer to the ethical principle that would be formulated in a general statement. It is unfortunate that English forces a choice between the linguistic entity and its expressed content.

35. '*Krisis*', '*krinesthai*', and related words, frequently translated as 'judgment' and 'judge', actually need not have this implication. They imply only the making of discriminations and selections. See Nussbaum, *De Motu* 334, with reference to an unpublished paper of J. M. Cooper.

36. The importance of harmony between general statements and the *kath' hekasta* is stressed by Aristotle in the sciences as well: for example, *MA* 698a11, *HA* 491a7–14, *GC* 316a5–14, *GA* 757b35ff., 760b28ff., 788b19ff., *DC* 306a5ff. In ethics, however, the nature of the 'matter of the practical' (cf. this ch., p. 302) makes the problem much more acute, the general statement much more potentially misleading.

37. See the excellent discussion of this passage in Wiggins, 'Deliberation'.

38. *Autoschediazein ta deonta*, Thuc. 1.138 (on Themistocles).

39. On *stochazesthai*, cf. also 1109a30, 1106b15, 28, 1109a23; and see the discussion of this word in Detienne and Vernant, *Mètis* 38, 297–300.

40. See also Essay 4, pp. 212–13.

41. See Wiggins's excellent account of this passage in 'Deliberation'. I follow his translation-cum-paraphrase to some extent here.

42. On *nous*, cf. Ch. 8, with references and bibliography.

43. Again, see Wiggins's discussion in 'Deliberation'.

44. See the exchange between Hilary Putnam and me on this point, in *NLH* 15 (1983).

45. See Ch. 12, with references.

46. See Ch. 12, and Ch. 7 n. 32.

47. On the mechanisms of this developmental process, see N. Sherman, *Aristotle's Theory of Moral Education*, Ph.D. dissertation, Harvard 1982.

48. *EN* 1113a9, 1139a23, b4–5, *MA* 700b23 (which says that *prohairesis* is *koinon dianoias kai orexeōs*, 'sharing in both reason and desire').

49. *EN* 1106b16ff. On this and related issues, see L. A. Kosman, 'Being properly affected', in Rorty, *Essays* 103–16.

50. *DA* 431b2ff. For valuable discussions of this passage, I am indebted to conversation with Christine Korsgaard and to an unpublished manuscript of hers on Aristotelian perception.

51. See my Essay 4 for a full account of these passages and a discussion of what the syllogistic vocabulary does and does not imply.

52. On this point see especially M. F. Burnyeat, 'Aristotle on learning to be good', in Rorty, *Essays* 69–92.

53. Cf. for example *EN* 1109b7–12.

54. Detienne and Vernant, *Mètis* 295ff.

55. Cf. Ch. 5, pp. 155–6.

56. J. Rawls, 'Outline of a decision procedure for ethics', *PR* 60 (1951) 177–97.

57. In that the view of language and reference that supports it is itself selected from the appearances, as the result of Aristotelian procedures.

58. I develop the connection between James and Aristotle in Nussbaum, 'Crystals'. Henry Richardson, in an unpublished paper, has developed an example from *The Ambassadors* to illustrate the nature of Aristotelian perception.

59. Trans. R. Lattimore, in *Greek Tragedies*, ed. D. Grene and R. Lattimore (Chicago 1956).

60. Sometimes, however, the constraint will be too severe to permit of action according to excellence: see the discussion of this issue in Ch. 11.

61. In my work on these issues, I am indebted above all to David Wiggins, with whom I have discussed them for years. I am also grateful for conversations with Larry Blum, Christine Korsgaard, Hilary Putnam, Henry Richardson, and Nancy Sherman.

11 The vulnerability of the good human life: activity and disaster

1. In discussing these issues I shall frequently make use of the *Magna Moralia*, which I believe to be an authentic work of Aristotle. My argument will not, however, rely on this material. The authenticity of the work is defended by F. Dirlmeier in his commentary, *Aristoteles – Magna Moralia* (Berlin 1958) and also by J. M. Cooper, 'The *Magna Moralia* and Aristotle's moral philosophy', *AJP* 94 (1973) 327–49; Cooper argues that the style is not Aristotle's own, but that the work is an accurate transcription of some early lectures of Aristotle's on moral subjects. For the opposing view, see D. J. Allan, '*Magna Moralia* and *Nicomachean Ethics*', *JHS* 77 (1957) 7–11; C. J. Rowe, 'A reply to John Cooper on the *Magna Moralia*', *AJP* 96 (1975) 160–72.

2. Although most of my discussion here will focus on the *Nicomachean Ethics*, since it contains the most extensive treatment of the issues, I shall supplement my discussion with material from the *Eudemian Ethics* wherever there is no serious problem of incompatibility of position. On the chronology of Aristotle's ethical thought, see A. Kenny's controversial *The Aristotelian Ethics* (Oxford 1978), and *Aristotle's Theory of the Will* (London 1979); also the fine review of the former by J. M. Cooper, *Nous* 15: 1 (1981) 381–92; and cf. also C. J. Rowe, *The Eudemian and Nicomachean Ethics* (Cambridge 1971).

3. The connection between *eudaimonia* and the praiseworthy is denied by those who think of *eudaimonia* as a psychological state of pleasure or contentment; but once we see that it *consists in* excellent activity we can understand why Aristotle stresses the connection as he does. See Ch. 10 n. 20.

4. I do not mean to claim that Plato is Aristotle's only opponent in passages in which he attacks this strategy; but our account of Plato's middle-period views should have

made it clear that he does argue this way. It is important to notice a salient difference between Plato and the character whom I have called the 'good-condition theorist': Plato always insists that the bearers of value are activities, not states; he pursues self-sufficiency not by denying the need for activity, but by picking out the activities that are maximally invulnerable.

5. It is not clear who these opponents are. They bear an obvious resemblance to Stoic thinkers who followed Aristotle. As in the case of Hellenistic skepticism, whose antecedents seem to be strikingly present in Aristotle's criticisms (see Ch. 8 and Long's article referred to there), so here we see evidence that a well-known Hellenistic view was around, in some form, in this earlier period.

6. This view is defended in certain poetic writers: especially by certain characters in dramas of Euripides (see for example the end of Hecuba's speech from the *Trojan Women*, discussed in Ch. 10). See also Ch. 4 n. 2 for works that discuss other examples of this view.

7. For a contemporary parallel, see Robert Nozick, *Philosophical Explanations* (Cambridge, MA 1981) 1–3.

8. Aristotle is going to conclude that the things under our control are *kurios* over *eudaimonia*, 'authoritative' or 'in charge'. On this important word and its function, see Ch. 9 nn. 44, 56. Hence (and cf. p. 332 and n. 25) it seems to mean 'the most important causal element in'.

9. For further discussion of ancient Greek views of self-refutation – especially of cases in which the very practice of engaging in argument refutes the view being argued for, see G. E. L. Owen, 'Plato and Parmenides on the timeless present', *The Monist* 50 (1966) 317–40, repr. in A. P. D. Mourelatos, ed., *The Presocratics* (Garden City, NY 1974); M. F. Burnyeat, 'Can the skeptic live his skepticism?', in M. Schofield *et al.*, eds., *Doubt and Dogmatism* (Oxford 1980) 20–53, and 'Protagoras and self-refutation in Plato's *Theaetetus*', PR 85 (1976) 172–95, 'Protagoras and self-refutation in later Greek philosophy', PR 85 (1976) 44–69.

10. I am making Aristotle's argument sound more systematic than it really is: in fact, the two groups of opponents are considered separately in different books of the *EN*; but there seems no reason not to bring them together in this way.

11. Aristotle's word (presumably the opponent's also) is *hexis*, frequently translated 'disposition'. I use 'state' or 'condition' to indicate that it is supposed to be something with psychological reality, that can be there in the person whether or not any action is going on. To call it a disposition would make the opponent's position seem even more paradoxical than it is; on the other hand, as we shall see, Aristotle believes that the criteria for ascription of a *hexis* are not present in the case of the totally inactive person.

12. It is not entirely clear whether Aristotle is saying (1) that the *hexis* might still be intact, but that we have an insuperable epistemological problem about telling whether it is; (2) that the notion of *hexis* is *logically* connected with activity, in such a way that it does not make sense to ascribe it apart from the presence of activity; (3) that *hexis* and action are *causally* interdependent, in such a way that an inactive person would be likely to lose her *hexis*. He certainly believes both (1) and (3); and (3) is, for him, not incompatible with (2), as we have seen in Ch. 9. But we know that he does not believe that a *hexis* goes away the minute no actual activity is being performed; it is a stable (or relatively stable) condition of the person. So whatever logical connection there is between *hexis* and activity, it cannot be this strong a connection.

13. See the excellent account of these matters in L. A. Kosman, 'Substance, being, and *Energeia*', *OSAP* 2 (1984) 121–49.

14. At this point, the good-condition theorist comes very close to the Platonist: for if what this person calls 'being' includes this sort of mental functioning, it will be *energeia*, as Plato's arguments understand it.

15. Although I have used 'his or her' in my own discussion, it seems inappropriate to translate Aristotle this way.

16. Contemplative activity is, of course, less vulnerable to reversal by the external than other activities; but, in Aristotle's view, it too has some external necessary conditions – cf. Ch. 12.

17. On this distinction, see Kosman, 'Substance, being'; J. L. Ackrill, 'Aristotle's distinct-ion between *energeia* and *kinesis*', in *New Essays on Plato and Aristotle*, ed. R. Bambrough (London 1965) 121–41; T. Penner, 'Verbs and the identity of actions', in *Ryle*, ed. G. Pitcher and O. Wood (New York 1970) 393–453. It is important to notice that Aristotle also uses '*energeia*' as a generic term to cover both species.

18. Cf. Ch. 10 n. 12.

19. Compare *Metaph.* 1091b15ff., 1022b22ff.

20. See the remarks on old age and *philia* in Ch. 12.

21. *Rep.* 388A–B (cf. Ch. 7), *Apol.* 41C–D, etc.; cf. Ch. 5. Here again, we need to point out that Plato differs from the good-condition theorist by requiring actual activity for *eudaimonia*; he will insist, however, that contemplative activity is altogether self-sufficient, requiring no special worldly conditions for its attainment beyond life itself.

22. Cf. for example, *Groundwork of the Metaphysics of Morals* (Berlin 1785), trans. H. J. Paton (New York 1960), Akad. p. 394, cf. Int. 2 n. 13.

23. H. H. Joachim, *The Nicomachean Ethics* (Oxford 1951) *ad loc.*; W. D. Ross, *The Works of Aristotle* (London 1923) 192.

24. For Aristotle's use of *en* ('in') in the sense of 'causally dependent on', see esp. *Ph.* 210b21–2; also *Metaph.* 1023a8–11, 23–5; *EN* 1109b23; and see my discussion in Nussbaum, *De Motu* Essay 3, p. 153.

25. The word used is *kurios* – see n. 8.

26. On the difficulties of interpretation on this issue, see Ch. 9, pp. 282–3, with references.

27. Cf. Ch. 2.

28. This seems to be the point of the difficult passage at 1199b36ff.; but 1188b15ff. does allow for circumstantial compulsion that will cause a person to forgo something of importance.

29. Cf. esp. *EN* IX.2; and also the remarks on number of friends and quarrels among one's friends – cf. Ch. 12.

30. For related remarks on conflict, cf. Nussbaum, *De Motu* Essay 4.

31. On development and its external conditions, cf. Chs. 9, 12.

32. Compare the use of these words by Euripides and Thucydides – cf. Ch. 13; Aristotle may be using a traditional metaphor.

33. For the *Rhetoric*, the only edition to use is that of R. Kassel (Berlin 1976); see my review in *AGP* 63 (1981) 346–50.

34. On *to euēthes* and its traditional association with excellence, cf. Ch. 13.

35. There is related material in the ethical works themselves: esp. *EN* 1124a20ff., on the contribution of goods of fortune to *megalopsuchia*; cf. also *MM* 1200a12ff.

36. On the *Politics* passage, cf. also Ch. 8. Related arguments about the context-relativity

of value are found in both Xenophanes and Heraclitus; see my '*Psuchē* in Heraclitus, ii', *Phronesis* 17 (1972), 153ff.

37. There is a difficulty about using this passage, in that it comes from the problematic passage in *EN* x whose incompatibility with the rest of the *EN* I discuss in the Appendix to Part iii. Aristotle goes on there to develop a non-anthropocentric and quite Platonic view of the good life that identifies *eudaimonia* with intellectual contemplation and relegates the moral virtues to second place, partly on account of their absence in the divine life of intellect. I argue in the Appendix that this passage is not in any sense the culmination of the argument of the *EN*, but is flatly incompatible with it in a number of important ways. I include the passage here only because the remarks about the context-relativity of the virtues are consistent elaborations of Aristotle's views of the virtues or excellences elsewhere (in the *Politics*, the other ethical works, and the *EN* itself); they forcefully and explicitly summarize views about the connection of the ethical excellences with a context of material limitation that can be found in the discussions of the specific excellences; and *EN* vii, as we have seen, also explicitly denies ethical *aretē* to divine beings. Throughout the *EN*, except in these three chapters (x.6–8), he defends activities according to these excellences, so understood, as valuable ends in themselves. In this context it is only what happens after the quoted passage – when these values are adversely contrasted to contemplation on grounds of their context-relativity – that poses a problem for a consistent overall interpretation of the *EN*. We can therefore draw on them cautiously in drawing a picture of the *nature* of ethical virtue that Aristotle consistently preserves even when he changes his account of the *ranking* of ethical excellence against other goods. It is worth stressing that in this sense even *EN* x is not Platonic: Plato, having decided to prefer activities that are non-context-relative (cf. Ch. 5), defends a picture of justice and the other traditional excellences that makes them like this as well, tying them tightly to contemplative activity. Aristotle cannot be convinced, even at his most Platonic, that there is a meaningful conception of the ethical outside of the practices and limits of human life.

38. For further discussion of this issue, see Appendix to Part iii, with references.

39. Heraclitus fr. DK b62; see Nussbaum, '*Psuchē* in Heraclitus, ii' (above n. 36).

40. This chapter was given as the first of the Eunice Belgum Lectures at St Olaf College (see Acknowledgements); in combination with material from Interlude 2, it was also read at the Institute for Classical Studies, London; at the Philosophy of Education Colloquia, Harvard University; at Brown University, Connecticut College, Smith College, Swarthmore College, and at conferences on Greek literary theory at Florida State University and Vassar College. I would like to thank those present, and especially Myles Burnyeat, Aryeh Kosman, Ruth Padel, and Charles Segal, for helpful comments.

12   The vulnerability of the good human life: relational goods

1. Cf. *EN* 1177a27ff., where this is said to be true of all of the excellences of character.

2. Aristotle's account of *phantasia* emphasizes this possibility – cf. *DA* iii.3, and Essay 5 in Nussbaum, *De Motu*.

3. *Metaphysics* xii.7; it is far from clear, however, just what 'thought of thought' would be, and whether such thought does or does not have objects for its content.

4. In these passages, Aristotle appears to use '*autarkēs*' in the Platonic way he has ruled

out at 1097b7–11 (cf. this ch., pp. 344–5). This is just one of the many problems involved in reconciling x.6–8 with the rest of the *EN*.

5. On the signs of such a project in x.6–8, see Ch. 11 n. 37.

6. The important topic of civic *philia* (which, in Aristotle's view, 'holds cities together' even more than justice does – 1155a22–7) has received little comment in the literature. The best general treatment is J. Hook, *Friendship and Politics in Aristotle's Ethical and Political Thought*, B.A. thesis *summa cum laude*, Harvard 1977.

7. As we shall see later, Aristotle will raise the Protagorean question whether such beings are in fact human.

8. On Aristotle's departure from Athens, see I. Düring, *Aristoteles* (Heidelberg 1966); G. E. L. Owen, 'Philosophical invective', *OSAP* 1 (1983) 1ff. For discussion of some of the passages in the *Politics* that bear on his relationship to the Macedonian court, see my 'Shame, separateness, and political unity', in Rorty, *Essays* 395–435. On Aristotle's status as *metoikos*, see Düring, *Aristoteles* 213ff., 232–6, 459ff., and D. Whitehead, 'Aristotle the metic', *PCPS* 21 (1975) 94–9 and *The Ideology of the Athenian Metic*, *PCPS* Suppl. Vol. 4 (1977). Whitehead and Düring argue persuasively that there is no good evidence that Aristotle was given any special privileges, such as were sometimes granted to *metoikoi* (Cephalus, for example, was allowed to hold property); thus he could not participate in the assembly, hold office, serve on a jury, own land, or build a house; he had to register and pay a tax, and to be supervised closely by a citizen *prostatēs*. Despite the evidence of *Pol.* 1278a (see this ch., p. 349), Whitehead argues from *EE* 1233a28–30 that Aristotle's attitude to this condition was 'phlegmatic'. The passage only says, however, that a lack of participation in civic affairs that would be blamed in a citizen can hardly be blamed in the case of the metic; this does not seem to me to show resignation.

9. See Diogenes Laertius ix. The conventional and legendary character of these reports is discussed in M. Frede, 'Des Skeptikers Meinungen', *Neue Hefte für Philosophie* 15/16 (1979) 102–29.

10. D. L. ix.68.

11. Epicurus was the first known philosopher to teach women; his school was notorious for its admission of women and slaves; and some women held positions of high respect.

12. See B. Frischer, *The Sculpted Word* (Berkeley 1982). Insofar as they make our encounter with the saving philosophy depend on circumstances not fully under our control, these opponents grant a part of Aristotle's point about the luck of development.

13. This becomes especially clear in *EN* ix – cf. this ch., pp. 350, 365–8.

14. On this passage, and on Aristotelian habituation generally, see: M. F. Burnyeat, 'Aristotle on learning to be good', in Rorty, *Essays* 69–92; N. Sherman, *Aristotle's Theory of Moral Education*, Ph.D. dissertation Harvard 1982; and Nussbaum, 'Aristophanes'.

15. 1180a18 and 29 refer to the superior *correctness* of such a scheme; 1180a21–2 to its origin in practical wisdom (*phronēsis*) and insight (*nous*).

16. On the craftsmen, see Nussbaum, 'Shame, separateness'. My argument that this is Aristotle's view of their situation depends upon combining his account of them with his general remarks about the importance of *prohairesis* for good living, the obligation of the *polis* to secure it to all those who are not naturally deprived.

17. See the more extensive discussion of these passages and issues in Nussbaum, 'Shame, separateness'.

18. See Nussbaum, 'Shame, separateness' n. 54; the most significant passages are *EN* 1161a34, *EE* 1242a28, *Pol.* 1255a12.

19. On the issues raised here, see Nussbaum, 'Shame, separateness' 419; cf. n. 8 above.

20. See *MM* 1194b5–23, *Pol.* 1255b20, 1261a39, 1277b7, 1279a20, 1288a12, 1274a22ff., 1275b18, 1276b38ff., 1277b7ff., 1317b2–3, 1332b32ff., *EN* 1134b15. *Pol.* 1328a18, however, says that metics are economically necessary for the city.

21. For discussion of various versions of this view, and criticism, see my 'Aristotle on human nature and the foundations of ethics', forthcoming.

22. On the connection between beliefs about essential nature and beliefs about value, see Chs. 4, 6, 7; my 'Aristotle on human nature' discusses related material from the *Philebus*.

23. On the Cyclopes and their importance for a tradition of thought on this issue, see Ch. 8; also Geoffrey Kirk, *Myth: its Meaning and Functions in Ancient and Other Cultures* (Cambridge 1970), and especially P. Vidal-Naquet, 'Valeurs religieuses et mythiques de la terre et du sacrifice dans l'Odyssée', in *Le Chasseur noir* (Paris 1981) 39–68.

24. The argument is discussed at greater length in my 'Aristotle on human nature'; the argument that follows this one, concerning the role of language in our ways of life, seems to me to tell the same story – it is discussed in detail in the same paper.

25. One part of this investigation is carried out through the comparative study of the stability and self-sufficiency of different types of political communities, in the *Politics* and in the various *politeiai* that were the results of a concerted research project in the Lyceum.

26. Cf. above n. 20.

27. On Aristotle's view of *philia*, see esp. J. M. Cooper, 'Aristotle on friendship', in Rorty, *Essays* 301–40; also W. F. R. Hardie, *Aristotle's Ethical Theory* (Oxford 1981, 2nd ed.).

28. On issues of translation, see also Cooper, 'Aristotle' n. 4. Cooper opposes translating *philein* as 'love', though he uses 'love' and 'friendship' for *philia* – on the grounds that there will be confusion when one comes to translate *eran* and *stergein*. For *eran* he recommends 'be in love' – compare our practice in Ch. 7 – and, for *stergein*, 'love'. For *philein* he chooses 'like'. This seems, however, much too affectively weak; and there seems to be no good reason to be worried about confusion with *stergein*, which is quite a rare word in Aristotle anyway. If 'love' is used for *philia*, it can only cause confusion to refuse to use 'love' for the verb.

29. Cf. however 1166a1ff. on self-love. A helpful treatment of this and related issues is J. Annas, 'Plato and Aristotle on friendship and altruism', *Mind* 86 (1977) 532–54.

30. The *Rhetoric* definition: '*Philein* is to wish for someone what one thinks to be good, for that person's own sake and not for one's own, and, insofar as one is able, to take action towards these things.'

31. We naturally wonder what happens to the case of blood relatives who are not personally acquainted; but this would be rare enough in the Greek *polis* not to be remarked on in an account such as this.

32. Cooper's ('Aristotle') discussion is especially persuasive on these points, and I am indebted to it.

33. It is not clear whether Aristotle really wants to accord to character the status of an essential property; his discussions of character-change certainly permit some change without a change of identity, and he never discusses sudden and sweeping changes. Elsewhere he certainly insists that the only essential characteristics are those that a being shares with all other members of its kind.

34. Cf. Ch. 9 on *orexis* and the lack of self-sufficiency.

35. Cf. *Rhet.* 1381a29ff.
36. *EN* 1099b3–4, *Rhet.* 1381b1.
37. Cf. also *EN* 1157a20ff., where Aristotle discusses the connection between trust and the resistance of *philia* to damage by slander.
38. Cf. 1158a10–11, and 1171a8–13, where Aristotle observes that the intensity of *philia* (*to sphodra*) is undercut by having too many *philoi*. Notice that intensity is an important element in *philia*.
39. Cf. *Rhet.* 1381a30ff.
40. On grief cf. Ch. 7, and Interlude 2 on related emotions.
41. Cf. I. Kant, *Critique of Practical Reason* (Berlin 1788), trans. Lewis White Beck (Indianapolis 1956), Akad. pp. 83ff.; I. Kant, *The Doctrine of Virtue* (Part III of *The Metaphysics of Morals*, Berlin 1797), trans. M. J. Gregor (Philadelphia 1969), Akad. pp. 500–1, 447ff.
42. Cf. Sherman, *Aristotle's Theory*.
43. See Cooper's good account of this argument ('Aristotle').
44. See Cooper's defense of the importance of this passage and his convincing interpretation, to which I am indebted. He does not, however, as I do, stress the cognitive role of the affective tie.
45. Here again (cf. n. 33 above) we notice that not just any member of one's own species will count as 'another oneself' for these purposes, although one would suppose that, according to the criteria of the *Metaphysics* and the biological works, any two normal species members would share all essential characteristics.
46. On the equivalence of *eudaimonia* and *makariotēs*, see Ch. 11, which discusses this passage.
47. See my 'Aristotle on human nature'.
48. Both of the charges that follow are made by Bernard Williams in 'Philosophy', *The Legacy of Greece*, ed. M. I. Finley (Oxford 1981) 202–55 – cf. Ch. 1.
49. Williams *op. cit.* 254.
50. The word *huperbolē* is used; this is the usual word for ethical excess in the books on the virtues. Cf. also *EN* 1157a6–10, where the relationship between *erastēs* and *erōmenos* is treated simply as an example of pleasure-love.
51. *Pol.* 1260a13, where he remarks cryptically that women have the deliberative faculty, but it is *akuros*, 'lacking in authority'. It is likely that he means 'lacking in authority over their irrational elements'; but some scholars have argued that it means 'lacking in authority over males in their social setting – in which case the argument against giving them political rights becomes hard to understand. G. E. R. Lloyd, in his excellent study of these issues (*Science and Speculation* (Cambridge 1983) 128–64) has shown to what extent Aristotle, in his work on women, is indeed echoing and supporting the pervasive ideology of his culture. His study makes clear, however, that there were other conflicting 'appearances' around, both from medicine and from social commentary, that might fruitfully have been explored and brought to bear on the issue. The near-unanimous cultural ideology of female inferiority might lead the method of appearances to incline *prima facie* in that direction; but there are other cases (cf. Ch. 8) in which beliefs just as prevalent are criticized through a patient scrutiny that is nowhere in evidence in Aristotle's work on *this* issue. Where physiology is concerned, it is even more obvious that the appearances required to correct his errors were well within reach: for he might have counted a few women's teeth, to see whether they in fact have a smaller number; he might have tested his claim that a menstruating woman who looks into a mirror turns it red; and so forth.

52. As we have seen, he does briefly mention the pair *erastēs/erōmenos* (above n. 50); but with no attempt to give a careful account of the relationship mentioned.

53. *EN* 1137b29ff., on which see the detailed discussion in Ch. 10.

54. This chapter was the second Eunice Belgum Lecture at St Olaf College. For discussion of the issues, I am also indebted to Nancy Sherman and Henry Richardson.

Appendix to Part III   Human and divine

1. See especially J. M. Cooper, *Reason and Human Good in Aristotle* (Cambridge, MA 1975); J. L. Ackrill, 'Aristotle on *eudaimonia*', *PBA* 60 (1974) 339–59. Repr. in Rorty, *Essays* 15–34; and David Keyt, 'Intellectualism in Aristotle', *Paideia* special Aristotle issue, 1980, ed. G. C. Simmons.

2. The arguments on this topic are set out in detail in my 'Aristotle on human nature and the foundations of ethics', forthcoming. Some are contextual, some philological (the meaning of expressions such as the -*ikē zōē*); put together, they are decisive in favor of an inclusive interpretation of human function.

3. I am grateful to Myles Burnyeat, whose criticisms prompted me to add this Appendix, and to Nancy Sherman and Miriam Woodruff for helpful discussion of the issues of *EN* x.6–8.

Interlude 2   Luck and the tragic emotions

1. On some of these points about Aristotle's *Poetics*, there is further discussion in my 'Aristotle', in *Ancient Writers: Greece and Rome*, ed. T. J. Luce (New York 1982) 377–416, with full bibliography. On the role of poetry in Aristotle's views about education, see N. Sherman, *Aristotle on Moral Education*, Ph.D. dissertation, Harvard, 1982. The best account of poetic 'imitation' I know, which sets Aristotle's views against the background of Greek discourse about *mimēsis* in an intelligent and fascinating way, is G. Sörbom, *Mimesis and Art* (Uppsala 1966).

2. The text I translate is: ἡ γὰρ τραγῳδία μίμησίς ἐστιν οὐκ ἀνθρώπων ἀλλὰ πράξεως καὶ βίου καὶ ἡ εὐδαιμονία καὶ τὸ ἐναντίον ἐν πράξει ἐστίν, καὶ τὸ τέλος πρᾶξίς τις ἐστίν, οὐ ποιότης· εἰσὶν δὲ κατὰ μὲν τὰ ἤθη ποιοί τινες, κατὰ δὲ τὰς πράξεις εὐδαίμονες ἢ τοὐναντίον. The following points require comment.

   (1) I have preferred the *praxeōs* of the Riccardianus to the *praxeōn* of most of the other manuscripts; however, nothing in my interpretation hangs on this.

   (2) Where the manuscripts read *eudaimonia* (or: -*as*) *kai hē kakodaimonia*, I have written *kai to enantion*. It has long been a major complaint against this passage that *kakodaimonia* is not an Aristotelian word (see, for example, Else, Lucas, *ad loc.*): neither it nor *kakodaimōn* is found elsewhere in the corpus. What has not been mentioned is that Aristotle's practice, in the absence of this word, is to indicate the opposite of *eudaimonia* by simply saying 'the opposite' – e.g. *EN* 1100b9–11, and immediately after this passage, *Poetics* 1450a19–20. Now this is just the sort of thing that is highly likely to produce a gloss in the Aristotelian manuscript tradition, in which manuscripts are heavily annotated and used as school texts. It could then easily have been incorporated into the text, displacing Aristotle's original locution. I suggest, then, that to write *to enantion* both removes the objectionable word and plausibly explains its presence. An alternative possibility is that the whole thing is a gloss: the sentence should read simply, *kai hē eudaimonia en praxei estin.*

(3) Most manuscripts read: *biou kai eudaimonias kai hē kakodaimonia*. The Riccardianus – and, apparently, the Arabic versions – show *biou kai eudaimonia* – which is probably to be preferred as better fitting the syntax of *kakodaimonia* (or whatever originally stood in its place). Some editors have supposed a lacuna. A popular solution of this type has been Vahlen's: *eudaimonias ⟨kai kakodaimonias· hē de eudaimonia⟩ kai hē kakodaimonia*, etc. This solution is accepted by Bywater and numerous others. I find it an attractive proposal; and I could happily accept it consistently with my interpretation. It seems, however, unnecessary.

The sequence of Aristotle's argument is: the plot is the most important – for what tragedy is is a representation of action and life, not just of character states; the reason why a whole course of life requires plot and not just character description for its adequate representation is to be found in the consideration that *eudaimonia* consists not in a characteristic but in *praxis*. The text of the Riccardianus requires, then, only a minimal further change: the addition of the article before *eudaimonia*.

I am not disturbed, as Else is, by the fact that the second half of the last of the disputed sentences (*kai to telos...poiotēs*) seems to say much the same as the first. Such repetitions are not uncommon; and it in fact clarifies the first half, both by introducing the contrast with *poiotēs* and by replacing 'is in [i.e. consists in] action' with the less ambiguous 'is a kind of action': Aristotle shows that 'is in' meant 'consists in', not 'is causally dependent on' (as it sometimes elsewhere does).

3. *Bios* in Aristotle always means a total way or mode of life. See J. M. Cooper, *Reason and Human Good in Aristotle* (Cambridge, MA 1975) 159–61, and my 'Aristotle on human nature and the foundations of ethics', forthcoming. See also G. Else, *Aristotle's Poetics: the Argument* (Cambridge, MA 1967) 256–7.

4. D. W. Lucas, *Aristotle's Poetics* (Oxford 1968) 102. Others who exclude the passage as irrelevant include R. Kassel (Oxford Classical Text) and Else, *op. cit.* 253–5. Else comments, 'The superiority of activities over states – e.g. virtue – is a commonplace in Aristotle's philosophy and so widely attested that we hardly need to document it. The question is how that superiority is exploited for his immediate purpose here, which is to prove the supremacy of the plot, i.e. the poetic action.'

5. J. Jones, *On Aristotle and Greek Tragedy* (London 1962) 30.

6. *EN* 1111b4–6; cf. *EE* 1228a3 *ek tēs proaireseōs krinomen poios tis*.

7. On this case and the problems it raises for Aristotle's views about action, see Chapter 9.

8. On this passage, see Ch. 7.

9. On *hamartia*, see especially T. C. W. Stinton, 'Hamartia in Aristotle and Greek Tragedy', *CQ* NS 25 (1975) 221–54; also J. M. Bremer, *Hamartia* (Amsterdam 1969); R. D. Dawe, 'Some reflections on *atē* and *hamartia*', *HSCP* 72 (1967) 89–123; E. R. Dodds, 'On misunderstanding the *Oedipus Rex*', *GR* 13 (1966) 37–49, repr. in Dodds, *ACP* 64–77; P. W. Harsh, 'Hamartia again', *TAPA* 76 (1945) 47–58. I discuss these issues further in 'Aristotle' (above n. 1) pp. 407–8.

10. For Plato's view of emotions, see Chs. 5 and 7 with references and bibliography. For related discussion of Aristotle, see Sherman, *Aristotle* and S. Leighton, 'Aristotle and the emotions', *Phronesis* 27 (1982).

11. *Rhet.* 1378a31. Aristotle actually complicates matters further by adding reference to the *orexis* for revenge.

12. On the transferral of 'false' from the grounding belief to the emotion or feeling,

compare the account of false pleasure in Plato's *Philebus*, 37Aff., on which see B. A. O. Williams, 'Pleasure and belief', *PASS* 33 (1959).

13. Something similar seems to be true for Kant – compare *Groundwork of the Metaphysics of Morals*, Akad. p. 394 with *Doctrine of Virtue* § 34. But the variety of terms used in his text for pity and related attitudes makes detailed comparison impossible in a brief discussion.

14. 'Outstanding' is too weak a translation for *diapherōn* here; the correct force is captured in Golden's translation (Englewood Cliffs, NJ 1968).

15. At 1452b35 Aristotle says that tragedy should not show *epieikeis andres* falling from good to bad fortune. This is odd, since *epieikēs* is usually more or less synonymous with *spoudaios*. Lucas *ad loc.* reviews the literature on the problem. The alternatives for reading the passage so that it will be consistent with those that follow seem to be: (1) to take *epieikēs* here to have not its usual sense, but, instead, the sense '*surpassing in justice*' (i.e. close to *diapherōn*); (2) to argue that what Aristotle objects to here is not the fall of the good man *per se*, but his *unexplained* fall. *Hamartia*, later introduced, would provide the requisite explanation. Since no indication in the text supports the latter reading, and since 1453a7, *ho metaxu toutōn loipos*, appears to support the former, we should probably choose it, charging Aristotle with inconsistency in vocabulary.

16. L. Golden, 'Catharsis', *TAPA* 93 (1962) 51–60; and 'Mimesis and catharsis', *CP* 64 (1969) 45–53.

17. On the word-group, see LSJ s.v., Chantraine, *Dict. Etym.*, s.v., Brandwood, *Lex. Plat.* s.v. (I have found the study of the function of the words in the *Phaedo*, esp. 65ff. and in the myth, of special interest); on the Hellenistic situation, the edition of Menander Rhetor by D. A. Russell and N. Wilson (Oxford 1981). For references to other interpretations of *katharsis*, and further critical discussion, see my 'Aristotle' (above n. 1); the classic defense of the purgation view is in J. Bernays, *Grundzüge der verlorenen Abhandlung des Aristoteles über Wirkung der Tragödie* (Breslau 1875, repr. Hildesheim 1970). The theory of humors in question appears in no genuine Aristotelian work, but only in the spurious and late *Problemata*. Aristotle's genuine work on psychological processes announces its opposition to physiological reductionism in no uncertain terms. (See Nussbaum, *De Motu* Essays 1 and 3; Ch. 9 above; also Nussbaum, 'Aristotelian dualism: a reply to Howard Robinson', *OSAP* 2 (1984) 198–207.) Aristotle would surely be strongly opposed to Lucas's conclusion that the psychological function of tragedy could be replaced by a dose of medicine, if only Greek physicians had not 'lacked confidence in their power to control black bile'.

A close English parallel is in the history of the word 'defecate' and its relatives. Here too, even a cursory study will show that the primary and continuous meaning is one of 'clearing up' or 'clarifying'; frequently it has an epistemological application (cf. *Oxford English Dictionary* s.v.). Its specific application to the voiding of feces is relatively late, and (until very recently) just one application of the general meaning. We could say that to read *katharsis* as medical purgation everywhere would be as inappropriate as to read every use of 'defecate' and 'defecation' in eighteenth- and nineteenth-century writers as having the meaning 'to void the feces' and to interpret any thinker who has a theoretical account of something called 'defecation' as talking about this particular type of clearing out or up. Consider what would become of the following, under such an interpretative principle:

> 1649 Jer. Taylor, 'a defecation of his faculties and an opportunity of prayer'
> 1751 Johnson, *Rambler* no. 177, 'to defecate and clear my mind'

1862 Goulburn, *Pers. Relig.*, 'to defecate the dregs of the mind'
1866 Lowell, 'a growing tendency to curtail language...and to defecate it of all emotion'
1867 F. Hall, *Hindu Philos.*, 'his judgment daily becomes more defecated'
1870 W. M. Rossetti, 'to defecate life of its misery'

If a student of ours made the interpretative move in question, we would patiently point out that the word simply *means* 'clarification', and that the application to feces is one special case of this, only to be discovered where the immediate context gives clear evidence that it is *that* sort of clarification, and no other, that is in question. (I am very grateful to E. D. Hirsch for bringing this parallel to my attention.)

18. Golden has informed me orally that he has modified this part of his view. Golden does not discuss *Pol.* 1341b32ff., which has sometimes been used to support the purgation view; nor shall I, in great detail. The discussion of musical education in *Pol.* VIII is at odds at a number of important points with the later mature doctrine of the *Poetics*; and this passage explicitly refers the reader to the later work (as to a work still unwritten) for a full and clearer discussion. The brief remarks are indeed unclear. *Katharsis* is linked in some way with medical treatment; but it is also linked to education. And the comparison of philosophical instruction to medical treatment was already common, too frequent to connote anything precise all by itself. (On this see my 'Therapeutic arguments: Epicurus and Aristotle', in *The Norms of Nature*, ed. M. Schofield and G. Striker (Cambridge 1985).) There is no obstacle to the translation 'clarification', and no reason to suppose that at this time Aristotle had any very precise view of what clarification, in this case, was.

19. For related discussion, see Nussbaum, 'Fictions'.
20. See Nussbaum, 'Consequences' 25–53.
21. Cic. *Acad.* II. 119; David the Armenian is the author of the second description (*Aphroditēs ennomou gemōn*). For other ancient encomia of Aristotle's style, see G. Grote, *Aristotle* (London 1872) 1.43. Salient examples (most noted by Grote) are Cic. *Top.* 1.3 (*incredibili copia, tum suavitate*), *De Or.* 1.49, *Brutus* 121, *Fin.* 1.14, *De Nat. Deor.* II.37; Dionysius Hal. *De Vet. Scr. Censura* (*to hēdu kai polumathes*), Quintilian, *Inst. Or.* x.1 (*eloquendi suavitas*).
22. Bernard Williams, for example, has frequently expressed this view to me in conversation.
23. For further discussion of these two alternatives, see Nussbaum, 'Crystals'; see also the comments by R. Wollheim, H. Putnam, and C. Diamond in the same (1983) issue of *NLH*.
24. On this motion, see M. F. Burnyeat, 'Aristotle on learning to be good', in Rorty, *Essays* 69–92.
25. A draft of this section was delivered at the Institute of Classical Studies in London; at Brown University; at a conference on Aristotle's Literary Theory at Florida State University; as a Eunice Belgum Memorial Lecture at St Olaf College; and at Connecticut College, Vassar College, Swarthmore College, and Smith College. I would like to thank those present for comments, and especially Julia Annas, Myles Burnyeat, Leon Golden, E. D. Hirsch, Jr, Eugene Kaelin, Ruth Padel, Charles Segal, and Richard Sorabji.

13   The betrayal of convention: a reading of Euripides' *Hecuba*

1. I have used the Teubner edition of S. G. Daitz (Leipzig 1973) and the Oxford Classical Text of Gilbert Murray (Oxford 1902). The critical discussions of the play that I have consulted include: Ernst L. Abrahamson, 'Euripides' tragedy of Hecuba', *TAPA* 83 (1952) 120–9; A. W. H. Adkins, 'Basic Greek values in Euripides' *Hecuba* and *Hercules Furens*', *CQ* NS 16 (1966) 193–219; W. Arrowsmith, introduction to translation in *Greek Tragedies* VI, ed. D. Grene and R. Lattimore (New York 1958) 84–9; D. J. Conacher, *Euripidean Drama* (Toronto 1967) 146–65; S. G. Daitz, 'Concepts of freedom and slavery in Euripides' *Hecuba*', *Hermes* 99 (1971) 217–26; G. M. A. Grube, *The Drama of Euripides* (London 1941) 93–7, 214–28; F. Heinimann, *Nomos and Phusis* (Basel 1945) 121–2; G. M. Kirkwood, 'Hecuba and *nomos*', *TAPA* 78 (1947) 61–8; H. D. F. Kitto, *Greek Tragedy* (London 1939) 216–23; A. Lesky, 'Psychologie bei Euripides', in Fondation Hardt, *Entretiens sur l'Antiquité Classique* VI (Geneva 1958) 123–50, esp. 151–68; L. Matthaei, *Studies in Greek Tragedy* (Cambridge 1918) 118–57; G. Méautis, *Mythes inconnus de la Grèce antique* (Paris 1944) 95–130; G. Norwood, *Greek Tragedy* (London 1929) 215–19; L. Pearson, *Popular Ethics in Ancient Greece* (Stanford 1962) 144ff.; M. Pohlenz, *Die Griechische Tragödie* (Göttingen 1954) 277–84; K. Reckford, 'Concepts of demoralization in Euripides' *Hecuba*', forthcoming; F. Solmsen, *Intellectual Experiments of the Greek Enlightenment* (Princeton 1975); W. Zürcher, *Die Darstellung des Menschen im Drama des Euripides* (Basel 1947) 73–84. I have considerable admiration for William Arrowsmith's translation of the play. I present my own more flat-footed rendering here for the sake of greater literalness, and also because in certain key passages Arrowsmith's renderings do not seem to me to catch the precise ethical emphasis of the text. (E.g. 799ff., where Arrowsmith informs me in conversation that he now would support a version similar to mine.)

2. It is clear that the shade, unlike the mangled corpse of which it tells us, retains the appearance of the living child, without decay or wound. Its aerial entrance, a privilege usually reserved for divinities, would not make us think, initially, of a dead human. (Polydorus explains his suspension by the fact that absence of burial forces the shade to hover, blown by the wind, about the scene of its death.) On the aerial entrance, see O. Taplin, *Greek Tragedy in Action* (Berkeley 1978) 12, 186 n. 20; W. Barrett, *Euripides: Hippolytus* (Oxford 1964) at line 1283.

3. Cf. *Inferno* XXX.16–18:

> Ecuba trista, misera e cattiva
>   poscia che vide Polissena morta
>   e del suo Polidoro in su la riva
> del mar si fu la dolorosa accorta,
>   forsennata latrò sì come cane;
>   tanto il dolor le fé la mente torta.

> Hecuba sad, wretched, captive, after she saw Polyxena dead
>   and recognized with anguish her Polydorus on the beach,
>   deranged, barked like a dog; so had grief twisted her mind.

It is significant that all modern English translations but one blunt the force of 'fé la mente torta', rendering it with some more innocuous phrase like 'wrung her heart'. (The exception is Allan Mandelbaum's new version.)

4. Influential, and characteristic, is Hermann's Preface to his 1831 (Berlin) edition. (I have only been able to locate his first edition (Leipzig 1806), which lacks this preface, so I cite these remarks from Matthaei's article.) The events of this play, he writes, are not 'tragica', they are 'nihil aliud quam detestabilia'. They would inspire tragic emotion only in the basest spectator: 'Non movent misericordiam nisi infimae plebis, tum maxime solitae et horrore et dolore perfundi cum oculis adspiciat atrocia.' Matthaei also notes that the *Hecuba* is one of three Greek tragedies that Racine did not annotate in the margins of his edition. For a twentieth-century rejection, see, for example, Norwood: 'The whole piece in its tone and method is far below the best of Eurpides' work... This pathos has no subtlety... We fall short of genuine tragedy and touch only melodrama.' After a review of such dismissals, Ernst Abrahamson, writing in 1952, makes an arresting historical judgment: 'It is possible that the horrible experiences of the last two decades were necessary to open our eyes again to the significance of this great and powerful tragedy. We have seen in our own day innumerable men and women dragged away from their devastated and burning homes, thrown into captivity and subjected to the most atrocious and infamous cruelty; we have seen them, as soon as their fortunes turned, betrayed by those whom they had called friends, and driven to the limits of abjection and despair.' Grube said something similar in 1941 (*Drama* 214).

5. Among three recent collections of papers on Euripidean drama, none includes an essay devoted to the *Hecuba*: E. Segal, ed., *Euripides* (Englewood Cliffs, NJ 1968); E. Schwinge, ed., *Euripides*, in the series *Wege der Forschung* (Darmstadt 1968) – which, however, reprints the Lesky article that contains a brief discussion of this play; *Euripide*, in the Fondation Hardt *Entretiens* VI (Geneva 1960) (the original home of Lesky's article). The play is similarly ignored by the recent collection *Greek Tragedy*, ed., T. F. Gould and C. J. Herington, *YCS* 25 (1977), most of which is devoted to Euripides. Also without discussion of the play are the influential books on Euripides by A. P. Burnett (*Catastrophe Survived: Euripides' Plays of Mixed Reversal* (Oxford 1971)), and Cedric Whitman (*Euripides and the Full Circle of Myth* (Cambridge, MA 1974)). In general works on tragedy or Greek literature the play is usually treated very briefly. Among the sources mentioned in n. 1, the strongest defenders of the play's importance include Arrowsmith, Matthaei, Abrahamson, Reckford.

6. It thus seems no accident that Hermann is in the first generation of scholars for whom Kant was a major influence; of course we should also recall that Kant was in many ways articulating an already prevalent ethical view.

7. Cf. Ch. 1 and Interlude 2. We can now add to our remarks about Kantianism in the interpretation of Greek literature the observation that Adkins's Kantian belief that circumstances beyond the agent's control cannot bring about *ethical* damage plays a regulative role in his decision about what a Greek text might and might not mean: see esp. his Appendix on the Scopas fragment of Simonides, *Merit* 357–8.

8. Although Hecuba's word for character is '*phusis*', which sometimes is connected with an idea of hereditary nature, Hecuba makes it clear that she is thinking primarily of the 'nature' that is formed by habituation and teaching. '*Phusis*' was still the only general word available for this notion, and it is used this way in other contemporary texts – cf. for example Sophocles' *Philoctetes*, 78, 88, 874, 902. Her position thus appears close to that of Protagoras's speech: cf. Ch. 4. On '*phusis*' and '*gennaios*' (Hecuba's word for 'noble', which implies fidelity to a stable nature or character), see Nussbaum, 'Consequences' 25–53; for further bibliography on '*phusis*', see Ch. 4, n. 30, among

which see esp. Heinimann, *Nomos und Phusis* (Basel 1945, repr. 1965) 89–109. The word '*charaktēr*', whose original meaning is 'distinctive mark' or 'seal', makes its first known appearance in this play, in connection with Polyxena's nobility (379).

9. Cf. Reckford, 'Concepts'. A similar view of the gods is ascribed to Hecuba in the *Troades* (415): Zeus may be 'the intellect of mortals', while Aphrodite is a name mortals invoke to justify their excesses (886, 989).

10. For much of this background, see Lloyd-Jones, *JZ*, who stresses the continuous importance, in early Greek thought about morality, of the idea that there is a stable world order that will eventually bring the offense to justice. Lloyd-Jones correctly observes that these early beliefs about cosmic justice are held in such a form that the transition to the anthropocentric conceptions of Protagoras and Democritus is 'easy and natural', and that such a transition is in many respects easier than the transition to a Platonic theory (pp. 162–3), since Zeus's justice, if not anthropocentric, is at least anthropomorphic, structurally similar to the judgments of a human judge. Without denying any of this, we can observe that the removal of the stable divine backing opens the agent to moral possibilities of a new kind. Reacting to these possibilities, which could not be guarded against by a simple return to the older theology, Plato felt that it was necessary to search for a new form of life-saving *technē*. (We can also agree with Lloyd-Jones in stressing the extent to which even the older conception itself left the agent fragile in the face of contingency, in ways that Plato found intolerable; see, for example, his remarks about conflict on p. 160, and further discussion of these in Ch. 2.)

11. Cf. esp. G. Nagy, *The Best of the Achaeans* (Baltimore 1981) 182ff., with references. On the anthropocentricity of this conception, see Nagy, *passim*, and also the Introduction by J. Redfield, p. xii. Other references are in Ch. 1, notes. For related discussion of water imagery in connection with human excellence and human *kleos*, see G. Nagy, *Comparative Studies in Greek and Indic Meter* (Cambridge, MA 1974) Ch. 3, and also my '*Psuchē* in Heraclitus, II', *Phronesis* 17 (1972) 153–70, at 160ff., where I argue that Heraclitus has an anthropocentric, or, rather, in general a species-centered ethical view, according to which value, for each kind of being, can be seen and judged only within the context of the ongoing needs and ways of life of that species.

12. On the role of relational excellence in earlier moral views, see the excellent arguments of A. A. Long, 'Morals and values in Homer', *JHS* 90 (1970) 121–39.

13. Cf. Ch. 5, pp. 148–9, for a related point about stability.

14. On the *nomos–phusis* debate in fifth-century ethical talk, cf. esp. F. Heinimann, *Nomos and Phusis*; Guthrie, *The Sophists* (= *History* III, Pt 1) 55–134; M. Pohlenz, '*Nomos* und *Phusis*', *Hermes* 81 (1953) 418–83; A. W. H. Adkins, *From the Many to the One* (London 1970) 110–26; Dover, *GPM*, 74–95, 256ff.; and my 'Eleatic conventionalism and Philolaus on the conditions of thought', *HSCP* 83 (1979) 63–108 and 'Aristophanes', with textual references and bibliography. On *phusis* see references in Ch. 4, n. 30. On *nomos*, see also P. Chantraine, *Dictionnaire étymologique de la langue grecque* III (Paris 1974) s.v., who argues that the earliest meaning of the word is 'ce qui est conforme à la règle, l'usage, les lois générales'. Cf. also the more detailed study in E. Laroche, *Histoire de la racine *nem- en grec ancien* (Paris 1949). Heinimann has an excellent detailed discussion (esp. pp. 59–85) of the evolution in the sense of '*nomos*' as it comes to be set over against '*phusis*' rather than used in close connection with it. Pp. 121ff. discuss the *Hecuba* as a salient example of this evolution.

15. The terminology of the debate is not altogether consistent. '*Phusis*', formerly associated

with the plant image and the emphasis on the growing, communal nature of anthropocentric value, becomes, gradually, opposed to '*nomos*' and associated with the view that stresses the extra-human permanence of value; so it is not altogether clear from the presence of these words alone what contrast is intended. It is interesting that Aristotle retains the more traditional usage of '*phusis*', associating the claim that excellence exists *phusei* with the idea that it is human and 'all mutable', but not, on the other hand, arbitrary or superficial; he sometimes uses '*nomos*' for the superficially conventional, or initially arbitrary (*EN* 1134b18–33).

16. I discuss criticisms of this inference in my 'Eleatic conventionalism'.

17. Cf. Critias DK 88 b25; Anon. Iambl. DK 89.

18. See Laroche, *Histoire, passim*.

19. Cf. esp. Heraclitus 102, 23; Aristotle, *EN* x.8 (which in many ways reflects motifs of the earlier literary tradition, especially with regard to its portrayals of the gods). See my '*Psuchē* in Heraclitus, ii', and Nagy, *The Best, passim*.

20. For related philosophical discussion of the relationship between human values and human ways of life, see esp. S. Cavell, *The Claim of Reason: Wittgenstein, Skepticism, Morality, and Tragedy* (New York 1980), esp. Ch. 5, and H. Putnam, *Reason, Truth, and History* (Cambridge 1980). Other references are in my 'Eleatic conventionalism'.

21. Trusting interpersonal relationships are essential to the functioning of Homeric society; it is not an exaggeration to say that the plot of the *Iliad* centers around the central ethical value of the *pistos hetairos*, 'trustworthy friend' (*cf.* xviii.235, 460, xvii. 557 of Patroclus; for other occurrences, see xv.437, 331, xvii.500, 589; *Od.* xv.539). Even enemies receive oaths and offers of hospitality without suspicious precaution, as the relationship of Achilles and Priam shows with especial clarity; this makes such violations of these bonds as the epics do depict particularly shocking. Aristotle emphasizes the importance of trust in beliefs about friendship and love at *EN* 1156b29, *EE* 1237b12, *MM* 1208b24, *Pol.* 1313b2.

22. This is now generally agreed. W. Schmid's conjecture of 417 (*Gesch. d. gr. Lit.* i Teil, 3. Band, 1. Hälfte (Munich 1949)) has long since been rejected.

23. Related Thucydidean issues are discussed in A. L. Edmunds, *Chance and Intelligence in Thucydides* (see Ch. 4). Méautis, *Mythes* links the play with Thucydides' observation of Thracian brutalities at Mycalessos in 415. Besides being anachronistic, this connection reflects Méautis's view that the *Hecuba* is a condemnation of barbarian brutality only, and a vindication of the distinction between Greek and barbarian; we shall criticize that view below. Further material on connections between Euripides and contemporary political thought can be found, for example, in Solmsen, *Intellectual Experiments* Ch. 2, esp. pp. 56ff., and J. H. Finley, Jr, 'Euripides and Thucydides', *Three Studies on Thucydides* (Cambridge, MA 1967); cf. also Daitz, 'Concepts' 219, Abrahamson, 'Euripides' tragedy' 121ff.

24. Thuc. iii.82–3. I have for the most part followed the translation of this extraordinarily difficult passage given by Gomme in his *Historical Commentary on Thucydides* ii (Oxford 1956). All changes but two are minor stylistic variations. (1) In the second sentence I accept the cogent argument of J. Wilson, '"The customary meanings of words were changed" – or were they? A note on Thucydides 3.82.4', *CQ* ns 32 (1982) 18–20. It is not the *meanings* of the ethical terms that are changed, but their applications to types of actions. (2) I diverge from Gomme (and agree with Hobbes) in the important sentence beginning 'Openness...' There is no agreement about the force of the construction with *metechei*. The sentence literally reads, 'The open [guileless], in which

above all the noble participates (*metechei*)...' Some translators understand the sense to be, 'Openness, of which noble character is the greatest part...' If, however, we compare the corresponding construction at 1.84.3, where the point must be to explain how Spartans came by their courage by saying that the greatest part of courage is a sense of shame, and the greatest part of the sense of shame is that moderation and orderliness which have just been said to be the products of Spartan law (rather than to explain the genesis of orderliness by tracing it to courage), we have strong reason to follow Hobbes. This clearly makes better sense in any case: it is very bizarre to speak of noble character as a *part* of trustfulness, whereas it is perfectly reasonable, and a sense borne out by the rest of the passage, to speak of trustfulness as a chief *part* of noble character. This accords, as well, with Plato' use of constructions with *metechei*. The thing *participated in* (viz. the form) is what explains the character of the things that participate. 'Justice, in which above all Socrates participates', would mean not that Socrates is the greatest part of what Justice is, but, obviously, that Justice is a big part of what Socrates is. Cf. also *Symp.* 211A, where 'face or hands or any other of those things in which body *metechei*' means not that body is a part of face and hands, but that these are parts of body.

25. Plato's Thrasymachus, asked whether justice is, in his view, a vice, replies that it is 'a very noble simplicity' (*panu gennaia euētheia*, 348C12): it is the way your character is when you are still trusting in communal agreements, before you discover that they are made by selfish people to secure power for themselves.

26. I have not found this point in the literature. The importance of the contrast between Polyxena and Hecuba is emphasized by Conacher, *Euripidean Drama* (Toronto 1967) 13, who, however, makes the contrast a contrast only of characters or personalities: it is because Hecuba has a less noble character than her daughter that she is corrupted. This approach, which ignores both Polyxena's own fears of corruption and the play's emphasis on the cumulative weight of Hecuba's discoveries, is well criticized by Abrahamson, 128–9. Cf. also Reckford, 'Concepts' n. 6 with further references.

27. On the connection between eyes and trust, see (for only a few among many examples) Pindar, *Nem.* VIII.40–4 (cf. Ch. 1), Aes. *Ag.* 795ff., *Cho.* 671, Soph. *Phil.* 110, Eur. *Ion*. For a full discussion of the eye and its symbolism in Greek and related cultures, see W. Deonna, *Le symbolisme de l'oeil* (Paris 1965). See also Ch. 3, pp. 70–2, 76–9 and n. 63.

28. Cf. Talthybius's wish to die before he encounters something shameful (497–8); see Abrahamson, 'Euripides' tragedy' 129.

29. The debate on this issue is comprehensively reviewed by Reckford, 'Concepts' n. 1. Outspoken critics of the play's structure in recent times include Kitto, *Greek Tragedy* (215, 268–9), Norwood, *Greek Tragedy*; some critics believe that the only substantial connection between the parts is that both present sufferings of Hecuba that contribute to her decline (see Grube, *The Drama*, Pohlenz, *Die Griechische Tragödie*). Matthaei, *Studies*, argues that this would not be unity enough; but her view of the connection – that there is a contrast between the requirements of a communal justice based on *nomos* and the demands of personal, private justice – seems unable to explain the decline itself.

30. Lines 7, 19, 26, 82, 710, 715, 774, 781, 790, 794, 852, 890, 1216, 1235, 1247.

31. Lines 1227, 794.

32. For the importance of *xenia* as a fundamental relational value, see for example *Iliad* VI.119ff., *Od.* IX.370 (where the Cyclopes' violation of *xenia* is the sign of their complete moral obtuseness and their distance from the human – compare Ch. 8). The entire issue

is well discussed in H. Bolkestein, *Wohltätigkeit und Armenpflege im vorchristlichen Altertum* (Utrecht 1939) 79–94, 111, 118–32, 214–31. Cf. also M. I. Finley, *The World of Odysseus* (London 1956), M. Nilsson, *Gesch. der gr. Relig.*, Erster Bd. (Munich 1955) 417–23; E. Benveniste, *Le Vocabulaire des institutions indo-européennes* (Paris 1969) I, 87ff., 341ff. On the Cyclopes, see G. Kirk, *Myth: its Meaning and Functions in Ancient and Other Cultures* (Cambridge 1970) 162ff.

33. The other male–female pair that figures prominently in the *Hecuba* is Helen and Paris. The crime of Paris, which also involves a violation of *xenia* and is responsible for destroying the city can be confronted, nonetheless, without moral disorientation, partly because the erotic motivation (cf. 635–7) makes it so predictable, and almost inevitable.

34. For discussion of Homeric and related views of the importance of according proper treatment to the corpse, see Nussbaum, '*Psuchē*', with references.

35. Kirkwood, 'Hecuba and *nomos*' argues that Hecuba's moral change occurs only later, when Agamemnon refuses her his aid. He needs, however, to distinguish two moral changes: (1) the change from trust in binding conventions to suspicious, solitary revenge-seeking; and (2) the change from the belief that other people can be used as instrumental means in this revenge to the belief that it is best to work alone. The second is the change that takes place in the scene with Agamemnon; and it seems far less important than the one that takes place here. Here she realizes that everything is 'untrustworthy'; here she decides that she must take up a new *nomos* in place of the old; here she announces her intention of being ruled by the revenge spirit. Conacher, *Euripidean Drama* (20), Pohlenz, *Die Griechische Tragödie* (291), and Grube, *The Drama* (222) all locate the crucial transition at the discovery of the murder; Méautis, *Mythes* agrees (116), adding that the 'derniers liens' are broken in the scene with Agamemnon.

36. It is impossible to convey in translation all the ambiguities of this answer. '*Apiston*' can mean either 'untrusted', 'un-looked-for', 'incredible', or 'untrustworthy', 'unreliable'. So Hecuba expresses in one word both her surprise and her sense of betrayal.

37. The play contains an unusually large number of references to *tuchē* through various connected words; see esp. 488–91, where Talthybius's response to the disorder he sees is to wonder whether the world of mortal beings is not governed by *tuchē* alone. See Reckford, 'Concepts' n. 9.

38. Notice that the word '*deinon*' is used here to signal Hecuba's shift: instead of the remarkable (*deinon*) firmness of good character, we have a new and more terrible wonder: the remarkable wrong done to this woman (694).

39. The importance of this pun as a sign of Hecuba's moral change is also emphasized by Reckford, 'Concepts' (n. 7, with bibliography). On the etymology, see Laroche, *Histoire*; Chantraine, *Dictionnaire* III s.v. *nomos*.

40. See n. 27 above.

41. This idea receives a remarkable development in Plato's *Alcibiades* I 132C–133B, where it is claimed that just as self-seeing requires seeing one's own image in the *korē* of the beholder, so self-knowledge concerning things of the soul requires knowing oneself in another's soul.

42. Cf. the discussion of Aes. *Eum.*, this ch., pp. 416–17.

43. Euripides was notorious in antiquity for this interest, which is parodied by Aristophanes both in *Frogs* and in *Thesmophoriazusae*, where Eurpides masquerades as a woman in order to gain entrée into restricted religious observances.

44. Lines 886ff. The first is the story that forms the basis for Aeschylus's *Suppliants*: the daughters of Danaus, outraged by the enforced marriage with the sons of Aegyptus,

kill their husbands on the wedding night. In the second, the women of Lemnos, having somehow offended Aphrodite, are afflicted by a disgusting odor that makes their husbands neglect them for foreign concubines. Enraged at this, they slaughter all the males. Both myths seem to express in opposed ways a woman's desire for bodily self-sufficiency, which expresses itself in vindictive violations of a situation of trust.

45. Although the women seem to act in concert, careful examination of their dialogue and of the choral lyrics reveals that there is no genuine cooperation or mutuality here, but only parallel projects of revenge. The choral lyrics, sometimes criticized for their dissociation from the action (cf. Kitto, *Greek Tragedy* 217), reveal, in their completely personal and solipsistic quality, the degree to which each woman, as an 'I', is obsessed with private dreams of revenge. Just following the inauguration of the revenge scheme is the most solipsistic lyric of all (905–52), in which each woman remembers herself 'gazing at the endless light deep in the golden mirror'. A mirror now substitutes for the eyes of another (cf. Aes. *Ag.* 839). Although they sing and act in unison, the vision of each is private.

46. See H. Scholz, *Der Hund in der griechisch-römischen Magie und Religion* (Berlin 1937) esp. 7ff.; Méautis, *Mythes*; Nagy, *The Best* 312–13; J. Redfield, *Nature and Culture in the Iliad* (Chicago 1975) 193–202; and now, R. Parker, *Miasma* (Oxford 1983).

47. On this speech, see Conacher, *Euripidean Drama* 22; Grube, *The Drama* 223–4; Méautis, *op. cit.* 127–8.

48. See Conacher, *op. cit.* 23–4 (who compares Aes. *Ag.* 385); Solmsen, *Intellectual Experiments* 56–7 – who strangely speaks of a 'utopian idea', an 'experiment of reason'.

49. Cf. *Cho.* 924, 1054; *Eum.* 132, 246, 253–4; also 106, 111, 117ff., 130, 326, 412; though they also have traits of other animals (cf. 48, where they are compared to Gorgons).

50. Recall the importance of good-will and well-wishing in Aristotelian *philia*.

51. Compare the discussion of Cyclopes and other solitary beings in Chs. 8 and 12.

52. Oedipus's blinding is self-inflicted and an act of insight and acknowledgment; he recognizes by and in pain the true significance of his act, therefore the extent to which horrible acts can become ours without our voluntary collaboration. Polymestor, too, is a victim of the world; but the victimization cuts, in his case as in Hecuba's, deeper; there is no dignity and no recognition, on either side.

53. Compare the excellent account of the meaning of bodily violence in Seneca in C. Segal, 'Boundary violation and the landscape of the self in Senecan tragedy', *Antike und Abendland* 29 (1983) 172–87.

54. I am thinking here primarily of the *Genealogy of Morals*. Nietzsche's position in *Zarathustra* is more complex. It appears there that all human beings are in need of being delivered from revenge; and this can be accomplished only by the acceptance of the idea of eternal return, therefore of the worldliness, temporality, and untrustworthiness of human existence.

55. Abrahamson, 'Euripides' tragedy' correctly emphasizes (128–9) that Hecuba's decline is not the fault of an especially weak character; indeed, even her choices can be defended as right within these terrible circumstances.

56. 'Perhaps it is easier, where you live, to kill guest-friends. For us Greeks, at any rate, this is a shameful thing.' Compare Odysseus's claims about barbarians at 328–31; his remarks about barbarian honor to their dead would be rejected by an audience whose central poetic text is the story of a 'barbarian' people's commitment to honor their dead. Nor does the play support his charges: it ends with the departure of Hecuba to bury her dead children. As for Agamemnon, the difference he alleges is nowhere

supported in literature or myth: only non-human Cyclopes lightly violate *xenia*. On Agamemnon, see also Matthaei, *Studies* 150, and Grube, *The Drama* 222, who oddly calls this behavior 'delightfully human'.

57. It is old, clearly, in relation to its own poetic tradition: compare the ending of Sophocles' *Philoctetes*, where the returning warriors will be escorted from the island in a ship conveyed by 'great destiny, and the judgment of friends, and the all-subduing *daimōn*, who brought this to fulfillment'. (See Nussbaum, 'Consequences'.)

58. In my work on this chapter, I am grateful to Kenneth Reckford, who first urged me to include a discussion of the *Hecuba* in this book; to audiences at Harvard University and the University of Iowa for a most helpful discussion; to Ruth Padel and to Harvey Yunis for extremely helpful comments.

Bibliography

Titles frequently cited in the notes are referred to only by author's surname and abbreviated title: the abbreviations are given at the conclusion of the relevant entries here.

Abrahamson, E. L. 'Euripides' tragedy of Hecuba', *TAPA* 83 (1952), 120–9.

Ackrill, J. L. 'Aristotle's distinction between *energeia* and *kinesis*', in R. Bambrough, ed., *New Essays on Plato and Aristotle*. London, 1965, pp. 121–41.

'In defense of Platonic division', in O. P. Wood and G. Pitcher, eds., *Ryle*. Garden City, 1970, pp. 373–92.

'Aristotle on "Good" and the Categories', in S. M. Stern, *et al.*, eds., *Islamic Philosophy and the Classical Tradition: Essays presented to Richard Walzer*. Oxford, 1972, pp. 17–25. Repr. in J. Barnes, ed., *Articles*, Vol. II, pp. 17–24.

'Aristotle on *Eudaimonia*', *PBA* 60 (1974), 339–59. Repr. in A. O. Rorty, ed., *Essays*, pp. 15–34.

'Aristotle on action', *Mind* 87 (1978), 595–601. Repr. in Rorty, *Essays*, pp. 93–103.

Adam, J., ed. *The Republic of Plato*, 2 vols. Cambridge, 1902, repr. 1969.

Adkins, A. W. H. *Merit and Responsibility*. Oxford, 1960. [*Merit*]

'Basic Greek values in Euripides' *Hecuba* and *Hercules Furens*', *CQ* NS 16 (1966), 193–219.

From the Many to the One. London, 1970.

'*Arete, Techne*, democracy and sophists: *Protagoras* 316B–328D', *JHS* 93 (1973), 3–12.

Allan, D. J. '*Magna Moralia* and *Nicomachean Ethics*', *JHS* 77 (1957), 7–11.

Allen, R. E., ed. *Studies in Plato's Metaphysics*. London, 1965.

Annas, J. *Aristotle's Metaphysics M and N*. Clarendon Aristotle Series. Oxford, 1976.

'Plato and Aristotle on friendship and altruism', *Mind* 86 (1977), 532–54.

'Truth and knowledge', in M. Schofield, *et al.*, eds., *Doubt and Dogmatism*, pp. 84–104.

An Introduction to Plato's Republic. Oxford, 1981.

Anton, J. 'Some Dionysian references in the Platonic dialogues', *CJ* 58 (1962–3), 49–55.

Anton, J. and Kustas, G., eds. *Essays in Ancient Greek Philosophy*. Albany, NY, 1972.

Arrowsmith, W. Introduction to and translation of Euripides' *Hecuba*, in D. Grene and R. Lattimore, *Greek Tragedies*. Vol. III, Chicago, 1959, pp. 488–554.

Austin, J. L. '*Agathon* and *Eudaimonia* in the ethics of Aristotle', in Austin, *Philosophical Papers*. Oxford, 1961, pp. 1–31. Repr. in J. M. E. Moravcsik, ed., *Aristotle*, pp. 261–96.

Philosophical Papers. Oxford, 1961.

Bacon, H. 'Socrates crowned', *Virginia Quarterly Review* 35 (1959), 415–30.

Bahmueller, C. *The National Charity Company: Jeremy Bentham's Silent Revolution*. Berkeley, 1981.

Bambrough, R., ed. *New Essays on Plato and Aristotle*. London, 1965.

Barnes, J., Schofield, M. and Sorabji, R., eds. *Articles on Aristotle*. Vol. I, London, 1975; Vol. II, 1977; Vol. III, 1979; Vol. IV, 1979. [*Articles*]

Barrett, W., ed. *Euripides: Hippolytus*. Oxford, 1964.

Beauvoir, S. de. *The Second Sex* (1949), trans. H. M. Parshley. New York, 1952.

Beazley, J. 'Some Attic vases in the Cyprus Museum', *PBA* 33 (1947), 195–244.

Becker, O. *Zwei Untersuchungen zur antiken Logik, Klassisch-philologische Studien* 17 (1957), 20ff.

Benardete, S. G. 'Two notes on Aeschylus' *Septem*', *Wiener Studien* 1 (1967), 22–30; 2 (1968), 5–17.

    'A reading of Sophocles' *Antigone*', *Interpretation* 4 (1975), 148–96; 5 (1975), 1–55, 148–84.

Benveniste, E. *Noms d'agent et noms d'action en indo-européen*. Paris, 1948.

    Le Vocabulaire des institutions indo-européennes, 2 vols. Paris, 1969.

Berlin, I. *Concepts and Categories*. New York, 1978.

Bernays, J. *Grundzüge der verlorenen Abhandlung des Aristoteles über Wirkung der Tragödie*. Breslau, 1857; repr. Hildesheim, 1970.

Berti, E., ed. *Aristotle on Science: the 'Posterior Analytics'*, Proceedings of the 8th Symposium Aristotelicum. Padua, 1981.

Boeder, H., 'Der frühgriechische Wortgebrauch von *Logos* und *Alētheia*', *Archiv für Begriffsgeschichte* 4 (1959), 81–112.

Bolkestein, H. *Wohltätigkeit und Armenpflege im vorchristlichen Altertum*. Utrecht, 1939.

Bolton, R. 'Essentialism and semantic theory in Aristotle', *PR* 85 (1976), 514–55.

Bowersock, G. W., Burkert, W. and Putnam, M. C. J., eds. *Arktouros: Hellenic Studies Presented to Bernard M. W. Knox*. Berlin/New York, 1979.

Bowra, C. M. 'Plato's epigram on Dion's death', *AJP* 59 (1938), 394–404.

Bradley, A. C. 'Hegel's theory of tragedy', *Oxford Lectures on Poetry*. London, 1950, pp. 69–95. Repr. in A. and H. Paolucci, eds., *Hegel on Tragedy*, pp. 367–88.

Brandt, R. B. 'The morality and rationality of suicide', in J. Rachels, ed., *Moral Problems*. New York, 1975, pp. 363–87.

Brandwood, L. *A Concordance to Plato*. Leeds, 1976.

Bremer, J. M. *Hamartia*. Amsterdam, 1969.

Bultmann, R. 'Polis und Hades in der *Antigone* des Sophokles', in H. Diller, ed., *Sophokles*. Wege der Forschung. Darmstadt, 1967, pp. 311–24.

Bundy, E. *Studia Pindarica*. Berkeley, 1962.

Burger, R. *Plato's Phaedrus*. Birmingham, 1980.

Buriks, A. A. *Peri Tuches: De ontwikkeling van het begrip tuche tot aan de Romeinse tijd, hoofdzakelijk in de philosophie*. Leiden, 1955.

Burkert, W. 'Greek tragedy and sacrificial ritual', *GRBS* 7 (1966), 87–121.

    Homo Necans: Interpretationen altgriechischer Opferriten und Mythen. Berlin, 1972.

Burnett, A. P. *Catastrophe Survived: Euripides' Plays of Mixed Reversal*. Oxford, 1971.

Burnyeat, M. F. 'Protagoras and self-refutation in Plato's *Theaetetus*', *PR* 85 (1976), 172–95.

    'Protagoras and self-refutation in later Greek philosophy', *PR* 85 (1976), 44–69.

    'The virtues of Plato', *NYRB* 26 (1979), 56–60.

    'Can the skeptic live his skepticism?', in M. Schofield, *et al.*, eds., *Doubt and Dogmatism*, pp. 20–53.

    'Aristotle on learning to be good', in Rorty, *Essays*, pp. 69–92.

    'Aristotle on understanding knowledge', in E. Berti, ed., *Aristotle on Science*. Padua, 1981, pp. 97–139.

    Review of M. C. Nussbaum, *Aristotle's De Motu Animalium*, *AGP* 63 (1981), 184–9.

Bury, R. G., ed. *The Symposium of Plato*. Cambridge, 1932; repr. 1966.

Camerer, L. *Praktische Klugheit bei Herodot: Untersuchungen zu den Beriffen Mechane, Techne, Sophie*. Tübingen, 1965.

Cavell, S. *The Claim of Reason: Wittgenstein, Skepticism, Morality, and Tragedy.* New York, 1979.

Chantraine, P. *Dictionnaire étymologique de la langue grecque*, Vol. III. Paris, 1974.

Clay, D. 'The tragic and comic poet of the *Symposium*', *Arion* NS 2 (1975), 238–61.
   'Socrates' prayer to Pan', in G. W. Bowersock, W. Burkert and M. C. J. Putnam, eds., *Arktouros*. Berlin/New York, 1979, pp. 345–53.

Cole, A. T. *Democritus and the Sources of Greek Anthropology.* New Haven, 1967.
   'The relativism of Protagoras', *YCS* 22 (1972), 19–46.

Conacher, D. J. *Euripidean Drama.* Toronto, 1967.

Connor, W. R. *The New Politicians of Fifth-Century Athens.* Princeton, 1971.

Cooper, J. M. 'The *Magna Moralia* and Aristotle's moral philosophy', *AJP* 94 (1973), 327–49.
   Reason and Human Good in Aristotle. Cambridge, MA, 1975.
   'Aristotle on friendship', in Rorty, *Essays*, pp. 301–40.
   Review of A. Kenny, *The Aristotelian Ethics*, in *Nous* 15: 1 (1981), 381–92.
   'Hypothetical necessity', forthcoming in A. Gotthelf, ed., Festschrift for David Balme. Pittsburgh, 1986.

Cornford, F. M. *Principium Sapientiae.* Cambridge, 1952.

Crombie, I. M. *An Examination of Plato's Doctrines.* Vol. I, London, 1962; Vol. II, 1963.

Cross, R. C. and Woozley, A. D. *Plato's Republic: a Philosophical Commentary.* London, 1964.

Crotty, K. *Song and Action: the Victory Odes of Pindar.* Baltimore, 1982.

Daitz, S. G. 'Concepts of freedom and slavery in Euripides' *Hecuba*', *Hermes* 99 (1971), 217–26.
   ed. *Euripidis Hecuba.* Teubner edition. Leipzig, 1973.

Davidson, A. *Religion and the Fanaticism of Reason.* Ph.D. thesis, Harvard University, 1982.

Davidson, D. 'How is weakness of will possible?', in J. Feinberg, ed., *Moral Concepts.* Oxford, 1969, pp. 93–113.

Dawe, R. D. 'The end of the *Seven Against Thebes*', *CQ* NS 17 (1967), 16–28.
   'Some reflections on *atē* and *hamartia*', *HSCP* 72 (1967), 89–123.

Denniston, J. D. and Page, D., eds. *Aeschylus: Agamemnon.* Oxford, 1957.

Deonna, W. *Le Symbolisme de l'oeil.* Paris, 1965.

Derrida, J. 'La pharmacie de Platon', *Tel Quel* 32, 33 (1968), 3–48. Repr. in Derrida, *La Dissémination*, Paris, 1972, pp. 69–197.

Detienne, M. *Les Maîtres de vérité en grèce ancienne.* Paris, 1967.
   Les Jardins d'Adonis. Paris, 1972.

Detienne, M. and Vernant, J.-P. *Les Ruses de l'intelligence: la Mètis des grecs.* Paris, 1974. [*Mètis*]
   eds. *La Cuisine du sacrifice en pays grec.* Paris, 1979.

Diamond, C. 'Having a rough story about what moral philosophy is', *NLH* 15 (1983), 155–70.

Dirlmeier, F., trans. *Aristotle: Magna Moralia.* Berlin, 1958.

Dodds, E. R. *The Greeks and the Irrational.* Berkeley, 1951. [*GI*]
   trans., and comm. *Plato: Gorgias.* Oxford, 1959.
   'Morals and politics in the *Oresteia*', *PCPS* 186 NS 6 (1960), 19–31. Repr. in Dodds, *The Ancient Concept of Progress*, pp. 45–63.
   'On misunderstanding the *Oedipus Rex*', *GR* 13 (1966), 37–49.
   The Ancient Concept of Progress and Other Essays on Greek Literature and Belief. Oxford, 1973. [*ACP*]

Donagan, A. 'Consistency in rationalist moral systems', *JP* 81 (1984), 291–309.

Dorter, K. 'The significance of the speeches in Plato's *Symposium*', *Philosophy and Rhetoric* 2 (1969), 215–34.

Dover, K. J. 'The date of Plato's *Symposium*', *Phronesis* 10 (1965), 2–20.

'Aristophanes' speech in Plato's *Symposium*', *JHS* 86 (1966), 41–50.

Lysias and the Corpus Lysiacum. Berkeley, 1968.

Aristophanic Comedy. London, 1972.

'Some neglected aspects of Agamemnon's dilemma', *JHS* 93 (1973), 58–69.

Greek Popular Morality. Oxford, 1974. [*GPM*]

Greek Homosexuality. Cambridge, MA, 1978. [*GH*]

'The portrayal of moral evaluation in Greek poetry', *JHS* 103 (1983), 35–48.

Düring, I. *Aristotle in the Ancient Biographical Tradition*. Göteborg, 1957.

Aristoteles. Heidelberg, 1966.

Düring, I. and Owen, G. E. L., eds. *Aristotle and Plato in the Mid-Fourth Century*. Proceedings of the 1st Symposium Aristotelicum. Göteborg, 1960.

Edelstein, L. *The Idea of Progress in Classical Antiquity*. Baltimore, 1967.

Edmunds, A. L. *Chance and Intelligence in Thucydides*. Cambridge, MA, 1975.

Edwards, M. 'Agamemnon's decision: freedom and folly in Aeschylus' *Agamemnon*', *California Studies in Classical Antiquity* 10 (1977), 17–38.

Ellendt, F. T. *Lexicon Sophocleum*. Berlin, 1872.

Else, G. *Aristotle's Poetics: the Argument*. Cambridge, MA, 1967.

Engberg-Pederson, T. 'More on Aristotelian epagoge', *Phronesis* 24 (1979), 301–19.

Erbse, H. 'Zur Exodos der Sieben', in J. L. Heller, ed., *Serta Turyniana*. Urbana, 1974, pp. 169–98.

Farnell, L. R., trans. and comm. *The Works of Pindar*. London, 1932.

Finley, Jr., J. H. 'Euripides and Thucydides', in J. H. Finley, *Three Studies on Thucydides*. Cambridge, MA, 1967.

Finley, M. I. *The World of Odysseus*. London, 1956.

Flashar, H. 'The critique of Plato's ideas in Aristotle's *Ethics*', trans. in Barnes, *Articles* II, 1–16.

Foot, P. 'Moral realism and moral dilemma', *JP* 80 (1983), 379–98.

Fraassen, B. van. 'Values and the heart's command', *JP* 70 (1973), 15–19.

Fraenkel, E., ed. *Aeschylus, Agamemnon*, 3 vols. Oxford, 1950.

'Schluss des *Sieben gegen Theben*', *Mus Helv* 21 (1964), 58–64.

Frede, M. 'Des Skeptikers Meinungen', *Neue Hefte für Philosophie* 15/16 (1979), 102–29.

'The original notion of cause', in M. Schofield, *et al.*, eds., *Doubt and Dogmatism*, pp. 217–49.

Freud, S. *Totem and Taboo: Some Points of Agreement Between the Mental Lives of Savages and Neurotics* (1912–13), trans. J. Strachey. New York, 1950.

Frischer, B. *The Sculpted Word: Epicureanism and Philosophical Recruitment in Ancient Greece*. Berkeley, 1982.

Fritz, K. von. 'The discovery of incommensurability by Hippasus of Metapontum', in D. Furley and R. E. Allen, eds., *Studies in Presocratic Philosophy*. Vol. 1, London, 1970, pp. 382–442.

Furley, D. and Allen, R. E., eds. *Studies in Presocratic Philosophy*, 2 vols. London, 1970.

Furley, D. 'Self movers', in G. E. R. Lloyd and G. E. L. Owen, eds., *Aristotle on Mind and the Senses*. Proceedings of the 7th Symposium Aristotelicum. Cambridge, 1978, pp. 165–80.

Gadamer, H. G. *Platons dialektische Ethik*. Hamburg, 1968.

Gagarin, M. *Aeschylean Drama*. Berkeley, 1976.
'Socrates' *hubris* and Alcibiades' failure', *Phoenix* 31 (1977), 22–37.
Geach, P. 'Plato's *Euthyphro*', *The Monist* 50 (1966), 369–82.
Gibson, M. 'Rationality', *PPA* 6 (1977), 193–225.
Goheen, R. F. *The Imagery of Sophocles' Antigone*. Princeton, 1951.
Golden, L. 'Catharsis', *TAPA* 93 (1962), 51–60.
   trans. *Aristotle's Poetics*. Englewood Cliffs, NJ, 1968.
   'Mimesis and catharsis', *CP* 64 (1969), 45–53.
Goldschmidt, V. *Les Dialogues de Platon*. Paris, 1947, 2nd ed., 1963.
Gomme, A. W. *A Historical Commentary on Thucydides*. Vol. I, Oxford, 1945; Vol. II and
   Vol. III, 1956.
Gomme, A. W., Dover, K. J. and Andrewes, A. *A Historical Commentary on Thucydides*. Vol.
   IV, Oxford, 1970.
Gosling, J. C. B. *Pleasure and Desire*. Oxford, 1969.
   'More Aristotelian pleasures', *PAS* 74 (1973–4), 15–34.
Gosling, J. C. B. and Taylor, C. C. W. *The Greeks on Pleasure*. Oxford, 1982.
Gould, T. *Platonic Love*. London, 1963.
Grice, H. P. 'Method in philosophical psychology', *PAPA* 48 (1974–5), 23–53.
Griswold, C. 'The ideas and criticism of poetry in Plato's *Republic*, Book 10', *JHP* 19 (1981),
   135–50.
   'Style and philosophy: the case of Plato's dialogues', *The Monist* 63 (1980), 530–46.
   'Self-knowledge and the "idea" of the soul in Plato's *Phaedrus*', *Revue de Métaphysique
   et de Morale* 26 (1981), 472–94.
Groag, E. 'Zue Lehre vom Wesen der Seele in Platons *Phaedros* und im x. Buche der
   Republik', *Wiener Studien* 37 (1915), 189–22.
Grote, G. *A History of Greece*. Vol. VII, London, 1888.
Grube, G. M. A. *The Drama of Euripides*. London, 1941.
Gundert, H. *Der platonische Dialog*. Heidelberg, 1968.
Guthrie, W. K. C., trans. *Plato, Protagoras and Meno*. London, 1956.
   'Plato's views on the nature of the soul', in G. Vlastos, *Plato*, II, pp. 230–43.
   A History of Greek Philosophy. Vol. III, Cambridge, 1969; Vol. IV, 1975. [*History*]
Hackforth, R. 'Hedonism in Plato's *Protagoras*', *CQ* NS 22 (1982), 39–42.
   trans., and comm. *Plato's Phaedrus*. Indianapolis, 1952.
Hammond, N. G. L. 'Personal freedom and its limitations in the *Oresteia*', *JHS* 85 (1965),
   42–55.
Hanslick, E. *The Beautiful in Music* (7th ed. Leipzig, 1885), trans. G. Cohen. Indianapolis,
   1957.
Hardie, W. F. R. *Aristotle's Ethical Theory*. 2nd ed., Oxford, 1981.
Hare, R. M. *The Language of Morals*. Oxford, 1952.
   Moral Thinking. Oxford, 1981.
Harsh, P. W. '*Hamartia* again', *TAPA* 76 (1945), 47–58.
Hartland-Swann, J. 'Plato as poet: a critical interpretation', *Philosophy* 26 (1951), 3–18,
   131–41.
Hatzfeld, J. 'Du nouveau sur Phèdre', *REA* 41 (1939), 311–18.
Havelock, E. *The Liberal Temper in Greek Politics*. London, 1957.
Heath, T. *A History of Greek Mathematics*. Oxford, 1921.
Hegel, G. W. F. *The Philosophy of Fine Art* (1835), trans. F. P. B. Osmaston. London, 1920.

Heinimann, F. *Nomos und Phusis*. Basel, 1945.

Henderson, J. J. *The Maculate Muse: Obscene Language in Attic Comedy*. New Haven, 1975.

Henrichs, A. 'Human sacrifice in Greek religion: three case studies', in *Le Sacrifice dans l'antiquité*, Fondation Hardt, *Entretiens sur l'Antiquité Classique* 27 (1981), 195–235.

Hermann, G. *Euripidis Opera*. 1st ed., Leipzig 1800; 2nd ed., 1831.

Hester, D. A. 'Sophocles the unphilosophical: a study in the *Antigone*', *Mnemosyne* 4th ser. 24 (1971), 11–59.

Hintikka, K. J. J. 'Deontic logic and its philosophical morals', in Hintikka, *Models for Modalities*. Dordrecht, 1969, pp. 184–214.

Hirzel, R. *Themis, Dike und Verwandtes*. Leipzig, 1907.

Holwerda, D. *Commentatio de vocis quae est φύσις vi atque usu*. Groningen, 1955.

Hook, J. *Friendship and Politics in Aristotle's Ethical and Political Thought*. B.A. thesis *summa cum laude*, Harvard University, 1977.

Hornsby, R. 'Significant action in the *Symposium*', *CJ* 52 (1956–7), 37–40.

Hume, D. *A Treatise of Human Nature* (1739), ed. L. A. Selby-Bigge. Oxford, 1888.

Hyland, D. 'Why Plato wrote dialogues', *Philosophy and Rhetoric* 1 (1968), 38–50.

Irwin, T. H. 'Aristotle's discovery of metaphysics', *RM* 31 (1977), 210–29.

Plato's Moral Theory. Oxford, 1977. [*PMT*]

trans. and comm. *Plato: Gorgias*. Clarendon Plato Series. Oxford, 1979.

'Reason and responsibility in Aristotle', in Rorty, *Essays*, pp. 117–56.

'Aristotle's concept of signification', in M. Schofield and M. C. Nussbaum, eds., *Language and Logos*. Cambridge, 1982.

Isnardi Parente, M. *Technē*. Florence, 1966.

Jebb, R. C., ed., and comm. *Sophocles: the Antigone*. Cambridge, 1900.

Joachim, H. H. *The Nicomachean Ethics*. Oxford, 1951.

Jones, J. *On Aristotle and Greek Tragedy*. London, 1962.

Kahn, C. H. *Anaximander and the Origins of Greek Cosmology*. New York, 1960.

The Art and Thought of Heraclitus. Cambridge, 1979.

'Drama and dialectic in Plato's *Gorgias*', *OSAP* 1 (1983), 75–121.

Kamerbeek, J. C. *Sophocles' Antigone*. Leiden, 1945.

Kant, I. *Groundwork of the Metaphysics of Morals* (Berlin, 1785), trans. H. J. Paton. New York, 1960.

Critique of Practical Reason (Berlin, 1788), trans. Lewis White Beck. Indianapolis, 1956.

Religion Within the Limits of Reason Alone (Berlin, 1791), trans. T. M. Greene and H. H. Hudson. New York, 1960.

The Metaphysical Elements of Justice. Part I of *The Metaphysics of Morals* (Berlin, 1797), trans. J. Ladd. Indianapolis, 1965.

The Doctrine of Virtue. Part II of *The Metaphysics of Morals* (Berlin, 1797), trans. M. J. Gregor. Philadelphia, 1969.

Kassel, R., ed. *Aristotelis Ars Rhetorica*. Berlin, 1976.

Kenny, A. *The Aristotelian Ethics*. Oxford, 1978.

Aristotle's Theory of the Will. London, 1979.

'A stylometric comparison between five disputed works and the remainder of the Aristotelian corpus', in P. Moraux and J. Wiesner, eds., *Zweifelhaftes im Corpus Aristotelium*. Berlin, 1983, pp. 345–66.

Kerferd, G. B. 'Plato's Account of the Relativism of Protagoras', *Durham University Journal* 42 NS 11 (1949–50), 20–6.

'Protagoras' doctrine of justice and virtue in the *Protagoras* of Plato', *JHS* 73 (1953), 42–5.

The Sophistic Movement. Cambridge, 1981.

Keyt, D. 'Intellectualism in Aristotle', in G. C. Simmons, ed., *Paideia: Special Aristotle Issue* (1978), 138–57.

Kirk, G. S. *Myth: its Meaning and Functions in Ancient and Other Cultures*. Cambridge, 1970.

Kirkwood, G. M. 'Hecuba and *nomos*', *TAPA* 78 (1947), 61–8.

Kitto, H. D. F. *Greek Tragedy*. London, 1939.

Knox, B. *The Heroic Temper: Studies in Sophoclean Tragedy*. Berkeley, 1964.

'The Socratic method', review of K. J. Dover, *Greek Homosexuality*, *NYRB* 25 (1979), 5–8.

Kosman, L. A. 'Predicating the good', *Phronesis* 13 (1968), 171–4.

'Explanation and understanding in Aristotle's *Posterior Analytics*', in Lee, *Exegesis*, pp. 374–92.

'Platonic love', in W. H. Werkmeister, ed., *Facets of Plato's Philosophy*, *Phronesis Suppl.* II. Assen, 1976, pp. 53–69.

'Being properly affected', in Rorty, *Essays*, pp. 103–16.

'Substance, being, and *energeia*', *OSAP* 2 (1984), 121–49.

Kranz, W. 'Diotima', *Die Antike* 2 (1926), 313–27.

Kraut, R. 'Reason and justice in Plato's *Republic*', in Lee, *Exegesis*, pp. 207–24.

Krentz, A. A. 'Dramatic form and philosophical content in Plato's Dialogues', *Phil Lit* 7 (1983), 32–47.

Krischer, T. '*Etymos* und *alēthēs*', *Philologus* 109 (1965), 161–74.

Kuhn, H. 'The true tragedy: on the relationship between Greek tragedy and Plato', *HSCP* 52 (1941), 1–40; 53 (1942), 37–88.

Kuhns, R. *The House, the City, and the Judge: the Growth of Moral Awareness in the Oresteia.* Indianapolis, 1962.

Kurz, D. *Akribeia: das Ideal der Exaktheit bei den Griechen bis Aristoteles*. Göppingen, 1970.

Laroche, E. *Histoire de la racine *nem- en grec ancien*. Paris, 1949.

Lebeck, A. *The Oresteia: a Study in Language and Structure*. Washington, Center for Hellenic Studies; distributed by Harvard University Press. Cambridge, MA, 1971.

'The central myth of Plato's *Phaedrus*', *GRBS* 13 (1972), 267–90.

Lee, E. N. '"Hoist with his own petard": ironic and comic elements in Plato's critique of Protagoras (*Tht.* 161–71)', in Lee, *Exegesis*, pp. 225–61.

Lee, E. N., Mourelatos, A. P. D. and Rorty, R. M., eds. *Exegesis and Argument: Studies in Greek Philosophy Presented to Gregory Vlastos*, *Phronesis Suppl.* I. Assen, 1973. [*Exegesis*]

Lefkowitz, M. R. *The Victory Ode*. Park Ridge, NJ, 1976.

Leighton, S. 'Aristotle and the emotions', *Phronesis* 27 (1982), 144–74.

Lemmon, E. J. 'Moral dilemmas', *PR* 71 (1962), 139–58.

Lesher, J. 'The role of *nous* in Aristotle's *Posterior Analytics*', *Phronesis* 18 (1973), 44–68.

Lesky, A. 'Psychologie bei Euripides', in Fondation Hardt, *Entretiens sur l'Antiquité Classique* 6 (1958), 123–50. Also in E. Schwinge, ed., *Euripides*, pp. 97–101.

'Decision and responsibility in the tragedy of Aeschylus', *JHS* 86 (1966), 78–85.

Levi, A. 'The ethical and social thought of Protagoras', *Mind* 49 (1940), 284–302.

Lewis, D. M. 'Who was Lysistrata?', *Annual of the British School of Athens* (1955), 1–12.

Linforth, I. M. 'Antigone and Creon', *University of California Publications in Classical Philology* 15 (1961), 183–260.

Livingstone, R. W., ed. *Portrait of Socrates*. Oxford, 1938.

Lloyd, G. E. R. 'Who is attacked in *On Ancient Medicine?*', *Phronesis* 8 (1963), 108–26.
   Magic, Reason, and Experience: Studies in the Origins and Development of Greek Science. Cambridge, 1981.
   Science, Folklore, and Ideology: Studies in the Life Sciences in Ancient Greece. Cambridge, 1983.
   'Measurement and mystification', forthcoming.
Lloyd, G. E. R. and Owen, G. E. L., eds. *Aristotle on Mind and the Senses:* Proceedings of the 7th Symposium Aristotelicum. Cambridge, 1978.
Lloyd-Jones, H. 'Notes on Sophocles' *Antigone*', *CQ* NS 7 (1957), 12–27.
   'The end of the *Seven Against Thebes*', *CQ* NS 9 (1959), 80–115.
   'The guilt of Agamemnon', *CQ* NS 12 (1962), 187–99. ['Guilt']
   The Justice of Zeus. Berkeley, 1971. [*JZ*]
   'Modern interpretation of Pindar', *JHS* 93 (1973), 109–37.
   'Women and love', review of K. J. Dover, *Greek Homosexuality. New Statesman* 6 (1978), 442. Repr. in Lloyd-Jones, *Classical Survivals: the Classics in the Modern World.* London, 1982, pp. 97–100.
   'Pindar', Lecture on a Master Mind, *PBA* 68 (1982), 139–63.
   'Artemis and Iphigeneia', *JHS* 103 (1983), 87–102.
Locke, J. *An Essay Concerning Human Understanding* (1690), ed. P. H. Nidditch. Oxford, 1975.
Loenen, D. *Protagoras and the Greek Community.* Amsterdam, 1940.
Long, A. A. 'Morals and values in Homer', *JHS* 90 (1970), 121–39.
   'Aristotle and the history of Greek skepticism' in D. J. O'Meara, ed., *Studies in Aristotle.* Washington, D.C., 1981, 79–106.
   'Pro and contra fratricide: Aeschylus *Septem* 653–719', in J. H. Betts, ed., volume in honour of T. B. L. Webster. Bristol, forthcoming.
Loraux, N. *Les Enfants d'Athéna: idées athéniennes sur la citoyenneté et la division des sexes.* Paris, 1981.
   L'Invention d'Athènes: histoire de l'oraison funèbre dans la 'cité classique'. Paris, 1981.
Lucas, D. W., ed., and comm. *Aristotle's Poetics.* Oxford, 1968.
Lyons, J. *Structural Semantics: an Analysis of Part of the Vocabulary of Plato.* Oxford, 1963.
Mackie, J. L. *The Cement of the Universe.* Oxford, 1974.
MacLeod, C. W. 'Politics and the *Oresteia*', *JHS* 102 (1982), 124–44.
Mansion, S., ed. *Aristote et les problèmes de méthode.* Proceedings of the 2nd Symposium Aristotelicum. Louvain, 1961.
Marcus, R. B. 'Moral dilemmas and consistency', *JP* 77 (1980), 121–36.
Matthaei, L. *Studies in Greek Tragedy.* Cambridge, 1918.
Méautis, G. *Mythes inconnus de la Grèce antique.* Paris, 1944.
Melden, A. *Free Action.* London, 1961.
Meritt, B. D. 'Greek inscriptions (14–27)', *Hesperia* 8 (1939), 48–90.
Meuli, K. 'Griechische Opferbräuche', in O. Gigon, ed., *Phyllobolia, Festschrift P. von der Mühll.* basel, 1960.
Meuss, H. *Tyche bei den attischen Tragikern.* Hirschberg, 1899.
Moraux, P. and Wiesner, J., eds. *Zweifelhaftes im Corpus Aristotelicum: Studien zu eininpen Dubia.* Proceedings of the 9th Symposium Aristotelicum. Berlin, 1983.
Moravcsik, J. M. E., ed. *Aristotle: a Collection of Critical Essays.* Garden City, 1967.
   'Reason and Eros in the ascent passage of the *Symposium*', in J. Anton and G. Kustas, eds., *Essays in Ancient Greek Philosophy.* Albany, 1972, pp. 285–302.

'Understanding and knowledge in Plato's dialogues', *Neue Hefte für Philosophie* 15/16 (1979), 53–69.

Moravcsik, J. M. E. and Temko, P., eds. *Plato on Beauty, Wisdom, and the Arts*, APQ Library of Philosophy. Totowa, 1982.

Morrison, J. S. 'The place of Protagoras in Athenian public life', *CQ* 35 (1941), 1–16.

'The shape of the earth in Plato's *Phaedo*', *Phronesis* 4 (1959), 101–19.

Moser, S. and Kustas, G. 'A comment on the "relativism" of Protagoras', *Phoenix* 20 (1966), 111–15.

Mourelatos, A. P. D., ed. *The Presocratics*. Garden City, NY, 1974.

Müller, G., ed. *Sophokles: Antigone*. Heidelberg, 1967.

Murdoch, I. *The Sovereignty of Good*. London, 1970.

The Fire and the Sun: Why Plato Banished the Artists. Oxford, 1977.

Murdoch, I. and Magee, B. 'Philosophy and literature: dialogue with Iris Murdoch', in Magee, ed., *Men of Ideas*. New York, 1978, pp. 264–84.

Murphy, N. R. *The Interpretation of Plato's Republic*. Oxford, 1951.

Murray, G., ed. *Euripidis Fabulae*, Vol. I. Oxford Classical Text. Oxford, 1902.

Nagel, T. 'War and massacre', *PPA* 1 (1972), 123–44. Repr. in Nagel, *Mortal Questions*, pp. 53–74.

'Moral luck', *PASS* 50 (1976), 137–51. Repr. in Nagel, *Mortal Questions*, pp. 24–38.

Mortal Questions. Cambridge, 1979.

Nagel, T., Irwin, T. H. and Burnyeat, M. F. 'An exchange on Plato', *NYRB* 27 (1980), 51–3.

Nagy, G. *Comparative Studies in Greek and Indic Meter*. Cambridge, MA, 1974.

The Best of the Achaeans. Baltimore, 1979.

Nietzsche, F. W. *The Birth of Tragedy* (1872), trans. W. Kaufmann. New York, 1976.

Thus Spoke Zarathustra (1883–5), trans. W. Kaufmann. New York, 1954.

The Will to Power (1883–8), trans. W. Kaufmann and R. J. Hollingdale. New York, 1967.

Nilsson, M. *Geschichte der griechische Religion*. Vol. I, Munich, 1955.

Norwood, G. *Greek Tragedy*. London, 1929.

Nozick, R. *Philosophical Explanations*. Cambridge, MA, 1981.

Nussbaum, M. C. '*Psuchē* in Heraclitus, II', *Phronesis* 17 (1972), 153–70.

'The text of Aristotle's *De Motu Animalium*', *HSCP* 80 (1976), 143–4.

'Consequences and character in Sophocles' *Philoctetes*', *Phil Lit* 1 (1976–7), 25–53. ['Consequences']

Aristotle's De Motu Animalium. Princeton, 1978. [*De Motu*]

Review of I. Murdoch, *The Fire and the Sun: Why Plato Banished the Artists*, *Phil Lit* 2 (1978), 125–6.

'The speech of Alcibiades: a reading of Plato's *Symposium*, *Phil Lit* 3 (1979), 131–72.

'Eleatic conventionalism and Philolaus on the conditions of thought', *HSCP* 83 (1979), 63–108.

'Aristophanes and Socrates on learning practical wisdom', *YCS* 26 (1980), 43–97. ['Aristophanes']

'Shame, separateness, and political unity: Aristotle's criticism of Plato', in Rorty, *Essays*, pp. 395–435.

Review of E. Hartman, *Substance, Body, and Soul*, *JP* 77 (1980), 355–65.

Review of R. Kassel, *Der Text der aristotelischen Rhetorik*, *AGP* 63 (1981), 346–50.

'Aristotle', in T. J. Luce, ed., *Ancient Writers: Greece and Rome*. New York, 1982, pp. 377–416.

'"This story isn't true": poetry, goodness, and understanding in Plato's *Phaedrus*', in J. M. E. Moravcsik and P. Temko, eds., *Plato on Beauty*. Totowa, 1982, pp. 79–124.

'Saving Aristotle's appearances', in M. Schofield and M. C. Nussbaum, eds., *Language and Logos*. Cambridge, 1982, pp. 267–93.

'The "common explanation" of animal motion', in P. Moraux and J. Wiesner, eds., *Zweifelhaftes im Corpus Aristotelicum*. Berlin, 1983, pp. 116–57.

'Fictions of the soul', *Phil Lit* 7 (1983), 145–61. ['Fictions']

'Flawed crystals: James's *The Golden Bowl* and literature as moral philosophy', *NLH* 15 (1983), 25–50. ['Crystals']

'Reply to Gardiner, Wollheim, and Putnam', *NLH* 15 (1983), 201–8.

'Plato on commensurability and desire', *PASS* 58 (1984), 55–80.

'Aristotelian dualism: a reply to Howard Robinson', *OSAP* 2 (1984), 198–207.

'Therapeutic arguments: Epicurus and Aristotle', in M. Schofield and G. Striker, eds., *The Norms of Nature*. Cambridge, 1985, pp. 31–74.

'Aristotle on human nature and the foundations of ethics', forthcoming.

'The discernment of perception: an Aristotelian conception of private and public rationality', in *Proceedings of the Boston Area Colloquium for Ancient Philosophy*, ed. J. Cleary. Vol. 1, New York, 1985, pp. 151–201.

O'Brien, M. *The Socratic Paradoxes and the Greek Mind*. Chapel Hill, NC, 1967.

Orwin, C. 'Feminine justice: the end of the *Seven Against Thebes*', *CP* 75 (1980), 187–96.

Owen, G. E. L. 'Logic and metaphysics in some earlier works of Aristotle', in I. Düring and G. E. L. Owen, *Aristotle and Plato in the Mid-Fourth Century*. Göteborg, 1960, pp. 163–90. Repr. in Barnes, *Articles*, Vol. III, pp. 13–32; in Owen, *Logic, Science, and Dialectic*.

'*Tithenai ta phainomena*', in S. Mansion, ed., *Aristote et les problèmes de méthode*. Louvain, 1961, pp. 83–103. Repr. in Barnes, *Articles*, Vol. I, pp. 113–26; in J. M. E. Moravcsik, ed., *Aristotle*, pp. 167–90; in Owen, *Logic*. ['*Tithenai*']

'The place of the *Timaeus* in Plato's dialogues', in R. E. Allen, ed., *Studies in Plato's Metaphysics*. London, 1965, pp. 329–36; in Owen, *Logic*.

'Plato and Parmenides on the timeless present', *The Monist* 50 (1966), 317–40. Repr. in A. P. D. Mourelatos, ed., *The Presocratics*, pp. 271–92; in Owen, *Logic*.

'Dialectic and eristic in the treatment of the forms', in Owen, ed., *Aristotle on Dialectic: the Topics*. Oxford, 1968, pp. 103–25; Repr. in Owen, *Logic*.

'Aristotelian pleasures', *PAS* 72 (1971–2), 135–52. Repr. in Owen, *Logic*.

'Philosophical invective', *OSAP* 1 (1983), 1–25. Repr. in Owen, *Logic*.

Logic, Science and Dialectic: Collected Papers on Ancient Greek Philosophy, ed. M. C. Nussbaum. London, 1986.

Page, D. L. *Actors' Interpolations in Greek Tragedy*. Oxford, 1934.

Paolucci, A. and H., eds. *Hegel on Tragedy*. New York, 1975.

Parker, R. *Miasma*. Oxford, 1983.

Patterson, R. 'The Platonic art of comedy and tragedy', *Phil Lit* 6 (1982), 76–93.

Pearson, A. C., ed. *Sophoclis Fabulae*. Oxford Classical Texts. Oxford, 1924.

Pearson, L. *Popular Ethics in Ancient Greece*. Stanford, 1962.

Penner, T. 'Verbs and the identity of actions', in O. Wood and G. Pitcher, eds., *Ryle*. New York, 1970, pp. 393–453.

'Thought and desire in Plato', in Vlastos, *Plato* II, pp. 96–118.

Peradotto, J. J. 'The omen of the eagles and the *ēthos* of Agamemnon', *Phoenix* 23 (1968), 237–63.

Perrotta, G. *Sofocle*. Messina–Florence, 1935.

Pfohl, G., ed. *Greek Poems on Stone*. Vol. 1 (Epitaphs), Leiden, 1967.

Plochmann, G. K. 'Supporting themes in the *Symposium*', in J. Anton and G. Kustas, eds., *Essays in Ancient Greek Philosophy*. Albany, 1972, pp. 328–44.

Podlecki, A. J. 'The character of Eteocles in Aeschylus' *Septem*', *TAPA* 95 (1964), 283–99.

Pohlenz, M. '*Nomos* und *phusis*', *Hermes* 81 (1953), 418–83.

  Die Griechische Tragödie. Göttingen, 1954.

Poschenrieder, F. *Die naturwissenschaftlichen Schriften des Aristoteles in ihrem Verhältnis zu der hippocratischen Sammlung*. Bamberg, 1887.

Prichard, H. A. 'The meaning of *agathon* in the ethics of Aristotle', *Philosophy* 10 (1935), 27–39. Repr. in J. M. E. Moravcsik, ed., *Aristotle*, pp. 241–60.

Putnam, H. 'There is at least one *a priori* truth', *Erkenntnis* 13 (1978), 153–70. Repr. in Putnam, *Realism and Reason: Philosophical Papers*, Vol. III, Cambridge, 1983, pp. 98–114.

  'Literature, science, and reflection', in Putnam, *Meaning and the Moral Sciences*. London, 1979, pp. 83–96.

  Reason, Truth, and History. Cambridge, 1981.

  'Taking rules seriously: a response to Martha Nussbaum', *NLH* 15 (1983), 193–200.

Raphael, D. D. 'Can literature be moral philosophy?', *NLH* 15 (1983), 1–12.

Rawls, J. 'Outline of a decision procedure for ethics', *PR* 60 (1951), 177–97.

  A Theory of Justice. Cambridge, MA, 1971.

Reckford, K. 'Concepts of demoralization in Euripides' *Hecuba*', forthcoming.

Redfield, J. *Nature and Culture in the Iliad*. Chicago, 1975.

  Foreword to G. Nagy, *The Best of the Achaeans*. Baltimore, 1981, pp. vii–xiii.

Rhees, R. 'Wittgenstein's lecture on ethics', *PR* 74 (1965), 3–26.

Riginos, A. *Platonica*. Leiden, 1976.

Robin, L. *La Théorie platonicienne de l'amour*. Paris, 1933.

  ed., and trans. *Platon: Phèdre*. Paris, 1939.

Robinson, R. *Plato's Earlier Dialectic*. Oxford, 1953.

Ronnet, G. *Sophocle: poète tragique*. Paris, 1969.

Rorty, A., ed. *Essays on Aristotle's Ethics*. Berkeley, 1980. [*Essays*]

Rose, P. 'Sophocles' *Philoctetes* and the teachings of the Sophists', *HSCP* 80 (1976), 49–105.

Rosen, S. *Plato's Symposium*. New Haven, 1968.

Rosenmeyer, T. G. 'Plato's prayer to Pan', *Hermes* 90 (1962), 34–44.

Ross, W. D., ed. *The Works of Aristotle Translated into English*. Oxford Translation. 12 vols., Oxford, 1910–52.

  The Right and the Good. Oxford, 1930.

  ed. *Aristotle's Physics*. Oxford, 1936.

  ed. *Aristotelis Fragmenta Selecta*. Oxford Classical Text. Oxford, 1955.

  Aristotle. London, 1923; 5th ed., 1960.

Rowe, C. J. *The Eudemian and Nicomachean Ethics*. Cambridge, 1971.

  'A reply to John Cooper on the *Magna Moralia*', *AJP* 96 (1975), 160–72.

Russell, D. A. and Wilson, N., eds. *Menander Rhetor*. Oxford, 1981.

Ryle, G. *Plato's Progress*. Cambridge, 1966.

Santas, G. 'Plato's *Protagoras* and explanations of weakness', *PR* 75 (1966), 3–33. Repr. in Vlastos, *Socrates*, pp. 264–98.

  'The form of the Good in Plato's *Republic*', *Philosophical Inquiry* 2 (1980), 374–403.

Santirocco, M. 'Justice in Sophocles' *Antigone*', *Phil Lit* 4 (1980), 180–98.

Sartre, J.-P. *L'Existentialisme est un humanisme*. Paris, 1946.

Schaerer, R. *Epistēmē et Technē: études sur les notions de connaissance et d'art d'Homère à Platon.* Lausanne, 1930.

La Question Platonicienne. Neuchatel, 1938; 2nd ed., 1969.

Schmid, W. 'Probleme aus der sophokleischen *Antigone*', *Philologus* 62 (1903), 1–34.

Schneewind, J. B. *Sidgwick and Victorian Morality.* Oxford, 1977.

Schofield, M., Burnyeat, M. and Barnes, J., eds. *Doubt and Dogmatism: Studies in Hellenistic Epistemology.* Oxford, 1980.

Schofield, M. and Nussbaum, M., eds. *Language and Logos: Studies in Ancient Greek Philosophy Presented to G. E. L. Owen.* Cambridge, 1982.

Schofield, M. and Striker, G., eds. *The Norms of Nature: Studies in Hellenistic Ethics.* Cambridge, 1985.

Scholz, H. *Der Hund in der griechisch-römischen Magie und Religion.* Berlin, 1937.

Schopenhauer, A. *The World as Will and Representation* (3rd ed., 1859), trans. E. J. Payne. 2 vols., New York, 1969.

Schwinge, E., ed. *Euripides.* Wege der Forschung. Darmstadt, 1968.

Searle, J. '*Prima Facie* obligations', in Z. van Straaten, ed., *Philosophical Subjects: Essays Presented to P. F. Strawson.* Oxford, 1980, pp. 238–59.

Seeskin, K. 'Is the *Apology* of Socrates a parody?', *Phil Lit* 6 (1982), 94–105.

Segal, C. 'The character of Dionysus and the unity of the *Frogs*', *HSCP* 65 (1961), 207–30.

'Sophocles' praise of man and the conflicts of the *Antigone*', *Arion* 3 (1964), 46–66. Repr. in T. Woodard, ed., *Sophocles: a Collection of Critical Essays.* Englewood Cliffs, NJ, 1966, pp. 62–85.

'"The myth was saved": reflections on Homer and the mythology of Plato's *Republic*', *Hermes* 106 (1978), 315–36.

Tragedy and Civilization: an Interpretation of Sophocles. Cambridge, MA, 1981.

'Boundary Violation and the Landscape of the Self in Senecan Tragedy', *Antike und Abendland* 29 (1983), 172–87.

Sherman, N. *Aristotle's Theory of Moral Education*, Ph.D. thesis, Harvard University, 1982.

Shorey, P. 'Note on Plato's *Republic* 488D', *CR* 20 (1906), 247–8.

Sidgwick, H. *The Methods of Ethics*, 7th ed. London 1907.

Sinaiko, H. *Love, Knowledge, and Discourse.* Chicago, 1965.

Smith, P. M. *On the Hymn to Zeus in Aeschylus' 'Agamemnon'*, American Classical Studies, No. 4. Ann Arbor, 1980.

Solmsen, F. 'The Erinys in Aeschylus' *Septem*', *TAPA* 68 (1937), 197–211.

Intellectual Experiments of the Greek Enlightenment. Princeton, 1975.

Sorabji, R. *Necessity, Cause, and Blame: Perspectives on Aristotle's Theory.* London, 1980.

Sörbom, G. *Mimesis and Art.* Uppsala, 1966.

Sparshott, F. E. 'Plato and Thrasymachus', *University of Toronto Quarterly* (1957), 54–61.

Stenzel, J. *Zahl und Gestalt.* Leipzig, 1933.

Stewart, Z. 'Democritus and the Cynics', *HSCP* 63 (1958), 179–91.

Stinton, T. C. W. '*Hamartia* in Aristotle and Greek tragedy', *CQ* NS 25 (1975), 221–54.

Striker, G. 'Antipater and the art of living', in M. Schofield and G. Striker, eds., *The Norms of Nature.* Cambridge, 1985.

Strohm, H. *Tyche: zur Schicksalsauffassung bei Pindar und den frühgriechischen Dichtern.* Stuttgart, 1944.

Sullivan, J. P. 'The hedonism in Plato's *Protagoras*', *Phronesis* 6 (1967), 10–28.

Taplin, O. Review of W. Arrowsmith, *The Greek Tragedy in New Translations*, *CR* NS 26 (1976), 168–70.

Greek Tragedy in Action. Berkeley, 1978.

Tarrant, D. 'Plato as dramatist', *JHS* 75 (1955), 82–9.

Taylor, A. E. *Plato*. London, 1926.

Plato, the Man and His Work, 4th ed. London, 1937.

Taylor, C. C. W., trans., and comm. *Plato: Protagoras*. Clarendon Plato Series. Oxford, 1976.

Trilling, L. 'The Princess Casamassima', in Trilling, *The Liberal Imagination: Essays on Literature and Society*. New York, 1950, pp. 58–92.

Tucker, T. G., trans., and comm. *The Seven Against Thebes of Aeschylus*. Cambridge, 1908.

Vernant, J.-P. 'Le travail et la pensée technique', in Vernant, *Mythe et pensée chez les Grecs*, vol. II, Paris, 1965, pp. 5–15.

'Remarques sur les formes et les limites de la pensée technique chez les Grecs', in Vernant, *Mythe et pensée chez les Grecs*, vol. II, Paris, 1965, pp. 44–64.

Mythe et pensée chez les Grecs: études de psychologie historique, 2 vols. Paris, 1965.

'Greek tragedy: problems of interpretation', in E. Donato and R. Macksey, eds., *The Languages of Criticism and the Sciences of Man*. Baltimore, 1970, pp. 273–89.

'Le moment historique de la tragédie en Grèce', in Vernant and Vidal-Naquet, *MT*, pp. 13–17.

'À la table des hommes', in M. Detienne and J.-P. Vernant, eds., *La Cuisine du sacrifice en pays grec*. Paris, 1979, pp. 37–132.

Les Origines de la pensée grecque. Paris, 1981.

'Tensions et ambiguités dans la tragédie grecque', in Vernant and Vidal-Naquet, *MT*, pp. 21–40.

Vernant, J.-P. and Vidal-Naquet, P. *Mythe et tragédie en grèce ancienne*. Paris, 1972. [*MT*]

Vidal-Naquet, P. 'Valeurs religieuses et mythiques de la terre et du sacrifice dans l'Odyssée', in Vidal-Naquet, *Le Chasseur noir: formes de pensée et formes de societé dans le monde grec*. Paris, 1981, pp. 39–68.

Vlastos, G., ed. *Plato's Protagoras*. Indianapolis, 1956.

ed. *The Philosophy of Socrates: a Collection of Critical Essays*. Garden City, NY, 1971. [*Socrates*]

ed. *Plato: a Collection of Critical Essays*, 2 vols. Garden City, NY, 1971. [*Plato*]

Platonic Studies. Princeton, 1973; 2nd ed., 1981. [*PS*]

'The individual as object of love in Plato's dialogues', in Vlastos, *PS*, pp. 1–34.

'Sex in Platonic love', Appendix II to 'The individual as object of love in Plato's dialogues', in Vlastos, *PS*, pp. 38–42.

'The virtuous and the happy', review of T. Irwin, *Plato's Moral Theory: The Early and Middle Dialogues*, *TLS* 24 Feb. 1978, pp. 230–1.

'Happiness and virtue in Socrates' moral theory', *PCPS* 210, NS 30 (1984), 181–213.

Walzer, M. 'Political action: the problem of dirty hands', *PPA* 2 (1973), 160–80.

Waterfield, R. A. H. 'The place of the *Philebus* in Plato's dialogues', *Phronesis* 25 (1980), 270–305.

Watson, G. 'Free agency', *JP* 72 (1975), 205–20.

'Skepticism about weakness of will', *PR* 86 (1977), 316–39.

Werkmeister, H., ed. *Facets of Plato's Philosophy*. Phronesis Suppl. II. Assen, 1976.

Whallon, W. 'Why is Artemis angry?', *AJP* 82 (1961), 78–88.

White, N. P. *A Companion to Plato's Republic*. Indianapolis, 1979.

Whitehead, D. 'Aristotle the Metic', *PCPS* 21 (1975), 94–9.

The Ideology of the Athenian Metic, *PCPS* Suppl. Vol. 4 (1977).

Whitman, C. H. *Sophocles: a Study of Heroic Humanism*. Cambridge, MA, 1951.
Euripides and the Full Circle of Myth. Cambridge, MA, 1974.
Wieland, W. *Platon und die Formen des Wissens*. Göttingen, 1982.
Wiggins, D. 'Deliberation and practical reason', *PAS* 76 (1975–6), 29–51. Repr. in Rorty, *Essays*, pp. 221–40. ['Deliberation']
'Weakness of will, commensurability, and the objects of deliberation and desire', *PAS* 79 (1978–9), 251–77. Repr. in Rorty, *Essays*, pp. 241–65.
Sameness and Substance. Oxford, 1980.
Wilamowitz-Moellendorf, U. *Platon*, 1. Berlin, 1920.
Williams, B. A. O. 'Pleasure and belief', *PASS* 33 (1959), 57–72.
'Ethical consistency', *PASS* 39 (1965), 103–24. Repr. in Williams, *Problems of the Self*, pp. 166–86.
Problems of the Self. Cambridge, 1973.
'Moral luck', *PASS* 50 (1976), 115–51. Repr. in Williams, *ML*, pp. 20–39.
'Conflicts of values', in *The Idea of Freedom: Essays in Honour of Isaiah Berlin*, ed. A. Ryan, Oxford, 1979. Repr. in Williams, *ML*, pp. 71–82.
Moral Luck: Philosophical Papers 1973–1980. Cambridge, 1981. [ML]
'Philosophy', in M. I. Finley, ed., *The Legacy of Greece: a New Appraisal*. Oxford, 1981, pp. 202–55.
Ethics and the Limits of Philosophy. Cambridge, MA, 1985.
Wilson, J. '"The customary meanings of words were changed" – or were they? A note on Thucydides 3.82.4', *CQ* NS 32 (1982), 18–20.
Winnington-Ingram, R. P. '*Septem Contra Thebas*', *YCS* 25 (1977), 1–45.
Sophocles: an Interpretation. Cambridge, 1980.
Wittgenstein, L. *The Blue and Brown Books*. Oxford, 1958.
Philosophical Investigations, trans. G. E. M. Anscombe,
Wollheim, R. 'Flawed crystals: James's *The Golden Bowl* and the plausibility of literature as moral philosophy', *NLH* 15 (1983), 185–92.
Wycherley, R. E. 'The scene of Plato's *Phaedrus*', *Phoenix* 17 (1963), 88–98.
Zeitlin, F. *Under the Sign of the Shield: Semiotics and Aeschylus' Seven Against Thebes*. Rome, 1982.
Zeyl, D. J. 'Socrates and hedonism in Plato's *Protagoras* 351B–358D', *Phronesis* 25 (1980), 250–69.
Zürcher, W. *Die Darstellung des Menschen in Drama des Euripides*. Basel, 1947.

General index

Index of passages